Sustainable Development in
Asia, America and Europe with
Global Applications

To My Father Yan-Cun Zhou
Mother Chu-Qin Wang
Supervisor Prof Stuart Holland and
Co-Supervisor Prof Domenico Mario Nuti

Sustainable Development in Asia, America and Europe with Global Applications:

A New Approach to Land Ownership

Jian-Ming Zhou

University of Florence
Italy

Edward Elgar
Cheltenham, UK • Northampton, MA, USA

Published by
Edward Elgar Publishing Limited
Glensanda House
Montpellier Parade
Cheltenham
Glos GL50 1UA
UK

Edward Elgar Publishing, Inc.
136 West Street
Suite 202
Northampton
Massachusetts 01060
USA

A catalogue record for this book
is available from the British Library

Library of Congress Cataloguing in Publication Data

Zhou, Jian-Ming.
  Sustainable development in Asia, America and Europe with global applications: a new approach to land ownership / Jian-Ming Zhou.
    p. cm
  Includes bibliographical references and index.
    1. Land tenure—Asia. 2. Land tenure—United States. 3. Land tenure—Europe. 4. Sustainable development—Asia. 5. Sustainable development—United States. 6. Sustainable development—Europe. I. Title.

  HD843.2.Z48 2000
  333.33'5—dc21   00–039371

ISBN 1 85898 965 5

Printed and bound in Great Britain by MPG Books Ltd, Bodmin, Cornwall

Contents

List of Figures viii
List of Tables ix
List of Abbreviations xiii
List of Transliterations xv
Glossary xvii
Acknowledgements xxi

PART ONE THEORIES 1

1. Introduction 3
  1.1 Monsoon Asia 3
  1.2 A Remaining Obstacle Unresolved by the Japanese Model . . . 4
  1.3 The Chinese Model 8
  1.4 The Agenda of the Book 11
  1.5 The Analytical Approach 16
  1.6 Tentative Contributions of the Book 20
2. Theories of Monsoon Asia Rice Economy and
  Variable Mixed Economies 31
  2.1 A Rice-Based Agriculture in Monsoon Asia 31
  2.2 The Prewar Vicious Circle of Poverty in Monsoon Asia 35
  2.3 The Postwar Initial Conditions for Development in
  Monsoon Asia 54
  2.4 Variable Mixed Economies 55
3. Theory of Property Rights 63
  3.1 Incentives under Private Ownership and
  Possession of Public Assets 64
  3.2 Achieving Pareto Efficiency according to Coase 71
  3.3 Relaxing Hypotheses of the Coase Theorem 82
  3.4 The Evolution of Property Rights Structures 100
  3.5 Relevant Concepts of Private Ownership 103

Appendix 3.1 How to Carry Out Land Consolidation
- An International Comparison 107

PART TWO THE JAPANESE MODEL AND A NEW MODEL .. 121

4. The Japanese Model versus the Last Obstacle 123
4.1 The Significance of the Japanese Model 123
4.2 Theoretical Discussion 126
4.3 The Remaining Obstacle 131
4.4 Theoretical Discussion 150
5. A New Model for Sustainable Rural Development 154
5.1 Conjectural Proposal 5.1 154
5.2 The Pioneering Chinese Elementary Cooperatives 166
5.3 A Possible Global Applicability of the New Model 176
5.4 Dynamic Determination of Farm Size 178
5.5 Theoretical Discussion 178
5.6 Other Rice-Based Economies under
Private Land Ownership in Monsoon Asia 184

PART THREE THE CHINESE MODEL 189

6. The Chinese Model and the Emergence of the Last Obstacle . 191
6.1 The Chinese Model in General 191
6.2 Theoretical Discussion 202
6.3 The Emergence of the Last Obstacle 209
6.4 Theoretical Discussion 221
7. Overcoming the Last Obstacle in the Chinese Model 223
7.1 A Large-Scale Farming and Collective–Individual
Mixed Economy 223
7.2 Functioning of Large-Scale Farming 248
7.3 Ascending a Higher Stage
- Preventing Food Overproduction and
Improving the Environment 277
7.4 Theoretical Discussion 288
8. Other Rice-Based Economies under Public Land Ownership
in Monsoon Asia 295
8.1 Different Levels of Land Tenure Reforms 296
8.2 An Analysis of the Nominal State - But *De Facto* Private -
Land Ownership 300
8.3 Conjectural Proposals 8.1, 8.2 and 8.3 308

PART FOUR APPLICATIONS OF THE NEW MODEL
BEYOND MONSOON ASIA 311

9.   The American Model and the Crowding Out of Small Farmers   313
     9.1 The General Trend in the USA 313
     9.2 The Underlying Economic Forces 333
     9.3 Government Interventions 344
10.   Application of the New Model in the USA 370
     10.1 Seeking a Possible Solution 370
     10.2 A Comparison among the American, Japanese, Chinese
          Models and the New Model 390
11.   Implementations of the New Model in the OECD, EU,
     CEECs, CIS, and Rest of the World 396
     11.1 In Rural Areas at Different Wage Economies 396
     11.2 In OECD and EU Countries in General 397
     11.3 In CEECs and the CIS (27 Countries) 399

Bibliography 434
Index 490

Figures

3.1   Formulas for Calculating General Grades of Farms   114
3.2   Before Consolidation — Fragmented Farms   117
3.3   After Consolidation — Each Farm Has *Two* Parcels   117
3.4   After Consolidation — Each Farm Has *One* Parcel   117

9.1   Economic Costs for Corn, Soybean and Wheat by
      Gross Income in the USA 1986—87   351
9.2   Economic Costs for Corn, Soybean and Wheat by
      Acreage in the USA 1986—87   352

Tables

2.1 Area Percentage and Yield of Rice, Wheat and
     Coarse Grains in Various Parts of the World in 1992   32
2.2 Agricultural Densities and Average Farm Sizes in
     Various Parts of the World in 1990   43

3.1 Ownership and Possession of Asset (Land)   68
3.2 Approaches to Assigning Property Rights for Eliminating or
     Efficiently Producing Negative Externalities with the
     Example of Slaves/Serfs Acquiring Freedom from
     Slave/Serf-Holders   92
3.3 Illustration of Assessing General Grade for Farm 1   115

4.1 Comparison of Rice Production Costs by
     Farm Size in Japan 1953—98   128
4.2 Farm Size 1950—98 and Fragmentation in 1988 in Japan   133
4.3 Proportions of Full-Time and Part-Time Farmers in
     Japan 1950—98   136
4.4 Abandonment of Cultivated Land in Japan 1975—95   139
4.5 Utilization Rate of Cultivated Land in Japan 1960—97   139
4.6 Senilization and Feminization of the
     Agricultural Labor Force in Japan 1965—98   140
4.7 Changes in the Number and Shares of
     Viable Farms in Japan 1960—96   143
4.8 Self-Sufficiency Rates of Foods in Japan 1960—97   144

5.1 Proportion of Distribution between Remuneration to
     Land Shares and Remuneration to Labor Contribution in
     Some Elementary Cooperatives of China 1954—55   169

6.1 Employment by Main Sectors in China 1978—98   202
6.2 Composition of Rural Social Labor Force in
     China 1978—98   203

6.3   Per Capita Output of Major Agricultural Products in
        China 1978—99   204
6.4   Years of Import Exceeding Export of
        Grain in China 1982—98   219

7.1   Area under the Dual Land System in China 1990—94   228
7.2   Areas of Self-Sufficiency Land and Responsibility Land
        under the Dual Land System in China 1990—94   228
7.3   Methods of Contracting Responsibility Land under the
        Dual Land System in China 1990—94   229
7.4   Progress in Overcoming Fragmentation in China 1986—92   236
7.5   Land Contracted per Individual Household
        in China 1986—92   237
7.6   Postwar Urban—Rural Population Changes
        in China and Japan   245
7.7   Land Contracted per Household in
        Specialized Teams of China 1986—92   254
7.8   Organizations of Large-Scale Farmers in
        Changshu City of China in 1989   256
7.9   Maximum Land Area per Laborer and
        Household under Different Degrees of
        Mechanization in China in the mid-1980s   266
7.10   Comparison of Economic Results under
        Different Farm Sizes in 586 Households of
        Six Counties and Cities of China 1990—91   268
7.11   Comparison of Economic Results under Different
        Farm Sizes in 236 Households of Beijing, China
        in the mid-1980s   269
7.12   Comparison of Economic Results under Different Farm
        Sizes in 240 Households of Wuxi County, China in 1986   270
7.13   Growth of Grain Production in
        Shunyi County, China 1985—89   274
7.14   Possession of Agricultural Machinery in
        Shunyi County, China 1987—90   276
7.15   Areas of Cultivated Land, That with a Slope at or over
        25 Degrees, and Other Types of Land
        in China by 31 October 1996   281

9.1   Number, Total and Average Acreage of Farms in
        the USA 1850—1992   316
9.2   Percentage in Farm Number by Farm Size in
        the USA 1910—92   318

9.3	Percentage in Farm Acreage by Farm Size in the USA 1910–92	319
9.4	Farm Number, Acreage and Value of Sales by Size of Sales in the USA 1949–92	322
9.5	Characteristics of the Minimum Number of Largest Farms Needed to Produce a Third of Total Gross Sales in the USA 1940–87	326
9.6	Farm Number, Acreage and Value of Sales by Type of Organization in the USA 1974–92	328
9.7	Characteristics of Corporate Farms in the USA 1974–92	330
9.8	Corn Costs of Farms and Operator Characteristics by Economic Class in the USA in 1987	345
9.9	Corn Costs of Farms and Operator Characteristics by Corn Acreage Class in the USA in 1987	346
9.10	Soybean Costs of Farms and Operator Characteristics by Economic Class in the USA in 1986	347
9.11	Soybean Costs of Farms and Operator Characteristics by Soybean Acreage Class in the USA in 1986	348
9.12	Wheat Costs of Farms and Operator Characteristics by Economic Class in the USA in 1986	349
9.13	Wheat Costs of Farms and Operator Characteristics by Wheat Acreage Class in the USA in 1986	350
9.14	Relationship among Deficiency Payment, Target Price, Loan Rate and Market Price in the USA up to 1996	354
9.15	Example of the Production Flexibility Contract Payment in the USA 1996–2002	366
10.1	Farm Number under Different Tenure of Operator in the USA 1900–92	371
10.2	Farm Acreage under Different Tenure of Operator in the USA 1900–92	372
10.3	Farm Number and Percentage by Tenure of Operator in Different Farm Acreage in the USA 1978–92	374
10.4	Average Variable Cash and Economic Costs for Corn (1987), Soybean (1986), Wheat (1986) Production by Tenure of Operator in the USA	375
10.5	Age, and Acreage Owned and Leased of Some Successful Black Farmers in the USA in 1976	379
11.1	Percentage in Agricultural Land of Collectively Operated Large Farms and Individual Farms in 13 CEECs 1991–98	402

11.2   Average Size of Collectively Operated Large Farms and
        Individual Farms in 13 CEECs 1991–98   403
11.3   Percentage in Agricultural Land by Collectively Operated
        Large Farms and Individual Farms in
        11 CIS Countries in the 1990s   404
11.4   Average Size of Collectively Operated Large Farms,
        Household Plots and Individual Farms in
        Eight CIS Countries in the 1990s   405
11.5   Percentage Change from Previous Year of Gross Agricultural
        Output in 12 CEECs and 12 CIS Countries 1990–98   410
11.6   Land Buy-Sale and Lease in Nine CEECs and Three CIS
        Countries 1996–98   417
11.7   Ownership and Use of Agricultural Land and
        Average Farm Size in Poland 1990–97   423

Abbreviations

ACP	-	Agricultural Conservation Program
ARP	-	Acreage Reduction Program
ASCS	-	Agricultural Stabilization and Conservation Service
CABI	-	Commonwealth Agricultural Bureau International
CCC	-	Commodity Credit Corporation
CCP	-	Conservation Compliance Provisions
CED	-	Committee for Economic Development
CEECs	-	Central and Eastern European Countries
CIS	-	Commonwealth of Independent States
CRP	-	Conservation Reserve Program
CUSTA	-	Canadian/United States Trade Agreement
DEIP	-	Dairy Export Incentive Program
EDMS	-	Electronic Distance Measuring System
EEP	-	Export Enhancement Program
ERP	-	Externality-Receiving Party
EU	-	European Union
EYP	-	Externality-Yielding Party
FAO	-	Food and Agriculture Organization of the United Nations
FCIC	-	Federal Crop Insurance Corporation
FIP	-	Forestry Incentive Program
FmHA	-	Farmers Home Administration
FSU	-	Former Soviet Union
GATT	-	General Agreement on Tariffs and Trade
GDP	-	Gross Domestic Product
GIS	-	Geographic Information Systems
GNP	-	Gross National Product
GPS	-	Global Positioning Systems
JMAFF	-	Japanese Ministry of Agriculture, Forestry and Fisheries
LURC	-	Land Use Right Certificate
NAFTA	-	North American Free Trade Agreement
NIS	-	New Independent States
OECD	-	Organization for Economic Cooperation and Development

PLD	-	Paid Land Diversion Program
SCS	-	Soil Conservation Service
TVE	-	Township and Village Enterprise
UK	-	United Kingdom
USA	-	United States of America
USDA	-	US Department of Agriculture
USSR	-	Union of Soviet Socialist Republics
WRP	-	Wetlands Reserve Program
WWI	-	World War I
WWII	-	World War II

Transliterations

bao   -   contract

bao *chan* dao hu   -   contracting output quotas to households and linking the fulfillment with workpoints which are then linked to remuneration

bao *gan* dao hu   -   contracting responsibilities to households and leaving the total residual output to them without the involvement of workpoints

bao *gong* dao lao (hu)   -   contracting *work* to laborers (households) and linking the fulfillment either directly to remuneration or indirectly through workpoints

Beida*cang*   -   a vast Northern *barn*

Beida*huang*   -   a vast Northern *wasteland*

Biyun   -   white clouds in a blue sky

cun ti liu (san ti)   -   village reserved fees (paid for three items)

fan zu dao bao   -   inverse leasing or contracting

ge ren du zi qi ye   -   individual single venture enterprise

ge ti gong shang hu   -   individual industrial or commercial household

kolkhozes   -   collectively owned farms

kou liang tian   -   self-sufficiency land, grain rations land

krom samaki   -   solidarity groups

lao dong ji lei gong   -   labor accumulation man-days

li tu bu li xiang   -   quit the land without quitting the countryside

nong cun yi wu gong   -   rural obligatory man-days

pai jia   -   quota prices

ping jia   -   parity prices

Shennong   -   magical agriculture

shun jia   -   streamline prices

si ying qi ye	-	private enterprise
sovkhozes	-	state owned farms
wu bao hu	-	childless and infirm old persons who were guaranteed food, clothing, medical care, housing and burial expenses
xiang tong chou fei (wu tong)	-	township unified finance fees (paid for five items)
xiao ye zhu	-	small or petty proprietor
yi gong *bu* nong	-	*subsidizing* agriculture by industry
yi gong *jian* nong	-	*constructing* agriculture by industry
ze ren tian	-	responsibility land
zhuan bao	-	sub-contracting
zhuan rang	-	making-over
zi liu di	-	family plot

Glossary

Nine Features of the Japanese Model of Rural Development

1. Institutional changes for an individual–cooperative mixed economy (1946–50).
2. Government policies supporting rice production and rural development.
3. Construction of rural infrastructure.
4. Higher yields and multiple cropping of rice and other grains.
5. Diversified cropping and non-crop agriculture.
6. Off-farm employment.
7. Peasant migration to cities and work in town and village firms.
8. Agricultural mechanization with small machinery.
9. Persistence of the fragmented small farms, due to inefficient land-holding by part-time and absent small farmers.

13 Features of the Chinese Model of Rural Development

1. Institutional changes for a small-scale farming and collective–individual mixed economy (1978–83).
2. Government policies supporting rice production and rural development.
3. Construction of rural infrastructure.
4. Higher yields and multiple cropping of rice and other grains.
5. Diversified cropping and non-crop agriculture.
6. Off-farm employment.
7. Peasant migration to cities and work in town and village firms.
8. Agricultural mechanization with small machinery.
9. Institutional changes for a large-scale farming and collective–individual mixed economy (starting roughly around 1985).
10. Agricultural mechanization with large machinery.
11. Earlier development in some (chiefly Eastern and coastal) rural areas, and its promotion in other (mainly Central and Western) areas especially from the early 1990s on.

12. Introduction of more advanced technology and management, larger investment, and domestic and international markets to agriculture by urban–rural joint enterprises, and external and foreign single and joint ventures.
13. Prevention of food overproduction, promotion in quality and perfectization in variety of agricultural products, and improvement of the environment, while strengthening development of the Central and especially the Western areas, mainly from mid-1999.

Eight Features of the American Model of Rural Development

1. Institutional changes for an individual land ownership (1783).
2. Government policies supporting agriculture.
3. Commercialization of the individual farming units promoting large farmers and driving small farmers to an inferior position.
4. Technological progress, managerial resources, rural development, procurement and marketing facilities further strengthening large farmers.
5. Government protective safety net (1933–96) failing to avert the trend towards fewer but larger farms since 1935 and prevent small farmers from being crowded out from agriculture.
6. Government market-driven measures since 1996 leaving small farmers more exposed to free market forces.
7. Part ownership of land tenure dominating since 1950 but never being promoted as a policy direction or a new round of institutional changes.
8. The development in recent decades of off-farm employment pursued as subordinate to the loss-making independent small farming resulting in inefficient land-holding by part-time and absent small farmers while only slowing but not halting small farmers' exiting farming.

Relevant Mixed Economies

Individual–cooperative mixed economy. Fragmented small farms under individual land ownership, which independently control the direct production process of agriculture, plus national rural service cooperatives, which socialistically collectivize forward and backward services and financing for the individual farming units. Established in Japan during 1946–50 and still prevails there.

Sub-village individual–collective mixed economy. Sub-village-wide cooperative/enterprise collective use of *physically withdrawable private* land shares, exercising collective–individual dual level operation of large land units, with the basic operation level at one household as the major form or at a farming unit including a small number of households as the minor form. Some elementary cooperatives in China before 1949 until April 1956, some agricultural production cooperatives and urban—rural joint farming enterprises in Japan since the 1970s have taken this form.

Village-wide individual—collective mixed economy. Extension of the individual—collective mixed economy from sub-village to village scope. Some elementary cooperatives in China before 1949 until April 1956, and some agricultural production cooperatives and urban—rural joint farming enterprises in Japan since the 1970s have taken this form.

Village-wide corporate—individual mixed economy. Collective use of *physically unwithdrawable private* (or publicly owned but privately possessed) land shares under corporate ownership, exercising village—individual dual level operation of large land units, with the basic operation level at one household as the major form or at a cooperative/enterprise including a small number of households as the minor form. Such a corporation could extend to cover a number of villages. Proposed by the author for Japan and other rice-based economies under private ownership (or public ownership but private possession) of land in monsoon Asia and other relevant economies in the rest of the world to overcome the fragmented small farms problem in both low wage and high wage economy, and also for CEECs and the CIS to facilitate the transition towards market economy of the collectively operated large farms.

Small-scale farming and collective—individual mixed economy. Land is collectively owned by the village, but contracted to households for fulfilling state procurement output quotas of grain and other major agricultural products and disposing of surplus output, which is called the *Household Contract System.* Land is equally distributed as fragmented small farms, hence the *Equal Land System.* The village has the duty of carrying out general management and providing services, thus village—household dual level operation of land, with the households as the basic level. Experimented during 1950s—70s and popularized during 1978—83 in China and still exists.

Large-scale farming and collective—individual mixed economy. Village—individual dual level operation of large land units under collective ownership and the Household Contract System, with the basic operation level at one household as the major form or at a cooperative/enterprise including a small number of households as the minor form. Exercised in China mainly since the mid-1980s under the *Dual Land System*, the *Leasing System*, the *Single Land System*, and the *Corporate-Holding System* as the major types.

Public—individual mixed economy. Land is under the state, municipal, collective or other forms of public ownership, but individually managed.

Nominal public—individual mixed economy. Land is (nominally) publicly (state, municipally or collectively) owned but individually possessed, and

exchangeable, transferable (salable), giftable and mortgageable. Adopted in
Cambodia in 1981 (with residential land privately owned), Laos in 1988,
Vietnam in 1993, and Kazakhstan (with household plots privately owned) in
the 1990s.

Large–small farmers mixed economy. Small farmers, being engaged in
off-farm activities, retain self-sufficiency land or family plots as small farms,
and lease production land to competent farmers as part owners to strengthen
the existing, or form new, large farms. Proposed by the author for the USA
and other relevant OECD countries with a large versus small bimodal farm
structure to strengthen large farmers while still preserving rather than
crowding out small farmers.

Acknowledgements

My sincere gratitude is hereby expressed to those nice persons in the European University Institute who have always been interested in and supported my work on the publication of this book; and to the University of Florence; the Italian government; the European Union; many friendly Italian and European people; some ardent Japanese and American scholars; and my Chinese compatriots.

Chapters 1 to 8 are built on my thesis 'Overcoming the Last Obstacle in Sustainable Rural Development of Monsoon Asia - The Japanese and Chinese Models and a Proposed New Model' for a PhD in economics of the European University Institute, defended in February 1998. Of the four jury members, Prof Domenico Mario Nuti was my first supervisor. He guided me to market socialism as a third way between the centrally planned economy and free market system, and property rights theory; supported me in initial research on China's economic reforms in industry, agriculture and banking; introduced me to academic associations and international organizations, in whose various conferences my papers were accepted (see the attached list 1). He also helped me to overcome a range of initial difficulties. After leaving the European University Institute, he became my co-supervisor and has extended great support. Prof Stuart Holland was initially my co-supervisor and then supervisor. He has made a particular contribution to my research. He introduced me to the taxonomy of variable mixed economies and development economics, encouraged the concentration of my research on China's economic reform in agriculture, supervised me in the whole process of writing, taught me writing skills, upgraded my English, supported my participation in academic activities, and helped me to surmount various academic and administrative difficulties. Prof Christopher Howe gave precious comments on the earlier version of the thesis, expanded my field of vision from China's agriculture to the whole rice-based economies of monsoon Asia, recommended essential literature, designed the outline of the new version, improved my writing techniques, and promoted an invaluable one-month visit to the School of Oriental and African Studies in London to research materials on China. His contribution was much beyond the call of duty. Prof Michael Artis democratically accepted my non-mathematical research approach, approved the outline of the new version, gave valuable comments on my research papers, improved my English, and sympathetically helped me with many other issues.

Dr Mirella Tieleman-Gargari continuously encouraged my study. Dr Jean Claude Marechal's important comments on my initial research promoted my concentration on Chinese agriculture later on. Prof Kirti Chaudhuri introduced me Prof Christopher Howe and his exceptional expertise on Asian and Chinese economy, including agriculture. Prof Alan Kirman and Prof Cyril Lin carefully read the earlier version of the thesis and gave constructive comments. Prof Norio Tsuge ardently presented me new developments of land tenure in Japan, and sent me updated materials and beneficial comments.

Dr Gustavo Gordillo, Prof Hans Meliczek, Dr James C. Riddell and Dr Paolo Groppo supported my research, gave me productive comments, provided me with the opportunities to make contributions at international level, and promoted the publication of my three articles before the defence and two afterwards by the Food and Agriculture Organization of the United Nations, which constituted the core of the thesis. Dr Janice Osborn and her team selected my six publications from the enormous amount of literature around the world for publishing their abstracts in *World Agricultural Economics and Rural Sociology Abstracts* of CABI (Commonwealth Agricultural Bureau International) (see the attached list 2).

After the defence, the thesis has been reworked with some contents condensed and new contents added for publication. Prof Domenico Mario Nuti introduced me the possible applicability of my proposed new model in CEECs and the CIS, Prof Stuart Holland encouraged me to extend research into the American agriculture, Prof Michael Artis, Mr Edward Elgar and Miss Dymphna Evans further supported me to write a new part, hence Chapters 9–11. On the US part, Dr James C. Riddell again extended valuable help, Ms Beverly R. Phillips introduced me to key literature, Dr Gene Wunderlich, Dr Janet Perry and Dr David Banker carefully read my lengthy draft and contributed very important comments. I received the honor of joining OECD's experts group on agricultural policies of emerging market and non-member economies and attending its forums in October 1998 in Paris, where I obtained opportunities to know more about the situations in the countries covered by this part from the nice and helpful participants and OECD staff. In particular, Prof Zvi Lerman, Dr Andrzej Kwiecinski, and Dr Eberhard Schulze patiently answered my various questions on CEECs and the CIS. I have also been greatly helped by Prof Augusto Marinelli and Prof Donato Romano.

Ms Ann Micheli voluntarily and carefully polished the whole manuscript.

An anonymous referee commissioned by the publisher gave constructive comments according to which the manuscript has been revised. University of Florence kindly afforded support for me to complete the preparation for the publication.

My parents raised me from childhood enduring much hardship. In order to carry out research in Italy, when successively they were seriously ill, I could not directly take care of them. Other members of our family had kindly borne this duty for me, and rendered me various support, thus made it possible for me to complete this work. A number of my relatives and friends in China also helped me.

Mr Xiao-Ping Deng (Deng, Xiao-Ping) was the chief designer of China's economic reforms and opening to the outside world. His historic contributions made it possible for Chinese farmers and officials to experiment with and find effective ways to overcome the inefficient land-holding by part-time and absent small farmers which, as a world-wide problem, has perpetuated the fragmented small farms as the last obstacle in sustainable rural development of monsoon Asia that the Japanese model under private land ownership has been unable to resolve ever since 1960; to promote appropriate large-scale farming while not crowding out small-scale farmers which is the target that the USA and many other OECD and EU countries have not achieved since the 1930s; to facilitate the transition of farm structure towards market economy which CEECs and the CIS have not yet succeeded since the late 1980s and early 1990s respectively; to eliminate rural poverty which is still the aim of numerous developing countries around the world; to prevent food overproduction which even developed countries have not realized; and further to improve the environment, and also for me to come abroad to carry out this comparative study and make possible contributions in these fields.

Needless to say, I take sole responsibility for my views in this book. Precious comments of all the distinguished readers are hereby cordially invited. Technical errors have been checked. But it would be possible that some may still remain in this over-500-page work, for whose disturbances to the eminent readers I would feel very sorry and should be most grateful if they could be conveyed to me.[1]

J.-M. Zhou
February 2001

---

[1] My email addresses are <Zhou@iue.it> and <Jmzhou46@hotmail.com>.

List 1: My Papers Presented in International Conferences (15 in total)

AISSEC — Italian Association for the Study of Comparative Economic Systems
EACES — European Association for Comparative Economic Studies
EARIE — European Association for Research in Industrial Economics
EEA — European Economic Association
FAO — Food and Agriculture Organization of the United Nations
USDA — US Department of Agriculture

1. 12—14 October 1989: 'China's Economic Reforms through Two Stages - The Case of the Industrial Enterprises', Sixth AISSEC Scientific Conference, in University of Urbino, Italy.

2. 2—4 September 1990: 'Short-Term Behavior of Chinese Industrial Enterprises', 17th EARIE Annual Conference, in Catholic University of Portugal, Lisbon.

3. 27—29 September 1990: 'The Inevitable Direction of China's Economic Reforms in Agriculture', First EACES Conference and Seventh AISSEC Scientific Conference, in University of Verona, Italy.

4. 30 August — 2 September 1991: 'The Trend of China's Economic Reform in Agriculture', Sixth EEA Annual Congress, in Department of Applied Economics, University of Cambridge, UK.

5. 3—5 October 1991: 'Why Is Lease System Successful in China?', Eighth AISSEC Scientific Conference, in Faculty of Economics and Commerce, University of Trieste, Italy.

6. 24—26 September 1992: 'Privatization, State—Private Mixed Economy or Improved Collective—Private Mixed Economy? Alternative Approaches for Further Agricultural Ownership Reform in China', Second EACES Conference, in Faculty of Economics, University of Groningen, the Netherlands.

7. 8—10 September 1994: 'A Third Way: Neither Collectivization Nor Full Privatization - Mixed Economy in Chinese Agriculture', Third EACES Conference, in Department of Comparative Economics, Budapest University of Economic Sciences, Hungary.

8. 9—13 April 1996: 'Agrarian Reform and Rural Development Strategies in China, Japan and Other Rice-Based Economies of Monsoon Asia', Rural Development: International Workshop, organized by FAO, in Department of Rural Sociology, University of Godollo, Hungary.

9. 12—14 September 1996: 'How to Overcome the Small Size Obstacle in Japan and Some Other Rice-Based Economies in Asia', Fourth EACES Conference, in Institute for Political Studies, University Pierre Mendes

France, Grenoble.

10. 10–12 September 1998: 'Is Nominal Public But *De Facto* Private Land Ownership Appropriate? - A Comparative Study among Cambodia, Laos, Vietnam; Japan, Taiwan Province of China, South Korea; China, Myanmar; and North Korea', Fifth EACES Conference, in Bulgarian Academy of Sciences, Golden Sands, Varna, Bulgaria.

11. 12–15 October 1999: 'Preserving Small while Strengthening Large Farmers in the USA and OECD', Second National Small Farm Conference, organized by USDA, St. Louis, Missouri.

12. 9–10 December 1999: 'Present Situation and Solution for Farm-Restructuring in the CIS and CEECs', Conference of 'The Present and the Future of the Russian Economy: Problems, Approaches, Solutions', organized by the Ministry of General Education and Vocational Training of Russian Federation, and Department of Economic Theory and World Economy, Faculty of Economics, Perm State University, Perm, Russia.

13. 16–18 December 1999: 'A New Proposal for Agricultural Transition in the CEECs and CIS', European Integration and Economies in Transition Conference, organized by East–West Cooperation in Economics of University of Crete, Department of Economics of University of Crete, and Department of Business Administration of University of the Aegean, Chios, Greece.

14. 5–7 January 2000: 'Land Consolidation and Expansion in China in the Reform Era', Sixth European Conference on Agricultural and Rural Development in China, organized by University of Leiden, the Netherlands.

15. 7–9 September 2000: 'A Third Way for Farm-Restructuring in the CIS and CEECs', Sixth EACES Conference, in Faculty of Economics, University of Barcelona, Spain.

List 2: My Publications (20 in total)

CABI   - Commonwealth Agricultural Bureau International
EACES - European Association for Comparative Economic Studies
EUI   - European University Institute, Italy
FAO   - Food and Agriculture Organization of the United Nations
USDA   - US Department of Agriculture

1. 1990: 'Le Due Fasi delle Riforme Economiche in Cina: il Caso delle Imprese Industriali' [China's Economic Reforms through Two Stages - The Case of the Industrial Enterprises], *Economia e Banca* [Economics and Banking], Banca di Trento e Bolzano [Bank of Trento and Bolzano], No. 3: 385–416. (In Italian)

2. 24–26 September 1992: Abstract of 'Privatization, State–Private Mixed Economy or Improved Collective–Private Mixed Economy?

Alternative Approaches for Further Agricultural Ownership Reform in China', *Proceedings of the Second EACES Conference*, in Faculty of Economics, University of Groningen, the Netherlands.

3. 9–13 April 1996: 'Agrarian Reform and Rural Development Strategies in China, Japan and Other Rice-Based Economies of Monsoon Asia', FAO (ed.) 1997 *Rural Development: International Workshop*: 44, 145–56; <http://www.fao.org>, search 'Jian-Ming Zhou'.

4. Abstract No. 3313 (of the above-mentioned publication), Vol. 40, No. 6, June 1998, *World Agricultural Economics and Rural Sociology Abstracts*, CABI.

5. 22 November 1996: *Proposals for Land Consolidation and Expansion in Japan*, EUI Working Paper ECO No. 96/36; <http://www.iue.it>, 'Department of Economics', 'Working Papers'.

6. Abstract No. 5508 (of the above-mentioned publication), Vol. 39, No. 10, October 1997, *World Agricultural Economics and Rural Sociology Abstracts*, CABI.

7. 1 October 1997: 'A New Proposal for Land Consolidation and Expansion in Japan and Other Economies', FAO *Sustainable Development Dimensions in the Internet* (voted *Internet's No. 1 website* - leading 78 top sites - on sustainable development by Lycos visitors, March 1998), <http://www.fao.org>, search 'Jian-Ming Zhou'.

8. 1998: 'Land Consolidation in Japan and Other Rice-Based Economies under Private Land Ownership in Monsoon Asia', *Land Reform, Land Settlement and Cooperatives*, FAO, No. 1: 123–34; <http://www.fao.org>, search 'Jian-Ming Zhou'.

9. 10 March 1998: *Is Nominal Public But De Facto Private Land Ownership Appropriate? - A Comparative Study among Cambodia, Laos, Vietnam; Japan, Taiwan Province of China, South Korea; China, Myanmar; and North Korea*, EUI Working Paper ECO No. 98/12; <http://www.iue.it>, 'Department of Economics', 'Working Papers'.

10. Abstract No. 1422 (of the above-mentioned publication), Vol. 41, No. 3, March 1999, *World Agricultural Economics and Rural Sociology Abstracts*, CABI.

11. January 1999: *How to Carry Out Land Consolidation - An International Comparison*, EUI Working Paper ECO No. 99/1; <http://www.iue.it>, 'Department of Economics', 'Working Papers'.

12. 12–15 October 1999 (forthcoming): Abstract of *Preserving Small while Strengthening Large Farmers in the USA and OECD*, proceedings of the Second National Small Farm Conference, organized by USDA, St. Louis, Missouri; text posted by University of Minnesota in its electronic library: <http://agecon.lib.umn.edu/>, search 'Jian-Ming Zhou'.

13. 16–18 December 1999 (forthcoming): *A New Proposal for*

Agricultural Transition in the CEECs and CIS, proceedings of the European Integration and Economies in Transition Conference, organized by the Journal *East–West Cooperation in Economics*, Department of Economics of University of Crete, and Department of Business Administration of University of the Aegean, Chios, Greece.

14. Abstract (of the above-mentioned publication, forthcoming), *World Agricultural Economics and Rural Sociology Abstracts*, CABI.

15. 7–9 September 2000 (forthcoming): *A Third Way for Farm-Restructuring in the CIS and CEECs*, proceedings of the Sixth EACES Conference, in Faculty of Economics, University of Barcelona, Spain.

16. 2000: 'Principal Forms of Land Consolidation and Expansion in China', *Land Reform, Land Settlement and Cooperatives*, FAO, No. 1: 88–107; <http://www.fao.org>, search 'Jian-Ming Zhou'.

17. Abstract (of the above-mentioned publication, 2001 forthcoming), *World Agricultural Economics and Rural Sociology Abstracts*, CABI.

18. 2001 (forthcoming): 'Functioning of the Appropriate Large-Scale Farming in China', *Land Reform, Land Settlement and Cooperatives*, FAO, No. 1; <http://www.fao.org>, search 'Jian-Ming Zhou'.

19. 2001: *Sustainable Development in Asia, America and Europe with Global Applications: A New Approach to Land Ownership*, Cheltenham, UK: Edward Elgar Publishing.

20. Abstract (of the above-mentioned publication, 2002 forthcoming), *World Agricultural Economics and Rural Sociology Abstracts*, CABI.

PART ONE

THEORIES

1. Introduction

1.1 Monsoon Asia

In general, the monsoon climate in Asia causes rains in May–October and dryness in November–April. Only rice best suits this climate. It has been the major crop for at least 4,000 years.1 Up to the end of World War Two (WWII), a system of feudal landlord ownership had been dominant: a few landlords owned large estates while most peasants owned little or no land and were either tenants or wage laborers, although a minority were also owner-peasants. Farm work had to be manual, using simple tools. Reclamation of new land had reached its limit. With such traditional institutions and technologies and physical constraints, in the rainy half of the year, rice cultivation required highly labor-intensive, sophisticated and coordinated work, resulting in labor shortage. This increased the demand for labor and caused high population growth, which in turn lowered the size of cultivated land per capita and reduced the size of individual (family) farming units, which were further fragmented mainly by equalized inheritance of land in terms of its quality, quantity and distance.2 In contrast, during the dry

---

[1] There are 19 rice-based economies in monsoon Asia: China (mainland), Japan, Democratic People's Republic of Korea (hereafter North Korea), Republic of Korea (hereafter South Korea) and Taiwan Province of China in East Asia; Cambodia, Indonesia, Laos, Malaysia, Myanmar (Burma), the Philippines, Thailand and Vietnam in Southeast Asia; and Bangladesh, Bhutan, India, Nepal, Pakistan and Sri Lanka in South Asia. Because little food is produced domestically in Hong Kong, Macao (whose sovereignties were returned to China in July 1997 and December 1999 respectively) and Singapore, these three monsoon Asia economies are not analyzed in this book. (Barker; Herdt & Rose 1985: 1. Oshima 1987: 9; 1993: 1)

[2] 'Farm' (or farming unit) means 'agricultural holding', which refers to all land that is used wholly or partly for agricultural production and *is operated by one person* - the holder - alone or with the assistance of others, without regard to title, size or location (livestock kept for agricultural purposes without agricultural land is also considered as constituting a holding) (FAO-PY 1972: 408).

Fragmentation of an agricultural holding is generally defined as the division of the holding into *many* discrete parcels in a village (Fre-Gov 1950: 56. Binns 1950: 5). But some just define

3

half of the year, the insufficient work opportunities led to serious unemployment, underemployment or disguised unemployment.3 (Oshima 1987: 18–27). These economies were dual economies, predominantly agricultural but with some industries in large cities.4 There was a widespread and persistent vicious circle of poverty within agriculture and between agriculture and industry.

Since then, with the same natural conditions, this economic situation has been transformed in some rice-based economies but still dominates in the others. In overcoming poverty, two basic models of rural development have been successful (although to different extent): the Japanese and Chinese models. While other economies under private land ownership may be at different stages along the Japanese model, those based on public land ownership may be at earlier stages of the Chinese one.

1.2 A Remaining Obstacle Unresolved by the Japanese Model

The Japanese model of rural development under private land ownership began in 1946 and progressed through nine major features or stages.

1. *Institutional changes for an individual–cooperative mixed economy (1946–50)*: introduction of land reform for individual ownership, which brought in huge incentives to peasants for production, but also maintained numerous fragmented small farms; and the setting-up of rural service cooperatives.

2. *Government policies supporting rice production and rural development.*

---

it as the situation in which a household operates *more than one* separate parcel of land (Blarel; Hazell; Place & Quiggin 1992: 233. Vander Meer 1982: 1).

A parcel is defined as all land in the holding entirely surrounded by land or water of other holdings or by land or water not forming part of any holding (FAO 1981: 92). It may also be called 'noncontiguous piece of land', 'plot' or 'land unit'.

Fragmentation is measured by the number of parcels of land in the holding in one village (the case of families holding land in several villages is excluded) (Heston & Kumar 1983: 199).

[3] Unemployment and underemployment are variously defined in labor force surveys, but the fundamental definitions are: (1) Those who are willing and able to work but cannot find work are *unemployed*. (2) Among those employed, those who are working less than full time and want more hours of work are *underemployed*. (Oshima 1993: 103). (3) The part of the population engaged in agriculture who could be removed without reducing agricultural output (hence their zero marginal product), even though the technical methods in use remain unchanged, are *disguisedly unemployed* (Nurkse 1953: 32).

[4] Although prewar Japan was developed, its industrialization was based on its import of foods from and export of industrial goods to colonies. Its agriculture was relatively stagnant. (Oshima 1987: 39, 109)

Besides institutional changes, technological progress also contributed to economic growth, which was embodied in features 3–8.

Five steps (3–7 below) were taken in order to achieve full employment:

3. *Construction of rural infrastructure*;

4. *Higher yields and multiple cropping of rice and other grains*;

5. *Diversified cropping5 and non-crop agriculture6*;

6. *Off-farm employment7* and

7. *Peasant migration to cities and work in town and village firms.*

As full employment was realized, wages rose. Hence a post-full employment step:

8. *Agricultural mechanization with small machinery.*

In 1960, rice self-sufficiency was attained, the first transition (agriculture to industry) completed, labor shortages appeared, and the second transition (industry to services) started.8 *Shattering the vicious circle of rural poverty by 1960 in the Japanese model could be regarded as the first breakthrough in sustainable rural development of monsoon Asia.9*

However, although most of the major obstacles imposed by the monsoon have been overcome, there has still been:

9. *Persistence of the fragmented small farms, due to inefficient land-*

---

[5] Diversified cropping implies a shift from a monoculture or a few crops (mainly grains) to a larger assortment of crops (roots and tubers, pulses, oil crops, vegetables, fruits, berries, treenuts, etc.) (Oshima 1993: 125. FAO-YP 1993: iv).

[6] Agriculture - depending on the context of the book - in a broad sense includes cropping (farming), animal husbandry, fishery, forestry and hunting (Oshima 1993: 152) (the importance of hunting has been in decline as environmental protection interests increase); but in a narrow sense may only refer to cropping (farming).

[7] Off-farm employment of farm families denotes their employment in non-agricultural sectors, i.e., industry and services. Industry includes mining, manufacturing, construction, public utilities, transportation and communication. Services comprise banking, real estate, public services which require the highest level of education and retail trade, restaurants, domestic and other personal services which only need minimal education. (Oshima 1993: 138, 152)

[8] In monsoon Asia, the first transition is said to be completed when the share of the agricultural labor force in the total labor force has fallen from about three-quarters to roughly one-third or one-quarter, while the share of the industrial labor force has risen. The second transition is said to be concluded when the service sector overtakes the industrial sector in size of labor force. But there are elements of arbitrariness in the definitions and some exceptions may be possible. (Oshima 1987: 56, 58)

[9] In 1991, FAO/Netherlands Conference on Agriculture and the Environment defined the essential and interdependent goals of sustainable agricultural and rural development as 'Food security, to be obtained by ensuring an appropriate and sustainable balance between self-sufficiency and self-reliance; employment and income generation in rural areas, particularly to eradicate poverty; and natural resource conservation and environmental protection' (SDD-FAO 1995: 1).

holding by part-time and absent small farmers.

In the high wage economy, income from rice production turned out to be much lower than that from non-grain agriculture and especially off-farm activities. As argued in detail later, in order to make full-time farmers viable,10 it was necessary to consolidate fragmented agricultural holdings and increase farm size,11 so that large machinery could be used, labor saved, costs reduced and increasing returns to scale gained. However, much land was held by part-time and absent small farmers with inefficient use, while the remaining full-time farmers could not obtain larger areas of land to till.

From the 1950s onwards various attempts were made to counteract the relevant aspects of the fragmented small farms problem. Efforts at promoting *land consolidation* since the 1950s were complemented by encouraging farm expansion through the *sale of land* in the 1960s, and, from 1970, *land lease*. All were not very successful. A number of further experiments followed: the introduction of *commissioned agricultural work* and *agricultural production cooperatives*12 (the collective use of private farmland as an individual—collective mixed economy, from sub-village to village-wide), and finally the promotion of *urban—rural joint farming* (this also involved the collective use of private farmland as an individual—collective mixed economy). In all these experiments, the private land ownership either hindered the achievement of economies of scale, or (in the case of village-wide collective use of private farmland) hampered the transformation of private parcels into non-farmland means of production (which refers to land-constituted assets other than farmland such as dam, road, canal, pond) while at the same time was unable to prevent the withdrawal of land and re-division of the amalgamated parcels.

---

[10] Farms that earn income per farm household member equal to, or above, that of non-farm employees who are living in rural areas are 'viable units' (Hayami 1988: 77).

[11] 'Farm size' may refer to the acreage of the land, or number of households, of the farm. The large farm size advocated in this book for monsoon Asia rice-based economies denotes the *large size in land acreage of a farm* under village—individual dual level operation, with the basic operation level at one household as the major form or at a unit including a small number of households as the minor form.

[12] There are various types of agricultural production collectives, cooperatives and enterprises in the world, many overlaps among them and much confusion in using these terms. It is impossible in this book to clarify them and put a 'correct' label on each. Nevertheless, a rough demarcation among them may be seen from the land ownership point of view: in a production collective, land is collectively owned; in a production cooperative, land is privately owned but collectively used to some extent; a production enterprise is a unit of accounting and operation assuming sole profits and losses, thus could be either a collective or cooperative or household.

In order to be viable and gain higher incomes, farmers and cooperatives lobbied for government *protection* of the domestic rice production. The ruling party yielded, fearing the loss of their votes. Thus costs and prices rose well above prevailing international levels. The government subsidies to farmers resulted in major budget deficits. Rice import prohibition during 1961−93 caused international protests. Following a natural disaster and loss of rice self-sufficiency in 1993, since 1994, cheap rice has had to be imported and rice self-sufficiency restored by continuous subsidies. In Japan, therefore, the critical issue remains that of how to consolidate and enlarge the fragmented small farms which have so far resisted restructuring.

The fragmented small farms were efficient in a low wage economy when there was little off-farm employment and labor was cheaper than large machinery, since they were conducive to the development and diffusion of land-saving and scale-neutral technology, dispersion of natural risks, and provision of employment to peasants. But in a high wage economy when large amount of labor has been absorbed by off-farm activities, and large machinery has thus become cheaper than labor, the inefficient holding of the fragmented small farms by part-time and absent small farmers hampers the achievement of land economies of scale, and is wasteful of land, labor, capital, management, and technology resources. This problem is common to all rapidly industrializing economies with limited land and reduced agricultural labor force, under private or public land ownership alike (though the degrees of fragmentation and smallness of farms may vary). Of the other rice-based economies under private land ownership in monsoon Asia, Taiwan and South Korea replicated the Japanese model (Hayami & Yamada 1991: 7). Malaysia, Thailand, Indonesia and the Philippines; Bangladesh, India, Pakistan, Sri Lanka; Bhutan and Nepal are generally at earlier phases of the model. Their fragmented small farm structure also would be harmful not only once the whole rural areas have entered the high wage economy, but also when some rural areas have, but others have not, reached the high wage economy, as many peasants at the low wage economy would go to those rural areas already at the high wage stage and cities to earn higher income, while still holding their land in inefficient use. (We will see that inefficient land-holding by part-time and absent small farmers has also appeared in China and other rice-based economies under public land ownership in monsoon Asia in Chapters 6−8, in the USA although the American small farmers' farm size is much larger than that in monsoon Asia and rice is not the major crop in Chapter 10, and in other parts of the world in Chapter 11.)

The fragmented small farms, owing to the inefficient land-holding by part-time and absent small farmers, therefore, has become the *remaining* or *last* obstacle imposed by the monsoon to sustainable agricultural and rural development in monsoon Asia (Oshima 1987: 65). This problem has also

been used as an argument against land reform of the feudal landlord
ownership systems prevailing in other rice-based economies of monsoon
Asia, on the grounds that the Japanese experience has demonstrated that the
benefits of scale economies will be lost if estate farming is dissolved
(Koppel 1993: 4. Takahashi 1993: 107). Although substantial analysis of this
problem has been made by many economists in this field for many years,
fundamental solutions have not yet been found (e.g., Bray 1986. Oshima
1987. Hayami 1988. Rothacher 1989. Hayami & Yamada 1991. Oshima
1993. OECD 1995. NIRA 1995. Francks 1996[13]).

1.3 The Chinese Model

The Chinese model of rural development which constitutes a third way
beyond the centrally planned economy and free market system, started in
1978 and has progressed through 13 major features or stages.

　　1. *Institutional changes for a small-scale farming and collective–
individual mixed economy (1978–83).* Land was collectively owned by the
village, but contracted to households in order to fulfil state procurement
output quotas of grain and other major agricultural products and dispose of
surplus output, which brought about huge incentives for peasants to increase
production. Land was distributed equally in terms of quality, quantity and
distance, hence the *Equal Land System*, creating numerous fragmented small
farms. The village had the duty of carrying out general management and
providing services, thus a village–household dual level operation of land,
with the households as the basic level.

　　2. *Government policies supporting rice production and rural development.*
(Technological progress was embodied in features 3–8 and 10–13).

　　3. *Construction of rural infrastructure.*

　　4. *Higher yields and multiple cropping of rice and other grains.*

　　5. *Diversified cropping and non-crop agriculture.*

　　6. *Off-farm employment.*

　　7. *Peasant migration to cities and work in town and village firms.*

---

[13] Bray (1986: 217) recommends an end to rice production as she concludes her book with
a statement that 'The chief problems of Japanese agriculture today seem largely to be caused
through Japanese farmers' reluctance to *abandon* growing rice'.

　　NIRA (1995: 173) claims that 'For the time being, our objectives should focus on easing
and on *partially* solving this issue'.

　　Francks (1996: 21) admits that her paper 'has done no more than raise' questions. In answer
to the author's question whether she knew of any solutions to this problem in her seminar in
the School of Oriental and African Studies, London, November 1995, she said: 'If I knew any
solutions, I would become someone like the Japanese Agricultural Minister.'

8. *Agricultural mechanization with small machinery.*

These eight features in general are similar to their counterparts in the Japanese model (the major differences being the individual land ownership in feature 1 and rice import protectionism during 1961—93 in feature 2 of the Japanese model) and had achieved similar positive effects by 1984 as had Japan by 1960.

Also similar to Japan, as the Eastern and coastal areas entered the high wage economy, increasing numbers of part-time and absent small farmers in not only these areas but also Central and Western areas held land in inefficient use, while the remaining full-time farmers were unable to contract enough land to be viable. Hence a second round of institutional changes was introduced around the mid-1980s (in some areas earlier, even at the beginning of the decade):

9. *Institutional changes for a large-scale farming and collective—individual mixed economy (starting roughly around 1985).* These changes took various forms: the *Dual Land System* (whereby self-sufficiency land was distributed to everybody, responsibility land was contracted to everybody, every labor force, every agricultural labor force, or expert farmers via tendering for higher output which was the standard form); the *Leasing System* (whereby responsibility land was leased to expert farmers via tendering for higher monetary rent, a special form of the Dual Land System); the *Single Land System* (in which ordinary households were sold grain for self-consumption at lower prices and given family plots for vegetables, but all the other land was contracted to expert farmers through a tendering system); and the *Corporate-Holding System* (in which ordinary households gave contracted land back to the village which then re-contracted it to expert farmers via tendering and paid dividends, sold grain for self-consumption at lower prices and distributed family plots for vegetables to ordinary households, which in practice also was a kind of the Single Land System). By these methods, land was distributed in more compact and larger units. The following results ensued.

10. *Agricultural mechanization with large machinery* now was possible.

11. *Earlier development in some (chiefly Eastern and coastal) rural areas, and its promotion in other (mainly Central and Western) areas*[14]

---

[14] There are in total 34 regional administrative units at provincial level in China, including 22 provinces, four municipalities, five autonomous regions, and two special administrative regions. 12 are in the Eastern part: (from south to north) Taiwan, Fujian, Zhejiang, Shanghai (Municipality), Jiangsu, Shandong, Hebei, Tianjin (Municipality), Beijing (Municipality, capital), Liaoning, Jilin and Heilongjiang provinces; 12 in the Central part: (from south to north) Hainan, Guangdong, Macao (Special Administrative Region), Hong Kong (Special Administrative Region), Guangxi (Zhuang Autonomous Region), Hunan, Jiangxi, Hubei, Anhui, Henan, Shanxi

especially from the early 1990s on could occur, and

12. *Introduction of more advanced technology and management, larger investment, and domestic and international markets to agriculture by urban–rural joint enterprises, and external15 and foreign single and joint ventures* also became feasible.

The evolutionary trend of land tenure may be seen as passing from the Equal Land System, through the Dual Land System, towards the Single Land System. While the development of non-grain agriculture and off-farm activities capable of absorbing surplus labor was a necessary condition for land consolidation and expansion, collective land ownership minimized the bargaining power of the part-time and absent small farmers who refused to give back land. Thus the Chinese model has found a number of effective ways to overcome the last obstacle imposed by the monsoon to sustainable rural development, i.e., the fragmented small farms, and may be considered superior to the Japanese model and therefore of relevance to other rice-based economies in the region.16 *Overcoming this final obstacle by public land ownership around the mid-1980s in the Chinese model could be perceived as the **second breakthrough** in sustainable rural development of monsoon Asia.*

Consequently, China was able to ascend a higher stage to fulfil a new task: 13. *Prevention of food overproduction, promotion in quality and perfectization in variety of agricultural products, and improvement of the environment, while strengthening development of the Central and especially the Western areas, mainly from mid-1999,* and has already achieved initial success. *Resolving food overproduction could be viewed as the **third***

---

[15] 'External' refers to Hong Kong, Macao and Taiwan, which are not 'foreign'.

[16] The superiority of the Chinese model upon public land ownership to the Japanese one under private land ownership may be arguably beyond the overcoming of this last obstacle. For example, China has generally prevented homelessness of people as those peasants who have lost jobs in off-farm activities could return to cultivate land while in Japan homeless people in cities who were mainly from rural areas have been increasing in the 1990s (see Chapter 5). In China, in order to achieve higher efficiency, enormous numbers of state employees previously under life-time employment have had to seek jobs in the market especially since the second half of the 1990s. A part of them has found jobs in reclamation and cultivation of waste mountain, hill, beach and gully (as four wastes), waste water and desert with contracts as long as up to 100 years, which was made possible by public land ownership. In contrast, in Japan, both unemployment and under-used/idled farmland have been increasing. But this book has to concentrate on showing the superiority of the Chinese model on overcoming the last obstacle.

breakthrough in *sustainable rural development of monsoon Asia and even of the world*, because this has not been fulfilled even by the USA and many other OECD, including EU, countries17 for decades.

Other rice-based economies under public land ownership in monsoon Asia - Myanmar; Cambodia, Laos, Vietnam; and North Korea - may be regarded as at earlier levels of the Chinese model of rural development.

1.4 The Agenda of the Book

Part 1 'Theories', which contains Chapters 1, 2 and 3, assesses economic theories in relation to practical issues.

Chapter 1 'Introduction' not only presents the structure of the book, but also examines the proximate sources and ultimate causes of the economic growth and analytical approach used in the book. In particular, it points out that *contrary* to Schultz's assertions, increasingly from at least the mid-1950s on, in (1) the low income countries still saddled with traditional agriculture, (2) the low income countries developing towards the high income economy, and (3) the high income countries, the part-time and absent small farmers are not so efficient in farming, and at least some of them are not so rational to the society's and their own fundamental interests, although the knowledge and other conditions are available for both them and the remaining full-time farmers to produce the same output with fewer resources or a larger output from the same resources; and the tenet 'that the costs of agricultural products fall as the size of the production unit in agriculture increases' does have logical basis, and have stood the test of time and empirical findings in the high income economy.

Chapter 2 'Theories of Monsoon Asia Rice Economy and Variable Mixed Economies' discusses theories of free market forces and the dual economy, with reference to monsoon Asia rice-based agriculture, the prewar vicious circle of poverty in monsoon Asia, the postwar initial conditions for development in monsoon Asia, and variable mixed economies. It argues that free market forces alone could not overcome the vicious circle of poverty and realize sustainable rural development in monsoon Asia, whereas variable mixed economy solutions have registered varying degrees of success.

---

[17] The Organization for Economic Cooperation and Development (OECD) includes 29 countries: Austria*, Belgium*, Canada, Denmark*, France*, Germany*, Greece*, Iceland, Ireland*, Italy*, Luxembourg*, the Netherlands*, Norway, Portugal*, Spain*, Sweden*, Switzerland, Turkey, UK*, USA (original members in 1960), Japan (joined in 1964), Finland* (1969), Australia (1971), New Zealand (1973), Mexico (1994), the Czech Republic (1995), Hungary, Poland and South Korea (1996), in which, 15 countries with * are members of the European Union (EU).

According to Holland, mixed economy refers to multiple structures of public and private ownership, and government intervention other than ownership, and variable mixed economies imply varying relations between the public and private sectors which dynamically change over time in relation to changing needs in economy and society. In particular, within the variable mixed economies, there is Nuti's model of market socialism which submits that the state-owned means of production could be leased to individuals to be operated efficiently according to market principles. The Chinese model actually is compatible with both Holland's concept of variable mixed economies and Nuti's model of market socialism.

Hence a *hypothesis* by the author: the fragmented small farms as the last obstacle imposed by the monsoon to sustainable rural development of Asia may be overcome by variable mixed economies, increasingly along three main phases.

Phase 1: sub-village individual—collective mixed economy (sub-village-wide cooperative/enterprise collective use of physically withdrawable private land shares, exercising collective—individual dual level operation of large land units, with the basic operation level at one household as the major form or at a unit including a small number of households as the minor form).

Phase 2: village-wide individual—collective mixed economy.

Phase 3: either large-scale farming public—individual mixed economy or corporate—individual mixed economy (collective use of either public land, or physically unwithdrawable private land shares under corporate ownership, exercising village—individual dual level operation of large land units, with the basic operation level at one household as the major form or at a unit including a small number of households as the minor form, as a third way beyond the centrally planned economy and free market system).

This three-phase hypothesis will be discussed in theory in Chapter 3 and tested in Chapters 4—8 with the *focus* on how to consolidate and enlarge the fragmented small farms in monsoon Asia under private and public land ownership with reference to the Japanese and Chinese models, and under village-wide corporate land ownership as a proposed new model.

Chapter 3 'Theory of Property Rights' reviews those theoretical viewpoints most relevant to the book's focus, i.e., (1) incentives under private ownership and possession of public assets (including property rights, ownership, possession, incentive and Pareto efficiency, and technological efficiency); (2) achieving Pareto efficiency according to Coase (containing externalities and the Coase theorem); (3) reaching Pareto efficiency when the hypotheses of the Coase theorem are relaxed (consisting of positive transaction costs, income effects, approaches in assignment of property rights, a transaction costs approach towards the choice among private, public and corporate land ownership, and Pio's puzzle); (4) the evolution of property rights structures (referring to the timing of, and general methods for, changing the existing property rights structures), and (5) relevant concepts of private ownership (capitalist, individual and capitalistic ownership).

Appendix 3.1 'How to Carry Out Land Consolidation - An International Comparison' makes a comparative international survey of general methods of land consolidation under private farmland ownership so as to show its very high transaction costs. The methods for assessment of the value of current farmland holdings will be used to calculate private land shares in the proposed new model in Chapter 5.

Part 2 'The Japanese Model and a New Model' comprises Chapters 4 and 5.

Chapter 4 'The Japanese Model versus the Last Obstacle' analyzes the significance of the Japanese model up to feature 8, and the remaining obstacle as feature 9, makes theoretical discussions, and tests the above-mentioned hypothesis.

Chapter 5 is 'A New Model for Sustainable Rural Development'. The book does not aim to repeat the analyses of the last obstacle already made by many economists, but *intends to solve it*. Hence conjectural *Proposal 5.1*: village-wide corporate ownership of physically unwithdrawable but financially salable private land shares. This conjectural *new model* on a variable mixed economies basis is different from both the Japanese and Chinese ones and may also be useful for other rice-based economies under private land ownership in monsoon Asia in both low wage economy where cooperatives and off-farm activities are not yet developed and in high wage economy where they are, to overcome inefficient land-holding, consolidate and enlarge fragmented small farms, increase farm competitiveness, realize food self-sufficiency, eliminate poverty, and further prevent food overproduction and improve the environment, so as to achieve sustainable rural development. Chapter 5 will state the principles of the new model and its potential applications in various forms in diverse areas of the world, under both private land ownership and private possession in public ownership of land, and undertake theoretical discussions.

Other rice-based economies under private land ownership in monsoon Asia will be categorized roughly into four groups according to their progress along the Japanese model: Group 1. Taiwan and South Korea together with Japan; Group 2. Malaysia, Thailand, Indonesia and the Philippines; Group 3. Bangladesh, India, Pakistan, and Sri Lanka; and Group 4. Bhutan and Nepal. Besides Proposal 5.1, conjectural Proposal 5.2 will be offered to Groups 2–4.

Proposal 5.2: Raising economies of scale of land should be gradual and follow the progress of non-grain agriculture and off-farm activities.

Part 3 'The Chinese Model' includes Chapters 6–8.

Chapter 6 'The Chinese Model and the Emergence of the Last Obstacle' studies general aspects of the Chinese model, and the appearance of the last obstacle (decreasing parcel size and increased fragmentation of land due to population growth, and inefficient use of land by part-time and absent small farmers), plus theoretical discussions.

Chapter 7 'Overcoming the Last Obstacle in the Chinese Model' inspects (1) a large-scale farming and collective–individual mixed economy (Dual Land System, Leasing System, Single Land System, Corporate-Holding System, selection of expert farmers, major problems, and trend of the evolution of the land tenure system); (2) the functioning of large-scale farming (organizations of large-scale farmers, agricultural mechanization with large machinery, optimal size of large-scale farms, subsidies and self-reliance, and related major problems); (3) ascending a higher stage - preventing food overproduction and improving the environment, followed by (4) theoretical discussions concerning, in particular, both overcoming individual bargaining power and avoiding officials' abuse of power by collective land ownership with villagers' democratic participation in order to achieve effective and appropriate large-scale farming.

Chapter 8 'Other Rice-Based Economies under Public Land Ownership in Monsoon Asia' classifies these economies roughly as at earlier levels of the Chinese model: Myanmar, whose land tenure system is quite similar to feature 1 of the Chinese model; Cambodia, Laos and Vietnam, whose newly established nominal state - but *de facto* private - land ownership has resulted in both newly landless and inefficient land-holding; and North Korea, which still retains a centrally planned economy. For these, conjectural proposals 8.1, 8.2 and 8.3 will be submitted.

Proposal 8.1: It is recommended that Cambodia, Laos and Vietnam abolish the nominal state - but *de facto* private - land ownership and pursue the Chinese model.

Proposal 8.2: In the revision of the present land tenure system for a more market-oriented rural development, it is suggested that Myanmar follow features 2–13 of the Chinese model, and avoid turning to a nominal state - but *de facto* private - land ownership.

Proposal 8.3: North Korea is the only country in monsoon Asia and the world which retains a centrally planned economy. It is advised to pursue the various successive features of the Chinese model.

Since Proposal 5.1 may be exercised not only for private land ownership, but also for private possession under public ownership of land, it could also be adopted in Myanmar; Cambodia, Laos and Vietnam; and North Korea. The Chinese model of rural development and Proposal 5.1 might be relevant to those economies based upon public land ownership *outside* monsoon Asia in the process of transition towards market economy as well.

Part 4 'Applications of the New Model beyond Monsoon Asia' is composed of Chapters 9–11.

Chapter 9 'The American Model and the Crowding Out of Small Farmers' demonstrates that in contrast to the Japanese model under which small farmers have hampered the formation of large farmers as one extreme, the American model is at the other extreme - small farmers have been crowded out by large farmers. It generates features 1–6 of the American model of rural development:

1. *Institutional changes for an individual land ownership (1783).*

2. *Government policies supporting agriculture.*

3. *Commercialization of the individual farming units promoting large farmers and driving small farmers to an inferior position.*

4. *Technological progress, managerial resources, rural development, procurement and marketing facilities further strengthening large farmers.*

5. *Government protective safety net (1933–96) failing to avert the trend towards fewer but larger farms since 1935 and prevent small farmers from being crowded out from agriculture.*

6. *Government market-driven measures since 1996 leaving small farmers more exposed to free market forces.*

Chapter 10 'Application of the New Model in the USA' further analyzes features 7 and 8 of the American model.

7. *Part ownership of land tenure dominating since 1950 but never being promoted as a policy direction or a new round of institutional changes.*

8. *The development in recent decades of off-farm employment pursued as subordinate to the loss-making independent small farming resulting in inefficient land-holding by part-time and absent small farmers while only slowing but not halting small farmers' exiting farming.*

Chapter 10 reveals that inefficient land-holding by part-time and absent small farmers has appeared not only in the rice-based economies of monsoon Asia, but also in the USA where corn, soybean and wheat are the major agricultural products. In order to preserve small farmers while still strengthening large farmers and also resolve the inefficient land-holding, conjectural *Proposal 10.1* as one of the various forms of the new model raised in Proposal 5.1 according to its principles will be afforded: to promote part ownership of land and off-farm activities with either a Dual Land System or Single Land System to form a large–small farmers mixed economy.

Chapter 11 'Applications of the New Model in the OECD, EU, CEECs, CIS, and Rest of the World' then briefly demonstrates the possible applications of the new model in various forms in other parts of the world at both low and high wage economy; in other OECD (including EU) countries which have a large versus small bimodal farm structure similar to the USA's; and in CEECs18 and the CIS19 where after land privatization or farm restructuring there have been two possible dilemmas: (1) persistence of both fragmented small individual farms, and unsuccessful collectively operated large farms, and (2) new landlessness owing to sale of land by some poor peasants and land concentration towards influential people at the low wage economy, and inefficient land-holding by part-time and absent small farmers earning higher off-farm income as the rural areas develop towards the high wage economy.

1.5 The Analytical Approach

Institutions versus other variables of growth. Agricultural production is a function of many variables including institutions, technologies, policies, prices, production structures, labor, capital, education, health, weather, etc. Not least, agriculture in China, Japan and many other rice-based economies of monsoon Asia is still vulnerable to bad weather. These variables, however, play different roles.

Oshima (1987: 47, 53) holds that development theories may be distinguished from growth theories in that they are concerned with structural changes.20 Hence, they are more pertinent to developing countries whose

---

[18] There are 15 Central and Eastern European countries (CEECs): Albania, Bosnia and Herzegovina, Bulgaria, Croatia, the Czech Republic, Estonia, Hungary, Latvia, Lithuania, Macedonia, Poland, Romania, Slovakia, Slovenia and Yugoslavia.

[19] In 1991 the USSR was broken up and 12 of the 15 former republics (excluding three Baltic states - Estonia, Latvia and Lithuania) set up the Commonwealth of Independent States (CIS): Armenia, Azerbaijan (joined in 1993), Belarus, Georgia (1993), Kazakhstan, Kyrgyzstan, Moldova (1993), Russia, Tajikistan, Turkmenistan, Ukraine and Uzbekistan, which are also called New Independent States (NISs). Armenia, Azerbaijan, Georgia, Kazakhstan, Kyrgyzstan, Tajikistan, Turkmenistan, and Uzbekistan are in Central Asia.

[20] According to Gillis, Perkins, Roemer and Snodgrass (1992: 8–9), *economic growth* refers to a rise in national or per capita income and product. Per capita income is measured a s the gross national product (the value of all goods and services produced by a country's economy in a year) divided by the population. *Economic development* implies not only economic growth but also fundamental changes in the structure of the economy and people's participation in these changes. The major structural changes are: (1) the rising share of industry, along with the falling share of agriculture, in the national product; (2) an increasing percentage of people who live in cities rather than the countryside; (3) passing through periods of accelerating, then decelerating, population growth, during which the nation's age structure changes dramatically; (4) consumption patterns change as people no longer have to spend all their income on necessities, but instead move on to consume durables and eventually to leisure-time products and services. People of the country must be major participants in the process that brought about these changes and in the production and enjoyment of the benefits of these

structures and underlying institutions are the product of centuries of tradition and lack the flexibility to change with the times. In previous studies of development theories and strategies, the growth of per capita product was explained as owing to either proximate *sources* or ultimate *causes*. There was a tendency to group various inputs into the category of sources (labor, capital, education, structural change, etc.); and to group the explanations o f changes in the productivity of inputs into the category of causes, the major ones being changes in institutions and technologies (broadly coinciding with ways or patterns of thinking and doing).

Oshima himself (1987: 5–6) studies the underlying long-term ultimate causes that sustain economic growth by assuming that growth is largely the outcome of the interplay of institutional and technological changes, as emphasized by Kuznets (1966), and finds that it is the *institutional component* that is the most important in the interaction of institutions and technologies underlying the growth of developing countries.

For example, the growth in agriculture, industry and service sectors of postwar Japan was all initiated by institutional reforms (Oshima 1987: 5– 6, 110–1, 116, 125–7, 134). The land reform was the most important factor among the postwar reforms in Japan in opening the path to rapid economic growth and in eliminating social unrest (Takahashi 1993: 106).

There are well known, typical and parallel examples in China. Since th e implementation of the combination of collective ownership and operation of land in advanced cooperatives during 1956–58, the production of Xiaogang Production Team of Liyuan Commune of Fengyang County of Anhui Province had been declining. All persons who could walk outside t o beg did so. By 1979, due to emigration to other rural areas, household numbers dropped from 34 to 18 and population from 175 persons to about 100. Annual per capita food ranged between 50 and 100 kg (i.e., an average of only 0.14–0.27 kg a day) and annual cash income 15–30 yuan. It became the smallest and poorest production team of the County. On 24 November 1978 - the first in the whole country to do so during the reform period - the Team Director and households initiated 'bao *gan* dao hu', the major form of the Household Contract System21 in the framework of the small-scale farming and collective–individual mixed economy. An area of 517 mu (34.46 ha)22 of collectively owned farmland was contracted

---

changes. The benefits should go to the whole people for equity rather than to a tiny wealthy minority.

[21] The major and minor forms of the Household Contract System will be elaborated in Chapter 6.

[22] 1 ha = 100 are = 10,000 square meters = 15 mu, 1 mu = 0.067 ha = 6.667 are = 666.667 square meters.

proportionately according to population to households equally, along with 10 draft cattle (one for every two households). The state tax and compulsory sale quotas, fees to collectives (commune, brigade and team), and repayment amount of credits were also allocated in the same way. Any surplus output would belong to the households. In the autumn of 1979, the total grain output jumped to over 66,000 kg, equivalent to the sum of the past five years; oil crops rose to 17,500 kg, equal to the total in the preceding 20 years; 135 pigs were raised in the current year, exceeding the number in any of the previous years. 15,000 kg of grain were sold to the state, the first of such sales since 1956, together with 12,466.5 kg of oil crops, as a new sale item. Credits were repaid for the first time by 800 yuan. As a result, annual per capita food reached 510 kg of grain (on average 1.4 kg a day), plus 50.335 kg of oil crops. Cash income averaged 200 yuan. (Yang & Liu 1987: 12–3, 112)

In the summer of 1979, Shannan District of Feixi County in the same Province implemented 'bao *chan* dao hu', the minor form of the Household Contract System. Although suffering from drought, high winds, pests and flood, some production teams achieved a total grain output equivalent to t he sum of the past five–six years. Some poor teams eliminated poverty in the same season even under such adverse conditions. (Chen; Chen & Yang 1993: 484). The Household Contract System proved to be a great success and enabled the provincial authority to convince other regions to adopt it (Kojima 1988: 709–10).

Thus, with the same technologies, government policies, prices and weather, farmers under different local institutions could achieve different production results. Institutional changes giving high incentives to farmers could raise production even in the same season and year.

Of course, in order to achieve sustainable rural development, institutional changes are not sufficient. They need to be followed by technological and structural changes, e.g., construction of rural infrastructure, higher yields a nd multiple cropping of rice and other grains, diversified cropping and non-crop agriculture, off-farm employment, peasant migration to cities and work in town and village firms, and agricultural mechanization with small machinery.

But once production has reached the frontier permitted by the established institutions, even though increases of production are still technologically possible (through agricultural mechanization with large machinery), it tends to be hampered by vested interests, just as feature 9 (persistence of the fragmented small farms, due to inefficient land-holding by part-time and absent small farmers) of the Japanese model has suggested. At this stage, another round of institutional changes is needed to allow sustainable rural development, just as feature 9 (a large-scale farming and collective–

individual mixed economy) of the Chinese model has shown.

Therefore, Barker, Herdt and Rose conclude that of so many variables for rural development, the institutional changes are the keystone (Barker; Herdt & Rose 1985: 157).

Narrative analysis versus econometric models. Oshima emphasizes that in development studies, while the proximate sources of the growth were quantifiable, the longer range ultimate causes were not easily quantified, a nd it was necessary to depend largely on *narrative analysis* or *analytical description* to understand the mechanisms involved. Thus, the 'bottom lines' in the studies of the growth experience of nations became rather ambiguous and indefinite since the major explanatory causes - institutions and technologies - were not measurable and their interactions difficult even to identify in a formal manner. (Oshima 1987: 53. Also see Matthews et al. 1982 for Britain; Carre, Dubois & Malinvaud 1975 for France; Ohkawa & Rosovsky 1973 for Japan; and Abramovitz and David 1973 for the USA). Econometric models thus proved to be of limited use as their results turned out to be highly unstable 'in the face of minor modifications in data specification, observation period and estimation method' (Matthews et al. 1982: 202).

All this meant that long-term analysis could not dispense with historical narrative analysis or analytical description of the development of institutions and technologies as these were important in understanding the role of the parameters, especially in long-term studies. To keep this type of analysis from becoming too diffuse, it was necessary to cast it in transition stages, to partition historical spans, facilitating the analysis of each portion. (Oshima 1987: 53–4)[23]

In Chapter 2, the prewar vicious circle of poverty in monsoon Asia will be assessed which implies historical narrative analysis. Also, keeping in mind

---

[23] Oshima gives two examples of what is meant by historical narrative analysis. (1) Contributing to the rise in total factor productivity in the USA in the early decades of the 20th century (in contrast to its slow growth in the previous century) was the rapid spread from the 1920s of new types of mechanical equipment powered by electric motors and internal combustion engines displacing large numbers of unskilled workers on farms and in industry. Contributing to the quick dissemination of this equipment were the wage increases following immigration restrictions enacted as a result of strong pressures from the American Federation of Labor, together with the pent-up demand for manufactured products from World War One (WWI). (2) In the case of postwar Japan, it was the new institutions introduced by the Allied Occupation and later modified by the Japanese that democratized and demilitarized basic economic and social institutions in the postwar years. Additional institutions were developed that succeeded in motivating peasants, workers, managers and bureaucrats to great heights of productivity as technologies were efficiently imported, adapted, disseminated and utilized. (Oshima 1987: 53–4)

that so many of the features of the Japanese and Chinese models are important, and taking into consideration that this book up to Chapter 8 has to focus on how to overcome the fragmented small farms in monsoon Asia, the emphasis of the analysis has to be on feature 9 of the Japanese and Chinese models, both concerning institutional changes. In Chapters 9 and 10, the historical evolution of the problem in the USA will be analyzed. In Chapter 11, the changes of farm policies and structures in the OECD, CEECs and CIS will be reviewed. Therefore, for the purpose of this book, *the Oshima approach of narrative analysis or analytical description* is used.

1.6 Tentative Contributions of the Book

Chapter 2 'Theories of Monsoon Asia Rice Economy and Variable Mixed Economies' reviews a number of postwar initial economic and social conditions faced by developing economies in monsoon Asia raised by Kuznets, Myrdal and Ishikawa. In contrast to these authors who include Japan with developed countries in the West, the author discovers that these conditions were also applicable to the immediate postwar Japan. This discovery paves the way for the later arguments that Japan had similar problems and tasks as in other rice-based economies of monsoon Asia, and that the Japanese model of rural development is highly relevant to them. According to the concept of variable mixed economies, the author summarizes and classifies various mixed economies later in Chapters 4–11. These include (1) individual–cooperative mixed economy; (2) sub-village individual–collective mixed economy; (3) village-wide individual–collective mixed economy; (4) village-wide corporate–individual mixed economy; (5) small-scale farming and (6) large-scale farming collective–individual mixed economy; (7) public–individual mixed economy; (8) nominal public–individual mixed economy, and (9) large–small farmers mixed economy. In the face of the global wave of privatization and blind worship of free market forces, the author stresses that only by variable mixed economies, rather than free market forces alone, can sustainable rural development and sustainable economic development in general be achieved. In this sense, the implication of the analysis would be beyond rural development and monsoon Asia.

Chapter 3 'Theory of Property Rights' analyzes the importance of negative pecuniary externalities and the relationship between the negative technological and pecuniary externalities. It notes that after most of the former centrally planned economies have adopted a market economy, and most capitalist countries have implemented deregulation, it is negative pecuniary externalities which would be the major negative externalities. They may outweigh negative technological externalities in the current real world but are unfortunately neglected in the literature. It identifies four kinds of negative externalities in time sequence; the definition of internalization of negative externalities, and the distinction between the elimination of negative externalities in financial terms and that in physical and psychological terms. It provides a more complete list of positive transaction costs, and systemizes five approaches in the assignment of property rights for eliminating or efficiently producing negative externalities. Using the Coase transaction costs approach, it discovers the 'secret' or fundamental reason why the consolidation and expansion of the fragmented small farms have been so difficult under the Japanese model but much smoother under the Chinese model, provides a solution to the century-old Pio's puzzle why capitalism has developed securitization for most commodities but not land and why cooperatives with private land shares have never succeeded, and explains that village-wide corporate land ownership could be a suitable way for overcoming this last obstacle in the rice-based economies under private land ownership in monsoon Asia. Accordingly, relevant views of the authorities in the property rights theory field such as Coase, Demsetz, Furubotn and Pejovich, Laffont, Milgrom and Roberts, and Varian are assessed.

Appendix 3.1 'How to Carry Out Land Consolidation - An International Comparison', in contrast to Binns's classic work (1950) on land consolidation upon private farmland ownership and many other similar studies, makes a much wider survey. It advocates the combination of land consolidation with overall rural development, stresses the importance of intervention of governments, education of public opinion, active participation of farmers, and application of modern technologies like satellite remote sensing and computers, and generates useful methods for assessment of the value of current farmland holdings, in order to reduce the transaction costs. Nevertheless, the transaction costs are still too high, hence the comparative advantage of the land consolidation under public land ownership as in the Chinese model and village corporate land ownership as in the proposed new model. The earlier version of it has been published by FAO - the Food and Agriculture Organization of the United Nations (Zhou, Jian-Ming 1998) and abstract by CABI - the Commonwealth Agricultural Bureau International in 'World Agricultural Economics and Rural Sociology Abstracts' (Zhou, Jian-Ming November 1996).

Chapters 4–8 synthesize the postwar rural development approaches to overcoming common obstacles imposed by the monsoon and prewar institutions and technologies in the 19 rice-based economies of monsoon Asia into two basic models: the Japanese and Chinese ones. They reveal that in the low wage economy, the two models have had similar successful features (1–8). However, in the high wage economy, these two models have shown sharp differences in feature 9: while the Japanese model failed to solve the inefficient land-holding by part-time and absent small farmers, and accordingly the last obstacle to sustainable rural development - the fragmented small farms, the Chinese model has succeeded in finding effective ways to surpass it and consequently introduced features 10–13. Hence the superiority of the Chinese model is argued. They then disclose that the success of the Japanese model up to 1960 was due to mixed economies among individuals, cooperatives and governments, rather than free market forces alone, and its failure since then owing to yielding to the free market forces, while the Chinese model can put its success down to the implementation of variable mixed economies via a second round of institutional changes. They further discover that, in general, those rice-based economies based on private land ownership may be regarded as at different stages of the Japanese model, and those on public land ownership at earlier levels of the Chinese one.

Understandably, Wickizer and Bennett are unable to anticipate the postwar paths of sustainable rural development in their 1941 book, which is regarded as the first comprehensive book on the rice-based economies of monsoon Asia (Barker; and Herdt with Rose 1985: xix).

Barker and Herdt with Rose (1985: xix) present their own work as the second comprehensive book on the rice-based economies of monsoon Asia. But they do not note that as early as in 1960 the fragmented small farms have already become an obstacle in the high wage economy of Japan, as they claim (1985: 33) that 'Small farm size is no absolute barrier to agricultural progress, however, as illustrated by Japan and Korea, which have the highest rice yields and fastest economic growth rates in Asia'.

Although Oshima in his book (1987: 65) has realized this last obstacle unresolved by the Japanese model, he is still unaware in his 1993 book that alongside the Japanese one there has been a Chinese model since 1978 which has found effective ways to overcome it even in the early 1980s.

Therefore, the discovery by this book, also trying to be comprehensive on the rice-based economies of monsoon Asia, is appreciated by both FAO and CABI, as its framework has been presented - under FAO's invitation - in its international workshop held in Godollo, Hungary, 9–13 April 1996 and published by FAO in Zhou, Jian-Ming [1996] (1997) with an abstract by CABI.

In Chapters 4 'The Japanese Model versus the Last Obstacle' and 5 'A New Model for Sustainable Rural Development', it is pointed out that the major efforts - and their limits - in overcoming the fragmented small farms obstacle in Japan since the 1970s are not actually 'a Japanese approach to land extensive farming' as acclaimed by Tabata, but a replication of those of the Chinese elementary cooperatives up to April 1956. A possible solution to Pio's puzzle is further provided and a new or *third* model proposed to overcome the last obstacle while still retaining private land ownership - a model which differs from both the Japanese and Chinese ones, as an endeavor for realizing the *second* breakthrough of overcoming the last obstacle in sustainable rural development of monsoon Asia and the *third* breakthrough of preventing food overproduction in not only monsoon Asia but also the world - this time under private land ownership, as they have already been achieved under public land ownership in the Chinese model around the mid-1980s and 2000 respectively. The major content of this new model has also been published by FAO (Zhou, Jian-Ming October 1997).

In Chapter 5, for other rice-based economies under private land ownership in monsoon Asia, this new model is proposed as well. In particular, for those where rural development is still at lower stages, it is stressed not only that the refusal to carry out a complete land reform against the feudal land ownership is wrong, but also that the establishment of large-scale farms with large machinery before rural industrialization can absorb surplus peasants thus making them landless and crowding them into city slums is incorrect, such as in India.24

In Chapter 7 'Overcoming the Last Obstacle in the Chinese Model', based on material relating to the period beginning in the late 1970s until 2000, the large-scale farming and collective−individual mixed economy to overcome the last obstacle in the high wage economy in China is systematically analyzed. Although some Western authors have observed some of the relevant practices, and been cited, such a comprehensive systematization is not found in the literature. A working paper analyzing the large-scale farming and collective−individual mixed economy has been presented in 'The Sixth European Conference on Agricultural and Rural Development in China' organized by the University of Leiden, the Netherlands (Zhou, Jian-Ming January 2000) and published by FAO (Zhou, Jian-Ming 2000), with abstract to be published by CABI. Another working paper inspecting the functioning of the appropriate large-scale farming has been accepted by FAO for publication (Zhou, Jian-Ming 2001) [It would be unusual for a non-FAO-staff to have achieved five publications there, and for this the author has received congratulations from various organizations and persons, including Amato (2000), Prime Minister of Italy and Johnston (2000), Secretary-General of OECD]. This chapter is also a harbinger in English literature for China's ascension of a higher stage to prevent food overproduction (a task unfulfilled even by many developed countries including the USA, many other OECD, containing EU, countries) and improve the environment since mid-

---

24 This book calls those positive models for others to follow as models. It does not call the various negative 'models' even unsuccessful in the low wage economy as models, simply because they should be for others to avoid rather than pursue, and for themselves to abolish.

1999 with initial success.

In Chapter 8 'Other Rice-Based Economies under Public Land Ownership in Monsoon Asia', for Cambodia, Laos and Vietnam, it is pointed out that their newly established nominal state - but *de facto* private - land ownership may not prevent the appearance of new landlessness in the low wage economy and inefficient land-holding by part-time and absent small farmers in the high wage economy, the views of its advocates including Hayami are assessed, and the abolition of such a nominal state - but *de facto* private - land ownership recommended. A working paper on this has been accepted by a conference of the European Association for Comparative Economic Studies, with abstract published by CABI (Zhou, Jian-Ming March 1998). The Chinese model of rural development and Proposal 5.1 might also be relevant to the economies based on public land ownership outside monsoon Asia.

Chapters 1–8 are built on the author's PhD thesis, which received the unanimous praise of an international jury of experts at the end of the defence: 'We recommend the award of the PhD and congratulate the candidate on a comprehensive analysis of a highly complex and significant problem and for his carefully considered suggestion for its solution.' Actually it was the second PhD thesis in economics receiving the jury's congratulations in the history of the European University Institute. Before the defence, two publishers had already accepted the entire text of the thesis. Of 167 theses defended in the Department of Economics of the European University Institute since its foundation in 1976 until 2 February 2001, only 13 or 7.8% have been published as books, including this one.

In the USA since 1935 there has been a trend towards fewer but larger farms. No solution has yet been found concerning how to preserve small farmers while still strengthening large farmers. The government has simply oscillated between protective safety net during 1933–96 which did not succeed in conserving small farmers, and free market forces since 1996 which have made them more vulnerable. Inefficient land-holding by part-time and absent small farmers has also occurred. Chapter 10 'Application of the New Model in the USA' thus contributes Proposal 10.1 as one of the various forms of the new model raised in Proposal 5.1 and as the application of its principles, which is not included in the huge amount of 145 recommendations for promoting small farmers in the comprehensive report 'A Time to Act' by the National Commission on Small Farms of the US Department of Agriculture in January 1998. A paper presenting Proposal 10.1 has been accepted by 'The Second National Small Farm Conference' organized by the US Department of Agriculture, 12–15 October 1999, St. Louis, Missouri, with abstract being published in the proceedings, and text posted by the University of Minnesota in its electronic library (Zhou, Jian-

Ming October 1999).

Chapter 11 'Applications of the New Model in the OECD, EU, CEECs, CIS, and Rest of the World' indicates that the new model in various forms according to its principles might be useful to other OECD (including EU) countries with the large versus small bimodal farm structure and problems similar to the USA's; to consolidate and enlarge the fragmented small farms persisting outside monsoon Asia in Central and West Asia, the Pacific, Africa, Latin America, and Central, Eastern and Southern Europe in both low and high wage economies; and to facilitate the transition towards market economy in Central and Eastern Europe and Central Asia where after land privatization or farm restructuring since the late 1980s/early 1990s two possible *dilemmas* have been encountered: (1) turning to individual farming would lead to fragmented small farms; but retaining collective operation of large farms would continue the low individual incentives of members and other problems of the old system, and (2) some poor peasants due to difficulties in production and living would have to sell land parcels or shares and become newly landless, and land has been concentrated towards powerful people at the low wage economy; and part-time and absent small farmers earning higher off-farm income in rural areas (including those still saddled with traditional agriculture) developing towards the high wage economy, or cities and abroad, may have little incentive to lease or sell land to the remaining full-time (or mainly agriculture-engaged) farmers, resulting in inefficient land-holding. No effective solution has yet been found - indeed, the (former) socialist economies in Central and Eastern Europe and Central Asia have been searching a proper land tenure system ever since the foundation of the Soviet Union in 1917 but still not succeeded. Applying Proposal 5.1 in farms of CEECs and the CIS would help them to find a way out of the dilemmas. In particular, it would assist them to stand on their own feet and promote EU enlargement, which has met a barrier as the EU, while unable yet to shed the burden of price protection and income subsidies to farms, faces the same burden to the incoming members in Central and Eastern Europe and Central Asia.

Papers proposing the new model to CEECs and the CIS have been accepted by three conferences on transition organized by the Russian Education Ministry (Zhou, Jian-Ming 9–10 December 1999), Greek universities with text being published in the proceedings and abstract to be published by CABI (Zhou, Jian-Ming 16–18 December 1999) and European Association for Comparative Economic Studies with text being published in the proceedings (Zhou, Jian-Ming 7–9 September 2000) respectively. The proposal has also received positive responses from the relevant governments and international organizations, some of which are shown below.

'Thanks for your fax. We looked through your interesting proposal. The question of land consolidation is an important issue at the moment for our country. This matter (land use policy) is complex and significant. We are interested in any experience.' Lapse (1999), State Secretary, Ministry of Agriculture, Latvia.

'The study findings have also been verified during the land and ownership reform in Estonia. We have had such former collective farms, where land users were not interested in privatization in fear of losing their jobs after the collapse of their former employer in case the majority of reform subjects withdrew their land from an agri-enterprise. By now, bankruptcy process has anyhow started in such enterprises, not initiated by landowners, but due to economic circumstances and poor management. By the middle of 1999, about half of the total area of the country was registered in the cadastre, thus passing the reform phase, where the decisions like specified in your proposal were possible. The German Law which is extremely strict in technical aspects of land ownership serves as legal basis of land legislation in Estonia. The implementation of your proposal would require significant modification of legislative base'; 'However, the topic is interesting and the comparison of reform processes very valuable from the scientific and analytical point of view.' Padar (1999), Minister of Agriculture, Estonia.

'Thank you for your proposal. We are planning to work more on agricultural issues at our research institute RECEP [the Russian European Center for Economic Policy] in Moscow, and I will take your proposal to the group. China's success in agricultural reform cannot be ignored.' Berglof (1999), Director, Stockholm Institute of Transition Economics and East European Economies (SITE), Stockholm School of Economics.

'I read with interest your message, on all these aspects of land restitution after the fall of the Berlin wall'; 'Your proposal would rather be of interest for people working on former USSR.' Beaumond (1999), Directorate-General for Agriculture (DG VI), EU Commission.

'Congratulations on the acceptance of your paper for the conferences in Russia and Greece'; 'The possible restructuring of large farms in the transition countries into a type of capital shareholding corporation . . . is legally possible, e.g. in Russia.' Kwiecinski (1999), Division on Non-Member Economies, Directorate-General for Agriculture, Food and Fisheries, OECD.

'Hereby I would like to thank you for your kind attention you pay for the changes in our region and for your offering your professional knowledge and help to solve the problems of transforming Hungarian agriculture. Your proposal to our Ministry has been studied by competent experts and has been found very useful. Please let me thank you again.' Beres (2000), Chef de Cabinet, Ministry of Agriculture and Regional Development, Hungary.

At this point, it would be crucial to mention Schultz's book *Transforming*

*Traditional Agriculture*25 ([1964] 1983) mainly for which he shared the 1979 Nobel Economics Prize - 'This is one of very small number of books that has made a difference. It has had a significant effect upon economic research and thinking about agriculture in low income countries, and it has had an effect upon what governments and international agencies have done with respect to agricultural policies. Schultz makes the very important point that farmers in low income countries are rational and make effective use of their resources. They are poor because their resources are very limited and because the knowledge is not available that would permit them to produce the same output with fewer resources or a larger output from the same resources. If this seems like a commonplace idea, it is so because of the writings of T. W. Schultz.' (Johnson 1983: back cover)**26**

Here, however, the low income countries are *closed* to the high income economy or high wage stage, as Schultz clarifies ([1964] 1983: 11, 15): 'A major new problem has arisen in a number of high income countries in which the agricultural sector has been most successful in adopting and using modern factors of production. It is the problem of adapting agriculture with its high rate of increase in labor productivity to a high income economy in which the demand for farm products is of slow growth. It becomes an acute problem when the labor force required for farming begins to decline at a substantial rate and many of the farm people . . . leave agriculture . . . for nonfarm jobs'. 'But countries still saddled with traditional agriculture are not up against this particular problem.' Thus, he puts aside the issue of 'the adaptation of the agricultural sector to growth in high income countries'.

But this book finds that at least from the mid-1950s on the low income countries still saddled with traditional agriculture have been increasingly open to the high income economy, as small peasants there would migrate to those rural areas already at the high wage stage, cities and abroad to earn higher income as part-time and absent farmers, thus also are up against the particular problem of adapting the agricultural sector to a high income economy.**27**

---

[25] 'Farming based wholly upon the kinds of factors of production that have been used by farmers for generations can be called traditional agriculture' (Schultz [1964] 1983: 3–4).

[26] Also here, 'Schultz systematically attacks the "zero marginal product" hypothesis' (Bowman 1983: back cover), which is closely related to the concept of disguised unemployment, of Lewis (who was however fairly and democratically awarded the other half of the same year's Nobel Economics Prize) and other economists. Because many debates between these two arguments have been made, this book does not discuss this theme a lot.

[27] For example, in Japan, of all farm households, full-time households accounted for 50% in 1950, 34.8% in 1955, 33.7% in 1960, and 20.5% in 1965; and of total farm household population, persons engaged mainly in farming (both those engaged exclusively in farming and

How then about the low income countries which are *open* to the high income economy? Schultz ([1964] 1983: 124) claims that 'in communities where nearby off-farm jobs are readily available on both a part-time basis and a full-time basis the contributions of a human agent become divisible and part-time farming becomes possible; and it can be efficient.'

Contrary to Schultz's claim, this book discovers, as a surmise, that in (1) the low income countries still saddled with traditional agriculture, (2) the low income countries developing towards the high income economy, and (3) the high income countries, the part-time and absent small farmers are not so efficient, as they hold land in inefficient use even though land property rights have been well defined and market transactions facilitated. This may be out of their rational concern over their direct interests in security. Thus if they could be guaranteed with a back-up basic social welfare and provided with appropriate remuneration, then some of them would be willing to transfer their inefficiently held land in various suitable forms to the full-time farmers for effective use, yet others would still be unwilling to do so. As a result, the remaining full-time small farmers, largely non-viable as the economy develops into the high wage stage, could not easily get the inefficiently held resources for effective use, although the knowledge and other conditions are available to both the full-time, and part-time and absent small farmers that would permit them to produce the same output with fewer resources or a larger output from the same resources. Government or community subsidies, budget burden, food shortage, unnecessary food import, higher domestic and international prices of agricultural goods, artificial food overproduction, land under-utilization or idleness, waste of other resources, environmental deterioration, etc. would also be incurred. Therefore at least some of the part-time and absent small farmers are not so rational to the society's and their own fundamental interests. Consequently proper land tenure systems in variable mixed economies should be devised to effect the transfer of their inefficiently held land. But this does not as yet seem like a commonplace idea.

Schultz ([1964] 1983: 9–10) also asserts that the tenet 'that the costs of agricultural products fall as the size of the production unit in agriculture increases' has 'no logical basis'. But even he himself ([1964] 1983: 122–3) has admitted that 'Where human effort (labor) is cheap relative to the price of other agricultural factors, a one-man (or family) farm may be efficient with a small garden-type tractor; on the other hand, where human

---

those engaged in farming for more days than in other jobs) took 53.2% in 1955, 42.3% in 1960, and 38.3% in 1965 (see Table 4.3). Schultz ([1964] 1983: 18) also cites that in Northwest Europe (Austria, Belgium, Denmark, France, West Germany, Ireland, the Netherlands, Norway, Sweden, and the UK) employment in agriculture declined over a fifth during 1950–59.

effort is relatively dear, a one-man farm may be efficient with a combination of two or even three tractors that differ in size and type.' However, 'It requires very special conditions for a fleet of big tractors to be efficient, conditions which in fact rarely exist.' Apparently, large farm size is such a condition. But the rare existence of such conditions does not mean that this tenet has 'no logical basis'. Actually, in 'a high income economy in which the demand for farm products is of slow growth', and 'the labor force required for farming begins to decline at a substantial rate and many of the farm people . . . leave agriculture . . . for nonfarm jobs', increase of farm size of the remaining full-time farmers would already be logically possible, and could be realized if the inefficient land-holding by the part-time and absent small farmers could be overcome, as this book discerns.

Schultz ([1964] 1983: 9–10, 17–8) further declares that this tenet has not 'stood the test of time' and 'empirical findings'. His empirical findings are that large-scale farming did not play a role in the excellent growth of agricultural production during 1952–59 in Western Europe, which was an 'old, crowded workshop with a population density much greater than Asia's'. However, as this book dynamically analyzes, the fragmented small farms were efficient in a low wage economy when there was little off-farm employment and labor was cheaper than large machinery, such as in Western Europe and Japan during the recovery period after WWII. But in a high wage economy when large amount of labor has been absorbed by off-farm activities, and large machinery has thus become cheaper than labor, that tenet would function, as evidenced by Japan, China, not to mention the USA and other developed members of OECD. Therefore, unfortunately, it would be Schultz's assertion that has not 'stood the test of time' and 'empirical findings' in the high income economy.

In short, under the Japanese model as one extreme, inefficient small farmers have hampered the formation of large farmers and maintenance of food self-sufficiency; under the American model as the other extreme, small farmers have been crowded out by large farmers and food overproduction could not be resolved; the Chinese model has achieved appropriate large-scale farming while not squeezing out small farmers, and overcome both food shortage and overproduction, but is based on public land ownership, which may not be acceptable to many other economies. In contrast, the new model, in its diverse forms, would avoid both the Japanese and American extremes, and reach the ends the Chinese model has accomplished, while still retaining private land ownership, thus would be more suitable to various economies around the world for achieving efficient land use and sustainable rural development.

CABI has ordered this book in order to publish its abstract (Zhou, Jian-Ming 2002) (it also would be rare for an author to have attained six CABI abstracts), while Franceschetti (2000), Professor, Department of Territory and Agro-Forest Systems, University of Padua, Italy, informed the author that 'I am happy to utilize your ample knowledge for our course of perfectization in rural development and cooperation in developing countries from January 2001 on'. The author also has had the honors to be invited to participate in the Emerging Market Economy Forum and Forum on Agricultural Policies in Non-Member Countries, OECD, Paris, October 1998; Working Group of FAO/University of Padua, Padua, November 1998; and Workshop on Sustainable Development of the Norwegian University of Science and Technology, Trondheim, Norway, March 2001.

2. Theories of Monsoon Asia Rice Economy and Variable Mixed Economies

2.1 A Rice-Based Agriculture in Monsoon Asia

A rice-based agriculture exists, not in Africa, North and Central America, South America, Europe and Oceania or the rest of Asia, but in monsoon Asia, as the much higher percentage of rice area in the total crop area in monsoon Asia shown in Table 2.1 indicates. This has been determined chiefly by the particular characteristics of Asian monsoon and rice.

Geography and climate. A monsoon climate is one that is dominated by seasonal winds that blow for half of the year in one direction and then reverse themselves (Barker; Herdt & Rose 1985: 22). Although each continent exhibits the seasonal reversal of winds and rains known as the monsoon effects, nowhere - in North America, South America, Africa, and Europe - are these reversals as notable as in Asia, where there are three distinct monsoon patterns: the Indian, the Malayan and the Japanese (Ginsburg; Brush; McCune; Philbrick; Randall & Weins 1958: 8. Spencer & Thomas 1971: 175). The Asian monsoon areas include nearly all of South, Southeast and East Asia but exclude Hokkaido of Japan; Mongolia; Manchuria in the Northeasternmost, Inner Mongolia in North-Central China; Afghanistan; Western Pakistan; the Southeastern islands of Indonesia; and India West and South of New Delhi (Oshima 1987: 20). In general, the monsoon climate in Asia causes rains in May—October and dryness in November—April. Commonly in Asia, the monsoon season is referred to as the wet season (Barker; Herdt & Rose 1985: 22).

Paddy and rice. Paddy is the term usually applied to (1) the rice plant as it grows in the field, (2) the cut and harvested stalks, (3) the grains that are detached by threshing (rice in the hull) and (4) the flooded field in which the plant grows. *Rice* is the name given to the grain of the rice plant from the time the hard, rather tight-fitting hull surrounding the kernel is removed by milling until it is ultimately consumed as cooked food or until it is otherwise

Table 2.1 Area Percentage and Yield of Rice, Wheat and Coarse Grains [a] *in Various Parts of the World in 1992*

	Percentage of harvested area in total crop-producing area [b]			Yield Kg/ha		
	Rice	Wheat	Coarse grains	Rice	Wheat	Coarse grains
World	10.3	15.3	22.9	3,557	2,550	2,625
Monsoon Asia	33.9	16.4	19.8	3,215	2,044	1,843
Rest of Asia	1.0	31.4	17.8	2,951	1,794	2,390
Africa	4.0	4.4	35.5	1,970	1,656	872
North & Central America	0.7	14.7	21.1	5,319 [c]	2,510	5,671
South America	5.6	6.3	19.2	2,597	2,109	2,462
Europe	0.3	18.5	28.1	5,849	4,543	3,582
Oceania	0.2	15.8	9.3	7,879	1,796	2,041

Notes:
a. Coarse grains include barley, corn, rye, oats, millet and sorghum.
b. Total crop-producing area refers to area of arable land and land under permanent crops. *Arable land* is land under temporary crops (double-cropped areas are counted only once), temporary meadows for mowing or pasture, land under market and kitchen gardens (including cultivation under glass) and land temporarily fallow (less than five years) (the abandoned land resulting from shifting cultivation is not included; the data are not meant to indicate the amount of land that is potentially cultivable). *Land under permanent crops* is land cultivated with crops that occupy the land for long periods and need not be replanted after each harvest, such as cocoa, coffee and rubber; this category includes land under shrubs, fruit trees, nut trees and vines, but excludes land under trees grown for wood or timber.
c. In 1979–81, 1991 and 1993, however, the yields of rice were all higher than those of coarse grains in North and Central America.

Source: FAO-YP 1993: vii, viii, xiv, 3, 6–7, 9–11, 68–74.

used. However, when referring to a type of agriculture, paddy, rice or paddy rice are often used interchangeably. (Wickizer & Bennett 1941: 9. Barker; Herdt & Rose 1985: 15)

There are several thousand more or less distinct cultivated varieties of rice, more than are known for any other cereal. It suffices here to distinguish between (1) common rice and (2) glutinous rice from the botanical perspective; and (1) upland rice, (2) irrigated lowland rice and (3) swamp lowland rice by cultural types. (Wickizer & Bennett 1941: 9—10)

Common rice and glutinous rice. Wickizer and Bennett (1941: 10) state that *common rice* comprises the varieties whose kernels can be cooked and still remain separate: sinica (indica and japonica) and javanica. It is the type of rice ordinarily referred to in discussions of rice production, trade and consumption. It constitutes the great bulk of production and consumption everywhere. *Glutinous rice* is far less important and mostly produced and consumed in restricted localities especially in China. When boiled it forms a gluey, sticky mass. This stickiness is not objectionable in the preparation of special foods such as pastries and confections, but detracts from the desirability of glutinous rice as a cereal for consumption as such.

Upland rice and lowland rice. Upland (dryland) rice (dry-rice) is grown without irrigation or not in surface water, hence known as 'hill' or 'mountain' rice. Upland methods of culture are mostly primitive; the yields obtained are characteristically small, and the crop uncertain. *Lowland (wetland) rice (wet-rice)* is grown with irrigation (as *irrigated lowland rice*) or in natural swamps (as *swamp lowland rice*) where there is standing water in the appropriate season, thus known as 'irrigated' and 'swamp' rice respectively. Commonly, the varieties grown as upland rice are not the same as those grown as lowland rice, for some varieties do relatively well in the drier environment, others relatively well in the moister environment. (Wickizer & Bennett 1941: 10—2. Barker; Herdt & Rose 1985: 15)

Very little of the world's and Asia's rice crop is upland rice, very little is glutinous rice, and very little is grown in natural swamps. Hence *common rice grown under artificial systems of irrigation is the outstandingly important type* of rice in the world economy. No other grain crop, and perhaps no other major crop of any sort, is grown under irrigation to the extent that is characteristic of rice. (Wickizer & Bennett 1941: 11)

Natural conditions for the rice economy. Although varieties differ one from the other, in general, the rice plant must have *high temperatures*, an *abundant supply of water* and *heavy soil* for germination and growth (Wickizer and Bennett 1941: 17—22. Bray 1986: 25—6, 28. Oshima 1987: 20. Copeland 1924: 50. Grist 1975: 20). Compared with rice, the yields of other cereals are lower, less suitable to the rainfall and humidity, or not superior in nutritional value. Therefore monsoon Asians had no option but to evolve paddy rice agriculture over many centuries (Oshima 1987: 18). Numerous archaeological investigations throughout Asia have established that rice was domesticated in and even before the fifth millennium BC (Lu & Chang 1980).1 In the zones of monsoon Asia where temperatures are high enough and rainfall abundant, the rice acreage lies mostly along the valley plains of great rivers and in deltas and other coastal plains. The construction of level, floodable and fertile rice fields here is simplest and least costly for reasons both of topography and soil. (Wickizer & Bennett 1941: 24)

Culture of other crops. Other crops are also produced in monsoon Asia where and when natural conditions are suitable for them but not for rice, such as millets, sorghums, wheat, less commonly corn, barley, and rarely oats and rye (Wickizer & Bennett 1941: 24).

Various cropping practices for rice. Cropping practices are determined by the availability of water and heat. Cropping systems based on rice are the most common form of agriculture in Asia, and a single crop of rice per year may be the most widely practiced land use pattern in Asia (World Bank 1976). There may be enough water in some places to produce two or three successive rice crops under irrigation. On the other hand, especially in the flood plains of rivers, the prevalence and duration of floods may preclude the cultivation of more than one crop in a year. Hence some of the land in a given region may be double-cropped to rice and some single-cropped. (Wickizer & Bennett 1941: 20)

Barker, Herdt and Rose (1985: 24) state that in the temperate areas, cold weather limits rice production to one crop per year. In the warmer areas, other crops are planted after or before rice on some fraction of land. Except for the high-latitude countries, the availability of adequate water is the main factor determining when rice is planted. Because of the pronounced monsoon and dry season, even the two-crop locations usually produce a second crop of rice only where irrigation is available. In most places, the cultivation season begins in May or June with the onset of the main monsoon showers.

It is common to find a wide range of upland crops planted in rotation with rice. This normally occurs where rainfall is not adequate for a second rice crop or where a third crop can be grown after the second rice harvest. However, in general, the area rice farmers use to plant crops after rice is much smaller than the area planted with the main rice crop. (Barker; Herdt & Rose 1985: 24)

Although various new techniques have been introduced in and innovations

---

[1] In 1996, a wet-rice field of 6,500 years ago was unearthed in Feng County of Changde City of Hunan Province, demonstrating not only the very long civilization history of China but also the self-origination of its rice culture (Zheng, Rong-Lai 2000).

made, the above-stated cropping practices for rice still prevail in general.

2.2 The Prewar Vicious Circle of Poverty in Monsoon Asia

There has been the well-known theory of dualism on modern industry mainly in cities and traditional agriculture in rural areas, started by Preobrazhensky in 1924 and re-discussed by Lewis, Jorgenson, Ranis, Fei and many others since the 1950s (Preobrazhensky [1924] 1965. Lewis 1954. Jorgenson 1961. Ranis & Fei 1961). It presents three characteristics of traditional agriculture: disguised unemployment, unlimited supply of labor, and wage gap (Nurkse 1953: 32–3, 35–6. Lewis 1954: 401–3. Agarwala 1983: 6–7). Following Nurkse's analysis (1952: 256; 1953: 4–5, 9) on the vicious circle of poverty in poor rural areas, and in capital formation in economically backward areas, Myrdal (1957: 26–34) and Holland (1976a: 56–9, 109–12, 118; 1976b: 97–110) further argue that if market forces were unhampered by policy intervention, then industrial production, commerce, banking, insurance, shipping and almost all those economic activities which in a developing economy tend to give a bigger than average return, and science, art, literature, education and higher culture, generally would cluster in certain localities and regions, leaving the rest of the country more or less in a backwater. The expansion in an advanced industrial locality tends to have not only '*backwash effects*' in other localities via 'economic factors' such as migration (resulting in senilization and feminization of the agricultural labor force and urban congestion), capital movements, trade, transportation,2 and 'non-economic factors' such as health and education, but also '*spread effects*' of expansionary momentum from the centers of economic expansion to other regions. The interaction of the 'backwash effects' and 'spread effects' would lead to *expanding, stagnating* or *regressing* localities interacting continuously on different levels, with multiple graduations between the extremes. While in rich countries the 'spread effects' are stronger, in poor countries 'backwash effects' are stronger. Thus, free play by the market forces and laissez-faire may not overcome the dual economy in underdeveloped countries; they will tend to reinforce it. A detailed review of this theory can be found in Chapter 2 of Zhou, Jian-Ming (December 1997).

This section is to try to show that free market forces alone could not

---

[2] Myrdal regards transportation as a non-economic factor, but it would be more appropriate to treat it as an economic factor.

overcome the vicious circle of poverty and realize sustainable rural development of monsoon Asia before WWII, and a number of underlying conditions still exist in various parts of the region today. It is analyzed as follows. Under natural monsoon conditions, there were (1) highly labor-intensive rice culture leading to labor force shortage in the peak seasons, population densities, and fragmented small farms; (2) little employment in the slack seasons; (3) unfeasibility of capitalistic large-scale farming, and (4) feudal landlord ownership reinforcing the poverty. While (1), (2) and (3) are mainly traditional productive and technological conditions, (4) is institutional.

Labor-Intensive Production

Highly labor-intensive nature of paddy rice culture. In the prewar period, very little machinery was used in monsoon Asian rice-producing economies. Tractor cultivation was attempted, but did not meet with much success in the places where it was tried. Tools and implements were generally of the simplest type. Under such *traditional technologies*, rice growing in the Orient was one of the most labor-intensive types of agriculture known. (Wickizer & Bennett 1941: 50)

Bray (1986: 149) argues that the nature of the inputs required to raise output in wet-rice cultivation in monsoon Asia was such that capital played a subordinate role to labor in developing the forces of production. The historical material shows clearly how over time Asian systems of wet-rice cultivation became progressively more intensive in their use of labor, while relying on relatively low levels of capital investment. In large part this is because the general trend in technological development has been towards the concentration of resources on raising the productivity of land. Ishikawa (1981: 2–3, 22) and Taylor (1981: 89) show that broadly speaking yields of wet-rice correlate positively with labor inputs.

Oshima (1971: 63–97; 1987: 24) indicates that labor requirements per ha of paddy rice grown varied from country to country in monsoon Asia, depending mainly on the extent to which work animals were used, the extent of irrigation and of available transportation, and so on. Labor required per ha in the prewar years was about 50 man-days in the Philippines, 80 in Thailand and Bombay, 100 in West Bengal, and 150 in Madras, China and Japan. The lower figures for Southeast Asia (except Java) reflected the more extensive use of work animals and the limited extent of irrigation and transportation, though even these figures were considerably higher than those for the wheat culture of the USA as early as 1800. For the USA in 1900, before mechanization, only five man-days for wheat and 10 days for corn were needed.

The major reasons for the heavy labor requirements could be seen throughout the three stages of rice cultivation. The first stage was planting. There was the need (in order to get high yields) to prepare seedling beds and to transplant seedlings instead of broadcasting or drilling seeds as in wheat. Typically, in Asian paddy fields, when the first rains came, the seedling beds were plowed and harrowed several times. The soil of the seed bed was hoed, plowed, or trampled into fine, soft mud before sowing. In most countries, the seeds were soaked in water and then sowed after the water was drained. The water was restored in the paddy after the seeds had germinated. After about a month, the young rice plants were pulled out, tied in bundles, top being cut, and taken to the fields to be planted. If the monsoons came too late, the seedlings became too old and might have had to be replaced with new ones. For example, in Japan, in 1954, before mechanization made headway, plowing per ha took 10 hours, preparing seedling beds and transplanting 17, weeding 15, reaping 18, threshing 10, and irrigating 11; transplanting and reaping/threshing were concentrated in a brief period. (Oshima 1987: 24)

The second stage was harvesting. The rice harvest usually began three—six months after transplanting, depending upon whether the varieties planted matured early or late (Wickizer & Bennett 1941: 53). The method of using a small knife or at best a sickle was time-consuming. Reaping with a larger cradle or scythe as in the Western wheat culture of the 19th century was not feasible in the wet or moist paddy soil: moisture could spoil the grain as it fell to the ground after scything. Moreover, with the long-stalk indica rice used extensively in Southeast Asia, lodging was a common problem, leading to uneven maturing so that the heads had to be cut singly with small knives to avoid heavy losses due to shattering, lodging and uneven maturing. Unlike other grains, the mature rice grain readily shattered. Thus, it is reported that before the war the Javanese peasant refused, despite strong urgings by the Dutch, to use the sickle in place of his small knife. (Oshima 1987: 24–5). Due to labor shortage, outside labor was imported in some areas especially for the harvest and the helpers commonly received compensation in the form of a certain portion of each day's harvest. For example, in Lower Myanmar, some 200,000–300,000 Indians came for the harvest each year, many remained and worked in the mills, and finally returned, mostly to the famine areas of Southern India. (Wickizer & Bennett 1941: 53)

The third stage was threshing. This was usually done by hand with some simple device. Bundles of harvested ears and attached stalks were carted to the threshing floor. In some areas bullocks, carabaos or oxen trod out the grain; in other places humans performed the same operations. In still other areas the grains were beaten with flails (long sticks - usually bamboo - at the end of which were attached stout reeds which swung freely as the operator alternately raised his pole and then brought it down hard on the threshing floor). The tramped or beaten material was winnowed by allowing it to fall gently from a platform while the wind carried away the chaff, dust, short pieces of straw and the lighter kernels. Sometimes threshing consisted only of pounding the rice heads on a log. (Wickizer & Bennett 1941: 50, 54–5)

Tight work schedule. For various operations in these stages, the monsoon rains which came and went at only certain periods of the year enforced a rigid work schedule. The early rains of the monsoon season were insufficient to soften the clay soils hardened by the dry months. The brick-hard earth could not be plowed even with buffalo power until the heavier rains began to flood the paddies. This called for timely and concentrated plowing, in addition to long hours of work with seed beds, so that transplantation would not be delayed beyond the optimal stage of seedling growth. Harvesting also must be carried out at the proper time; otherwise large losses would be incurred as over-ripe grain was more liable to shatter. (Oshima 1987: 26)

Labor force shortage in peak seasons and increasing population densities. The heavy concentration of labor required during the few months of the monsoon and the tight work schedule meant that labor required for optimal yields typically exceeded by a wide margin the available adult male working population. (In areas where labor was available, both labor inputs and yields were highest, as in China, Japan and Java; they were lowest in countries like Thailand where labor was not available for intensive cultivation.) This called for the use of young, old, and female workers. *These heavy labor requirements must have contributed to the rapid rise of population* in the major, more temperate Asian regions such as China, India and Japan, as the technology of monsoon paddy culture became increasingly labor-intensive in the centuries of the second millennium, with deeper and more careful plowing, more intensive transplanting, multiple cropping and more intensive reaping. None of these operations (except for plowing) could use work animals, so that the demand for working hands increased. Two rice crops on the same land during the year meant that with the same labor force much more could be produced and more people could be fed. But increased hands could lead to more intensive cultivation to get higher yields per crop, so that in the latter case population and food supply went up more or less simultaneously. (Oshima 1987: 26)

Fragmented small farms. Oshima (1987: 25) points out that high population densities in the rural areas with limited availability of new land and the labor intensity of agricultural operations meant that farms were small. Moreover, the small farms were fragmented (which Oshima does not point out). In Japan, many farmers had their pieces of farmland scattered over the village (Nishimura & Sasaki 1993: 74–5). In China, the average size of most farms was about 15 mu (1 ha). Such a small farm was composed of many irregular (so-called fish-scale shaped) parcels smaller than 1 mu (0.067 ha) especially in the mountain and hill areas. (Huang, Xi-Yuan 1986: 371). In India it was common to find a holding of 4–5 ha scattered into 20–30 parcels (Menon 1956: 597). For example, in Uttar Pradesh, a village with an area of 60.705 ha contained more than 1,000 parcels, on average 0.06 ha each, and a cultivator with 0.8094 ha of paddy land possessed more than 150 parcels, on average 0.005 ha (Sahi 1964). The same situation existed in Malaya (since 1963 Malaysia), Pakistan, the Philippines, Sri Lanka (Ceylon), Taiwan Province of China as well as other rice-based economies of monsoon Asia (Wilson 1958: 82. Ahmed & Timmons 1971: 59, 63. BCS 1965: 205. Michael 1953: 40. Vander Meer & Vander Meer 1968: 147). The major specific causes of fragmentation of small farms and its disadvantages and advantages perceived in monsoon Asia may be summarized as follows.

Supply-side causes of fragmentation. Reclamation. When a new area was reclaimed, only the best pieces of land were exploited and the intervening areas left unoccupied. Subsequently, when pressure on land increased, the poorer soils were also taken over but usually by others than the pioneers. The original cultivator or his successor in such a case found new cultivators in occupation of areas in between his parcels of land. (Zaheer 1975: 87)

Inheritance. Limited land, increasing population, and little off-farm employment made peasants dependent on tilling land. This led to the property right to freely subdivide the existing land (rather than primogeniture). Fair division of the parents' farm among heirs concerning land productivity (fertility, acreage, access to water, distance to village, flatness, etc.) resulted in fragmentation. Inheritance in this way generation after generation contributed to more and more fragmented farms. (Binns 1950: 10–2, 14)

Division. When a large united family disintegrated, the sub-families tended to insist on fair and equitable division of the assets of the family, thus parcelling out land with various levels of productivity (Zaheer 1975: 87).

Acquisition. The existence of property rights to freely transfer or add to existing agricultural holdings also caused fragmentation. Marriage could bring dowry land (Vander Meer 1982: 1). An owner-peasant, due to limited financial resources, might not be able to afford to buy large estates in single lot and would therefore have to purchase cheaper land piece by piece. A peasant who owned land but also rented in land might have had to surrender his owned land to a feudal landlord if he were unable to pay the rent. A moneylender could acquire the land of a debtor if he could not repay the debt. The newly gained parcels were generally located in different places. (Binns 1950: 11–2)

Lease. Some feudal landlords (especially warlords) could seize large areas of land by forced occupation or cheap purchase, but they then had to rent it out in small pieces (Huang, Xi-Yuan 1986: 171) since large-scale farming was not feasible (as analyzed below). There also were owners who were loath to rent out land and would do so only in small parcels when absolutely necessarily (Fals-Borda 1955: 160—1). Owners of land generally had a right to resume land and also to re-let land to others. Thus, a cultivator might be divested of the parcel he rented in earlier and the same parcel might be leased to another tenant. Consequently a tenant could possess parcels in different places. (Zaheer 1975: 87). A tenant also might not have enough family labor force to justify renting in more land. After his children became part of the labor force, he could rent in more, but only parcels in different places, since those contiguous to his were already rented out to others.

Sale. Due to debt or other reasons, some owner-peasants might be compelled to sell parcels of land. These were usually choice areas which could readily command a good price with the minimum area being parted. (Zaheer 1975: 87)

Use. Under some communal or feudal serf-holder land systems, members or villeins were given fragmented subsistence parcels on an equal basis in terms of fertility, acreage, access to water, distance, etc. (Binns 1950: 12)

Construction. Construction of infrastructure such as roads, canals, railways, and other rights-of-way might separate land (Wilson 1958: 84—5).

Incomplete irrigation also could contribute to land fragmentation. For example, in Pul Eliya Village of Sri Lanka, the channels extended downslope from the water tanks, and the fields lay on one or both sides of the channels so that they could receive water. In some years, however, the water was insufficient to reach the lower fields. To insure a harvest, thus, farmers had to have both higher and lower fields. To hold land only in the lowest areas would have been extremely hazardous. (Leach 1961: 171)

Demand-side causes of fragmentation. Risk diversification. To diversify risks, peasants needed varieties of soil and different locations to avoid being dependent on a single parcel or product (Binns 1950: 22, 31. Heston & Kumar 1983: 200).

Natural needs. One of the factors promoting excessive fragmentation was the wide variation in the fertility or productivity of land. Farmers needed land suitable for seed nurseries and land for growing of rice. There were seasonal reasons for working both an upland parcel and a parcel on river banks and islands at different times of the year. (Binns 1950: 22, 31). Many farms in mountain regions consisted of three separate estates - in the plains, on the middle levels and on the high levels (Swi-Gov 1950: 90).

Disadvantages of fragmentation. Diseconomies of scale were bound to apply: below the optimal size, the smaller the size the higher the cost of raising crops on it, and the lower the income (Zaheer 1975: 87—8).

Waste of time and energy was typical in transporting material inputs to the parcels and in bringing the output to the threshing ground. Workers on the land had to make long and unnecessary trips from one parcel to another for various agricultural operations. (Zaheer 1975: 87–8)

Sub-optimization of land use. If parcels were widely separated or some were distant from the farmstead, the demands on available time and energy might force the farmer to cultivate a lower labor-demanding crop, especially on more distant fields, or devote less time to such work as weeding and fertilizing. Under such circumstances, the land was not optimally utilized and profits were less than their full potential. (Chisholm 1962: 59)

Prevention of use of machinery and animals. The use of machinery would be impracticable on such small fields even if it were available. Where animals were plentiful, their use for plowing was often precluded because of small parcel size. In the more densely populated areas of monsoon Asia, per capita land was so small that no land was available for growing both food and feed; hence working beasts tended to be relatively scarce. Most of the work in connection with the production of rice and its preparation for consumption had to be done manually. (Wickizer & Bennett 1941: 50–1)

Obstacles to land improvement. Making physical improvements was generally more costly on a scattered farm than on a single-parcel farm. Longer fences to control stray livestock movements were needed per unit of area enclosed (Smith 1959: 149), whose higher cost prevented farmers from building fences in monsoon Asia. Individual initiative in the construction of irrigation facilities was discouraged by the high unit costs of the area served. (Buck [1937] 1964: 185). Soil conservation on the tiny parcels was also difficult (Zaheer 1975: 87–8).

Waste of land was typical because of the plethora of demarcation boundaries (Zaheer 1975: 87–8).

High cost of supervision. In fragmented farms, the cost of inspection of crops was high and even then uniform supervision became almost impossible due to the dispersed locations of the parcels. In areas where crops were subject to the depredations of animals and birds, keeping them free from this menace became very difficult. (Zaheer 1975: 87–8). As the harvest period approached and crops required protection from insects or thieves, more field watchers were needed (Fals-Borda 1955: 156).

Difficult coordination. Devising a practical drainage system became difficult since any such scheme had to be coordinated with numerous other land-holders (Zaheer 1975: 87–8). Individual farm management practices were hard to improve. The farmer who used insecticides on his several parcels could be discouraged if even a few of his many field neighbors failed to control insects on their land, so that his insecticide application was ineffective. (Fals-Borda 1955: 152). In general, the smaller the parcels worked by a farmer, the more he was bound by and locked into the cropping pattern and time schedules of the other farmers in his locality, and the more he was hampered in his ability to change his ways in response to changing technological and market conditions (Floyd 1964: 101).

Neighbor problems. That the cultivator of a fragmented farm had more field neighbors naturally increased opportunities for conflict (Smith 1959: 149). It was difficult to keep one's animals from disturbing the crops of other farmers (Buck [1937] 1964: 185). Access of fields to roads or to irrigation water sources was complicated by the presence of intervening landowners (Fals-Borda 1955: 152). Construction of irrigation facilities also was extremely difficult because channels had to extend long distances past neighbors' fields (Buck [1937] 1964: 185).

Advantages of fragmentation. Diversification. Different parcels located in different soils or micro-climates could support a greater diversity of crops (Lehrer 1964: 31), which could provide the farmer with both greater income and security of income (Fals-Borda 1955: 158–9). Working parcels in several places also spread the risks of natural disasters (Abler; Adams & Gould 1971: 482–3. Lehrer 1964: 31).

More exchanges of ideas could occur as a farmer met other farmers adjacent to his many parcels of land (Lehrer 1964: 31).

It was more socially desirable, with little off-farm employment and insufficient rural infrastructure especially irrigation, to provide peasants with relatively equitable access to farmland and facilities than to concentrate them on a few farmers.

Development of intensive farming techniques was promoted in monsoon Asia due to increasing population pressure and decreasing field size (Huang, Xi-Yuan 1986: 20–2), which will be analyzed later on.

In comparison with the disadvantages, the advantages were minor. All of these reflected backward economic, technological and social conditions. In other words, farmers were forced to accept the fragmented small farms because they had no other choice. In fact, *wet-rice farmers in monsoon Asia generally preferred having all their land in one contiguous parcel* (Vander Meer 1982: 93).

In sum, the wet monsoons imposed on Asians a labor-intensive form of agriculture which over the centuries created greater and greater demand for labor during the peak seasons. The increasing population densities meant decreasing size and fragmentation of farms, as crop land began to be scarce and diminishing returns set in. As a result, during the first half of the 20th century, agricultural productivity grew slowly. (Oshima 1987: 26–7, 45)

In the postwar period, although this highly labor-intensive culture has been replaced by agricultural mechanization in some economies like Japan and Taiwan, it is still dominant in the others. Agricultural population densities, and fragmented small farms prevail. In Japan and China, fragmentation is more serious (see Chapters 4–7 respectively). Table 2.2 shows that in 1990, among all parts of the world, the ratios of agricultural population to agricultural land and agricultural population to arable land in

Table 2.2 Agricultural Densities and Average Farm Sizes in Various Parts of the World in 1990

Region/ Continent	Agri popula- tion/ agri land *	Agri popula- tion/ arable land (per- sons/ ha)	Area of agricultural holdings (ha)	Number of agricultural holdings	Average area of agricul- tural holdings (ha/ holding)
World	0.508	1.822	1,918,712,863	173,902,231	11.033
Monsoon Asia	2.130	4.885	227,839,882	122,989,378	1.853
Rest of Asia	0.203	1.204	40,779,157	7,442,478	5.479
Africa	0.348	2.258	29,336,264	18,118,095	1.619
North & Central America	0.188	0.198	649,063,996	7,468,472	86.907
South America	0.114	0.753	288,394,014	4,048,875	71.228
Europe	0.217	0.385	198,257,579	13,503,896	14.682
USSR	0.093	0.248	–	–	–
Oceania	0.011	0.106	485,041,971	331,037	1,465.220

* Agricultural land = Arable land + Land under permanent crops + Permanent meadows and pastures. Permanent meadows and pastures are land used permanently (five years or more) for herbaceous forage crops, either cultivated or growing wild. Other definitions see Table 2.1.

Sources: *Definitions of land*: Oshima 1987: 23; FAO-YP 1993: viii. *Agricultural population, arable land and land under permanent crops*: FAO-YP 1996: 3–13, 19–35. *Permanent meadows and pastures*: FAO-YP 1991: 3–13. *Area and number of agricultural holdings*: FAO-SDE 1997: 30–33 (based on 1990 agricultural census in various countries).

monsoon Asia were the highest, and the number of agricultural holdings the largest, implying the high agricultural population densities and scarcity of land; as a result, the average farm size was one of the smallest (second only to Africa in this sample survey).

If those parts not influenced by the monsoon climate (Western Pakistan, Western and most of Northern China, about half of India and parts of Indonesia) are excluded, the monsoon Asian densities will rise to nearly 10 persons per ha of agricultural land, or about 30 times that of Africa, 40 times that of Europe and over 100 times that of the Americas (in 1975). In those parts influenced by the monsoon climate, if the less labor-intensive plantation crop areas are not taken into account, i.e., if agricultural population is divided by arable land (with temporary crops) only, densities will rise further because most of the population is concentrated in the valleys and basins of the great and small rivers where paddy rice is grown. (Oshima 1987: 19–21)

Seasonal Employment

The seasonality of the monsoon limited the use of the tiny holdings to about half of the year only, unless irrigation brought water during the dry seasons. Therefore, according to Oshima (1987: 17, 25), the majority of Asian peasants traditionally undertook non-crop agricultural work (animal husbandry, fishery, hunting and forestry) or off-farm activities (such as handicraft production) when the dry months came, and some also after the busy months of planting and before harvesting, as crops growing in water did not require as much care as those crops grown in dry fields, such as wheat. However, neither the non-crop agricultural work nor off-farm activities could provide sufficient employment for them.

In Western countries, the sparsely settled, low-density rural areas, together with the evenness of rainfall throughout the year, permitted farmers to complement their agricultural production with livestock raising as land (when wheat or other cereals were not being grown) was sufficient to allow growing of crops to feed livestock during the winter months. Beginning with enclosures for sheep raising, and then livestock raising for food, increasing amounts of land were put into the growing of livestock feed (grasses, turnips and clover). The growing of crops for winter feeding of livestock enabled English farmers to combine farming with animal husbandry - a combination which generated economies of scale as labor requirements per ha diminished. The rise of capitalistic agriculture, especially in England from the 18th century, hastened the combination of agriculture with animal husbandry. Agriculture also separated from handicraft which promoted the growth of industries to provide sufficient jobs for farmers leaving agriculture. In contrast, such combination and separation did not occur in monsoon Asia.

(Oshima 1987: 25, 36)

The impossibility of combining agriculture with animal husbandry. The high population densities and the dry season precluded the development of animal husbandry from becoming a seasonal complement to crop culture even in areas with year-round warm weather. As mentioned above, in the more densely populated areas, land was not available for growing both food and feed; hence working beasts tended to be relatively scarce. Thus, the great population densities demanded that all arable land be devoted to the growing of food for human beings. Whatever feed was available had to be fed to the oxen and buffaloes used in plowing. In places as densely settled as Java, the amount of available feed for buffaloes was insufficient, and most plowing had to be done by hand. And everywhere the average Asian had to pull his own cart or carry produce on his back before the advent of bicycles, railways and other modern means of transport. As one foreign observer in Japan noted in the 1880s, when the Meiji government3 ordered the raising of a horse on each farm, the farmers complied at the sacrifice of food for the family. (Oshima 1987: 25, 36—7). Therefore, animal husbandry could not provide sufficient jobs to peasants in the slack seasons.

Non-separation and the lack of handicraft development. As Oshima argues, traditional handicraft did not develop into modern industries as in the West, since it did not separate from agriculture. Further, neither urban factories nor rural handicraft could offer enough work to peasants in the dry half of the year.

In terms of the demand for labor, due to the high cost and low productivity of machines and other overheads of the steam-powered machines of the First Industrial Revolution of the 18th/19th century, the factories had to be operated year-round to be profitable, unlike hand spindles and looms (Oshima 1987: 40).

In terms of the supply of labor, however, as long as the basic traditional village structure remained largely intact, the vast peasant population was needed for the peak seasons of agricultural work, and traditional transportation was inadequate for commuting to work in the cities during the seasonal slack. Therefore, the *unlimited supply of labor* was only in the dry half year. For example, the Dutch used to interpret the backward-sloping supply curve of Indonesian workers as indolence, but it was largely a reflection of workers going back to the villages during the busy seasons. (Oshima 1987: 38, 40)

To attract the labor for year-round work, the factories would have had not

---

[3] The Meiji Reformation (Restoration) of Japan started in 1868 and the Meiji era lasted until 1912 (CEDIC 1980: 799. NECD 1985: 716).

only to pay wages equal to those for cloth making but also to make up the cost of food production. Until the factories became much more productive, with more and better machines - such as the electricity/gas-driven ones of the Second Industrial Revolution in the early decades of the 20th century - and greater economies of scale, the *wage gap* offered was not sufficiently attractive to tempt village laborers to abandon the farms.4 Therefore, despite the lower productivity of hand-operated spindles and looms, the opportunity- cost of working on them in the village was low. There was no choice for the peasants but to carry on with traditional off-farm work, principally hand spinning and weaving. (Oshima 1987: 38–40). Until the spurt of rapid growth beginning in the mid-1950s, the labor emigration to urban occupations had not been large enough to significantly reduce the absolute size of the agricultural labor force (Hayami & Yamada 1991: 4).

Such a slow release of workers from agriculture impeded industrialization. For example, Japan emerged from feudalism in the 1880s. The first textile factories in the early Meiji period had to turn to the daughters of the unemployed samurai who found no place for their traditional warrior skills, as their labor force. But due to the low agricultural productivity, not enough food could be prepared for industrial workers, so the pace of industrialization was sluggish. Around 1900, the acceleration of Japan's industrialization was possible only by the importation of large amounts of rice from its colonies *Taiwan* and *Korea* which it occupied in 1895–1945 and 1910–45 respectively. Compared with Japan, there was little or no industrial growth in the rest of Asia. Thus, the growth of modern industry was hampered and Asia fell behind in industrial production. (Oshima 1987: 38–40, 44–5, 106; 1993: 5)

But although handicraft was not separated from agriculture, with the importation of cheaper products made by Western machines in the last few centuries, the peasants lost their urban markets, and their production of handicraft was confined to village needs (Oshima 1987: 25). Therefore, village handicraft provided much less employment than before during the slack seasons.

Even today, in most monsoon Asian economies, this separation has not yet occurred, except in plantation crops such as rubber and tea which require labor all year around. The growing rural population found less to do during the dry months as the larger population sought more work. Much of the

---

[4] The migration of Chinese to Malaya was for full-time work in the tin mines, and that of Indians was for full-time work on the rubber plantations of Malaya and tea plantations in Sri Lanka - all of which paid more than part-time work in the rice paddies of China and India (Oshima 1987: 40).

available work was marginal, intermittent, irregular, of short duration, and of low intensity; and with so much labor competing for so little work in the dry months, remuneration was low. In Indonesia, per capita incomes were lower in the rural areas of Java and Bali (where densities were much higher) than in Sumatra, Kalimantan and Sulawesi; similarly, in the Philippines incomes were higher in Mindanao, which was less densely settled, than in most parts of the country. (Oshima 1987: 25, 27). Therefore, in monsoon Asia, though at the peak seasons all the available labor was needed and active at work, there were serious underemployment, unemployment and disguised unemployment in the slack time, which gravely contributed to poverty.

The Obstacles to Large-Scale Farming

In Western Europe, the favorable climate - more even rainfall - and abundance of land made it easy to convert small strip farms into large capitalistic farms even with *simple* technologies such as multiple-horse-driven iron plows in the 16th century. Technological progress, especially in England after the 15th/16th century, displaced labor-intensive production. The combination with animal husbandry generated economies of scale as mentioned before. Using the technologies of the First Industrial Revolution represented by steam-powered machines and those of the Second Industrial Revolution led by electricity/gas-driven ones, the West grew rapidly with capitalistic agriculture and industry. (Oshima 1987: 35–6, 38, 41, 45)

In contrast, although the civilizations of China and India were second to none during most of the first millennium AD and in the first half of the second millennium AD, they began to fall behind the West afterwards. By the end of the 19th century, monsoon Asia had become one of the poorest regions in the world, densely packed with tiny farms and traditional handicraft and, eventually, falling prey to the stronger West. Monsoon Asia's rice farms were not transformed into capitalistic operations, remaining essentially peasant agriculture dependent on family labor. Oshima holds that the reason for this was that agriculture of these countries was a different type from that of the West, and that for this type of agriculture capitalism was not a suitable form of organization. It was the *complexity* of Asian agricultural systems that blocked the transfer of the technology and institutions emerging in the post-medieval centuries in Europe to Asian rice farms. (Oshima 1993: 4; 1987: 35–6). Similarly, Bray (1986: xiii–xiv) argues that the reason must lie in the conditions of rice production. To monsoon Asia, the following trend might be applied: (1) the monsoon climate led to a sophisticated rice culture; (2) the technological innovations of the West up to the First Industrial Revolution were almost entirely irrelevant; (3) therefore, capitalistic large-scale farming was not feasible before WWII.

Sophisticated rice culture. Oshima (1987: 36) points out that even in the centuries BC, the technological movement of paddy rice cultivation was towards sophistication, with deep plowing, terracing, green and organic manuring, ratooning5 and small- and large-scale irrigation and drainage appearing in Northern China. Then, in the early centuries of the first millennium, transplanting began raising not only yields but also labor requirements, as seedling beds, transplanting, thorough land preparation, water management, careful cultivation and time-consuming reaping called for more labor. The first century of the second millennium saw the advent of multiple cropping with the use of short-duration, drought-resistant seeds from Vietnam, raising even further the complexity (and labor intensity) of land and seedling-bed preparations, transplantation, water management, reaping and threshing with tight schedules as one crop was harvested and the next put in immediately and with greater crop diversification. Elvin (1973: 129) believes that by the 13th century China thus had what was probably the most sophisticated agriculture in the world, India being the only conceivable rival. In the centuries following, each of these was further improved, largely by the use of more labor. These improved technologies and methods were diffused over wider areas of China and beyond. (Chang; Vegara & Yoshida 1976)

Bray (1986: 16–7, 25–6) argues that the techniques were as such that farmers themselves have been able to select for desirable traits through the centuries, so a very wide range of cultivation could be developed. By keeping a range of varieties in stock the farmer could protect himself in fair measure against the risk of drought or flood. Actually, rice farmers usually grew several different varieties of rice in any one season, partly to provide for different requirements and partly as a means of minimizing risks. The farmer could also increase his income, either by producing more rice, or by combining rice cultivation with more profitable activities like cash-cropping.

King went to China, Japan and Korea in the early 1900s to find out how people could farm the same fields for 4,000 years without destroying their fertility and how farmers could support families of 12 to 15 people on less than 2 acres, and do it generation after generation without buying fertilizer. What King saw was an essentially intensive and sophisticated agriculture and a farm system where nothing was wasted, with canals, multiple and diversified cropping, combination of irrigation and dry farming methods, and biological fertilizers. (King 1911: covers, 8–11)

Therefore, Oshima argues that it is the *complexity*, rather than 'the

---

5 Ratooning is to let a plant (usually sugarcane) send up new shoots after being cut down or cropped (OED 1989: 221).

simplicity (as Marx holds) of the organization for production in these self-sufficing communities that constantly reproduce themselves in the same form . . . that supplies the key to the secret of the unchangeableness of Asiatic societies, an unchangeableness in such striking contrast with the constant dissolution and refounding of Asiatic States, and the never-ceasing changes of dynasty.' (Oshima 1987: 34–6. Marx [1887] 1977: 338–9)

Unsuitability of the Western technologies. The technological innovations of the West up to the First Industrial Revolution were almost entirely irrelevant to monsoon agriculture. Oshima writes that drilling in place of transplanting would have caused yields to fall substantially; drainage systems were far more advanced and intricate in Asia; and it was multiple cropping rather than either fallowing or crop rotation systems that Asia needed. Nor were improvements in scythes and cradles of any use as the easily shattered and lodged rice plant required knives and smaller sickles. The steam-powered machines of the First Industrial Revolution were not suitable either. They require large boilers, shafts, transmission lines, and other equipment, which the Asian factories and farms were too small to afford. (Oshima 1987: 37; 1993: 4–5). Therefore, the Western technologies up to the 19th century could not be adopted in the monsoon Asia rice economy.

Unfeasibility of capitalistic large-scale farming. The most important Western institutional innovation - capitalistic large-scale farming - was not feasible before WWII. Oshima states that the rice culture of monsoon Asia was too complex. To feed the enormous population with so little arable land, the technology that evolved became not only intensive but intricate: deep and thorough plowing several times over, fine puddling and harrowing, elaborately seedling bed preparing, properly spaced transplanting, finely tuned watering, weed and insect controlling, careful reaping of a crop prone to lodge and shatter - and all this was carried out within a tight schedule imposed by the coming and going of monsoon rains. This was not the kind of work which could be done well by low-paid wage workers or adequately supervised by a few managers on a large farm. Nor could work animals and the steam-powered machines of the First Industrial Revolution be substituted for the highly labor-intensive operations of transplanting and reaping. With the traditional technologies, only on small farms with close coordination and cooperation of highly motivated family workers who received all the returns after paying taxes, rents and costs could productivity per ha rise to high levels in the arduous and demanding husbandry of monsoon paddy agriculture. (Oshima 1987: 37)

Bray (1986: 150) writes that rice yields are directly related to the efficacy of management of the water supply and until very recently this imposed restrictions on the size of wet-rice fields and was an important barrier to mechanical rationalization of the European type. Given the large investment in labor and time required to develop a productive rice field, there was instead a strong incentive to evolve land-saving skills in both technical and managerial terms. Effective supervision of such skilled work was highly demanding, and as rice cultivation systems became more productive there was a marked tendency for units of management to become smaller rather than larger, usually taking the form of family farms supplying the bulk of their own labor.

Oshima (1987: 37–9, 42) further indicates that large-scale agriculture (capitalistically managed or otherwise) could not produce the necessary yields per ha and capitalistic rice-growing was a low-productivity undertaking, as the Japanese found to their dismay when they attempted to introduce Western technologies after the Meiji Restoration. During the 1870s–80s, the new Meiji government sought to establish Western agricultural methods in Japan but found that the large machines were not suited to small farms and had to abandon the efforts, although some successes were achieved in spacious Hokkaido, Japan's Northernmost island, which lies outside the monsoon zone. As a result, Japan went to colonize Taiwan (1895) and Korea (1910) in order to produce rice for its industrial workers and create markets for its industrial products. In the Philippines beginning in the 19th century, plantations were operated capitalistically with a hired labor force for the growing of less labor-intensive commercial products like sugar, coconut, rubber and banana, but the large rice estates of the Spanish friars and Filipino oligarchies were rented out to tenants in small parcels for their families to work on.

Berry and Cline (1979), Binswanger, Deininger and Feder (1993) claim that there is an inverse relationship of farm size to land productivity in monsoon Asia which is evidence that large-scale farms are less productive than the small ones under the traditional technologies.

Thus, with the traditional technologies or the steam-powered machines of the First Industrial Revolution, large-scale farming was impossible. The electricity/gas-driven machines of the Second Industrial Revolution of the 20th century were suitable to both the fragmented small farms and large farms of monsoon Asia, but their introduction to the region was mainly after WWII. Even in the present era, the traditional technologies still dominate the agriculture of most rice-based economies in monsoon Asia, which together with other factors determine the dominance of the small farm size.

Feudal Landlord Ownership and Persistent Poverty

The three previous sections have dealt with the vicious circle of poverty in prewar monsoon Asia mainly in terms of the productive and technological conditions. This section touches its institutional aspects, and in particular, the feudal landlord ownership. It will be relatively brief, granted that (1) it is already well-known that feudal landlord ownership was one of the major causes of rural poverty and that most monsoon Asian economies have undertaken land reform; and (2) there is also already a huge literature on this topic and it would be difficult to fully analyze this issue for so many economies in a single section.

As Oshima (1987: 42) points out, with the old structure of the peasant production unchanged, the traditional structure of power (with the imperial system on top, the bureaucracy downwards, and the gentry in the towns and villages) remained intact through most of the latter half of the second millennium. This power structure did everything to preserve the old mode of production of which it was part and parcel and without which it would have become redundant. Thus, it was inconceivable that the agricultural revolutions of the West be transplanted to Asian soil in prewar times.

Up to the end of WWII, the feudal landlord ownership had been dominant: a few landlords owned large estates while most peasants owned little or no land and had to be tenants or farm workers. The poverty of rice growers and the hopeless position under the feudal landlord ownership were mainly caused by tenancy and loss of land ownership; usury and growing debt; and unfavorable marketing machinery, for which, Wickizer and Bennett cite examples and believe that they have properly indicated the desperately poverty-stricken condition of farmers in many monsoon Asian economies (Wickizer & Bennett 1941: 168–9). Ash (1976: 1, 50–1) holds that the feudal tenancy system constituted a serious barrier to agricultural growth, and such barriers inherent in the institutional framework of the rural sector were considerable.

Since WWII, the feudal ownership has been completely reformed in *Cambodia, mainland China, Japan, North Korea, South Korea, Myanmar, Taiwan* and *Vietnam*, but remained incompletely changed, or even intact in some other economies.

In *India*, in most areas, although the largest land-holdings were redistributed, relatively smaller but large enough landlords still exist (Barker; Herdt & Rose 1985: 35). They are very powerful and have their own security forces (Oshima 1987: 226; 1993: 246).

In the *Philippines*, after the 1972 land reform, relatively few rice farmers owned their land (Barker; Herdt & Rose 1985: 35). The landed oligarchy was even more powerful, as they owned private armies and dominated local politics (Oshima 1993: 246–7). In 1988, new land reform to cover all land was introduced, but was criticized for its vulnerability to manipulation at local level. Consequently, in 1995 the program was significantly behind the target (Hodgkinson 1996: 913). Harassment and, at times, murder occurred. Many of those who have been issued land titles were not physically given

land while those who had secured ownership of their farms were not
receiving the support and resources they were supposed to get. Despite the
farmers' grave situation, big landowners continue to threaten reform
beneficiaries and explicitly mock the agrarian reform law. (ANGOC 1997)

In *Bangladesh*, land reform has been pursued, the largest estates were
turned to individual peasant ownership, land-holding ceilings established and
minimum wages for agricultural labor determined (Hussain 1995: 79, 91,
112). But the ownership pattern is still characterized by considerable
inequality in land-holding (Khan 1997: 122).

In *Sri Lanka*, the 1972 Land Reform Act fixed a ceiling of 10.1 ha on
paddy holdings per family, which was so large that the previous paddy
ownership was left practically untouched (De A. Samarasinghe 1997: 990).

In *Malaysia*, while Malays and other indigenous people concentrate on the
traditional subsistence agriculture, other races hold larger areas of land (Bray
1986: 185. Edwards 1997: 572–4, 579).

In *Thailand*, in many rural areas, there is an acute shortage of land, with
a few rich owning large holdings alongside many landless people (Dixon
1997: 1028. Richardson 1997: 1).

In *Pakistan*, there have been only very limited steps taken to reduce the
size of the largest holdings and to transfer land rights to the actual cultivators
(Taylor 1997: 875).

In *Indonesia*, land reform laws of 1960 and 1961 were not implemented
after 1966 and landlessness was increasingly severe (Bray 1986: 187–8,
191). There is a variety of distributional imbalances (Hobohm 1997: 372).

In *Bhutan* and *Nepal*, the serf-holder and landlord systems remain largely
intact. The rural poverty in these countries is related to such systems.
(Oshima 1993: 247. Khanal 1995: 41–4)

Moreover, *slavery* - a system historically more backward than feudalism -
still is flourishing, especially in South Asia. Poverty drives peasants to usury
which in turn makes them debt-bonded. Bonded workers agree to sell their
labor in exchange for a lump sum to pay, e.g., a large medical bill. But the
line is easily crossed into slavery, when low wages, high interest rates and
cheating make the debt impossible to repay. In South Asia, many people are
illiterate, ignorant of their rights, and thus easily deceived. For example, in
Nepal and Pakistan, millions of bonded laborers work in farming. Bonded
debts can be passed on to the next generation. Those who are deemed not to
have paid their debt can be sold to another landlord. If a person escapes his
place of slavery, his family can be held until he returns, or sold if he does
not. Bonded peasants can be sold into marriage. Slavery can be found in
prostitution and industry too. Although laws have been passed to prohibit
slavery, little has been done to enforce them. (*Economist* 1996: 45–6). This
phenomenon also exists in India (Thomas 1993: 7. FEER 1999: 16).

Vicious Circle of Poverty within Agriculture and between Agriculture and Industry

In sum, as Oshima (1993: 4) indicates, before the end of WWII, there was a vicious circle of poverty in monsoon Asia. It existed not only within agriculture but also between agriculture and industry.

Vicious circle of poverty within agriculture. Heavy monsoon rains fall for six months of the year, while there is little rain during the other six months, giving rise in monsoon Asia to an agriculture different from that of the West and other regions, i.e., paddy rice culture, which over the centuries has become very labor-intensive. Up to the end of WWII, for maximum yields, many workers were needed for planting, harvesting and threshing. As population increased faster than available land, farm size diminished and densities rose to the greatest in the world, rice culture became more and more labor-intensive and sophisticated, which demanded even more labor. But in the dry half year, this enormous labor force was unable to find sufficient work. Some found work in handicraft which was never separated from agriculture but also declined facing the cheaper products made by machines from the West. (Oshima 1993: 3). The more labor force was needed in the wet seasons, the more the labor force was underemployed, unemployed or disguisedly unemployed in the dry seasons, which in turn called for even more labor force in order to produce more food for the population to survive the dry seasons or 'spring hunger', which again caused smaller and more fragmented farms, greater densities and higher underemployment, unemployment and disguised unemployment in the dry half year. *Hence a vicious circle of poverty within agriculture.*

Vicious circle of poverty between agriculture and industry. The development of industry required a year-round supply of labor, but the unlimited supply of labor was only available in the dry half year. In order to induce peasants to abandon farming, a sufficiently high wage gap was needed, which the factories, with the steam-powered machines of the First Industrial Revolution and low productivity, were unable to provide. Even if it could be provided, the consequent labor force shortage in the peak seasons would reduce the agricultural output. And even if industry could acquire labor from other sources (e.g., the daughters of the unemployed samurai in Japan after the Meiji Restoration), agriculture could not provide enough food due to its low productivity. The industrial sector also needed a huge rural market for its products, but the poverty of peasants impeded the establishment of such a market. Therefore, the emergence of a modern industry was hampered. The slow growth of industry could not generate enough wealth which might then be used to aid agricultural development.

Hence a vicious circle of poverty between agriculture and industry.

Capitalistic large-scale farming was not feasible, because the technological innovations of the West up to the First Industrial Revolution were almost entirely irrelevant to the highly labor-intensive and sophisticated rice culture. The electricity/gas-driven machines of the Second Industrial Revolution were suitable but they needed education and technological help, of which the illiterate peasants themselves could not partake. More serious was the institutional and power structure, especially the feudal landlord ownership system, which strengthened the vicious circle of poverty.

Free market forces alone could not shatter the vicious circle of poverty and realize sustainable rural development. Therefore, it was necessary to resort to a mixed economy in the postwar era.

2.3 The Postwar Initial Conditions for Development in Monsoon Asia

In the initial postwar period, the above-mentioned three traditional productive and technological conditions - i.e., (1) highly labor-intensive rice culture leading to labor force shortage in the peak seasons, high population densities, and fragmented small farms; (2) little employment in the slack seasons; (3) unfeasibility of capitalistic large-scale farming - still prevailed. Furthermore, one institutional condition - feudal landlord ownership - still remained in many economies. These were particular to monsoon Asia and different from the characteristics of Europe.

Besides, there were a number of initial economic and social conditions which were also very important and of which Kuznets ([1954] 1958: 144, 147–55; 1960), Myrdal (1972: 49–55) and Ishikawa (1967: 1, 4, 8–13, 18–22, 26) have done special analyses. Those most relevant to rural development (not including culture, politics, industry and foreign trade) were (1) *low per capita income*, (2) *vast population and a huge labor force*, (3) *low productivity in peasant agriculture*, and (4) *new institutional settings* (colonialism renounced and the feudal landlord system criticized or reformed, hence new markets and sources of investment had to be found).

These authors' common view is that these initial conditions facing the postwar developing economies in monsoon Asia were different from those in the advanced countries (including Japan) at their past comparable stages of economic development and unfavorable to these economies' development. In contrast, *the author's major finding in this section is that these initial conditions were also applicable to the immediate postwar Japan, which these authors do not note.* In the immediate postwar period: (1) Japan's per capita income was also low as it suffered from devastation. With acute food shortages and hyperinflation the majority of Japanese people were barely able to maintain a subsistence standard of living (Hayami 1988: 43). (2) The territory reduced by almost one-half and population increased by repatriates from colonies. Moreover, up to the mid-1950s, as the repatriates and demobilized soldiers did not have sufficient employment opportunities in cities, agricultural population increased by 200–300‰ over the prewar figure and the rural community became overcrowded. (ESJ 1955–56: 95–6. Hayami & Yamada 1991: 83). (3) It became evident in the 1910s that the technological potential in agriculture exhausted when the rate of growth in agricultural output and productivity began to decelerate. During the interwar era, agriculture was relatively stagnant. New technological potential emerged, but militarism diverted the resources to wage WWII to invade other countries and stagnation lasted to the immediate postwar period. (Hayami 1988: 43. Hayami & Yamada 1991: 77–83). (4) Colonialism was given up and the feudal landlord system reformed. This finding would pave the way for the argument in later chapters that the postwar Japanese model of rural development would also be relevant to other rice-based economies in monsoon Asia.

Myrdal (1972: 54) stresses that all of the differences in initial conditions made the problem of economic development more difficult for the nations of South and Southeast Asia than it once was for the Western nations. Ishikawa (1967: 28–9) also holds that there were no ready measures to solve the difficulties caused by the initial conditions, and any possible measures may be conflicting in front of the interactions of the initial conditions.

But, although very difficult as Ishikawa anticipates, the tasks of raising per capita income, employing a huge labor force, increasing productivity in peasant agriculture, finding new growth and investment sources under the new institutional settings, etc., would have to be fulfilled by the postwar monsoon developing economies (as well as Japan with a stagnant agriculture). Now that free market forces alone could not overcome the dual economy and realize sustainable rural development as the prewar experience had shown, it was logical to turn to and strengthen the mixed economy.

2.4 Variable Mixed Economies

Holland's Concept of Variable Mixed Economies

Mixed economy. Multiple structures of public and private ownership. Holland (1993: 8) has illustrated multiple ownership in the postwar Western welfare states. He writes that the postwar increases in welfare did not always take the form of growth plus redistribution through state welfare policies. Much of it came from structural shifts (i.e., shifts out of agriculture into industry and services) which had major social effects and especially the historic one-off transition from a peasant-based to an industrial economy. In Italy (as in Japan, Taiwan and South Korea) the increases in welfare were accompanied by a significant degree of land reform. Such changes in the ownership base in agriculture, rather than nationalization of industry or utilities, were important to the context within which welfare gains could be achieved.

The postwar models of economic and social cohesion in Europe have depended on a nexus of cooperative horizontal and vertical links which have been crucial to ensuring that small and medium firms and farms have been able to survive and by and large flourish for decades. In France and Italy this has included a major role for agricultural cooperatives in both production and distribution. In Italy, cooperative associations of small producers in Tuscany, Emilia Romagna and Veneto formed interest groups which worked in successful symbiosis with local and regional governments and local trade unions. Social partnerships in such cases, at the micro and local level, reinforced the sense of purposeful interaction between private interest groups and public institutions. This included not only regional public credit institutions, but also mutual credit institutions between small producers. In France and Italy, the mixed economy also included more public ownership in industry and services. (Holland 1993: 6–8)

Intervention other than ownership. Holland (1993: 6–8) points out that while postwar France and Italy used more public ownership and planning, Germany adopted a model which was different - on ownership - but more effective - on planning. The German reconstruction involved extensive economic planning through the Kreditanstalt fur Wiederaufbau (KfW or KW - Reconstruction Loan Corporation). The underlying strength of the German economy lay in its big business groups, its network of medium sized firms (*Mittelstand*) and public institutions. Through the chairmanship of Deutsche Bank President Herman Abs and with the representation in the KfW of all the main banks, which in turn were shareholders in all the leading companies in the economy, the KfW arguably was able to plan the allocation of Marshall Aid and counterpart finance as effectively - albeit with virtually no public profile - as did the much publicized First French Plan under the high profile leadership of its first director, Jean Monnet. (Shonfield 1969: 242, 253, 262, 276–82). Such planning for German reconstruction needed major public spending through Marshall Aid. But it did not need public ownership. Nor did it need a formal planning structure within the state rather than a symbiosis between a key public credit agency (the KfW) and the main private banks which, through their supervisory board membership in leading firms, knew where the strengths were which should be reinforced and the bottlenecks which needed widening. (Holland 1993: 6–8)

Variable mixed economies. According to Holland (1993: 5–6), there is a matrix of the mixed economy which includes *varying* relations between public and private economic power; public and private economic interest groups; public and private institutions; public and private credit and finance; public and private regulations; public and private planning; public and private spending; public and private enterprises; public and private management. The relative balance and effectiveness of such factors in the public and private sectors varied both *between* economies and societies, and *within* them over time. The result was not one, two or three models but a range of discrete outcomes in a general paradigm of the mixed economy. In this sense, Nuti's model of market socialism as outlined below also belongs to variable mixed economies.

Holland's concept of variable mixed economies not only implies varying relations between the public and private sectors, but also means that dynamically, they should change over time in relation to changing needs in the economy and society. For example, in Japan, the Meiji dynasty achieved basic industrialization through public ownership, including some manufacturing firms. It was only with evidence of economic take-off that some of these were privatized. The model in this respect was similar to that of the USA after independence, when the post colonial states in several cases not only owned banks and financed infrastructure but also owned manufacturing companies. In fact, the USA was one of the first countries to exhibit the modern tendency to extend the activity of the state into industry. (Holland 1994: 75, 188; 1976b: 114–20. Callender 1902: 111)

In the postwar era, the South Korean government implemented what Wade (1990: 297) calls a 'Governed Market' policy. It fundamentally reshaped ownership through land reform and a publicly owned banking system. It created an enclave of relative stability for long-term investment decisions through its control of key parameters (foreign exchange rates, interest rates and aggregate demand). It modulated the economy's exposure to international competitive pressures in the domestic market through protection and exchange control. It imposed conditions on the activities of foreign companies in the country so as to gain benefits in terms of trade and technology transfer. It subsidized and promoted national champions. (Hamilton 1986). It also planned outcomes through the Economic Planning Board (Wade 1990: 200). Not least, an ostensibly private enterprise economy utilized public ownership to an extent which parallelled that of many countries advocating a socialist pattern of society (Jones & Sakong 1980: 141). In 1972, 12 of the 16 biggest industrial enterprises were public ones (Jones & Mason 1982: 38).

From the mid-1970s to early 1980s, the government promoted petrochemicals and other heavy and chemical industries (HCIS) including petrochemicals, steel, nonferrous metals, machinery, automobiles, shipbuilding and electronics (Wade 1990: 309–20).

But this too changed over time. During the 1980s, the South Korean government moved towards a follower rather than leader role with companies, as they showed themselves capable of casting global shadows. It since has been concentrating more on basic research and development (R&D), leaving commercialization and marketing to the firms and setting its R&D agenda in consultation with them. (Wade 1990: 312–9)

Nuti's Model of Market Socialism

Of the various arguments in Nuti's model of market socialism, the one most relevant to this book is as follows.

Nuti (1992: 22) criticizes Mises's belief that private ownership of the means of production was a precondition of markets, because only ultimate owners have the incentive to control their efficient use (Mises 1951). Hence, for Mises there is the dilemma: either socialism or markets, and there could be no such a thing as market socialism. Nuti believes that Mises is both right and wrong. He is right in that the appropriation of all, or a sizable fraction, of the capital gains deriving from successful enterprise seems a necessary precondition for the mobilization of entrepreneurial initiatives; but he is wrong in that this is all that is needed.

Nuti (1992: 22–3) suggests a pluralist ownership. There can be a large but not exclusive or even necessarily predominant public ownership of productive capacity (state, local and cooperative) coexisting and competing on equal terms with a non-public sector. One form of privatization of management is the maintenance of a large state stake in national capital through state shareholdings in private companies.

Nuti (1992: 17, 19–20, 22–3) also imagines an economy where the ownership of all means of production and their further reproduction are in the hands of the state, but these means are leased in competitive leasing markets to private entrepreneurs who retain a residual claim to both income and capital gains and are able to transfer these claims. Capital leasings - present on a small scale under the New Economic Policy during 1921–26 in the USSR - have reappeared widely in the recent reforms in Eastern Europe, unfortunately on too small a scale. There is a model of 'entrepreneurial socialism' by Liska (1963) based precisely on the competitive leasing of state assets and their compulsory surrender to the highest tenderer (however, with the additional tenders belonging to tenderers, not to the state), all citizens having a capital stake to invest or to use to exercise entrepreneurship (Barsony 1982. Nuti 1988: 2–6). Leasings, instead of privatization, are worthy of greater consideration than they have attracted in economic reform to date. Nuti stresses that this model of market socialism is a 'Third Way' between the centrally planned economy and a free market system. The exploration of such a model should be of interest to socialists and non-socialists alike, also in the West.

Incentive from competitive leasing, not necessarily from ownership, is the *core* of Nuti's model of market socialism. Market socialism may have different models. In this book, it refers to that in Nuti's model. Actually, as introduced in Chapter 1 and further in Chapters 5–7, the Household Contract System of China, invented in the elementary cooperatives (contracting collectively used private land shares to households for operation) in the 1950s, continued in the advanced cooperatives and the people's communes (contracting collectively owned land to households for operation) in the 1950s–70s, and popularized and theorized since 1978, was already a long-term successful practice of market socialism.

Hence a *hypothesis* is presented here: the fragmented small farms as the last obstacle imposed by the monsoon in sustainable rural development of monsoon Asia may be overcome by variable mixed economies, increasingly along three main phases. *Phase 1*: sub-village individual–collective mixed economy (sub-village-wide cooperative/enterprise collective use of physically withdrawable private land shares, exercising collective–individual dual level operation of large land units, with the basic operation level at one household as the major form or at a unit including a small number of households as the minor form). *Phase 2*: village-wide individual–collective mixed economy. *Phase 3*: either large-scale farming public–individual mixed economy or corporate–individual mixed economy (collective use of either public land, or physically unwithdrawable private land shares under corporate ownership, exercising village–individual dual level operation of large land units, with the basic operation level at one household as the major form or at a unit including a small number of households as the minor form, as a third way beyond the centrally planned economy and free market system). Hence also the *focus* of Chapters 3–8: how to consolidate and enlarge the fragmented small farms in monsoon Asia under private and public land ownership with reference to the Japanese and Chinese models respectively, and under corporate land ownership as a proposed new model.

The Role of Government in Economic Development

Kuznets (1971: 346–7) points out that the role of the nation-state in modern economic growth with its continuous technological and social innovations and its rapid rate of structural change is an important factor in modern economic growth, and asks whether the delay in the rise of a modern nation-state was a factor in the failure of underdeveloped countries to enter the modern growth process.

Abramovitz (1981: 2) indicates that the process includes the displacement and redistribution of the population among regions, the abandonment of old industries and occupations, the qualification of workers for new and more skilled occupations and extension of education. The growth of very large-scale enterprise establishes new types of market power and alters the relations of workers and employees. These imply a great change in the structure of families and in their roles in caring for children, the sick and the old. These and other changes transform the positions, prospects and power of established groups. Conflict and resistance are intrinsic to the growth process. To resolve such conflict and resistance in a way that preserves a large consensus for growth, yet does not impose a cost which retards growth unduly, a mechanism of conflict resolution is needed. The national sovereign state necessarily becomes the arbiter of group conflict.

Oshima (1993: 226) further stresses that it is abundantly clear that the role of government in monsoon Asian development is of the utmost importance, especially during the agro—industrial transition. Governments in monsoon Asia have a greater role to play in agriculture than in other regions: land is scarce, and many farmers own little or no land, so agrarian reform is needed. Rents charged to tenants and interest rates on loans tend to be high, requiring regulation. But often governments fail to intervene, fearing the landowning class. Irrigation is needed to supply water during the dry season, and drainage is needed in the wet season.

During the early stages of the agro—industrial transition, there are other functions to be performed by government. Government is crucial in the construction of modern physical infrastructure, the import and supervision of technologies, the development of human and natural resources, the mobilization and channeling of savings, and the reduction of unemployment and poverty. Moreover, traditional institutions must be modernized, and the foundations of new organizations, such as labor unions, farmers' cooperatives, industrial and commercial associations, and banks, must be laid. (Oshima 1993: 227)

Bray (1986: 158—61) holds that the state has several areas in which it may invest to foster agricultural growth. The first is infrastructure: land reclamation; provision of transport facilities; and most importantly water conservancy. The second is capital including capital inputs especially fertilizers; and capital goods such as tilling, harvesting and processing machinery. The third is provision of credit facilities.

Oshima (1993: 227) notes that there are some who are impatient with the inefficiencies of government and want to shift to the market, which they consider the most efficient allocator of resources. But the market is only as efficient as the forces making up the market. It took some time for the West to evolve and nurture these forces. It is well known that the (former) socialist countries are encountering difficulties in shifting from a planned to a market economy. It will take some time before market forces are developed, especially the ability of entrepreneurs to finance and market their production. Indeed, an important historical function of government in the process of development is to mold these forces so that the market becomes an efficient resource allocator. One reason for the rapid growth of East Asian economies was the efficiency of their governments. They were more effective in raising productivity, promoting saving, generating employment through agricultural diversification, multiple cropping, and off-farm employment, and developing human resources. In addition, they supplied the necessary urban infrastructures such as roads and public utilities, secured political and social stability, and motivated the populace to work energetically to develop the economy. The governments of East Asia regulated the market deeply without disturbing the market unduly or weakening market forces.

Gordillo de Anda (1997: 1–3, 7–8) argues that markets do not function by themselves. It is naive to assume that the removal of government interventions will result in reasonable approximations of perfect markets. It does not follow that social welfare will rise as a consequence of the removal of some or all government interventions. On the contrary, the impact of structural reform and liberalization has negatively affected the poorest. The virtues of the market are exaggerated in line with the vices of the state. Markets must be managed and market failures compensated for. For development to work, people have to feel that they directly benefit; and for that to work, there has to be a *mix* of market, civic society (such as farmers' cooperatives or associations) and government. Each of these three parts needs the other. Such a mix could release something far more powerful than the energy of each: the synergy of 'collective imagination and action' that results in sustainable development. Riddell (1997: 2) further presents that there exists a wide range of examples of public sector and private sector cooperation. The challenge that all nations are facing is to identify and implement solutions that respond to their own situation.

Dreze and Sen (1991: 28–9) warn that 'A purist strategy - relying only on the market or only on State action - can be awfully short of logistic means. The need to consider the plurality of levers and a heterogeneous set of mechanisms is hard to escape in the pursuit of social security.' In 'famine prevention', there are 'both the possible failure of the market mechanism to provide adequate guarantee of entitlements and the possibly helpful role of markets in meeting demands generated by public relief programs.' In 'the elimination of systematic and persistent deprivations and the promotion of living standards in general', there is 'the part that economic growth - even when promoted by market-related processes - can play provided that the fruits of growth are sensibly used for the purpose of social security. In this context we have to guard against two rather disparate and contrary dangers. One is to ignore the part that the market mechanism can play in generating growth efficiency (despite its various limitations as an allocative device), with the State trying to do it all itself through administrative devices. The other is to be over-impressed by what the market mechanism can do and to place our reliance entirely on it, neglecting those things that the government can effectively undertake (including various policies for the promotion of health and education).' Moreover, 'Public action must not be confused with State action only. Public action includes not merely what is done for the public by the State, but also what is done by the public itself. We have to recognize inter alia the role of non-governmental organizations in providing social security (particularly in times of distress), and the part that social, political, and humanitarian institutions can play in protecting and promoting living conditions.'

These viewpoints are in accordance with the variable mixed economies.

However, systematically reviewing and discussing all patterns of mixed economy in agriculture, industry, finance, trade, etc. and their interrelationship in all countries of the West and East in their developing and developed stages would not be feasible here. Thus, Chapters 4–8 will concentrate on the two variants of the mixed economy in agriculture in postwar monsoon Asia: the Japanese one and the Chinese one, examining whether they could overcome the last obstacle to sustainable rural development in monsoon Asia. A new model will also be proposed.

3. Theory of Property Rights

Modern property rights theory was mainly formed at the beginning of the 1960s. Of its many branches, this chapter can only review those most relevant to one of the major tasks of this book, i.e., how to overcome the inefficient land-holding by part-time and absent small farmers, and consolidate and enlarge the fragmented small farms. They will be applied into economic analysis in later chapters, although some brief reference will also be made in this chapter to show their relevance to the Japanese and Chinese models of rural development and the proposed new model.

Not surprisingly, the literature contains a range of different views and perspectives. There is no single universally accepted statement of the theory (Weitzman & Xu 1993: 5). This chapter adopts those which are perceived here as most appropriate, while criticizing incorrect views, especially those in some widely-used economics textbooks and dictionary.1

---

[1] In the literature, the terminology differs but some of the main concepts are similar. For example, the authors variously use terms such as 'property rights' (Demsetz [1967] 1974: 31), 'property relations' (Furubotn & Pejovich 1974: 2), 'rights', 'entitlements' (Alchian 1974: xiii). Few explicit differences are explained clearly in the literature and there is no substantive difference in the main conceptual framework of the various authors. Therefore, in the text, when expressing a *general* concept of property rights, the author will use the term 'property rights'.

Similarly, although different authors use 'ownership', 'ownership rights', 'ownership title' (Demsetz 1988: 12; [1967] 1974: 33), 'right of ownership' (Furubotn & Pejovich 1974: 4), this book will use the term 'ownership' to represent the concept of ownership of an asset.

The author also finds that the terms 'property rights (or ownership) assignments', 'property rights (or ownership) system', 'property rights (or ownership) structures', 'property rights (or ownership) configurations', 'patterns of property rights (or ownership)' (Furubotn & Pejovich 1974: 1, 3), sometimes even 'property rights (or ownership)' (Demsetz [1967] 1974: 32) are used by different authors to express the same concept, i.e., property rights (or ownership) structures. Thus, in this book, when presenting the concept of property rights (or ownership) structures, the author will mainly use the term 'property rights (or ownership) structures', but sometimes also use the term 'property rights (or ownership) assignments' as it is relevant in a specific context.

3.1 Incentives under Private Ownership and Possession of Public Assets

Property Rights, Ownership and Possession

Property rights. Furubotn and Pejovich (1974: 3) define the concept of property rights as the sanctioned behavioral relations among people that arise from the existence of goods and pertain to their use.

These relations, as Demsetz ([1967] 1974: 31—2) emphasizes, convey the right to benefit or harm oneself or others. For example, harming a competitor by producing superior products may be permitted, while shooting him may not. They specify the norms of behavior with respect to goods that each and every person must observe in his (her) daily interactions with other persons, or bear the cost of non-observance (Furubotn & Pejovich 1974: 3). They also specify ways in which persons may be benefited and harmed, and, therefore, who must pay whom to modify the actions taken by persons (Demsetz [1967] 1974: 32).

Furubotn, Pejovich and Demsetz indicate the basic implications of the concept of property rights as follows.

Property rights are an instrument of society. In the world of Robinson Crusoe, they play no role. (Demsetz [1967] 1974: 31). This applies to all scarce goods and includes both the rights over material things (to sell my computer) as well as human rights (the right to vote, to publish, etc.). Here, the term 'good' refers to anything that yields utility or satisfaction to a person. The prevailing property rights structure in the community is the sum of economic and social relations with respect to scarce resources in which individual members stand to each other (Furubotn & Pejovich 1974: 3).

Ownership. Furubotn and Pejovich (1974: 4) claim that ownership of an asset is the best known of the many sub-categories of the general concept of property rights. It implies the following three elements.

First, the right to use the asset (Furubotn & Pejovich 1974: 4). Especially, as Milgrom and Roberts stress, it includes the right to residual control - that is, the right to make any decisions concerning the asset's use that are not explicitly controlled by law or assigned to another by contract (Milgrom & Roberts 1992: 289). For example, Japanese owner-peasants can decide whether or not to produce, what product and how much to produce on their own land, which are not explicitly controlled by law.

Second, the right to appropriate returns from the asset (Furubotn & Pejovich 1974: 4), or the right to refuse use of the asset to anyone who will not pay the price the owner demands. Particularly, it contains the right to residual returns - the net income an asset brings after all revenues have been collected and all debts, expenses and other contractual obligations have been paid. Thus, the owner of an asset is the residual claimant - the one who is entitled to receive any net income the asset produces. (Milgrom & Roberts 1992: 290–1)

Third, the right to change the asset's form and/or substance. This element, the right to bear the consequences from changes in the value of an asset, is the fundamental component of ownership. It implies that the owner has the legal freedom to transfer all rights (e.g., to sell a piece of land), or some rights (e.g., to lease the land), in the asset to others at a mutually agreed-upon price. (Furubotn & Pejovich 1974: 4)

Ownership is an exclusive but not unrestricted right in the sense that it is limited only by those restrictions that are explicitly stated in the law; or, sometimes, in the customs and mores of a society (Demsetz [1967] 1974: 31). Such restrictions may range from substantial to minor. For example, on one hand, there is the serious case where an individual's ownership of an asset cannot be transferred for a price higher than the ceiling price established by the government; on the other, there is the situation where a landowner is constrained for building a fence within two feet of the property line. (Furubotn & Pejovich 1974: 4)

This statement is especially relevant to this book. As shown in Chapters 1 and 4, the land reform in Japan during 1946–50 restricted the acreage of private land ownership, protected tenants from eviction and controlled land rent. In China, as presented in Chapter 6, villages own the land but cannot sell it without the state's permission.

Possession. Possession of an asset refers to the holding of an asset either by ownership control or in other ways. Three relevant features are considered here.

1. The owner also is possessor. If the owner holds the asset completely with him (her), he (she) is also its possessor. Here, ownership is also possession. For example, those Japanese small farmers who till their own land are both owners and possessors of the land.

2. The owner is not possessor. Two cases are considered here. (1) *Leasing* of land. If the owner (as lessor) leases the asset (land) to another party (as lessee), then, during the lease period, the owner is no more its possessor, nor is the possessor its owner. This is the case under the leasing of private land in Japan. (2) *Contracting* output for using land. If the owner (as contractee) contracts a complete task using the asset (land) to another party (as contractor), and the owner has the duty to provide the contractor with services, then, during the contract period, the owner is no more its possessor, nor is the possessor its owner. (There are numerous forms of contracting. Here it refers to that under the Chinese Household Contract System as outlined in Chapters 1, 6 and 7. 'Contracts a complete task' means to

contract the whole agricultural production process, rather than a part or parts of the task, e.g., harvesting only.)

The major difference between leasing and contracting is that the lessor has no duty to provide services while the contractee has.

3. The ordinary owner is not direct possessor. There has been cooperative/ enterprise engaging in both Chinese and Japanese agriculture with land shares by landowners, capital shares by investors, distributing revenue among land shares, capital shares and labor contribution. Here, if there are many landowners, then possession is by the board of directors (representing all landowners and capital shareholders, making major decisions) and managers. Some of the landowners may operate land as employees of the cooperative/ enterprise, but not as land owners. In this book, such a cooperative/enterprise is referred to as 'Shareholding', if land is physically withdrawable when a member quits; and 'Corporate-Holding' (under public land ownership) or 'Corporate-Ownership' (under private land ownership), if land is physically unwithdrawable. In Table 3.1, only the case of shareholding is illustrated.

Incentive and Pareto Efficiency

Milgrom and Roberts (1992: 288, 291) point out that the institution of ownership accompanied by secure property rights is the most common and effective institution for providing people with incentive to create, maintain and improve assets. Tying together residual returns and residual control is the key to the incentive effects of ownership. These effects are very powerful because the decision maker bears the full financial impact of his choices.

Suppose a transaction involves several people supplying labor, physical inputs, and so on. If some of the parties involved receive fixed amounts of value specified by a contract and there is only one residual claimant, then maximizing the total value received by the residual claimant is just the same as maximizing the total value. If the residual claimant also has the residual control, then just by pursuing his own interests and maximizing his own returns, the claimant will be led to make the decisions reaching *Pareto efficiency*. (Milgrom & Roberts 1992: 291–2)

Efficiency usually means not wasteful, or doing the 'best' one can with available resources. An allocation of resources in the economy is Pareto efficient if there is no other productively feasible allocation which makes all individuals in the economy at least as well off, and at least one strictly better off, than they were initially. (Pareto [1927] 1971. Lockwood 1987: 811). Efficiency is always defined relative to a specific set of individuals and available options - this is what 'economy' means in the definition. Efficiency criteria cannot be applied to resolve ethical questions about whether it is justified or worthwhile to help one person at another's expense (this point will be further discussed later). (Milgrom & Roberts 1992: 22)

When it is possible for a single individual to both have the residual control and receive the residual returns, the residual decisions made will tend to be Pareto efficient ones. For example, the owner of a car receives both the residual control and residual returns. If he exercises his right not to maintain his car, then he suffers the diminished services it provides and the reduced selling price it eventually commands. (Milgrom & Roberts 1992: 291–2). Thus, he will have incentive to maintain the car well.

In contrast, if only part of the costs or benefits of a decision accrues to the party making the decision, then that individual will find it in his personal interest to ignore some of these effects, frequently leading to inefficient decisions. Milgrom and Roberts give a striking example in the case of car hire. In the case, there is extreme difficulty in performance measurement - the virtual impossibility of establishing exactly how much the car's value has depreciated during any particular rental. For this reason, the rental company is unable to base its charges on its actual costs. Instead, it bases them on the things it can observe (such as days and hours of the rental, miles driven and obvious collision damage). Such a charge is necessarily less than perfectly sensitive to any single actual use and its effects, so careful use is not fully rewarded and rough use is not fully charged. The one who decides on how the asset is actually used - the person renting in it - has residual control (for a time) but is not the residual claimant. Therefore, he will not have much incentive to do his best in caring for the car during its use. For general assets, as long as performance measurement is imperfect, a user who does not receive the residual returns is unlikely to take the value-maximizing level of care in maintaining its value and even more unlikely to do much to add to the asset's value. (Milgrom & Roberts 1992: 291–2)

As Table 3.1 shows, not only private ownership and possession of an asset, but also possession (leasing, contracting, shareholding in cooperatives/ enterprises) of an either public or private asset (e.g., land), may tie residual control and residual returns together, thus giving incentives to producers (as possessors) for profit-maximization to reach Pareto efficiency. In leasing, contracting and shareholding, although the possessors (lessee, contractor and manager) have no ownership of the physical asset (e.g., land), they have the ownership of the enterprise which uses that asset. The appropriation of both profits as residual returns and any increment in the value of the enterprise gives incentive to the possessor. (Of course, the minimum amount of the residual returns should not be lower than the subsistence. Otherwise, the possessor would not be able to make a living, as is the case under the exploitative feudal landlord–tenant system). Free transfer of long-leasing, contracting and shares of land in the market is a sufficient condition for the functioning of a market economy. This is in accordance with the core of

Table 3.1 Ownership and Possession of Asset (Land) [a]

Right	The owner is possessor of land.		The owner is not possessor and the possessor is not owner of land. The owner (lessor/contractee) leases/contracts the land to another party (lessee/contractor).		Ordinary owner is not direct possessor of land. Cooperative/enterprise with land shares by landowners, capital shares by investors, distributing revenue among land shares, capital shares and labor contribution. Possession is by a board of directors (representing all land and capital shareholders, making major decisions and managers).	
	Landowner is land possessor		Landowner (lessor/contractee)	Land possessor (lessee/contractor)	Landowner	Land possessor (board of directors and managers)
1. Use the asset/ residual control	Yes		No	Yes	Use - no (if yes, only as employee). Residual control - yes, through board of directors	Yes

Right	Landowner is land possessor	Landowner (lessor/contractee)	Land possessor (lessee/contractor)	Landowner	Land possessor (board of directors and managers)
2. Get return/ residual from the asset	Yes	Yes	Yes	Yes	Yes
		Fixed rent as return, without residual	Residual above fixed rent		
		Proportionate rent as return, without residual	Residual above proportionate rent		
		In contracting, output in contracted quota as return, without residual	Residual above contracted quota		
3. Change the form and/or substance of the asset	Yes	Change to non-farmland requires agreement of possessor; [b] Sale of land yes, but the ongoing lease/contract should not be affected without compensation	Change to non-farmland requires agreement of owner; [b] Sale of land no; Transfer of lease/contract possible; Improvement of quality yes; Destruction no	Change to non-farmland requires agreement of possessor; [b] Sale of land shares yes; Quit with land from cooperative/enterprise yes	Change to non-farmland requires agreement of owner; [b] Sale of land no; Leasing/contracting yes; Improvement of quality yes; Destruction no
Application	Japan	Leasing mainly in Japan, contracting chiefly in China.		Japan and China	

Notes:
a. This table is the author's own formulation.
b. Non-farmland means of production refers to land-constituted assets other than farmland (such as dam, road, canal, pond).

Nuti's model of market socialism - incentive from competitive leasing, not necessarily from ownership of the means of production.

Relevance to Japanese and Chinese agriculture. The nine main features of the Japanese model of rural development (identified in Chapters 1 and 4) and 13 main features in the Chinese counterpart (introduced in Chapters 1, 5–7) are relevant in this context. The huge incentive to efficient production after the land reforms by owner-peasants and tenants in the late 1940s and 1950s in Japan, and by owner-peasants in the late 1940s and early 1950s in China, and by peasants contracting collectively owned land in the late 1970s and the first half of the 1980s in China; and experiences in shareholding agricultural cooperatives/enterprises as efforts for large-scale farming in the elementary cooperatives up to April 1956 in China and since the 1970s in Japan, are evidence for the above-discussed property rights theory. This theory also supports Holland's concept of mixed economy and Nuti's model of market socialism introduced in Chapter 2. It is compatible with the author's hypothesis raised in both Chapters 1 and 2 - the fragmented small farms as the last obstacle imposed by the monsoon in sustainable rural development of monsoon Asia may be overcome by variable mixed economies, increasingly along three main phases. *Phase 1*: sub-village individual–collective mixed economy (sub-village-wide cooperative/ enterprise collective use of physically withdrawable private land shares, exercising collective–individual dual level operation of large land units, with the basic operation level at one household as the major form or at a unit including a small number of households as the minor form). *Phase 2*: village-wide individual–collective mixed economy. *Phase 3*: either large-scale farming public–individual mixed economy or corporate–individual mixed economy (collective use of either public land, or physically unwithdrawable private land shares under corporate ownership, exercising village–individual dual level operation of large land units, with the basic operation level at one household as the major form or at a unit including a small number of households as the minor form, as a third way beyond the centrally planned economy and free market system).

Technological Efficiency

A production plan is (technologically) efficient if there is no way to produce more output with the same inputs or to produce the same output with less inputs, as Varian argues (1992: 4). This is actually a kind of Pareto efficiency. Putting parentheses around 'technologically' implies that technology is more important in this respect than in the classic Pareto condition, although the role of the institutional changes is not excluded.

Static or short-run technological efficiency could be attained without changing technologies but with higher incentives and/or better division and coordination of labor through institutional changes. It could also be reached by adopting already invented more advanced technologies which were not used before peasants gained incentives and/or achieved better division and coordination of labor.

For example, as presented in feature 1 of both the Japanese and Chinese models, the land reform and setting-up of cooperatives in Japan in the late 1940s gave huge incentives and better division and coordination of labor to peasants, and the land tenure reform in China in the late 1970s also highly motivated farmers. They increased production quickly with the original technologies, and then also adopted the existing more advanced technologies unused before.

Dynamic or long-run technological efficiency needed for achieving sustainable growth depends heavily on the technological progress embodied in construction of rural infrastructure, higher yields and multiple cropping of rice and other grains, diversified cropping and non-crop agriculture, off-farm employment, peasant migration to cities and work in town and village firms, agricultural mechanization with small or large machinery (features 3–8 in the Japanese model and features 3–8 and 10 in the Chinese one respectively), as well as regional transfer of development and environmental improvement (features 11–13 in the Chinese model), which would take longer time (e.g., finding a higher yielding variety of rice, building a big dam, transform a desert, or educating peasants may cost several years).

Institutional changes still play a critical role in this long-run process. In a high wage economy, it is only by consolidating and enlarging fragmented small farms that large machinery can be used and labor saved, so that increasing agricultural output with the same inputs or producing the same output with less inputs becomes possible. Institutional problems may inhibit the achievement of technological efficiency in this respect as much land is inefficiently held by part-time and absent small farmers, even though the knowledge and other conditions are available for both them and the remaining full-time small farmers to produce the same output with fewer resources or a larger output from the same resources. It is on this (feature 9 in the Japanese and Chinese models) that the relevant chapters of the book focus. The theory of technological efficiency, especially the dynamic or long-run one, is consistent with Holland's concept of variable mixed economies indicated in Chapter 2 and the author's hypothesis outlined earlier.

3.2 Achieving Pareto Efficiency according to Coase

In the context of Pareto efficiency, inefficiency means that there is an alternative allocation of resources that would improve one party without harming any other in the economy. The existence of negative technological externalities which have no market, causes inefficiency. The Coase theorem provides one of the several approaches to the achievement of Pareto efficiency with the introduction of market mechanisms, so that the (future) negative externalities could be either eliminated or efficiently produced, just like ordinary goods. But after the introduction of market mechanisms, there may be negative pecuniary externalities which also will lead to inefficiency.

Externalities

Concept of externalities. Demsetz finds that externality is an ambiguous concept (Demsetz [1967] 1974: 32). Some important relevant definitions are reviewed briefly here.

Externalities are positive (beneficial) or negative (harmful) effects that one economic agent's consumption activity or production activity has on another's welfare (including the consumption set of a consumer, the utility function of a consumer, the production function of a producer, or the production set of a producer2) which are not regulated by the market system of prices (*technological externalities*) or function with the price system (*pecuniary externalities*). Such an externality on the consumption set or utility function of a consumer is called *consumption externality*. That on the production function or production set of a producer is a *production externality*. (Varian 1992: 433).3 For the purpose of the book, major attention is paid to negative externalities hereafter.

Negative technological externalities. The typical example of negative technological externalities is pollution: normally, there exists *no market* to buy and sell noise, smoke or other pollution. Suppose there are two firms. Firm 1 (say, a steel mill) produces an output which it sells in the market. However, the production yields pollution on firm 2 (say, a fishery). Firm 1

---

[2] Consumption set refers to a set of possible consumption bundles which are objects of consumer choice. Utility function is a way of assigning a number to every possible consumption bundle such that more-preferred bundles get assigned greater numbers than less-preferred bundles. Production function shows the maximum possible output for a given level of input. Production set indicates a set of all combinations of inputs and outputs that comprise a technologically feasible way to produce. (Varian 1987: 33, 53, 310; 1992: 94)

[3] Definition transformed by the author from those by Varian (1987: 542–3; 1992: 432), Milgrom and Roberts (1992: 75), Demsetz ([1967] 1974: 32) and Laffont (1987: 264). Varian, Milgrom and Roberts exclude pecuniary externality while it should be included as done by Demsetz and Laffont. Varian also inappropriately omits consumption set and production function.

takes into account the internal cost (private cost) - the cost it imposes on itself - but ignores the external cost - the cost it imposes on the other firm. (Varian 1987: 542–3, 549; 1992: 433).4 A similar case is that a chemical dye factory pollutes water and deposits chemicals on agricultural land which uses the water for irrigation.

Pareto efficiency implies that competitive equilibrium would yield an efficient allocation of resources. His arguments were much refined and extended over the years by Barone, Lerner, Hicks, Samuelson, etc. The current version of the proposition is essentially based on the work of Arrow and Debreu who generalized and clarified the mathematics of the result. They indicate that it is in fact a two-fold proposition: an equilibrium allocation achieved by a set of competitive markets will necessarily be Pareto efficient (the First Theorem of Welfare Economics); and if all agents have convex preferences, then there will always be a set of prices such that each Pareto efficient allocation is a market equilibrium for a proper assignment of endowments (the Second Theorem of Welfare Economics). (Arrow 1963. Debreu 1959. Varian 1987: 495, 499–500. Lockwood 1987: 811)

'Competitive' in the present context means that resources can move smoothly in response to prices (i.e., without being monopolistically or oligopolistically held with bargaining power); all firms or agents take prices as given; firms maximize profits and consumers maximize personal utility (Milgrom & Roberts 1992: 62). Under such circumstances, the sufficient conditions for the First Theorem are (1) that there are *no* externalities (because they have no market) and (2) that there are contingent markets for all commodities, i.e., markets at all present and future dates and states in all contingencies. Implicit in (2) is the assumption that all agents are equally and perfectly informed about all aspects of their environment. The reason why the first condition is sufficient (and generally, necessary) is simply that externalities are in this framework products for which no markets exist, so there is no mechanism for the marginal benefits of the externality-producing activities to be equated to the marginal damages they impose on others. (Lockwood 1987: 811–2)

Internalization of negative externalities is a process of taking into account the external cost by the externality-yielding party (therefore, strictly speaking, taking into account *partial* external cost by the externality-yielding party can only be called *partial internalization* of negative externalities). If

---

[4] Varian (1992: 433) states that Firm 1 'ignores the *social costs* - the private cost plus cost that it imposes on the other firm'. This may be inaccurate since Firm 1 does not ignore the private cost - the internal cost, but only ignores the 'cost that it imposes on the other firm' - the external cost.

the polluting firm could do that, then Pareto efficiency would be reached. One way of internalizing externalities is for the two firms (polluting and polluted) to merge, so that social costs which now equal private costs will be computed to determine the efficient output of both products (steel and fish) and efficient amount of pollution. In this way, the new firm may produce less steel thus less pollution, but more fish, so that it would not be worse off. (Varian 1987: 549–50). (Other ways of internalization will be discussed later.)

Internalizing externalities is necessary in order to establish the sufficient conditions for Pareto efficiency, i.e., introducing market mechanism into the production of externalities. Before the market mechanism has been established, Pareto efficiency may not always be applicable. In the process of establishing market mechanism, the externality-yielding party may have to bear the external cost it imposes on others and thus be worse off than before [e.g., rather than merging, the steel firm may be imposed a tax equal to its external cost on the fishing farm, called Pigouvian tax (Pigou 1920)].

It is important to note that Pareto efficiency excludes externalities because they have no market. If market mechanism has been introduced into their production, then Pareto efficiency does not exclude them but sets them at levels such that their social marginal benefit equates their social marginal cost. (Laffont 1987: 264)

When there are externalities, however, even if the private market economy has been introduced in, equilibria will not be in general Pareto efficient since the private decentralized optimizations of economic agents lead them to take into account only private costs through the price system (Laffont 1987: 264). Thus, it is essential to examine negative pecuniary externalities as below.

Negative pecuniary externalities. One example of the negative pecuniary externalities is that consumer A affects consumer B's welfare by increasing A's consumption of whisky which leads to the increase in price (Laffont 1987: 264). Another example is that some firms decrease output of a product, resulting in its higher price.

However, according to competitive market equilibrium, prices only equate supply and demand. Therefore, pecuniary externalities do not matter as long as they are temporary and can be removed by the market price mechanism. (Laffont 1987: 264). If some firms have reduced the output of a product, the resulting higher price would lead other firms to increase their production of that product until market equilibrium is reached.

But, recall that Pareto efficiency is based on the assumption that market is competitive which means that resources can move smoothly in response to prices, all firms or agents take prices as given, firms maximize profits and consumers maximize personal utility. In contrast, in many cases of reality, as well known, the market is not perfect or competitive; especially, the bargaining power of some agents plays a strong role in transactions (Milgrom & Roberts 1992: 316). Under such circumstances, by affecting prices, some agents affect the welfare of other agents. If pecuniary externalities are lasting and could not be eliminated by the market price mechanism, then they do matter for welfare economics and Pareto efficiency cannot be attained. (Laffont 1987: 264). Hereafter, pecuniary externalities denote those lasting ones.

The relationship between technological and pecuniary externalities. For technological externalities, there exists no market; while for pecuniary externalities, the market is there, but cannot function properly. Therefore, once the market mechanism has been introduced into the production of technological externalities, if they still cannot be eliminated or efficiently produced as ordinary goods, they become pecuniary externalities. (This relationship is not noted in the literature reviewed.)

Not enough importance, if any, however, has been attached to pecuniary externalities in the literature reviewed. For example, in Varian's textbooks (1987; 1992), the term is not used at all. In the textbook by Milgrom and Roberts, the definition for externalities is limited to technological externalities. Accordingly, only pollution is cited as an example of what externalities an incomplete and imperfect market, and bargaining power, in reality will result in. (Milgrom & Roberts 1992: 75, 316). In *The New Palgrave - A Dictionary of Economics*, after mentioning pecuniary externalities in only two paragraphs, Laffont focuses on technological externalities in the following 19 paragraphs (Laffont 1987: 264–5). Since these textbooks and dictionary are widely used, readers, especially economics students, are misled into believing that pecuniary externalities are not so important. Here, the opposite is argued.

Demsetz ([1967] 1974: 32) stresses that in a lawful society, the prohibition of voluntary negotiations makes the cost of transacting infinite. He actually means that negative technological externalities cannot be eliminated because market exchange is not permitted. His implication is that once voluntary negotiations are allowed, the cost of transacting would be abundantly less. However, he does not note that once voluntary negotiations are legalized in a lawful society, the externality-yielding party can still impose negative *pecuniary* externalities, thus making the cost of transacting infinite *as well*. Indeed, after most of the former socialist centrally planned economies have adopted a market economy, and most capitalist countries have implemented deregulation, it is negative *pecuniary* externalities which would become the major negative externalities. They may outweigh negative technological externalities in the current real world.

In Japanese and Chinese agriculture, for example, the part-time and absent small farmers had no incentive to maximize profits on farming due to seeking higher off-farm income and/or psychological reasons.5 In Japan, farmers had the right of neither tilling their land, nor earning rent or revenue from land shares by leasing or joining cooperative/enterprise. This had been a negative technological externality since there was a land-holding ceiling before 1962 and permanent tenancy and rent control before 1970. But in these two years, they were lifted respectively. Now that it still could not be eliminated by voluntary negotiations, it became a negative pecuniary externality.

In China (before the Dual Land System was introduced), after fulfilling the quota (by either producing on the land or simply purchasing products from the market), contractors could not only stop production but also refuse to sub-let their land to full-time farmers, though they were allowed to sub-let. Thus right from the start, it was already a negative pecuniary externality.

This would raise the prices of rice as well as other agricultural products if cheap foreign food were not imported; but if it were imported, food prices in the world market would rise, as already happened in the first half of the 1990s. If land were not scarce, or if idle land could be transferred easily to the full-time farmers, the latter could operate larger areas of land and increase output, so that such pecuniary externalities could be removed and Pareto efficiency achieved.

But land is extremely scarce. In Japan the land was privately owned and in China the public land was contracted to households. Thus full-time farmers could not easily obtain more land from the earth because there is a finite area of land in any country, nor had they the right to till the idle land of the others. Because the market of land transfer is not perfect or competitive, the pecuniary externalities could not be removed and Pareto efficiency could not be achieved. Therefore, it is negative pecuniary externalities that have played the major role in hampering the efficient use of land and achievement of large-scale farming. Here we can see that, as surmised in Chapter 1, and opposite to Schultz's claims, the part-time and absent small farmers are not so efficient in their use of land, and at least some of them are not so rational to the society's and their own fundamental interests, as government or community subsidies, budget burden, food shortage, unnecessary food import, higher domestic and international prices of agricultural goods, artificial food overproduction, land under-utilization or idleness, waste of other resources, environmental deterioration, etc. would be

---

5 Although the goal most commonly ascribed to firms in economic analyses is profit maximization, for the self-interested owners of a firm would seem to unanimously favor such a goal, actually, there are many cases in which owners might have other objectives (Milgrom & Roberts 1992: 40).

incurred. As a result, the remaining full-time small farmers, largely non-viable as the economy develops into the high wage stage, could not easily get the inefficiently held resources for effective use, although the knowledge and other conditions are available for them to produce the same output with fewer resources or a larger output from the same resources.

How to solve this problem? We start from the Coase theorem which provides one of the approaches.

Coase Theorem

In his theory of social cost, Coase assumes that transaction costs are zero; income effects of different distributions of wealth are neglected; and property rights are well defined. Then the output mix that results when the exchange of property rights is allowed (1) is Pareto efficient; (2) is independent of who is assigned the relevant property rights initially and (3) the (future) externalities are either eliminated or efficiently produced. (Coase 1960: 1–44. Varian 1987: 546–7. Demsetz [1967] 1974: 33; 1988: 262. - Demsetz does not notice that the externality can be efficiently produced; and none of these authors pays attention to the point that it is the *future* externality that is eliminated or efficiently produced, as discussed below.)

The smoking example. Due to its simplicity and clarity, this example is preferred in the literature. The reference is from Varian (1987: 543–6), but with modifications and suggestions for new and potentially significant applications made by the author here.

Suppose persons A and B share a room. A likes smoking but B does not. When A smokes, he imposes a (negative technological) externality on B. Now, assume B is assigned the right to clean air, and A is given $20. If A prefers to keep $20 for other purposes without smoking, then this externality will not be produced. But A may prefer to pay B $1 for smoking one cigarette and up to $20 for a full pack of 20 cigarettes. In so doing, the externality is eliminated (internalized) by A because he has borne the social cost: the private (internal) cost - A pays to buy cigarettes, plus external cost - A's payment to B. A is better off but B is not worse off, so that Pareto efficiency is attained.

In this case, B may ask for more payment from A until he feels fully compensated, just as in free market negotiations. But in reality, wealth is always limited to a certain amount. Thus, for the sake of simplicity, here it is limited to $1 for one cigarette and $20 for 20 cigarettes.

B may also refuse to exchange at all, for believing that no amount of money - no matter how much - can eliminate the damaging negative externality of smoking on his lungs and life span in *physical* and *psychological* terms. In free market transactions, A cannot force B to exchange. But here, let us just suppose B is willing to accept up to $20 for A's smoking up to 20 cigarettes and regard the externality as eliminated in *financial* terms. (Attention is not paid by Varian on the distinction between elimination of negative externalities in physical, psychological terms and financial terms.)

Alternatively, suppose A is awarded the right to smoke a pack of cigarettes, and B is distributed $20. B may prefer to keep $20 and bear the externality from A's smoking. In so doing, the externality is Pareto-efficiently produced, because no one can be made better off without harming the other (this case is not considered by Varian). B may also prefer to trade money with A for reducing/removing A's smoking, by paying A $1 for reducing one cigarette and up to $20 for A's no smoking at all (in a free market negotiation, A may refuse to exchange; but here we suppose A is willing to exchange). In so doing, the cost of A's externality on B is also borne by B (this seems unfair, but Pareto efficiency does not necessarily imply social justice). In this sense, *the externality is not eliminated* since it only changed its form from smoke to money. *Nor is it internalized*, because the external cost by A on B (in smoke form) is borne by B (in monetary form). But it is now Pareto-efficiently produced because B is better off while A is not worse off. The payment of B to A is a kind of *redemption fee* for B's temporary freedom from A's smoking (Varian does not note the temporary redemption fee either, which is the author's concept).

If everyday B prefers to pay A up to $20 for less or no smoking, then everyday, the externality by A on B is Pareto-efficiently produced, *but, again, neither eliminated nor internalized*: it still exists, although in the form of B's daily or temporary redemption fee. If B prefers and could manage to pay A a much larger sum for A's no longer smoking in the future, the payment is a redemption fee for B's permanent freedom from A's smoking. Pareto efficiency is achieved. After the permanent redemption, new or future externalities will not be created either in smoking form or monetary form. But the permanent redemption fee is also an externality of A on B, because it simply transformed A's future externality on B in smoking form to the present externality in monetary form borne by B (again, Varian neglects the permanent redemption fee, which is also the author's concept).

Four kinds of negative externalities in time sequence. The significance of the temporary and permanent redemption fees exceeds the smoking example. The temporary and permanent redemption fees are here referred to as *redemption externalities*, which are not found in the literature reviewed.

As mentioned above, the definition here of internalization of negative externalities is a process of taking into account the external cost by the externality-yielding party (and hence, strictly speaking, partial internalization of negative externalities means taking into account partial external cost by the externality-yielding party). But Demsetz defines it as a process that enables the external cost 'to bear (in greater degree) on *all* interacting persons'. He gives the following example. 'It might be thought that a firm which uses slave labor will not recognize all the costs of its activities, since it can have its slave labor by paying subsistence wages only. This will not be true if negotiations are permitted, for the slaves can offer to the firm a payment for their freedom based on the expected return to them of being free men. The cost of slavery can thus be internalized in the calculations of the firm.' (Demsetz [1967] 1974: 32)

However, Demsetz's definition may not be correct and his explanation in this example may lead to some confusion. 'Internal' is relative to 'external'. Among 'all interacting persons', someone (the externality-yielding party) has imposed an external cost on others (the externality-receiving party). Internalization should mean withdrawal of such a cost by the yielding party. If it were still borne by the receiving party (in greater degree or not), it would remain external, which is contradictory to the term 'internalization'.

In general, four kinds of externalities over time are perceived here: present, historical, redemption (either temporary or permanent, but in this example permanent) and future externalities. Such a division was absent in the literature reviewed.

(1) *Present externality* is the external cost that the externality-yielding party is currently imposing on the receiving party (which, for avoiding confusion, does not include redemption externality that is actually a future externality but is turned to a present one). It may have started recently (e.g., being unable to repay a usury, a person has just fallen into the hands of the usurer) or a long time ago (e.g., a person born to a slave family who has inherited the slave status for decades). The present externality will be turned to historical externality once the yielding party has stopped imposing it on the receiving party (due to, e.g., personal redemption or social liberation).

(2) After the slaves have got freedom through redemption or liberation, the *historical externality* or external cost on the slaves before the redemption or liberation still remains with them and has been neither eliminated nor internalized by the firm (or, more appropriately, farm). But this does not mean that the historical externality could not or should not be internalized by the externality-yielding party. For example, during WWII, the Japanese invading troops forced numerus women of other Asian countries to be their sexual slaves. This historical externality has remained with the 'Asian comfort women' after WWII. But they have had no reason to bear it, although required to do so by the definition of Demsetz because they were 'interacting persons'. Thus, they have been demanding compensation from the Japanese government (as the German government paid to people in the

countries Germany had invaded). If the payment were sufficient, this historical external cost could be eliminated, internalized, fully compensated or fully borne in financial terms by the externality-yielding party. (If the payment were not sufficient, it would be partially eliminated, internalized or compensated.)

Here, one question arises: can such a historical externality like sexual slavery be eliminated? If a worn ordinary car has been damaged but then replaced by a new one, the historical externality may be regarded as eliminated, internalized, fully compensated or fully borne by the car damager in physical, psychological and financial terms. In contrast, if a person has been made blind, then no matter how much money is paid to him by the destroyer of his sight, this historical externality, in both *physical* and *psychological* terms, can never be eliminated, internalized or fully compensated. But if a compensation payment were sufficient (obviously always limited to a certain amount), then *in financial terms* the externality might be considered as eliminated, internalized or fully compensated. Therefore, it is in financial terms (neither physical nor psychological terms) that we may say that if the Japanese government sufficiently paid the 'Asian comfort women', this historical externality would be regarded as eliminated, internalized or fully compensated.

(3) The permanent redemption fee is also an externality (*redemption externality*), which has transformed the future slavery externality into the present monetary form, borne by the slaves rather than being eliminated or internalized by the firm/farm, although it was Pareto-efficiently produced since the slaves preferred to pay it for buying freedom. (Of course, a slave might pay a temporary redemption fee for a freedom of a short period. But here, we concentrate on permanent redemption.) Again, this does not mean that the slaves must always bear a redemption externality to get freedom. For example, the US Civil War and the War of Anti-Japanese Invasion liberated the Southern slaves and 'Asian comfort women' respectively without requiring them to pay redemption fees to their masters, although they were 'interacting persons' and should have paid according to Demsetz's definition.

(4) After the slaves have paid a permanent redemption fee for future freedom, if the firm/farm wants to continue production, it will have to take into account the social costs: the internal (private) cost - the cost it imposes on itself, and external cost - the cost on the former slaves which was previously ignored but is now eliminated or internalized by the firm/farm through paying them normal wages. Thus *future externality* actually includes two parts. The first part is the permanent redemption fee already borne by the slaves. The second part is the external cost which exceeds the permanent redemption fee, which will be borne, internalized or eliminated by the firm/farm, rather than being imposed on the former slaves anymore. Because the

first part has been transformed into the present monetary form as redemption externality, it is the second part which is called future externality hereafter.

Bearing the historical and redemption externalities by the slaves is not internalization, nor a necessary pre-condition of internalizing the future externality by the slave-holders, although in some cases the slaves either 'preferred' or had to do this. Therefore, internalization of negative externalities should be defined as a bearing of the external cost by the externality-yielding party, rather than by '*all* interacting persons'.

Similarly, for solving the pollution problem, the fishing farm could be given the right to clean water and let the steel firm pay it for its pollution, so that the negative externality is eliminated in financial terms. Alternatively, the steel firm could be given the right to pollution, and let the fishing farm pay it to produce less or no pollution, thus the negative externality is Pareto-efficiently produced. Both would reach Pareto efficiency via market exchange according to the Coase theorem. (Varian 1987: 555–6). The latter choice is not fair, but, again, Pareto efficiency does not necessarily imply social justice. Sometimes, this might even be the only efficient choice. For example, in some regions controlled by gangsters, the incompetence of police actually gives them a 'right' to charge shopkeepers a regular 'protection fee' or to kill them. The shopkeepers 'prefer' to pay a 'protection fee', under which the negative externality is Pareto-efficiently produced. Similarly, an unarmed pedestrian may prefer paying a couple of armed bandits to being slain in the night, under which the negative externality is also Pareto-efficiently produced. These two realistic examples show that despite criticism to the contrary, the Coase theorem is not always unrealistic.

Proper definition of property rights. Varian (1987: 546) claims that the practical problems with externalities generally arise due to poorly defined property rights. In the smoking case, if A believes that he has the right to smoke and B believes that he has the right to clean air, then who should pay whom? The negotiation is difficult. Cases where property rights are poorly defined can lead to inefficient production of externalities - which means that there would be at least one way to make one party better off while another party not worse off by changing the production of externalities.6 If property rights are well defined, and mechanisms are in place to allow for negotiation between people, then people can trade their property rights to produce externalities in the same way that they trade rights to produce and consume

---

6 Varian (1987: 546) claims 'inefficient production of externalities - which means that there would be ways to make both parties involved better off'. This statement seems inaccurate. Thus the author modified 'ways' into 'at least one way' and 'both parties involved better off' into 'one party better off while another party not worse off'.

ordinary goods.7

Hence, for reaching Pareto efficiency, there is *Approach 1: permission for the relevant parties to exchange property rights through a political or legal process, followed by market exchange* (Demsetz [1967] 1974: 33).

Relevance to Japanese and Chinese agriculture. Applying Approach 1 to the problem of pecuniary externalities imposed by the Japanese part-time and absent small farmers, we may see that, as presented in Chapter 4, in 1962, the land-holding ceiling was lifted, so that peasants acquired the right to buy more land (exchange between money and land). In the 1970s, protection of tenants from eviction and rent control were removed, so that landlords did not need to worry about losing leased land to tenants and could charge higher rent (exchange between rent and land use). They could also join a shareholding cooperative/enterprise to earn revenue from land shares. Thus, voluntary sale or lease, if carried out, could eliminate the negative technological externalities which existed before such market exchanges were allowed, so that Pareto efficiency could be achieved. Full-time farmers and the whole society would be better off, but the part-time and absent small farmers would not be worse off. They might even be better off since, e.g., they could now earn rent through leasing or revenue from land shares through joining cooperatives/enterprises.

Applying Approach 1 to the problem of negative pecuniary externalities imposed by the Chinese part-time and absent small farmers, we could see that, as shown in Chapters 1 and 6, the right to voluntarily transfer contract was already established from the start. In those cases where it was carried out, the part-time and absent small farmers could be discharged from fulfilling quotas, while the full-time farmers could contract more land - also an exchange. Pecuniary externalities could be eliminated and Pareto efficiency attained: full-time farmers and the whole society would be better off, but the part-time and absent small farmers would not be worse off. They might also even be better off since they could now concentrate on off-farm activities to earn higher income.

3.3 Relaxing Hypotheses of the Coase Theorem

Coase himself admits that in the real world, transaction costs are positive, and distribution of wealth has income effects. Therefore the assignment of

---

[7] Should property rights be well defined in *all* economic activities of *all* societies? Weitzman and Xu (1993) say no because they find that the Chinese township and village enterprises (TVEs) as vaguely defined cooperatives have been quite successful. But this topic is not directly related to this book.

property rights matters. None of this, however, is taken into consideration in the Coase theorem. (Coase 1960: 15–6). Therefore, Milgrom and Roberts warn that it is important to remember that the Coase theorem and its various implications depend on restrictive hypotheses regarding preferences and the ability to make transfer payments between the parties. The implications do not hold when some of the parties have very limited capital to make payments. Thus, although it would be reasonable to apply this analysis to study the terms of a contract between General Motors and Toyota, it would be a mistake to apply it uncritically, for example, to study land tenure in a developing country or the institutions of slavery in the pre-Civil War American South. (Milgrom & Roberts 1992: 39). The question of how to *achieve Pareto efficiency when the hypotheses of the Coase theorem are relaxed* should thus be considered.

Positive Transaction Costs

Assignment of property rights matters because transaction costs are positive. According to Coase, Furubotn, Pejovich and North, the major positive costs in transacting property rights are: (1) the costs of discovering who it is that one wishes to deal with; (2) the costs of informing the people one intends to deal with; (3) the costs of defining property rights (determining who owns what property, and who holds which rights); (4) the costs of measuring property rights (assessing precisely the specific attributes of the properties to be exchanged); (5) the costs of bargaining over property rights (negotiating on what terms to make the transaction, refusing to exchange or demanding unbearable prices by the externality-yielding party and overcoming the bargaining power of the yielding party by the receiving party and society); (6) the costs of drawing up the contract for transacting property rights; (7) the costs of exchanging property rights (exercising physical transactions); and (8) the costs of policing property rights (enforcing the newly established property rights). (Coase 1960: 15. Furubotn & Pejovich 1974: 46. North 1990: 28–33, 48–9). Each of these authors, however, has only noted part of this list. Coase does not note the costs of defining, measuring and exchanging, and Furubotn and Pejovich only mention the costs of defining, exchanging and policing. Moreover, they have neglected some important costs. There would be (9) the costs of *organizing* transactions (sometimes even some special organizations may have to be set up to organize all or a part of the above eight steps); (10) the costs of time (all transactions cost time; to achieve the same results, under some property rights structures, certain transactions may either be avoided or cost less time, hence Pareto efficiency); and (11) the opportunity costs (for obtaining the same results, under other property rights structures, certain transactions may either be unavoidable or cost more time, whose costs could otherwise be saved and used on other productive activities, hence inefficiency). (Further more transaction costs may not be excluded. But for the purposes of this book, they are not dealt with here.)

Relevance to Japanese agriculture. For example, in Japan, land consolidation under private farmland ownership leads to (1) the costs of discovering who it is that one wishes to deal with, e.g., finding who holds fragmented small farms in a village or district; (2) the costs of informing the people one intends to deal with, e.g., notifying all farm households that the village or local government intends to launch land consolidation; (3) the costs of defining property rights, e.g., examining the current farmland cadastral records to determine who owns which parcels; (4) the costs of measuring property rights, e.g., assessing each parcel's value; (5) the costs of bargaining over property rights, e.g., educating public opinion and discussing the necessity of land consolidation and voting to decide whether to carry it out in the village or area concerned [this may be done after step (2)]; refusing to exchange or asserting too high a value for one's parcels by some landowners, which will hinder the process of land consolidation and thus incur costs to the society; and obliging them to exchange at reasonable valuation of land by the authorities, which will also tend to incur legal and possibly enforcement costs to society; (6) the costs of drawing up the contract for transacting property rights, e.g., designing and finalizing the scheme of land redistribution; (7) the costs of exchanging property rights, e.g., physically reorganizing parcels to form compact land units, removing and/or re-constructing buildings on land; and (8) the costs of policing property rights, e.g., notarizing the newly established land-holdings; (9) the costs of organizing transactions, e.g., legislation, setting up special committees at administrative levels, and their activities; (10) the costs of time, e.g., each of the above steps costs abundant time; and (11) the opportunity costs, e.g., if farmland were turned to village-wide corporate ownership to be reorganized into compact form and operated under a Dual Land System or Single Land System as suggested in Proposal 5.1 of Chapter 5, then most of the above costs could be saved and used on other productive activities.[8]

The following example also shows the importance of transaction costs. Measuring the size of transaction costs that go through the market (such as

---

[8] In Appendix 3.1, a comparative international survey of the general methods of land consolidation under private farmland ownership is undertaken, which discloses its very high transaction costs compared with the land consolidation under public land ownership and corporate land ownership.

costs associated with banking, insurance, finance, wholesale, and retail trade; or, in terms of occupations, with lawyers, accountants, etc.) in the US economy, Wallis and North find that more than 45% of national income was devoted to transaction and, moreover, that this percentage had increased from approximately 25% a century ago (Wallis & North 1986. North 1990: 28).

Income Effects

Assignment of property rights matters also because different property rights assignments have different income effects. According to Demsetz, the income effects include three basic aspects.

First, altering the assignments of property rights changes the distribution of wealth, because under different assignments of property rights, different persons are made richer or poorer (Demsetz 1988: 15).

In the example of a chemical dye factory polluting farmland, if the dye factory is given the right to pollution, then the farm has to pay to the factory for reducing or stopping pollution. Thus the factory is relatively made richer. If the farm is given the right to clean water, then the factory has to pay the farm for its pollution. Thus the farm is relatively made richer.

Second, because each person's propensity to consume or save may differ, a different distribution of wealth may result in different levels of consumption and saving. Thus, the total mix of consumption and saving in the economy must change if the distribution of wealth changes. (Demsetz 1988: 15)

In the above example, if the chemical dye factory is made richer, it may spend more. If the farm is made richer, it may save more.

Third, even if each person's propensity to consume or save were the same, because their marginal rates of substitution between goods may be different, the persons made wealthier may purchase goods in different proportion from that of the persons made poorer. Thus, the total mix of outputs in the economy must change if the distribution of wealth changes. As long as those who are made wealthier and those made poorer, taken as two groups, have different marginal rates of substitution, alternative distributions of wealth imply different efficient mixes of output. (Demsetz 1988: 15)

In the above example, even though the chemical dye factory and farm have the same propensity to consume or save, once the factory is made richer, it would purchase more chemical materials; once the farm is made wealthier, it would buy more agricultural inputs. Accordingly, the society would have different mixes of production of chemical materials and agricultural inputs.

Approaches in Assignment of Property Rights

Due to the positive transaction costs and income effects, assigning property rights or changing property rights structures is not negligible, but plays a major allocative function in internalizing externalities (Demsetz [1967] 1974: 34) or efficiently producing externalities (Demsetz does not note this point) so as to reach Pareto efficiency. Hence the following five approaches to assigning property rights under different circumstances of positive transaction costs and income effects. Some elements of these approaches could be found here and there in the literature. But the summarization and systematization are made by the author.

Approach 1. If both externality-yielding and receiving parties are willing to exchange their relevant property rights, and could afford their respective transaction costs and income effects, the above-mentioned Approach 1 could be adopted, i.e., permission for the relevant parties to exchange property rights through a political or legal process, followed by market exchange. The examples include voluntary land sale, lease, and joining cooperatives/enterprises in Japan, and voluntary transfer of contracts for using public land in China, as already cited.

Approach 2. Under some circumstances, market mechanism has been introduced, but the externality-yielding party, by its stronger social, political, or economic bargaining power, may refuse to make an exchange, and thus keeps imposing negative externalities on others. As Milgrom and Roberts emphasize, even if a Pareto efficient allocation of resources has been identified, it is still necessary to ensure that the parties involved play their part in bringing it about. The problem is that there will often be inefficient allocations that are better for one person or a subgroup than the target efficient allocation, and these people may be able to effect the inefficient outcome that they prefer. (Milgrom & Roberts 1992: 23). For example, slave/serf-holders could refuse to accept payment by slaves/serfs to buy their freedom and land according to the prevailing market prices.

Thus, although the market mechanism has been set up for the production of negative technological externalities, it may not function. Consequently, they become pecuniary externalities. However, there are other social institutions such as the legal system, or government intervention, that can 'mimic' the functioning of the market mechanism and thereby reach Pareto efficiency (Varian 1987: 543). This is consistent with the theoretical views that free market forces alone could not overcome the vicious circle of poverty and realize sustainable rural development.

Hence, if both the externality-yielding and receiving parties could afford the respective transaction costs and income effects, there is *Approach 2: implementation of social actions (law, tax, etc.) to oblige the externality-*

yielding party to exchange property rights, followed by market exchange.

In so doing, in some cases, the externality-receiving party would have to bear a redemption fee (or redemption externality) and the historical external cost in exchange for not creating the future externality by the yielding party. Examples could be the forced agreement of slave/serf-holders to accept full payment at market prices to redeem permanent freedom by slaves/serfs; or obligatory sale of extra land at market prices by slave/serf-holders to slaves/serfs. Here, the negative externality is Pareto-efficiently produced.

Moreover, Furubotn and Pejovich claim that if the existing property rights structures are to be modified by social action to reduce or eliminate an externality, taxes must be imposed on those who will gain from the proposed legal change, and compensation paid (also as an incentive) to those who will suffer capital loss as a result of the new law. Presumably, agreement on the terms of the tax−compensation scheme can be reached through a political process, but the *basic mechanism* here is one of trade, a market process (Furubotn & Pejovich 1974: 46), although apparently not a pure one. In so doing, the negative externality is Pareto-efficiently produced at the expenses of not only the slaves/serfs, but also other people who pay the taxes and the *government* which pays compensation to the externality-yielding party (slave/serf-holders).

Then the questions arise: Could the possession of slaves/serfs by slave/serf-holders be justified? If not, why should such externality-yielding parties be fully compensated at market prices by the externality-receiving parties? Furubotn and Pejovich do not give reasons. But for this, a basic reason must be to keep social stability in the process of elimination of future externalities, so that the losers may not resist in a manner jeopardizing the outcome.

In other cases, there will be no capital losers after the exchange. For example, in *Proposal 5.1*, private landowners could turn land over to village corporate ownership, in exchange for private land shares which could earn permanent remuneration (housing land, self-sufficiency land or family plot would be owner-used, while shares of production land for market could earn revenue from the village), be inherited, or sold in financial terms in the market, while the village could physically possess land and reorganize land into compact form and contract land to full-time farmers, expert farmers or cooperatives/enterprises for large-scale farming. The part-time and absent small farmers may even be capital-gainers, for the remuneration to land shares could financially exceed what they could get from the land in the status quo - part-time farming or no farming at all.

Approach 3. Approach 1 is a pure free private market exchange at market prices. Approach 2 is socially enforced but also based on market exchange, sometimes even with compensation higher than market prices paid by the externality-receiving party to the yielding party as an incentive. By these approaches, both parties should bear the respective transaction costs and income effects. However, some people, especially those within the externality-receiving party, may not be able to afford the high transaction costs and unfavorable income effects. Thus, Furubotn and Pejovich further argue that whenever the private terms of exchange fail to account for some harmful or beneficial effects to the contractual parties or to others, the market solution will appear inconsistent with the social value of the bundle of property rights that is exchanged. Such private–social divergences tend to arise due to high transaction costs. Government intervention may be required if transaction costs are so high as to prevent private exchange. (Furubotn & Pejovich 1974: 46)

Thus, when the externality-yielding party, by bargaining power, refuses to exchange and/or demands unbearable prices, or market prices are too high for the externality-receiving party to bear, there is *Approach 3: reform of property rights structures through a political or legal process, followed by exchange at prices lower than the market levels.* In this case, only partial compensation will be paid by the externality-receiving party to the yielding party, and the latter will have to partially internalize the redemption externality, for not creating the future externality.

For example, slaves/serfs could be allowed by law to acquire freedom from the slave/serf-holders by a partial redemption fee and purchase land from them at prices lower than the market levels. During the Japanese land reform of 1946–50, the state compulsorily purchased and resold the farmland of the feudal landlords to peasants at prices which soon became minimum due to inflation, so that the landlords were actually not fully compensated. In Italy and some other countries, private land can be bought by the authorities for public projects at prices lower than the market levels.

Relevance to Japanese and Chinese agriculture. In Proposal 5.1 for Japan and other economies under private land ownership, although from the financial point of view part-time and absent small farmers would not be capital-losers and may even be capital-gainers after joining the village corporation to earn permanent remuneration for their physically unwithdrawable private land shares, they might be psychological losers, since there existed a strong envy towards any specific villager who became competitive in the market by expanding his farm. Thus in their personal interest the best way would be to keep the status quo, which however would perpetuate their negative externalities on the full-time farmers and society. Paying them permanent remuneration in exchange for using their land would eliminate the future negative externalities, but they might psychologically be worse off; or the remuneration would be regarded as not enough to compensate their psychological loss, or as lower than their 'psychological market value' which is to keep the status quo. However, it would be better than collectivizing their private land ownership. Actually, as surmised in Chapter 1 and elaborated in Chapter 4, the part-time and absent small farmers may have some rational concern over their direct interests in security. Thus if they could keep a back-up basic social welfare (such as the private land ownership) and receive proper remuneration, then some of them would be willing to transfer their inefficiently held land in various suitable forms to the full-time farmers for effective use, but others would still be involuntary to do so even though land property rights have been well defined and market transactions facilitated. Therefore, government intervention, education of public opinion, and active participation of all peasants are necessary so as to make all of them realize that a balance or compromise between collectivization and the status quo, with some psychological loss not fully compensated according to their 'psychological market value' but financially with no capital loss and even with capital gains, should be the best for them and the society. After the elimination of the future negative externalities, Pareto efficiency could be reached. Similarly, in China, under public land ownership, some part-time and absent small farmers also would be voluntary to transfer the inefficiently held land to the full-time farmers for effective use, if they are guaranteed a back-up basic social welfare and afforded appropriate remuneration, although others would still be reluctant to do so. The Dual Land System, based on the villagers' majority agreement, accordingly provided them with self-sufficiency land, and effected the transfer of the remaining land to the full-time farmers.

Approach 4. When the externality-yielding party, by bargaining power, refuses to exchange and/or demands unbearable prices, or market prices are too high for the externality-receiving party to afford even partial compensation to the externality-yielding party, or due to reasons of ethics the society regards it unfair to ask the receiving party to pay the yielding party, there is *Approach 4: reorganization of property rights structures without market exchange through a political or legal process*, i.e., the authorities award the relevant property rights to the externality-receiving party (Demsetz [1967] 1974: 33).

An illustration would be an obligatory merger of the polluting and polluted firms - in our example, the steel firm and fishing farm (obligatory because the steel firm may have no incentive to merge the fishing farm); imposition on the polluting firm of a Pigouvian tax equal to its external cost on the polluted firm and society; or compulsory payment directly by the polluting to the polluted firm - all of which would force the polluting firm to internalize the external cost. Other examples are the US Civil War and the War of Anti-Japanese Invasion which liberated the Southern slaves and 'Asian comfort women' respectively without requiring them to pay a redemption fee. A further case was distribution to peasants of extra land from feudal landlords without compensation in the Chinese land reform of 1949—53. There was also obligatory transfer of inefficiently used land from part-time and absent small farmers to full-time farmers in the Chinese Dual Land System since the 1980s.

Approach 5. In Approaches 1—4, the externality-yielding party is not required to internalize its historical external cost on the externality-receiving party. This could be changed by *Approach 5: re-establishment of property rights through a political or legal process requiring the externality-yielding party to fully or partially internalize its historical external cost on the externality-receiving party without market exchange.* Again, this is mixed economy.

For example, if person A has wrecked person B's land, the court could oblige A to not only cease destroying B's land (eliminating the future externality) but also cover B's expenses on restoring the land and income loss (internalizing the historical externality). After WWII, Germany had to pay the invaded countries war compensation. The Japanese government should officially do the same to the 'Asian comfort women'.

The above five approaches to assigning property rights are generalized in Table 3.2 with the example of slaves/serfs acquiring freedom from slave/serf-holders.

These approaches may be used in different combinations. For example, voluntary land consolidation (100% agreement by landowners) uses Approach 1, compulsory consolidation (0% consent by landowners) adopts Approach 2, while the partly voluntary one is a mixture of Approaches 1 and 2.

Relevance to Japanese agriculture. In Japan, although the 1949 Land Improvement Law prescribed that agreement by 50% of landowners representing 50% of land acreage of the village was sufficient for launching land consolidation and the 1992 new policies raised it to two-thirds majority, due to the efforts of officials and peasants, in most cases 100% consent was attained before starting it, hence a mixture of Approaches 1 and 2.

In some cases, the externality-receiving party may not be able to afford the positive transaction costs and unfavorable income effect. Thus, the government may have to bear some and even a major part of the transaction costs. For example, in the US Civil War, to force the Southern slave-holders to emancipate slaves, the government and society bore huge and bloody bargaining costs to overcome the bargaining power of the slave-holders. The same argument holds for the War of Anti-Japanese Invasion to liberate the 'Asian comfort women' and Japanese occupied countries.

Even in a purely or primarily private market exchange (as in Approaches 1 and 2 respectively) in which the externality-yielding and receiving parties are supposed to bear the respective transaction costs, the government should also financially help the receiving party. For example, the government could give subsidies and long-term credits to slaves/serfs to buy extra land from the slave/serf-holders, so as to facilitate the process.

These five approaches and the government sharing of transaction costs are in accordance with the thesis that free market forces alone cannot realize sustainable rural development in monsoon Asia and that variable mixed economy outcomes are needed.

Private, Public or Corporate Land Ownership?
A Transaction Costs Approach

What is the major factor that determines which of the aforementioned approaches to assigning property rights should be used? The above analysis has shown that it is the transaction costs. (Of course, transaction costs reflect income effects. The more the income of a party is affected, the more strongly it will resist the exchange of relevant property rights or the more compensation it will demand for such an exchange. While bearing this in mind, the discussion can focus on transaction costs.)

Originally, Coase (1937: 392–3; 1960: 16–7) finds that it is the transaction costs which determine whether a product should be produced by a firm or procured through market transactions. Coase stresses that within the firm, individual *bargains* between the various cooperating factors of production are *eliminated* and that for a market transaction is substituted an administrative decision by an 'entrepreneur' who directs resources with authority. It does not follow that the administrative costs of organizing a transaction through a firm are inevitably less than the costs of the market transaction which are superseded. But where contracts are peculiarly difficult to draw up and an attempt to describe what the parties have agreed to do or not to do (e.g., the amount and kind of a smell or noise that they may make or will not make) would necessitate a lengthy and highly involved document, and where, as is probable, a long-term contract would be desirable, a firm could be a solution to deal with the problem of harmful effects of individual bargains among market transacting parties. This solution would be adopted whenever the administrative costs of the firm were less than the costs of the market transactions that it supersedes, and the gains which would result from the rearrangement of activities greater than the firms' costs of organizing them.

Coase (1937: 393, 396–7) further indicates that transaction costs also determine whether a firm should become larger or smaller. A firm becomes larger as additional transactions (which could be exchange transactions coordinated through market price mechanism) are organized by the

Table 3.2 *Approaches to Assigning Property Rights for Eliminating or Efficiently Producing Negative Externalities with the Example of Slaves/Serfs Acquiring Freedom from Slave/Serf-Holders* [a]

Approach	Right assigned to	Historical externality	Redemption externality		Future externality
			Permanent	Temporary	
1. Permission for the relevant parties to exchange property rights, followed by market exchange	EYP [b] (slave/serf-holder) [c]	Borne by ERP [b] (slave/serf)	Borne by ERP (slave/serf)		No
				Borne by ERP (slave/serf)	Borne by ERP (slave/serf)
2. Implementation of social actions to oblige the externality-yielding party to exchange property rights, followed by market exchange	EYP (slave/serf-holder)	Borne by ERP (slave/serf)	Borne by ERP (slave/serf)		No
				Borne by ERP (slave/serf) [d]	Borne by ERP (slave/serf) [d]

3. Reform of property rights structures, followed by exchange at prices lower than the market levels	EYP (slave/serf-holder), restricted to receive partial redemption	Borne by ERP (slave/serf)	Partly borne by ERP (slave/serf)	Partly borne by ERP (slave/serf) [d]	Borne by ERP (slave/serf) [d]	No
4. Reorganization of property rights structures without market exchange	ERP (slave/serf)	Borne by ERP (slave/serf)	No - waived for ERP (slave/serf)			No
5. Re-establishment of property rights requiring the EYP to fully or partially internalize its historical external cost on the ERP without market exchange	ERP (slave/serf)	Borne by EYP (slave/serf-holder) fully or partly	No - waived for ERP (slave/serf)			No

Notes:

a. This table is the author's own formulation.

b. EYP - Externality-yielding party, ERP - Externality-receiving party.

c. Alternatively, right might be assigned to the slave/serf so that he could be waived from redemption. But under the assumption of Approach 1 that both parties could afford the transaction costs, there would be no need to do so. If he were regarded as not capable of paying it and given the right to freedom, it would become Approach 4 which takes into account the unbearable transaction costs.

d. If the aim of the social actions is to terminate slave/serf-holding forever, temporary redemption may not be allowed.

entrepreneur and becomes smaller as he abandons the organization of such transactions. A firm will tend to be larger (1) the less the costs of organizing and the slower these costs rise with an increase in the transactions organized; (2) the less likely the entrepreneur is to make mistakes and the smaller the increase in mistakes with an increase in the transactions organized; and (3) the greater the lowering (or the less the rise) in the supply price of factors of production to firms of larger size.

Relevance to monsoon Asia agriculture. Using the Coase transaction costs approach, and comparing the transaction costs incurred in land consolidation and expansion to overcome the fragmented small farms as the last obstacle imposed by the monsoon under private and public land ownership, the answers to the following two questions may be given: 1. Should rural land in monsoon Asia be privately, publicly or corporately owned? 2. If it should be publicly or corporately owned, then in Japan and other rice-based economies still under private land ownership, should rural land be converted to public or corporate ownership?

With regards to the first question, section I of this chapter has already noted that not only private ownership and possession of an asset, but also possession (leasing, contracting, shareholding in cooperative/enterprise) of an either public or private asset (e.g., land), may tie residual control and residual returns together, thus giving incentives to producers (possessors) for profit-maximization to reach Pareto efficiency. In fact, features 1–8 in the Japanese and Chinese models of rural development show that both private and public land ownership could succeed in overcoming most obstacles imposed by the monsoon in rural development of monsoon Asia (one may argue that public land ownership may have a certain superiority over private ownership even in this process in a large economy such as China, but this is not the topic of this book). However, in overcoming the last obstacle - the fragmented small farms - a sharp difference has been exhibited between private and public land ownership.

Japan established the system of family-managed fragmented small farms under individual land ownership during 1946–50, and China popularized them upon village land ownership during 1978–83. As much agricultural labor force transferred to off-farm activities, inefficient land-holding by part-time and absent small farmers happened in Japan at the end of the 1950s and in (some areas of) China at the beginning, and especially in the middle, of the 1980s. The part-time and absent small farmers became rich with higher off-farm income, while the remaining full-time farmers found it difficult to be viable in a high wage economy. Thus, it would seem logical that the part-time and absent small farmers should let the full-time farmers use their land, so that from both a resource optimization and social justice point of view, full-time farmers could enlarge farm size, gain returns to scale and increase their incomes. In terms of the national economy, waste of land, labor, management, capital, machinery resources, etc. could be avoided, sufficient rice and other agricultural products produced, their prices lowered, stabilized or not much raised, and government subsidies reduced or saved. In the context of the international economy, no or less import of grain (rice) would lead to no or less increase of grain prices which would benefit other grain-importing countries, especially the poor ones.

However, as already briefly mentioned in Chapter 1, and to be elaborated in Chapters 4–7 respectively, the progress of consolidation and expansion of the fragmented small farms in Japan and China has been conspicuously different. In Japan, the process started in 1950 and was promoted by the central government especially from 1960 on. But, after more than four decades, not much progress has been achieved, and effective ways feasible to Japan have not yet been found or confirmed (meanwhile there have been costs of government subsidies, costs of time, and opportunity costs - hence the comparative advantages of Proposal 5.1). In China, in contrast, mainly due to the efforts of grass-roots officials and peasants themselves, as early as at the beginning of the 1980s, the Dual Land System, then also Leasing System, Single Land System and Corporate-Holding System were already invented. Of course, since China is so large, the progress of land consolidation and expansion has been gradual and uneven especially in the Central and Western parts, where off-farm activities are less developed. But at least suitable ways have been found and are successful when properly implemented. There are various causes (also in non-agricultural sectors but related to agriculture) which have contributed to the increase of prices and import of grains at times. But this book focuses on the fragmented small farms issue.

So, why have land consolidation and expansion been so difficult in Japan? The 'secret' or fundamental reason is that *private land ownership incurs higher transaction costs chiefly because private landowners exert a strong bargaining power from ownership.* They can refuse to sell or lease their inefficiently used dispersed parcels or join cooperatives/enterprises. For carrying out land consolidation, the governments and villages have made enormous efforts. The process led to high transaction costs mainly owing to individual bargains. After land consolidation, owners could still resist land expansion in the forms of leasing or joining cooperatives/enterprises, which again requires great endeavor by governments and villages to resolve, if at all. The experience of Taiwan Province of China is similar. Land expansion through individual lease may lead to new fragmentation since the compact land units of the lessor and lessee may not be contiguous. Termination of lease may reduce farm size again. A cooperative/enterprise with physically withdrawable private land shares is not a typical or real 'firm' in which individual bargains are eliminated and everybody follows the authority of the entrepreneur as Coase supposes, but a peculiar 'firm' composed by individual landowners with strong bargaining power. When problems arise within a cooperative/enterprise, rather than settling them within the 'firm' which may also incur high transaction costs to them, some members may choose to use their right to quit so as to operate land individually or form another cooperative/enterprise which may re-fragment the once unified land and would certainly reduce the farm size.

In comparison, the 'mystery' or major reason why China could achieve much smoother land consolidation and expansion is that *public land ownership leads to lower transaction costs mainly because private land users do not have strong bargaining power.* The village as the landowner could behave like a real 'firm' to reduce/eliminate individual bargains between the various cooperating factors of production. Under the (standard) Dual Land System, self-sufficiency land was given to all households including those of the part-time and absent small farmers as a back-up basic social welfare, but responsibility land was contracted only to the expert farmers for production for the state and market. Land was not only consolidated, since both these types of land could be reorganized into compact form, but also enlarged because each of the remaining expert farmers could now contract larger areas of land. Once the off-farm jobs of the part-time and absent small farmers had been secured, then even their self-sufficiency land could be given to the expert farmers whose farm size was thus further enlarged under such a Single Land System. Under the Corporate-Holding System, households gave their contracted land back to the village which re-contracted land in compact form to full-time farmers or expert farmers and paid households dividends. Cooperatives/enterprises could also be formed among full-time or expert farmers, even together with urban, industrial, external and foreign companies which could introduce investment, improve technology and widen domestic and international markets. The revenue could be distributed among land shares of the village, capital shares of the internal and external investors, and internal and external wage laborers.

Of course, there may also be problems with public land ownership. In China, under the initial Equal Land System (each household contracted equal dispersed parcels in terms of quality, quantity and distance according to its population for both self-consumption and the state and market), those households which have increased their family size could be given additional land which had to be taken away from the village reserved land (if any) or from other households, thus violating contracts. This method, although perhaps not opposed by villagers on equality grounds, would discourage long-term land improvement by the contractors and encourage a higher birth rate. The Dual Land on Account System provided a solution to such frequent land redistributions: as family size became larger (smaller), the ratio of the self-sufficiency land to responsibility land of the household would be increased (reduced), while the whole land of the household was not changed.

Village officials as the 'entrepreneur' of the 'firm' may also improperly use their directing authority under the Dual Land System. For example, some officials were so eager to expand farm size that they contracted the responsibility land only to the expert farmers, making the less skilled full-time farmers who could not yet find off-farm jobs subsist on self-sufficiency land. One case was reported that in 1993 the leader of a village did not select expert farmers via tendering, hence corruption could be involved (see Chapter 7). But because the village officials are only representatives of the public land but not landowners, their 'bargaining' power, although stronger than that of the ordinary villagers, is also limited. Starting from 1988, the state has been popularizing the direct election of the villagers' committee members including the director and vice director(s) by all villagers of 18 years old and over. Peasants could also appeal to the media and the governments or sue the officials in the courts. Some officials of the lower level governments may be involved in corruption or bureaucracy as well, but they are also supervised by the higher governments which oblige them to eradicate rural poverty and promote development as the means of keeping their posts and gaining promotion. The 'Administrative Procedural Law' announced on 4 April 1989 and implemented on 1 October 1990, for the first time empowered citizens, legal persons and other organizations to sue government administrative organs and staff if the latter have injured the former's legal rights and interests (APL 1989). The 'State Compensation Law' promulgated on 12 May 1994 and enforced on 1 January 1995, further *specified* the right of the victims to get state compensation (SCL 1994), which had been written only as a principle in Article 97 of the 'Constitution' adopted on 20 September 1954 thus unimplementable (Constitution 1954). These two laws have indeed been practiced increasingly. Therefore, the government officials have incentives to correct the wrongdoings of the village officials and their own.

Moreover, in order to curb the excessive charges of the collective fees on the peasants by villages and townships, the state has decided in 1999 to replace the collective fees (village reserved fees, township unified finance fees and other relevant fees) as well as labor services to collectives (rural obligatory man-days and labor accumulation man-days) with unified agricultural tax, tax on special agricultural products and additional agricultural tax. Determined through more serious procedures by and paid to the higher governments, taxes are more compatible with a lawful society and matured market economy. Villages and townships do not have the power to create or increase them, or charge them into their own pockets. Exercises have started in Anhui Province as experiments in 2000 and dependent on their successes will be spread to all the other rural areas. (See Chapter 6)

Although not surprisingly, corruption cannot be underestimated in the young market economy of China just as in many other developing (and even developed) countries, it should not be overestimated either, for the corruption anyway has been combated to a degree that has permitted continuous buoyant economic growth recognized world-wide. As the market economy, democratic and judiciary systems become more mature, it may be more effectively controlled and the legal rights of peasants more soundly protected. Indeed, the amended 'Land Management Law' exercised on 1 January 1999 (which stipulated that the contractee should stop the contract and withdraw the land if the contractor has idled it continuously for two years; required a two-thirds majority agreement by villagers or their representatives and county government approval, and allowed court judgement, for adjusting individual land within its contractual period) was a mature and effective measure to prevent not only the inefficient land-holding by part-time and absent small farmers but also the arbitrariness and corruption by officials in altering contracted land with villagers' democratic participation (for details see Chapters 6 and 7).

For Japan, Proposal 5.1 recommends the collective use of physically unwithdrawable private land shares under village *corporate* ownership, in which private shares for housing land, self-sufficiency land or family plots would be owner-used, while shares of production land for market could earn permanent revenue from the village. Shares could be inherited, and sold in financial terms in the market. But shareholders could not withdraw land physically or claim financial reimbursement from the village. The village *physically* possesses land and could reorganize and operate land in a Dual Land System or Single Land System. Under such an institution, the village - as entrepreneur - could reduce or remove individual bargains just as in a real 'firm', as under public land ownership.

Therefore, the answer to question 1 is that, according to the Coase transaction costs approach, granted that transaction costs incurred in land consolidation and expansion for overcoming the fragmented small farms as the last obstacle imposed by the monsoon are much higher under private land ownership than under either public or corporate land ownership, rural land in monsoon Asia should be either publicly or corporately owned (of course, managed at village level).

As far as regards question 2, if rural land in monsoon Asia should be publicly or corporately owned, then in Japan and other rice-based economies under private land ownership, should rural land be converted to public or village corporate ownership? The answer again depends on the transaction costs involved. Rural land may be taken into public ownership (state, regional or village collectives) with or without compensation and operated at village level in either a Dual Land System or Single Land System. In the contemporary era, facing increasing land prices and a global wave of privatization, under the scheme with compensation, the public institutions may not be able to afford to pay (high exchange costs), while private landowners may not wish to sell (strong bargaining power). Under the scheme without compensation, owners may not agree either (also mighty bargaining power). In contrast, in converting land to village-wide corporate ownership as mentioned above, it is not necessary for villages to buy land while private land shareholders could get permanent remuneration. This would incur much lower transaction costs and be more feasible. Hence the answer to question 2 is that, in Japan and other rice-based economies under private land ownership, rural land should indeed be converted to village corporate ownership.

Pio's Puzzle

In 1871, Pio already proposes to organize agricultural cooperatives based on private land shares - the individual peasant households of a village or parish in Denmark were to pool their land to form a single big farm in order to cultivate it for common account and distribute the yield in proportion to the land, money and labor contributed (Pio 1871).

However, although capitalism has developed all sorts of commodities up to derivatives and stock is what real capital and other firm assets are made into the form of commodities, it has not developed securitization of land. In fact, cooperatives with private land shares have never succeeded in the history. Why? Because the practices have met serious difficulties Pio has not expected: members may not agree to transform their private parcels into non-farmland means of production (dams, roads, canals, ponds, etc.); and more severely, when members quit with land, the amalgamated parcels would be re-split, which made the cooperatives physically unable to function. (Indeed, it was the incompetence of the elementary cooperatives to solve these problems that prompted China to turn to collectivizing land ownership in 1956; the similar problems remain with the Japanese village-wide production cooperatives since the 1970s, see Chapters 4 and 5.). As analyzed above, such a production cooperative is not a real 'firm' as Coase supposes and cannot eliminate the internal individual bargains between the various cooperating factors of production.

In contrast, in a modern capital shareholding corporation, it is the 'entrepreneur' who directs resources with authority; and when a shareholder quits, he cannot pull out any equipment, nor get reimbursement for his shares from the corporation, but can sell them in the market, therefore the corporation can still physically function.

Proposal 5.1, by recommending a village-wide corporation with physically unwithdrawable but financially salable private land shares, may resolve the century-old Pio's puzzle, and pave the way for cooperatives with private land shares to succeed.

3.4 The Evolution of Property Rights Structures

Earlier in this chapter it has been shown that in order to eliminate (internalize) or efficiently produce externalities, the property rights structures may have to be changed. According to Furubotn and Pejovich (1974: 46) and also to common sense, at any given moment, there is a legally sanctioned structure of property rights in force. This section will first discuss *when* to change the existing property rights structures so as to eliminate (internalize) or efficiently produce (mainly negative) externalities. This reflects the views of Demsetz, Furubotn and Pejovich (however, they have only mentioned internalizing externalities and have no concept of efficiently producing externalities which is introduced here). General methods of *how* to alter the existing property rights structures are then considered.

Timing of Changing Existing Property Rights Structures

Demsetz claims that every cost and benefit associated with social interdependencies is a potential externality. One condition is necessary to make a potential externality a real one: the cost of a transaction of property rights between the parties concerned must exceed the gains from internalization [Demsetz (1967) 1974: 32] or efficient production of externality.

Furubotn and Pejovich argue that there is no basis for believing that all existing externalities should be corrected. Only when the gains of correction exceed its costs, should the existing externalities be internalized (Furubotn & Pejovich 1974: 46) or efficiently produced.

Therefore, the evolution, adjustment or change of property rights structures, can be best understood by their association with the emergence of new or different beneficial and harmful externalities.9 Changes in

---

9 Demsetz ([1967] 1974: 34) states that 'the *emergence* of property rights can be best understood by their association with the emergence of new or different beneficial and harmful externalities' as if there existed *no* property rights before the latter emergence. Therefore, the author has amended 'the *emergence* of property rights' into '*evolution, adjustment or change* of property rights'.

knowledge and innovation result in changes in production functions, market values, and aspirations. New techniques, new ways of doing the same things, and doing new things - all invoke either harmful or beneficial (or both) externalities to which the society has not been accustomed. The property rights structures evolve in response to the desires of the interacting persons to internalize or efficiently produce externalities for adjustment to new benefit–cost possibilities when the gains of internalization or efficient production become higher than its cost. (Demsetz [1967] 1974: 34)

Demsetz ([1967] 1974: 35) cites Leacock's following finding as an example (Leacock 1954). Primarily, in the American Indians, the land was commonly owned. Hunting was basically for the family's need of food and a few furs, and could be carried out freely. Under this ownership structure of land, overly intensive hunting exerted external costs on the subsequent hunters. Thus it was in no person's interest to invest in increasing or maintaining the stock of game. But people did not care much about these external costs, because the value of furs was so low that there was no need to husband fur-bearing animals.

Following the advent of the fur trade at the beginning of the 18th century, the value of furs increased considerably, so the scale of hunting rose sharply. Thus the Indians established private ownership of land so that each group of families could hunt and husband fur-bearing animals in their private territory. They did this gradually, from the first step - temporary allocation of hunting territories, to the second - seasonal allotment, and by the middle of the century the third - permanent distribution. Under the new ownership structure, people could no more hunt freely except on their own land (internalization of negative externalities), although a starving Indian could kill and eat another's beaver if he left the fur and tail (efficient production of negative externalities). (Demsetz [1967] 1974: 35–6)

The principle that associates the changes of property rights structures with the emergence of new, and reevaluation of old, harmful and beneficial externalities suggests in this example that the fur trade made it economic to encourage the husbandry of fur-bearing animals. Husbandry requires to prevent poaching and this, in turn, suggests that changes in the ownership structure in hunting land would occur (Demsetz [1967] 1974: 36), hence a new legal framework for respect and enforcement of such rights.

Thus, we can see the following trend: (1) the development of production, technology and markets, which induces (2) new benefit–cost possibilities, which in turn shows (3) gains of internalization (or efficient production) of negative externalities that exceed its costs, which subsequently raises (4) the need for internalization (or efficient production) of negative externalities, which finally requires (5) a change of the existing property rights structures and (6) a new institutional and legal framework for enforcement.

Relevance to Japanese and Chinese agriculture. The fragmented small farms, although with many disadvantages, were more suitable for the monoculture of rice in the low wage economy of Japan and China. The steam-powered large agricultural machinery reflecting the technologies of the First Industrial Revolution was technically not workable in monsoon Asia at all. The electricity/gas-driven large machinery representing the technologies of the Second Industrial Revolution, although technically feasible, was not economical since labor cost was lower than large machinery cost. However, as diversified cropping, non-crop agriculture and off-farm employment developed, wages rose. The agricultural labor force diminished. Thus large-scale farming with the electricity/gas-driven large machinery became profitable. The construction of rural infrastructure especially irrigation strengthened the ability of peasants to resist natural disasters. Therefore the gains of consolidating and expanding the fragmented small farms exceeded its costs. In turn this promoted the case for large-scale farming and land tenure reform in these two countries.

General Methods for Changing Existing Property Rights Structures

There are two general methods in the evolution, adjustment or change of property rights structures.

The first general method is to make *gradual* changes in social mores and common law precedents. At each step of the adjustment process, it is unlikely that externalities per se are consciously related to the issue being solved. The moral, practical and legal experiments may be hit-and-miss procedures to some extent but in a society that weighs the achievement of efficiency heavily, their viability in the long run will depend on how well they modify behavior towards the externalities related to major changes in technology or market values. (Demsetz [1967] 1974: 34)

The second general method is to make a *conscious* (collective) endeavor (Demsetz [1967] 1974: 34), such as a major reform or revolution at a certain stage of the gradual changes in the first general method.

The five approaches outlined earlier are actually *specific* methods of assigning property rights, and could be either moral and legal experiments in the first general method or conscious collective endeavor in the second.

In the above American Indian example, the temporary allotment of private hunting territories was a change in social mores and common law precedents, while the permanent distribution was a conscious collective endeavor. It used Approach 4 - reorganization of property rights structures without market exchange. Rights were directly assigned to households, historical externality was not repaid, redemption externality was waived, but future externality was internalized.

The US Civil War, as a conscious collective endeavor, was at least in part the result of change in moral attitudes - slave-holding was gradually and increasingly regarded as immoral.

Relevance to Chinese and Japanese agriculture. Resolving the last obstacle - the fragmented small farms perpetuated due to inefficient land-holding by part-time and absent small farmers in the high wage economy in China and Japan was also a process combining these two general methods: the realization by the society of the negative externalities of the inefficient land-holding and fragmentation, then the local experiments in seeking solutions, and finally the conscious collective endeavor - the establishment of the Dual Land System, Leasing System, Single Land System and Corporate-Holding System, as in China during the 1980s. In Japan, as early as since 1960, the society has already experimented with large-scale farming but did not achieve much success. This shows that the first general method is not sufficient and the second is necessary. Hence Proposal 5.1 for land consolidation and expansion as conscious collective endeavors in Japan.

The timing of and general methods for changing the existing property rights structures examined in this section are also consistent with the theory of dynamic efficiency discussed in the first section, Holland's concept of variable mixed economies reviewed in Chapter 2 and the author's hypothesis outlined earlier.

3.5 Relevant Concepts of Private Ownership

Private ownership may be divided into slave-holder ownership, feudal ownership, individual ownership and capitalist ownership. For the purpose of the book, it is perhaps useful to discuss the relationship between the individual ownership and capitalist ownership.

Concept of Capitalist Ownership

Capitalist ownership or capitalist private ownership (often just called private ownership in the reform period in China so as to avoid sensitive political problems) has both qualitative and quantitative dimensions, both of which are appreciated by Marx.

The *qualitative dimension* includes *two basic factors*: 1. private ownership of the means of production, and 2. employment of wage laborers.

In the *quantitative dimension*, a certain minimum amount of money or of exchange-value must be presupposed in the hands of the individual possessor of money or commodities, in order that the number of laborers simultaneously employed by him the whole year through, day in, day out, and consequently, the amount of surplus-value produced, might satisfy *three conditions* so that he can become a capitalist: (1) to liberate him from manual labor, (2) to enable him to live better than an ordinary laborer (say, twice as well) and (3) to increase the production by turning a part (say, half) of the surplus-value produced into capital. (Marx [1887] 1977: 291–2, 312)

In qualitative terms, factors 1 and 2 are related each other. If someone owns the means of production but does not employ wage laborers, then he cannot earn surplus-value, so that it is not a capitalist private ownership. If someone employs wage laborers but does not own the means of production, so that his wage laborers can work upon nothing and produce no surplus-value, this is not a capitalist private ownership either. Nevertheless, such a situation should be noted: *private possession*, without ownership, of the (public or private) means of production (through leasing, contracting, etc.) plus employment of wage labor can also extract surplus-value, and thus is also capitalist behavior. In practice, however, capitalist private possession without ownership is put under the general title of capitalist private ownership, because the latter is more typical.

In quantitative terms, the three conditions form a *direct criterion* to judge whether a person is a capitalist or not. However, there are also *two alternative indirect criteria.*

Marx ([1887] 1977: 291–2) supposes that (at his time) eight working-hours a day are sufficient for the reproduction of the means of subsistence for an ordinary laborer, and a capitalist needs to employ eight laborers simultaneously, each working for 12 hours each day, or totally 96 hours each day. Among them, 64 hours are for the reproduction of their means of subsistence (i.e., eight hours for each of the eight laborers); 32 hours for the surplus-value, in which, 16 hours are for the means of subsistence of himself (i.e., he can live twice as well as an ordinary laborer), and 16 hours for the increase of his production (i.e., he can turn half of the surplus-value produced into capital).

Thus, not every sum of money, or of value, is transformable at pleasure into capital. In order to meet the three conditions, a minimum initial amount of money should be held as capital which should include variable capital to pay for 64 working-hours each day for the reproduction of the means of subsistence of eight ordinary laborers, and constant capital to buy means of production sufficient for 96 working hours each day. (Marx [1887] 1977: 291–2)

Hence come two alternative indirect criteria to define a capitalist: 1. He owns such a minimum amount of money as capital, or 2. He employs a certain number of wage laborers, so that he can meet the three conditions.

Concerning the first criterion, in order to metamorphose himself into a capitalist, the minimum of the sum of value that the individual possessor of money or commodities must command, changes with the different stages of development of capitalist production, according to their special and technical conditions. (Marx [1887] 1977: 293)

Concerning the second criterion, Marx says ([1887] 1977: 167–8), the value of labor-power is the value of the means of subsistence necessary for the maintenance, continuation and development of this special article. Particularly, in contradistinction to the case of other commodities, there enters into the determination of the value of labor-power a historical and moral element. Nevertheless, in a given country, at a given period, the average quantity of the means of subsistence necessary for the laborer is in practice known.

Relevance to Chinese agriculture. In China, until 1956, criterion 1 was adopted in industry and commerce: an industrial capitalist had to own 3,000 yuan and a commercial capitalist 2,000 yuan (Huang, Qiang-Hua 1980a: 99; 1980b). Criterion 2 was adopted in handicraft and agricultural sectors: in handicraft, a capitalist must employ at least four wage laborers (Bo, Yi-Bo 1991: 439); in agriculture, as long as a person himself labored and hired one laborer, he was classified as a rich peasant (Huang, Xi-Yuan 1986: 150) or an agricultural capitalist (more properly, quasi-capitalist since he also labored). This was mainly because capitalism in handicraft and agriculture was much weaker than in industry and commerce, so that employment of even less than eight laborers was still regarded as capitalist.

In China's present economic reform, capitalist ownership has been allowed (although called private ownership). Due to inflation, criterion 1 has not been adopted into law. Although some researchers used it, there has been no consensus on the minimum requisite to define a capitalist. Instead, criterion 2 has been taken into law.

However, in present China, how many working-hours a day are sufficient for the reproduction of the means of subsistence for an ordinary laborer? And, therefore, how many wage laborers has one to employ simultaneously so as to become a capitalist? Rather than 'in practice known', there is no consensus, because no one could convince others that his calculation is applicable all over the country. Therefore, the readiest benchmark in China was that put forward by Marx over a century ago: eight wage laborers to be employed simultaneously. In the event, this was stipulated in Articles 2 and 3 of 'Temporary Regulations on Private Enterprises' promulgated on 25 June and implemented on 1 July 1988 by the State Council (TRPE 1988: 17). Accordingly, an enterprise which hired eight or more wage laborers has been called 'private enterprise' (si ying qi ye).

The management activity by a capitalist is regarded as exploitative (Marx [1887] 1977: 292. Xu, He 1973: 92). Thus, as long as one employs eight wage laborers, he is regarded as a capitalist, no matter whether he himself is the manager or he hires a manager. However, the management activity by a manager who is not a capitalist but hired by a capitalist is viewed as labor.

Concept of Individual Ownership

Individual ownership or non-capitalist individual ownership (often just called individual ownership in China) refers to such an ownership whereby a person (or persons) individually or privately owns the means of production and employs *no* wage laborer - type 1, in which there is no capitalist factor, or employs *less than eight* wage laborers - type 2, in which the difference between such an employer and a capitalist is the quantity of the wage laborers employed and the means of production owned sufficient for the use of the wage laborers. Because quantitatively he has possessed some, but not enough, capitalist factors, qualitatively he is not yet a capitalist but still belongs to the laboring class. However, citing Hegel's 'Logic', Marx argues, merely quantitative differences beyond a certain point pass into qualitative changes: once the wage laborers he employs and the means of production he owns have become enough for him to meet the three conditions, he becomes a capitalist. Thus, Marx calls such a person 'small master' - a hybrid between capitalist and laborer. (Marx [1887] 1977: 292). In China, such a person (in either type 1 or 2) was called 'xiao ye zhu' ('small proprietor' or 'petty proprietor') before the reform and 'ge ti gong shang hu' ('individual industrial or commercial household') since the reform. Here the author refers a person employing one to seven wage laborers to 'quasi-capitalist'.

Individual ownership has existed in all the slave, feudal, capitalist, and socialist societies (in China during 1956–78 only type 1 was allowed). The central point in the individual ownership is that the owner of the means of production does not (in type 1), or cannot yet (in type 2), live upon the surplus-value of the wage laborers he hires.

In other rice-based economies of monsoon Asia, hiring how many wage laborers simultaneously could be regarded as capitalist? Apparently, there is no consensus. Therefore, in this book, the term *'capitalistic'* is used to refer to either capitalist or quasi-capitalist or both. In fact, as China's economic reform widens and deepens, 'Law on Individual Single Venture Enterprises' promulgated on 30 August 1999 and executed on 1 January 2000 uniformly refers to any enterprise under single person ownership as 'individual single venture enterprise' (ge ren du zi qi ye) no matter how many wage laborers it hires, thus ceasing the practice of calling enterprises hiring less than eight wage laborers as 'individual industrial or commercial households', and those hiring eight or more as 'private enterprises', and diluting the difference between capitalist and individual ownership (LISVE 1999).

Appendix 3.1
How to Carry Out Land Consolidation
- An International Comparison [10]

Readers are recommended to consult this appendix before reading Chapter 4, not only since it reveals the very high transaction costs incurred in land consolidation under the system of private farmland ownership, thus demonstrating the comparative advantage of that under public land ownership (as in the Chinese model) and corporate land ownership as in the proposed new model in Proposal 5.1, but also because the methods for assessing the value of current farmland holdings will be used to calculate private land shares in the proposed new model in Chapter 5.

This appendix does not discuss the causes, disadvantages and advantages of fragmented farms, nor the desirability, suitability of or need for land consolidation, which have been the topics of many other papers and books and also other chapters of this book. Rather it focuses on *how* to carry out land consolidation. Moreover, such land consolidation is based on a mixed economy combining private ownership of farmland with public ownership of infrastructure land. Land consolidation in areas where there is complete public ownership of rural land is not discussed since it belongs to another land tenure system.

Definition of Land Consolidation under
Private Land Ownership

Land consolidation is an exchange of the private ownership and location of spatially dispersed parcels of farms to form new holdings containing a single (or as few as possible) parcel(s), with the same (or similar) value as the original areas. No landowner should be made a loser through consolidation. (Oldenburg 1990: 183). It is not, however, a measure for social justice. It neither changes the status of the large and small landowners, nor gives farmland to the landless. (Trivedi & Trivedi 1973: 180). Therefore, it could be implemented with no or incomplete land reform [e.g., in India since 1900

---

[10] The earlier versions of this appended text have been published by the Food and Agriculture Organization of the United Nations in Zhou, Jian-Ming (1998), abstract by CABI (Zhou, Jian-Ming November 1996), and Zhou, Jian-Ming (January 1999).

(Zaheer 1975: 92–5, 118)11], or in conjunction with land reform, which distributed land of landlords to peasants with equity in consolidated forms [e.g., in Denmark during 1770s–1835 and Ireland during 1870–1940s (Skovgaard 1950: 43, 45. Ire-Gov 1950: 64–76)], or after land reform [e.g., in Switzerland during 1840–1940s, Russia during 1906–17, Japan since 1950, and Taiwan Province of China since 1959, which preserved equity in land ownership (Swi-Gov 1950: 82, 85. OECD 1998d: 75. Tsuge 1997. Huang, Chieh 1967: Foreword. Myers 1996: 260))].

General Procedure of Land Consolidation

There has been little difference between developing and developed countries as far as collective action for consolidation is concerned (Sharma 1986: 716). Programs of land consolidation differ in various respects: from voluntary to compulsory; from dealing only with farmland to being linked to overall rural development; from farmers alone bearing the cost to sharing it with the authorities (Oldenburg 1990: 183); and, from using primitive methods to advanced satellite remote sensing and computer technologies. Here is the general procedure.

Administrative preparations. Government guidance committees at national and local levels (province, prefecture, county, municipality, district) should be set up; education of public opinion about the disadvantages of fragmentation and advantages of land consolidation made; laws, statutes and regulations concerning the major aspects of land consolidation established; and special tribunals at primary and appellate courts formed. In particular, it should be decided whether land consolidation should be started upon the consent of landowners by 100% (voluntary), or 0% (compulsory), or between these two extremes (partly voluntary or partly compulsory).

Once a village has decided to carry out land consolidation, it should set up an executive committee consisting of representatives of officials, large and small landowners and tenants, and under which a technical group composed of experts on survey, appraisal, land records, computer, rural infrastructure and development, as well as some officials. An expected time

---

11 Even in the 1980s, in some areas of India, poor farmers with small parcels of low-value land might only be able to trade in them for an even smaller but better land unit which merely allowed them to grow some vegetables (Oldenburg 1990: 189). The lack of a complete land reform for equity in land ownership may be one reason why rural poverty is still widespread in this country.

limit for implementing the consolidation should be announced.12 Landholders (owners and tenants) would thereafter be prohibited from taking any action which might lower the value of their land property without the permission of the village executive committee. Infringers of this rule are liable to a fine. (Vanderpol 1956: 552). New construction in the fields and transfer of land would not be allowed (Elder 1962: 23).

Technical preparations. The technical group should correct the current farmland cadastral records, and produce a provisional consolidation scheme with maps of assessing the value of the current land-holdings, setting aside land for communal use, and assigning new holdings to each household (Bonner 1987: 21). It should then present the scheme with the maps to the village executive committee which in turn should inform all households of this for discussion. In case of disagreement, households could appeal for re-arrangement to the village executive committee, the guidance committees of the local governments, the primary court and appellate court whose judgement should be final. (Trivedi & Trivedi 1973: 183. Oldenburg 1990: 185).

Implementation. Once the appeals have been handled, the consolidation scheme could be fixed. After the main (autumn) harvest, it could be implemented. The new land cadastral records should then be established by public notary. The consolidation is thus completed. (Bonner 1987: 22. Vanderpol 1956: 553)

Some Major Issues

Consent of peasants. The process of exchange of private parcels for consolidation would not be easy. There are indefinite individual obstacles to land consolidation. The resulting farms differ considerably in size, type, and topography. Some farmers get better bargains than others - and a still larger number will probably fear that others may do so. Some households may receive poorer land than they had before. It may not be possible to cater to the need of all the farmers. This would be compounded by the inertia of peasant tradition. For example, one family could claim that its parcels belong to heritage of its ancestors and could not be given away. Another may feel unfamiliar with the new parcels. There also will be financial concerns. For instance, some farmers may worry that permanent crops, buildings, etc., in the old parcels would not be sufficiently compensated. (Binns 1950: 22–3).

---

12 For example, it took two–three years in France and three–four years in the Netherlands in the 1940s–50s, and six–nine months in some areas of India in the 1980s (Roche 1956: 543. Van Rossem 1956: 555. Oldenburg 1990: 186, 193).

Such realities imply that - to fulfil its objectives - consolidation may have to be voluntary, compulsory or partly voluntary.

* *Voluntary consolidation* is one when 100% of landowners of the village (or area concerned) agree to carry it out. It could be through the spontaneous efforts of farmers in the form of cooperatives or personal exchanges, and should be assisted and encouraged by governments. However, for the above reasons, such operations are slow and unsatisfactory. Anything like complete success is unlikely to result from purely private enterprise. (Binns 1950: 24–5. Zaheer 1975: 92–3. Clout 1984: 104)

For example, consolidation was practiced in the village fields of Oster Hjermitslev, Denmark, in 1820 by the freehold farmers (owner-peasants) themselves. Having been unable to agree on a rational consolidation scheme, the farmers' land remained split up in 12 different places all over the village. In 1917, nearly 100 years after, though some amalgamation of the parcels of land had taken place, the situation remained unchanged. The experience in Denmark has been that where the consolidation process has been left entirely to the peasants, it has been ineffectual. (Skovgaard 1950: 45–6, 50–1). Slow progress under voluntary consolidation was also evident in France (1697–1888), Switzerland (1884–1911), India (1900–51), and the Netherlands (before 1920) (Roche 1956: 539. Swi-Gov 1950: 83. Zaheer 1975: 92–3. Clout 1984: 104. Vanderpol 1956: 549). Therefore, government intervention was called for.

* *Compulsory consolidation*, at the other extreme, is imposed by the authorities even if 0% of landowners of the village (or area concerned) wish to start it. The authorities normally listen to landowners - but not through mass voting - before making decisions, and landowners could also appeal although they have to accept the decision of the higher authorities. This approach may result in uncooperation, resentment and resistance of peasants. It might succeed in relatively less democratic times or areas relatively easier for consolidation [e.g., there were positive cases in Denmark during 1770s–1835 and France during 1935–80s (Skovgaard 1950: 43–5. Fre-Gov 1950: 59–60. Roche 1956: 539–43. Clout 1984: 105–10)], but not enjoy much success, if at all, in an increasingly democratic era or regions comparatively more difficult for consolidation. For example, in the 1950s, in the village of Manovan, Uttar Pradesh, India, opposition to compulsory consolidation took a political turn when the Jan Sangh Party led a campaign to obstruct consolidation and evicted farmers who took the newly assigned parcels. Police had to arrest seven local leaders before consolidation could proceed. (Elder 1962: 27). In France, such schemes have been criticized as being over costly, bureaucratic and paying too much attention to the interests of landowners, especially in areas where tenancy was important. Fragmentation was still a severe problem in the 1980s, particularly in vine and fruit

growing regions. (Harrison 1982: 41–2). In 1996, small farmers in Slovenia resisted the government's decision to proceed with compulsory consolidation (Riddell 1996). Therefore, democracy and sufficient participation by peasants in deciding whether to carry out consolidation are important.

* *Partly voluntary consolidation* is one started with the consent of some landowners of the village (or area concerned) and approval of the authorities, while others, although disagreeing, have to follow. On one hand, there is accord by *substantial majority* (two-thirds of landowners representing two-thirds of land). For example, before 1861, all agricultural land in Russia was owned by the Tsar as state ownership but its use granted to nobles or communities of 'state peasant' households with the duty to serve the state. Serfs providing labor for serf-holders were allowed to use a part of the land held by the serf-holders. The land was used on a communal basis with three-field crop rotations, each peasant household using some strips of land in each field determined jointly by the whole village. Under the *1861 Emancipation Act* serfs were de jure freed from their serf-holders. The land they used was allocated to them, similar to a land reform. After the 1905 uprisings, the government further encouraged the reorganization of agricultural holdings. By a law of *9 November 1906* peasants were given the right to change their communal strips of land into fully enclosed farms outside the village or consolidated holdings within it. The village could make this transformation by a two-thirds majority vote of the heads of households. (OECD 1998d: 75). However, substantial majority is similar to a voluntary scheme and therefore difficult to obtain. In Russia, by the time of the October Revolution in 1917, about 15% of all the peasant households in the European part had consolidated their land, raising the share of family farms in hereditary tenure to 27–33% (Figes 1996). However, most individual farms were created in the West, South and Southeast. The majority of the peasants in the Central part did not change the land layout based on three-field crop rotations. (OECD 1998d: 75–6). On the other hand, there is consent by *simple minority* (one-third of landowners representing one-third of land, or even less) which is close to compulsory action and thus could not always achieve the cooperation of other farmers in a democratic era.

Agreement by *simple majority* (51%) or half would be more effective. Therefore, on one side, the Netherlands transformed the requirement for agreement ratio from 100% to 66.7% in 1920, further to 51% in 1938 (Vanderpol 1956: 549); on the other, Sweden changed from requiring the agreement of only one landowner in a village in 1757 to that of majority in 1926 (Ytterborn 1956: 560). Taiwan and Portugal adopted 51% in 1936 and 1962 respectively, while Greece stipulated 50% in 1948 [Huang, Chieh 1967: (Appendix) 1, 37–8. Monke; Avillez & Ferro 1992: 69. Keeler & Skuras 1990: 74] [in India, rules vary among states from compulsory, simple minority, to substantial majority (Agarwal 1971: Appendix II)]. In general, once 51% of landowners representing 51% of land in the area concerned have agreed, land consolidation could be started.

Here, governmental intervention to forward consolidation has aimed at encouraging voluntary action and supporting it by financial and other inducements, as well as providing technical assistance. Such activities need to educate public opinion, with very careful and intensive preparation. For instance, in Japan, although the 1949 Land Improvement Law prescribed that agreement by 50% of landowners of a village (or area concerned) was sufficient for carrying out land consolidation and the 1992 new policies raised it to a two-thirds majority, in most cases 100% consent was attained before starting it, but great efforts had to be made by officials to overcome serious difficulties in adjusting interests among peasants (Hyodo 1956: 559. Tsuge 1997. NIRA 1995: 174). Nevertheless, *legal power for compulsory action should be reserved in special cases* (Binns 1950: 25). For example, the Netherlands empowered the Ministry of Agriculture in 1938 to impose consolidation schemes when they were urgently required in the public interest even if the necessary votes had not been obtained; and Greece prescribed in 1948 that consolidation could be compulsory if it was needed to successfully complete drainage and irrigation projects - both of them have facilitated land consolidation (Vanderpol 1956: 550, 552. Keeler & Skuras 1990: 74–5).

Assessment of the value of current farmland holdings. The most critical phase of the entire process is the evaluation of the farmlands. Only an impartial and accurate valuation can assure a fair and equitable redistribution. Three major methods for valuing land could be considered. These are valuation by (1) market price; (2) rental value; and (3) land productivity. The main disadvantage of the first method is that the market price of some parcels (e.g., those near the main village residential site) may be very high as reflecting industrial or housing demand for land rather than agricultural profits. The major disadvantage of the second is that rental system varies from fixed rent to proportionate rent in cash or kind, which renders the determination of exact rental value difficult. Therefore, the third method is more suitable. Under this system, the value of a parcel of land is based on an assessment of its agricultural productivity. A variety of natural factors should be considered, including the acreage, fertility, access to water, flatness and distance to the main village residential site, etc. After touring the village land, the technical group selects some parcels which are, by common agreement, the best in the village in terms of one or some of these factors, thus becoming the standard of others. (Bonner 1987: 22. Roche 1956: 541). Below is an illustration [The principle in the following method has been used in practice (e.g., in India - Oldenburg 1990: 186). But the mathematical generalization is made by the author as it was not found in the literature reviewed. It could be adapted to local conditions and expanded to more complicated models using econometric tools and computer techniques. The numbers are hypothetical. The sizes of farms in figures are not proportionate to the grades].

Suppose: A village has m (say, five) household farms:

F_m: $m = 1, 2, \ldots, 5$;

Each farm has up to n (say, 10) parcels located in different places:

P_n: $n = 1, 2, \ldots, 10$;

Also suppose F_1 has 6 parcels, F_2 7 parcels, . . . , F_5 10 parcels (see Figure 3.1).

Each parcel can be assessed on i factors (say, five: acreage, fertility, access to water, flatness, distance to the main village residential site):

Q_i: $i = 1, 2, \ldots, 5$;

The best parcel in one factor could be assessed as 1 (e.g., in Figure 3.1, P_1 is valued as 1 in Q_2 — fertility, and P_4 is given 1 in Q_5 — distance to the main village residential site), parcels inferior to it could be given numbers smaller than 1.

Each factor could be given different weight:

W_j: $= (0, 1)$, $j = 1, 2, \ldots, 5$;

Total $W = 1$ (acreage and fertility may receive higher weights, and in general a smaller area of good land could be exchanged with a larger area of poor land; in Figure 3.1, these five factors are given weights of 0.35, 0.35, 0.15, 0.05, 0.1 respectively) (see formulas in Figure 3.1 and illustration in Table 3.3).

Following the assessment, general grade could be given to each farm, say, $F_1 = 2.48$, $F_2 = 3.26$, $F_3 = 4.37$, $F_4 = 5.93$, $F_5 = 6.12$.

The fixed capital assets (permanent crops, orchards, vineyards, buildings, wells, etc.) on the parcels are not natural but artificial factors. Those which have to be destroyed should be reimbursed or rebuilt in the new place by the village; those which will be reserved but transferred to another owner should be paid for by that owner (offsetting between owners may be arranged), or be valued as extra grade to the parcels.

Promotion of rural development. Among the newly established larger land units, major infrastructure items (main roads among farms and linked to other villages, water conservancy, irrigation and drainage network linking lakes-rivers-canals-ditches-drains, electricity facilities, etc.) should be built, so that each land unit could have easy access to roads, large machinery, irrigation and other facilities. A scientific design for the facilities to process and store agricultural products, schools, hospitals, cultural halls, sport grounds, post and telecommunications office, village administrative offices, housing, land for industrial use, land reserved for future construction, etc., in the village should be made. Environmental protection (forest, nature reserves, tourist resorts, etc.) should be taken into consideration.

Thus, a number of villages in a district could coordinate their consolidation plans or even create a general one. Migration of some peasants from the congested to less populated rural districts could be arranged, so that both the remaining and outgoing peasants could acquire larger land units. Apparently, government coordination is necessary.

Each farm should contribute a small percentage (e.g., 3–5%) of farmland for the communal use. The removal of numerous boundaries would make this possible without (significant) reduction of farm size. (Zaheer 1975: 113). Nominal compensation could be paid to the contributors by the village (Trivedi & Trivedi 1973: 183–4). Exchanges between farmland and non-farmland means of production, and between private and public land could

$$\textit{Grade for } F_1 = P_1(Q_1W_1 + Q_2W_2 + \ldots + Q_5W_5)$$
$$+ P_2(Q_1W_1 + Q_2W_2 + \ldots + Q_5W_5)$$
$$+ \ldots$$
$$+ P_6(Q_1W_1 + Q_2W_2 + \ldots + Q_5W_5)$$
$$= \sum_{n=1}^{6} P_n \sum_{i,j=1}^{5} Q_iW_j = 2.48, \ W_j = (0,1), \ \sum_{j=1}^{5} W_j = 1$$

$$\textit{Grade for } F_2 = \sum_{n=1}^{7} P_n \sum_{i,j=1}^{5} Q_iW_j = 3.26$$

$$\textit{Grade for } F_3 = \sum_{n=1}^{8} P_n \sum_{i,j=1}^{5} Q_iW_j = 4.37$$

$$\textit{Grade for } F_4 = \sum_{n=1}^{9} P_n \sum_{i,j=1}^{5} Q_iW_j = 5.93$$

$$\textit{Grade for } F_5 = \sum_{n=1}^{10} P_n \sum_{i,j=1}^{5} Q_iW_j = 6.12$$

Note: This figure is the author's own formulation.

Figure 3.1 Formulas for Calculating General Grades of Farms

Table 3.3   Illustration of Assessing General Grade for Farm 1 *

	Q_1	W_1	Q_1W_1	Q_2	W_2	Q_2W_2	Q_3	W_3	Q_3W_3	Q_4	W_4	Q_4W_4	Q_5	W_5	Q_5W_5	Sub-grade
P_1	0.05	0.35	0.0175	1	0.35	0.35	0.9	0.15	0.135	0.8	0.05	0.04	0.5	0.1	0.05	0.5925
P_2	0.1		0.035	0.8		0.28	0.3		0.045	0.9		0.045	0.3		0.03	0.435
P_3	0.15		0.0525	0.6		0.21	0.7		0.105	0.7		0.035	0.7		0.07	0.4725
P_4	0.2		0.07	0.4		0.14	0.5		0.075	0.3		0.015	1		0.1	0.4
P_5	0.2		0.07	0.3		0.105	0.4		0.06	0.4		0.02	0.6		0.06	0.315
P_6	0.3		0.105	0.2		0.07	0.3		0.045	0.7		0.035	0.1		0.01	0.265
																2.48 Total general grade

Q_1, W_1: acreage (ha); Q_2, W_2: fertility; Q_3, W_3: access to water; Q_4, W_4: flatness; Q_5, W_5: distance to the main village residential site

Sub-grade = $Q_1W_1 + Q_2W_2 + Q_3W_3 + Q_4W_4 + Q_5W_5$

* This table is the author's own formulation.

also be organized.

The land accommodating major infrastructure should be publicly owned by governments (central, local) or by the village - hence a mixed economy of private ownership of farmland and public ownership of infrastructure land. The main reasons for this are that private landowners may inhibit others from getting access to the infrastructure (Oldenburg 1990: 188) and also have the right to withdraw their land if they wish, which would exert harmful externalities on other peasants and the whole community. The infrastructure itself could belong to the governments or village and individual investors according to their respective investment shares. [There have been good experiences in combining land consolidation with the overall rural development in Belgium, France, Germany, Greece, India, Japan, the Netherlands, Taiwan, etc. (Clout 1984: 108–16. Keeler & Skuras 1990: 75. Zaheer 1975: 112–3. Tsuge 1997. Huang, Chieh 1967: 91–5)]

Assignment of new farmland to each household. The land assigned to each farm should be given the most practical shape possible (in general *rectangular* - the length of the parcel should not be more than three or four times its breadth, and *square* for larger parcels) (Skovgaard 1950: 44. Roche 1956: 541). In contrast to the fragmented farms as shown in Figure 3.2, after the reorganization, each household would privately own one or a few (preferably no more than three) compact farmland unit(s), as illustrated in Figures 3.3 and 3.4). The total farm size is more or less the same as before, but the size of land unit (parcel) is larger. For example, a farm previously composed of 10 dispersed parcels (on average 0.1 ha each) can now hold one compact parcel of 1 ha.

Some discreteness of parcels may be rational due to differences in geography, ecology, etc. For example, a farmer may need both summer and winter pasture in certain hill areas, or land suitable for seed nurseries and land for growing of rice, or varieties of soil and situation in certain types of mixed farming to avoid risk of being dependent on one product. There is also local custom of working both an upland parcel and a parcel on river banks and islands where work is done in entirely different seasons. (Binns 1950: 31. Heston & Kumar 1983: 213). Many farms in mountain regions consist of three separate estates - in the plains, on the middle levels and on the high levels. The solution may be to lighten the task and the expense of the peasants by regrouping to the greatest possible extent the fields which they possess at the various levels, and by reducing to a minimum the capital invested in construction. (Swi-Gov 1950: 90). In a village with very distinct qualities of land, exchanging a smaller area of good land with a larger area of poor land to form just one compact land unit for each farm might be difficult. Under such circumstances, different qualities could be classified into a few (e.g., three) classes, and a farmer could retain consolidated parcels

F_1P_1	F_4P_1	F_3P_1	F_2P_1	F_5P_1	F_1P_2	F_2P_2	F_5P_2
F_2P_3	F_5P_3	F_2P_4	F_4P_2	F_3P_2	F_4P_3	F_5P_4	F_1P_3
F_3P_3	F_1P_4	F_4P_4	F_5P_5	F_4P_5	F_5P_6	F_2P_5	F_3P_4
F_4P_6	F_3P_5	F_5P_7	F_1P_5	F_2P_6	F_3P_6	F_4P_7	F_5P_8
F_5P_9	F_4P_8	F_3P_7	F_2P_7	F_3P_8	F_5P_{10}	F_1P_6	F_4P_9

Note: This figure is the author's own formulation.

Figure 3.2 Before Consolidation − Fragmented Farms

F_1P_1	F_3P_1	F_5P_1	F_2P_2	F_4P_2
F_2P_1	F_4P_1	F_1P_2	F_3P_2	F_5P_2

Note: This figure is the author's own formulation.

Figure 3.3 After Consolidation − Each Farm Has Two Parcels

F_1	F_2	F_3	F_4	F_5

Note: This figure is the author's own formulation.

Figure 3.4 After Consolidation − Each Farm Has One Parcel

of each quality, whose original fragments were in each class. (Heston & Kumar 1983: 209–10, 213). In general, most farms should contain only one parcel, with a few farms holding two or three (Oldenburg 1990: 186. Trivedi & Trivedi 1973: 186. Skovgaard 1950: 43–4).

Application of modern technologies. A cadastre, which registers not only the boundaries but also the value of real estate, is fundamental to land redistribution. Previously, with hundreds of tiny parcels to delineate, it could take years, often decades, for surveyors to draw and redraw maps to come up with an equitable form of consolidation. Mistakes occurred,[13] disputes increased, farmers felt imposed on and were reluctant to cooperate. (Nelson 1993: 24)

Now, this work can be much simplified. The government could organize satellite remote sensing for national land cover mapping as a component within a Geographic Information Systems (GIS), providing land data to each village (Haack & English 1996: 845). An ordinary personal computer equipped with the right program can create a cadastre from aerial photographs and digitalized field notes gathered with high speed by an Electronic Distance Measuring System (EDMS). Values of parcels resulting from assessment can also be put in. Using the computer, a surveyor can produce a cadastre in minutes and redraw it just as quickly in response to any number of 'what if' scenarios. It can be done on the spot with the participation of the local farming community. People whose land boundaries are in question can consider the alternatives and explain exactly what they want and do not want at each step. Each household could see the new map including its own future farm in the computer screen and make appeals if necessary before the consolidation scheme is finalized. Once the final version is ready, the information is fed into a larger, more powerful micro-computer capable of drawing the fine lines needed for boundaries and producing a map on durable, high-quality paper. (Nelson 1993: 24). In this way, survey, valuation, calculation, design, allocation, expenditure, etc., could be much facilitated, mistakes reduced, disputes decreased, unfair distribution due to corruption of officials supervised and time shortened.

Control of corruption. Corruption could present a major problem during land consolidation. It is reported that in some areas of India, large landowners paid bribes to the consolidation officials and got land of better quality, near the village and with fewer parcels, while the small owners could not afford to bribe, thus received the opposite and became poorer

---

13
     In the land consolidation of some areas of India, irrigation experts had to rely on guesswork and conjecture, and consolidation officials made channels on paper which were later discovered to be unworkable when demarcated on the spot (Zaheer 1975: 117).

(Elder 1962: 36). Factions in the villages are commonplace and can stimulate corruption. Except for using a computer as mentioned above, thorough and intensive inspection, investigation of appeals on the spot before the whole village assembly and removal of the corrupt officials are necessary for combating this problem. (Trivedi & Trivedi 1973: 185)

Appeals. Appeals should thus be handled, at a maximum of three levels in administrative system (village executive committee, guidance committees in two levels of the local governments above the village), plus two levels in judicial system (primary and appellate courts). A time limit for processing is necessary, because once consolidation has been promulgated, farmers would not improve the original land but wait for the new one (Trivedi & Trivedi 1973: 185). Administrative processing of appeals should take no more than three months. Courts would take a much longer time and cost much more money. Thus either special tribunals should be set up to speed the processing, or peasants be persuaded not to sue for small bargains (Oldenburg 1990: 185–6) and administrative processing be strengthened accordingly.

Expenses. Expenses are incurred in the above process. For private landholders, some permanent crops, buildings and other infrastructure in the old parcels would have to be removed and compensated, new buildings and other infrastructure in the new farms be built and subsidized. Some peasants might be asked to migrate to other areas and be subsidized as well. There was the SAFER (Societe d'Amenagement Foncier et d'Etablissement Rural - Society for Rural Settling and Country Planning) model in France which involved buying land from some farmers and reallocating it to others by the governments (Csaki & Lerman 2000: 37). Public infrastructure may imply public finance. Fees for organizational purposes occurred for setting up ad hoc committees, inviting external experts, etc. and carrying out their activities. These expenses should be borne by the central and local governments, village and landholders in the form of government grants and loans, bank credits, and personal payments. The village and landholders should be involved in decision making and allocation concerning the funds.

Population control. Population control should be strengthened. Otherwise, due to inheritance and other factors, not only the present fragmented small farms would be further fragmented, but also the already consolidated farms would be re-fragmented. For example, in India, although land consolidation has been pursued, the problem of re-fragmentation is not prevented (Trivedi

& Trivedi 1973: 186).**14** In fact, the average farm size has dropped from 2.3 ha in 1970–71 to 1.6 ha in 1990–91 (Kanda 1998: 3).

Conclusion

Based on a mixed economy of private ownership of farmland and public ownership of infrastructure land, dispersed parcels of farms could be consolidated through exchange of private ownership and reallocation in compact land units. In this process, intervention of governments, education of public opinion, active participation of farmers, and combination with overall rural development are necessary, and application of satellite remote sensing and computer technologies is beneficial. Nevertheless, the transaction costs involved are still very high, and population growth would lead to re-fragmentation.

14
There are tribes and areas in both Southern and Northern states of India still practicing a polyandry-like system whereby the parents' land is inherited by one of the sons only so as to prevent division (and successive divisions) of land among children (and grand and consecutive great-grand children). The sons share one wife, and the family's land can only be further inherited by one of their sons from the same wife. (PD 1999. Thamilarasan 1999). But even if polyandry could control population growth and prevent land fragmentation to some extent, whether it is acceptable to the modern civilized societies remains a question.

PART TWO

THE JAPANESE MODEL AND A NEW MODEL

4. The Japanese Model versus the Last Obstacle [1]

4.1 The Significance of the Japanese Model

The Japanese model of rural development began in 1946.[2] It combines nine major features or stages.[3]

1. Institutional changes for an individual—cooperative mixed economy (1946–50):

(1) The land reform during 1946–50 (Hayami & Yamada 1991: 83) was imposed by the General Headquarters of the Supreme Commander for the Allied Powers. The government compulsorily purchased the farmlands of resident landlords over 1 ha and those of absentee landlords, and resold them to peasants for individual ownership, at prices 40 times the annual rent in kind in lowland paddy fields and 48 times in upland fields, the rents being evaluated by the commodity prices of November 1945, which became negligible due to rapid inflation in 1945–49. The government also protected tenants from eviction, set land rents at very low levels; and imposed a 3 ha ceiling on land-holding in order to prevent the revival of landlordism through repurchasing (Hayami 1988: 45. Hayami & Yamada 1991: 84–5. Rothacher 1989: 16–7). This gave huge incentives for peasants to increase output.

In the land reform, farmlands were generally sold to the former tenants

---

[1] The earlier versions of this chapter have been published by the Food and Agriculture Organization of the United Nations in Zhou, Jian-Ming [1996] (1997) with abstract by CABI; (October 1997); and (1998).

[2] The Meiji era (1868–1912) had already carried out some land reform on the feudal landlord ownership. Technological progress and rural development had been made even in the Tokugawa period (1600–1868) and continued thereafter. (Smith 1966. Francks 1984). They all exerted important impacts on the postwar progress. But due to the length limit, this chapter has to concentrate on the postwar era.

[3] Summarized by the author from Oshima (1987: 60–5) and others indicated below. Oshima, however, does not indicate fragmentation.

who already possessed, and thus were familiar with, them. This was conducive to keeping production order, but also maintained the fragmentation of small farms which had existed before (as presented in Chapter 2). On average, the farm size was 0.8—1 ha, number of parcels per farm 10—20, parcel size 0.06 ha, and the total one-way distance to parcels about 4 km (Hyodo 1956: 558)4 - also see Table 4.2.

(2) The setting-up of national rural cooperatives left the direct production process to the individual farms, but *collectivized* forward linkage, backward linkage and finance. In forward linkage, farm machinery, chemical fertilizers, agricultural chemicals, market information and seeds were supplied, and technical guidance given. In backward linkage, farm produce, marine products, forestry goods, etc. could only be sold through the agricultural, fishery, forestry cooperatives respectively, as they controlled ties with the consumer markets. Rural financing was provided for forward linkage, the direct production process, and backward linkage. (Kojima 1988: 725—6)

In particular, the national rural cooperatives supplied superior seeds, semen and seedlings for improving productivity and increasing value added. To raise the quality of farm produce and livestock, establish uniform standards and win markets, the cooperatives designated certain species for cultivation by individual farms, distributed manuals for farms to follow, and eliminated sub-standard farm produce found at the grading sites before shipment. Farms which failed to follow the policies of the cooperatives could not operate successfully. Thus, although being mainly service cooperatives, they were extremely powerful. Individual farms had almost no self-management rights in these aspects at all. In other words, with the exception of the private land ownership, Japanese agriculture was organized more 'socialistically' than the Chinese counterpart after the dismembering of the people's communes. (Kojima 1988: 725—6)

However, because the individual farming units were based on private land ownership and controlled the direct production process, they also held the power of producing less or not producing at all. It was this, plus the formidable demand for labor from rural areas by industry, that contributed to the later inefficient land-holding by part-time and absent small farmers.

The author summarizes this form of mixed economy as an *individual— cooperative mixed economy*.

2. Government policies supporting rice production and rural development included rice self-sufficiency, rice price support, farm credit and subsidies, technological research and extension services, rice import

---

[4] The farm size and fragmentation data in this chapter exclude those of Hokkaido which is outside the monsoon region and has much larger farm size and fewer fragmented parcels.

protection during 1961—93, and policies supporting features 1 and 3—8.

Besides institutional changes, technological progress also contributed to economic growth and rural development, which was embodied in features 3—8. Five steps (3—7 below) were taken in order to reach full employment in rural areas:

3. Construction of rural infrastructure - mainly irrigation, land improvement, transportation, communication, electrification, education - established the technical basis for further rural development.

4. Higher yields and multiple cropping of rice and other grains (much of this was made possible by high-yielding varieties and fertilizers) raised both land and labor productivity and released labor from grain culture.

5. Diversified cropping and non-crop agriculture increased peasants' income, changed agricultural structures, and necessitated the establishment of rural enterprises for processing, transporting and marketing crop, livestock, fishery and forestry products.

6. Off-farm employment offered peasants jobs in both urban and rural enterprises, further raised peasants' income, changed rural structures, and promoted urbanization.

7. Peasant migration to cities and work in town and village firms were mainly by able-bodied males, leaving the aged and women in agriculture.

As peasants could get jobs also in the dry half year, full employment was achieved and wages rose. Hence a post-full employment step:

8. Agricultural mechanization with small machinery. Chapter 2 pointed out that the steam-driven machines of the First Industrial Revolution of the West in the 18th/19th century, were not suitable to the tiny paddy farms of monsoon Asia. But the electricity/gas-powered machines of the Second Industrial Revolution developed since the early 20th century were, because of their size, cheapness, efficiency, and the ease of connection to electricity. The gas-driven internal combustion engines could be inserted into small cultivators and used to run the small harvesters of Asian farms. (Oshima 1984: 44. Oshima 1993: 4—5)

As full employment was approached and reached, the widespread use of power cultivators, threshers, sprayers, pumps, weeders, driers, and motorized transport saved farm work. As the young people left for urban jobs, even the most labor-intensive operations of monsoon paddy farming - transplanting and reaping, began to be mechanized. Mechanical transplanters and reapers released a large number of workers at the busiest time of monsoon rice growing, so that the labor force on the farms began to shrink sharply without reducing output, another landmark event in monsoon Asia.

In 1960, rice self-sufficiency was achieved, per capita product raised, equity in income distribution reached, and poverty eradicated. The first transition (from agriculture to industry) was completed, and shortage of labor appeared. (JSY 1993/94: 272. ESJ 1960–61: 70. YLS 1963: 38–9. Oshima 1987: 115. Oshima 1993: 112, 125). At this high stage of rural development, all the major obstacles imposed by the monsoon have been overcome except for **9. persistence of the fragmented small farms, due to inefficient land-holding by part-time and absent small farmers** (Kristof 1996: 4) which will be analyzed later. Thus, shattering the vicious circle of poverty by the Japanese model around 1960 was regarded as the **first breakthrough** in sustainable rural development of monsoon Asia (Oshima 1993: 4). Features 1–8 continued to function beyond 1960. The second transition (industry to services) was concluded in 1974 (FEA 1975–76: 824). Except for rice import protection in feature 2, they are significant for other economies.

4.2 Theoretical Discussion [5]

The success of the Japanese model of rural development in features 1–8 i s consistent with the theory of the long-term ultimate causes for economic growth examined in Chapter 1, theories of dualism, monsoon Asia rice ec onomy and variable mixed economies reviewed in Chapter 2 and theory o f property rights discussed in Chapter 3.

At the end of WWII, under natural monsoon conditions, Japan, like other Asian rice-based economies, inherited (1) a highly labor-intensive rice culture leading to labor shortage in the peak seasons, population density, a nd fragmented small farms; (2) little employment in the slack seasons with unemployment, underemployment and disguised unemployment, and unli mited supply of labor; (3) unfeasibility of capitalistic large-scale farming, as three traditional productive and technological conditions, and (4) feudal landlord ownership as an institutional condition. There were also initial po stwar economic and social conditions, i.e., (1) low per capita income, (2) vast population and a huge labor force, (3) low productivity in peasant agr iculture, (4) denunciation of colonialism and feudalism. The Japanese eco nomy was a dual economy dominated by traditional agriculture, which wa s compounded by the destruction of the once strong and invasion war-oriented industry. Even during the prewar period, the rural areas did not enjoy many 'spread effects', but suffered from 'backwash effects' from the advanced big cities. Free market forces alone had been unable to overcome the vicious circle of poverty and realize sustainable rural development, thus

---

[5] All the theoretical points of view examined in Chapters 1, 2 and 3 are relevant to issues analyzed in Chapters 4–11. But writing all of them into the theoretical discussion sections is not permitted by the length limit of the book. Thus, only some major theoretical views are referred to.

agriculture was stagnant.

By 1960, with the same natural monsoon conditions, such an economic situation had been fundamentally changed in Japan by a mixed economy s olution - multiple structures of public and private ownership, and government intervention. The General Headquarters of the Supreme Commander for th e Allied Powers imposed the land reform, which was a conscious collective endeavor for changing the legally sanctioned structure of property rights i n force - the feudal landlord ownership. It used Approach 3: reform of pr operty rights structures through political or legal process, followed by exc hange at prices lower than the market levels. The state, overcoming the ba rgaining power of the feudal landlords, forcibly bought and resold their land to peasants at prices which soon became minimal due to inflation, so that the landlords were not fully compensated in real terms. The externality-yielding party had to partially internalize the redemption externality, for not creating the future externality, so as to establish the sufficient conditions for Pareto efficiency. The land reform instituted an equitable individual land ownership which brought huge incentives to peasants for production. The government set up powerful national rural cooperatives which not only collectivized overall services to the individual farming units, but also 'socialistically' restricted them from buying, producing and selling inferior products. Such institutional changes, as one of the long-term ultimate causes, played a keystone role in sustaining economic growth.

In order to sustain economic growth, there are not only institutional ch anges, but also technological progress as another long-term ultimate cause, and proximate sources (labor, capital, education, and structural changes, et c.). Thus, the government further promoted technological efficiency, in pa rticular dynamic efficiency, by supporting technological progress. Although 'backwash effects' were not completely avoided (e.g., senilization and fe minization of the agricultural labor force as indicated in Chapter 2), 'spread effects' were strengthened by constructing rural infrastructure, developing higher yields and multiple cropping of rice and other grains, diversified cr opping, non-crop agriculture and off-farm employment, which led to full e mployment of peasants also in the slack seasons and significantly lowered the wage gap. Peasants' migration to cities and work in town and village firms further raised their income. The development of towns strengthened the 'spread effects', constrained the 'backwash effects' and lessened urban congestion. Agricultural mechanization with small machinery reduced labor-intensity in rice culture, released more labor and paved the way for capital istic large-scale farming. The vicious circle of poverty in monsoon Asia was shattered for the first time in Japan.

Table 4.1 Comparison of Rice Production Costs by Farm Size in Japan 1953–98

Cost item	Farm size (ha)	Index of production cost per kg (below 0.3 ha = 100)										
		1953	55	60	65	70	75	80	84	89	94 [a]	98 [a]
Total costs	Below 0.3	100	100	100	100	100	100	100	100	100	100	100 [b]
	0.3–0.5	96	103	106	102	95	93	93	90	94	92	
	0.5–1											83
	1.0–1.5	89	98	96	88	78	75	70	67	71	72	72
	1.5–2											65
	2.0–3	79	88	92	82	67	61	57	54	63	59	61
	Above 3	75	90	87	93	69	60	51	51	54		
	3.0–5										51	53
	5.0–10										53	50
	10 & over										50	46
	15 & over											47

Cost item	Farm size (ha)	Index of production cost per kg (below 0.3 ha = 100)										
		1953	55	60	65	70	75	80	84	89	94 [a]	98 [a]
Labor costs	Below 0.3	100	100	100	100	100	100	100	100	100	100	100 [b]
	0.3–0.5	93	100	106	100	98	93	92	92	95	83	
	0.5–1											80
	1.0–1.5	83	91	91	87	79	72	66	62	67	66	68
	1.5–2											60
	2.0–3	66	74	83	80	63	52	50	49	55	48	56
	Above 3	60	73	78	90	68	50	42	43	46	38	
	3.0–5											47
	5.0–10											42
	10 & over											34
	15 & over											33

Table 4.1 continued

Cost item	Farm size (ha)	Index of production cost per kg (below 0.3 ha = 100)										
		1953	55	60	65	70	75	80	84	89	94 [a]	98 [a c]
Machinery & power costs	Below 0.3	100	100	100	100	100	100	100	100	100	100	100 [b]
	0.3–0.5	87	138	135	134	104	102	103	91	96	93	
	0.5–1											98
	1.0–1.5	92	156	146	127	89	90	81	72	86	85	95
	1.5–2											92
	2.0–3	89	143	137	108	72	82	64	54	77	86	96
	Above 3	89	144	121	123	69	76	55	51	63	71	
	3.0–5											89
	5.0–10											92
	10 & over											93
	15 & over											104

Notes: a. Index of production cost per 60 kg. b. Below 0.5 ha. c. Light, heat and power costs.
Sources: *1953 & 1989*: Nishimura & Sasaki 1993: 77. *1955–84*: JMAFF (c); Hayami 1988: 98. *1994*: JMAFF 1994. *1998*: JMAFF 1998.

4.3 The Remaining Obstacle

The ninth feature of the Japanese model of rural development is the persistence of the fragmented small farms, due to inefficient land-holding by part-time and absent small farmers. In Japan, as people became richer, rice consumption, although still necessary, declined. In the high wage economy, the income from rice production turned out to be much lower than that from diversified cropping, non-crop agriculture and off-farm employment. If rice farmers could not be viable, they would have to abandon rice production, so that rice self-sufficiency could not be maintained. In order to make them viable and gain international competitive strength, the income from rice production should be raised by *removing fragmentation and enlarging farm size* so that large machinery could be used, labor saved, cost reduced and increasing returns to land scale gained, as Table 4.1 shows.

Large machines like riding tractors, combines and rice transplanters were introduced into agriculture in the late 1960s. As Table 4.1 reveals, before 1955, when there was still abundant and even excessive agricultural labor force, larger farm size registered lower labor, machinery and power, and total costs. A possible explanation by the author is that as farm size increased, the primarily disguisedly unemployed labor could now be utilized to raise output so that the costs per kg could be reduced. During 1955–65, as agricultural labor force decreased and wages rose, small machinery prevailed. It could save labor, so that it maintained lower labor and total costs (although they were higher than those in the same farm size categories before 1955), but incurred higher machinery and power costs for larger farms. From 1970 on, however, by using large machinery, larger farms significantly lowered labor, machinery and power, and total costs - the total costs of farms over 3 ha were nearly one-half those of farms below 0.3 ha. This contrast shows that the agricultural mechanization with large machinery is characterized by increasing returns to land scale.[6] (Hayami 1988: 97). Hence the empirical evidence to the tenet 'that the costs of agricultural products fall as the size of the production unit in agriculture increases' and the logical necessity of increasing farm size following the substantial decline of the labor force required for farming and the engagement in nonfarm jobs by many of the farm people, just counter to Schultz's beliefs as mentioned in Chapter 1.

Concerning supervision of labor, when farm work had to be done by hand with simple tools, or by small machinery, it was difficult to standardize and

---

[6] The observations in Table 4.1 are not large enough for running regressions. More detailed data, however, are unavailable.

supervise the varied work of individual farmers. Thus, the head of a farm could not use or hire many farm workers, and hence could not run a large farm. Family farms would be more suitable. This was one of the major reasons why even a large feudal landlord had to lease land to tenants in small parcels as household farms, rather than employing the same number of tenants as his (her) wage laborers in a capitalistic farm of large acreage to be managed by himself, as Chapter 2 already indicated.

With large machinery, however, it became much easier to standardize farm work and supervise workers. Thus, enlarging farm size and employing more wage laborers to run a large capitalistic farm became technically possible (as farm size increases, more wage laborers would be hired, although not many, in order to save labor costs).

Therefore, land consolidation to resolve fragmentation was promoted since the 1950s and other attempts were made to increase the farm size from the 1960s onwards.

Major Efforts on Land Consolidation and Expansion

The first major effort. Land consolidation under private farmland ownership, as defined in Appendix 3.1, was sporadically carried out in Japan in ancient times before the 20th century. In 1901, the law on cultivated land consolidation was established to enable owners of agricultural land to organize cooperatives for the consolidation of their land. But the feudal landlords hampered the progress. The postwar government decided to promote land consolidation after the land reform. Thus, in June 1949, the Land Improvement Law was introduced. (Hyodo 1956: 558–9). Between 1950 and 1992, of the total 3,957,000 ha of farmland outside Hokkaido (data for 1992), 1,880,000 ha or 47.51% had been consolidated in Honshu (major part of Japan) (JSY 1993/94: 225. Tsuge 1997). It was strengthened in 1992 as a part of the *new policies*, for 'The Basic Direction of New Policies for Food, Agriculture and Rural Areas' of the Japanese Ministry of Agriculture, Forestry and Fisheries (JMAFF) declared that 'To foster farm management bodies that will operate on large-scale, aggregated farmland, methods to promote land improvement projects will be implemented that *allow land to be exchanged*' (JMAFF 1992: 15). The aim was to create compact land units of 1, 2 or 3 ha. Since 1993, of the total 3,879,000 ha of farmland outside Hokkaido (data for 1994), 50,000 ha or 1.29% per year have been consolidated in Honshu (JSY 1996: 229. Tsuge 1997). Although the 1949 Law prescribed that agreement by 50% of landowners of the village was sufficient for carrying out land consolidation and the 1992 new policies raised it to two-thirds majority, in most cases 100% consent was attained before starting it, but great efforts had to be made by officials to overcome

Table 4.2 Farm Size (ha) 1950–98 and Fragmentation in 1988 in Japan (in percentage) *

Year	Under 0.5	0.5–1	1–2	2–3	3–5	Over 5	Total %	Average farm size
1950	41.0	32.0	21.7	3.4	1.2	0.8	100	1.0
1960	38.3	31.7	23.6	3.8	1.5	1.0	100	1.0
1970	38.0	30.2	24.1	4.8	1.7	1.3	100	1.1
1980	41.6	28.1	21.2	5.3	2.2	1.5	100	1.2
1985	42.7	27.1	20.4	5.5	2.5	1.7	100	1.2
1990	41.7	28.1	20.9	9.3			100	1.1
1995	24.6	35.9	26.5	13.1			100	1.5
1997	22.7	36.3	26.8	14.2			100	1.5
1998	22.7	36.1	26.7	14.5			100	1.5

Parcels per farm over 5 ha			
1988	1–4	5–8	9 and more
100%	28.4	39.1	32.5

* Excluding Hokkaido.

Sources: *1950–85*: Kayo 1977; JMAFF (a); JMAFF (d); Hayami 1988: 27. *1990*: JSY 1992: 161; JSY 1996: 223. *1995*: JSY 1997: 225, 231. *1997*: JSY 1999: 223, 228. *1998*: JSY 2000: 219, 224. *1988*: JMAFF 1988: 250.

serious difficulties in adjusting interests among peasants (Hyodo 1956: 559. Tsuge 1997. NIRA 1995: 174. Zhou, Jian-Ming January 1999: 7).

The second major effort was to encourage *land sale* in order to increase farm size. From 1961 on, the purchase of land by farmers was subsidized by the government. In 1962, the land-holding ceiling was relaxed. However, not enough land sales occurred. On the supply side, part-time farming became dominant. Many able-bodied males commuted to off-farm employment, while their wives and old parents farmed. But the part-time and absent small farmers had no incentive to sell land: off-farm income was high and a rural place for their retirement was preserved. For the part-time farmers, the distance between towns and villages was short, transportation convenient. They had no need to pay high rent for city dwellings and enjoyed less pollution. Moreover, as industrialization proceeded, land prices soared. Land sales in the future would be much more profitable than now. On the demand side, because land prices went well over income surplus from rice production, it became unprofitable for full-time farmers to enlarge farm size through land purchase. (Hayami 1988: 80–9. Oshima 1993: 172–3). In effect, it was the shortcomings of private land ownership which hampered land sales.

Hence the resort to *land lease* as *the third major effort* which was also aimed at promoting large-scale farming. In 1970, rent control was removed, and land could be returned to landlords upon termination of contracts of more than 10 years. In 1975 and 1980, leases for shorter period were also legalized. Land lease occurred more than sale and formed some large-scale farms.7 The progress was initially slow but has been quicker since 1985, as not only older farmers in mountainous areas but also part-time farmers in lowland regions increasingly faced the lack of young successors for farming, and have been more willing to lease land (Tsuge 1997), which is the major cause of the decline of farms under 0.5 ha and the increase of those of 0.5 ha and over during 1985–98 in Table 4.2.

But there also exist unfavorable factors. On the supply side, landowners were rich enough from off-farm income and did not have much incentive to rent out land. If the rent was not sufficiently high, the part-time and absent small farmers had no incentive to lease land; but if it was high enough to satisfy the lessors, the full-time farmers could not afford it. Tenants might over-exploit the soil, which might not be detected soon nor even at the end of the lease contract. Law disputes could be incurred, costing much time, energy and money as well beyond the rent incomes. There was a strong equalitarianism among village people, who felt uncomfortable if a specific villager expanded his farm and became competitive in the market. This resulted in entrenched inefficiency and vested interests. (Hayami 1988: 86–8, 108, 126). Farm households had a solid preference for permanent residence which has continued for generations, and regarded agricultural land as a valuable asset handed down from the ancestors which should be passed on as it is to the offspring. They still feared that once let, land would be lost, as happened in the land reform. Thus, people tended to avoid renting out land. (Tabata 1990: 18, 22)

On the demand side, because the small farm was composed of many fragmented parcels located in different parts of the village, it was not always possible for the lessee to join them into large land units (because the parcels

---

7 For example, in Saitama Prefecture, some large-scale rice/wheat farms were formed by owned and leased lands with the acreage from 3 ha to 27 ha and on average 10 ha, but operated by senior farmers often without young successors (Kurita 1994: 511, 519).

of other landowners could be interspersed among them) or change them to non-farmland means of production (dams, roads, canals, ponds, etc.) (as the ownership belonged to the lessor) for using large machinery (Tabata 1990: 18, 22). Even if the owned and leased parcels were adjacent, once the lease was ended, the lessor may shift the lease to another lessee, hence re-splitting the unified land and reducing farm size. Here, private land ownership and free market forces constrained both land lease and the efficient use of leased land.

Land consolidation as the above-mentioned first major effort could turn farms from fragmented to compact units, expand parcel size, and make sale, lease, and other forms of joint use of land physically easier. But it did not enlarge farm size [e.g., a farm previously composed of 10 dispersed parcels (on average 0.1 ha each) could now hold one compact parcel of 1 ha]. Nor did it ensure efficient use of the consolidated land by the full-time farmers. A part-time or absent small farmer who previously had no incentive to sell or lease his fragmented farm may now still be unwilling to do so for his compact farm.

The fourth to sixth major efforts. Since the 1970s, the fourth major effort to achieve large-scale farming was *commissioned agricultural work* (also called custom work) - commissioning or contracting a part or the whole process of rice cultivation primarily by small households holding land up to 0.5 ha to other farmers for using the latter's machinery, labor and management. (This was at the threshold to start collective use of private land). The fifth major effort was *agricultural production cooperatives* - groups of farm households mainly holding land of 2–5 ha and over, accomplishing all or a part of agricultural production process by jointly using machinery and assigning members to commissioned work (this was collective use of private land.) Some production cooperatives were joined by farm households of a whole village, exercised village-wide collective use and management of private farmland and machinery, eliminated boundaries among parcels, thus enlarged farming scale - 'a result of measures collectively taken on the village level to preserve a region's agricultural activity', which implied education of peasants to reach consensus or follow the majority agreement (NIRA 1995: 172–4, 176–7). The sixth major effort was *urban–rural joint farming* - enterprises other than farm households organized joint management, joint venture, production corporation and limited companies in farming including receiving commissioned work (this was also collective use of private land), which have achieved a considerable share in certain sectors but not much in land-extensive farming. These three major forms all had advantages in tilling otherwise idle land, achieving economies of scale in using machinery, labor and management, and reducing the cost of machinery. (Tabata 1990: 20–2). There have been various other

Table 4.3 *Proportions of Full-Time and Part-Time Farmers in Japan 1950-98* [a]

Year	Farm households	Full-time [b] %	Part-time 1: mainly farming [b] %	Part-time 2: mainly other jobs [b] %	Farm household population	Persons engaged in farming [c] %	Persons engaged mainly in farming [d] %	Principal persons engaged mainly in farming [e] %	Male principal persons engaged mainly in farming %
1950 [f]	6,176,419	50.0	28.4	21.6	–	–	–	–	–
1955 [f]	6,042,945	34.8	37.6	27.5	36,347,290	–	53.2	39.1	–
1960	5,822,996	33.7		66.3	34,411,187 [f]	–	42.3 [f]	38.1 [f]	14.2 [f]
1965	5,465,794	20.5		79.5	30,083,252 [f]	–	38.3 [f]	32.0 [f]	11.0 [f]
1970	5,175,866	14.5		85.5	26,281,780 [f]	–	39.0 [f]	32.1 [f]	10.8 [f]
1975	4,818,808	11.6		88.4	23,197,451 [f]	–	34.1 [f]	28.3 [f]	9.3 [f]
1980	4,541,740	12.6	21.2	66.2	20,834,025	–	32.2	27.8	9.4
1985	4,266,698	13.6	17.4	69.0	19,367,000	58.5	31.6	18.1	9.1
1990	3,739,295	14.7	13.4	71.9	16,891,000	59.8	32.2	17.5	9.1
1992	2,806,070	14.8	14.8	70.4	13,065,000	60.0	33.1	20.0	10.2
1993	2,755,270	14.9	14.5	70.6	12,758,000	59.9	33.0	19.9	10.1
1994	2,709,870	15.2	13.2	71.6	12,455,000	59.7	33.0	19.8	10.1

1995	2,577,815	15.3	18.2	66.5	11,725,000	61.4	33.8	20.6	11.0
1996	2,534,390	15.8	16.8	67.4	11,465,000	60.5	33.2	20.3	10.9
1997	2,497,470	16.1	15.4	68.5	11,255,000	60.6	33.5	20.6	11.1
1998	2,453,610	16.3	14.6	69.0	11,031,000	61.0	33.9	20.6	11.1

Notes:

a. Excluding Hokkaido.

b. *Full-time* farm households refer to those farm households whose all members are exclusively engaged in farming. *Part-time* ones denote those whose one or more members are engaged in jobs other than farming. *Part-time 1* (mainly farming) mean those part-time households earning income mainly from farming. *Part-time 2* (mainly other jobs) indicate those gaining income chiefly from jobs other than farming. (JSY 2000: 213)

c. Called *persons engaged in own farming* in JSY 1983–90, and *persons engaged in family operated and custom farming* in JSY 1991–99; but unlisted in earlier JSY; representing those household members 15 years of age and older who have been engaged in any work in farming for one day or more in the year preceding the survey date (JSY 2000: 213).

d. Labeled as *population engaged in agriculture* in JSY 1977–83, and *population engaged in farming* in JSY 1984–99, but referring to *persons engaged mainly in farming*, containing both those engaged exclusively in farming and those engaged in farming for more days than in other jobs (JSY 2000: 213).

e. Identified as *population in agriculture only* in JSY 1977, *population in agriculture exclusively* in JSY 1978–82, and *principal persons engaged in own farming* in JSY 1983–84, *principal persons engaged in farming* in JSY 1985–99, also called *core farmers*,[8] signifying *core or principal persons engaged mainly in farming* - those mainly engaged in farming for over 150 days per year (Hayami 1988: 82).

f. Including Hokkaido.

Sources: *1950–55*: JSY 1981: 109, 113. *1960–75*: JSY 1977: 100; JSY 1981: 113. *1980*: JSY 1981: 111, 113. *1985*: JSY 1986: 150, 152. *1990*: JSY 1991: 152, 154. *1992*: JSY 1993/94: 220, 222. *1993*: JSY 1995: 224, 226. *1994*: JSY 1996: 224. *1995*: JSY 1997: 226. *1996*: JSY 1998: 226. *1997*: JSY 1999: 224. *1998*: JSY 2000: 220.

---

8 It is important to note that core farmers include but do not equal full-time farmers since the non-full-time core farmers still spend a part of their time on other jobs which could otherwise be used on agriculture as well. Therefore, this book recommends the promotion of full-time farmers, rather than that of core farmers as advocated in Japan (e.g., by Saito; Fukukawa; Tada & Kajiya 1995: 81).

forms of collective use of private land, which could also be classified as at sub-village and village-wide scope. According to Tsuge (May 1998), the village-wide ones are still in small numbers. Here we can see that as long as a back-up basic social welfare (such as the private land ownership) could be kept and appropriate remuneration afforded so as to relieve their rational concern over direct interests in security, then some part-time and absent small farmers would be agreeable to transfer their inefficiently held land in various suitable forms to the full-time farmers for effective use, although not all of them would be voluntary to do so, as surmised in Chapter 1.

But except for the village-wide collective use of private land, these forms were less successful in achieving economies of scale of land. Without the agreement of all landowners concerned, they were unable to form large land units or change parcels to non-farmland means of production. Fragmentation was still a barrier. In the case of village-wide collective use of private land, cooperative members could agree to remove boundaries among parcels. But as long as private land was physically withdrawable, there could be three problems. (1) If the village needed to change parcels into non-farmland means of production, members may disagree or demand high compensation. At enough transaction costs, the village may succeed in persuading them to accept other parcels as an exchange, but may also not succeed. (2) Due to various personal and organizational reasons/problems, some members may quit to operate land individually or organize another cooperative. Thus, the joined land would be re-split. At high transaction costs again, the cooperative may make a quitting member agree to accept a parcel on the periphery in exchange for his original land so as to keep all fields of the remaining members together, but he may also refuse to accept. (3) Quitting with land would certainly reduce the farm size operated by the remaining full-time farmers of the cooperative, to which no solution may be ready. Therefore, as Tabata (1998) notes, setting up of land use cooperatives and their subsequent breaking down have repeatedly occurred.9

Consequences

Land under-utilization and idling. Table 4.2 shows that the progress in economies of scale of land was slow. Although farms of 0.5 ha and over have increased especially since 1985 through leasing prompted by the lack of young successors to farming, fragmentation was still preserved (hence the

---

9 NIRA (1995) provides a number of examples at local including village levels in detail. But they are in Japanese. No example is given in English in other literature reviewed in this chapter. But the statements by the Japanese authors should be dependable.

major shortcoming of land lease). Table 4.3 further demonstrates a predominance of part-time farming - of all farm households, the full-time ones have declined from 33.7% in 1960 to lower than 20% ever since 1970; although they increased from 14.5% in 1970 to 16.8% in 1998, this was accompanied by the decrease of part-time 1 from 21.2% in 1980 to 14.6% in 1998, and the full-time and part-time 1 together dropped from 33.8% in 1980 to 30.9% in 1998, while part-time 2 remained around 70% since 1985, under which much land has been in inefficient use, i.e., under-utilization or idling. In fact, abandonment of cultivated land has been increasing during 1975–95 as Table 4.4 presents (the landowners abandoned the operation rather than ownership of land, thus non-owners still could not use the abandoned land) and utilization rate of cultivated land has decreased from 133.9% in 1960 to 95.3% in 1997 as Table 4.5 indicates. There are even rural areas where there have been no farmers to operate agricultural land at all (JMAFF 1992: 15). Such phenomena would obviously contribute to the deterioration of the environment. In particular, land abandonment might lead to desertification.

Senilization and feminization of the agricultural labor force. As Table 4.6

Table 4.4 Abandonment of Cultivated Land in Japan 1975–95

	1975	1980	1985	1990	1995
Abandoned cultivated land (1,000 ha)	99	92	97	151	162
Cultivated land abandonment ratio % *	2.0	1.9	2.0	3.3	3.8

*   Cultivated land abandonment ratio = Area of abandoned cultivated land / (Area of utilized cultivated land + Area of abandoned cultivated land)

Source: JMAFF 1997: Chapter 1 - II 2 (4).

Table 4.5 Utilization Rate of Cultivated Land in Japan 1960–97 (in percentage)

1960	70	80	85	90	93	94	95	96	97
133.9	108.9	104.5	105.1	102	100	99.3	97.7	95.8	95.3

Sources: *1960*: JSY 1986: 159. *1970–90 and 1994–96*: JSY 1999: 231. *1993*: JSY 1997: 235. *1997*: JSY 2000: 227.

Table 4.6 *Senilization and Feminization of the Agricultural Labor Force in Japan 1965–98 (1,000 persons)*

Year	Total	Male						Female					
		Total	15–29	30–49	50–59	60–64	65 & over	Total	15–29	30–49	50–59	60–64	65 & over
							Persons engaged in farming [a]						
1965	15,443	7,490	1,522 [b]	4,451		1,517		7,954	1,533 [b]	5,124		1,297	
1975	13,732	6,877	1,415 [b]	2,681	1,242	530	1,008	6,855	1,067 [b]	2,878	1,437	589	884
1985	11,629	6,031	807 [b]	2,110	1,462	585	1,067	5,597	506 [b]	1,938	1,501	647	1,005
1995	7,398	3,960	380	1,381	681	473	1,044	3,438	207	1,077	716	476	962
1997	7,013	3,757	326	1,282	614	434	1,100	3,256	178	999	622	448	1,010
1998	6,914	3,706	324	1,221	620	410	1,131	3,208	174	945	611	433	1,044
							Persons engaged mainly in farming [c]						
1965	11,514	4,565	748 [b]	2,528		1,290		6,949	1,186 [b]	4,521		1,242	
1975	7,907	2,975	446 [b]	845	544	319	821	4,932	575 [b]	1,878	1,122	520	839
1985	6,363	2,478	204 [b]	459	563	353	899	3,885	238 [b]	1,045	1,086	559	956
1995	4,140	1,767	119	263	227	276	883	2,372	95	490	468	404	916
1997	3,931	1,704	94	248	196	248	919	2,227	76	436	390	371	954
1998	3,892	1,688	94	232	189	232	942	2,204	74	408	374	360	989

Principal persons engaged mainly in farming [d]

1965	8,941	4,191	574 [b]	2,490			1,127	4,750	807 [b]	3,379			564
1975	4,889	2,298	211 [b]	1,343			743	2,591	180 [b]	1,968			443
1985	3,696	1,870	95 [b]	526	443	290	518	1,826	52 [b]	599	636	261	278
1995	2,560	1,372	31	218	253	246	625	1,188	10	255	299	232	392
1997	2,456	1,318	28	188	237	223	643	1,137	9.7	240	268	217	402
1998	2,408	1,293	27	181	223	207	654	1,115	8.3	225	256	215	412

Notes:

a. Called *persons engaged in family-operated and custom farming* in the original table.

b. 16–29 years old.

c. Labeled as *population engaged in farming* in the original table.

d. Listed as *principal persons engaged in farming* in the original table.

Sources: *1965*: JSY 1992: 153. *1975–98*: JSY 2000: 213, 221.

reveals, during 1965–98, there has been a general trend of a decrease of the total agricultural labor force and those males and females aged between 15–64, and an increase of those aged 65 and over. While the aging of the agricultural labor force is a common feature to OECD countries, the high proportion of women in farming in Japan is particular. This trend, in part, may reflect the role of the elderly or retirees (formerly engaged in off-farm work) in farm households who take on the responsibility for the daily maintenance of small rice farms on a full-time basis. The proportion of elderly workers returning to the farm sector has increased since the general slowdown in growth rates of the economy from the late 1970s. (OECD 1995: 16)

The lack of young successors to farming has strengthened the labor shortage in agriculture. A number of reasons may explain the decline of young farmers: the lower per capita incomes from farming; more onerous working conditions and longer hours of work than those of urban workers; and the difficulties of finding suitable marriage partners in the more remote areas which have experienced continuing migration. The continuation of the trend may finally result in a reduction in agricultural production and the size of some rural communities. (OECD 1995: 17)

Non-viability of and protection for farmers. As a result, the number of viable farms diminished (see Table 4.7), and farmers and cooperatives organized political lobbying for *protection*. The ruling party had to yield, fearing loss of votes. (Hayami 1988: 49, 51). In 1960, a 'cost-of-production and income-compensation scheme' was designed. The government as the monopsonist buyer (through the national cooperatives) bought rice at a predetermined price and sold it at a lower price, thus subsidizing rice farmers. The 1961 Agricultural Basic Law prohibited rice imports. Rice prices increased to 10 times the world level in the 1980s. Stimulated by the price distortion, rice was overproduced until 1992. (Rothacher 1989: 162–3. Schaede 1994: 388. Schaede 1997: 427)

Consequently, in the 1980s, the budget deficit on rice rose to more than US$7,000 million. Internationally, protests flowed, especially from the USA. The GATT Uruguay Round of 1993 stipulated that rice imports gradually increase up to 10% of the total consumption size per year until 2005. Following a disastrous harvest and loss of rice self-sufficiency in 1993, cheap rice had in 1994 to be imported for the first time since 1960, from Australia, China, Thailand and the USA (Schaede 1997: 427). In 1996, two-thirds of what the Japanese consumed was imported cheaper food. Further liberalization is expected (Kristof 1996: 4). This contributed to the rising of the world market rice prices. During 1995–96, the world grain prices rose to record highs and the post-sale grain stocks fell to their lowest levels in 25 years, as global consumption outpaced production. (Stuart & Runge 1997:

129). This affected other grain importing countries especially the poor ones of the Third World. Domestically, with the fragmented small farms, it is difficult for rice farmers to subsist and for the government to establish a competitively surviving rice self-sufficiency. Subsidies have to continue. In late 1994, the government decided to spend 6,000 billion yen over six years from 1995–96 to 2000–01 for farmers to adjust to the new regime. The government purchase price was maintained at the same high level as before in 1994–95, and three–five times higher than the price of the imported rice in 1998–2000, which has again caused overproduction that, together with the imported cheap rice, led to a glut in inventories. The government has then again used subsidies to encourage farmers to cut young crops or turn rice to forage. It has also set up non-tariff barriers to restrict rice import. (Schaede 1997: 427. FEA 1997: 435. CVJ 2000). In contrast, the self-sufficiency rates

Table 4.7 Changes in the Number and Shares of Viable Farms in Japan 1960–96 *

	1960	1970	1980	1985	1990	1994	1996
Total farms (1,000)	6,057	5,342	4,661	4,376	3,835	2,787	2,606
Viable farms (1,000)	521	353	242	232	253	198	149
Share of viable farms (%) in							
Household number	8.6	6.6	5.2	5.3	6.6	7.1	5.7
Agricultural output	23	25	30	31	39	32	31
Arable land	24	18	19	21	26	23	20
Agricultural labor force	16	19	21	22	29	26	24
Agricultural fixed capital	19	19	21	24	29	23	23

*   Including Hokkaido.

Sources: *1960–85*: JMAFF (a); (b); JSY 2000: 219; Hayami 1988: 81. *1990–94*: JSY 2000: 219; JMAFF 1995: 179. *1996*: JSY 2000: 219; JMAFF 1996.

Table 4.8 Self-Sufficiency Rates of Foods in Japan 1960–97 (fiscal year, in percentage) *

	1960	65	70	75	80	85	90	91	92	93	94	95	96	97
Cereals														
Rice	102	95	106	110	100	107	100	100	101	75	120	103	102	99
Wheat	39	28	9	4	10	14	15	12	12	10	9	7	7	9
Barley	104	57	28	8	13	14	12	10	10	10	8	8	8	7
Naked barley	112	123	73	98	98	100	92	70	92	100	86	70	78	85
Miscellaneous cereals	21	5	1	1	0	0	0	0	0	0	0	0	0	0
Potatoes & sweet potatoes	100	100	100	99	96	96	93	91	91	89	88	87	85	87
Starches	76	67	41	24	21	19	13	12	13	12	12	12	10	11
Pulses	44	25	13	9	7	8	8	7	6	4	5	5	5	5
Vegetables	100	100	99	99	97	95	91	90	90	88	86	85	86	86
Fruits	100	90	84	84	81	77	63	60	59	53	47	49	47	53

Meat (excluding whale)	91	90	89	77	81	81	70	67	65	64	60	57	55	56
Whale	100	107	100	72	46	47	67	67	100	100	100	100	100	100
Hen eggs	101	100	97	97	98	98	98	98	97	96	96	96	96	96
Cow's milk & milk products	89	86	89	81	82	85	78	77	81	80	72	72	72	71
Fish & shellfish	110	109	108	102	104	96	86	86	83	76	70	75	70	72
Seaweeds	92	88	91	86	74	74	72	70	75	70	70	68	67	66
Sugar	18	31	22	15	27	33	33	36	35	33	29	35	32	31
Fats & oils	42	31	22	23	29	32	28	24	19	17	15	15	14	14
Mushrooms	—	115	111	110	109	102	92	91	87	81	78	78	80	76

* Fiscal year: 1 April of the stated year – 31 March of the following year (JSY 2000: vi).

Sources: JSY 1993/94: 272; 1997: 276; 2000: 268.

of other agricultural products, being given less or no subsidies, all declined to below 100% in 1994 (most of them have been so even since the 1960s), as Table 4.8 demonstrates, with the only exception being whale, whose self-sufficiency has been maintained at the expense of this scarce and diminishing sea animal despite the continuous international protests. In 1997, even rice self-sufficiency was not reached and whale became the unique agricultural product to be self-sufficient. Thus, how to *effectively* overcome the inefficient land-holding in order to consolidate and enlarge the fragmented small farms has become a critical issue in the sustainable rural development of Japan.

Repetition by Taiwan Province of China

Similarly, Taiwan completed the first (agriculture–industry) and second (industry–services) transitions during 1970–73 and 1994 respectively (SYAP 1970: 77. FEA 1977–78: 342; 1997: 267). Land consolidation under private farmland ownership was promoted into law in 1936, started in 1959 [Huang, Chieh 1967: (Appendix) 1, 37–8, Foreword] and strengthened in 1975 as 'the second land reform'. By 1982, 300,000 ha, or two-thirds of 446,000 ha farmland planned for consolidation had been reorganized into large, rectangular fields more suitable for mechanized farming. By 1989, however, 88.6% of farming households were still part-time farms, which earned 62.8% of their income from off-farm activities. (Myers 1996: 260). In 1994, 4.4 ha were the rice farming area that enabled a full-time farm family to earn an income from its farming to balance off its consumptive expenditure. But those who held this or larger land scale accounted for only 7% of all the farm families. (Cheng, Shy-Hwa 1994: 94–5). This and the above-mentioned Japanese case clearly show how free market forces could lastingly constrain farm expansion.

Unsuitable Alternative Solutions

Facing the largely unsuccessful functioning in Japan of the free market solutions such as land sale and lease, which have worked well to some extent in some Western European regions, one may wonder, given that the fragmented small farms problem has been prevented, resolved or much improved in various (although not all) regions of Western Europe, whether some of their other solutions could be transplanted to Japan and monsoon Asia.

A market solution - *emigration* - played a major part in Western Europe in the previous centuries and the first half of the 20th century, and in some countries even after WWII. When peasants left on a large scale for South

Africa, North America, South America, Australia, New Zealand, etc., they naturally transferred land ownership to the fewer remaining farmers in their own countries. Presently, however, the West has largely blocked this market solution by immigration control. Now that it is so difficult for peasants in monsoon Asia to emigrate, they naturally hold land ownership within their own economy even after they have become part-time or absent farmers.

A non-market solution - *primogeniture*, as the rule or law for inheritance whereby land descends to the oldest son - was legally practiced in England in the middle ages and is still customary there (Chernow & Vallasi 1993: 2219). In Australia, Canada, Ireland, New Zealand and the USA, it is the common law without legislative intervention which allows an heir to be designated by testator's will as a single successor to a whole farm without obligation to pay monetary compensation to other heirs. Similarly, the legislations in Austria, Denmark, Finland, Germany, Greece, Norway, Sweden, and Switzerland allow one heir to inherit a whole farm, although by paying monetary compensation to other heirs. They have effectively prevented fragmentation from inheritance. It is noteworthy, however, that the single heir system has not been accepted in France, Belgium, Italy, Luxembourg, the Netherlands, Portugal, Spain and Turkey which have adopted the principle of equalitarian inheritance, hence fragmentation from inheritance is not excluded but can be abated by decreasing children. (OECD 1998a: 18–20). In comparison, in monsoon Asia, land is the basic and even unique income source when peasants are poor and is still a precious asset after they have become rich. Therefore, it is generally unpractical to exclude other children from inheriting their parents' land. Even though, the civil law in the Meiji era of Japan adopted primogeniture, which was changed after WWII into equalitarian inheritance, but undivided inheritance by one child (usually a son) through consensus within a family has still been a commonly observed practice (OECD 1998a: 20), although divided inheritance is gradually increasing due to the decrease of children (Tsuge December 1998). The practice in Japan shows that primogeniture, though it does not exacerbate, may not improve fragmentation.

There was another non-market solution - *enclosure of land* in Britain. Between the 12th and 14th century, land formerly subject to common rights was enclosed by landlords on the condition that they left sufficient land for free tenants. Thereafter, however, owing to the rapid expansion of the Flemish wool trade, landlords either made agreements with or just illegally expelled tenants, in order to enclose large areas for sheep pastures. The hardship of dispossessed tenants, increasing vagrancy, and social unrest resulted in statutes designed to limit the practice under the autocratic rule of the Tudors. Ironically, however, under the so-called parliamentary democracy established after the 1604 revolution, the process continued actually uncontrolled, reaching its peak in the late 17th century. Hence no democracy for ordinary peasants. This discloses that the establishment and perfectization of democracy have experienced a historical process at least in the UK. Although there was little enclosure in the early 18th century, it increased dramatically from 1750 to 1800 as strengthened by the private act of Parliament. The General Enclosure Act of 1801 standardized much of the process, and an act of 1845 provided for the incorporation of all enclosures in a single act each year. By this time, the movement towards general enclosure was largely completed. The process of forcing small farmers out of agriculture, although harsh, met the increasing demand for labor by the First Industrial Revolution, and promoted more efficient farming which was able to produce an ever-increasing agricultural output during the 19th century when the population was growing rapidly. (Chernow & Vallasi 1993: 1320). However, such a solution is apparently unacceptable in the increasingly democratic contemporary era.

A further non-market solution - *tax on waste of land* - was proposed by, e.g., Schiller (1956: 563) among others. However, such a tax might be implementable in some Western countries where rural population, after enormous emigration, is lower than 10% of the total population, thus holding less votes to block the parliaments from adopting it. But in Japan, in 1995, of the total population, that in towns and villages still accounted for 21.95% (see Table 7.6), of which, male principal farmers (excluding Hokkaido) accounted for only 11% (see Table 4.3). The ruling party may not dare to initiate such a tax, fearing the loss of the votes of the large number of part-time and absent small farmers. Even if such a tax were imposed, part-time and absent small farmers could easily evade it by symbolically planting some crops, and thus claiming that their land is not 'wasted', but actually not taking care of them in the rest of the year. Moreover, it may not be possible to impose a tax on those full-time farmers who quit a cooperative/enterprise to individually operate (hence also strengthening) fragmented parcels. These factors may explain why such a tax has not been imposed thus far.

In Chapter 1, it was cited that in Northwest Europe (Austria, Belgium, Denmark, France, West Germany, Ireland, the Netherlands, Norway, Sweden, and the UK) employment in agriculture declined over a fifth during 1950–59. Those leaving agriculture treated land mainly in there ways: (1) some part-time and absent farmers maintained farming by wives and old parents, (2) other peasants sold land near cities or communication lines since their expansion raised land prices to levels much higher than its value in agricultural terms, and (3) many even sold distant land because they wanted to quit farming and the backward rural areas (Milward 2001). Would (3) happen nowadays in such a scope as in the 1950s? Unlikely, because the present rural areas may enjoy the similar facilities as in the cities (e.g., electricity, tap water, gas and microwave ovens, refrigerators, fixed and mobile phones, fax machines, computers, Internet), transportation and services become convenient (cars, coaches, trains, planes, schools, medical service, entertainment, etc.), and most importantly, people attach much more value to the precious and primitive rural environment since the publication of *The Limits to Growth* in 1974 (Meadows; Meadows; Randers & Behrens).

The above analysis has shown that in Western Europe, not only market solutions but also non-market solutions, government interventions, and different social, economic and environmental conditions and values have played a strong part in both the historical and contemporary process of resolving fragmentation and increasing farm size.

As an opposite solution to private land ownership, rural land may be turned to *public ownership* (state, regional or village collectives), just as in Cambodia, China, North Korea, Laos, Myanmar and Vietnam. But facing increasing land prices and a global wave of decollectivization and privatization, under a scheme of paying compensation, the public institutions may not be able to afford to buy and landowners may not wish to sell; under a scheme without compensation, owners may not agree either.

Bray (1986: 217) simply recommends Japan to *abandon rice production and rely on import*. Apparently rice is much cheaper abroad and thus import is compatible with the theory of comparative advantage of Ricardo ([1817] 1973: Chapter VII) of which Marshall says ([1887] 1926: 65) 'I do not know that any person has shaken it in the least'. However, though perhaps unknown to Marshall, List in the 1820s–30s counters Ricardo's view of free trade and advocates *protection to 'infant industries'*, as he believes that commercial freedom was a doctrine which erroneously generalized the situation of Britain to the rest of the world, and for it to dominate the world economy, thanks to the development of its economy. Free trade and economic liberty were highly desirable for the world economy, but were only appropriate to a world of economic equals. Such a world could be created only if those countries which were in the development process could protect their key industries against premature competition. (Tribe 1987: 217). Therefore, even Portugal wanted to establish its own industries rather than remaining an agricultural country and relying on the lower costs of industrial goods of England as in Ricardo's favorite wine versus cloth example. Would Ricardo's theory be fully adopted by countries *with matured industries*? Still not. Agriculture and industry in today's European Union are not infant. But the EU has still set high tariffs. One may suggest that the EU keep the landscape for tourism and import everything else, e.g., cheaper agricultural goods from Australia and the USA and less expensive industrial products from the USA and Japan. Would the EU agree? *In terms of national security*, if a country relied on import for its staple food, then it might be threatened in diplomatic conflicts and have its throat cut during wartime. Thus, Japan could tolerate under-self-sufficiency and rely on import for all the other agricultural goods but not for rice (and, of course, whale), whose self-sufficiency has been artificially kept with heavy government subsidies ever since 1960. Like Japan, China 'does not want to be dependent on imports of grain' (Oi 1999: 622). *Importing food may also be denounced* as pushing up world prices, just as refusing to do so would be criticized as not opening domestic markets - hence a dilemma. For example, China's agricultural output declined in 1994 which led to grain import exceeding export in 1995–96 (see Table 6.4). Immediately the question of China's capacity to feed itself has become an international issue following claims that China's food needs will destabilize world markets (Howe 1998: 232). 'Some worry that China might empty the world's food basket' (Oi 1999: 621). Thus importing food may not be so welcome in the world market as it seems to be. As a result, 'The Chinese authorities consider that food security can only be achieved if China is self-sufficient for 95% of its food (grain) needs' (Aubert 1999: 14). Moreover, *resources are scarce* on the earth and could not afford wasting. In many countries there is much land being under-utilized or idled while food security has not been reached/maintained. If they were asked to rely on importing food rather than fully using land, this would amount to wasting resources. Not to mention that land idling would lead to desertification. These reasons may partly explain why FAO defines sustainable agricultural and rural development as including food security to be obtained by self-sufficiency and self-reliance, and natural resource conservation in parallel with environmental protection as cited in Chapter 1.

Therefore, the fragmented small farms, due to the inefficient land-holding by part-time and absent small farmers, has become the *remaining* or *last* obstacle imposed by the monsoon to sustainable agricultural and rural development in monsoon Asia.

4.4 Theoretical Discussion

In Chapter 2, it was pointed out that in the prewar era, in comparison with the disadvantages (negative externalities) of the fragmented small farms, their advantages were much less and all related to the backward economic, technological and social conditions. In other words, farmers were forced to accept them because they had no other choice. In fact, wet-rice farmers in monsoon Asia generally preferred having all their land in one contiguous parcel. During the postwar period up to 1960, however, due to the implementation of features 1–8 of the Japanese model, farmers could overcome poverty with fragmented small farms. According to the arguments in Chapter 3, there is no basis for believing that all existing negative externalities should be corrected. Only when the gains of correction exceed its costs, should they be internalized. Therefore, there was no urgent need to change this land tenure situation as the legally sanctioned structure of property rights in force. Accordingly, there was only an effort to gradually improve fragmentation by land consolidation in the 1950s which used both Approaches 1 (permission for the relevant parties to exchange property rights through a political or legal process, followed by market exchange) and 2 [implementation of social actions (law, tax, etc.) to oblige the externality-yielding party to exchange property rights, followed by market exchange], but no efforts on increasing the farm size.

In the 1960s, however, on one hand, part-time and absent small farming developed further, resulting in senilization and feminization of the agricultural labor force and leading to waste of land and other resources, and the high wage economy made it difficult for small rice farmers to be viable; on the other, the introduction of large agricultural machinery made large-scale farming profitable and it could reach technological Pareto efficiency by producing more output with the same inputs or producing the same output with less inputs. Thus, the gains of correction of the fragmented small farms exceeded its costs, and the time was ripe to change the existing property rights structures to internalize their negative externalities.

According to the Coase theorem, with the introduction of market exchange, negative technological externalities could be internalized and Pareto efficiency reached. Thus, during the 1960s–80s, Approach 1 was adopted by the Japanese government. The land-holding ceiling was relaxed, rent control removed, land could be returned to landlords upon termination of contracts, and the first general method of changing the existing property rights structures (gradual changes in social mores and common law precedents including moral, practical and legal experiments) was used to encourage voluntary land sale, lease, or joining cooperatives/enterprises. In those cases where they were carried out, the negative externalities of the fragmented small farms could, to some extent, be eliminated and large-scale farming achieved.

Chapter 3, however, also stressed that when there are externalities, even if the private market economy has been introduced, equilibria will not be in general Pareto efficient since the private decentralized optimizations of economic agents lead them to take into account only private costs through the price system. Thus, after the market exchange had been allowed, the externality-yielding party might refuse to exchange relevant property rights, so that the previous negative technological externalities now became negative pecuniary ones. Because of private land ownership, part-time and absent small farmers could exert strong bargaining power by either refusing to exchange or demanding high prices, which in turn incurred higher transaction costs, especially huge costs of government subsidies derived from taxpayers and consumers for farmers to not only produce rice but also reduce its overproduction, costs of time (four decades since 1960), opportunity costs, plus otherwise unnecessary food import, higher domestic and international prices of agricultural goods, land under-utilization or idleness, waste of other resources, environmental deterioration, etc. Therefore, as surmised in Chapter 1, and antithetic to Schultz's arguments, the part-time and absent small farmers are not so efficient in their use of land, and at least some of them are not so rational to the society's and their own fundamental interests, even though land property rights have been well defined and market transactions facilitated.

Farm expansion through both land sale and individual lease was constrained by private land ownership and free market forces even after land consolidation which made farm enlargement physically easier. As stressed in Chapter 2, this shows that free market forces alone, or *private use of private land*, may not realize sustainable rural development.

As Chapter 1 indicated, of the many variables for rural development, the institutional changes are the keystone. It is the institutional component that is the most important in the interaction of institutions and technologies as the underlying long-term ultimate causes that sustain economic growth of developing countries. Once production has reached the frontier permitted by the established institutions, even though the increase of production is technologically possible, as the knowledge and other conditions are available for both the part-time and absent small farmers and the remaining largely non-viable full-time small farmers to produce the same output with fewer resources or a larger output from the same resources, it would be hampered by the vested interests, just as the case of the persistence of the fragmented small farms due to inefficient land-holding by part-time and absent small farmers - the ninth feature of the Japanese model - has suggested. At this stage, another round of institutional changes should take place to allow sustainable rural development. Hence variable mixed economies were needed - varying relations between the public and private sectors, and their dynamic change over time in relation to changing needs in economy and society - for reaching dynamic or long-term Pareto efficiency.

In fact, variable mixed economies have been spontaneously practiced by village officials and peasants, using the first general method and proceeding from the first to the second phase of the author's hypothesis outlined earlier. Education of villagers was carried out and measures were taken collectively on the village level in order to preserve a region's agricultural activity. In the fifth major effort (agricultural production cooperatives), the sub-village collective use of private land was actually at *phase 1*: sub-village individual—collective mixed economy (sub-village-wide cooperative/

enterprise collective use of physically withdrawable private land shares, exercising collective—individual dual level operation of large land units, with the basic operation level at one household as the major form or at a unit including a small number of households as the minor form). The fourth major effort (commissioned agricultural work) was at the threshold of phase 1. Once the commission receivers were organized, it became the fifth major effort. The sixth major effort (urban—rural joint farming) was the inclusion of urban enterprises into phase 1. These and various other forms at sub-village level all had advantages in tilling otherwise idle land, achieving economies of scale in using machinery, labor and management, and reducing cost of machinery, but were less successful in achieving large-scale farming as they were still seriously constrained by the private land ownership and free market forces.

In order to overcome the shortcomings at phase 1, the sub-village collective use of private land was extended to be village-wide, just as in *phase 2*: village-wide individual—collective mixed economy. It could remove boundaries among parcels and achieve large-scale farming, but still kept three major shortcomings, due to the withdrawability of private land.

Thus, a higher phase of the variable mixed economies, combination of the first general method with the second (conscious collective endeavor), and joint use of Approaches 1 and 2 are needed to eliminate or efficiently produce the negative pecuniary externalities imposed by the part-time and absent small farmers.

5. A New Model for Sustainable Rural Development

In order to overcome the fragmented small farms obstacle perpetuated by the inefficient land-holding of part-time and absent small farmers and achieve sustainable rural development, a new model based on private land ownership is proposed as follows.

5.1 Conjectural Proposal 5.1: Village-Wide Corporate Ownership of Physically Unwithdrawable But Financially Salable Private Land Shares.1

The general design. Proposal 5.1 is designed not only for economies at the high wage stage, but also for those at the low wage stage; and not only for rice-based economies in monsoon Asia, but also for relevant economies in the rest of the world, although the basic reference here is drawn from Japan.

Whereas all the other means of production could be privately, publicly or jointly owned, land of each household could be turned into private land shares to earn permanent remuneration. While private land shareholders still own land, the village corporation possesses land physically and could reorganize it. Private land shares could be inherited. They could also be sold in financial terms in the market. But shareholders could not withdraw land physically or claim financial reimbursement from the village (although if the village wished, it could buy private land shares when offered, and convert them into collective land shares). Such a corporation could also be extended to include more villages.

Private land could be classified into two types: housing land and agricultural land (divided between either self-sufficiency land or family plots, and production land for market). *Housing land shares would not receive revenue* from the village because the owner gets remuneration from using the

---

[1] The main content of the proposal has been published by the Food and Agriculture Organization of the United Nations in Zhou, Jian-Ming (October 1997).

154

land.

* *Dual Land System. Agricultural land* could be operated in a *Dual Land System* where non-grain agriculture and off-farm activities are not yet very highly developed and most peasants working there have not yet secured jobs.

(1) *Self-sufficiency land* could be distributed in compact form equally to each household on a per capita basis for self-sufficiency production of grains and vegetables, as a back-up basic social welfare (its significance may be seen from the recent reappearance of homeless people in Japanese cities who were mainly from rural areas2). *Shares for self-sufficiency land would not receive revenue* from the village because the owner gets remuneration from using the land. Absentees could decide not to retain a self-sufficiency land, which would be added into their shares of the production land for market.

(2) *Production land for market* should be contracted or leased in compact form to households on the conditions of fulfilling output quotas or monetary rent for the village corporation. The contractors/lessees could dispose of the surplus products on the market. *Shares of production land for market would receive revenue* (dividends) paid by the village corporation from the output in quota or monetary rent it obtained from the contractors/lessees of the production land for market. In general, the higher the degree of development of the village's non-grain agriculture and off-farm activities, the more competitive the distribution of the production land for market. There could be four basic categories.

Category 1: In areas where non-grain agriculture and off-farm employment are *little* developed and peasants almost completely rely on grain production for their living, production land for market should be equally contracted/leased to households on a *per capita* basis.

Category 2: In areas where non-grain agriculture and off-farm employment are *modestly* developed, production land for market could be equally contracted to every *labor force*. Here, some laborers have already

---

[2] For years, affluent Japan prided itself on the tiny numbers of people living on its streets and never envisaged 'An Army of Homeless Rises Up in Tokyo'.

The first record of homeless people dates from the Nara Period in the eighth century. They remained a common sight in big cities for more than 1,000 years. But they largely disappeared between the early 1950s and the late 1980s, when Japan experienced its economic 'miracle'.

Since the collapse of real estate and share prices in the early 1990s, however, Japan has experienced acute economic changes. The unemployment rate reached 3.4% in early 1997, a record high. Although this rate is still low by international standards, the number of homeless people in Tokyo has already risen by about four-fold, to 10,000. They have also appeared in small cities recently for the first time. Thus, government officials, activists and academics expect that homeless people may soon become a common sight.

The bulk of the homeless are poor, old, ill and unskilled people who were absorbed by the previous brisk economic growth from *rural areas* (Kattoulas 1997: 2).

started to work in non-grain agriculture and off-farm activities. But jobs there are not secure, so that they are not yet willing to transfer their production land for market. Such areas are richer than those in Category 1, thus non-laborers (the old, children, etc.) should be entitled to self-sufficiency land only but not to production land for market so as to make the use of the latter more efficient. As the production land for market is distributed among fewer people, each laborer could equally get more land so that the economies of scale could be raised.

Category 3: In areas where non-grain agriculture and off-farm employment are *fairly* developed, production land for market could be equally contracted/leased to every *agricultural* labor force in grain production. This means that those laborers who have left grain agriculture are no longer entitled to production land for market, though still to self-sufficiency land. Because only the remaining grain-producing labor force could equally contract/lease land, they could get more land and the economies of scale would be further raised.

Category 4: In areas where non-grain agriculture and off-farm employment are *highly* developed, production land for market should be contracted/leased to agricultural labor for grain production by *competition* of tendering. Here, because many peasants would like to concentrate on non-grain agriculture and off-farm activities to earn higher income, it would be possible for the village to contract/lease the production land for market to *expert* farmers. The contract would be given to the tender(s) with best expertise and strongest ability for the highest quality and output of products and investment, and best management. Expert farmers could be chosen from non-villagers with priority to villagers. Land would be divided according to its suitability to a specific product (rice, wheat, etc.) and the relevant expertise and ability of the expert farmers. Economies of scale of land would be greatly increased.

Contracts could be transferred (with the approval of the village) and renewed according to market principles of competition. If, within the contract period, other than owing to natural disaster, the output target is not reached, the land quality diminished, production abandoned, or environment polluted, etc., the contract could be stopped and sanctions engaged. In order to avoid arbitrariness and corruption, the agreement of 51% or two-thirds of village members or their representatives should be reached to adjust individual land within its contractual period or change its major content. Law suits and settlement by courts should be allowed before implementing the adjustment or change. If the land has been improved, awards could be given. The basic operational level should be at one family as the major form, and at units with a small number of households in cooperatives/enterprises as the minor form. Urban companies could participate. Wage laborers could be hired, but normally not many by a farming unit, except in the busy seasons.

The output-in-quota or monetary rent handed to the village by the contractors/lessees of the production land for market could be distributed as remuneration to village managers, other village management expenses, village infrastructure construction costs, a common accumulation fund for further development, a common welfare fund for aiding the poor, dividends to shares of the private production land for market, dividends to private and collective capital shares, etc.

The residuals above the quotas from the production land for market retained by the contractors/lessees could be distributed as remuneration to hired labor, capital and services; self-owned capital and family labor, etc.

* *Single Land System*. Alternatively, where non-grain agriculture and off-farm work are *very highly* developed and most peasants have secured their jobs there, a *Single Land System* could be adopted for the agricultural land.3

(1) A *family plot* (or a few family plots) much smaller than the self-sufficiency land could be given in compact form to each household for growing some vegetables to accommodate the peasant tradition of not buying them from the market. *Shares for family plots would not receive revenue* from the village because the owner gets remuneration from using the land. Absentees or retirees could choose not to keep a family plot, which would be added into their shares of the production land for market.

(2) Production land for market should be contracted to expert farmers via competition of tendering as mentioned above. Self-sufficiency land is no longer needed since expert farmers could operate production land for market for both self-sufficiency and market, and peasants on non-grain agriculture and off-farm work could earn income there; the family plot is negligible from quantitative point of view. Thus agricultural land is no longer divided into the Dual Land. Hence it is a Single Land System. Reducing self-sufficiency land to family plots correspondingly makes the farming scale of the production land for market much larger than under the Dual Land System.

Under the Single Land System, if those peasants on non-grain agriculture and off-farm work have lost jobs there, they should have priority to regain full-time employment as farmers to independently contract production land for market or join production cooperatives/enterprises, as a back-up basic social welfare.

---

[3] The terms of 'little', 'modestly', 'fairly', 'highly' and 'very highly' refer to the degrees of development of non-grain agriculture and off-farm activities, and will be explained in Chapter 7, since case studies will be cited there.

The Dual Land System and Single Land System could also be mixed, if some peasants are already willing to concentrate on off-farm activities and only retain the smaller family plots, while others still wish to keep the larger self-sufficiency land. The village could actively encourage, mobilize or organize peasants to leave grain agriculture for developing non-grain agriculture and off-farm production, so as to promote the transition from the low to the high wage economy and from agriculture to industry and further to services, and the Dual Land System to the Single Land System.

As a result of preventing the inefficient land-holding and achieving economies of scale of land, food production may become surplus. At this higher stage, food overproduction would replace food shortage as the new and major problem. Externally, export of food should be promoted. But it may not always be able to fully absorb the surplus food, as the world demand is fluctuating and other countries are also trying to realize food self-sufficiency. Thus, internally, a strategic adjustment in agricultural structures should be carried out, i.e., to prevent food overproduction and improve the environment. (1) The village could establish a contract with the owners of the erodible cultivated land shares. The owners should convert such land back to forestry, grassland, lake land, and wetland, and plant and maintain trees and grasses, produce fruits, livestock or fish. In recognition of their contribution to the improvement of the environment, the village should remunerate them with a food subsidy from the surplus food produced on the normal cultivated land, until they could earn a living from forest fruits, tourism and services, animal husbandry, and lake fishery on their own land. At that time, they would be able to buy food. Owners could transfer such a contract to a non-owner and divide the benefits between them. (2) Surplus food should be continuously produced on the normal cultivated land, and inferior varieties replaced by superior ones. The allocation of the surplus food to the owners of the erodible land shares would eliminate the food overproduction of the village. (3) If some regions have abundant normal cultivated land, while others ample erodible one, a macro policy would be required in order to allocate the surplus food from the former to the latter so that the erodible cultivated land there could be converted back to the nature, and a national or regional balance between food supply and demand be reached, and overproduction avoided.

Further optional measures to prevent a bubble economy and poverty.
* *Sale of a zone.* At both low and high wage stages, a belt of agricultural land may be sold for industrial or urban use either owing to normal industrial or urban development, or due to speculative purposes. Under these circumstances, two solutions are recommended here.

(1) In order to avoid a bubble economy from happening, turning agricultural land over to industrial or urban use should be approved by the

government, and capital gains tax be imposed on the sellers.

(2) Having sold land shares and turned a zone of agricultural land over to industrial or urban use, the former peasants may also have lost their last resort of living. In order to prevent them from falling into destitution in the future after they have spent the earnings but could not find or have lost jobs, the land shares of the former village agricultural corporation, rather than being sold, could be turned to the land shares of the new industrial or urban enterprises which should pay them dividends permanently.

 * *Individual land transfer* includes two types.

 - *Forced sale* of land due to debt-servicing caused by serious natural disasters, diseases, business failures or even gambling losses may happen, more possibly at the low wage economy when peasants are generally poor (as in Japan and China in the early 1950s), but also at the high wage economy. Thus, an additional measure might be considered, i.e., members may not be allowed or forced to sell land shares up to a minimum amount even though they still owe debt, so as to maintain a permanent source of basic income for them.

 - *Voluntary transfer* (not due to debt-servicing) could also happen at both low and high wage economy (e.g., when migrating to cities, some peasants may sell land shares or donate them to relatives/friends), although once peasants have become rich from off-farm income (as in Japan since the late 1950s), usually they may not have much incentive to sell land shares. Selling these claims for relatively low but constant and permanent revenue may bring the sellers high but short-term earnings. In a future time, however, the sellers may fall into destitution if they have spent the earnings and also lost jobs. The above-mentioned additional measure might also be considered, i.e., members may not be allowed to transfer land shares up to a minimum amount, in order to maintain a permanent source of basic income for them.

The restriction on land share transfer in these two cases would serve as a protection for peasants to prevent them from falling into destitution and causing a social problem and burden for the government social welfare which is weak in many developing and even developed countries. Such a restriction on free market exchange at the side of sellers/transferrers is comparable to that at the buyer's side implemented in Japan before 1962, i.e., land-holding ceiling of 3 ha. This ceiling made it difficult (although still possible) for land sellers to find buyers and thus successfully contributed to the prevention of new landlessness after the land reform in Japan. Similarly, under China's collective land ownership, if a household has fallen into debts, then all of its properties could be taken away but not its housing land and contracted agricultural land because they belong to the village, so that it could still build a poor but livable house and produce food for state quotas, self-sufficiency and market. This provides an explanation why China has avoided the landless and homeless problem.

The obligation and also the right to keep land shares up to a minimum amount may be applied to original holders only, i.e., it could be relaxed for the subsequent holders (who have acquired the land shares through purchase, inheritance, etc.). But it could also be extended to the subsequent holders.

The additional measure of obliging, and also giving the right to, members to keep some minimum land shares would generate a permanent source of basic income for them even though some of them live outside of the village, so as to realize sustainable rural development - achieving food security based on self-reliance and generating income in rural areas to eradicate poverty. Of course, over that minimum amount, land shares could be freely transferred in the market.

In Japan, if the proposed village corporations with private land shares physically unwithdrawable but financially salable *over a minimum amount* had been set up in the 1950s, then many peasants migrating to cities would not have sold or relinquished their land ownership, could have enjoyed dividends as a permanent source of basic income, and thus would not have ended up living on city streets and causing a serious welfare problem to society and government after having lost the previously so-called permanent jobs in the 1990s. Indeed, the lifetime employment in Japan, once admired world-wide, has gone with the breaking up of the bubble economy in the 1990s, just to be followed by South Korea and other East and Southeast Asian rice-based economies after the Asian financial crisis since the summer of 1997. No government social welfare could afford to sustain them (bearing in mind that even Western countries have also been shedding the heavy social welfare burdens in the recent decades albeit homeless people have been increasing).

Whether the additional measure of obliging members to retain some minimum land shares should be implemented or not; and if so, it should be applied only to the original holders or be extended to the subsequent holders, would have to be decided locally through experiments, taking into account the welfare system of the specific economy (nation, state, province, county, etc.). Similarly, the minimum amount of land shares members are obliged to keep would also have to be determined locally in the practices of each economy, taking into consideration the average annual revenue a land share can bring and the poverty line. Of course, if an economy has a well-established welfare system which could take care of the jobless people and prevent them from homelessness and hunger, there would be no need to oblige village members to retain any minimum land shares.

Technical aspects. * *Cadastre of the original land.* As pointed out in Appendix 3.1, a cadastre, which registers not only the boundaries but also the value of real estate, is fundamental to land redistribution.

In terms of how to compute the shares of the current private agricultural land, methods for assessment of the value of current farmland holdings, and Figure 3.1 and Table 3.3 in Appendix 3.1 could be used and consulted. Using the example there, after the assessment, general grade could be given to each farm as $F_1 = 2.48$, $F_2 = 3.26$, $F_3 = 4.37$, $F_4 = 5.93$, and $F_5 = 6.12$.

After the assessment of the value of current farmland holdings, the original map as Figure 3.2 would be kept forever, from which the pre-consolidation fragmented farms of each household could always be seen.

In terms of the current private housing land, its acreage, location and ownership should be registered in the cadastre. But because it is used by households and not going to receive dividends in the new village corporation, it would not be necessary to give grades to it. If a household wants to sell it, its price could be determined in the market. In the coming reorganization of land, the village corporation may need to exchange some farmland with housing land. Under such circumstances, it would not be difficult to measure the fertility and other factors of the housing land in question.

* *Redistribution of land.* Once the cadastre of the original land has completed, the fragmented farms should be reorganized in compact form into self-sufficiency land or family plots, and production land for market. After the consolidation, the previous fragmented farms could no more be found in the field, but still registered under each household's private ownership and always kept in the original map.

Under the Dual Land System, each household should be assigned self-sufficiency land in compact form according to family size which would not receive dividends from the village. The grade of the self-sufficiency land (Fs) could be determined in the same way as for the general grade, say, $Fs_1 = 0.8$, $Fs_2 = 1.1$, $Fs_3 = 0.9$, $Fs_4 = 0.7$, and $Fs_5 = 1.0$, which would be deducted from the general grade. The remaining grade for the production land for market (Fp), $Fp_1 = 1.68$, $Fp_2 = 2.16$, $Fp_3 = 3.47$, $Fp_4 = 5.23$, and $Fp_5 = 5.12$, is the basis of the share of the production land for market, which could obtain dividends from the village corporation.

Under the Single Land System, each farm household could be allotted a family plot (or a few family plots) in compact form much smaller than the self-sufficiency land also according to family size, which would not get dividends from the village either. The grade for family plot (Ff), say, $Ff_1 = 0.12$, $Ff_2 = 0.15$, $Ff_3 = 0.13$, $Ff_4 = 0.11$, and $Ff_5 = 0.14$, would be deducted from the general grade. The remaining grade for the production land for market (Fp), $Fp_1 = 2.36$, $Fp_2 = 3.11$, $Fp_3 = 4.24$, $Fp_4 = 5.82$, and $Fp_5 = 5.98$, is the basis of the share of the production land for market, which could enjoy dividends from the village corporation.

As already indicated in Appendix 3.1, among the newly established larger land units, major infrastructure items (main roads among farms and linked to other villages, water conservancy, irrigation and drainage network linking lakes-rivers-canals-ditches-drains, electricity facilities, etc.) should be built, so that each land unit could have easy access to roads, large machinery, irrigation and other facilities. A scientific design for the facilities to process and store agricultural products, schools, hospitals, cultural halls, sport grounds, post and telecommunications office, village administrative offices, housing, land for industrial use, land reserved for future construction, etc., in the village should be made. Environmental protection (forest, natural reserves, tourist resorts, etc.) should be taken into consideration.

In order to prevent corruption and unfairness in redistribution of land to ordinary households and to expert farmers through tendering, appeals should be allowed and handled at administrative and judicial levels as stated in Appendix 3.1.

Comparison with a capital shareholding corporation. The proposed village agricultural corporation with physically unwithdrawable but financially salable private land shares is similar to a modern capital shareholding corporation whose shareholders can earn dividends and sell shares in the market but cannot reimburse them, nor withdraw any equipment physically, from the corporation. But they are also different. (1) Selling capital shares of a capital shareholding corporation would reduce the capital value of the corporation, but selling land shares in financial terms would not affect either the physical value of the land, or its productivity. (2) Capital equipment can be out-moded easily, but land is always productive (as long as it is properly maintained). (3) The poor management of a capital shareholding corporation may be unimprovable, lead to its bankruptcy and render its capital shares worthless even overnight (thus free sale of capital shares should not be restricted). But land is scarce and the prices tend to be high and stay high. The management of such an agricultural corporation, as long as it still holds land, is improvable, because the contracts the village gave to contractors/lessees could be stopped/dis-renewed if they did not operate land properly (thus incentive from competitive leasing). Therefore the value of land shares would not be reduced to zero and could recover even after a corporation has been bankrupt and taken over by another (hence obliging members to keep certain land shares brings no harm but only benefits to them).

The village agricultural corporation could set up a supervisory board composed of some representatives of land shareholders, capital shareholders and laborers. The supervisory board would be responsible for making major decisions, appointing chief managers for ordinary management, controlling corruption, etc. But more fundamental decisions should be based on the agreement of 51% or two-thirds of village members or their representatives. Owing to the incentive from ownership, it should work well.

The result is summarized here as a *village-wide corporate–individual mixed economy*, exercising village–individual dual level operation of land, with the basic operation level at one household as the major form or at a unit including a small number of households as the minor form, public infrastructure land, corporate ownership of agricultural and housing land with physically unwithdrawable but financially salable private land shares, private/public ownership of other means of production, corporate/individual/cooperative management and capitalistic wage labor employment.

Some comparative advantages of the new model. There is no need to collectivize private land ownership, because there is no need for the village to take private land without compensation or buy it. But the merits of collectivization would still be achieved, since all fragmented small farms could now be joined and re-splitting prevented.

There is no need to sell land in order to increase the farm size, as encouraged by the Japanese government in the 1960s but failed. Accordingly, the government subsidies to full-time farmers for purchasing land could be saved. The rational concern of losing private land could also be relieved, as private landowners could earn permanent remuneration from private land shares generation after generation, and enjoy a back-up basic social welfare if they were to lose their employment in non-grain agriculture and off-farm activities. This would be more acceptable to part-time and absent small farmers, and old farmers without young successors in farming than land sale. The village would pay dividends to private land shares from productive earnings of the village itself, rather than relying on government subsidies, hence income generation within rural areas - an important factor of sustainable rural development. The additional measure of obliging members to keep some minimum land shares from transferring would protect them from falling into poverty (acquiring another merit of public land ownership but not by collectivization) and the freedom of transferring land shares over the minimum amount would promote the market economy.

Land lease, as encouraged by the Japanese government since the 1970s but hampered by private land ownership, could be organized systematically as the village could contract/lease production land for market equally to each household on a per capita basis, labor force, grain-producing labor force or competitively to expert farmers.

The aim of land consolidation under private farmland ownership could be reached, but there is no need to make exchanges of the private ownership and location of spatially dispersed parcels of farms, thus avoiding a huge amount of transaction costs as reviewed in Chapter 3 and especially Appendix 3.1.

The shortcomings in consolidating and expanding the fragmented small farms related to private land sale, private use of private land through individual lease, sub-village and village-wide collective use of private land with physically withdrawable private land shares could be overcome.

This model could be adopted not only in the high wage economy as in Japan since 1960, but also in the low wage economy when non-grain agriculture and off-farm production have not yet developed. In the low wage economy, if the fragmented small farms were tilled and there were cooperative services to help the weak single household operation of land, then the small farmers could prosper. However, having all their land in one contiguous parcel would be even better, as generally preferred by wet-rice farmers in monsoon Asia and pointed out in Chapter 2. Also, where land was partially or completely idled/abandoned as peasants left for cities or other rural areas which had entered the high wage economy earlier, or there were no or little cooperative services, such a village corporation would be more advantageous. Preventing land idling/abandonment would contribute to the protection of the environment.

Moreover, once food overproduction has appeared as a result of overcoming the inefficient land-holding by part-time and absent small farmers and achieving economies of scale of land, this model could be used to prevent it from becoming chronic and further improve the environment, bearing in mind that food overproduction has never been resolved in developed countries.

This is actually at *phase 3* of the author's hypothesis outlined earlier for overcoming the fragmented small farms by variable mixed economies: collective use of either public land, or physically unwithdrawable private land shares under corporate ownership, exercising village–individual dual level operation of large land units, with the basic operation level at one household as the major form or at a unit including a small number of households as the minor form, as a third way beyond the centrally planned economy and free market system.

Needless to say, appropriate intervention of governments, education of public opinion, and active participation of peasants, are necessary. Details (specific ways of establishing village-wide corporate land ownership; land contract/lease length and fees; proportions for dividing revenue among shares of production land for market, capital shares and labor; whether or not to implement the additional measure of obliging members to keep some minimum land shares from transferring, etc.) should be determined through experiments, public discussions, and expert consultations.4 Just as with

---

[4] One of the major 'secrets' why China has achieved successes in its economic reforms has been 'trying first, concluding later', 'experimenting first, popularizing later', 'practicing first, theorizing later', and 'crossing the river by groping stones'. For only by putting a foot into the

carrying out land consolidation under private farmland ownership, majority agreement by landowners in the village should be sufficient for establishing corporate land ownership, but great efforts should be made to try to reach consensus.

The village-wide corporate land ownership with private land shares physically unwithdrawable but financially salable for consolidating and expanding the fragmented small farms is different from both the Japanese and Chinese models and may be regarded as a new model.

A proposal is a proposal. It might be adopted either in the exact form or revised forms, and either immediately, in the near future, remote future, or never. Nonetheless, the task of scientific research is to seek possible solutions. An idea might first be rejected as being of 'no value at all' but later prove to be invaluable. In contrast, a measure might seem valuable but then be demonstrated as not quite so (e.g., land sale in Japan was encouraged and subsidized in the 1960s but then failed). Therefore, experiments are necessary. Proposal 5.1 could be practiced in parallel with other experiments. However, even though other experiments may be somehow different from this proposed new model, some aspects would have to be in common: (1) The scope should be village-wide, because if only some village households participated while others not, then it would be difficult to join the parcels of members together since they may be interspersed across the village and mixed with those of the non-members. Thus although the experiments could start from sub-village-wide range, they would then have to be extended to village-wide scope. (2) Physically withdrawing land should be prevented. Otherwise, re-splitting of joined land may not be effectively precluded. (3) While promoting land transfer in the market, an effective mechanism should be established to prevent peasants from falling into destitution after they have sold land, lost jobs, but the government could not afford to provide them with some basic social welfare. These are essential to the fundamental success of any experiments.

The principles of the new model are: implementing variable mixed economies; combining market economy with appropriate interventions by the central and local governments and rural communities and participation by farmers; keeping private ownership of farmland and housing land; holding public land ownership for major infrastructure; strengthening large while preserving small farmers rather than crowding them out; dividing small farmers' farmland into production land for market and self-sufficiency land

---

river, can one find the first stone; and then another foot, the second; and so on and so forth. Only by experiments can one find errors, appropriate methods, laws and specific mechanism; and test, modify or repeal the existing theories and practices, and create new ones.

(under the Dual Land System) or family plots (under the Single Land System) for household's own use; joining the production land for market for the use of each household on a per capita basis, labor force, grain-producing labor force, and finally competitively expert farmers to gain economies of scale and more efficient use of land, capital, labor, technology, and management resources and paying dividends to small landowners; retaining the self-sufficiency land or family plots by small farmers; promoting off-farm employment for small farmers to speed the transition from agriculture to industry and further to services; progressing from the Dual Land System to Single Land System following the transfer of small farmers to off-farm activities; sustaining agricultural and rural development by generating income and food security within rural areas rather than relying on the government welfare subsidies and food import; allocating surplus food produced on the normal cultivated land to the owners of the erodible cultivated land in order for them to convert it back to forestry, grassland, lake land and wetland, so as to both prevent food overproduction and improve the environment.

5.2 The Pioneering Chinese Elementary Cooperatives

In Japan, the village-wide collective use of private farmland (as a production cooperative with physically withdrawable land shares) was a spontaneous effort by village officials and peasants to resolve the last obstacle. This form could remove boundaries among parcels and reach large-scale farming. It has been hailed by Tabata as 'a *Japanese approach* to land extensive farming' and recommended by NIRA to be 'actively' promoted (Tabata 1990: 22. NIRA 1995: 173). But neither author notes that the three problems as mentioned in Chapter 4 may still remain. Moreover, Tabata is not aware that it is not a 'Japanese' approach, but is what the *Chinese elementary agricultural producers' cooperatives* had experienced up to April 1956 (during May 1956 — 1957 withdrawing land was actually forbidden).5

In China, the land reform (already carried out in the earlier liberated smaller areas since the 1920s, and implemented in large scope during May 1946 — June 1950 in the Northeasternmost part and from then to the spring of 1953 in the rest of the country) turned the feudal landlord ownership to individual land ownership, and maintained fragmented small farms: 7.05—25.05 mu (0.47–1.67 ha) per household, divided into several parcels, each

---

[5] The following paragraphs about the elementary cooperatives and relevant institutional changes in China are based upon the author's preparatory work for this book. The references exceed 100 and are thus not all listed here.

smaller than 1.005 mu (0.067 ha) (ER 1965: 13. Huang, Xi-Yuan 1986: 410). It brought peasants huge incentives to production and raised their living standard. But the fragmented small farms were too weak for the farmers to sustain rural development. Thus the period of December 1954 — April 1956 was dominated (covering more than 50% of rural households) by what summarized here by the author as an *individual–collective mixed economy*, including *temporary mutual aid teams* (private land ownership; labor exchange; common use of labor, private animals and tools; quasi-mixed economy), *permanent mutual aid teams* (plus collective ownership of some assets; mixed economy to a higher extent) and elementary cooperatives (collective use of private land; typical mixed economy). All the three forms started before 1949,6 but the mutual aid teams were predominant during December 1954 — autumn 1955, and the elementary cooperatives prevailed during December 1955 — April 1956 and existed also in 1957, so that much experience *in individual cases* had been gained.7 The major features and achievements of the elementary cooperative and its main shortcomings most relevant to the Japanese practice are briefly discussed below.

Ownership and possession. Members kept individual ownership of land but gave land to the cooperative for reorganization. Wasteland reclaimed by the cooperative was in collective ownership. Members kept individual ownership of farm animals and large tools but could lease or sell them to the cooperative. The cooperative could also buy non-land assets from other sources into collective ownership.

The cooperative provided family plots for vegetables to households according to family size, and exercised collective–individual dual level operation on the rest of farmland with the household as the basic operation level. The cooperative established Production Responsibility Systems, i.e., contracting work or output quotas to groups, laborers or households, linking workpoints with the fulfillment, of which, contracting output to households was the superior (this was the origin of 'bao *chan* dao hu' - the minor form of the Household Contract System popularized since 1978). Land (including those units owned by other members) and other means of production could be distributed to the contractor for fulfilling the quotas. The cooperative was

---

[6] The first mutual aid team was organized in the summer of 1931 in Caixi Township of Shanghang County of Fujian Province (Huang, Xi-Yuan 1986: 340–1), while the first elementary cooperative was in March 1944 in Wugong Village of Raoyang County of Hebei Province (Yao, Shi-An et al. 1952).

[7] For example, Walker (1966: 29) notes that 'An unrivalled collection of materials, on how cooperatives of every province had handled all kinds of problems, an instruction book for cadres, is *The Socialist High Tide in the Chinese Countryside*, 3 volumes (GO 1956). Many of the reports were first published separately between 1954 and 1956'.

responsible for investment, procurement, sale, machinery, technology and other services, construction of infrastructure, wasteland reclamation, and general management. An example is given below.

Siyi Cooperative of Anguang County of Jilin Province was established in the spring of 1952. In 1953, because of the waste of over 300 and over 100 man-days in the summer hoeing and autumn harvest respectively as well as other inefficient performances, some members quit. In 1954, contracting work and output systems were adopted. After the hoeing, it was recognized by the whole village that the Cooperative's land was the cleanest. The quitters returned and others joined. Inspired by the better performances, three more elementary cooperatives were set up. (RWDAC [1955] 1956: 419–25)

The scope of an elementary cooperative was about 25–50 households. Some cooperative spanned a whole village. Even in cases where not all households of a village belonged to the cooperative, where parcels of the cooperative members were adjacent, boundaries could be eliminated (although members could at least still roughly recognize their original parcels), so that the individual farming units were amalgamated into relatively larger land units.

Payment. Revenue was distributed (in the following order of priority) for general costs of production; remuneration to leased privately owned non-land assets (farm animals, large tools, etc., as capital shares); agricultural taxes to the state; a common welfare fund for aiding the poor; a common accumulation fund for increasing the collectively owned non-land assets; management expenses including managing costs and payment to managers as a kind of remuneration to labor; remuneration to land shares; and remuneration to laborers (non-managers). The remuneration to labor was according to the workpoints the laborer earned during the year. Workpoints were linked to the fulfillment of the contractual work or output quotas in grain agriculture, non-grain agriculture and off-farm production. Men and women enjoyed equal pay for equal work. As a result, more women participated in productive activities.

After the deduction of revenue for other items, the distribution between remuneration to land shares and that to laborers varied across regions, as shown in Table 5.1. In the rural areas (such as Hebei and Fujian provinces) where population was relatively more and land less, the land shares could get more remuneration. In the suburbs of cities (such as Beijing) where peasants produced more vegetables and other industrial crops which required more labor, the labor could get more remuneration.

By adopting the above-mentioned mechanism, the elementary cooperatives achieved initial success. Below are only some of the numerous examples.

More efficient organization of land. For instance, in Qijiazi, Hecheng and Fanshen villages of Fuyu County of Jilin Province, land was originally

Table 5.1 Proportion of Distribution between Remuneration to Land Shares and Remuneration to Labor Contribution in Some Elementary Cooperatives of China 1954–55

Year/ Region	Elementary cooperatives	Remuneration to land share (RLS) vs. remuneration to labor contribution (RLC)
1954 31,000 elementary cooperatives Hebei Province [a]	70.82%	50 : 50
	7.32%	RLS > RLC
	17.29%	RLS < RLC
	4.50%	Other distribution ways
1954 Fujian Province [b]	Kanxia, Liancheng County	34.4 : 65.6
	Jingxing, Minhou County	32.1 : 67.9
	Jianshe, Jian-ou County	29.4 : 70.6
	Sancun, Yong-an County	29.2 : 70.8
	Average	31.275 : 68.725
1955 Xishan Township Beijing [c]	Shengli (1954)	8.5 : 91.5
	Xishan	11.1 : 88.9
	Beixinzhuang	11.3 : 88.7
	Wuxing	16.4 : 83.6
	Average	11.825 : 88.175

Sources: a. Shi, Jing-Tang 1957 II: 655.   b. RWDFJ [1954] 1980 : 116.   c. Fan, Hong (1980): 113.

divided into 3,440 pieces. The cooperatives joined them into 650 pieces, so that the area of cultivation was increased by 1,017 mu (67.8 ha). (Zhao, Fang-Chun 1955)

In Chadian District of Ninghe County, Hebei Province, under individual operation, upon small parcels of 4–5 mu (0.27–0.33 ha), one new type horse-drawn plow could only plow 6–8 mu (0.4–0.53 ha) per day. The cooperatives eliminated the boundaries among parcels and established large land units of 50 mu (3.33 ha) or so. Then, the same tool could plow 12–14 mu (0.8–0.93 ha) per day. (DGAA 1952)

More scientific use of land. For example, in Chibao Village of Qin County of Shanxi Province, the lowland was shady, damp and suitable for corn, while the upland sunny, dry and fit for millet. But individual households needed to plant both crops even if they owned only one type of land. In 1953, Cao Lan-Mu Cooperative was set up, which planted corn only in the shady and damp lowland, with millet solely in the sunny and dry upland. In the same year, the per mu output of corn of the Cooperative reached 232.5 kg, while that of the individual households only 60 kg. (Lu, Sheng 1953)

Development of features 3–7. Due to more efficient organization and more scientific use of land, and better division and coordination of labor, some of the labor force, previously under 'disguised unemployment', was now released from low-yielding monoculture of grain to promoting construction of rural infrastructure (feature 3), higher yields and multiple cropping of rice and other grains (feature 4), diversified cropping and non-crop agriculture (feature 5), off-farm employment (feature 6), peasant work in village firms (feature 7) which are common to both the Japanese and Chinese models of rural development. (But peasants' work in commerce and other services - parts of feature 6, and migration to cities and work in towns - parts of feature 7, were restricted by the centrally planned economy, while feature 8 - agricultural mechanization with small machinery, was constrained by the then relatively backward economic and technological conditions. These features themselves were not exclusive to the elementary cooperatives.) The labor force remaining in grain agriculture was thus less than before and could operate larger areas of land per laborer.

For example, in Yu Luo-Shan Cooperative, Gedan Village, Xisha District, Ji County, Hebei Province, before the setting-up of the Cooperative, in order to sow cotton seeds in their farmland of 70.5 mu (4.7 ha), divided into 22 parcels (on average 3.20 mu or 0.21 ha each), dispersed within 1.5 square km, these (future member) households had to use 36 able-bodied persons with several drills for one and a half days. The Cooperative reorganized cotton culture into farmland of 57.3 mu (3.82 ha), divided into 11 parcels (on average 5.21 mu or 0.35 ha each) in a concentrated area. Then three able-bodied persons could fulfil the sowing by using one drill for one day only. (Geng, Yan-Ling 1952). In this case, not only economies of scale of land were raised, but also much of the labor force was released. The surplus laborers could be transferred to develop infrastructure construction, non-grain agriculture and off-farm activities, as the following examples show.

In 10 elementary cooperatives of Changzhi Prefecture of Shanxi Province, due to the increase in agricultural productivity, much of the labor force was moved from 'disguised unemployment' to infrastructure construction, non-grain agriculture and handicraft. In 1951, 2,523 man-days were devoted to infrastructure construction (feature 3). They built weirs of 3,683 meters, canals of 1,233 meters and two modern kilns, adjusted and improved land of 341 mu (22.73 ha), and reclaimed some parts of flooded land and abandoned land. The income from non-grain agriculture and handicraft increased to 22.5% of the total income of the cooperatives. (CPCOSP 1952)

Qingchun and Chenci elementary cooperatives of Luchen Township of Feidong County of Anhui Province were established in the winter of 1954 and spring of 1955 respectively. Of 34 male and female laborers of Qingchun Cooperative, 11 could be dispensed with, while in Chenci Cooperative, 18 became redundant. Then, seven laborers were used to collect green manure (crop-turned manure) for more intensive farming, which could raise 2.5 kg of grain per mu (0.067 ha), or 935 kg of grain for 374 mu (24.93 ha) in total (higher yields of grain - feature 4); three laborers to expand cotton production by 18 mu (1.2 ha) (diversified cropping - feature 5); four to enlarge fruit planting by 3 mu (0.2 ha) and five to increase pig raising (non-crop agriculture - feature 5); 10 to develop flour milling (off-farm employment and village firms - features 6 and 7). Thus, all the 29 surplus laborers found jobs. These achievements attracted five households to join Chenci Cooperative. (Shitang [1955] 1956: 578–80)

In Xiangyin County of Hunan Province, during 1954–55, the surplus labor force of the elementary cooperatives in the plain areas was transferred to constructing rural infrastructure; enlarging areas of multiple cropping and increasing intercropping8 of rice, buckwheat, broad beans, milk vetch, oil crops; raising pigs and fish; transporting; processing; etc. In lake areas, to fishing, raising ducks and shellfish, planting lotus roots, etc. And in mountainous areas, to planting tea trees, lumbering, extracting oil; baking bricks, burning lime, excavating feldspar, mica and other ores; manufacturing umbrellas, writing brushes (a tool made of animal hair to write Chinese characters), straw or palm-bark rain capes, thin bamboo strips, bamboo hats and other goods woven of thin bamboo strips; spinning, weaving cotton cloth and socks, twisting hempen threads, etc. (Ren, Pei-Wu [1955] 1956: 889–91)

Increase of living standard of members. The then rural areas were still at a low wage economy with little off-farm employment opportunities. Land sale and tenancy were allowed so that many impoverished farmers, owing to difficulties in production and living caused by natural disasters, diseases,

---

[8] Intercrops are two or more crops planted at regular intervals in the same field, so as to make use of positive externalities between them and use land more efficiently. For example, one or two drills of green gram (a kind of bean) can be planted between each two drills of corn.

debts, etc., re-lost land ownership and became tenants again, while a small number of wealthier peasants gathered more and then leased land. In contrast, within the elementary cooperatives, land sale and tenancy were banned. Therefore the possibility of selling land by peasants and their becoming newly landless was precluded.

The elementary cooperatives further raised the living standard of members. Below is an example (Zhang, Shi-Rong [1955] 1956: 541–3).

In 1953, Ren-Huai Zhang and Ming-Yi Kai organized an elementary cooperative, with Ming-Yi Kai as the Director, on the basis of two mutual aid teams in Shihe Township of Tongcheng County of Anhui Province. 11 households of middle peasants and 11 households of poor peasants joined.[9] But 10 middle peasant households subsequently quit because they feared that the poor peasant members who did not have draft cattle, large tools and capital would pull them down to poverty too. Ming-Yi Kai only succeeded in persuading his middle peasant uncle to remain.

After the establishment, however, 11 poor peasant member households ran out of food. Some of them wanted to quit and even Ming-Yi Kai's wife complained. He tried to persuade his middle peasant brother who owned draft cattle to join but was to the contrary rebuked. County officials asked them to change back to mutual aid teams, worrying that its expected failure would mar the fame of the elementary cooperatives. Under such unfavorable circumstances, Ren-Huai Zhang and Ming-Yi Kai convinced all the members to carry on.

First, during the winter of 1953 and early spring of 1954, Ming-Yi Kai led most of the able-bodied laborers out to be engaged in off-farm activities such as carrying lime, cutting firewood to sell, and processing grain in the grain company. Their earnings of 240 yuan enabled them not only to provide food for the poor member households and add some small tools, but also, plus bank credits, to buy a draft ox and rent in a set of plow and harrow.

---

[9] Definitions for relevant classes pre-land reform are: landlords did not labor and lived by renting out land, rich peasants as agricultural capitalists hired wage labor but also labored, middle peasants as owner-peasants normally tilled their own land, poor peasants generally rented in land as tenants, and farm laborers mainly worked as wage laborers (Mao, Ze-Dong [1926] 1967: 4–10; [1933] 1967: 113–5). During the land reform, land, farm animals, tools and housing were equitably distributed to all of them, with the quantity to each of them increasing in the order of landlords, farm laborers, poor peasants, middle peasants, rich peasants, hence the resultant order of their wealth. Their titles remained except for farm laborers who were included with poor peasants. Landlords were ranked as class enemies, from 1956 so were rich peasants, but since 1978 both as normal citizens. In the economic development after the land reform, there appeared new rich peasants, and middle peasants evolved into upper middle peasants and lower middle peasants. Thus the new wealth distribution was in the order of landlords, poor peasants, lower middle peasants, upper middle peasants, new rich peasants, and rich peasants.

They also bought on credit 250 kg of bean cake as manure. Meanwhile Ren-Huai Zhang directed semi-able-bodied workers in manure collection and soil preparation for the spring plowing.

Second, they used advanced technologies such as selecting fine seeds through diluted form of mud, adopting higher yielding varieties, close planting, multiple cropping by growing additional late autumn rice, etc.

As a result, production increased. In 1954, grain output reached 16,119.5 kg, higher than that in 1953 by over 7,000 kg. After paying 1,852.5 kg as agricultural tax in kind, selling 3,817.5 kg to the state, members, regardless of age, received grain, 288 kg on average. Credits for draft cattle and bean cake were fully repaid, waterwheels, plows and harrows bought, a fertilizer store cellar constructed, and three new houses built. Members said: 'We stood up only half via the land reform, but fully through the Cooperative within just one year.' Thus they renamed the Cooperative as *Standing-Up* Cooperative. In 1955, per mu yield of grain further increased to 448.5 kg from 293 kg in 1954. With all the 10 former middle peasant households rejoining, plus other new households, the Standing-Up Cooperative was enlarged to include 102 households.

Remaining shortcomings. One of the major shortcomings, just as in Japan, was that building of infrastructure over private land (changing parcels into non-farmland means of production) was hampered by private land ownership. The economies of scale of land and construction of infrastructure were hence limited. Joining cooperatives was voluntary and quitting with land free (until April 1956), and the latter could cause re-fragmentation.

For example, in 1955, in Neiqiu County of Hebei Province, Daleidong Village intended to construct a dam to save more than 200 mu (13.33 ha) of good land from flood. But because the members who owned relevant land did not agree, it could not be realized. Heinao Village planned to build a road that could be used by carts so that 10 man-days could be saved. However, no single member allowed it to be built on his land. (Li, Ji-Ping 1956). Also in 1955, Zheng Nong-Mu Elementary Cooperative of Houyu Township of Fuzhou City owned a two-wheeled double-shared plow. Since the members did not agree to build broader paths on their own fields, it could not be used. (Ye & Liu 1956)

Even if this shortcoming could be resolved by land exchange to consolidate private parcels, another relevant shortcoming remained, i.e., quitting with land from the cooperative was free (before May 1956), which could obviously result in re-fragmentation.

According to the relevant regulations, when quitting, a member could either withdraw his original land or land with equivalent quantity and quality. But even if a quitting member could be persuaded to accept land on the periphery of the unified land of the cooperative in exchange for his original land, so as to avoid re-fragmentation of the cooperative, the farm size to be operated by the remaining members of the cooperative would still be reduced, to which there was no ready solution.

The above examples and analysis have demonstrated that production cooperatives with private land shares could be established even in the low wage economy where cooperative services, non-grain agriculture and off-farm activities are not yet developed, and thus foster the transition from the low to the high wage economy and from agriculture to industry. If the remaining shortcomings could be overcome, then, sustainable rural development of achieving food security based on self-sufficiency and self-reliance and eradicating poverty could well be realized.

Exploratory transformations. However, because the ways of overcoming these remaining shortcomings were not found within the private land ownership framework, the elementary cooperatives, under the initial generally speaking proper guidance of the government, voluntarily turned private land without compensation to collective ownership of the *advanced agricultural producers' cooperatives* which also started before 1949[10] and had slowly developed since, accounting for 4% of the total households in December 1955. But speeded by the government's rash and immature compulsory action in mid-1956 on those elementary cooperatives which were not yet ready to transit to the advanced cooperatives and those households which had not yet even joined the mutual aid teams or elementary cooperatives, the advanced cooperatives (containing about 150 households) swiftly became dominant in May 1956. Since then, free quitting with land, which was allowed before, was actually forbidden. Those who quit from the advanced cooperatives or the remaining elementary ones were criticized in a class struggle way. But even in the advanced cooperatives, Production Responsibility Systems including 'bao *chan* dao hu' had also been successfully implemented, although less widely than in the elementary cooperatives. Thus the collectivization had been achieved 'without triggering massive resistance, large-scale slaughtering of livestock, or a general decline in output' (Putterman 1993: 28). This encouraged the government to further replace the advanced cooperatives by the *people's communes* (including several townships or even one county) in August 1958, which together with the Great Leap Forward campaign resulted in a sharp output decrease in 1959–60. As a rectification, in September 1962, a three-level system of ownership of the means of production was set up, i.e., ownership by the commune (lowered to comprise one township), by the production brigade

---

[10] The first advanced cooperative was established in Ansai County of Shaanxi Province during 1937–45 (Mao, Ze-Dong [1955] 1977: 170).

(covering one administrative village or about 150 households) and by the production team (containing one natural village or about 25—50 households), with the team as the basic ownership and also operation unit of land.11

Putterman (1993: 348) stresses that 'In the 1960s and 1970s, China's agriculture did not perform badly, overall, compared to the agricultures of other densely populated Asian countries. Yields were increased sharply through intensification of input application. Extension of irrigation, increasing use of chemical fertilizer, and dissemination of improved seeds, the hallmarks of what has been known elsewhere as the "green revolution", were successfully promoted, in part on the basis of indigenous technical innovation. The commune system safeguarded a minimal welfare standard for most residents where more conventional regimes generated vast numbers of landless and destitute. The comparison of achieved life expectancies with those of similarly poor countries is especially telling. Even the figures on farm production in the narrowest sense are not consistent with the belief that group farm institutions guaranteed universal and totally unchecked loafing. In a significant minority of cases, achievements went beyond bare "survival with equity": substantial local capital formation occurred and rural industry made a healthy start.' Ahmad, Dreze, Hills and Sen (1991: ix—x) also affirm the 'post-revolutionary China's outstanding success in substantially protecting the population from deprivation in spite of a relatively low level aggregate opulence', and hold that 'Guaranteed access to land in the rural areas, guaranteed employment in urban areas, and public provisioning of basic commodities and services appear to have been the pillars of this success.'

Nevertheless, China fell behind more rapidly developing neighbors such as Japan and South Korea (Putterman 1993: 15). One of the major responsible factors was the replacement of the Household Contract System by the unique collective land operation (labor was given workpoints which could not exactly reflect one's marginal productivity on the varied farm work). In cases in which the collective land ownership was operated under the Production Responsibility Systems, especially the Household Contract System, i.e., lowering the operation unit to the family level, it worked well. Such operations were exercised widely during 1959—62 and from time to time in the 1960s—70s before the economic reform in Anhui, Gansu, Guangdong, Guizhou, Hebei, Henan, Hubei, Hunan, Shaanxi, Shanxi provinces and Guangxi Zhuang Autonomous Region, etc. (Gao, Yi 1983: 41—4. Hao & Duan 1984: 545. Hu, Sheng 1991: 396. Du, Run-Sheng 1985:

---

[11] An administrative village may include just one natural village if the latter is very large or several smaller natural villages. Hereafter, unless specified, 'village' in the Chinese context refers to an administrative one.

15. Huang, Xi-Yuan 1986: 555). This has also been noted by Putterman (1993: 11–2), Kojima (1988: 709), and Nolan (1988: 50). In particular, 'bao *gan* dao hu' - the major form of the Household Contract System was invented in 1960 in Su County of Anhui Province and adopted widely (Liu & Zhou 1983: 35–6). Therefore, the collectivization of land ownership itself was not misguided.

Finally, as Chapter 6 will elaborate, in 1978, China started the economic reform which, drawing both positive and negative lessons from the past, kept collective land ownership at village level, but introduced the Household Contract System. This again brought huge incentives to peasants for production upon the numerous newly established fragmented small farms.

But although some rural areas (especially in the Central and Western parts) still remained in the low wage economy, more and more of the others have successively moved into the high wage economy where this farming structure also hampered sustainable rural development. Thus, in the 1980s, the Dual Land System, Leasing System, Single Land System and Corporate-Holding System were invented. Where properly practiced, they achieved appropriate large-scale farming and hence overcame the last obstacle while did not crowd those small farmers who still relied on land out of agriculture. This also is a third way beyond the centrally planned economy and free market system. It is based on collective land ownership so that land cannot be taken away by individuals. Under the village-wide corporate land ownership proposed here, private land shares could not be physically withdrawn, thus the same goal would be reached.

Similarly, in Japan, the collective use of private land by production cooperatives (from sub-village to village-wide) is a measure to overcome the shortcomings of the private use of private land. But some major shortcomings still remain mainly owing to the withdrawability of private land. Therefore it may be a temporary or transitory solution as the Chinese elementary cooperatives, and not a fundamental one. Turning private land to village-wide corporate ownership with physically unwithdrawable but financially salable private land shares would thus be a not only suitable, natural and logical but also critical further step for finally solving the last obstacle.

5.3 A Possible Global Applicability of the New Model

The new model, either in its specific form as presented in Proposal 5.1, or in other forms adapted to varied local conditions according to its principles, may have a global applicability.

The new model could be exercised in various forms under the conditions that land consolidation upon private land ownership has not been conducted, cooperative services are very weak, off-farm activities are not yet developed, rural areas are still in the low wage economy, the first transition has not been completed, the fragmented small farms have not yet emerged as the last obstacle (e.g., as a possible step-forward replacement of the Chinese elementary cooperatives in the 1950s). At this stage, although the fragmented small farms may prosper, consolidated land structure would be better. That is why China, India, Japan, etc. all tried to consolidate land even at the low wage economy in the 1950s.

The new model could be used in different methods under the situation that many peasants are seeking higher off-farm income in their own rural areas which are still in the low wage economy but developing towards the high wage economy, in other rural areas which have already entered the high wage economy, or cities and abroad, while still holding land in inefficient use.

The new model might be applied in diverse patterns under the circumstances that land consolidation upon private land ownership has been tried or conducted (either partially or completely), cooperative services are sound, off-farm activities are developed, rural areas have entered the high wage economy, the first transition has been completed, the fragmented small farms have become the last obstacle, large farmers are weak but part-time and absent small farmers strong (e.g., as a possible advanced displacement of the Japanese village-wide production cooperatives since the 1970s).

The new model may be adopted in revised forms for preserving small farmers while still strengthening large farmers, such as in the USA and many other OECD, including EU, countries.

The new model may be employed in varied types for the transition of collectively operated large farms in CEECs and the CIS where on one hand the newly established individual farms are generally fragmented and small, and on the other many farmers have joined their privately owned or publicly owned but privately possessed land shares for collective (rather than family) operation.

The new model could also be implemented to prevent food overproduction which has never been solved by developed countries, and further improve the environment.

It should be pointed out that this new model may also be practiced under *public* land ownership. In order to raise individual incentives for production, publicly owned land can and should be distributed for private use or possession. In such cases, the term '*private* land shares' in the new model is replaced by '*individual* land shares'.

The applications of the new model in various forms in other rice-based economies under private land ownership in monsoon Asia will be discussed later in this chapter, while those in the USA, OECD, EU, CEECs, CIS, and rest of the world in Chapters 9–11.

5.4 Dynamic Determination of Farm Size

To what extent should a farm be enlarged? This is a practical question to which the answer varies across time and location. For example, in 1994, in Saitama Prefecture of Japan, the critical size for a viable rice farm has been established at 15 ha or more (Kurita 1994: 511), while in Taiwan Province of China a survival area for a full-time rice farm was 4.4 ha as mentioned in Chapter 4. Starting from the survival area, farm size could be increased further until an optimal amount beyond which there would be no economies of scale. But the data for the optimal farm size in Japan and Taiwan are unavailable (for such data on mainland China see Chapter 7). As time passes, the economic structures (urban–rural, industry–agriculture, import–export, etc.), technologies, managing and tilling skills as well as the ratio of cost/profit in rice and other agricultural production will change. Thus, farm size could be adjusted accordingly by joining compact farms for expansion or separating them for contraction.

5.5 Theoretical Discussion

Combination of public and private factors a necessity. In terms of the historical evolution of land tenure system, we can see that in order to promote sustainable rural development, variable mixed economies as sub-village individual–collective mixed economy and village-wide individual–collective mixed economy at phases 1 and 2 in the author's hypothesis had been experimented with in China in the 1940s–50s in the form of the sub-village and village-wide elementary cooperatives. But they were rejected by main-stream Western economists and politicians as 'communist collectivization'. However, apparently without even being aware of the Chinese precedents, the similar sub-village and village-wide collective use of private land have been practiced spontaneously and independently in such a strong and leading capitalist country as Japan under the Liberal Democratic Party or its short-term coalition with the Social Democratic Party since the 1970s in a direction entirely opposite to the overwhelming global wave of decollectivization and privatization. This is a surprise for the advocates of free market forces. The village-wide collective use of private land has been acclaimed and its active promotion recommended in the 1990s at a time when the global decollectivization and privatization reached its peak as most former socialist countries in Central and Eastern Europe and Central Asia have all privatized agricultural land ownership. Therefore, without political or ideological preconception, it could be claimed that variable mixed economies combining varying public and private economic factors, including collective use of private farmland, may be a necessary condition for realizing sustainable rural development at least in monsoon Asia, irrespective of the political system or ideology in any specific country or economy.

Resolution of Pio's puzzle. For overcoming the fragmented small farms obstacle, although sub-village collective use of private land is better than private use of private land, and a village-wide one even better than the sub-village one, three major shortcomings still remain. These mainly are due to the withdrawability of private land from the cooperative.

Here, the Coase transaction costs approach can be applied. Private land ownership incurs higher transaction costs chiefly because private land owners hold strong bargaining power. A cooperative/enterprise with physically withdrawable private land shares is not a typical or real 'firm' in which individual bargains are eliminated and everybody follows the authority of the entrepreneur as Coase supposes, but a peculiar 'firm' composed of individual landowners all with strong bargaining power. Due to various problems within a cooperative/enterprise, rather than settling them within the 'firm' which may also lead to high transaction costs, some members may choose to use their right to quit so as to operate land individually or form another cooperative/enterprise which may re-fragment the unified land and would certainly reduce the farm size.

Thus once village-wide collective use of private land has reached its production frontier, the negative externalities imposed by private land ownership may hamper the achievement of dynamic or long-run (technological) Pareto efficiency. Being unable to find a solution to Pio's puzzle as reviewed in Chapter 3, the Chinese peasants had to turn private land to collective ownership in 1956 as a new round of institutional changes, which, through a series of exploratory transformations, finally evolved into a successful small-scale farming and collective–individual mixed economy in 1978–83 and a large-scale one in the mid-1980s as higher phases of variable mixed economies.

However, turning private land to public ownership after the cold war since the 1990s may also face high transaction costs, as the public institutions may not be able to afford to pay compensation (exchange costs) and private landowners may not wish to sell (strong bargaining power); landowners may not agree with a scheme without compensation either (also mighty bargaining power). Applying the Coase transaction costs approach again, it would be desirable to find a solution within the framework of private land ownership, which, however, requires the resolution of the century-old Pio's puzzle as analyzed in Chapter 3: Now that capitalism has developed all sorts of commodities up to derivatives, and stock is what real capital and other firm assets are made into the form of commodities, why has not it developed securitization of land? In fact, cooperatives with private land shares have never succeeded in the history.

It is perceived here that this is because the practices (as in the Chinese elementary cooperatives until April 1956 and Japanese village-wide production cooperatives since the 1970s) have met severe problems Pio did not expect: members may not agree to transform their private parcels into non-farmland means of production (dams, roads, canals, ponds, etc.); and more seriously, when members quit with land, the amalgamated parcels would be re-split, which made the cooperatives physically unfunctionable.

In contrast, in a modern capital shareholding corporation, it is the 'entrepreneur' who directs resources with authority; and when a shareholder quits, he cannot pull out any equipment, nor get reimbursement for his shares from the corporation, but can sell them in the market, therefore the corporation can still physically function.

Towards these problems, a village-wide corporation with private land shares physically unwithdrawable but financially salable is proposed. This may resolve Pio's puzzle, pave the way for cooperatives with private land shares to succeed and thus provide a possible solution to overcome the last obstacle while still keeping private land ownership.

Considerations on the village-wide corporate ownership. Now that a possible solution under private land ownership has been found, turning private land to such a village-wide corporate ownership would be more suitable. The corporate ownership could be established at both low and high wage economy. In applying Approaches 1 (permission for the relevant parties to exchange property rights through a political or legal process, followed by market exchange) and 2 [implementation of social actions (law, tax, etc.) to oblige the externality-yielding party to exchange property rights, followed by market exchange] to assigning property rights in mixture to eliminate or efficiently produce negative externalities and reach Pareto efficiency, agreement by the majority of landowners in the village should be sufficient for establishing corporate land ownership but great efforts should be made to reach consensus.

Just like public land ownership, corporate land ownership leads to lower transaction costs mainly because physically unwithdrawable private land shareholders do not have strong bargaining power. The corporation as the physical land possessor could behave like a real 'firm' to reduce or eliminate individual bargains between the various cooperating factors of production so as to smoothen land consolidation and expansion. The Dual Land System and Single Land System based upon either public or corporate land ownership are compatible with both capitalist markets, market socialism and incentive mechanism presented in Chapters 2 and 3.

Although from financial point of view, part-time and absent small farmers would not be capital-losers and may even be capital-gainers after joining the village corporation to earn permanent remuneration for their physically unwithdrawable private land shares, they might become psychological losers, since there existed a strong envy towards any specific villager who became competitive in the market by expanding his farm. Thus it was in their personal interest to maintain the status quo, which however would perpetuate their negative pecuniary externalities on the full-time farmers and society. Paying them permanent remuneration in exchange for use of their land would eliminate the future negative pecuniary externalities, but they might psychologically be worse off, or the remuneration would be regarded as not enough to compensate their psychological loss, or as being lower than their 'psychological market value' which is to maintain the status quo. However, it would be better than collectivizing their private land ownership. Therefore, from the psychological point of view, Approach 3 (reform of property rights structures through a political or legal process, followed by exchange at prices lower than the market levels) would be appropriate. Government intervention, education of public opinion and active participation of all peasants are necessary in order to make them realize that something between collectivization and the status quo, with some psychological loss not fully compensated according to their 'psychological market value' but financially with no capital loss and even with capital gains, should be the best for both them and the society as a whole. Now that education of peasants could function in obtaining consensus for land consolidation upon private farmland ownership and setting up the village-wide production cooperatives with physically withdrawable private land shares in Japan, it should also be able to work in establishing the village-wide production cooperatives with physically unwithdrawable but financially salable private land shares. Only after the elimination of the future negative pecuniary externalities, could Pareto efficiency be reached.

In such a village corporation, it is in the interest of the land and capital shareholders to supervise the performance of the administration, which is out of the incentive from ownership. But there is also incentive from competitive leasing - the core of market socialism - the contract would be given to the tenderer for the highest investment, quality and output, and best management, and could be stopped or dis-renewed for inefficient performance.

In this model the full-time or expert farmers would operate larger areas of land to become competitive, thus the government subsidies could be reduced or terminated. It is the village corporation which would pay dividends from production profits to private land shareholders. Thus, this model would achieve the essential and interdependent goals of sustainable agricultural and rural development as reviewed in Chapter 1 which include food security, to be obtained by ensuring an appropriate and sustainable balance between *self-sufficiency* and *self-reliance*; and employment and income generation in *rural areas*, particularly to eradicate poverty.

The recommended government approval of, and imposition of capital gains tax on, selling land shares for industrial or urban use in order to prevent speculative activities reflect government intervention as a part of mixed economy framework. Alternatively, the suggested conversion of land shares of the former village agricultural corporation to those of the new industrial or urban enterprises for peasants to receive permanent dividends would avoid their falling into poverty after they have lost agricultural land as their last resort of living, thus matching the principles of sustainable rural development.

The additional measure of obliging members to keep some minimum land shares in order to generate a permanent source of basic income for them would restrict the negative effects of free market forces, and prevent them from becoming landless, jobless, homeless, helpless and an unaffordable burden of the government social welfare, hence also sustainable rural development. Free transfer of land shares over the minimum amount would promote the market economy.

A similar minimum level of restriction could be found in the case of education. In all developed countries and many developing countries, children are obliged to receive education up to lower middle school. Education beyond that level is not obligatory. But suppose there is no this restriction. Then, people could enjoy the freedom of spending all their time. This, however, would exert harmful externalities to the society because it would end up with many illiterate people and to these people themselves since they could not master relevant knowledge in order to earn decent or even subsisting incomes. Therefore, free-spending of time up to a certain minimum level must be controlled but beyond that level allowed.

Another minimum level of restriction could be perceived in the case of pension finance. In many countries, during working period, a minimum percentage of worker's salary is obligatorily retained by the state constantly, which accumulates into a larger sum as pension to support the worker's living after retirement. But if this restriction were lifted, and workers were allowed to receive their entire salary during the working period, then some of them would spend it without any saving, nor receiving any other income, for old age, which would be both a personal and social problem.

The minimum education level, pension finance, and additional measure of obliging members to keep some minimum land shares from transferring are in accordance with the point of view discussed in Chapter 2 that free market forces should be regulated in order to avoid their negative effects and market economy should be fostered by government intervention.

Chapter 3 has reviewed two general methods in the evolution, adjustment or change of property rights structures. The first general method is to make *gradual* changes in social mores and common law precedents. The moral, practical and legal experiments may be hit-and-miss procedures to some extent. The second general method is to make a *conscious* (collective) endeavor, such as a major reform or revolution at a certain stage of the gradual changes in the first general method. Therefore, for finding the specific mechanism of the village-corporate ownership with physically unwithdrawable but financially salable private land shares and popularizing it, experiments are essential, and should be made in villages across the country or economy, modified and gradually extended.

The above-analyzed evolution from private use of private land to sub-village, then village-wide, collective use of physically withdrawable private land shares, as well as its remaining shortcomings in China and Japan, further to collective use of collective land in China, and prospective collective use of physically unwithdrawable private land shares under village-wide corporation ownership in Japan, is consistent with the following trend indicated in Chapter 3: (1) the development of production, technology and market, which induces (2) new benefit–cost possibilities, which in turn shows (3) gains of internalization (or efficient production) of negative externalities that exceed its costs, which subsequently raises (4) the need for internalization (or efficient production) of negative externalities, which finally requires (5) a change of the existing property rights structures and (6) a new institutional and legal framework for enforcement.

It has also provided evidence for the author's hypothesis that the fragmented small farms as the last obstacle imposed by the monsoon in sustainable rural development of monsoon Asia may be overcome by variable mixed economies, increasingly along three main phases. *Phase 1*: sub-village individual–collective mixed economy (sub-village-wide cooperative/enterprise collective use of physically withdrawable private land shares, exercising collective–individual dual level operation of large land units, with the basic operation level at one household as the major form or at a unit including a small number of households as the minor form). *Phase 2*: village-wide individual–collective mixed economy. *Phase 3*: either large-scale farming public–individual mixed economy or corporate–individual mixed economy (collective use of either public land, or physically unwithdrawable private land shares under corporate ownership, exercising village–individual dual level operation of large land units, with the basic operation level at one household as the major form or at a unit including a small number of households as the minor form, as a third way beyond the centrally planned economy and free market system).

Transaction costs determined farm size. As for the dynamic determination of farm size, Coase's transaction costs approach may also be applied. A firm becomes larger as additional transactions (which could be exchange transactions coordinated through market price mechanism) are organized by the entrepreneur and becomes smaller as he abandons the organization of such transactions. A firm will tend to be larger (1) the less the costs of organizing and the slower these costs rise with an increase in the transactions organized; (2) the less likely the entrepreneur is to make mistakes and the smaller the increase in mistakes with an increase in the transactions organized; and (3) the greater the lowering (or the less the rise) in the supply price of factors of production to firms of larger size. As time passes, the economic structures (urban—rural, industry—agriculture, import—export, etc.), technologies, managing and tilling skills as well as the ratio of cost/profit in rice and other agricultural production also will change in a specific locality, economy or country. Thus, farm size could be adjusted dynamically according to the transaction costs.

5.6 Other Rice-Based Economies under Private Land Ownership in Monsoon Asia [12]

Other rice-based economies under private land ownership in monsoon Asia may be generally regarded as at different stages along the Japanese model of rural development. To examine their performance along all the nine features of the Japanese model is not feasible here, although the situation concerning land reform in these economies has been reviewed in Chapter 2.

Group 1: Taiwan and South Korea together with Japan

Japan completed the first transition in 1960 (when the share of the agricultural labor force in the total labor force fell to one-third) and the second transition in 1974 (when the service sector overtook the industrial sector in size of labor force). Taiwan concluded them during 1970—73 and 1994 respectively. South Korea finished the first in 1980 (FEA 1981—82: 666), and its labor force in services was more than that in industry during (data unavailable before 1974) 1974—76, 78—87, 89—95, and less only in

---

[12] An earlier version of this section has been published by the Food and Agriculture Organization of the United Nations in Zhou, Jian-Ming [1996] (1997), with abstract by CABI.

1977 and 1988 (FEA 1975–76: 917; 1976–77: 904; 1977–78: 605; 1979–80: 645; 1980–81: 652; 1981–82: 666; 1982–83: 676; 1986: 557; 1989: 585; 1992: 483; 1997: 512. YLS 1978: 100–1). But to determine when it finished the second transition is not the task of this book (similarly this book is not involved in explaining the phenomenon that the labor force in services was/is already more than that in industry even during the first transition in some other rice-based economies of monsoon Asia). Taiwan and South Korea as 'newly industrialized economies' have repeated the Japanese rural development process - and problems, especially feature 9, and may thus be put together with Japan in Group 1.

Group 2: Malaysia, Thailand, Indonesia and the Philippines

Malaysia, Thailand, Indonesia and the Philippines are at the lower stage of the Japanese model and may be classified as Group 2. The speed of industrialization of Malaysia, Thailand and Indonesia since the mid-1970s, 1986 and 1988 respectively has been so high that they have been called 'newly industrializing economies', and, together with Group 1, 'high-performing Asian economies' (Edwards 1997: 572. Dixon 1997: 1020. Hobohm 1997: 380. World Bank 1993: 1). In particular, Malaysia finished the first transition in 1985 (FEA 1989: 642). The Philippines entered this group in 1994 (Hodgkinson 1997: 920). They have made various great efforts in strengthening rural development. But income disparity unfavorable to rural areas and within rural areas still persists (unlike Group 1 which achieved equity during rapid growth) (Edwards 1997: 572–3. Dixon 1997: 1028. Hobohm 1997: 380. Hodgkinson 1997: 922. Handley 1993: 46–8. Giordano & Raney 1993: 136–8. Hjort & Landes 1993: 62. Levin 1993: 11). In some areas (especially Malaysia), much of the rural labor force has been induced to abandon agriculture to go to cities (Edwards 1997: 574). Thus fragmented small farms have started to become an obstacle even before the overcoming of other obstacles to rural development (a difference from Group 1). Here we can see that the low income economies still saddled with traditional agriculture have been increasingly open to the high income economy, as small peasants there migrate to those rural areas already at the high wage stage, cities and abroad to earn higher income as part-time and absent farmers, thus also are up against the particular problem of adapting the agricultural sector to a high income economy, as pointed out in Chapter 1. The Asian financial crisis since the summer of 1997 has affected not only Group 1, but also the speed of industrialization and social stability of Group 2, although at different degrees. But after their recovery, peasant migration from rural areas still at the low wage economy to rural areas which have entered the high wage economy, cities and abroad would be strengthened, as will the inefficient holding of the fragmented small farms by part-time and absent small farmers. Therefore they should strengthen rural development according to domestic emphases along features 1–8 (except for rice import protection) and start to overcome the fragmented small farms obstacle in feature 9 of the Japanese model.

Group 3: Bangladesh, India, Pakistan and Sri Lanka

Bangladesh, India, Pakistan, and Sri Lanka are at the further lower stage of the Japanese model and may be placed in Group 3. Industrialization has been pursued but less speedily than in Groups 1 and 2. Thus the order of sequencing them is alphabetical. Serious instability (social, political, religious, ethnical, or territorial) has been continuous [unlike Groups 1 and 2 (though grave unrest has been experienced in Indonesia and the Philippines since the 1997 Asian financial crisis) and Group 4 (albeit small groups of rebels exist in Bhutan and Nepal)]. Although they have also made various endeavors to promote rural development, the majority of Asia's poor are in this group (and Group 4) and inequity in income distribution is severe. (Khan 1997: 122. Baru 1997: 320, 323. Taylor 1997: 873. De A. Samarasinghe 1997: 989. Levin 1993: 11)

In particular, as Dreze stresses, 'India's record of famine prevention in recent decades has often been presented as a highly impressive one, and several attempts have been made to draw out the possible lessons of this experience for other countries'. However, since independence in 1947, per capita food production levels have not dramatically increased, but remain lower than the late 19th century levels, and the net consumption of food has stayed remarkably stagnant. In fact, it is the relief system which has played the crucial role in averting large-scale starvation. Thus, 'This alleged success arguably needs to be put in proper perspective, and it has to be remembered that the various influences which combine to ensure the sustenance of the people in times of crisis do little more than keep them barely alive'; 'In fact, it can be argued that the diagnosis of success in crisis management is contingent upon the existence of acute and lasting famine vulnerability in the first place. The disappearance of large-scale famines in India has indeed coexisted with the resilient persistence of mass poverty and hunger'; 'the government of India can and should be criticized for having gone little further than espousing the earlier colonial view that "while the duty of the Government is to save life, it is not bound to maintain the laboring community at its normal level of comfort"'. (Dreze 1990: 13, 97–9). In recent years, India has achieved a fast development of IT (information technology) industry, especially computer software exports. This, however, is a knowledge-intensive activity. How to reduce the massive rural poverty and urban unemployment is still a task to be fulfilled. 'The government has now embarked upon an ambitious target of doubling food production and making India hunger-free in 10 years' (Kanda 1998: 2). But even with mass poverty and hunger, large amount of land is idled by absent landowners who have no intention of renting it out (Kanda 1998: 7).

Therefore, these countries should overcome social instability and strengthen rural development along features 1–8 of the Japanese model (except for rice import protection) and solve the fragmented small farms when they have emerged as an obstacle as fossilized by the inefficient land-holding of part-time and absent farmers.

Group 4: Bhutan and Nepal

Bhutan and Nepal, two of the world's poorest nations, are at the bottom of the Japanese model and may be joined into Group 4. They are also listed here alphabetically. Although progress in road-building was achieved, rural development remains behind that in other groups. Inequality in wealth is grave. (Brown 1997: 672–3, 676. Shaw 1997: 146). Thus they need to accelerate the progress along features 1–8 of the Japanese model (except for rice import protection).

Applications of the New Model

As already pointed out, the new model in various forms could be applied under the circumstances that land consolidation upon private land ownership has been conducted (either partially or completely), cooperative services are sound, off-farm activities are developed, rural areas have entered the high wage economy, the fragmented small farms have become the last obstacle, large farmers are weak but part-time and absent small farmers strong. It may also be adopted under the conditions that land consolidation upon private land ownership has not been conducted, cooperative services are very weak, off-farm activities are not yet developed, rural areas are still in the low wage economy, the fragmented small farms have not yet become an obstacle. Therefore, it would be applicable in the other rice-based economies under private land ownership in monsoon Asia.

Conjectural Proposal 5.2

Raising economies of scale of land should be gradual and follow the progress of diversified cropping, non-crop agriculture and off-farm activities. If, before the absorption of surplus peasants by the development of these sectors, much land were already transferred to large-scale farmers using large machinery and hiring fewer laborers, small peasants would be hard put to survive. Such a situation has unfortunately appeared in, for example, India, to which, however, the Indian government did not want to intervene (Baru 1997: 320. Byres 1995). Those peasants who have been crowded out from their small-scale subsistence farms had to become vagrants, slaves, or city slum dwellers. Thus, Ahmad, Dreze, Hills and Sen (1991: x) point out that 'Land reform, employment generation, and public provisioning are also the main instruments of action . . . in social security in South Asia [Bangladesh, India, and Sri Lanka]. In sharp contrast with China, the experience of this region with each of these three routes to the reduction of insecurity has been, so far, rather unproductive. . . . the prospects for guaranteeing minimal living standards [are] severely limited by economic constraints and political circumstances.'

Some of the other economies seem to be making their own way out of the Japanese model. But such a program is hazardous. A complete land reform with a limit on land-holding and rent and protection of tenants from eviction is needed. As these sectors developed, such controls could be gradually relaxed and appropriate large-scale farming promoted.

Although the Japanese model has not overcome the last obstacle imposed by the monsoon in sustainable rural development, its features 1–8 represent the correct stages in overcoming all the obstacles before the last one, which are common to the whole monsoon Asia. Needless to say, other rice-based economies in monsoon Asia have the right to create their own models of rural development. But deviation from these features (e.g., rejecting a complete land reform, failing to set up a village–household mixed economy to provide services to individual households, promoting unmatured large-scale farming before non-grain agriculture and off-farm activities could absorb surplus peasants) would only result in slowing the progress of rural development.

PART THREE

THE CHINESE MODEL

6. The Chinese Model and the Emergence of the Last Obstacle

6.1 The Chinese Model in General

The Chinese model of rural development, a third way beyond the centrally planned economy and free market system, started in 1978, although much work had been done before as stated in Chapter 5. It combines 13 major features or stages as summarized in Chapter 1. Since the focus of the analysis is on feature 9, other features are presented relatively briefly.

1. Institutional changes for a small-scale farming and collective– individual mixed economy (1978–83).

A 'System of Contracted Responsibilities on the Household Basis with Remuneration Linked to Output', briefly 'Household Contract System', was set up. After experiments on various forms, the following two prevailed.

The major form: 'bao *gan* dao hu' - contracting responsibilities to households and leaving the total residual output to them without the involvement of workpoints.

(1) *Ownership.* Land was owned by the village (equivalent to the former brigade) and could not be sold without the state's permission and could never be turned to individual ownership, all the other means of production could be either privately, collectively or jointly owned.

(2) *Land use.* Normal farmland (as opposed to wasteland) was divided into two parts under two systems respectively.

* *Equal Land System.* i. *Family plot* (zi liu di) was given to each household equally on a per capita basis for production of vegetables for self-consumption. ii. *Responsibility land* (ze ren tian) was contracted to households for production for the state, family and market equally either on a per capita basis (adopted by the majority of villages) *or* according to the ratio of labor force to population of each household (L/P): larger amounts went to those with higher L/P ratio, so that households with more laborers could contract more land [implemented by a minority of villages - 25% of 280 villages in a country-wide investigation (He, Dao-Feng et al. 1992: 100)].

The distribution of land to households was by equal assignment of parcels in terms of quality, quantity and distance, hence an *'Equal Land System'*, resulting in numerous fragmented small farms composed of parcels of different quality and size at different places in the village.

* *Dual Land System* (preliminary form): i. *Self-sufficiency land* (kou liang tian - grain rations land) was equally given to each household on a per capita basis for producing food for self-consumption; ii. *Responsibility land* was equally contracted to labor force for fulfilling tasks for the state and market. It was the preliminary form of the Dual Land System, and adopted by only a few areas mainly in the Eastern part of China. (Zhang, Chao-Zun 1991: 66. Wang & Ma 1990: 33). Even under this system, parcels were fragmented because they were assigned equally in terms of quality, quantity and distance (RWDWX 1984: 30. Prosterman; Hanstad & Li July 1996: 14).

There were villages which distributed hog land for producing pig feed on a per hog basis to households (Zou; Yan & Shi 1984: 22). There were also villages which reserved land to meet the future demand by increased population or rural development, and assigned it to expert farmers for temporary use [in an investigation of 280 villages of the whole country, 37.9% did so (He, Dao-Feng et al. 1992: 100)]. Self-sufficiency land, responsibility land, together with either hog land or reserve land were called a *Trio Land System*. But because hog land could be regarded as either self-sufficiency land or responsibility land (if there were quotas to sell pigs to the state), and reserve land was temporarily used as responsibility land, it was still a Dual Land System.

In 1986, the per household area of cultivated land was 9.2 mu (0.65 ha), scattered into nine parcels as revealed by one investigation (Wu, Wei-Han 1989: 22) (also see Table 7.4). In 1988, the per capita area of cultivated land of peasant households was 2.06 mu (0.137 ha), including 1.82 mu (0.121 ha) (88.35%) as land under contract and 0.18 mu (0.012 ha) (8.74%) as family plot (CSY 1989: 156). By calculation, an average peasant household had four—five people (9.2/2.06 = 4.47).

(3) *Responsibilities.*

* *State quotas.* Households should contract the annual production quotas of major agricultural products (e.g., grain, cotton, oil crops, sugar crops) and sell them to the state at state-decided prices (quota prices, pai jia). In the event of a natural disaster, the quota could be reduced or exempted and the households would get relief from the governments or collectives.

The state decided the national quotas [e.g., in 1988 it accounted for 12.7%

of China's grain output and 41.7% of its commodity grain1 (RCRD [1989] 1993: 448. SYC [1989] 1993: 448–50) and provincial quotas which were different across provinces. The provinces further broke down quotas to prefectures, and in turn to counties, townships, villages and finally to households. According to a national sample survey on the state compulsory purchase system, grain sold at the quota prices, depending on location, accounted for 13.5–21.6% of the total grain output in 155 sample villages in 1988. (RCRD [1989] 1993: 448–9)

The length of contracts of the first round was initially about three to six years, but decided locally. This was extended by the state in 1984 to 15 years (i.e., 1978–93) (CCCPC [1984] 1992: 224), and for poor areas, 30 years (CCCPC & SC [1984] 1992: 297). That of the second round was established in 1993 as 30 years (i.e., 1994–2024) for all areas (CCCPC [1993] 1996: 17; [1994] 1996: 17). The contracts were renewable. Notarization of the contracts has been gradually implemented. For example, Luliang Prefecture of Shanxi Province2 stipulated that all contracts in the second round of renewal be notarized. (Niu & Yu 1998)

* *Collective quotas.* The village collective could contract wasteland [waste mountain, hill, beach, gully - as four wastes (Wang, Xue-Xi 1995: 23)] and waste water for reclamation, either to households equally, or to expert farmers through competitive tendering for higher quotas to the collective up to 100 years (Prosterman; Hanstad & Li November 1996: 94–5). The quotas could be waived during the period of reclamation and then phased in (Peng; Zhang & Yang 1988: 18). Such reclamation was encouraged by the state for developing unused resources and improving the environment. Collective quotas would also be demanded at those households or individuals who contract reserve land. But not every village has wasteland or waste water to be reclaimed and reserve land.

* *State tax.* Upon contracted responsibility land, households should also pay agricultural tax to the state in monetary form. The averaged state agricultural tax was 3.7 yuan per mu (0.067 ha) in 1988, as up to about 4% of the net income per mu (SYC [1989] 1993: 174, 663. RCRD [1989] 1993).

* *Collective fees.* The State Council stipulated in 1991 the following two kinds of fees.

i. *Village reserved fees* (cun ti liu) are paid for three items (san ti):

(i) *Common accumulation fund* for capital construction of farmland and water conservancy, afforestation, purchase of productive fixed assets and

---

[1] Commodity grain refers to the grain sold to the state at both quota prices and negotiable prices (explanation see blow) and to the market at free prices, rather than self-consumed.

[2] Shanxi Province is in the North-Central part of China.

establishment of collective enterprises. Some villages also charged a contractual fee.

(ii) *Common welfare fund* for supporting households enjoying the five guarantees (i.e., wu bao hu: childless and infirm old persons who were guaranteed food, clothing, medical care, housing and burial expenses), subsidizing households with special difficulties, cooperative medical and health care and other collective welfare facilities or services.

(iii) *Management expenses* for remuneration to village officials and management costs.

ii. *Township unified finance fees* (xiang tong chou fei) are collected for five items (wu tong): (i) schools at townships and villages, (ii) family planning, (iii) special care given to disabled servicemen and to family members of revolutionary martyrs and servicemen, (iv) militia training, (v) road construction in townships and villages, and other undertakings run by the local people and subsidized by the state.

These collective fees should not exceed 5% of last year's per capita net income of peasants of the village and township in question. In developed areas, this percentage could be appropriately raised, subject to the approval of the provincial government. The amount of these fees paid by land contracting peasants was subject to the area of contracted land or the numbers of the family labor force. (RFSBP [1991] 1992: 12–3). (In reality, the forms, titles, amounts of the collective fees varied across the country and many areas incorrectly exceeded the 5% ceiling after 1984.)

* *Labor services to collectives.* The State Council also prescribed in 1991 the following two types of labor services.

i. *Rural obligatory man-days* (nong cun yi wu gong) were mainly for afforestation, flood-prevention, road construction, schoolhouse repair, etc. Each rural laborer should provide 5–10 man-days of this kind annually. Local governments could increase such man-days in the event of natural disasters.

ii. *Labor accumulation man-days* (lao dong ji lei gong) were chiefly for capital construction of farmland and water conservancy, and afforestation. Each rural laborer should deliver 10–20 man-days of this type each year. Under some conditions, subject to the approval of the county government, such man-days could be appropriately increased. They were mainly taken in slack seasons of farming. (RFSBP [1991] 1992: 13)

(4) *Remuneration.* During 1979–84, after selling products in quota to the state at quota prices and fulfilling other responsibilities, households could dispose of the residual output for self-consumption or sale to the state at higher state-decided prices. The state purchasing prices for in-quota output of 18 staple and non-staple products were on average raised by 24.8%, and those for above-quota output of grain, cotton and oil crops by 50% (Zuo &

Song 1988: 431). From 1985 on, besides the quota prices (as one price track), above-quota output could be sold to the state at negotiable prices or to the market at free prices (the other price track) - hence a Dual Track Price System. The quota prices were often lower than the market prices by 50–100% (Zhu & Jiang 1993: 449). In poor years the state negotiable prices were higher than the quota prices, and usually equivalent to or slightly lower than the market prices. But after a very good harvest, the market prices may fluctuate towards lower prices than the pre-determined quota prices and negotiable prices.3 Such a trend was clear after the brilliant summer harvest of grain in 1997, as the then Vice Prime Minister Rong-Ji Zhu claims on 7 July 1997 (Zhu, Rong-Ji 1997). As a result, while the quota prices lower than the market prices in poor years would lead peasants to incur losses, the quota prices higher than the market prices in good years could make them earn profits with the losses being passed to the state agencies. Thus the quota prices have also been called parity prices (ping jia). There were, however, two major shortcomings: in poor years, peasants would still suffer from losses; while in good years, some state agencies, in order to avoid their own losses, might refuse to procure grain from peasants, who would then be forced to sell grain to private agencies at the lower market prices, which would in turn have interest to press market procurement prices further down. Thus on 6 June 1998, the State Council issued 'Regulations on Grain Procurement' stipulating that all grain sold by peasants (i.e., both grain in quota and above quota) was to be procured only by state agencies at the market prices when they were higher than the procuring prices, and at the procuring prices when the market prices fell below them, as a protection for peasants; the state agencies, after filling in the state grain reserve, could then sell grain in the market at the procuring prices; private agencies could not buy grain directly from peasants but only from the state agencies; the losses of the state agencies due to the accumulation of inventory, etc. would be borne by the state treasury. As the state agencies bought all grain at prices not lower than the procuring prices and sold it at the procuring prices as if forming a streamline, the procuring prices were also called streamline prices (shun jia). This has prevented the market prices from falling further below the procuring prices. (XHNA 1998. XHD 1998). Such an overall protection, however, also led peasants to produce products of low quality without good marketing prospects while the state agencies had to buy all of them. Thus in June 1999 the government turned to selective protection: the above-mentioned protective streamline prices would be used to procure those

---

[3] The fluctuating procurement situations in 1979–85 have been described by Oi (1989: 162–81) and afterwards to 1995 by Aubert (1996: 321–8).

products with high quality and good marketing prospects; for those with low quality and bad marketing prospects, lower and eventually no protective prices would be exercised; those large agro-food processing enterprises and big forage producing firms could, with the provincial government's approval, buy high quality grain directly from peasants according to pre-determined contracts, so as to offer peasants sales guarantee before their starting to produce grain. The selective protection would encourage peasants to produce products according to market demand and adjust structures of products while still enjoying appropriate protection. (Wang, Chun-Zheng 1999: 2). In May 2000, the State Council further eased its policies by allowing and encouraging food-use and -sales enterprises (no matter whether large or small), with the provincial government's approval, to directly procure those foods still under the protective prices; permitting food-use and -sales firms, with the prefectural and county government's approval, to purchase those foods no longer under the protective prices; and encouraging farmers to sell foods produced by themselves, without amount limit, in the rural fair markets (XHNA May 2000). In January 2001, the state specified that public, private and individual food-use and -sales firms could procure foods in rural fair markets and wholesale markets (or deep further, directly in the rural areas without convenient transportation) with the provincial government's approval (Du, Deng-Bin 2001). The State Council stressed the need to further implement and perfectize the reform of the food circulation system and accelerate the strategic adjustment of the structures of agriculture and food production (XHNA May 2000).

Households could produce and sell minor agricultural goods to the free market, and also dispose of the products above the collective quotas if they contracted wasteland or waste water.

The above responsibilities - state quotas (around 20% of grain output), agricultural tax (up to 4% of the net income per mu), collective fees (no more than 5% of per capita net income), labor services to collectives (about 30 man-days) - were not very heavy. Thus the residuals as remuneration to peasants were high, hence also their incentives.

(5) *Land transfer.* Not only official transfer (returning the land to the village for redistribution) but also personal transfer [sub-contracting (zhuan bao) of land while retaining the title of contractor in front of the village, and making-over (zhuan rang) of the contractor's title to another household] could be done on a voluntary basis and with the village's approval. The investment and improvement made by the transferor could be reasonably reimbursed. (CCCPC [1984] 1992: 224)

(6) *Disciplines.* It was forbidden to desolate the household contracted land, build housing and graves on, or take away earth from it. Compensation should be paid if the fertility were lowered due to over-exploitation.

Abandoned or desolated land should be withdrawn by the village. Land should also be returned to the village if the household in question was not able to till it or had shifted to other jobs. (Summary [1981] 1992: 119. CCCPC [1984] 1992: 225). These regulations, however, were widely ignored in practice.4

(6) *Capitalistic operation.* Quasi-capitalist (hiring less than eight laborers) or capitalist (hiring eight or more) operation of land was allowed (CCCPC [1982] 1992: 172; [1984] 1992: 225), but in fact not necessarily needed by the small farms. For instance, when an average household had four people and operated 8.24 mu (0.549 ha) of land, two laborers using farm animals could suffice for effective operation and still have some seasonal surplus labor (SY [1989] 1991: 97). Therefore, the individual farming units prevailed.

(7) *Village duties.* The village had the duty to fulfil the general management of the contract system and provision of services, hence a village —household dual level operation of land with the household as the basic operation level. The village also was responsible for managing social welfare, infrastructure construction, natural disaster control, overall rural development, etc.

Gradualism was used in popularizing this system upon the willingness of peasants. By the end of 1983, over 94% of households had adopted 'bao *gan* dao hu' (CSY [1984] 1988: 131).

The minor form: 'bao *chan* dao hu' - contracting output quotas to households and linking the fulfillment with workpoints which were then linked to remuneration.5

(1) *The main features* were that the village undertook planning of planting, paid basic production costs, disposed of products (including paying tax and selling grain to the state), with the remuneration to households based on a basic income mainly in kind (grain and other products) subject to a bonus or fine (CEST 1996: 38).

The village as the contractee, and a laborer (representing a household) as the contractor, signed a contract, stipulating the annual quotas of i. output of certain kinds of products the contractor had to fulfil, ii. man-days (workpoints) related to the output quota and iii. production investment the contractee should provide to the contractor (i.e., the contractor had to bear

---

[4] For example, by early 1998, 50,000,000 mu (3,333,333.33 ha) or 2.56% of 1,951,000,000 mu (130,066,666.67 ha) of cultivated land of the whole country had been occupied by graves (SQD 1998. National Survey [1996] 2000).

[5] A further minor form of the Household Contract System 'bao *gong* dao lao (hu)' - contracting *work* to laborers (households), whose fulfillment could be related either directly to remuneration or indirectly through workpoints, will be dealt with in Chapter 7.

the extra production costs).

The household could use a certain amount of land, farm animals, and tools distributed to it by the village. The village should also provide other means of production to the contractor within the production investment quota, and was responsible for procurement, sale, machinery, technology and other services, construction of infrastructure and general management. Thus, the land was under village—household dual level operation with the household as the basic operation unit.

If contractors could fulfil the output quota, they could get the normal workpoints related to that quota. If they overfulfilled it, they would be rewarded by more workpoints or a part (e.g., 20—80%) or total of the above-quota output. If they underfulfilled it, they would get less workpoints, or had to reimburse the loss of the production investment of the village, or compensate a part (e.g., 40%) or whole of the unfulfilled gap. In the distribution of payment at the end of the year, they might still get a minimum payment for subsistence, but the above-subsistence payment would be reduced in proportion to the loss. (Liu & Hu 1982: 30, 38)

(2) *Major merits.* In terms of the village, a merit of the system was that it could achieve better scientific organization, improvements in agriculture and rural development and ensure relatively easily that the tasks for the state and collective could be fulfilled by households (by contrast, under 'bao *gan* dao hu', households had more autonomy but the village less). Land consolidation and expansion were also easier. In terms of the households, because contractors were responsible for fulfilling the output quotas to earn correspondent workpoints, they had to attach importance to the quality of the daily farm work as it would affect the final output. Since overfulfillment of the quota would bring more workpoints as a bonus and underfulfillment incur less workpoints as a fine, both incentive and responsibility were introduced directly to the households. Shirking in terms of work quality could thus be minimized. Family members including the aged, children and women also had an incentive to fulfil the common tasks of their family.

(3) *Principal remaining problem.* The system used workpoints as a linkage between output quota and remuneration. It thus was different from 'bao *gan* dao hu', which abolished them. During the year, the contractors accumulated workpoints. At the end of the year, the general cost of production of the whole village and management expenses including subsidies to managing officials, among other items, had to be deducted from the total final revenue. Only the residual could be divided by the total workpoints and distributed to the contractors accordingly. But village officials might manage production less efficiently, which would lead to higher general cost. They could also claim that they had worked harder and deserved more subsidies. It was not so easy for the ordinary members to

exert day-to-day monitoring on their performance. Therefore, the remaining revenue to contractors was affected by the general cost of production and management expenses. In other words, the payment to contractors did not necessarily match their marginal productivity.

Only those villages with very efficient and fair cadres could adopt the system. Thus it was not popular. During 1990–94, on only 0.23% of the total farmland of the country, about 7,000 villages which accounted for 0.15% and 0.2% of all villages in 1990 and 1992–94 respectively still implemented it. (CEST 1991: 33; 1996: 38). For this reason, the following analysis will concentrate on the major form of 'bao *gan* dao hu'.

The previous commune–brigade–team system was formally abolished between October 1983 and the end of 1984 (Hu, Sheng 1991: 511–2). The commune was altered to township as the lowest level government, brigade changed to village, and team became villagers' group.6 But before the formal change, this system was already being replaced by the village–household collective–individual mixed economy.7 Nevertheless, the government allowed peasants to keep the team mechanism as they wished. Thus, the Fourth Production Team of Liming Village of Shuangcheng County of Heilongjiang Province8 became the last team of the whole country to replace the team mechanism with the Household Contract System in the form of 'bao *gan* dao hu' on 12 January 1998 as the members finally realized its superiority, almost 20 years after the first one - Xiaogang Production Team of Liyuan Commune of Fengyang County of Anhui Province9 on 24 November 1978 as mentioned in Chapter 1 (Xie & Gao 1998).

2. Government policies supporting rice production and rural development. These included making market-oriented policies, establishing laws and regulations, adjusting state agricultural taxes, purchasing quotas and prices, providing financial, technological and material support, importing

---

[6] Each village is governed by a villagers' committee. Starting from 1988, the state has been popularizing the direct election of the committee members including the director and vice director(s) by all villagers of 18 years old and over, with the 'Law on the Organization of the Villagers' Committees (Tentative)'. The township government is the guider (rather than leader) of the villagers' committees. An amended version of the Law was enforced on 4 November 1998. (Ni & Li 1998)

[7] There have been also state-owned farms. The 'Household Contract System', farm–household dual level operation of land with the household as the basic level, and transition from small-scale farming to large-scale farming are relevant to them too. Due to the length limit, except for citing a few examples, Chapters 6 and 7 do not analyze them.

[8] Heilongjiang Province is in the Northeasternmost part of China.

[9] Anhui Province is in the Central part of China.

grain when necessary, promoting export of agricultural goods, combating corruption and crimes, and policies supporting features 1 and 3–13.

Besides institutional changes, technological progress also contributed to economic growth, which was embodied in features 3–8 and 10–13.

3. Construction of rural infrastructure.

4. Higher yields and multiple cropping of rice and other grains.

5. Diversified cropping and non-crop agriculture.

6. Off-farm employment.

7. Peasant migration to cities and work in town and village firms. Compared with previously being bound within the countryside, peasants could now enter cities to be employed. Both villages and individuals could also set up enterprises in cities. But in order to avoid urban congestion, peasants (except for being approved to live in cities as university graduates, newly recruited employees of state enterprises, etc.) were not entitled to permanent city residence, commodity grain at prices subsidized by the governments, housing allocated by the governments at subsidized rent, government subsidies for inflation, labor insurance by the state, or other social welfare which city residents could enjoy.**10** Instead, peasants were encouraged to industrialize and urbanize rural areas by establishing in both industry and services collective township and village enterprises (TVEs),**11** individual, capitalist (called private),**12** urban–rural joint, external and foreign single or joint enterprises, and developing small and medium towns.**13**

8. Agricultural mechanization with small machinery.

---

[10] As Putterman (1993: 5) notes, 'while constraints on temporary movement of labor among localities and from countryside to cities had been loosened, the gap between rural and urban incomes and entitlements remained large, and most farmers remained tied to their land and to their status as peasants thanks to the persistence of the residence permit system and the denial of a range of public benefits to those holding agricultural classification.'

[11] Since the 15th National Congress of the Communist Party of China in September 1997 which emphasized the pluralist ownership structures, 80–90% of the TVEs had actually been turned from collective to joint or private ownership by the end of 1999 (Chen, Jian-Bo 2000).

[12] Private (capitalist) ownership of the means of production was preserved after the socialist transformations in 1956, prohibited during the Cultural Revolution of 1966–76, re-permitted at the end of the 1970s, treated as '*a complement to the socialist economy under public ownership of the means of production*' in the amendment of the Constitution on 12 April 1988, and further raised to the status of '*an important component of the socialist market economy*' in the revision of the Constitution on 15 March 1999 (Xiang, Zhen-Hua 1999: 6). Therefore the acceleration of the development of private (capitalist) enterprises can be expected.

[13] As Aubert (1999: 18) notices, the government prefers such 'kind of rural industrialization process where the laborer would "quit the land without quitting the countryside" (li tu bu li xiang)'.

Features 1–8 in general were similar to their counterparts in the Japanese model (the major differences being the individual land ownership in feature 1 and rice import protectionism during 1961–93 in feature 2 of the Japanese model) and have had positive effects similar to Japan.

Also, analogous to Japan, the fragmented small farms began to be non-viable for rice and other grain production as the low wage economy moved to the high wage economy, hence a second round of institutional changes (which will be studied in the next section):

9. Institutional changes for a large-scale farming and collective–individual mixed economy (starting roughly around 1985) to achieve economies of scale of land, which resulted in

10. Agricultural mechanization with large machinery.

The following features reflected regional transfer of development.

11. Earlier development in some (chiefly Eastern and coastal) rural areas, and its promotion in other (mainly Central and Western) areas14 especially from the early 1990s on.15 This feature was not so conspicuous in Japan probably because it is not very large in size and such a transfer was much quicker.

12. Introduction of more advanced technology and management, larger investment, and domestic and international markets to agriculture by urban–rural joint enterprises, and external and foreign single and joint ventures. In Japan, the introduction of foreign technology was marked, but foreign investment and venture in agriculture were not so, because private land ownership even constrains land lease to Japanese.

There is still much room to improve in all the features. Features 3–12 cannot be regarded as completed. Nevertheless, some real success has been achieved. Table 6.1 demonstrates that during 1978–98, China has been steadily progressing in the transition from agriculture to industry and further to services, as the labor force in agriculture declined while that in industry and services increased. Table 6.2 indicates that in the same period, the *rural* labor force in farming, forestry, animal husbandry and fishery decreased whereas that in industry and services increased. Off-farm employment and peasant migration to cities and work in town and village firms have been promoted. Thus the transition from agriculture to industry and further to

---

[14] This is a general statement. It does not exclude different speeds of development within the Eastern and costal rural areas. For example, Jiangsu Province is in East-Central part of China and coastal. But its Southern part - the Sunan region - has been much more developed than the Northern one - the Subei region.

[15] Putterman (1993: 364) praises that 'It does indeed seem the better part of wisdom to let the forces of diffusion from the other high-growth centers of East Asia work their way through China's proximate coastal regions in a more or less natural fashion'.

services has been based upon overall rural development, rather than on unique industrialization which neglected rural areas. Table 6.3 shows that during 1978–99, per capita output of grain and cotton was higher in later years than in 1978, indicating success in agriculture. The per capita output of oil crops and meat rose, demonstrating positive results from diversified cropping and non-crop agriculture (numbers in italic and bold display the lowest and highest levels respectively in the production fluctuation).

Thus Aubert (1999: 14) concludes: 'During the 1960s and 1970s, the high increases in grain production were mostly absorbed by the population growth (more than 2% a year). The boom that followed the decollectivization of the early 1980s, combined with the effects of family planning, resulted in big increases in grain availability (for the first time the level of 400 kg per capita was reached in 1984). At the same time, farm households enlarged their meat output and consumption. At last, the risk of famine was disappearing from the Chinese countryside.'

Furthermore, China has entered a higher phase to fulfil a new task, as embodied in feature **13. Prevention of food overproduction, promotion in quality and perfectization in variety of agricultural products, and improvement of the environment, while strengthening development of the Central and especially the Western areas, mainly from mid–1999.**

Features 11–13 really need a detailed analysis. But, since they are not the focus of the book, only some examples will be given in Chapter 7.

6.2 Theoretical Discussion

After WWII, in order to overcome dualism and the vicious circle of poverty

Table 6.1 Employment by Main Sectors in China 1978–98 (in percentage)

Year	Primary (agriculture)	Secondary (industry)	Tertiary (services)	%
1978	70.5	17.3	12.2	100
1985	62.4	20.8	16.8	100
1990	60.1	21.4	18.5	100
1995	52.2	23.0	24.8	100
1998	49.8	23.5	26.7	100

Sources: CSY 1999: 134.

Table 6.2 Composition of Rural Social Labor Force in China 1978–98 (in percentage)

| Year | Farming, forestry, animal husbandry & fishery | Industry * | | | Transportation, storage, post & communication | Wholesale, retail & catering | Other off-farm acti-vities | % |
		Total	Mining, manufacturing & public utilities	Construction				
1978	92.41	–	–	–	–	–	–	–
1985	81.89	11.62	7.40	3.05	1.17	1.25	5.25	100
1990	79.35	12.82	7.69	3.62	1.51	1.65	6.17	100
1995	71.79	15.89	8.82	4.89	2.18	2.60	9.72	100
1998	70.27	15.96	8.46	5.15	2.34	3.15	10.63	100

* In CSY 1999, 'industry' is parallel with 'construction' and 'transportation & communication', thus is a narrower concept of 'industry' equivalent to 'mining, manufacturing & public utilities'.

Sources: *1978:* CSY 1991: 76, 80. *1985–98:* CSY 1999: 380.

Table 6.3 Per Capita Output of Major Agricultural Products (kg) in China 1978–99

Year	Total grain	Rice	Cotton	Oil crops	Meat
1978	*316.61*	142.25	2.25	5.42	8.90 *
1979	340.49	147.37	2.26	6.60	10.89 *
1980	324.77	141.75	2.74	7.79	12.21 *
1981	324.79	143.86	2.97	10.20	12.60 *
1982	348.73	158.97	3.54	11.62	13.29 *
1983	375.97	163.94	4.50	10.24	13.61 *
1984	**390.30**	170.82	6.00	11.41	14.76 *
1985	358.15	159.25	3.92	14.91	18.20
1986	364.17	160.19	3.29	13.71	19.65
1987	368.69	159.43	3.88	13.98	20.27
1988	*354.94*	152.32	3.74	11.89	22.33
1989	361.61	159.83	3.36	11.49	23.32
1990	**390.30**	165.60	3.94	14.11	24.99
1991	375.82	158.70	4.90	14.14	27.14
1992	377.79	158.93	3.85	14.01	29.28
1993	385.17	149.78	3.15	15.22	32.41
1994	*371.38*	146.79	3.62	16.60	37.54
1995	385.25	152.93	3.94	18.58	43.43
1996	**412.24**	159.41	3.43	18.06	48.33
1997	399.73	162.37	3.72	17.45	41.67
1998	410.46	159.21	3.61	18.54	45.86
1999	403.47	–	3.04	20.65	47.28

* Pork, beef and mutton only.

Sources: *1978–84*: CSY 1993: 65, 330, 341. *1985–94*: CSY 1993: 330; 1995: 354; 1999: 111, 395–6. *1995–98*: CSY 1997: 390; 1999: 111, 395–6, 401. *1999*: SBNESDC [1999] 2000.

inherited from the prewar period, both China and Japan undertook land reform and established individual land ownership. With an individual–cooperative mixed economy, plus features 2–8, Japan had succeeded by 1960. China guided peasants to an individual–collective mixed economy through temporary mutual aid teams, permanent mutual aid teams and elementary cooperatives, and then collectivized land ownership in 1956. Thereafter until 1978, China abandoned the mixed economy but exercised a combination of collective ownership and operation of land under the centrally planned economy. 'In this period the Chinese rural economy performed only moderately in terms of its pace of growth of output, of factor productivity and farm income' (Nolan 1988: 47–8) and China then fell behind Japan. However, this period was not completely wasted since it provided valuable experiences. During 1978–83, China founded a small-scale farming and collective–individual mixed economy with success. Thus, the achievement in both Japan and China was brought about by a mixed economy, as stressed in Chapter 2: multiple structures of public and private ownership plus government intervention other than ownership.

Chapter 2 presented market socialism as a third way between the centrally planned economy and free market system: an economy where the ownership of all means of production and their further reproduction are in the hands of the state, but these means are leased in competitive markets to private entrepreneurs who retain a residual claim to both income and capital gains and are able to transfer those claims. In the Chinese case, the land was owned by the village collective, but contracted to households which retained a residual claim to both income and capital gains and were able to transfer those claims. Thus market socialism is in accordance with the small-scale farming and collective–individual mixed economy in China as a third way between the centrally planned economy and free market system.

Chapter 3 noted that in the case of a transaction involving several people supplying labor, physical inputs, etc., if some of the parties involved receive fixed amounts of value specified by a contract and there is only one residual claimant, then maximizing the total value received by the residual claimant is just the same as maximizing the total value. If the residual claimant also has the residual control, then just by pursuing his (her) own interests and maximizing his own returns, the claimant will be led to make the decisions reaching Pareto efficiency: in an economy there is no other productively feasible allocation which makes all individuals at least as well off, and at least one strictly better off, than they were initially. Under the Chinese Household Contract System, a household as a single individual both had the residual control and received the residual returns after fulfilling the state and collective tasks, thus the residual decisions made would tend to be Pareto efficient ones, just as under private land ownership in the Japanese model.

Approach 1 to assigning property rights (permission for the relevant parties to exchange property rights through a political or legal process, followed by market exchange) was used in establishing the small-scale farming and collective–individual mixed economy: households were given land for producing products to be sold to the state at quota prices (in general lower than the negotiable and market prices) and fulfilling other responsibilities in exchange for the right to dispose of the residual for self-consumption and sale to the state at negotiable prices and to the market.

Both of the two general methods in the evolution, adjustment or change of property rights structures, as reviewed in Chapter 3, were adopted in establishing the Household Contract System. The first general method is to make *gradual* changes in social mores and common law precedents. At each step of the adjustment process, it is unlikely that externalities per se are consciously related to the issue being resolved. The moral, practical and legal experiments may be hit-and-miss procedures to some extent. In a society that weighs the achievement of efficiency heavily, their viability in the long run will depend on how well they modify behavior towards the externalities associated with important changes in technology or market values. Indeed, not only in the elementary cooperatives, but even during 1956–78, the Household Contract System was already being implemented by peasants and grass-roots officials time and again in different areas, which showed its superiority over the combination between collective ownership and operation of land.

The second general method is to make a *conscious* collective endeavor, such as a major reform or revolution at a certain stage of the gradual changes in the first general method. Finally in 1978–80, as a part of feature 2 of the Chinese model, the state decided to legalize and popularize the Household Contract System as the beginning of an overall economic reform.

Chapter 1 cited the definition of the essential and interdependent goals of sustainable agricultural and rural development which includes 'Food security, to be obtained by ensuring an appropriate and sustainable balance between self-sufficiency and self-reliance; employment and income generation in *rural areas*, particularly to eradicate poverty'. Under China's collective land ownership, if a household has fallen into debts owing to natural disasters, diseases, business failures or even gambling losses, then all of its properties might be taken away but not its housing land and contracted agricultural land because they belong to the village, so that it could at least still build a poor but livable house and produce food for the state, self-sufficiency and market. Therefore, the combination between collective ownership and household operation of land not only leads peasants to richness on one hand but also prevents them from falling into destitution on the other, rather than making them rely on government subsidies or crowding them out to city slums, hence sustainable development within the rural sector itself.

The government set compulsory quotas on the basic agricultural goods to be bought by the state from peasants at quota prices, and above-quota output at higher state-decided prices during 1979–84. Subsequently in 1985–98, the above-quota output could be sold to the state at negotiable prices or to the market at free prices. From mid-1998 on, both in-quota and above-quota grain products were bought by the state which could then sell a part to the private traders. Since mid-1999, such protection of peasants' interest has been continued to those grain products with high quality and good marketing prospects, but phased out to those without. This combination of both protection and flexibility was not only conducive to the improvement of the varieties and structures of grain and agricultural production but also preventive against such grain (rice) overproduction as incurred under the excessive protection of the Japanese government as indicated in Chapter 4. Sufficient storage and food security against poor harvests and disasters have accordingly been established. For example, the grain storage could feed the whole population for two years (Xu, Hui 1998: 5).

China's success upon the establishment of the Household Contract System also supports the thesis emphasized in Chapter 1 that it is the institutional component that is the most important in the interaction of institutions and technologies underlying the growth of developing countries, and of so many variables for rural development, the institutional changes are the keystone. This has been confirmed by Putterman's observation (1993: 343) that 'decollectivization bore a greater responsibility for the period's growth than did price changes or changes in cropping patterns'.

The first round of the institutional changes paved the way for technology, as another long-term ultimate cause, and labor, capital, education, structural change, etc., as proximate sources of economic growth to play important roles. They exerted positive impact on the later features of the Chinese model.

However, as Nolan stresses (1988: 98, 112), despite the revolution-like institutional changes, there were continuities from pre-1978 to the mid-1980s more than many Western accounts allow. China's policy makers and economists did not shift to the view that a completely individualistic, free market rural economy was desirable either for growth or distribution. On the contrary, they emphasized that many activities necessary to the success of the farm economy require public intervention in the market.

Without collective and local state agencies such as the villagers' group, village, township and county, many activities vital to the prosperity of the rural economy (e.g., irrigation and drainage; technical services including accounting, seeds selection and supply, planting techniques and plant protection; power and road construction; communications; research) would not have occurred at as high a level as they did in the mid-1980s (Nolan 1988: 99—100, 112).

A high (although declining) proportion of rural plant and equipment (including industrial enterprises, transport and spraying equipment, tractors, power stations, etc.) was owned by villages, townships, and counties, though with much altered methods of operation for higher efficiency. The income generated by the collective industry continued to play a vital role in subsidizing agricultural and other activities. For example, in 1984, of the total funds invested in rural production activities, just 1% came from the state, compared to 6% from the 'new economic associations' (different forms of non-collective cooperation) and 40% from peasant households, while 54% still from the collective. (Nolan 1988: 100, 108)

Collective institutions also remained centrally important in welfare provision such as education, health and old-age care which has been a national policy. Contributions from peasants were required to the common welfare fund, although in some very rich areas with high income from collective enterprises, they often were waived or reduced. (Nolan 1988: 101). Just opposite to a completely individualistic system, as Oi (1989: 223) notes, 'Some township party committees and governments have decided that each township and village cadre should contract (bao) to help one poor household develop production.' Consequently, wealthier peasants also assisted the poor households - 'bring them gifts, help them build houses without payment, and sometimes give them shares in their enterprises and partial profits without their investment or work.'

Nolan (1988: 172—3) further notes that albeit growth of labor productivity and incomes in the 1980s was quite uneven between different rural parts, most areas experienced at least some real growth. The institutional reforms released untapped production potential in poor areas as well. There were major advances even in the poorest provinces with the smallest increases in average per capita net income. The state (at different levels) also used the extra incomes contributed by the advanced areas to raise the level of labor productivity and incomes in the poorer areas (as part of features 11 and 13). Hence a national uneven growth rather than polarization.

Thus Oi (1989: 10) concludes that 'The once highly centralized command economy is now . . . a mixed economy.' In particular, 'The dislocations of transition to a market economy found in Eastern Europe and the former Soviet Union have been attenuated to an extensive degree in China by the redistributive socialism . . . This is yet another reason why the state may want to maintain collective ownership of land' (Oi 1999: 625).

However, Friedman (1990: 36) incorrectly summarizes the new system as a free-market economy, as he claims: 'Talk about the "enormous costs of moving to a free-market economy" is much too gloomy. There is no reason why total output cannot start expanding rapidly almost immediately after the totalitarian restrictions of people's activities are removed. That certainly was the case in agricultural sector of China after the major reforms of the late 1970s.' Thus, if Friedman's statement has puzzled many Eastern Europeans a year (or indeed even a decade) after the collapse of communism, it should not be a surprise (Putterman 1993: 3).

Chapter 2 indicated the many disadvantages and few advantages of the fragmented small farms. Nevertheless, they succeeded during 1978–84 in China, just as in the 1950s in Japan, because they were suitable to the then relatively backward economic, social and technological conditions. This affirms the point of view in Chapter 3 that there is no basis for believing that all existing externalities should be corrected. Only when the gains of correction exceed costs, should the existing externalities be internalized or efficiently produced.

Features 1–8 in the Chinese and Japanese models are analogous. This reflects the fact that the rice-based economies in monsoon Asia have common features and tasks in overcoming the common obstacles imposed by the monsoon.

The theoretical discussion in Chapter 4 on the significance of the Japanese model is applicable to that of the Chinese model, and therefore does not need to be repeated here.

6.3 The Emergence of the Last Obstacle

Table 6.3 showed that China's per capita output of grain, rice and cotton reached a peak in 1984, but declined by a large margin in 1985–88. Many factors were responsible, including the over-optimism on the part of the central and local governments that China's agricultural problems had been solved once for all, thus failing to support agriculture continuously; the improper shift of priority by many local governments from grain production to developing non-grain agriculture and off-farm activities; the reduction of farmland acreage due to rural industrial and housing construction; the exorbitant charge of collective fees well over peasants' capacity (5% of last year's net income) for rural development (corrupt misuse also occurred);**16**

---

[16] In order to curb the excessive charges of the collective fees, the state has decided in 1999 to replace the collective fees (village reserved fees, township unified finance fees and other relevant fees) as well as labor services to collectives (rural obligatory man-days and labor accumulation man-days) with unified agricultural tax, tax on special agricultural products and additional agricultural tax. This is because taxes are more compatible with a lawful society and

the insufficient services by villages, resulting in weak operation of land by single households; the starting of economic reform in industry and granting of autonomy to industrial enterprises for partially deciding prices in 1984, leading to higher expenditure by peasants on buying more expensive industrial materials for agricultural use and higher costs for grain production; the reduction in rice and grain consumption as people became richer and demanded more vegetables, fruits, meat, aquatic products, just as happened in Japan, etc. But, here, the focus is on the non-viability of the fragmented small farms for rice and grain production in the high wage economy.

Decreasing Parcel Size and Increased Fragmentation of Land due to Population Growth

Under the Equal Land System, land should be returned to the village from those who have left due to death, marriage, etc., and newcomers from birth, marriage, etc. were entitled to an equal share of land (Yang, Zuo-Hua 1995: 48). Births outnumber deaths since China's population has been increasing, while farmland acreage decreasing. The Equal Land System put no control on and even encouraged higher fertility of population.

Village reserve land, which was kept not only for increased population but also for overall rural development, had to be assigned to new people and was gradually exhausted. For example, in 1986, Luoshui Town of Shifang County of Sichuan Province17 had 220 net increased people, including 158 as the newly-born and 120 immigrants. In 1987, 26% or 16 of 61 villagers' groups had exhausted their supply of reserve land. Still, it had to register the marriages of more than 200 people, receive a number of immigrants, and provide a quota for 50 births, a part of whom, however, could not be given any land. (Zhou, Da-Fu 1987: 29)

Redistribution of previously assigned land had to be conducted which made the fragmented small farms smaller (Wang, Gui-Chen 1989: 16. Yang, Wen-Bo 1995: 43). Minor redistribution - involving only the land of those households whose size was changed - could be done either at the time the family size altered or over several years. Major redistribution - whereby the land of all households was returned to the village for redistribution - was

---

matured market economy, determined through more serious procedures by and paid to the higher governments. Villages and townships do not have the power to create or augment them, or charge them into their own pockets. Exercises have started in Anhui Province as experiments in 2000 and dependent on their successes will be popularized to the whole rural areas. (AD 2000. JFEC 2000)

[17] Sichuan Province is in the Southwest part of China.

performed every three–six years. (Prosterman; Hanstad & Li 1995: 40). According to Chinese sources cited by Oi (1999: 618), nation-wide, during the late 1970s – late 1990s, at least 80% of villages had adjusted land allocations at least once, and some even five times or more. Such a redistribution of land, although generally accepted by peasants for equality consideration, violated the land use contracts, led to instability and low confidence in keeping contracted parcels, discouraged long-term investment and encouraged the short-term behavior [i.e., getting the highest output in the short-run by depleting land fertility in exploitative ways, such as applying large amount of chemical fertilizers and reducing or abandoning organic ones, resulting in the hardening of soil (Wang, Song-Pei 1989: 32). Oi (1989: 199) and Putterman (1993: 39) have also noted it]. A major redistribution involving a whole county would incur huge costs, e.g., 2 million yuan in Lulong Country of Hebei Province18 (Yang, Wen-Bo 1995: 43). In those areas where land was not readjusted for a long time, contracted land was not proportionate to changed family size, hence serious imbalances of interests among households of the village (Qin & Wang 1995: 42).

Inefficient Land Use by Part-Time and Absent Small Farmers

Income from grain production declined relatively, while that from diversified cropping, non-crop agriculture and off-farm activities grew quickly, due to development in these lines. According to an investigation, in 1984–88, net income per mu increased by 12.1% in growing grain, but 213% in cash crops; net income per yuan investment decreased by 15.6% in planting grain but increased by 171% in cash crops and 10.1% in forestry, animal husbandry and fishery; net income per man-day increased by 15.1% in producing grain, but 96.5% in cash crops, 73.8% in forestry, animal husbandry and fishery and 45.9% in off-farm activities. (RSO 1990: 19).

Thus, peasants naturally wanted to produce less grain, and be engaged more in other agricultural lines and off-farm activities. Hence also peasant migration to cities and work in town and village firms. As Table 6.2 illustrates, during 1978–95, the rural labor force was in decline in agriculture but increasing in industry and services. This has led to feminization and senilization in agriculture. Apparently, in the high wage economy, it was difficult for the remaining full-time farmers to survive on rice and grain

---

[18] Hebei Province is in the Northeast part of China and coastal.

production by tilling the fragmented small farms.**19**

Low willingness to transfer land. In order to make the remaining full-time farmers viable and maintain/increase rice and grain production, the land inefficiently used by other peasants should be transferred to them, so that they could enlarge farm size, use large machinery, reduce costs, and gain increasing returns to scale. But under the Equal Land System, land transfer was voluntary. In the areas where the off-farm activities were relatively developed and many peasants had been enticed into jobs there to earn higher income, an investigation showed that, of 3,366 households whose income from grain production was lower than 20% of the whole income, only 4.5% were willing to officially transfer land (RCSC 1996: 17). Another investigation revealed that 10.8% of households were willing to do so (Lu, Xiu-Jun 1989: 52).

In contrast, a questionnaire to 1,039 workers of rural firms in Changshu City of the Sunan region of Jiangsu Province where off-farm activities were highly developed demonstrated that 33% of them were willing to till self-sufficiency land only and return responsibility land, and 20% willing to leave farming completely, as long as their land was taken over by someone else (Jiang, Zhong-Yi et al. 1992c: 77–8). An investigation of 4,015 peasant households in the suburbs of Shanghai Municipality**20** where off-farm activities were the most developed, indicated that 45.7% were willing to partially or completely transfer land (Meng, Fan-Qi 1988: 13). But regions like Shanghai and Sunan were few.

The major concern of peasants was that land was the last resort for peasants' living and served as a back-up basic social welfare in case they lost jobs in off-farm activities. Peasants who had transferred to work in rural off-farm enterprises in general could not enjoy job security. The majority of firms were small. Closures and bankruptcy were frequent. For example, during 1979–87, about 1 million TVEs had gone bankrupt (ED [1988] 1989). In Yanbei Prefecture of Shanxi Province, during 1981–86, the total rural labor force increased by 77,000. In 1983–84, employees of rural firms increased by 130,000. Due to difficulties met by the firms, however, 54,900 and 11,000 had to return to agriculture in 1985 and 1986 respectively. (Shen,

---

[19] Aubert (1996: 322, 332; 1999: 15) has also observed that as off-farm incomes rose, agricultural activities were not lucrative enough for farmers, and there was huge migration of temporary peasant workers into towns and cities. Putterman (1993: 348) concludes that households remaining in agriculture were main losers in the race towards higher living standards. Oi (1999: 620) points out that as the economy has become more diversified and peasants have more freedom of choice and movement, increasing numbers of peasants are becoming part-time and absent farmers.

[20] Shanghai is in the Southeast part of China and coastal.

Shou-Ye 1987: 28). But no rural instability was caused since they could still till the household contracted land.

80% of peasants who left their localities to earn income outside (mainly in cities) during periods of economic expansion were manual labor (Zhang, Shi-Yun 1996: 17). During economic contraction, they both needed and also could return to the countryside to till land. Primarily due to the back-up social welfare function of the household contracted land, the problem of city slums which are common in many developing and even developed countries does not exist in China (recall the reappearance in the 1990s of jobless and homeless people in Japanese cities originating from rural areas indicated in Chapter 5). (Zhang & Hou 1995: 27)

Low occurrence of personal land transfer. Chiefly as a result of this concern on the supply side, during 1984–92, of 7,012 households across the country, 93.8% did not make any personal transfer of farmland; 4.2% did a partial transfer; and only 1.99% transferred their whole farmland (ED [1994] 1996: 17). In 1994, a mere 1.06% of households of the whole country carried out personal land transfer (CEST 1996: 38–9).**21**

Inefficient use of personally transferred land. In cases where such transfers were čarried out, they were mainly done spontaneously among relatives, so that parcels were often non-contiguous and still fragmented, and in short-term, seasonal and unstable arrangements (Zhang, Shi-Yun 1996: 17). An investigation of 1,879 households which were engaged in personal land transfer in Langfang Prefecture of Hebei Province before 1987 showed that even the longest contract did not exceed four years (Cao & Liu 1987: 36) (of course, when the village implemented minor or major land redistribution following the changes in family sizes, transferred parcels would not be excluded, which shortened the holding of them). Accordingly, receivers had little incentive in long-term investment in land (Liu, Zong-Xiao 1987: 64).

On the demand side, where income from grain production was much lower than that from other activities, quite often no villager wanted to accept

---

[21] Similarly, Nolan (1988: 93) observes that bankruptcy was already a real threat to TVEs in the early 1980s, Aubert (1999: 18) perceives that a slowdown in the economy could force millions of 'peasant workers' back to their villages, and Oi (1999: 622) points out that as the reforms to the state-owned enterprises have been deepened and massive lay-offs created, returning to farming would be an economic cushion for the millions of peasants once they have lost jobs in urban and rural factories. Thus, most farmers want to keep their land as an insurance policy even if they do not farm it (Oi 1989: 192). Because farming serves as the last resort (Kung & Liu 1997) and land is the basic form of rural security, even in areas with plenty of off-farm employment, some peasants were reluctant to sub-let land, afraid that this might be the first step to losing control over it completely (Nolan 1988: 147).

a personal land transfer (RWDWX 1984: 31). Those who transferred a part of their land normally singled out poor land (as reported in Yanbei Prefecture of Shanxi Province and the Sunan region), which almost nobody was interested in. This promoted careless farming or even led to desolation of land. (Shen, Shou-Ye 1987: 28–9. Qiu, Wei-Lian 1988: 63)

Some peasants engaging in off-farm activities sub-let land to outside farmers who were mainly from poorer rural areas. The lessors charged a small or no sub-letting fee, or even paid some fee to the lessees for fulfilling state quotas. The length varied (e.g., from two to seven years in the Pearl River Delta of Guangdong Province22). The lessors retained the title of contractor within the village. The outside farmers could earn higher income and learn more advanced technologies, farming skills and new ideas. But many of them changed to producing cash crops or turned land over to ponds for fishery, thus affecting grain output. They were also engaged in the local off-farm activities, hence part-time farming too. Moreover, many left their original rural areas to escape family planning rules and to have more children in other areas. (Tao, Xiao-Yong 1986: 16–8)

Part-time farming prevailed. Many peasants only farmed in busy seasons, without taking care of the plants in the rest of the year. A lot of able-bodied males worked in cities, while their old parents and wives cultivated the land. Because the farms were tiny, it was possible for peasants who worked in nearby firms to just till the land in the early morning, midday and evening during slack seasons, and to concentrate on farming during the short busiest periods by leaving the firms temporarily. They were satisfied with producing for self-sufficiency (so that they did not need to buy grain and vegetables) and fulfilling state quotas (which was not their aim but a condition), unwilling to produce more for the state and market, to transfer land or make more effort in farming. (Zou; Yan & Shi 1984: 23. Ding; Wei; Yang & Sang 1995: 23. Yang, Wen-Bo 1995: 43. Zhu, Qi-Zhen 1996: 35–6)23

For example, in Suzhou City of the Sunan region, during 1978–85, the ratio of the agricultural labor force to the total rural labor force dropped from 76% to 38%. The total rural labor force increased by 340,000, but labor in farming decreased by 780,000. Most agricultural laborers were either aged, weak, female or children. In order to let workers attend to farming in the two busiest periods, the firms had to stop working half a month each

---

[22] Guangdong Province is in the South-Central part of China and coastal.

[23] Nolan (1988: 143) observes that a large proportion of rural off-farm workers still lived in the villages, and at the peak season typically returned to work on the family farm; Aubert (1999: 18) notes that many migrant workers still return to till the land at some point of the year; and Oi (1999: 621) notices that little land actually lies fallow, but an increasing amount is not worked with the care and investment of time and inputs that would produce maximum yields.

time, their revenue being directly affected. (Qiu, Wei-Lian 1987: 28). In Lulong Town of Lulong County of Hebei Province, the family of Shu-En Ji had three members including one laborer, and contracted more than 3 mu (0.2 ha) of land. He was engaged in off-farm activities in the slack seasons and in farming only in the busy time. (Lu, Nong 1988: 42). The family of the head of the Industrial Company of Lianglukou Township of Shifang County of Sichuan Province had seven members, four in firms. With his wife aged over 50 and two children in home, they had to hire somebody for farming. In the busy spring season of 1987, they could find nobody to employ. Thus the transplanting for 2.8 mu (0.187 ha) of wet rice land was delayed by 10 days. (Zhou, Da-Fu 1987: 29)

Both off-farm work and farming require increasing knowledge of sciences and technology (recalling that technological progress also contributes to economic growth and is embodied in features 3–8 and 10–13). Objectively, it would be difficult for the part-time farmers to learn such knowledge in both jobs. Subjectively, they were not interested in learning more to improve farming beyond the goal of self-sufficiency.

Even worse, some farmers planted cash crops on their land to earn more money and purchased grain in quota from the market - at higher prices - to sell to the state - at lower prices, thereby creating a false output. Or they just paid cash equivalent to bridge the gap between the quota price (lower) and state negotiable price (higher) of grain to fulfil the contract so as to save the cost of transporting grain back from the market (Zhu & Jiang 1993: 449). Some others even refused to sell grain in quota or pay tax to the state at all (Qian; Shi & Xie 1996: 27). In Shifang County of Sichuan Province, 10% of peasant households did not pay collective fees for common accumulation fund and common welfare fund in 1984. In 1985, this ratio increased to 30%. (Ma, Bing-Quan 1988: 48)

Desolation of farmland. Further and far more serious was the fact that much farmland was partially or even completely desolated by part-time and absent small farmers, occupied by new housing, or used for burial (Ran & Yang 1985: 15–6. Qin & Wang 1995: 42). Partial desolation (called careless farming) was dominant, because farmers feared that the villages would punish them by withdrawing land. Thus they either just planted crops, without taking care of them afterwards; or grew a bit in the summer and a bit in the winter, pretending they were still tilling the land. (Ran & Yang 1985: 15).

For example, in 1984, in Langfang Prefecture of Hebei Province, 50% of land was operated by 50% of peasants who were also engaged in 113,000 firms. In seven villages of Wen-an County, 20–50% of households were careless farmers. In some villages, more than 5% of land was completely desolated. In Xinglonggong Township, nearly 10,000 mu (666.67 ha) of land was carelessly farmed, and over 2,000 mu (133.33 ha) desolated. Four of the seven villages paid cash equivalent to bridge the gap between the quota price and the state negotiable price of grain to fulfil the contracts. (Cao & Liu 1987: 32, 36)

In 1986, in Jing-an Village of Lianglukou Township, there were 486 households, 1,677 people, and 1,006 laborers. 60% of the labor force had shifted to off-farm activities, but the Equal Land System was still held with 1.14 mu (0.076 ha) of farmland per capita. 10—20% of land were carelessly farmed, and over 3 mu (0.2 ha) idled. (Zhou, Da-Fu 1987: 28—9)

One estimate is that 2—3% of farmland was idled in 1986—87 by families who preferred not to farm but were unwilling to sub-contract (Nolan 1988: 147).

Shipai Town of Zhongxiang County of Hubei Province24 was famous for its bean curd. By 1988, of 8,829 peasant households, 1,800 had left in whole families for other places in the bean curd business, but only 57 transferred the whole of their land. 11,000 laborers, or 62.6% of the total labor force had left the Town, but they only transferred 3,820 mu (254.67 ha), as 15.3% of their contracted land. (Peng; Zhang & Yang 1988: 19)

In the winter of 1993, in Zhejiang Province,25 about 466,900 ha of farmland were idled, and the multiple cropping ratio of grain dropped to 214.9% from 223.5% in 1980 (Ding; Wei; Yang & Sang 1995: 23).

In Feidong County of Anhui Province, of the total labor force, more than 40% went outside, 20% were engaged in local off-farm activities, leaving less than 40% in agriculture; of the whole farmland, 8% or 100,500 mu (6,700 ha) were at some stage idled. But during the major redistribution of land in 1994, many peasants who during several years had never returned home also came back to 'contract' land. (Zhang & Hou 1995: 24)

Desire for more land by full-time and expert farmers. While the part-time and absent small farmers held land without efficient use, there were some full-time farmers who were good at farming and wished to contract more land. Even in the areas where income from grain production was much lower than that from non-grain agriculture and off-farm activities, some farmers were willing to contract more land if the scale was large enough for them to earn an income equivalent to or higher than that from off-farm employment. (Gao & Liu 1984: 20. Yang, Wen-Bo 1995: 43). For example, in the above-mentioned questionnaire in Changshu City, 72.6% of the 1,039 rural firm workers expressed willingness to till land if the income from farming rose to 3,000 yuan, or 125% of the average net income per local household

---

[24] Hubei Province is in the Central part of China.

[25] Zhejiang Province is in the Southeast part of China and coastal.

around 1990 (Jiang, Zhong-Yi et al. 1992c: 77).

Possibility of transferring land by part-time and absent small farmers. As long as a back-up basic social welfare could be reserved/provided for them, many (but not all) of part-time and absent small farmers were willing to transfer their land partially or even wholly.26 Some of them have spontaneously done so.

For example, the family of Zheng-Xiang Li of Qianli Brigade of Caiji Commune of Quanjiao County of Chuxian Prefecture of Anhui Province had six members including two laborers in 1980. They contracted 10 mu (0.667 ha) of farmland from which they could earn a net annual income of 1,300 yuan only. They also raised 13 hives of bees. Because they could not manage both agriculture and apiculture, bees escaped eight times, causing a loss of 400 yuan. In 1981, they earned an income of over 2,000 yuan from raising 20 hives. In 1982, they raised more hives and income approached 4,000 yuan. Thus, they retained 4 mu (0.267 ha) as grain-rations land for self-sufficiency and returned 6 mu (0.4 ha) to the Production Team. (Qu; Chen & Bao 1982: 56–8)

Lack of mechanism. The Equal Land System lacked an effective mechanism to systemize and organize the transfer of land from part-time and absent small farmers to full-time farmers.

For example, in 1982, in Zhongshan City of Guangdong Province, rural firms competed for labor, leaving the aged and female in farming. Peasants have preferred to transfer the land bearing contracts for grain, sugarcane and mulberry, and retain some land for self-sufficiency without obligations. Since there was no mechanism to organize it, in Beiqu Village of Xiaolan Town, of 190 mu (12.67 ha) of sugarcane land, 150 mu (10 ha) were desolated. 170 mu (11.33 ha) of mulberry fields were left unfertilized, unweeded or unharvested. (GT 1988: 17)

By 1988, in Tielou Village of Guanyindang Town of Jiangling County of Hubei Province, 48 households had left to live in the nearby Town to earn higher incomes from commerce and transportation. They wanted to transfer 1,000 mu (66.67 ha) of land but could find no villager to accept. (Peng; Zhang & Yang 1988: 19)

An obstacle. Therefore, in those areas (mainly Eastern and coastal parts) which had entered the high wage economy, the fragmented small farms had emerged as the last obstacle in sustainable rural development at as early as the onset of the 1980s, just as in Japan at the beginning of the 1960s. In some Central and Western parts (e.g., Anhui and Sichuan provinces), off-

---

[26] Oi (1989: 190) also notes that where off-farm activities are booming, some peasants have wanted to dispose of, or at least decrease, the land they originally contracted.

farm employment was not yet developed and the local economy has not reached the high wage stage. But many peasants there migrated to the Eastern and coastal areas to earn higher income, while still holding land use contracts and leaving land resources to waste. (Yang, Yong-Zhe 1995: 17). For example, in Dachuan Prefecture of Sichuan Province, over 40% of agricultural labor transferred to work in rural off-farm activities or cities. In one county of this Prefecture, more than 12,000 mu (800 ha) of farmland were desolated (Yang, Zuo-Hua 1995: 50). Where this has happened, the fragmented small farms became an obstacle alongside other obstacles *even in the low wage economy.*

Thus while China required more grain to support its growing population and economy, much land was held by part-time and absent small farmers in inefficient use. This contributed to the situation that in most years during 1982–98, grain imports exceeded exports, as shown in Table 6.4. {During 1979–81, 15 million tons of grain were imported each year, but the trade balance data are unavailable (Chen, Yun [1978] 1992: 6. Wan, Li [1982] 1992: 135)}. This has in turn pushed up grain prices in the world markets and affected other, especially poor, grain importing countries as indicated in Chapter 4.

Direct subsidies did not work.[27] Facing the situation that the costs of grain production were increasing and that many peasants did not use their land efficiently, many rural areas where TVEs were developed diverted a part of their profits as direct subsidies to farming mainly in the form of a certain amount of money per mu. This, however, did not stimulate the part-time and absent small farmers to invest and work more in land, but was used by them on consumption. Moreover, now that holding land itself could earn direct subsidies, their tendency to hold on to the land without transfer to full-time farmers was strengthened. At the same time, it seriously weakened the strength of the newly established TVEs. (Tao, Xiao-Yong 1986: 18, 61. Lin, Cong-Jun 1987: 18. Zhou, Xin-Jing 1988: 8)

Conclusion. The above analysis has shown that, as surmised in Chapter 1, and opposite to Schultz's argumentation, as the labor force required for farming began to decline at a substantial rate and many of the farm people left agriculture for nonfarm jobs, it would be logical to increase farm size of the remaining full-time farmers and benefit from the functioning of the tenet

---

[27] The aim of subsidies to grain-producing households was to raise their income near, equivalent to or higher than that of non-grain agriculture and off-farm workers. Direct subsidies were a certain amount of money directly paid to them. Indirect subsidies were expenditure on the indirect means, e.g., improvement of services, infrastructure, technology and purchase of machinery, to promote their competitive strength so as to earn a higher income through their own better performance.

'that the costs of agricultural products fall as the size of the production unit in agriculture increases'. However, the part-time and absent small farmers

Table 6.4 Years of Import Exceeding Export of Grain in China 1982–98 (1,000,000 tons)

Year	Export (cereals, cereal flour, pulses, etc.)	Import (cereals, cereal flour, pulses, etc.)	Import exceeding export
1982	0.81	16.15	15.34
1983	1.15	13.53	12.38
1984	3.19	10.41	7.22
1985	9.33	5.97	
1986	9.42	7.73	
1987	7.37	16.28	8.91
1988	7.17	15.33	8.16
1989	6.56	16.58	10.02
1990	5.83	13.72	7.89
1991	10.86	13.45	2.59
1992	13.64	11.75	
1993	15.35	7.52	
1994	13.46	9.20	
1995	2.14	20.81	18.67
1996	1.98	12.23	10.25
1996 *	1.24	10.83	9.59
1997 *	8.34	4.17	
1998 *	8.89	3.88	

* Cereals and cereal flour only.

Sources: SYC 1984: 388, 393; 1986: 487, 490. CSY 1988: 649, 652; 1990: 608, 611; 1992: 583, 586. SYC 1994: 515, 518. CSY 1996: 589, 592; 1997: 597, 600; 1998: 629, 632; 1999: 586, 589.

would hold land in inefficient use even though land property rights have
been well defined and market transactions facilitated. They did have some
rational concern over their direct interests in security. Thus if they could be
guaranteed with a back-up basic social welfare and given appropriate
remuneration, then some of them would be voluntary to transfer their
inefficiently held land in various suitable forms to the full-time farmers for
effective use, but others would still be reluctant to do so. This would make
it difficult for the remaining full-time small farmers to be viable as the
economy develops into the high wage stage, and to obtain the inefficiently
held land for effective use, even if the knowledge and other conditions were
available for them to produce the same output with fewer resources or a
larger output from the same resources. Government or community subsidies,
budget burden, food shortage (even artificial food overproduction at a later
stage), unnecessary food import, higher domestic and international prices of
agricultural goods, land under-utilization or idleness, waste of other
resources, environmental deterioration, etc. would also be incurred. Thus at
least some of the part-time and absent small farmers were not so rational to
the society's and their own fundamental interests. Consequently, according
to variable mixed economies, a new round of institutional changes for a new
land tenure system should be called for, which would provide a back-up
basic social welfare and appropriate remuneration to those peasants who
were or would be engaged mainly in non-grain agriculture and off-farm
production and effectively expand farm size for the full-time and expert
farmers.

Summary. Xiao-Ping Deng (Deng, Xiao-Ping [1990] 1997) points out in
1990: 'From a long-run point of view, there should be two leaps in the
reform and development of China's socialist agriculture. *The first leap* was
to abolish the people's communes, and implement the responsibility system
mainly in the form of household contract with remuneration linked to output.
This was really a big advance, and should be maintained for a long time. *The
second leap* is to develop *appropriate economies of scale on land operation*
and collective economy, according to the need of scientific cultivation and
socialization of production. This is another very great advance, and of
course, needs a rather long process.'

As Howe (1997: 222–3) correctly indicates, during the economic reform,
attention from the mid-1980s to the mid-1990s tended to focus on industry,
foreign trade and foreign direct investment. There was a tendency to assume
that food and agricultural problems were no longer serious. This was partly
because the rise in Chinese incomes diverted demand away from grain; and
partly because in the first phase of reform (1978–84), the agricultural sector
did grow impressively. In recent years, however, the situation has become
more serious. It is clear that the 'once for all' gains from raising peasant

incentives have been made and that the trajectory of production is being affected by lack of investment and other problems. In the *People's Daily* one can find stories about the shortage of rural labor, while there was also unemployment. The problem is that the right people with the appropriate skills are not where they are needed. Thus, the government is encouraging a further transformation of agriculture, this time towards large-scale farming rather than the small-scale one that produced positive results in the first phase of reform. This larger scale will be accompanied by improvements in water control, *greater mechanization* and a higher quality of managerial expertise.

6.4 Theoretical Discussion

The theoretical discussion on the emergence of the fragmented small farms as the last obstacle to sustainable rural development imposed by the monsoon in Japan in Chapter 4 is also applicable in this context and therefore not repeated here.

However, one major difference between Japan and China is worthy of note. In Japan, there was a land-holding ceiling until 1962, land rent control until 1970, tenancy protection from eviction in long-term lease until 1970 and in short-term lease until 1975 and 1980. Before such restrictions on market exchange were removed, the negative externality imposed by the part-time and absent small farmers was technological; and thereafter, pecuniary. But in China, voluntary transfer was allowed even at the beginning. Therefore, such an externality was immediately pecuniary.

Another major difference was that China, due to its large size, the regional difference in development was much more conspicuous than in Japan. In Japan, at the low wage economy stage, fragmented small farms could prosper. Only in the high wage economy, did they become an obstacle to sustainable rural development. When the whole of China was in the low wage economy, this farming structure also prospered. But once the Eastern and coastal parts have entered the high wage economy, although the Central and Western areas still remained in the low wage economy, many peasants there already started to migrate to the Eastern and coastal areas to earn higher income, leaving their land idle. Where this phenomenon has appeared, before the overcoming of other obstacles and earlier than in Japan, the fragmented small farms had already become an obstacle. This is similar to Group 2 (especially Malaysia) reviewed in Chapter 5 where much of the rural labor force has abandoned backward agriculture to move to the cities. This has given evidence to the author's indication in Chapter 1 that the low income countries (economies) still saddled with traditional agriculture are also open to the high income economy, as small peasants there shift to those rural areas already at the high wage stage, cities and abroad to earn higher income as part-time and absent farmers, thus also are up against the particular problem of adapting the agricultural sector to a high income economy.

Nevertheless, in the sense that the fragmented small farms, as long as they are tilled and the weak single household land operation receives help from villages, could prosper while overcoming other obstacles in the low wage economy, they can still be regarded as the last obstacle.

For eliminating the above-mentioned negative pecuniary externality in China, on one hand, free market forces or laissez-faire could not work, because voluntary land transfer by peasants themselves was not effective. On the other, any obligatory scheme of land transfer should provide peasants with a back-up basic social welfare, so that even in cases of closure of rural firms and economic contraction, peasants would not be squeezed out to city slums, but could always have a last resort of living in agriculture.

Thus, variable mixed economies (varying relations between the public and private sectors, and their dynamic change over time in relation to changing needs in economy and society, as reviewed in Chapter 2) should be adopted for reaching dynamic or long-term Pareto efficiency (as indicated in Chapter 3) not only in the Eastern and coastal parts where the fragmented small farms have become the last obstacle, but also in those Central and Western areas where they have become one of the obstacles, both due to the inefficient land-holding by part-time and absent small farmers.

7. Overcoming the Last Obstacle in the Chinese Model

7.1 A Large-Scale Farming and Collective–Individual Mixed Economy [1]

This section is intended to show that efficient large-scale farming could be achieved in a collective–individual mixed economy (different from the low productive large-scale farming with the combination of public ownership and operation of land under the centrally planned economy which had failed). From as early as the beginning of the 1980s, in those areas where the fragmented small farms had emerged as an obstacle, experiments on reaching *appropriate* economies of scale of land operation or large-scale farming had already been made and success achieved. 'Appropriate' in this context meant to raise the scale gradually in accordance with the extent to which the surplus peasants were transferred to non-grain agriculture and off-farm activities, rather than squeezing out peasants who were still relying on land. Cases before 1985 will be cited in order to stress the much smoother transition in comparison with the slow progress in Japan.

There have been *four principal forms* in this new land tenure system.

Dual Land System (formal form)

Self-sufficiency land (grain-rations land) was equally contracted in compact form to households on a per capita basis for planting mainly grain for self-consumption. Contractors were required to pay either (1) both a contractual

---

[1] A working paper based on the earlier version of this section has been presented in 'The Sixth European Conference on Agricultural and Rural Development in China' organized by the University of Leiden, the Netherlands (Zhou, Jian-Ming January 2000) and published by the Food and Agriculture Organization of the United Nations (Zhou, Jian-Ming 2000), with abstract to be published by CABI.

fee to the village and agricultural tax to the state, or (2) only a contractual fee (Wang & Ma 1990: 33), or (3) only an agricultural tax (CEST 1991: 33), or (4) no fee at all (Wang & Ma 1990: 33).

The use of self-sufficiency land was almost free of charge (as a basic social welfare) because the contractual fee and agricultural tax (if imposed) were low. In general, the higher the degree of development of the village's non-grain agriculture and off-farm activities, the less the payment required for using the self-sufficiency land.

Large-scale farming was not excluded on self-sufficiency land. For example, in 1987, 24 households in Yanhe Villagers' Group of Hujiadu Village of Yanqiao Township of Wuxi County of the Sunan region contracted their 72.5 mu (4.83 ha) of personal self-sufficiency land in compact form to four expert farmers to set up a farm. All of the grain was sold to the Village, which retained seeds for next year's production, then sold grain in self-sufficiency amounts to all the member households (including the four experts') at prices lower than the quota prices, and the rest to the state (the sale could be at negotiable prices). This revenue went to these experts. In so doing, although the 24 households had to buy grain, they could save time and energy and thus earn higher income in other jobs. (Hu; Yu et al. 1988: 63). By 1995, some villages in Xishan City of the Sunan region had also amalgamated self-sufficiency land for large-scale farming (Lu; Gao & Li 1995).

Responsibility land was also contracted in compact form on the conditions of fulfilling output quotas of the state, paying agricultural tax to the state and all collective fees. The contractors could dispose of the surplus products on the market.

In general, the higher the degree of development of the village's non-grain agriculture and off-farm activities, the more competitive the distribution of the responsibility land. There were four basic categories.

Category 1. In areas where non-grain agriculture and off-farm employment were *little* developed and peasants almost completely relied on grain production for living, responsibility land was equally contracted to households on a *per capita* basis.

Under the Equal Land System, the increase of population was actually encouraged and led to land redistributions which made the parcels of land smaller and more fragmented, in addition to the other problems indicated in Chapter 6.

Under the Dual Land System, the contracted land of each household was divided into two. The increase in household members would lead to the reduction of its responsibility land but an increment of its self-sufficiency land (children born beyond the family planning limit were not taken into account). A decrease in household size would lead to the increment of its responsibility land but deduction of its self-sufficiency land. Thus, as the family size changed, the area and location of the household's land remained the same, only the proportion of the two kinds of land was changed on the account. This was called *the Dual Land on Account System*. Households were thus encouraged to produce less children in order to gain more responsibility land within their total contracted land so that they could produce more to sell in the market. The economies of scale of land would at least not be lowered due to further reduction in size and fragmentation. Indeed it may even be raised. (Wang & Ma 1990: 34)

Category 2. In areas where non-grain agriculture and off-farm employment were *modestly* developed, responsibility land was equally contracted to every *labor force*. Here, some laborers already worked in non-grain agriculture and off-farm activities. But jobs there were not secure, so that they were not yet willing to transfer their responsibility land. Such areas were richer than those in Category 1, thus non-laborers (the old, children, etc.) were only entitled to self-sufficiency land but not to responsibility land so as to make the use of the latter more efficient. As the responsibility land was distributed among fewer people, each laborer could equally obtain more land so that the economies of scale were raised. (Wang & Ma 1990: 34)

Some villages set aside reserve land for both overall rural development and newly increased population. To those households without laborers, if the population grew and their self-sufficiency land was not enough, a part of the reserve land could be given to the new population. (Zhang; Liu & Zhang 1989: 34–6). To those households with laborers, the 'Dual Land on Account System' was also applied.

Category 3. In areas where non-grain agriculture and off-farm employment were *fairly* developed, responsibility land was equally contracted to every *agricultural* labor force in grain production. That implied that those laborers who had left grain agriculture but still held their permanent residence in the village were no longer entitled to responsibility land, although they still had a right to self-sufficiency land. Because only the remaining grain-producing labor force could equally contract more land, the economies of scale were further raised. (Wang & Ma 1990: 34)

Here, for adjusting the ratio of self-sufficiency land to responsibility land of the households of agricultural labor force, the Dual Land on Account System could still be applied. To the households of non-grain agriculture and off-farm laborers, if their self-sufficiency land was not enough due to population growth, a part of the reserve land could be given.

Category 4. In areas where non-grain agriculture and off-farm employment were *highly* developed, responsibility land was contracted to agricultural labor (for grain production) by *competition* in a system of tendering. Here, because many peasants wished to concentrate on non-grain agriculture and off-farm activities to earn higher incomes, it was possible for villages to contract the responsibility land to *expert* farmers. Only those who tendered for higher output could win the contract. The land was divided according to its suitability to a specific product (rice, cotton, etc.). Expert farmers, who could also be non-villagers, were given land according to their relevant expertise and ability. Economies of scale of land were raised considerably.

As the villages became rich, they could provide the newly increased population with food at quota prices, rather than self-sufficiency land.

This was regarded as the optimal standard Dual Land System, for the self-sufficiency land was distributed equally as a back-up basic social welfare, but responsibility land was contracted through competition of tendering (Wang & Ma 1990: 33–4). It combined both competition and cohesion, and both efficiency and equity.

For example, in 1982, Changyuan Brigade of Linxiang County of Hunan Province[2] arranged for 27 households which were competent and active at non-grain agriculture and off-farm activities to till self-sufficiency land only, and for 138 households which were good at farming to produce grain on responsibility land (RO 1984: 14).

Rural industry in the Sunan region began a long time before the economic reform and developed much faster since then. The implementation of the Household Contract System was completed with the Dual Land System in its preliminary form in 1983. The average area of household contracted land was 2–3 mu (0.13–0.2 ha) but divided into 7–8 parcels, forming various individual farming units (RT 1991: 23). In 1987, an able-bodied laborer was sufficient for operating a 4-mu (0.267 ha) farm earning 600 yuan, much lower than the annual per capita income of 853 yuan and that in rural industry of 1,000 yuan (Fei, Xiao-Tong 1990: 5). Peasants swarmed to non-grain agriculture and off-farm activities but were not yet willing to transfer all of their contracted land. Thus, since 1983, the preliminary form was gradually transformed into the standard type.

For example, in Wuxi County, in the autumn of 1983, an expert household contracted 22.56 mu (1.504 ha) of land in Dongge Town; in the spring of 1984, 529 mu (35.267 ha) or 77.8% of the total responsibility land in Rongnan Village of Yuqi Town were contracted to 70 laborers of 60 households, raising contracted land area per laborer from 1.16 mu (0.077 ha) to 7.56 mu (0.504 ha) and that per household from 1.57 mu (0.105 ha) to 8.8 mu (0.587 ha). In 1986, 386 mu (25.73 ha) or 77.8% of the total cultivated land of Yuanhe Village of Qinnan Township of Changshu City were

---

[2] Hunan Province is in the South-Central part of China.

contracted to an agricultural labor force of 19, with contracted land area per laborer as 20.3 mu (1.353 ha); in Wuxi and Wu counties, 115 households contracted 15–20 mu (1–1.33 ha) each, and 75 households contracted more than 20 mu (1.33 ha) each. (RT 1991: 23)

In 1986, in Wuxi County, the number of farming units contracting more than 5 mu (0.333 ha) was 4,080, holding a total of 28,800 mu (1,920 ha) or 11.09% of the total responsibility land of the County. In 1989, this number reduced to 3,820, holding a total of 34,600 mu (2,306.67 ha) or 13.8%; within this group, 6.5% or 248 farming units contracted more than 15 mu (1 ha) each, holding in total 9,260 mu (617.33 ha) or 26.6% of the total responsibility land of the group. In 1989, in Suzhou City, there were 970 farming units each contracting over 15 mu and in total 43,300 mu (2,886.67 ha) or 3.6% of all responsibility land of the City. (RT 1991: 23)

In 1989, Changshu City transformed the preliminary Dual Land System into a *mixture of Categories 2, 3 and 4* of the formal Dual Land System. Self-sufficiency land was assigned as per capita 0.5 mu (0.03 ha); the average area of responsibility land was 1.88 mu (0.125 ha) per laborer, which was not given to those who had secured off-farm jobs, but 50–100% of which could be distributed to those who had not yet secured such jobs, while an area larger than that allocated to the expert farmers via tendering (non-villagers were included with priority to villagers). By the end of the year, 11,046.4 mu (737.63 ha) or 1.06% of the total farmland had been contracted to 536 expert farmers to form 190 large-scale farms (according to the criterion of minimum area of 15 mu per laborer), with 20.7 mu (1.38 ha) per laborer as 11 times the average, and the largest over 50 mu (3.33 ha) per household. (Jiang, Zhong-Yi et al. 1992c: 74–6, 80)

During 1990–94, both the area under the Dual Land System and its percentage in the total household contracted land in China rose, and this system was also adopted in the Western part where non-grain agriculture and off-farm production were less developed than in the Eastern and Central parts, as Table 7.1 shows. As revealed in Table 7.2, the area of self-sufficiency land decreased, and that of responsibility land increased, leading to a lower ratio of self-sufficiency land to responsibility land, and implying that land was more efficiently used. Table 7.3 further indicates that, in terms of the methods of contracting responsibility land under the Dual Land System, both the percentages on a per capita basis and via tendering rose but that on the per laborer basis declined, suggesting not only the population pressure on land, but also an increase in market competition.

Active education of villagers was necessary since their majority agreement was needed to implement the Dual Land System (Jiang, Zhong-Yi et al. 1992b: 68).

For example, three villages in Wu County (Wuxian) of the Sunan region began to establish large-scale farming in 1987 and 1988. The village leaders started by talking with the villagers about the importance of large-scale farming. At least some villagers openly opposed it in all the three villages. In village 1, only one or two households did so because they would lose responsibility land, but the leaders obliged them to give it up with the rest of the villagers. In village 2, many were against it but were persuaded to accept it. In village 3, opposition was stronger and initially only 15% of the farmers gave up their responsibility land. In this case, a gradual approach was adopted. The leaders then took back all the arable land and divided it into two consolidated portions for self-sufficiency land and responsibility land respectively. Self-sufficiency land was allocated in one consolidated parcel to households on a per capita basis by drawing lots. The responsibility land was distributed to large-scale farmers immediately in villages 1 and 2 in 1987 or 1988, but gradually over the following years in village 3 as other farmers also gave up responsibility land voluntarily or under collective persuasion. (Prosterman; Hanstad & Li July 1996: 15–6). This was in

Table 7.1 Area under the Dual Land System in China 1990–94 (1,000,000 ha)

	1990	Of total household contracted land	1994	Of total household contracted land
Country	37	38.2%	42	47.8%
Eastern	15	–	14	–
Central	16	–	20	–
Western	5	–	7	–

Sources: CEST 1991: 34; 1996: 39.

Table 7.2 Areas of Self-Sufficiency Land and Responsibility Land under the Dual Land System in China 1990–94 (1,000,000 ha)

1990			1994		
Self-suffi- ciency land	Responsi- bility land	S:R	Self-suffi- ciency land	Responsi- bility land	S:R
18	36	1:2	13	29	1:2.23

Sources: CEST 1991: 33; 1996: 39.

Table 7.3 Methods of Contracting Responsibility Land under the Dual Land System in China 1990–94 (1,000,000 ha)

Per capita				Per laborer				Tendering			
Area		%		Area		%		Area		%	
1990	1994	1990	1994	1990	1994	1990	1994	1990	1994	1990	1994
15.5	19	63.9	68	7.3	8	29.9	25	1.5	2	6.2	7

Sources: CEST 1991: 34; 1996: 39.

Category 4.

Leasing System

The village may also lease land in compact form to expert farmers via tendering for higher monetary rent, which was different from contracting output. However, such a leasing still stipulated that the lessees should produce a certain type and amount of products (e.g., grain) and the village had the duty to provide services, hence it was still a kind of village—household dual level operation of land. This was distinctive from typical leasing for monetary rent under which the lessees may produce whatever they wish and the lessor did not have the duty to provide services. A village usually leased its reserve land, although some other land might also take this form. Here, the land under leasing was a kind of responsibility land too, hence a special form under the Dual Land System.

For example, Bai Village of Baicun Township of Dingxiang County of Shanxi Province had 3,073 mu (204.87 ha) of farmland. It reserved 112 mu (7.47 ha) of saline-alkali land for leasing to produce sorghum in the mid-1980s. The contract was for one year and renewable. The rent was 8,000 yuan in total, 71.43 yuan per mu (0.067 ha) in 1987, but raised in 1988 to 11,000 yuan, 98.21 yuan per mu, by tendering among six farmers representing 20 households. (Wu; Xu; Tian & Bai 1988: 36—8)

In contrast, Yujiazhuang Village of Shoulu Township of the above-mentioned County had exhausted its reserve land. It then divided all land into five classes according to productivity, and leased 290 mu (19.33 ha) of the highest class to expert households with more labor to produce grain, the rent being 80—100 yuan per mu. (Wu; Xu; Tian & Bai 1988: 37)

Single Land System

In areas where non-grain agriculture and off-farm production were *very highly* developed, many peasants secured their jobs there, and were not only *voluntary* but also felt the *imperative* to formally transfer both their self-sufficiency land and responsibility land to expert farmers.3 They thereby

---

3 The terms of 'little', 'modestly', 'fairly', 'highly' and 'very highly' are used to refer to the degrees of development of non-grain agriculture and off-farm activities. The reference for measuring them would be the proportion of labor force inside and outside grain agriculture, recalling that in monsoon Asia, both the first and second transitions are measured by the share of labor force in agriculture, industry and services according to Oshima as introduced in Chapter 1. As for which ratio of labor force inside and outside grain production corresponds to which

left (grain) agriculture although most of them still lived in rural areas, even in the same villages. Their voluntary action was, however, also based on the active promotion of the villages, which sold them grain for self-consumption at quota prices and might also allow them to keep some family plots for producing vegetables to accommodate the peasant tradition of not buying them in the market. These measures were both an incentive for them to hand in land and a basic social welfare provision. The expert farmers could operate much larger areas of land than under the Dual Land System, upon which they were to fulfil tasks for the state and collective and could then dispose of the residual for their own living and on the market. There was no more division between self-sufficiency land and responsibility land. 'Dual Land' became 'Single Land'. (Wang & Ma 1990: 36). The Single Land could also be either contracted for output, or leased for monetary rent, via tendering to expert farmers.

In the above-cited example in Wu County of the Sunan region which established a Dual Land System in 1987 or 1988, some farmers then voluntarily gave up their self-sufficiency land for allocation to large-scale farmers in all the three villages. In one village, about 20% of households did so. Two villages offered 450 kg of paddy rice per year at about 50% of the market price for each mu of self-sufficiency land given up by households. (Prosterman; Hanstad & Li July 1996: 16)

By 1988, in the Sunan region, some other villages, even townships, had gathered all their land to be contracted through tendering to some expert farmers (Fei, Xiao-Tong 1990: 6).

The Dual Land System started in Qianzhou Village of Qianzhou Town of Xishan City of the Sunan region at the end of the 1980s. As off-farm employment quickly developed, it became no longer suitable, since rural firms had to close for half a month in each of the two busiest farming periods, thus seriously affecting their business. In a 1991 referendum, all villagers unanimously agreed to give up self-sufficiency land. Thus, all the land of the Village was joined to form a collective farm, which contracted

---

of these terms, not only do they vary among localities, but also systematic data are unavailable. But they could be observed in case studies, as cited in this chapter. According to such ratios, local officials and peasants decided to adopt which category of the Dual Land System or Single Land System. Thus Chinese literature uses these terms as rough representations of the degrees of development of non-grain agriculture and off-farm employment in general. To gather systematic data and make econometric analysis would be desirable, but is beyond the physical and financial possibility the author has had in Italy. Here by using these rough terms, it suffices to make a comparison with the Japanese model under which land has still been largely held by part-time and absent farmers, while under the Chinese model, as more and more peasants left grain agriculture, increasing amount of land could be transferred to the remaining full-time farmers for more efficient use.

land to seven member households, on the conditions that they sell 575 kg of rice and 125 kg of wheat per mu at quota prices each year to the Village, in return for being able to dispose of the residuals. The Village then sold grain to the state according to quotas, and 147 kg of rice and 28 kg of wheat to each of the other villagers at prices even lower than the state-subsidized prices to city residents. Then, Mixiangqiao Village and Lidong Village of Dongxiang Town, Tan Village of Chaqiao Town and Taoshu Village of Xuelang Town also adopted the Single Land System. As a result, rural firms now could shorten considerably or even put an end to the closing. Unified seed supply, plant protection and agricultural mechanization were achieved and high-yielding varieties and advanced technologies introduced, in which Qianzhou Village became a demonstration village in the Town. The net income of farming households (whose laborers were usually husband and wife) in Mixiangqiao Village reached 22,000–25,000 yuan, 100% higher than that of households in off-farm activities. (Lu; Li & Zou 1996)

In the areas where local off-farm activities were very highly developed, the Single Land System could also be set up directly upon the abolition of the Equal Land System.

For example, Matou Village was in the suburbs of Zhongshan City of Guangdong Province. In 1984, it had 60 households, 170 laborers, 132 mu (8.8 ha) of land for grain, 38 mu (2.53 ha) for vegetables, 8.4 mu (0.56 ha) for fishery and 40 mu (2.67 ha) for fruit trees. The local industry and services were very highly developed and could absorb all the surplus labor force, but peasants were still unwilling to transfer their farmland. The Village then changed the Equal Land System directly to the Single Land System by assigning all land to expert farmer Zhi-Hua Huang's household, and achieved the agreement of other households by offering to sell them grain at quota prices, and allowing them to keep some family plots for producing self-consumed vegetables. Zhi-Hua Huang was to hand in 600 kg of grain per mu to the Village to fulfil its obligations to the state and sell grain to other villagers for self-consumption. Huang could dispose of the surplus as he chose. (Lu & Li 1987: 33)

Shunyi County of Beijing Municipality4 started the Equal Land System at the end of 1983 with three-year contracts [with some villages implementing the preliminary Dual Land System in 1985 (Zhong & Cai 1997: 54)], each household operating 3–5 mu (0.2–0.3 ha) of fragmented land. Although over 70% of the rural labor force shifted to non-grain agriculture and off-farm production, personal transfer of land was scarce. It diverted profits of TVEs to subsidize costs on grain production of all peasant

---

4 Beijing is in the Northeast part of China.

households, 50 yuan per mu per annum, but the money was simply used on consumption and little output was stimulated. Thus, in the autumn of 1986, taking the opportunity offered by the renewal of contracts, the County implemented the Single Land System. It first made experiments in the developed areas between August 1986 and August 1987, then popularized this in most other areas by the autumn of 1989. New contracts were not given to those who had gained stable jobs and income from non-grain agriculture and off-farm production, or been engaged in house work (cooking, cleaning the house, etc.) for a long time, or were unable to till land. Those who were not good at grain-production but had not yet got other stable jobs were either recruited into TVEs, or into activities in diversified cropping and non-crop agriculture (for vegetables, fruits, fish, cattle, chickens, pigs, etc.) newly created for them by the special investment of townships and villages. Those part-time farmers who were neither active in grain production nor willing to give up land were required to meet conditions for carrying out large-scale farming. As a result, those who could not do so voluntarily handed land back. More than enough grain was guaranteed to be sold at prices lower than the market levels to those laborers who were no longer engaged in grain production and their family members for self-consumption. Direct subsidies were abolished. Land for grain production was successfully transferred to the expert farmers who earned higher income not through direct subsidies but by their own economic performance. (Pei, Chang-Hong et al. 1992: 87–9, 92)

However, in general, the Dual Land System was a transitory stage between the Equal Land System and the Single Land System, as rural industrialization proceeded and could absorb more and more surplus labor force. Surpassing this stage may not be viable. For example, in 1984, Zijing Village of Jiangling County of Hubei Province established three companies, each for agriculture, industry, livestock and fish farming respectively and each took about one third of the total labor force. It implemented the Single Land System by subsidizing those who left land to buy grain at market prices and those who contracted larger areas of land with the profits of village enterprises of 41,000 yuan per year. Thus 77% of over 400 laborers left the land altogether, and farmland per laborer was expanded from 3.8 mu (0.25 ha) to 16.5 mu (1.1 ha). In order to get more direct subsidies, some households contracted 60–100 mu (4–6.67 ha) of land, 30 mu (2 ha) per laborer, exceeding their operating ability. In 1986, however, two major enterprises were closed due to unprofitability and other enterprises had to rationalize. Thus, on one hand, half of the workers became surplus and had to return to agriculture; on the other, an end of subsidies from the enterprises made farmers unable to maintain large-scale farming. In 1987, the Village had to change to the Dual Land System, which proved to be suitable. (Li, Wan-Dao 1988: 57–8. Peng; Zhang & Yang 1988: 17–8)

By 1996 the Single Land System was still not widespread in the country.

Corporate-Holding System

The *typical form* of the Corporate-Holding System was one whereby households transferred their land contracted under the Equal Land System to the village in exchange for land shares. The village, as a collective corporation, contracted land through tendering in compact form to expert farmers who were to fulfil tasks for the state and collective and could then dispose of the surplus products as they saw fit. The village then distributed a part of the revenue to land shareholders as dividends. The village also sold grain at quota prices, and made available family plots for producing vegetables to ordinary households for self-consumption. These households could then concentrate on non-grain agriculture and off-farm activities. Land shareholders could not withdraw land physically from the village but could transfer (including bequeath) the shares in financial form. A change in family size of the land shareholders could not affect their number of shares, which discouraged rather than encouraged births. (Chen, Dong-Qiang 1996: 23–4)

This was similar to the functions of a modern capital shareholding corporation whose shareholders can earn dividends and sell shares in the market but cannot claim reimbursement for them by the corporation (as already analyzed in Proposal 5.1 in Chapter 5). The major difference between the Chinese system and the proposed system is that, under the former, land is collectively owned but was previously contracted to households equally, hence the title Corporate-*Holding* System, while under the latter, land is privately owned, hence Corporate-*Ownership* System.

For example, Shatou Village of Jun-an Town of Shunde County of Guangdong Province initially contracted farmland of 460 mu (30.67 ha) equally to over 600 households, each holding about 0.767 mu (0.051 ha), yielding only 2–3 tons of sugarcane per mu. At the beginning of 1986, in response to popular demand, the Village took back the land, invested 210,000 yuan and assigned special farmers to plant lizhi (or litchi, lychee - a fruit). In the same year, the revenue from the intercrops already reached 210,000 yuan, over twice the previous income of sugarcane. In the lizhi harvesting year, the land would be contracted to expert farmers via tendering. A part of the revenue was to be distributed to the original households according to their previously contracted areas. (Lu & Li 1987: 34)

Although this example was about fruit production, the same approach was applicable to grain. For instance, by 1995, 70% of peasants in Nanhai City of Guangdong Province had given up their contracted land, accounting for about 45% of the total contracted land, to the villages to be contracted to expert farmers, in exchange for revenue (dividends) to their land shares (PD

[1995] 1996: 51). The expert farmers who contracted larger areas of land could earn an income higher than that of the off-farm workers (Yang, Yong-Zhe 1995: 16).

Inverse Leasing or Contracting (fan zu dao bao) as an *untypical form*. The original contractors under the Equal Land System leased/contracted their land to the village which paid rent or gave grain for self-consumption to them, and then leased/contracted the land in compact form to expert farmers for large-scale farming. Since, in so doing, it was the original contractors who leased/contracted their land to the village, it was called Inverse Leasing or Contracting. (Chen, Dong-Qiang 1996: 24). It may be regarded as an *untypical form* of the Corporate-Holding System, because the rent - or grain for self-consumption - given by the village to the original contractors would be a part of the gross revenue of the new lessees/contractors as large-scale farmers, just as dividends for land shares under the typical form. This system has been implemented in Leqing City and other areas of Zhejiang Province, Linquan County of Fuyang Prefecture and Dawang Town of Nanqiao District of Chuzhou City of Anhui Province (Wu & Hu 1995: 43. Huang; Xu; Zhang & Ni 1996: 60. Qin & Wang 1995: 43. Fan & Zhou 1994: 16).

The Corporate-Holding System is actually also a kind of Single Land System (although a special one) and its implementation requires a high development of rural industrialization to absorb surplus labor. Thus, relatively fewer regions have adopted it.

Table 7.4 shows that during 1986–90, the number of parcels contracted per household already decreased, while the area per parcel (except for Central China) and the area contracted per household still reduced; but during 1990–92 (numbers in bold), the number of parcels contracted per household declined significantly, the area per parcel grew to be beyond the 1986 levels, and the area contracted per household increased to the 1986 levels (in whole and Eastern China) or beyond (in Central China), although still diminished in Western China, suggesting a general improvement of fragmentation as a result of implementing the above-stated forms of large-scale farming. Similarly, Table 7.5 indicates that the percentage of the smallest-scale farms (under 0.333 ha) in land contracted per individual household augmented during 1986–90, but fell in 1990–92 (numbers in bold) to even below the 1986 levels.

The implementation of these four principal forms of the new land tenure system has given evidence to the author's surmise in Chapter 1 that if the part-time and absent small farmers could be guaranteed with a back-up basic social welfare and rendered appropriate remuneration to relieve their rational concern over direct interests in security, then some of them would be voluntary to transfer their inefficiently held land in various suitable forms to the full-time farmers for effective use, while others would still be disinclined

The Chinese Model

*Table 7.4 Progress in Overcoming Fragmentation in China 1986–92 ***

Whole country	Area contracted per household (ha)	No. of parcels contracted per household	Area per parcel (ha)
1986	0.466	5.85	0.08
1988	0.446	5.67	0.079
1990	0.42	5.52	0.076
1992	0.466	**3.16**	**0.147**
Eastern			
1986	0.333	5.32	0.063
1988	0.32	5.19	0.062
1990	0.306	5.03	0.061
1992	0.333	**3.35**	**0.099**
Central			
1986	0.666	5.20	0.128
1988	0.653	5.07	0.129
1990	0.62	4.70	0.132
1992	0.806	**4.58**	**0.176**
Western			
1986	0.8	7.60	0.105
1988	0.706	7.10	0.099
1990	0.646	6.80	0.095
1992	0.466	**2.15**	**0.217**

* Samples from 7,983 villages of over 200 counties in 29 provinces, municipalities and autonomous regions (without Tibet Autonomous Region and Taiwan Province of China5).
Source: CEST 1993: 48.

5 Tibet Autonomous Region is in the Southwesternmost, and Taiwan Province (island) Southeast part of China.

*Table 7.5 Land Contracted per Individual Household in
China 1986—92 (in percentage)* *

Country	%	Under 0.333 ha	0.4– 0.666 ha	0.733– 1.0 ha	1.066– 1.333 ha	1.4– 3.33 ha	3.4 ha and over
1986		51.1	–	–	–	–	–
1988		52.7	–	–	–	–	–
1990		54.2	–	–	–	–	–
1992	100	**48.0**	31.2	11.3	5.7	3.4	0.4
Eastern							
1986		61.7	–	–	–	–	–
1988		65.4	–	–	–	–	–
1990		66.2	–	–	–	–	–
1992	100	**60.4**	25.2	10.4	3.3	0.6	0.1
Central							
1986		30.8	–	–	–	–	–
1988		38.0	–	–	–	–	–
1990		40.4	–	–	–	–	–
1992	100	**26.1**	44.7	12.0	8.2	7.8	1.2
Western							
1986		51.7	–	–	–	–	–
1988		50.4	–	–	–	–	–
1990		51.8	–	–	–	–	–
1992	100	**42.9**	32.7	12.0	7.4	4.8	0.2

*   Samples from 7,983 villages of over 200 counties in 29 provinces, municipalities and
autonomous regions (without Tibet and Taiwan).

Source: CEST 1993: 47.

to do so even though land property rights have been well defined and market transactions facilitated, which shows that at least some part-time and absent small farmers are not so rational to the society's and their own fundamental interests; and accordingly proper land tenure systems in variable mixed economies should be devised to effect such a transfer.

Selection of Expert Farmers

As above-presented, the selection of expert farmers to be large-scale farmers was through tendering. Some specific aspects of this mechanism follow. Chapter 2 indicated that as a result of at least 40 centuries of development, farmers in monsoon Asia have mastered sophisticated intensive farming techniques, even if they might not have attended formal schools, although schooling is important. Villagers usually recognize who are expert farmers and who are not. The process of tendering to fulfil contracts also helps to identify expertise. The more competent can contract more land. Priority was given to villagers, but non-villagers could also be selected.6

The conditions of contracts stipulated not only the output and varieties of grain and other products to be fulfilled for the state and village, but also requirements for the maintenance and improvement of land quality.

For example, in 1983, noticing the reduction of agriculture due to the development of off-farm activities, Zhangjiabian Town of Zhongshan City of Guangdong Province decided to investigate. They found that 90% of peasants were only willing to keep a small amount of land. Thus, it called for tenders to contract 56,000 mu (3,733.33 ha) of grain and sugarcane land. The amount of land allocated depended on the ability and willingness of tenderers. Due to shortage of local agricultural labor, 16,000 mu (1,066.67 ha) were not taken up. The Town therefore called for further tenders from outsiders, and 223 outside expert farmers were contracted land. The largest contracted area by one household was 448 mu (29.87 ha), and the smallest 30 mu (2 ha). (GT 1988: 18)

In order to avoid re-fragmentation of farms, Nanwen Village of Dayong

---

6 Nolan (1988: 127) finds plenty of press reports that rich areas in agricultural labor shortages attracted workers from distant poor parts to take over land contracts, especially in suburban areas of big cities in Eastern China. Oi (1989: 191–2) cites an example that an agricultural research station in Jiangsu Province contracted land to a peasant from Hebei Province to produce a total of 13,750 kg of grain, with a minimum of 225 kg per mu. The station provided him with access to fertilizer, insecticide, and other agricultural inputs; technical support; and investment. He produced 50,000 kg and yielded a net profit of over 50,000 yuan in just one year. This profitable arrangement prompted him to sell his newly-built house in his home village, build one at the station, and concentrate on grain production.

Town in the same region and same period stipulated in tendering that the smallest contractable area was limited to 10 mu (0.67 ha), but that several households could make a joint tender (GT 1988: 18).

The conditions set for expert farmers to contract responsibility land under the Dual Land System since 1985 in Luyang Town of Kunshan County of Suzhou City of the Sunan region were that they should be able-bodied; with a certain educational level, scientific and technological knowledge, and practical experience; they should be fond of farming, competent in operation, good at management, and hardworking. In 1986, the candidates were short-listed first by villagers' groups and villages, then selected by the Town. Compared with heads of the 29 households in 1985, of those of the 40 selected in 1986, 70% were under 40 years old (12% higher than in 1985); 32.5% had been educated at junior middle school level and over (1.5% higher); 52% were former production team directors, accountants, agricultural technicians, or mechanics (who were usually more competent than ordinary peasants) (1% higher). (Shi & Zhang 1987: 24). In 1993, facing the situation where the attendance rate of senior middle schooling was 15.36%, and only 42.41% of labor force was educated to junior middle school and over in the rural areas of the six counties and cities within the jurisdiction of Suzhou City, the governments stipulated that new contractors must receive special training and obtain a 'Green Certificate' (eligibility to be farmers). Thus, training and lectures on technologies and policies have been provided regularly by relevant government organs, grain administrations, machinery and electricity stations, credit cooperatives, supply and marketing cooperatives, etc. for large-scale farmers. Associations of large-scale farmers also periodically organized live demonstrations and exchanges of experience. (Sun, Yong-Zheng 1996: 24)

The length of contracts. The contracts ranged from one to 10 years and were renewable (Prosterman; Hanstad & Li July 1996: 25). Although the state stipulated in 1984 that the length was to be extended to 15 years and, in 1993, to 30 years, local officials normally preferred a shorter period for the responsibility land in Category 4 of the Dual Land System and Single Land System, so that they could use the renewal as an incentive to the contractors. The contract could be either stopped or dis-renewed, and the contractor would even be punished if, with the exception of natural causes, the farming season were missed, fields desolated, land quality reduced, or superior varieties mixed with the inferior ones and degraded, and the contract therefore not fulfilled (Shen, Shou-Ye 1987: 32).

Attention has to be paid to the possibility that short-term contracts may affect the incentive of the contractors to make long-term improvements to the land. However, there were offsetting factors. (1) Because the contract was renewable, the incentive of the present contractor might be stimulated so as to earn a good reputation and win the next contract. This was different from the situation under the Equal Land System in which the actually short period of contract discouraged long-term investment, because the parcels would almost certainly be redistributed to others due to population change, rather than being kept or renewed. (2) In order to win the next contract, the present contractor and his competitors must tender for higher output, or rent, by proposing improved measures conducive to land fertility, and, once won, implement them. (3) The basic requirement of contractors was that the land fertility should not be reduced. This could be disciplined even by a short-term contract and thus provided the basis for the long-term use of the land. Then, for large long-term infrastructure construction, the village could rely on TVEs for their financial strength and collectively mobilizing and organizing peasants, more than on the individual contractors whose financial and physical abilities were relatively weak. The village could also invest the revenue (or rent) paid by the winner in long-term improvements to the land. Actually, even large-scale farms in monsoon Asia are quite tiny compared with those in Europe and the USA. Investment by a farmer, no matter how long the term, never reaches beyond the geographic boundaries of his own parcel of land. Construction of infrastructure for the whole village was dependent on collective action. (4) If the winner proved unable to operate a large land unit as he had expected, he would not be obliged to hold the contract for too long. (5) A short-term contract to be won via tendering would also be helpful in controlling corruption of village officials who might have interest in giving a long-term contract to a relative/friend even if his performance could not justify it. (6) How long a contract should be is not yet concluded but still being tried through active local experiments. If short-term contracts were indeed to prove harmful, local officials/peasants would have an interest in prolonging them.

For instance, in the above-mentioned one-year lease of 112 mu (7.47 ha) of saline-alkali land of Bai Village of Baicun Township of Dingxiang County of Shanxi Province, in 1987, one of the lessees, Wan-Nian Gao, operated 56 mu (3.73 ha), applied 50 kg of chemical fertilizer and one cart of superior chicken manure per mu, and reached a sorghum yield of 375 kg per mu, 2.5 times the 1982 level. In 1988, four households of Gui-Lan Gao et al. won the contract and immediately renovated the land. They decided to build a ditch of 112 meters to transform it into an irrigated land, apply 100 kg of chemical fertilizer and 50 kg of farm manure per mu, to raise the yield to 500 kg per mu. (Wu; Xu; Tian & Bai 1988: 38)

Yang Town of Shunyi County of Beijing started the preliminary Dual Land System in 1985. In changing to the Single Land System in 1986, its Tianjiayin Village first introduced in a *one-year* lease system via tendering. Its success made it possible for the Town in the early 1990s, and the County in 1995, to popularize it in suitable villages. By 1996, 21 of the total 27 villages of the Town had adopted it on 26,000 mu (1,733.3 ha), or 65% of 40,000 mu (2,666.67 ha) of the total grain land of the Town. (Zhong & Cai 1997: 54–6)

In their practices, tenders were called for each year on 18 August. Grain land was divided into compact units of 7 mu (0.467 ha), 15 mu or 30 mu (2 ha) depending on which village. According to the quality and distance, a bottom (minimum) contract fee (or rent), of 100–200 yuan per mu, for each unit was announced three days earlier. A tenderer could be one or several households, and, in order to tender, should pay a deposit of 300–500 yuan, which would not be reimbursed if the tenderer failed to till the land after winning the contract. The units were contracted to the tenderers offering the highest contract fees. About 60–70% of households could get land, the rest would seek other jobs or be offered posts in firms by the villages. (Zhong & Cai 1997: 55)

The contractors must pay the contract fee (on average 265 yuan per mu), deposit for selling output in quota (30 yuan per mu), production costs on unified collective services for seeds, fertilizer, pesticide, machinery, plowing, irrigating, harvesting, land clearing, etc. (90 yuan per mu) within two days of winning the contracts, and would reap the economic results after fulfilling them. Because some 385 yuan were already inputted, contractors were naturally motivated to gain rather than lose, which encouraged them to learn and apply more science and technology, carry out intensive farming and increase investment. As a result, there was indeed a surplus. For example, in 1996, the average yield of grain was 750 kg (double cropping), gross income 1,100 yuan, and net income 500–600 yuan for each mu. More than 10 years of experience have not only shown that no short-term or predatory behavior occurred, but also, to the contrary, more land was efficiently used. For example, in 1987, Tianjiayin Village still had 400 mu (26.67 ha) of wasteland, which were then all turned to farmland via tendering for the one-year contracts. Agriculture was further strengthened by the village collectives through feeding back the contract fees. By 1996, the collectives of the Town owned 406 motor-pumped wells, 168 sets of spraying irrigation facilities, and 23,808 kilowatt of agricultural machinery power, 0.595 kilowatt per mu of grain land, with a total investment of over 45 million yuan, mainly from the contract fees. The collective water, electricity and machinery services charged lower fees. For example, in Tianjiayin Village, the cost of irrigating 1 mu of land was 20 yuan, but the collective only charged 10 yuan, the rest being borne by the contract fees. Hence 'from the peasants and to the peasants'. (Zhong & Cai 1997: 55–6)

Major Problems

The major problems discussed in this context concern the process of promoting the new land tenure system, rather than the general aspects of agricultural and rural development of China.

Both the problems of not promoting large-scale farming where land was already inefficiently held by part-time and absent small farmers, *and* of promoting it prematurely have occurred. While in the early 1980s, the former presented the main problem (Gao & Liu 1984: 21), in the 1990s, the latter outweighed it.

As early as in 1984, as Oi (1989: 192) cites, Chinese journals already criticized the wrongdoings of some cadres who created large specialized households, such as 5,000-kg-grain-producing ones, by arbitrarily reducing the already meager holdings of the other peasants in the village while the local off-farm activities were not yet developed.

In many areas where rural firms could not yet absorb enough peasants, quite a few villages, under the pretext of 'introducing market mechanism', without the majority agreement of villagers, enforced Category 4 of the Dual Land System by reducing self-sufficiency land and enlarging responsibility land, and allocating the latter through tendering, so as to charge more village reserved fees. Those peasants who could neither win responsibility land nor find jobs in other lines had to subsist on the tiny plots of self-sufficiency land allocated to them. This caused strong resentment. (CEST 1993: 46; 1996: 39)

One extreme case was reported. Hougu Village of Shendan Town of Dengta County of Liaoyang City of Liaoning Province[7] had 2,100 persons and 5,028 mu (335.2 ha) of farmland. In 1983, each household contracted land and had gained considerably from this. In 1993, however, despite the requirement of further prolonging contracts by the central government, the Village, without seeking the agreement of peasants, took back all the land and implemented a mixture of partial Dual Land System and partial Single Land System. Only 28 peasants obtained self-sufficiency land, while a few farmers contracted all the responsibility land, as decided by the leader personally. The contract fee per mu for self-sufficiency land and dryland was as high as 120–130 yuan, while that for the profitable wetland only 40 yuan. Most peasants had no land to till, and had to sub-rent in land from these 'large-scale farmers' with high rent, or rent in land at other villages, or do odd jobs, resulting in a steady decline in their living standard year after year.

---

[7] Liaoning Province is in the Northeasternmost part of China and coastal.

(LD 1996). In this case, corruption might be involved.

Such wrongdoings attracted the attention of the media. The government has repeatedly stressed the *appropriateness* of promoting large-scale farming following the degree to which peasants have found jobs in other sectors, established new regulations and laws and launched campaigns to combat corruption. For example, on 7 July 1997, the then Vice Prime Minister Rong-Ji Zhu (Zhu, Rong-Ji 1997) publicly calls on provincial leaders to stop wrong practices in some rural areas whereby responsibility land was withdrawn from peasants and re-distributed via tendering for the purpose of charging high contract fees, regardless of whether surplus peasants could find other jobs or not, thus causing increased financial burden on peasants.

Trend of the Evolution of the Land Tenure System

The evolutionary trend of the land tenure system towards overcoming the fragmented small farms as the last obstacle imposed by the monsoon in China may be from the Equal Land System, through the Dual Land System (including Leasing System), towards the Single Land System (including Leasing System and Corporate-Holding System). The necessary condition is the development of rural industrialization to absorb surplus peasants. The Dual Land System is more significant. Self-sufficiency land equally contracted to all households on a per capita basis would serve as a back-up basic social welfare or last resort for peasants' living and remove their major concern in case they lost jobs in off-farm activities as indicated in Chapter 6, thus is inherently desirable. This back-up basic social welfare provided by the Dual Land System does not need peasants to buy grain for self-consumption, while that afforded by the Single Land System requires them to buy it albeit at prices below the higher market levels. Meanwhile, the Dual Land System could also raise economies of scale of land even in those areas where rural non-grain agriculture and off-farm activities are less developed, as responsibility land, i.e, land beyond self-sufficiency need, is to be contracted to everyone, every labor force, every agricultural labor force, or expert farmers following the development of non-grain agriculture and off-farm activities. Thus it would be more suitable to China and would last for a longer time.

At the beginning of the 1980s, the state had already raised the issue of promoting appropriate large-scale farming wherever relevant conditions were ripe (Yang, Yong-Zhe 1995: 17). In 1982 and 1983, the state and Xiao-Ping Deng himself supported the emerging large household contractors (CCCPC [1982] 1992: 169. Deng, Xiao-Ping [1983] 1992: 184). In 1984, the state called for the concentration of land towards the expert farmers (CCCPC [1984] 1992: 224). Practices across the country have shown that the *ideal* conditions for appropriate large-scale farming by expert farmers (i.e., Category 4 under the Dual Land System, Leasing System, Single Land System and Corporate-Holding System) were that 70% of rural labor force have shifted to non-grain agriculture and off-farm activities, generating 80% of the local revenue and 90% of peasant households' income; the village had strong economic strength, competent leadership and an overall service system to farmers. However, not many rural areas could meet these desirable conditions. Thus, as long as some households were no more interested in grain production, a *basic* condition was already present, whereby the village could mobilize or oblige the transfer of their land to the full-time farmers, rather than relying passively on their voluntary personal transfer. (Yang, Yong-Zhe 1995: 17). This could be done even before adopting the Dual Land System throughout the whole village. Here, opposed to Schultz's reasoning introduced in Chapter 1, increasing farm size of the remaining full-time farmers in order to apply the tenet 'that the costs of agricultural products fall as the size of the production unit in agriculture increases' is quite logical. As the local conditions gradually approach the ideal ones, economies of scale of land operation could be raised accordingly.

As Table 7.1 shows, by 1994, still less than 50% of total household contracted land had adopted the Dual Land System. In other words, more than half were still under the Equal Land System (mainly in the Western part). This is primarily because both the urban and rural population of China was increasing during 1949–99 respectively, as Table 7.6 shows, while farmland area was decreasing and the speed of rural industrialization especially in the Central and Western parts has not been fast enough to absorb the surplus peasants. According to a national survey, by 31 October 1996, per capita cultivated land of China was 1.59 mu (0.106 ha), smaller than half of that of the world. In 12 provinces of the Northeasternmost, Northwest, Northwesternmost, Southwest and Southwesternmost, per capita cultivated land was larger than 2 mu (0.133 ha), but the natural conditions there are worse and grain yields were lower than normal. By contrast, in four provinces of the Southeast and Beijing, Shanghai, and Tianjin municipalities, 8 grain yields were higher, but per capita cultivated land was smaller than 1 mu. (National Survey [1996] 2000). The Dual Land System was popularized generally in the areas with per capita farmland of 1.2 mu (0.08 ha); where it was smaller than 1 mu, responsibility land (if divided out from self-sufficiency land) would be too small to be profitable (CEST 1996: 39). Even in the Eastern part, although on one hand its rural industrialization was more rapid, on the other it also held the densest population, which would certainly

---

8 Tianjin Municipality is in the Northeast part of China and coastal.

Table 7.6 Postwar Urban–Rural Population Changes in China and Japan (1,000 persons)

China	Urban (cities & towns)	%	Rural	%	Total	%
1949	57,650	10.64	484,020	89.36	541,670	100
1995	351,740	29.04	859,470	70.96	1,211,210	100
1999	388,920	30.89	870,170	69.11	1,259,090	100
Japan	Cities		Towns & villages *			
1945	20,022	27.81	51,976	72.19	71,998	100
1995	98,009	78.05	27,561	21.95	125,570	100

* Division of population between rural towns and villages unavailable.

Sources: CSY 1991: 61; 1999: 111. SBNESDC [1999] 2000. JSY 2000: 36.

constrain the development of large-scale farming. For example, at the beginning of the 1980s, some densely populated villages in Wuxi County of the Sunan region already lacked responsibility land to be contracted to laborers (Prosterman; Hanstad & Li July 1996: 20). The criterion for appropriate large-scale farming varied across the country, but many regions determined it as about 15 mu per laborer. In 1994, the area under appropriate large-scale farming was 90,844,500 mu (6,056,300 ha) and accounted for only 6.5% of the total farmland area of the country. (CEST 1996: 40)

Nevertheless, some effective ways to overcome the last obstacle have been found. Where they were properly implemented, quick progress was achieved. For example, by the end of 1986, of 2,347 villages in the peripheral plain of Beijing, 30% or 706 villages had carried out large-scale farming; under further government intervention, in just two months of 1987, an additional 45% or 1,051 villages did so, reaching 75% of the total; in Shunyi County, 94% did so (Meng, Fan-Qi 1988: 13). By 1996, in the Yangtze River Delta, large-scale farming units had become the backbone of agricultural production. In Zhejiang Province, two-thirds of grain in state quotas was sold by large-scale farmers. (Shi; Zhu & Zhang 1996).[9]

As population growth may reach its peak sometime in the 21st century and then decline, and as the development in the Central and Western parts has been accelerating since the early 1990s, the prospect of overcoming this obstacle should be bright. By comparison, in Japan, the population in towns and villages has decreased during 1945–95 as Table 7.6 demonstrates and off-farm activities were already highly developed by 1960. Thus hardly any excuse could be found for the persistence of the last obstacle in Japan.

In 1993, in order to overcome the frequent redistribution of contracted land due to changes in family size and the use of farmland for housing construction, the state stipulated that at the start of the second round of contracts (1994–2024), farmland might be redistributed, but persons born over the family planning limit were not eligible to be given land; housing construction was to be regulated and standardized. Then, the land of a household would not be reduced with a decrease in family size (thus

---

[9] Nolan (1988: 95, 147, 184) also notes that the government encouraged the gradual concentration of farmland to expert farmers as early as in the first half of the 1980s. In those areas where off-farm employment has absorbed surplus peasants, a high degree of concentration in land operation emerged, fragmentation was overcome and mechanization reached. An example is cited by Oi (1999: 622) that as early as in the 1980s, Daqiuzhuang (Village) of Tianjin Municipality designated only a few households to farm but they were able to produce sufficient grain to feed the entire community and allowed the village to meet its grain sales quotas to the state. But in districts where off-farm activities were less developed, the concentration of holdings was hardly developing and fragmentation remained (Nolan 1988: 147).

encouraging family members to quit agriculture and leave the remaining members more land), or increased in the case of its expansion (hence discouraging new births and obliging the new arrivals to seek non-grain agriculture and off-farm employment). A proper land transfer mechanism also was to be established in order to achieve appropriate large-scale farming. (Zhang & Hou 1995: 23–4. Zhang, Shi-Yun 1996: 17)

'Land Management Law' amended on 29 August 1998 and enforced on 1 January 1999, prescribed by the first time in the form of law that a land contract is valid for 30 years (renewable); the contractor is obliged to protect and appropriately use the land according the contract; the contractee should stop the contract and withdraw the land if the contractor has idled it continuously for two years; for adjusting individual land within its contractual period among land contractors, the agreement by two-thirds of villagers or villager representatives, and approvals by the township government and agricultural administration of the county government are required; law suits are allowed and before their settlement by courts, the present situation of land use cannot be changed (LML [1998] 1999: 3–5, 11). These rules not only guaranteed stability in land use, but also showed flexibility in preventing inefficient land-holding. They gave local officials power in adjusting land while promoting democracy and peasants' participation so as to avoid arbitrariness and corruption of officials. This law reflects that, through over a decade of experiments, China has reached a more matured stage in overcoming the last obstacle.

In July 2000, the state further decided that from the same year on, all those peasants who have acquired legal and immobile housing, and stable jobs or living sources in small towns at or below county level, could out of their own will change their rural residence to town residence, and enjoy the same treatments received by the town residents in schooling children, joining the military, and obtaining employment, without being discriminated. Those farmers who have got the town residence could according to their own wish either retain the right of operating the contractual land or transfer it legally in exchange for remuneration. (CCCPC & SC 2000). This measure would promote part-time and absent small farmers' leaving agriculture and the transfer of their land to the remaining full-time farmers.

Moreover, as China has been developing towards richness, a minimum living standard guarantee system has gradually been established, whereby residents are paid the difference between their incomes and the local minimum living standard. It was first tried in some cities in 1994, and popularized to all the 668 cities, and 1,638 towns where the county governments are situated between September 1997 and the end of 1999. From 1997 to March 2000, 4.98 billion yuan were paid by the governments to 3.01 million urban poor, about 2.35 million or 78% of whom were employed, unemployed, or retired staff and workers. Between September 1997 and March 2000, it has also been spread to rural areas. In 2,687 counties (including cities and districts at the county level) of all the 30 provinces, municipalities and autonomous regions (without Hong Kong, Macao10 and Taiwan), nearly 2,000 have adopted it to different extent. Among them, 14 provinces, municipalities and autonomous regions have implemented it for all their rural poor. In 1997, 0.93 billion yuan (including aid in kind) were paid to 3.16 million rural poor, over 20 yuan per capita per month, about half by the provincial, county and township governments and half by the village collective common welfare funds. China's social relief system has thus been upgraded from one with aid of fixed quantity and duration, or temporary nature, to a more standard one. (Zhai, Wei 2000. Wang, Jing 2000. CSY 1999: 3). Such a constant and sounder back-up basic social welfare to all the urban and rural poor would further boost the transfer of inefficiently used land from part-time and absent small farmers to full-time large-scale farmers.

Of course, the last obstacle has not yet been completely resolved in China since its rural areas are so vast. For example, in early 2001, it was found that land desolation seriously appeared in recent two years in nine townships and towns of Dingyuan County, Chuzhou City, Anhui Province mainly due to small peasants' increasing engagement in off-farm activities and the ineffective land transfer to full-time farmers (Chui, Rong-Hui 2001). Thus further experiments and more effective work will still have to be carried out.

7.2 Functioning of Large-Scale Farming [11]

Organizations of Large-Scale Farmers

Once expert farmers had been selected to be large-scale farmers, various forms of organization were created, as each rural area was allowed and encouraged to make experiments to find the form of organization most suited to it. The principal forms are presented below.

Individual household farm. This was the dominant form across the country (RG 1987: 17). In 1995, in Zhejiang Province, it accounted for about 90%

10
    Hong Kong and Macao special administrative regions (islands) are in the South-Central part of China.

11
    A working paper based on the earlier version of this section has been accepted for publication by the Food and Agriculture Organization of the United Nations (Zhou, Jian-Ming 2001).

of the area under large-scale farming (Zheng, Ke-Feng 1996: 67). In the same year, in Wu County of the Sunan region, it included 94% of the large-scale farms (Prosterman; Hanstad & Li July 1996: 13).

A much earlier example is as follows. In 1976, Jingwang Brigade (Village) of Yanlu Commune (Township) of Lingbi County of Anhui Province assigned 60 mu (4 ha) of farmland to expert farmer Xue-Rong Jing to lead 10 farmers for scientific experiments. But, due to collective operation, neither experiments nor normal production succeeded. Only 7,500 kg of grain were harvested, just offsetting the costs. At the end of the 1970s, the land was divided and contracted to a number of households, and in *1981*, contracted to Jing's household alone (with six members including three laborers). Just in the same year, it harvested 14,000 kg of grain and sold 10,000 kg to the state. In 1982, although suffering from floods, it produced over 28,000 kg and sold over 22,500 kg to the state, more than twice the quota of the Brigade. In 1983, by further enlarging farming scale and applying scientific methods of multiple cropping, it reaped 22,560 kg of wheat on 70 mu (4.67 ha), 6,000 kg of soybeans on 40 mu (2.67 ha), 19,500 kg of dried white sweet potato on 30 mu (2 ha), 250 kg of sorghum on 1 mu and 125 kg of peanuts on 1 mu, sold over 40,500 kg of grain to the state, and earned an annual income of more than 13,000 yuan - over 2,100 yuan per capita, which was above the average local level. Its 48,310 kg of grain were equal to 128% of the grain output of the whole Brigade in 1978. (Gao & Liu 1984: 21)

Songke Brigade (Village) of Xiaomiao Commune (Township) of Feixi County of Anhui Province had an area of low-lying wasteland of 93 mu (6.2 ha). Under the Equal Land System, it was divided to be contracted to a number of households, but could never be tilled well, resulting in a loss of several hundred yuan each year. In 1983, the Brigade auctioned its use to anyone who could pay 700 yuan as collateral. De-Ming Gao's household contracted it, planted rice, harvested 36,500 kg, sold 32,500 kg to the state, and earned 11,225 yuan in the same year. (Gao & Liu 1984: 21)

In Shunyi County of Beijing, in 1989, 22,000 mu (1,466.67 ha) of responsibility land were contracted to the individual household farms, with 12.1 mu (0.807 ha) per laborer (Pei, Chang-Hong et al. 1992: 93).

Joint households farm as a cooperative. This was also one of the forms of organization of large-scale farming across the country (Liang & Wang 1988: 17). At its preliminary stage, they were unstable, mainly due to difficulties in supervising and calculating remuneration to manual labor in the varied farm work within the member households. For example, there were 29 joint households farms in grain production in Jiangsu Province in 1984. Owing to such difficulties, most of them were dissolved later. (Jiang, Ji-Fen 1986: 23). However, what evolved was a shareholding system by some households in *operating* land. Land was owned by the village and contracted to the joint households who won the tender. They mainly used large machinery so that farm work could be standardized and supervised. Remuneration was distributed among their respective shares of working capital, machinery and labor. For example, in Leqing City of Zhejiang Province, in 1994, of 67 large-scale farms operating over 100 mu (6.67 ha), eight were shareholding joint households farms. Xian-Yu Wan, Xian-Jian Wan and Yao-Xi Chen contracted 380 mu (25.33 ha) of paddy fields in 1993 and 403 mu (26.87 ha) in 1994, being the largest farm of grain production in the City. (Wu & Hu 1995: 42)

There were also cases in which there was a small number of members of a joint households farm, all with relevant expertise and hardworking, led by one household which could supervise work and distribute remuneration according to each one's labor contribution, although large machinery was not necessarily relied on. For example, in the mid-1980s, in the areas formerly flooded by the Yongding River and areas with more sandy soil and fruit trees of Langfang Prefecture of Hebei Province, the village collectives could not provide effective services while single household operation was too weak, 1,135 joint households farms emerged, on average contracting 55 mu (3.67 ha) per farm. In 1986, nine households of Si-De Ren et al. contracted 160 mu (10.67 ha) of land. All the nine principal laborers were experts, three for fruit trees, two for melons and vegetables, and four for grain. They gathered funds of 11,000 yuan, dug a motor-pumped well, built six farm houses, planted 4,000 fruit trees, produced grain and oil crops on 100 mu (6.67 ha), melons and vegetables on 60 mu (4 ha), and could earn 18,000 yuan, 2,000 yuan per laborer. (Cao & Liu 1987: 34–5)

Collective farm 1: operating and accounting unit at household level. In such a collective farm, the operating and accounting unit was still at household level, the farm being a managing unit only. The village appointed and paid one or two managers who were then responsible for unified planning in planting, coordinating and managing those farm works which required collective work, and arranging technical services to the member households. The households were to fulfil the whole process of farm work and the contracted output quotas, be responsible for their own profits and losses and could dispose of surplus products. (Bai; Zhao & Pei 1988: 41). Such a household was actually also an individual farm (although not so called in practice) and was not much different from the above-stated individual household farm, except for its collective coordination, which could provide the member households with special services and help them to solve specific problems in order to be competent in large-scale farming (Zhang; Wang & Guo 1987: 15).

For example, in Shunyi County of Beijing in 1989, there were totally 497 collective farms, with 43,656 laborers, operating 648,000 mu (43,200 ha) of farmland, on average 1,304 mu (86.93 ha) per farm and 15 mu per laborer; 63.78% or 317 of them were collective farms of this first type (Pei, Chang-Hong et al. 1992: 93).

Collective farm 2: operating unit at household level, accounting unit at both collective and household levels. In the first section of Chapter 6, 'bao chan dao hu' as the minor form of the Household Contract System was reviewed. It was also adopted as way of organizing expert farmers for large-scale farming.

The village assigned a few managers to organize a farm and contracted a large area of land and output quotas to it (which could also be attached to a rural collective firm - TVE - as its agricultural workshop), the farm was thus not only a managing unit but also an accounting unit. The farm further contracted output quotas to the member households. The same farm undertook planning of planting, paid basic production costs, could dispose of products, with the remuneration to households based on a basic salary in money (although it also could be in kind) subject to bonuses and fines. The household was to fulfil the whole process of farm work and the contracted output quotas, hence functioning as both an operating and accounting unit (such a household was actually also an individual farm, although not so called in practice). (Bai; Zhao & Pei 1988: 41)

For example, in the above-presented 497 collective farms in Shunyi County of Beijing in 1989, 36.22% or 180 were collective farms of the second type (Pei, Chang-Hong et al. 1992: 93).

In some of the collective farms of Wu County of the Sunan region, there was an internal responsibility system called 'five certains' - a certain person, certain land, certain yield, certain expense, and certain salary. Members were assigned certain parcels, given a certain target yield, and allowed a certain amount of expenses. If they met the target yield while staying within the target expenses, they could receive a fixed salary. The annual salary was 5,200 yuan in one village and 10,000 yuan in another, both exceeding the average pay for a village factory worker. If members exceeded the target yield, they could receive a bonus, and if they exceeded the target expenses, they would be penalized. If the collective farm as a whole earned a profit, 50% of it would be given to the members. (Prosterman; Hanstad & Li July 1996: 18–9)

In some areas where TVEs were very strong and income from grain production was low, such a farm would be attached to a TVE as a workshop for agriculture. The TVE could use its profits to pay expert farmers a salary equivalent to or higher than that of a firm worker, as an incentive for them to concentrate on grain production and a direct subsidy and support to agriculture. It was called 'integration between agriculture and industry' (Ran

& Yang 1985: 17) or 'management of agriculture by industry' (RWDWX 1984: 31).

For example, during 1982–84, Xinxu Brigade (Village) of Huangtang Commune (Township) of Jiangyin County of Wuxi City of the Sunan region set up an agricultural workshop and recruited laborers of 16 households which had previously produced 1,500 kg of grain (as commodity sold to the state) on 3 mu (0.2 ha) of responsibility land (as opposed to self-sufficiency land) to be its agricultural workers. A worker should produce an annual yield of 650 kg of grain per mu, and the workshop paid him costs of 80 yuan, agricultural tax 12 yuan, and salary 160 yuan per mu. He could retain straw, surplus grain output and cost savings, but inversely was liable for excess costs and had to reimburse reduced output. The workshop took his revenue from selling target grain and direct subsidies to his grain production by the Commune, and paid 8 yuan per mu to his Production Team as his dues for the common accumulation fund and common welfare fund. (RWDWX 1984: 31)**12**

Collective farm 3: both operating and accounting unit at collective level. In this case the village designated some managers to set up a farm (which could also be attached to a TVE as its agricultural workshop) to contract large areas of land and output quotas. The farm employed some laborers to conduct *partial* farming (their family members could always help). The collective was thus not only a managing and accounting unit but also an operating unit, while a laborer (or his family) no longer constituted an actual individual farm. The internal responsibility system was 'contracting *work* to laborers (households) - bao *gong* dao lao (hu)', a further minor form of the Household Contract System (the fulfillment of the contracted work could be related either directly to remuneration or indirectly through workpoints). If the workers could fulfil the work requirement, they could earn a fixed salary. Better or worse performance would lead to a bonus or penalty respectively. However, this type of collective farms was still relatively rare.

For example, Songjiang County of Shanghai started large-scale farming in 1984. Miaobang Village of Xinqiao Township set up a farm by gathering together 205 mu (13.67 ha) of grain land from its three villagers' groups, the director of the Village at the same time also being the manager. Through investment by the Village and Township, in 1989, the whole process of wheat production and sowing of rice were mechanized, and irrigation facilities completed. Farm laborers were responsible for the work which still could not be done by machinery, such as taking care of field and harvesting

---

    12
       Some similar examples of agricultural workshop of TVEs have also been cited by Oi (1989: 196–7).

rice under single cropping systems. The average income of members of the farm was a bit higher than that per local laborer. (Jiang, Zhong-Yi et al. 1992a: 51, 58)

In Wu County of the Sunan region, one collective farm of 303 mu (20.2 ha) had four member farmers and one manager. Another collective farm of 250 mu (16.67 ha) had three member laborers, a manager and a deputy manager. Each member farmer did the weeding and irrigation on his assigned land, but the plowing, transplanting, fertilization, pesticide application and harvesting were done jointly on a uniform basis. The managers also had oversight and technical advice duties. The member farmers were obliged to follow their direction or risk being replaced by others who would. (Prosterman; Hanstad & Li July 1996: 19)

In general, these collective farms were also called *specialized teams*.13 Possessing the collective help, such farms (teams) developed relatively quickly. Table 7.7 shows that in terms of contracted land area per household in specialized teams, the smallest (under 0.666 ha) decreased during 1986–92, except in the Western part in 1990–92; and the average land area increased during 1986–92, except in the Eastern part in 1990–92. The ratio of the area contracted by the specialized teams to the total contracted farmland area of the country was 1.6% in 1990 and increased to 2.6% in 1992 and 5.9% in 1994 (CEST 1991: 37; 1993: 45; 1996: 38).

Nevertheless, in 1994, of 90,844,500 mu (6,056,300 ha) of land under appropriate large-scale farming, 83.8% or 76,111,500 mu (5,074,100 ha) were under individual household farms (including the joint form), and only 16.2% or 14,733,000 mu (982,200 ha) under collective farms (CEST 1996: 40) (Table 7.8 shows the similar ratio in Changshu City in 1989). The collective farms were also based on households as the operating and accounting unit (in types 1 and 2) or on internal responsibility system closely related to the individual worker's performance (in type 3), and thus were different from the previous collective farms under the unique collective operation of land before the economic reform. In Songjiang County of Shanghai, Yuyao City of Zhejiang Province and Changshu City of the Sunan region, there existed all the above-mentioned forms of individual household farms, joint households farms, and collective farms. Farmland operated by a farming unit in each form varied from 15 mu to 1,000 mu (66.67 ha).

---

13 In some areas, e.g., Shunyi County of Beijing (Pei, Chang-Hong et al. 1992: 93), only collective farm type 1 was so called. In some others, e.g., Langfang Prefecture of Hebei Province (Cao & Liu 1987: 35), collective farm type 2 was also so named. In some further others, e.g., Jiangsu Province (Jiang, Ji-Feng 1986: 23), only those not attached to TVEs were so labeled. But they were all described as such by CEST.

Table 7.7 Land Contracted per Household in Specialized Teams of China 1986–92 (in percentage) *

Country	Average area (ha)	%	Under 0.666 ha	0.666–1.333 ha	1.4–3.333 ha	3.4–6.666 ha	6.733–13.333 ha	13.4–33.333 ha	33.4 ha and over
1986	4.5	100	16.5	–	–	–	–	–	–
1988	5.17	100	12.5	–	–	–	–	–	–
1990	5.68	100	11.5	–	–	–	–	–	–
1992	6.8	100	10.3	82.1	1.2	1.5	2.7	2.1	0.1
Eastern									
1986	4.53	100	18.6	–	–	–	–	–	–
1988	5.47	100	13.0	–	–	–	–	–	–
1990	6.4	100	11.4	–	–	–	–	–	–
1992	5.34	100	10.6	84.2	1.3	0.7	1.8	1.3	0.1

Central									
1986	3.93	100	22.5	–	–	–	–	–	–
1988	5.47	100	18.1	–	–	–	–	–	–
1990	6.2	100	11.9	–	–	–	–	–	–
1992	12.94	100	8.3	70.7	2.1	10.0	6.2	2.7	0
Western									
1986	3.87	100	8.6	–	–	–	–	–	–
1988	4.07	100	8.6	–	–	–	–	–	–
1990	3.87	100	8.4	–	–	–	–	–	–
1992	8.526	100	10.3	80.1	0.5	1.1	4.0	3.6	0.4

* Samples from 7,983 villages of over 200 counties in 29 provinces, municipalities and autonomous regions (without Tibet and Taiwan).

Source: CEST 1993: 48.

Table 7.8 Organizations of Large-Scale Farmers in Changshu City of China in 1989

	Individual household		Joint households		Collective farm 2	
	No.	%	No.	%	No.	%
Total large-scale farming units: 190	145	76.32	9	4.74	36	18.95
Total area: 1,1046.4 mu (736.43 ha)	8,037.1 (535.81)	72.76	564 (37.6)	5.11	2,445.3 (163.02)	22.14
Total laborers: 536	343	63.99	27	5.04	166	30.97
Area per unit: mu (ha)	55.4 (3.69)		62.7 (4.18)		68 (4.53)	
Area per laborer: mu (ha)	23.4 (1.56)		20.9 (1.39)		14.7 (0.98)	

Source: Jiang, Zhong-Yi et al. 1992c: 80–1.

(Jiang; He; Wang et al. 1992: 15–6)

Urban—rural joint enterprise. This is not strictly within the focus of the chapter. However, in order to show that public land ownership could allow the participation of urban enterprises in agriculture for large-scale farming in such a scope that *cannot be expected under the present private land ownership system of Japan*, some examples are given.

In 1995, dozens of enterprises in construction, textile, breweries, etc. of Shaoxing County of Zhejiang Province started to invest in agriculture, including farming, forestry, animal husbandry, fishery and related off-farm activities. They all made large investments (over 1 million yuan once in each item), used high technology and implemented economies of scale. As a result, they all gained profits and then reinvested them in agriculture. Yongli Group - a large enterprise of textile machinery - of Yangxunqiao Town planted rice in over 100 mu (6.67 ha) of land and achieved an output of over 50,000 kg. Xianheng Group, a brewery, took over Jiefang Reservoir of Lanting Town, developed water conservancy projects which ensured stable yields despite drought or excessive rain to nearly 1,000 mu (66.67 ha) of farmland in the nearby nine villages, and gained profits from fish farming in an area of water spanning 800 mu (53.33 ha). Green Group signed contracts with 3,000 peasant households to produce pollution-free vegetables and sell them to the Group for export. In total 4,000 mu (266.67 ha) of waste mountain and 1,000 mu (66.67 ha) of waste water were reclaimed. (Xin & Zhao 1996)

Since the beginning of 1995, over 50 large and medium industrial enterprises of Guangdong Province so far have, with the long-term plan of investing in total several billions of yuan, invested more than 1 billion yuan in agriculture not only in the Province itself which is situated in the South, but also across the country to the North in Heilongjiang Province, Jilin Province, Xinjiang Uighur Autonomous Region, Hexi Corridor (in the West of the Yellow River) of Gansu Province, and the plain between the Yellow River and Huai River.14 Through investment, cooperation, purchase, etc., Shennong (meaning 'magical agriculture') Development Corporation Ltd established by Sanjiu Group of Shenzhen City (a Special Economic Zone near Hong Kong) has entered the agricultural sector. The assets of the agricultural enterprises it held surpassed 1 billion yuan in 1996, yielded taxes and profits of 100 million yuan from agricultural products, and increased the income of over 300,000 peasant households in 1995. In Heilongjiang

---

14 Jilin Province is in the Northeasternmost, Xinjiang Uighur Autonomous Region Northwesternmost, Gansu Province Northwest, and the plain between the Yellow River and Huai River North-Central part of China.

Province, Haowei Group of Shenzhen City invested 220 million yuan in developing Zhenbaodao Farm of 385,000 mu (25,666.67 ha) of land together with several local partners. This was the largest overall agricultural development project invested by urban enterprises of the whole country. Once completed, it could produce over 58 million kg of grain and soybeans, 10,000 cattle for meat, 350,000 kg of fish, and over 500,000 kg of vegetables. (Wang, Yun-Feng 1996)

External and foreign venture. Chinese public land ownership could permit external and foreign ventures into domestic agriculture on a large-scale, *which is unimaginable under the private land ownership system of Japan.*

In Panshidian Village of Panshidian Town of Haiyang County of Shandong Province,15 there was a land area of 300 mu (20 ha), in which the peasants had been reluctant to invest more so that the yield of taro could not be raised for many years. In the spring of 1995, the Village signed a contract with Zong-Tong Chen of Singapore who had established the Tongda Food Company Ltd under single venture in nearby Yantai City: the Village leased it to the Company for 10 years to set up Tongda Farm for producing grain, oil crops or vegetables only; land could not be idled and no buildings were to be built on it. The annual rent of 100,000 yuan, plus salary to farmers in the Farm, could bring a net revenue of 200,000 yuan to peasants, equivalent to over three times average revenue under normal harvest years. The rent was used in establishing off-farm projects and welfare services to villagers. The Farm invested in the renovation of water conservancy facilities, applied sufficient base fertilizer before sowing, and invited highly qualified agricultural scientists and technicians to guide farmers in the scientific management of taro cultivation. Yield would be over 2,500 kg per mu, 70% higher than the average local yield. Taro would be sent to the Company to be processed and then exported. After examining the Farm in August, foreign businessmen were very happy with the quality and orders already extended to August 1996. Meanwhile peasants not only learned advanced technologies, but also gained a new idea 'In order to earn high revenue from planting taro, large investments are needed'. (Gong & Wang 1995)

In the Yangtze River Delta (including Shanghai, a part of Zhejiang Province and Jiangsu Province) which has the best natural conditions, densest population, highest output of commodity grain, and highest living standard in China, companies from over 20 external regions (including Hong Kong and Taiwan) and foreign countries (Australia, Brazil, Germany, Japan, Singapore, Thailand, the USA, etc.) have invested in agriculture in recent

---

15 Shandong Province is in the East-Central part of China and coastal.

years. During 1994–96, in the state farms in its Southern part - Hangjiahu plain of Zhejiang Province, over 40 external and foreign ventures, with a total investment nearing US$100 million, were set up; while in its Northern part - the Sunan region, 700 ventures, over US$200 million. In its further Northern part, Nantong City of Jiangsu Province, an external overall agricultural development zone with 420,000 mu (28,000 ha) of sea shore was founded in October 1995. The plan was to develop it for the production, process and export of grain, cotton, oil crops, and fishery products by 2001. The state has given incentives in terms of taxes, land use, etc. By June 1996, over 10 joint ventures had been established, with total investment of 17 million yuan. (Zhang; Zhu & Shi 1996)

In sharp contrast, Xinjiang Uighur Autonomous Region is one of the areas with the most unfavorable natural conditions, scarcest population, largest wasteland (150 million mu or 10 million ha of reclaimable land plus mountains and the Gobi Desert), and lowest living standard in China. At the beginning of the 1990s, the state decided to develop the Region into the largest base for cotton and an important base for grain production of the country. It implemented various favorable policies (including long-term land leasing) to attract domestic, external and foreign investors to reclaim wasteland, with the first 7,500,000 mu (500,000 ha) to be achieved by 2001. Since 1994, businessmen from Hong Kong, Canada, Israel, the USA, etc., together with Chinese domestic industrial and commercial companies from the Eastern and Central parts, have invested on a large scale. Compared with the previous reclaimers, they have made heavier investments and carried out much larger-scale farming with higher level of mechanization and more advanced technologies. (Li, Da-Dong 1996)

The above examples in urban–rural joint enterprises and external and foreign ventures, and their diffusion into the Central and Western parts of China also reflected *feature 11 - earlier development in some (chiefly Eastern and coastal) rural areas, and its promotion in other (mainly Central and Western) areas especially from the early 1990s on,* and *feature 12 - introduction of more advanced technology and management, larger investment, and domestic and international markets to agriculture by urban– rural joint enterprises, and external and foreign single and joint ventures,* of the Chinese model of rural development.

In terms of the trend in the organization of large-scale farmers, according to Table 7.5, small-scale farms in both individual household farms and collective farms would appear to be decreasing and large-scale farms increasing. But even in the long run, individual household farms may still be the major form country-wide, although collective farms may grow more quickly. Urban–rural joint enterprises and external and foreign ventures in China's agriculture may well develop further.

Agricultural Mechanization with Large Machinery

After obtaining more land to farm, the family labor force of the large-scale farmers was usually not enough. Take for example a household in Tanjia Village of Lulong Town of Lu County of Hebei Province which contracted 95 mu (6.33 ha) of land in 1987. Due to the persistent use of draft cattle and manual hoes by family members only without the help of either machinery or extra labor for the large-scale farming, net income per mu reduced to 80 yuan, less by over 100 yuan than that in small-scale farming. (Lu, Nong 1988: 42)

Thus, wage labor employment by large-scale farmers had been widespread across the country by the early 1990s (Zeddies 1992: 165). In some areas, 70% of such farmers did so (Liang & Wang 1988: 18).

Various problems occurred. For example, in some individual large-scale farms in Xinzhou Prefecture of Shanxi Province, hired labor force accounted for 60.2−80% of their total labor force, thus *labor productivity was not raised*. Most of them were hired for the busy seasons, few for the whole year. Due to shortage of local skillful able-bodied laborers who were mainly engaged in off-farm production, most of the local employees were *aged, female, weak, less skilled*, and were only available after they had finished farm work on their own land, thus missing the best timing, and harming the output for the employers. It was *difficult to supervise* varied manual farm work with simple tools, which led to careless farming. *Labor costs rose quickly* and reached 31.2%, even 45.7%, of the total costs. (Zhang & Xing 1985: 54). *Laborers from outside also were at lower quality*, because most of them were from poorer rural areas, with low literacy levels, and highly mobile, as reported, e.g., in Suzhou City of the Sunan region (Shi & Zhang 1987: 23).**16**

Thus it became necessary for the large-scale farmers to use large machinery to reduce costs, especially labor costs. Dividing land into compact forms (rectangular or square) and constructing roads among them made large machinery usable. Table 4.1 'Comparison of Rice Production Costs by Farm Size in Japan 1953−98' in Chapter 4 showed that as farm size increased, with the use of large machinery since 1970, total costs, labor costs, and machinery and power costs decreased significantly. Such data for China as a whole are unavailable. But individual reports indicate the same trend. For

---

16 Nolan (1988: 97) also reports that due to problems of labor supervision, expansion of hired labor in farming proper was quite limited, and Oi (1989: 191) notices that grain-specialized households farm the land themselves, and hire laborers, mostly other peasants from the village, during the busy season, according to Chinese sources.

example, labor costs continuously rose year after year in the Sunan region. In 1987, manual transplanting of rice seedlings per mu cost 20 yuan, while a transplanter worth 4,000 yuan could serve 200 mu (13.33 ha). Therefore, if it were bought, the investment could be offset within one year by savings in manual labor costs. On the basis of this calculation, Ouqiao Village of Miaoqiao Town of Zhangjiagang City bought five transplanters in 1986, and achieved positive results. In 1987, 50 were bought in the whole Town. In the same year, Zhengyi State Farm of Kunshan County decided to use mechanical transplanters for all transplanting. Moreover, during the busy seasons, inviting relatives and friends to help with farm work meant incurring entertainment costs. A table of good meals for several guests could set a family back some 40–50 yuan. Thus peasants were willing to pay fees for machinery services. (Qiu, Wei-Lian 1987: 29)

Owning machines was better for farmers than having none at all. For example, an investigation of nearly 200 expert grain farmers in over 310 counties of 27 provinces, municipalities and autonomous regions in 1983 showed that on average those households which owned motive power machines [some of them even operated over 500 mu (33.3 ha) of farmland] could sell over 1,450 kg of commodity grain and earn 720 yuan per capita, while those without any machines could only sell over 1,100 kg and earn 558 yuan per capita, the former being 32% and 29% higher than the latter respectively (Zhou, Xiao 1984: 35).

However, there also were constraints in owning machines. For example, it was found in Suzhou City of the Sunan region and Beijing that households could not afford large investments, especially in buying complete sets of large machinery; the use of self-owned machinery was limited, resulting in diseconomies of scale and high cost; it was difficult for farmers to both till land and manage and maintain machines, a task which required special knowledge and was time consuming (Fan, Kun-Tian 1987: 63. Bai; Zhao & Pei 1988: 41–2).

Therefore, while (1) encouraging those large-scale farmers who could afford to buy and efficiently use large machinery to do so, many areas also promoted (2) specialized individual households, or (3) joint households, or (4) collectives to give machinery services to large-scale farms. For example, Lingkuang Town of Zhongxiang County of Hubei Province had all four of these forms (Wang, Wei-Jia 1987: 35). An investigation of 2,277 specialized households in over 310 counties of 27 provinces, municipalities and autonomous regions in 1983 revealed that 66% or 1,500 of them were specialized in providing machinery services to farming, livestock raising, repairing, transporting and processing (Zhou, Xiao 1984: 35). In 1989, Jiangxiang Village of Changshu City of the Sunan region invested 465,000 yuan in setting up a collective general agricultural service station, which employed 47 technicians and provided services in agricultural machinery, technology, irrigation and plant protection to all households, priority being given to large-scale farms. Overall 80% of transplanting and 99% of harvesting were mechanized. By charging fees, the station earned a gross revenue of 120,000 yuan and a net income of 4,000 yuan in 1991. During 1989–91, the investment in agricultural machinery in the whole City was 9,320,000 yuan which added 1,675 sets with 14,000 horse-power to the existing machinery. (Jiang, Zhong-Yi et al. 1992c: 82–3)

As large-scale farming proceeded, in Zhejiang Province in 1994, there was a 'hot wave' of purchasing large machinery including irrigating and draining equipment, trench diggers, walking tractors, manure vehicles, manure spreaders, plowing machines, sowers, factory-style plants and equipment for raising rice seedlings, motor transplanters, spraying equipment, ordinary harvesters, combine harvesters, electric threshers, motor boats, trucks, etc., mechanizing the whole process of grain production including plowing, irrigating, draining, rice seedling raising, transplanting, plant protecting, fertilizer applying, harvesting, threshing and transporting (Ding; Wei; Yang & Sang 1995: 25). In 1995, on 650,000 mu (43,333.33 ha) of land in Jiangyin County of the Sunan region, there were 1,500 sets of large and medium tractors and combine harvesters. The degree of machinery plowing and threshing reached almost 100%. Each village had machinery service team. (Liu; Kong & Liu 1995)

As a result, large-scale farmers were able to achieve agricultural mechanization. For example, as early as in late 1984, 40% of the total area of farmland and fishponds in Zhongshan City of Guangdong Province had already been contracted by only one-eighth of the rural population (Fewsmith 1985: 53). In such areas, the degree of mechanization of farm work was high (Kung 1986: 20).

Although the state farms as a whole are not analyzed in this chapter, it may be beneficial to cite some more examples here. In the summer of 1978, American farmer Handing (English surname in Chinese pinyin pronunciation) introduced to China the fact that each American farm worker could produce over 100,000 kg of grain to feed several hundred people annually, and a set of large agricultural machinery advanced at the world level from the American John Deere Company to the Second Team of the Fifth Branch of the Friendship Farm of Heilongjiang Province which is a relatively sparsely populated region due to cold weather. The Team had 23,000 mu (1,533.33 ha) of land and 20 farm workers, 1,150 mu (76.67 ha) each. Immediately in 1979, over 100,000 kg of cereals and soybeans were produced per farm worker, an unprecedented miracle. The farm was hence nicknamed 'Handing Farm'. During 1979–98, with the same amount of land and number of farm workers, each worker on average produced annual output of 245,000 kg of cereals and soybeans, in the peak year 331,000 kg, and could feed 800 persons (supposing each consumes 400 kg per annum), catching up with or even surpassing the American level. (Wang & Wang 1998)

Inspired by this successful example, in 1980 China's first modern farm Honghe Farm was established with advanced large agricultural machinery from Japan, and in 1983, Erdaohe Farm and Yaluhe Farm were founded also with imported modern large machinery. Nowadays, farms with each worker producing 100,000–200,000 kg of cereals and soybeans yearly are popular in the vast area of Heilongjiang Province. (Wang & Wang 1998)

Special attention should be paid to the new development that peasants in China have started to use computers and the Internet in the 1990s in agricultural production with both small and large machinery, procurement, marketing, and off-farm activities. In fact, China (data not including Hong Kong, Macao and Taiwan) has been at the 17th place in countries with the most computers at the end of 1993, but jumped to 10th at the end of 1996; eighth in PCs-in-use at the end of 1998, and computers-in-use at the end of 2000 (estimate); and 14th in the Internet use at the end of 1998, and 13th at the end of 2000 (estimate) (C-I-A 1994; 1997; September 1998; November 1998; March 1999; April 1999). In the South - Zhejiang Province, in 2000, the Internet users have exceeded 200,000, a considerable part of whom are peasants, mainly members of specialized agricultural households and businessmen. During 1996–2000, the Association of Sciences of the Province has held training courses for computers and the Internet in rural areas, and nearly 30,000 peasants have learned computer operation and been trying to create their own webpages or websites. In its Jiangshan City, there are already almost 2,000 peasant Internet users, selling in the website established specially for agricultural products by the City. In 1999, the website received virtually 10,000 visitors, and sold goods of over 1 million yuan, accounting for 10.4% of the total agricultural output of the City. In its Haining City, Li-Zhong Wang operated a breeding farm for scorpions, toads, centipedes and snakes, and sold all products through the Internet. In 1999, he concluded transactions of over 1.3 million yuan. Similarly, in the North - Heilongjiang Province, 32 villages in Mudanjiang City have set up information boards in the Internet, providing the newest information on the international supply of and demand for fruits and vegetables, and gratuitously helped peasants to create their own homepages. As a result, more and more farmers have been selling products in the Internet, and the annual export of fruits and vegetables to Russia has exceeded 440,000 tons in 2000. (Cao, Yin-Kang 2000). An example more relevant to this section is stated below, and another later in this chapter.

Grain farmer Mei Li of Hebei Province has built three websites and edited five web-based electronic journals, and established connections with many agricultural scientists in Beijing, Tianjin, Henan Province[17] and his own province. Once new varieties have been bred, he would try them in his own responsibility land, and upon success, spread them through the Internet. For example, he found and grew a variety of wheat with higher yield and protein special for bread. Its stalk is thicker and stronger, leaf wider and larger, and ear bigger and denser than his neighbors' - with 103 grains per ear, while his neighbors' 57. Farmers of Mei County, Hu County, Suide County and other counties of Shaanxi Province planted the varieties of dry-rice and sugarcane introduced in his websites so successfully that their products were exhibited in the Yangling Agricultural Fair at the national level. He also popularized agricultural machinery to several other provinces. (Chen; Cai & Jin 2000)

Hence *feature 10 of agricultural mechanization with large machinery* in the Chinese model of rural development.

Optimal Size of Large-Scale Farms

Various practices in China have shown that large-scale farms have been better than small-scale ones in achieving lower costs, higher labor productivity, higher output, higher commodity grain rate,[18] higher income per worker/household and higher yield per land unit, or higher overall appraisal combining all these indicators (even if taken individually some of the indicators show poorer results than the small-scale farms). By gradually hiring less wage labor, and using more machinery on larger land, the running costs of large-scale farms could be lowered from the initial higher level as one of the key indicators of the better economic results of large-scale farms. But labor productivity, output, commodity grain rate, and income per farm would be raised even with the same yield, as long as the expansion rate of land exceeded that of the labor force. Thus, another of such key indicators was higher yield. These practices have also demonstrated that if farms were larger than an *optimal* size, the above indicators would be sub-optimal. The optimal farm size, however, varied across time and place, and was dynamically determined by the degree of agricultural mechanization, infrastructure, services, the operating and managing skills of large-scale farmers, the economic structures (urban—rural, industry—agriculture, import—export, etc.), cost/profit ratio, etc.

For example, Table 7.9 shows that as the degree of agricultural mechanization was enhanced, farm size could be enlarged. It also indicates

---

[17] Henan Province is in the Central part of China.

[18] Commodity grain rate is the ratio of commodity grain quantity to the total grain output. For example, if of 100 kg of grain, 80 kg were sold, then the commodity grain rate was 80%.

the optimal size of large-scale farms under different degrees of mechanization in three major areas of grain production of the country in the mid-1980s.

Tables 7.10, 7.11 and 7.12 demonstrate that while large-scale farms were better than small-scale ones, there was also an optimal size per household. This was 20–30 mu (1.33–2 ha) in six counties and cities (for rice, wheat and corn) across the country in 1990–91 in Table 7.10, 35–39.9 mu (2.33–2.66 ha) in the suburbs of Beijing (for wheat and corn) in the mid-1980s in Table 7.11, and 10.1–15 mu (0.673–1 ha) in Wuxi County in 1986 in Table 7.12 (other numbers in bold along with them display the best results they have achieved). Table 7.10 does not provide data on costs. In Table 7.11, the optimal size gave the highest per mu cost of all farm sizes, but its overall appraisal combining all indicators was also the highest. In Table 7.12, the optimal size carried the highest per mu yield, and the highest per mu income without direct subsidy. Its highest income per kg per mu without direct subsidy implies the lowest cost per kg. (The observations in Tables 7.9–7.12 are not large enough for running regressions. More detailed data, however, are unavailable.). Such data have given empirical evidence to the tenet 'that the costs of agricultural products fall as the size of the production unit in agriculture increases', just diametric to Schultz's observations as raised in Chapter 1.

The optimal size of large-scale farms should be ascertained by practice and experiment. For instance, in 1993, large-scale farmer Ying-Gan Wan of Xintang Village of Lecheng Town of Leqing County of Zhejiang Province operated 120 mu (8 ha) of grain land. In 1994, however, rather than expanding farm size gradually, he immediately doubled it to 240 mu (16 ha), leading to the decline of his net income from 16,800 yuan to 16,000 yuan. In 1995, he reduced the size to 105 mu (7 ha), resulting in a net income of 75,000 yuan. (Wu; Yu & Zhu 1996: 15)

Subsidies and Self-Reliance

As already stated, in the high wage economy, income from grain (and other major agricultural products such as cotton, oil crops) production upon small farms was very low in comparison with that from other lines. Raising income of expert grain farmers by enlarging their farm size was, however, constrained by not squeezing out those peasants who could not yet find jobs in non-grain agriculture and off-farm activities, insufficient services (irrigation, machinery, etc.), inferior infrastructure, the operating and managing skill of the expert farmers themselves, etc. Under such circumstances, large-scale farmers should be helped.

Initially, *as the first stage*, villages and local governments (townships,

Table 7.9 Maximum Land Area per Laborer and Household under Different Degrees of Mechanization in China in the mid-1980s

	Mechanization item	Maximum area per laborer				Maximum area per household		Data source
		Summer busy time		Autumn busy time				
		mu	ha	mu	ha	mu	ha	
Wuxi City & Suzhou City, Sunan region, Jiangsu Province, (Southeast China)	Plowing, harrowing, levelling, irrigating, plant protecting, wheat harvesting, threshing, ditching	6.83	0.46	7.90	0.53	13.7	0.91	Huazhuang Town & Youyi Town, Wuxi
	Ditto plus sowing	6.32	0.42	8.37	0.56	12.6	0.84	Dongxiang Town, Wuxi
	Ditto plus rice seedling raising in factory methods, transplanting, rice harvesting, field transporting	12.11	0.81	15.94	1.06	24.2	1.61	Luyang Town, Suzhou
		11.96	0.80	15.30	1.02	23.9	1.59	Huazhuang Town & Youyi Town, Wuxi
		11.59	0.77	16.23	1.08	23.2	1.55	Dongxiang Town, Wuxi

Region	Operations mechanized	mu	ha	mu	ha	mu	ha	Location
Huabei (Northeast & North-Central China)	Plowing, harrowing, levelling, threshing, transporting	6.52	0.43	9.64	0.64	13.0	0.87	Jin County, Hebei Province
	All mechanized except for corn harvesting	25.51	1.70	16.92	1.13	33.8	2.25	Fangshandou Town, Beijing
Liaoning Province & Heilongjiang	(A) Plowing, harrowing, levelling & (B) threshing	24	1.6	48	3.2			Shuangcheng County, Heilongjiang
Liaoning Province, (Northeasternmost China)	(A) plus (C) sowing, transporting plus partial (D) harvesting & partial (B) threshing	45 (sowing in small tractors)	3	90	6			Changtu County, Liaoning
		70 (sowing in large tractors)	4.67	140	9.33			
	(A) (C) plus (D) harvesting & (B) threshing	200	13.33	400	26.67			Fujinjianshan State Farm, Heilongjiang

Source: JRG 1987: 30—1.

Table 7.10 Comparison of Economic Results under Different Farm Sizes in 586 Households of Six Counties and Cities [a] of China 1990–91

mu	ha	Household No.	Persons per household	Laborers per household	Income per capita (yuan)	Yield per mu (0.067 ha) of grain (rice, wheat, corn, etc.) (kg)	Yield per mu of rice [b] (kg)			
							Jiangsu	Shaanxi	Shanghai	Zhejiang
Under 5	Under 0.33	269	3.4	2.0	980	625	–	–	922	712
5–10	0.33–0.67	196	3.9	2.5	805	609	972	–	989	835
10–15	0.67–1	61	5.1	2.7	805	615	–	610	973	752
15–20	1.00–1.33	22	5.8	3.0	1,506	657				
20–30	1.33–2	20	5.2	2.2	2,589	689	–	675	1,024	–
Over 30	Over 2	18	5.6	2.9	2,838	666	810	641	950	814

Notes:
a. Six counties & cities: (summer rice, winter wheat) Lingui County of Guangxi Zhuang Autonomous Region, Changshu City of Jiangsu Province, Songjiang County of Shanghai, and Yuyao City of Zhejiang Province; (wheat & corn) Shunyi County of Beijing, and Wugong County of Shaanxi Province.[19]
b. Data of some rice producing households among the above 586 households. Household No. unspecified.

Sources: Jiang; He; Wang et al. 1992: 17–8, 25. G & G 1992: 129.

[19] Guangxi Zhuang Autonomous Region is in the South-Central part of China and coastal, and Shaanxi Province Northwest part of China.

Table 7.11 Comparison of Economic Results under Different Farm Sizes in 236 Households of Beijing, China in the mid-1980s

mu / ha		Cost per mu (0.067 ha) (yuan)	Man-day per mu	Investment on mechanization per mu (yuan)	Overall degree of mechanization	Yield per mu (kg)	Labor productivity (kg)	Commodity grain rate %	Income per laborer (yuan)	Overall appraisal	Ordinal No.
Weight		0.1	0.1	0.1	0.1	0.2	0.15	0.15	0.1		
Under 5	Under 0.33	57.53	23.78	80.95	49.85	473.735	1,536.33	7.38	425.66	0.647	9
5– 9.9	0.33–0.66	75.21	13.33	80.86	50.06	457.735	3,112.96	42.84	685.15	0.770	8
10–14.9	0.67–0.99	79.89	11.73	74.88	51.77	478.11	5,114.64	52.14	1,136.81	0.864	7
15–19.9	1.00–1.33	76.39	10.21	81.27	56.28	476.92	7,801.59	52.40	1,761.25	0.945	6
20–24.9	1.33–1.66	79.14	10.36	99.69	64.04	471.785	9,969.82	58.77	1,943.23	1.000	5
25–29.9	1.67–1.99	78.09	8.29	96.63	64.42	403.03	11,105.81	69.18	2,135.28	1.143	4
30–34.9	2.00–2.33	90.88	5.67	108.86	68.85	475.87	14,916.825	78.31	2,434.58	1.220	2
35–39.9	2.33–2.66	104.48	4.00	183.53	100.00	530.015	19,354.5	92.06	2,407.25	1.420	1
40–50	2.67–3.33	79.89	5.39	102.87	62.42	440.525	18,761.375	46.84	2,481.64	1.202	3

Source: JRG 1987: inside back cover.

Table 7.12 Comparison of Economic Results under Different Farm Sizes in 240 Households of Wuxi County, China in 1986

mu	ha	Household No. total 240	Area per farming laborer mu	Area per farming laborer ha	Yield per mu (0.067 ha) (kg)	Output per farming laborer (kg)	Commodity grain rate (%)	Income per mu without direct subsidy (yuan)	Income per kg per mu without direct subsidy (yuan)	Income per farming laborer without direct subsidy (yuan)
5.0–10	0.33 –0.67	92	8.91	0.594	744	6,630.5	60.7	217.52	0.292	1,938
10.1–15	**0.673–1**	97	10.41	0.694	**762.5**	7,933	68.39	**229.02**	**0.300**	2,383
15.1–20	1.01 –1.33	23	13.88	0.925	729.5	10,121	79.41	201.99	0.277	2,803
Over 20	Over 1.33	28	13.79	0.919	691.5	9,537.5	87.77	182.36	0.264	2,515
Average			11.02	0.735	735.5	8,101.5	71.75	210.71	0.286	2,321

Source: Liu & Song 1987: 27.

counties, prefectures) might have to use *direct subsidies* gained from non-grain agriculture and off-farm activities to promote the formation of large-scale grain farmers, so that by contracting larger responsibility land, grain producers could earn an income equivalent to, or higher than that from other lines. An investigation into 253 villages in 26 provinces and municipalities around 1990 showed that 23.7% of them implemented a policy of *subsidizing* agriculture by industry (yi gong *bu* nong). The forms varied from giving a certain amount of money to grain farmers on the basis of *per laborer* engaged solely in farming (6.7% of the villages, on average 26.5 yuan per month), or *per mu* of responsibility land (16.7%, 42.7 yuan), or in proportion *to the output in quota sold* (26.7%, 13.6 yuan per 100 kg), or *to the extra output sold to the state* (6.7 %, 22.5 yuan per 100 kg); to charging less or no fees on providing collective services (68.3%), in which 3.8% of poor villages (annual per capita income up to 300 yuan) subsidized 6 yuan per mu, 1.9% of lower-middle income villages (300–450 yuan) 2 yuan per mu, 12.8% of middle income villages (450–650 yuan) 6.18 yuan per mu, 20% of upper-middle income villages (650–900 yuan) 13.5 yuan per mu, 43.2% of high income villages (900 yuan and over) 13.66 yuan per mu. Therefore, by contracting larger areas of land and producing higher output one could obtain more direct subsidies, hence an incentive to become large-scale grain farmers. (Jiang; He; Wang et al 1992: 31–2). Other forms were to charge more collective fees (village reserved fees and township unified finance fees) from non-grain agriculture and off-farm activities, but less or no fees from large-scale grain farmers; give direct subsidies to them in proportion to their yield per mu; or divert a part of profits of TVEs to them (as in the above-mentioned agricultural workshop of TVEs).

For example, in 1983, the communes, brigades and teams of Yanbei Prefecture of Shanxi Province charged more collective used fees from non-grain agriculture and off-farm activities, but less or no fees from large-scale grain farmers. In the same year, 2–3 million yuan as part of the financial resources in reserve of the Prefecture, counties and communes were utilized as direct subsidies to large-scale grain farmers. (Lin & Tao 1983: 7)

At the second stage, as the large-scale farmers became able to stand on their own feet to earn an income equivalent to or higher than that from other lines in a competitive way, the direct subsidies could and should be phased out, so that they would not rely on them.

For example, Huangjiabu Town of Yuyao City of Zhejiang Province started the Dual Land System (although called trio land system: self-sufficiency land, responsibility land, plus reserve land which before being used for other purposes in rural development was treated as responsibility land) in two villages in 1993 and four in 1994–95. Responsibility land was contracted for five years to expert farmers. Initially, it was distributed without tendering to the best tenderer, but larger areas of land to farmers with more expertise and smaller areas to those with less expertise, according to their previous performance. Villages subsidized them by offering a sum of money per mu and machinery services for plowing and irrigating free of charge. Then, tendering was introduced in Huajia Village and Xihua Village which allowed non-villagers to participate, although with priority to villagers. In order to beat the competition, some expert farmers not only did not need the direct subsidies per mu, but also offered to pay contract fees (or rent) per mu and fees for machinery services, thus won. In early 1996, in the whole Town, 1,288 mu (85.87 ha) of farmland were operated by expert farmers, with 20 households contracting over 10 mu (0.67 ha) and 10 households over 100 mu (6.67 ha). (Qian; Shi & Xie 1996: 27−9, 32)

During 1985−86, large-scale farmers in Jintan County of the Sunan region voluntarily contracted larger areas of land without direct subsidies, achieved grain production better than that by small-scale farmers and earned an income higher than that of off-farm workers (Qian, Wei-Zeng 1987: 16−7).

At both the first and second stages, villages and local governments could also divert a part of profits of non-grain agriculture and off-farm activities, as *indirect subsidies*, to the improvement of services, infrastructure and technology in agriculture, which could significantly reduce costs in grain production, help large-scale grain farmers to get rid of direct subsidies earlier and upgrade the overall rural development. This was usually called *constructing* agriculture by industry (yi gong *jian* nong, as opposed to the above-mentioned *subsidizing* agriculture by industry - yi gong *bu* nong). The indirect subsidies were more significant, fundamental, long-term and wider benefiting than the direct ones. Much importance should be attached to and emphasis put on them by villages and local governments over a long period. Villages could also reinvest gains contributed by large-scale grain farmers themselves (e.g., contract fee, rent) in the improvement of services, infrastructure and technology in agriculture.

Take an example of the indirect subsidies at the first stage. In the above-cited Yanbei Prefecture of Shanxi Province, Liaohuozhuang Brigade realized a revenue of 200,000 yuan from non-grain agriculture and off-farm activities in 1982. Besides giving direct subsidies, it spent 60,000 yuan as indirect subsidies on farmland infrastructure, built three irrigation stations and 6,000 meters of canals, and levelled 6,000 mu (400 ha) of land. (Lin & Tao 1983: 7)

Such an example at the second stage was the aforementioned Huajia Village and Xihua Village of Huangjiabu Town of Yuyao City of Zhejiang Province where large-scale farmers did not need direct subsidies and paid fees for contracting land and receiving services in 1994−95. Nevertheless, the Town and Villages still gave indirect subsidies to the improvement of services, construction of infrastructure (including ditches, canals, roads), adoption of new technology and techniques, and purchase of large machinery by these large-scale farmers. (Qian; Shi & Xie 1996: 29)

A more significant example was Changshu City of the Sunan region where the large-scale farmers formed via tendering under the Dual Land System in 1989 could not enjoy direct subsidies and had to pay a contract fee per mu plus other collective used fees which were then reinvested in the promotion of services, infrastructure and technology in agriculture. During 1989–91, the City invested 9,320,000 yuan in agricultural machinery, which increased by 1,675 sets with a total of 14,000 horse-power. In 22 large-scale farming units of eight demonstration villages situated around Xiaoshan Village of Dayi Town, the whole process in rice and wheat production was basically mechanized. Mechanized sowing of rice was carried out on 76.5% of the total farmland, and combine harvesters for both rice and wheat were used on 82.6%; for realizing modern irrigating and draining system, 1,325,000 yuan were invested, 128,600 man-days put in and 312,000 cubic meters of earth work completed in constructing 30 km of underground cement pipelines for carrying water, covering 7,337 mu (489.13 ha) or 60% of the whole area of these villages. As a result, *higher yield* was achieved. The average annual per mu yield of grain was 727 kg, higher than that of these villages and of the City by 4.1% and 11% respectively during 1989– 91. In 1990, due to unfavorable natural conditions, the average per mu yield of wheat of the City dropped to 184 kg, lower than that in 1989 by 21.7%, but that of these large-scale farming units reduced to 230 kg, lower than that in 1989 by 1.9% only. In 1991, the average per mu wheat yield of these units recovered to 281.5 kg, 4.8% and 9.8% higher than that of these villages and of the City respectively. *Higher labor productivity* was reached, as the average annual output of grain per laborer went to 11,300 kg, 9.7 times that of the City. *Higher commodity grain rate* was realized. Their average annual rate of 90.4% was higher than that of the City by 65.2%. Thus they were no more traditional self-sufficient small farmers, but modern commodity grain producers. *Higher income per laborer* was earned. Their average annual net income per laborer increased to 4,148 yuan, 2.2 times that of TVEs of the City and 2.48 times that of the City. *A low input–output ratio* was gained. Although they had to pay for machinery services, due to economies of scale, the ratio was still as low as 1:1.82 (the authors omit to provide the local average ratio as a comparison, but the implication is that the ratio achieved by the large-scale farms was lower). (Jiang, Zhong-Yi et al. 1992c: 81–4). Albeit other factors also contributed to the above achievements, the policy of constructing agriculture by industry played an important part.

At the third stage, the large-scale farmers became more competent and could even give up the construction fees by the industry. Of course, there is still a long way to go before the whole country is able to reach this stage. In 1990, however, Shunyi County of Beijing was already near it, which is illustrated below as an example.

Every year before 1986–87, under the Equal Land System, the County, townships and villages had to divert 30 million yuan of off-farm profits to agriculture, which were dispersed in direct subsidies to agricultural tax, collective fees, irrigation, tillage, electricity, fertilizer, etc. Each year since then, under the Single Land System, the large-scale farms could accumulate 40–50 million yuan, thus the direct subsidies were changed to indirect ones on improving services and infrastructure like agricultural machinery and water conservancy. As the large-scale farms could become stronger and stronger standing on their own feet, they could gradually reduce and even finally waive the 'blood transfusion' from off-farm profits. (Liaison 1989: 38). The strength of the large-scale farms, as some of the major benefits of the large-scale farming and collective–individual mixed economy, is indicated below.

* *Increase of income of agricultural labor force.* Compared with the annual income per laborer of 400–600 yuan by contracting 3–5 mu (0.2–0.33 ha) under the Equal Land System, it was raised to 1,800–4,100 yuan by contracting 26.2 mu (1.75 ha) in 1988. (Liaison 1989: 36)

* *Growth of grain production.* During 1985–89, although the area of grain land continuously declined, the total output, per mu yield, and sale of commodity grain to the state successively increased as Table 7.13 shows. In 1989, the commodity grain rate of the large-scale farms reached 56%, accounting for 93% of the total commodity grain of the County. In 1990, the total output and per mu yield continued to increase. (Pei, Chang-Hong et al.

Table 7.13 Growth of Grain Production in Shunyi County, China 1985–89

Year	Area of grain land (ha)	Total output (ton)	Yield per mu (0.067 ha) (kg)	Sale to state (ton)
1985	48,216.9	426,520	589.5	96,245
1986	46,785.3	431,505	615	107,370
1987	46,801.3	471,590	671.5	158,785
1988	46,769.5	496,000	707	160,000
1989	46,468.9	512,110	734.7	200,000

Source: Pei, Chang-Hong et al. 1992: 87. Liaison 1989: 36.

1992: 94). Their sale of grain to the state grew by a big margin, because they wanted to contribute to the state by selling more grain (even though compared with the free market prices, the quota prices were much lower and negotiable prices might also be lower), so that the state could strengthen its position in grain reserves and stabilize the grain supply situation of the country.

* *Progress in agricultural mechanization with both small and large machinery.* During 1986–88, 200 million yuan were invested in agricultural machinery by the County, townships and villages. 384 large and medium tractors, and 1,053 small ones, 1,252 trucks for agricultural use, 459 combine harvesters, 150 corn harvesters, 136 large, medium and small sowers, 146 precision corn drills, and nine grain dryers were purchased. Motive power of the agricultural machinery and that per 100 mu (6.67 ha) of grain land were raised from 516,000 h.p. (horse-power) and 73.7 h.p. in 1985 to 642,000 h.p. and 91.7 h.p. in 1988 respectively. Machinery sowing and harvesting for wheat reached 100% and 87%, and for corn 63% and 14% respectively. The period for major farm work such as planting, tilling and harvesting in the summer and autumn was reduced from about two months to 15–20 days. (Liaison 1989: 37). The composition and procurement of machinery aimed at completing both harvesting and planting in the summer in seven days, and those in the autumn within 10 days (Pei, Chang-Hong et al. 1992: 94). Table 7.14 provides a general picture.

* *Popularization of advanced technology.* The area of *chemical weeding* was enlarged from 256,000 mu (17,066.67 ha) in 1985, 333,000 mu (22,200 ha) in 1986, 626,000 mu (41,733.33 ha) in 1987 to 740,000 mu (49,333.33 ha) in 1988, and that for wheat from 40% in 1985 to 97% in 1988. Compared with canal irrigation, *spraying* could increase yield by 20–30%, save water by 30–50% and raise the utilization rate of land by 7–10%. The area using *airplanes* to prevent plant disease and insect pests was maintained at about 400,000 mu (26,666.67 ha), which accounted for 63.5% of the wheat land. Plastic film, fertilizer in prescription, stoving of grain, returning of straw to land, bacteria to increase yield, fine seeds, etc. were also popularized by a big margin. (Liaison 1989: 36–7)

In 2000, it has become normal that large-scale farmers in Shunyi, Tongzhou, Fangshan and other counties of Beijing use the Internet to find solutions for their cultivation problems. The Agricultural Information Technology Research Center of Beijing has set up a website of wheat management expert wisdom system, which provides technologies for the whole cultivation process from sowing to harvesting, and prescriptions for problems in all links and aspects of the production, as part of the 'precision agriculture'. Its services could be so exact as to match the demand of a small area of land of 10 square meters (0.015 mu or 0.001 ha). For example, if

Table 7.14 Possession of Agricultural Machinery (set) in Shunyi County, China 1987–90

Machinery	1987 quantity	1988 increment	1990 increment	1990 quantity
Large & medium tractors	1,898	500	600	2,998
Wheat combine harvesters	574	200	250	800
Corn harvesters	55	300	450	800
Corn drills	61	140	50	250
Wheat rotary drills	123	297	–	420
Grain dryers *	4	30	16	50
Trucks for agricultural use	1,378	500	1,000	2,878
Irrigating sprayers	300	400	1,300	2,000
Spraying area: mu	70,000	100,000	330,000	500,000
ha	4,666.7	6,666.7	22,000	33,333.3

* Drying 15 tons per set per hour.

Source: Pei, Chang-Hong et al. 1992: 94–5.

such land had certain plant diseases or insect pests, or lacked certain chemical elements, the system would give accurate prescriptions of when, what and how much pesticides, insecticides or fertilizers to be applied, so that a larger area of their applications could be avoided and pollution minimized. The use of agricultural machinery like sowing machines, harvesters, sprayers could be adjusted and rationalized according to the specific requests of small land and its plants. (Liu, Wei 2000)

  * *Promotion of non-grain agriculture and off-farm activities.* Since the implementation of the Single Land System, of the total 223,000 laborers of the County, only 23,800 remained in grain production. 40,000 were released to non-staple foodstuff production, 10,000 to commerce and 150,000 to TVEs. In 1988, the output of egg, poultry, meat, and vegetables reached one quarter of the whole output of Beijing. The total income of the rural firms

increased from 1 billion yuan in 1986 to 2.2 billion yuan in 1988. (Liaison 1989: 38)

Major Problems

In technical terms, the problems relating to the promotion of large-scale farming were mainly insufficient services and technological progress. It is therefore necessary to strengthen them, especially by improving infrastructure and machinery. For example, in 1995, in one village of Wuxi County of the Sunan region, the large-scale farmers did not use machinery to harvest rice, because the fields were too wet for the domestically manufactured combines owned by the village, while the Japanese combines which would do the job were prohibitively expensive for the village even with the indirect subsidies on machinery purchases. They had to hire migrant workers to fulfil this task. (Prosterman; Hanstad & Li July 1996: 22). In 1995–96, in Yuzhuang Village and Xikong Village of Tengzhou City of Shandong Province, per mu yield of wheat had been raised to over 600 kg. But the existing combine harvesters of various trade marks could not work in the fields with per mu yield higher than 500 kg. (CCJ 1996)

7.3 Ascending a Higher Stage
- Preventing Food Overproduction and
Improving the Environment

Due to the implementation of the above-presented 12 features of the Chinese model of rural development, especially the overcoming of the last obstacle, China has achieved five years (1995–99) of continuous good harvests (see Table 6.3), and advanced from a chronic under- to a temporary over-supply of food (as well as some other major agricultural products), hence entering a new phase of development, as Ze-Min Jiang, President of the State, declares in March 2000 (Jiang, Ze-Min 2000). On one hand, such an overproduction of food is structural, i.e., with a mixture of over-supply of low, but under-supply of high, quality of varieties (Lu & Zhao 2000). China's agriculture is generally speaking still vulnerable to weather, and output could fluctuate owing to heavy natural disasters. Thus Jiang stresses that one should never claim that the agricultural problem has been fundamentally resolved, and agriculture's status as the foundation of the national economy should never be neglected and shaken even in dozens of years (Jiang, Ze-Min 2000). This shows that the government has become more matured, and avoided the type of mistakes as in 1985–88 when agricultural problem was regarded as having been solved once for all and thus overlooked (as mentioned in Chapter 6). On the other hand, China has indeed resolved the problem of feeding the population of the whole country by and large, and ascended a higher stage in which its major task would not be to increase food output, but to prevent the temporary overproduction of food from becoming chronic, and to improve the environment (SC 2000). Thus Jiang proclaims that the central task in this new stage is to carry out strategic adjustment in the agricultural structures (Jiang, Ze-Min 2000).

Although this new stage has just started, the author has tentatively perceived a new feature of the Chinese model - *feature 13: prevention of food overproduction, promotion in quality and perfectization in variety of agricultural products, and improvement of the environment, while strengthening development of the Central and especially the Western areas, mainly from mid-1999*. Feature 13 is not the focus of the book, and deserves a special study. Thus only a brief presentation with a few examples are given here.

Reduction in quantity of grain and some other major agricultural products. From 1998 on, the state has replaced planned targets for agricultural production, which represent the centrally planned economy, by forecasting targets, that reflect market economy and a respect to producers' autonomy and could guide local governments and peasants in production. Following the decreased forecasting targets, in 1999, the area of early rice in the whole country was actually reduced by 3,300,000 mu (220,000 ha), that of winter wheat in the South by 5 million mu (333,333.33 ha), spring wheat in Heilongjiang, Liaoning and Jilin provinces and Inner Mongolia Autonomous Region[20] 3 million mu (200,000 ha), low-yielding cotton in scattered fields 9,700,000 mu (646,666.67 ha), and sugar crops 4,100,000 mu (273,333.33 ha) (Zhao, Cheng May 2000). At the beginning of 2000, the Ministry of Agriculture issued forecasting targets of the year, cutting down output of grain by about 1.97% (10 million tons), cotton by 16.45% (630,000 tons), and aquatic products by more than 2.44% (over 1 million tons) from their 1999 levels (Lu & Zhao 2000. SBNESDC [1999] 2000). The area of early rice in 2000 declined by nearly 8% (over 9 million mu or 600,000 ha) compared with 1999 (Zhao, Cheng May 2000). In fact, in 2000, without causing any food shortage, the grain sown area reduced by 90 million mu (6 million ha) from the 1999 level to 1,607 million mu (107.13 million ha) - the *least* since the foundation of the People's Republic of China in 1949, though population grew by 132% from 1949 to 1999 (see Table 7.6), hence the healthy growth of yield. It is estimated that according to the current production capacity of China, 1,650 million mu (110 million ha) of grain

---

[20] Inner Mongolia Autonomous Region is in the North-Central part of China.

sown area would be appropriate for meeting the demand. Thus, in 2001, the state has guided all regions to stabilize such area. (CNA 2001). Further adjustment would depend on the increase of the production capacity in, and demand for, grain.

Promotion in quality and perfectization in variety of agricultural products. Chapter 6 has already mentioned that in June 1998, the state stipulated that all grain sold by peasants was to be procured by the state at the protective streamline prices. Such an overall protection would however lead peasants to produce products of low quality without good marketing prospects. Thus in June 1999 a selective protection was initiated: the protective prices would be used to procure those products with high quality and good marketing prospects; for those with low quality and bad marketing prospects, lower and eventually no protective prices would be exercised. This selective protection would prompt farmers to produce goods according to market demand and adjust structures of products while still enjoying appropriate protection. At the beginning of 2000, the state further decided to pick certain unsuitable varieties of grain from the range of state procurement under the protective prices, as promulgated by Prime Minister Rong-Ji Zhu (Zhu, Rong-Ji 6 March 2000). In fact, the area of high quality early rice rose by 8,500,000 mu (566,666.67 ha) in 1999 over 1998; and will expand by 9,800,000 mu (653,333.33 ha) in 2000, reaching more than 53 million mu (3,533,333.33 ha), and accounting for about 50% of the whole area of early rice, 14% higher than in 1999. Since 1999, the ratios of cattle, sheep, and pigs with more lean in the livestock have been raised; the productions of eggs and milk have grown by large margins; and famous, superior, special and new aquatic products have increased by a considerably big margin. (Zhao, Cheng May 2000). In reducing output of grain, cotton and aquatic products in 2000, it has been emphasized that it is certain inferior varieties of them which should be eliminated as soon as possible, while those superior ones would be promoted (Lu & Zhao 2000).

The agricultural structures will accordingly be adjusted, as Vice Minister of Agriculture Cheng-Guo Liu pronounces (Liu, Cheng-Guo 2000). The Eastern regions and suburbs of large and medium-sized cities will develop export- and city-oriented modern agriculture, producing more high value-added cash crops and export-used distinctive goods. The Central zones are to give full play to their superiority in food production, establishing large production bases for commodity grain, and food special for processing and forage, with top quality, stable yields and superior economic, social and ecological results. The Western and ecologically weak areas should accelerate the development of agriculture with distinct features, superior economic, social and ecological results, and xerophilous and water-efficient products conducive to protecting the environment. Animal husbandry will be attached special importance, so as to promote the transformation of grain products, structural adjustment of farming, and development of foodstuff, wool spinning, leather, forage and other related industries.

Improvement of the environment all over the country, especially in the Central and Western areas where the ecological system is much weaker. In June 1999, President Jiang has announced the strategy of developing the Central and Western areas in a vast scale (Li, Jian-Guo 2000), and in January 2000 the State Council further stressed to implement this strategy by seizing the opportune moment that China has solved the problem of feeding the population of the whole country by and large and faced a temporary over-supply of food (SC 2000). All sectors of the national economy in the Central and Western areas should be developed, but in agriculture the major task is to improve the environment, and this task should also be fulfilled in the Eastern areas.

* *Converting erodible cultivated land back to forestry, grassland, lake land and wetland.* In China, there are more mountains and grasslands in the Central, further more in the Western, than in the Eastern, part. In over 5,000 years, human beings have been cutting trees and grasses and occupying lake land and wetland for producing grain (Zhu, Rong-Ji 15 March 2000). In fact, a national survey found that by 31 October 1996, 4.66% of the cultivated land had a slope at or over 25 degrees, distributed with 6.4%, 17.1%, and 76.5% in the Eastern, Central and Western areas respectively (see Table 7.15). As a result, soil erosion and desertification have been very serious in the Central, even more in the Western, areas. For example, Sichuan Province is at the upper reaches of the Yangtze River and full of high mountains and steep hills. 70% of its total cultivated land are on the slopes, and its soil erosion accounts for 40.87% of that in the whole Yangtze River valley. (Liang, Xiao-Qin 2000)

During the 11 years from 1989 on, in the upper reaches of the Yangtze River, over 9 million mu (600,000 ha) of the sloping cultivated land, and over 70% of the steeply sloping cultivated land had already been converted back to forestry and grassland respectively. By the end of 1998, in the middle and upper reaches of the Yellow River where the soil erosion was the most serious and the ecological environment the weakest in China and even in the world, conversion of the erodible cultivated land back to forestry and plantation for water- and soil-conserving forests on waste mountains and hills had covered 132 million mu (8,800,000 ha), while grassland converted from the erodible cultivated land and with artificially planted grasses reached 36 million mu (2,400,000 ha). (Jia, Quan-Xin 2000)

At the end of the 1990s, when China had reached the historic landmark - gaining temporary food overproduction, the state further decided that peasants in the ecologically weak areas, while receiving grain subsidy,

Table 7.15 Areas of Cultivated Land, That with a Slope at or over 25 Degrees, and Other Types of Land in China by 31 October 1996

	Country	Eastern	Central	Western
Cultivated land	1,951,000,000 mu (130,066,666.67 ha)	28.4%	43.2%	28.4%
Cultivated land with a slope at or over 25 degrees	91,000,000 mu (6,066,666.67 ha) 4.66% of all cultivate land	6.4%	17.1%	76.5%
Garden plot	150,000,000 mu (10,000,000 ha)	–	–	–
Forestry	3,414,000,000 mu (227,600,000 ha)	–	–	–
Pasture	3,991,000,000 mu (266,066,666,67 ha)	–	–	–
Residential, industrial, & mineral land	361,000,000 mu (24,066,666.67 ha)	–	–	–
Transportation land	82,000,000 mu (5,466,666.67 ha)	–	–	–
Sub-total	9,949,000,000 mu (663,266,666.67 ha)	–	–	–
Waters & unused land	–	–	–	–

Source: National Survey [1996] 2000.

gradually in a planned way convert cultivated land including that with a slope at or over 25 degrees back to forestry, grassland, lake land and wetland (Zou, Qing-Li 2000). In so doing, other areas could continue to produce surplus grain which would be allocated to the ecologically weak areas, and the national food overproduction would accordingly be eliminated.

In March 2000 the state specified to convert 5,150,000 mu (343,333.33 ha) of erodible cultivated land back to forestry in the same year in 174 counties of 13 provinces and autonomous regions around the upper reaches of the Yangtze River and the middle and upper reaches of the Yellow River (most of them are in the Western, some in the Central, areas). For each mu, the state will, calculated according to the grain output and costs per mu, subsidize 150 kg of grain at the upper reaches of the Yangtze River and 100 kg of grain at the middle and upper reaches of the Yellow River (each kg equivalent to 1.40 yuan), plus cash 20 yuan for medical, education and other expenses to peasants. The expenses of allocating and shipping the grain subsidy will be borne by the local governments. The state will also subsidize 50 yuan per mu for seeds and seedlings of trees and grasses to their producing firms; peasants, rather than being imposed the varieties, may be given subsidies to buy them at their own choices in the market (Zhu, Rong-Ji 31 July 2000). The length of subsidizing peasants is according to the need, i.e., without time limit until they can stand on their own feet by the returns from the forest fruits or other activities. The farmers should plant and maintain trees on the previous cultivated land, and where the conditions exist, also reclaim 2 mu (0.133 ha) or more of four wastes (waste mountain, hill, beach and gully) for forestry. The Household Contract System applies, i.e., contractors own all trees and fruits, and can retain all the residuals after fulfilling their responsibilities for the state and collectives. The contract is for 30 years and renewable. (CNA March 2000. Liang, Xiao-Qin 2000. PD 2000)

In addition to the state actions, many provinces, municipalities and autonomous regions have made their own endeavor from their own budget. For example, Guangxi Zhuang Autonomous Region converted 76,666 mu (5,111.07 ha) and 230,000 mu (15,333.33 ha) of erodible cultivated land back to forestry for quick-growing fruits with good marketing prospects in 1998 and 1999 respectively (Chen, Rui-Hua 2000).

* *Halting excessive grazing in order to protect pastures*. During the past decades, increasing pastures have been desertified. Take the example of Inner Mongolia. By the end of the 1990s, 145,800,000 mu (9,720,000 ha) or 23.5% of the whole area of pastures have been destroyed. The area of usable pastures was less than that in the 1980s by 124,200,000 mu (8,280,000 ha). The main causes - all related to population growth - were: (1) Overload by excessive grazing. The effective area of pastures per sheep declined from 49.5 mu (3.3 ha) in the 1950s, to 13.05 mu (0.87 ha) in the mid-1980s, and 6.3 mu (0.42 ha) in the 1990s. The hunger sheep ate young grasses and turned pastures to barren. (GD 2000). The destroying ability of goats to pastures is 20 times that of sheep, since they can dig and eat the roots of grasses even in precipices. (2) Reclamation for grain production of pastures unsuitable for cultivated land. Without the protection of grasses, such land was vulnerable to the invasion of desert. (3) Cutting grasses for fuel. As a result, the northern deserts have approached Beijing, and the 12 sand storms - the most serious of the decades - in the spring of 2000 have even threatened Shanghai in the South. (Shi, Yu-Wen 2000)

In 2000, farmers and herdsmen have been mobilized to not only convert the erodible cultivated land back to grassland, and but also halt excessive grazing by slaughtering over raised livestock, and adopting animal husbandry in pens and stables. Quickly growing and high quality varieties of sheep, goats and cattle have been introduced in to replace the slowly growing and low quality ones, so that herdsmen could decrease the numbers of livestock, but increase their sales, and also incomes. (GD 2000. Li & Tang 2000. Nie & Tang 2000)

   * *Stopping reclamation of forestry, wetlands and grasslands.* For example, Heilongjiang Province started reclamation of a region nicknamed 'Beida*huang*' (meaning a vast Northern *wasteland*) at the beginning of the 1950s. By 1999, the region had acquired 30 million mu (2 million ha) of cultivated land, and produced 8.5 billion kg of grain per year, hence becoming a 'Beida*cang*' (a vast Northern *barn*). In that year, the regional authority resolutely decided to stop reclamation, so as to preserve the remaining forests, grasslands, wetlands, and wild lives; to convert 2,700,000 mu (180,000 ha) of sandy, semi-sandy and inferior cultivated land back to forestry, grasslands or fallow fields within three years; to appropriate 5 million yuan for enlarging and constructing the natural reserves; and to establish training and monitoring programs for improving wetland ecology in joint venture with Japan. The grain output of the region will not be affected because the authority has meanwhile also carried out market-oriented adjustment of the agricultural structures and promoted technological progress to raise yield. In fact, its grain output in 1999 has reached another historic record - 9.05 billion kg. (Gao & Wang 2000)

   Qinghai Lake in Qinghai Province[21] is the largest inland salty lake of China. Its water level was lowered, and the numbers of Huang fish (a special fish) and birds decreased in recent decades. The Province started a seven-year fishing-forbidden period in 1994, prohibited reclamation of grasslands around the Lake in recent years, and implemented other environmental protection measures. As a result, in 1999 the water level increased the first time since 1993, the numbers of Huang fish started to restore in recent two years, and those of birds grew by 400% since 1990. From the beginning of 2000, the Province has started conversion of erodible cultivated land back to grasslands, and a project invested by the state in over 5 million yuan to improve the ecology by planting 5,000 mu (333.33 ha) of trees in the islands for birds, and ameliorating retrograded grasslands of 20,000 mu (1,333.33 ha). (Liang, Juan 2000)

---

[21] Qinghai Province is in the Northwest part of China.

Guizhou Province22 is at the watershed of the upper reaches of the Yangtze River and Pearl River. Its ecological environment is therefore vital to the middle and lower reaches of these long rivers. Due to population growth, some peasants at outlying districts carried out large areas of land reclamation for grain production, and thus seriously destroyed vegetation, and strengthened soil erosion and natural disasters. In August 2000, the Province decided to completely prohibit land reclamation for grain production; convert cultivated land with a slope at or over 25 degrees back to forestry and grassland; and transform medium or low-yielding cultivated land with a slope below 25 degrees to high- and stable yielding one. (He & Ding 2000)

  * *Establishing natural reserves for wild animals and plants.* Contrary to reclaiming forests, grasslands, lakes, and wetlands for grain production, by the end of 1999, China had established 1,118 natural reserves of various types including over 240 of those on wetlands, the total area being 1.2 billion mu (80 million ha or 800,000 square km), accounting for about 8.3% of the whole territory 9,600,000 square km. They have protected 85% of the total types of land ecological systems, 85% of the entire races and colonies of wild animals, and 65% of the whole plant communities at higher degrees. (XHNA January 2000). In Qinghai Province, the area of the natural reserves has reached 50% of the whole area by mid-September 2000 (Chen & Zhang 2000).

  * *Recompensing cultivated land occupied by non-agricultural constructions with reclaimed wasteland.* At the mid-1990s, the state already prescribed that a dynamic balance between the amount of cultivated land turned over for non-agricultural constructions and that of cultivated land newly reclaimed from wasteland must be reached in every province, municipality and autonomous region. At the beginning of 2000, the Ministry of Land and Natural Resources criticized seven provinces and municipalities which still had not achieved such a balance in 1999, and requested them to realize so in 2000. It reiterated that provincial governments must hold responsibility to reject any application for non-agricultural construction by any working unit without funding and feasible planning for reclaiming wasteland whose amount and quality would be equivalent to those of the cultivated land to be occupied; to supervise the reclamation; and to dig the cultivated land surface and move it to the reclaimed wasteland if possible.

---

[22] Guizhou Province is in the Southwest part of China.

(CNA April 2000).**23** In February 2001, the Ministry further proclaimed to implement the practice of recompensing cultivated land with reclaimed wasteland *before* its occupation by non-agricultural constructions, by establishing cultivated land reserves at provincial level (SQD 2001).

China has a great quantity of mining. Mining would ravage land not only because its facilities would occupy land, but also, when the mineral has been dug out, the land surface would cave in. Thus Article 18 of 'Land Management Law' adopted on 25 June 1986 and enforced on 1 January 1987, stipulated that any land which is restorable after mining or its surface has been taken, should be restored by the working units or individuals that have used it (LML [1986] 1989: 29). The State Council further issued detailed 'Regulations on the Restoration of Land' on 21 October 1988, to be exercised on 1 January 1989 (RRL [1988] 1989: 194–9). By 1999, 8% of the land ruined by mining has been restored. But this ratio was still much lower than the prevailing one - about 50% - in the advanced countries. China has thus strengthened work in this field in recent years and established over 20 successful demonstration sites, e.g., Huaibei City of Anhui Province, Tangshan City of Hebei Province and Feicheng City of Shandong Province. (Qin, Jing-Wu August 2000)

Since July 1999, the Ministry of Land and Natural Resources has used the data from the US and French satellites with resolving power of 30 and 10 meters respectively to monitor - in an accuracy of over 90% - the dynamic change in land use of 66 cities with 500,000 or more inhabitants (which account for 78.6% of such cities and whose area of the cultivated land makes up 19.5% of that of the whole country). Applying the remote sensing data to check the land change investigation results of 10 provinces and municipalities, the Ministry found that, while most results were correct, a few districts hid the truth or did not make thorough investigations. In one city, over 2,800 mu (186.67 ha) of cultivated land had been occupied without approval. Now, all the 66 cities are utilizing the remote sensing data to check their land use situation and correct errors. The Ministry will extend remote sensing to larger areas. (Qin, Jing-Wu July 2000. Wang, Shi-Yuan 1999). In February 2001, this Ministry has announced to take the strictest measures (including both those already and to be adopted) to protect the cultivated land, and ensure that its area will not be below 1,920 million mu (128 million ha) during the Tenth Five-Year Plan period (2001–05) (SQD 2001).

---

[23] As it may no longer be possible to reclaim wasteland with a slope at or over 25 degrees for cultivated land, a corresponding adjustment of this regulation would be to reach a balance between the amount of cultivated land turned over for non-agricultural constructions and that of cultivated land newly reclaimed from wasteland with a slope below 25 degrees as well as that of forestry and grassland newly reclaimed from wasteland with a slope at or over 25 degrees.

* *Preventing idleness of farmland transferred for non-agricultural development.* Article 21 of 'Regulations on the Protection of the Main Farmland' promulgated on 18 August and implemented on 1 October 1994 by the State Council prescribed that, if a piece of *main* farmland already approved for non-agricultural construction is not to be used so within one year, it should be cultivated and harvested (if this is possible) by the original collective or individuals, or by other farmers organized by the constructing unit; if it has been idled for more than one year, the constructing unit should pay an idling fee; if it has been continuously idled for two years without proper approval, the land should be withdrawn to the original collective by the county government (RPMF [1994] 1995: 14). Article 37 of 'Land Management Law' amended on 29 August 1998 and exercised on 1 January 1999 further extended its application to *all* farmland and ordained that such withdrawal of land is free of remuneration to the constructing unit (LML [1998] 1999: 11).**24**

* *Strengthening afforestation.* At the beginning of 2000, China declared that in contrast to the downsizing trend of the forest resources of the whole world, both area and storage quantity of forests in China have been continuously increasing (Wang, Zhi-Bao 2000), and 12 provinces and autonomous regions have made all their afforestable waste mountains green. The ratio of land covered by forests to the whole land has been raised from 8% in 1949 (Li, Liu & Zhang 2000) to 15.12% in 1993 and 16.55% in 1998 (Zhao, Cheng June 2000). After the heavy flood in the summer of 1998, the state firmly stopped lumbering in the upper reaches of the Yangtze River. At the beginning of 2000, the state further put forward that (1) in the upper reaches of the Yangtze River and the middle and upper reaches of the Yellow River, natural forests should be protected, afforestable waste mountains and land made green, and cultivated land on steep hills converted back to forestry and grasslands; (2) in the dry, windy and sandy Northwest and Northwesternmost zones, anti-desertification projects strengthened; (3) in the Northeasternmost and Inner Mongolian regions, lumbering changed to forest maintenance; and (4) in the Eastern and Central areas, quick-growing and high-yielding timber, forests for industrial use, and famous, special, new and superior varieties of cash fruit forests developed (Zhao & Zhou 2000).

* *Substituting tree-cutting with forest tourism and services.* For example,

---

[24] Similarly, the state has also prohibited idleness of the state-owned urban land transferred for real estate development. Article 25 of 'Management Law on Urban Real Estate' announced on 5 July 1994 and enforced on 1 January 1995, decreed that the government can impose an idling fee on the real estate developer if the construction has not started one year after the date decided in the contract, and withdraw the land free of payment if it has been idled for two years (MLURE 1994: 23).

Li-Min Zhang of Tiantang Zhai Tree Farm of Luotian County of Hubei Province lived by tree-cutting before 1999. In that year, he turned to guide tourists and sell them foods in the Farm and earned over 3,000 yuan. In the same year, the Farm received 20,000 tourists, gaining economic benefits equivalent to those from tree-cutting in a whole previous year. In the Province, there are already nearly 100,000 persons like Li-Min Zhang who have left poverty for richness through forest tourism and services. (Liu, Hui 2000)

  * *Developing green agriculture.* For instance, Jiangxi Province25 enjoys suitable temperature, full of sunshine, and abundant rainfall as favorable natural conditions to develop pollution-free green agriculture. Under the promotion of all levels of governments, in recent years, water- and soil-conserving forests and grasses have been grown, cash fruit forests planted, and terraced fields re-arranged in scientific ways. In 1999, 343,000 mu (22,866.67 ha) of land with soil erosion were harnessed; firewood- and coal-efficient stoves popularized; and methane-generating pits (in which human and livestock excrements are kept to yield methane for heating, cooking and lighting thus saving firewood, coal and electricity, and then used as manure for fruits, vegetables and fish, that in turn would be consumed by human beings and livestock, hence a sanitary ecological chain) kept by 8.92% of the total rural households. These pits could per year lead to the production of 660,000 domestic animals, 200,000 tons of vegetables, and 190,000 tons of fruits, direct economic benefits of about 1 billion yuan, and saving of firewood equivalent to a quantity yielded by 3 million mu (200,000 ha) of fuel forests. As a result, the ratio of land covered by forests to total land reached 53%, leading in the whole country. Peasants further changed from highly poisonous to biological, slightly or non poisonous new pesticides, and used advanced technology to reduce the times of pesticide application, thus greatly cutting down their remnants. At the beginning of 2000, farmers eagerly purchased special fertilizers, composite fertilizers, and new pesticides, increasing their sales by more than 10%. Transformations of the present varieties of grain, oil, pigs, vegetables, melons, fruits, etc. have been made in order to produce new brands of high quality, local, special, pollution-free green agricultural products. In 1999, 21 types of green foods were developed, equivalent to the sum in the previous 10 years. The pollution-free vegetables of Yangzizhou High Technology Garden of Nanchang City entered the supermarkets of the City. Biyun (meaning white clouds in a blue sky) japonica rice won a large share of the coastal markets. The price of Dazhang Mountain Tea was three—four times that of ordinary

---

[25] Jiangxi Province is in the South-Central part of China.

ones, but sold well even in the European Union. (Ou & Yan 2000)

7.4 Theoretical Discussion

In merely about 20 years from 1978 to 1999, China has not only overcome food shortage, a challenge still facing many developing economies and even developed ones like Japan which once reached food self-sufficiency in 1960 but has fallen from - or artificially maintained - it ever since, but also prevented food overproduction, a task even developed countries have never fulfilled. Schultz's observation ([1964] 1983: 20–1) 'The breakthrough in agricultural production centers on Japan. China, despite its massive program to expand agricultural production, is in real trouble' should be correct for the first breakthrough in sustainable rural development of monsoon Asia in 1960 (shattering the vicious circle of rural poverty). Since the mid-1980s, however, China has achieved the second and third breakthroughs (overcoming the fragmented small farms maintained by the inefficient land-holding of the part-time and absent small farmers as the last obstacle; and preventing food overproduction). Thus, the same observation would still be true as long as the names of the two countries are exchanged. Indeed, rural poor people (those under subsistence level) reduced sharply from 250 million as 30.7% of the rural population in 1978 to 34 million as about only 4% by the end of 1999 in China (POSC 2000: 6. Guo, Wei 2000: 2). Here, a theoretical consideration would be desirable.

Elimination of individual bargains. Compared with the situation in Japan, the process of land consolidation and expansion to overcome the fragmented small farms as the last obstacle imposed by the monsoon in sustainable rural development of Asia was much smoother in China. The fundamental reason was the land tenure system. Under the village collective form of land ownership of China, the bargaining power of the part-time and absent small farmers who held contracted land for inefficient use and imposed negative pecuniary externalities on the full-time farmers and the society was much weaker. Thus, the village could function as a typical or real firm within which, as Coase supposes, the individual bargains between the various cooperating factors of production are eliminated/reduced and a market transaction is substituted by an administrative decision by an entrepreneur who directs resources with authority. The inefficiently used land could be transferred to full-time and expert farmers for efficient use at much lower transaction costs - educating villagers on the importance of efficient use of land and large-scale farming; providing them with self-sufficiency land for establishing the Dual Land System, and selling them self-consumed grain at prices lower than market levels plus family plots for vegetables for setting up the Single Land System, which could provide them with a back-up basic social welfare and win the majority and even unanimous agreement of them; and obliging those part-time and absent small farmers who still refused to give up land to participate in tendering together with expert farmers, thus either winning or losing the contract. Approach 1 to assigning property rights for eliminating negative externalities (permission for the relevant parties to exchange property rights through a political or legal process, followed by market exchange) and Approach 2 [implementation of social actions (law, tax, etc.) to oblige the externality-yielding party to exchange property rights, followed by market exchange] were applied. Both were applications of mixed economy: multiple structures of public and private ownership, and government intervention other than ownership.

It is because the collective land ownership could eliminate the bargaining power of land users that the inefficient land-holding by part-time and absent small farmers and the fragmented small farms as the last obstacle could be overcome, food self-sufficiency maintained, and furthermore surplus food produced on normal land (mainly in the Eastern and Central parts) and allocated to the ecologically weak areas (chiefly in the Western and Central parts). It is also because of this reason that the possessors of the erodible cultivated land could be mobilized or obliged to convert it back to forestry, grassland, lake land and wetland so as to prevent a national food overproduction and improve the environment.

Collective land ownership has always been despised as anti-market economy by the main stream Western economists (represented by Hayek and Friedman). Since the end of the 1980s, decollectivization has been in fashion in Central and Eastern Europe and former USSR countries. Interesting enough, under private land ownership in Japan, land could not be operated according to market principles of competition (recalling that 'competitive' means that resources can move smoothly in response to prices, i.e., without being monopolistically or oligopolistically held with bargaining power, as reviewed in Chapter 3), creating thus indeed an anti-market economy; but under collective land ownership in China, it could, hence a pro-market economy. Therefore, collective land ownership not only does not exclude a market economy, it can even strengthen it under a collective–individual mixed economy.

Government intervention has also been regarded as being too closely related with public ownership of the means of production by the mainstream Western economists. This therefore implies that private land ownership should require less government intervention. Ironical enough, however, in order to promote land consolidation and expansion, the Japanese government intervened on a much wider scale, spent much more money, time and effort than the Chinese government which mainly relied on the initiatives of local officials and peasants and financial resources of villages and townships, plus issuing guidance to them. The major problem with the Japanese government intervention was that it remained outside the land tenure system, regarding private land ownership as untouchable, which thus resulted in even more government intervention and still little progress. By contrast, to achieve the same aim, collective land ownership in a collective–individual mixed economy in China required far less government intervention.

Therefore, the key question is not whether government should intervene or not, but with what and how it should intervene. A major reform of private land ownership and introduction of relevant public factors into it may result in much less government intervention.

Hence the possible value of Proposal 5.1 as elaborated in Chapter 5 - village-wide corporate ownership of physically unwithdrawable but financially salable private land shares, which, by preserving private land ownership but adding public factors to it, would weaken the bargain power of the private landowners in land consolidation and expansion and later in conversion of erodible cultivated land to the original nature, thus introducing a competitive market economy into land use and greatly reducing (although not abolishing) government intervention.

Appropriateness of large-scale farming. The large-scale farming and collective–individual mixed economy in China pursued *appropriate* large-scale farming, i.e., it expanded the farming scale from the Equal Land System first to the Dual Land System (self-sufficiency land to everybody; responsibility land to everybody, every labor force, every agricultural labor force, and finally expert farmers via tendering) then to the Single Land System (responsibility land to expert farmers; self-consumed grain at lower prices and family plots for vegetables to everyone else), according to the extent to which the development of non-grain agriculture and off-farm activities could absorb surplus peasants, rather than squeezing out those peasants who still relied on the land. Holland's concept of variable mixed economies - varying relations between the public and private sectors, and their dynamic change over time in relation to changing needs in economy and society - actually reflects this process. This was also exhibited in the theme of the timing of changing existing property rights structures - following the development of production, technology and market, which induces new benefit–cost possibilities, that in turn shows gains of internalization (or efficient production) of negative externalities that exceed its costs, which subsequently raises the need for internalization (or efficient production) of negative externalities, that finally requires a change of the existing property rights structures and a new institutional and legal framework for enforcement.

Although the village could function as a typical or real firm with an entrepreneur directing resources with authority, the leaders (entrepreneurs) could not do it arbitrarily. In order to introduce and manage the Dual Land System, majority agreement had to be gained, while the Single Land System required majority or even unanimous consent. There have been cases in which village officials, in order to charge more collective fees for rural industrialization or probably also for personal gains, violated the appropriateness of large-scale farming and forced the mass of peasants who could not yet find jobs in non-grain agriculture and off-farm activities to subsist on tiny self-sufficiency land or, in one extreme case, gave them no land. But such wrongdoings would exert negative externalities on the farmers and society as a whole, tending to be reported and sued by villagers, exposed by the media and penalized by the government which attaches extreme importance to the maintenance of rural stability and eradication of poverty.

The successful practices and the amended 'Land Management Law' enforced on 1 January 1999 (which stipulated that the contractee should stop the contract and withdraw the land if the contractor has idled it continuously for two years; required a two-thirds majority agreement by villagers or their representatives and county government approval, and allowed court judgement, for adjusting individual land within its contractual period) have demonstrated that the large-scale farming and collective–individual mixed economy based on public land ownership in China, could on one hand eliminate the negative pecuniary externalities by the part-time and absent small farmers on the full-time farmers much more easily than in Japan, and on the other with the villagers' democratic participation control the speed of expansion of large-scale farming so as to prevent the negative externalities by the large-scale farmers (and arbitrary officials) on the mass of peasants who still needed land, thereby also avoiding such a situation as in India (as reviewed in Chapter 5) from happening in China.

Functioning of large-scale farming. Under the Chinese model of rural development, not only fragmented small farms could thrive at the low wage economy just as under the Japanese model, but also large-scale farmers could prosper at the high wage economy, which has been constrained under the Japanese model.

Nuti's model of market socialism as a third way between the centrally planned economy and free market system, in which incentives from competitive leasing and Pareto efficiency could be achieved, in fact is in accordance with the mechanism whereby various organizations of large-scale farmers (individual household farms, joint households farms, collective farms 1, 2 and 3, urban–rural joint enterprises, external and foreign ventures) could work well within a framework of public land ownership in China.

Again, of the many variables for rural development, institutional changes are the keystone. It is the institutional component that is the most important in the interaction of institutions and technologies as the underlying long-term ultimate causes that sustain economic growth of developing countries. But once production has reached the frontier permitted by the established institutions, even though the increase of production is technologically possible, it would be hampered by the vested interests - the part-time and absent small farmers who held land for inefficient use in both Japan and China. At this stage, variable mixed economies were needed in order to reach dynamic or long-term Pareto efficiency, and another round of institutional changes required to allow sustainable rural development. It did not take place in Japan, hence feature 9 of the Japanese model (persistence of the fragmented small farms due to inefficient land-holding). But it did take place in China, thus feature 9 of the Chinese model (large-scale farming and collective– individual mixed economy), which made its feature 10 (agricultural mechanization with large machinery) possible, and facilitated its features 11 (successive promotion of development in poorer areas), 12 (urban–rural joint enterprises and external and foreign ventures in agriculture) and 13 (prevention of food overproduction and improvement of the environment). Hence the arguable superiority of the Chinese model over the Japanese.

Agricultural mechanization with large machinery became necessary because as more and more able-bodied male peasants went to work in non-grain agriculture and off-farm activities, labor costs exceeded machinery costs in grain culture. It would be generally unprofitable for large-scale farms to hire many wage laborers to form *capitalist* farms, although it was allowed. Rather, by using large machinery, participating in labor by large-scale farmers themselves, and hiring a few laborers when necessary, large-scale *quasi-capitalist* farms would be more suitable. Therefore, in general, the large-scale farms could be regarded as *capitalistic* farms, as defined in Chapter 3.

After agricultural mechanization with large machinery became both necessary and possible, there existed the problem that ordinary individual farming households might not be able to afford to buy machines and, even if they could, might not use them in economies of scale. Thus, economies of scale in holding large machinery were also applied and promoted: machinery services to large-scale farms were provided by specialized individual households, or joint households, or collective service stations.

The optimal size of large-scale farming reflected technological Pareto efficiency by which there is no way to produce more output with the same inputs or to produce the same output with less inputs. But the optimal size varies across time and place and changes as the economic structures change, hence also dynamic efficiency.

The three stages in providing direct and indirect subsidies from industrial profits to large-scale farmers give evidence for the thesis that market forces should be fostered. As reviewed in Chapter 2, there are some who are impatient with the inefficiencies of government and want to shift to the market, which they consider the most efficient allocator of resources. But the market is only as efficient as the forces making up the market. It took some time for the West to evolve and nurture these forces. It is well known that the (former) socialist countries are encountering difficulties in shifting from a planned to a market economy. It will take some time before market forces are developed, especially the ability of entrepreneurs to finance and market their production. Indeed, an important historical function of government in the process of development is to mold these forces so that the market becomes an efficient resource allocator. Therefore, the large-scale farmers initially required both direct and indirect subsidies. As they became stronger, they could relinquish the direct subsidies first, and even indirect subsidies in the future.

But even the subsidies by industry to agriculture were mainly from villages and township governments, less from the higher local governments, and virtually not from the central government. Likewise, the grain subsidies for peasants to convert erodible cultivated land back to forestry, grassland, lake land and wetland, in order to both prevent a national food overproduction and improve the environment, are from surplus food produced on normal land.26 Therefore under the Chinese model based on

---

[26] According to the World Trade Organization (WTO 2000), the agricultural package of the Uruguay Round has fundamentally changed the way domestic support in favor of agricultural producers was treated under the GATT 1947. A key objective has been to discipline and reduce domestic support while at the same time leaving great scope for governments to design domestic agricultural policies in face of, and response to, the wide variety of the specific circumstances in individual countries and individual agricultural sectors. The approach agreed upon is also aimed at helping ensure that the specific binding commitments in the areas of market access and export competition are not undermined through domestic support measures.

There are basically two categories of government domestic support. 1. 'Green Box' subsidies are support with no, or minimal, distortive effect on trade. They have to be government-funded (not by charging consumers higher prices) and must not involve price support. They include government service programs (e.g., agricultural research or training), environmental protection and regional development programs, programs that are not directed at particular products, direct income supports for farmers that are not related to current production levels or prices (e.g., natural disaster relief), etc. They are allowed without limits, provided they comply with relevant criteria. ('Green Box' subsidies are roughly equivalent to the indirect subsidies referred to in Chapters 6 and 7 of this book.)

In addition, certain direct payments under production-limiting programs ('Blue Box' subsidies) and certain developmental measures in developing countries are also allowed.

2. 'Amber Box' subsidies (trade-distorting support) include market price support measures (government buying-in at a guaranteed price), direct production subsidies, input subsidies, etc. The minimum allowed level is 5% of the total value of production of the agricultural product in question for developed countries, and 10% for developing countries. ('Amber Box' subsidies

collective land ownership, by implementing variable mixed economies, self-reliance within the rural sector could be achieved, matching the definition of sustainable agricultural and rural development as reviewed in Chapter 1, which includes 'Food security, to be obtained by ensuring an appropriate and sustainable balance between self-sufficiency and self-reliance; employment and income generation in rural areas, particularly to eradicate poverty; and natural resource conservation and environmental protection.' In contrast, in the Japanese model under private land ownership, due to yielding to free market forces, large-scale farming could not be realized, and small-scale farmers could not survive without huge government subsidies derived from non-agricultural sectors, which then led to rice overproduction, that further required government subsidies to reduce, hence an unsustainable agricultural and rural development.

The evolution from the small-scale to the large-scale farming collective–individual mixed economy apparently followed the two general methods of changing existing property rights structures: the first is to make *gradual* changes in social mores and common law precedents, and the second to make a *conscious* collective endeavor, such as a major reform or revolution at a certain stage of the gradual changes in the first general method.

Chapter 7, together with Chapters 4–6, has provided evidence for the author's hypothesis outlined earlier that the fragmented small farms as the last obstacle imposed by the monsoon against sustainable rural development in Asia may be overcome by variable mixed economies, increasingly along three main phases. *Phase 1*: sub-village individual–collective mixed economy (sub-village-wide cooperative/enterprise collective use of physically withdrawable private land shares, exercising collective–individual dual level operation of large land units, with the basic operation level at one household as the major form or at a unit including a small number of households as the minor form). *Phase 2*: village-wide individual–collective mixed economy. *Phase 3*: either large-scale farming public–individual mixed economy or corporate–individual mixed economy (collective use of either public land, or physically unwithdrawable private land shares under corporate ownership, exercising village–individual dual level operation of large land units, with the basic operation level at one household as the major form or at a unit including a small number of households as the minor form, as a third way beyond the centrally planned economy and free market system).

---

are similar to the direct subsidies referred to in Chapters 6 and 7 of this book.)

China is the largest developing country of the world. By January 2001, however, the government 'Amber Box' subsidies have been at only 2% (EIN 2001).

8. Other Rice-Based Economies under Public Land Ownership in Monsoon Asia

Agricultural land has been under public ownership in Cambodia, Laos, Myanmar, North Korea and Vietnam. They have all adopted market-oriented rural development measures, although to distinctly different degrees. In the sense that they still retain public land ownership, they could be regarded as within the Chinese model. According to the criteria that China has achieved the fastest economic development with average annual growth rate of gross domestic product (GDP) of 9.71% during 1990—99 (CSY 1999: 57. SBNESDC [1999] 2000), avoided new landlessness in the low wage economy and controlled inefficient land-holding in the high wage economy, China might be considered as being at *level 1*. Myanmar, whose average annual growth rate of GDP reached 5.55% during 1991/92—98/99 (Vokes 2000: 761), and whose land tenure system has avoided new landlessness in the low wage economy and could also control inefficient land-holding in the high wage economy, may be regarded as being at *level 2*. The average annual growth rate of GDP was 4.5% during 1992—98 in Cambodia (Summers 2000: 218— 20), 6.24% during 1991—98 in Laos (Gainsborough 2000: 643—4), and 8.26% during 1990—98 in Vietnam (Demaine 2000: 1243). But following the establishment of a nominal state - but *de facto* private - land ownership, both new landlessness and inefficient land-holding have immediately appeared. Therefore they are placed at *level 3*. North Korea in principle still retains the centrally planned economy, its average annual growth rate of gross national product (GNP) was –4.76% (note *negative*) during 1991—97, and growth rate of GDP –1.1% in 1998 (Chung 2000: 578), but achieved positive growth in 1999—2000 (Ai, Chen 2001). Hence it is classified at *level 4*. The following review focuses on their land tenure reforms.1

8.1 Different Levels of Land Tenure Reforms

Level 2: Myanmar

The Constitution of 24 September 1947 of *Myanmar* which gained independence on 4 January 1948 established a state land ownership with the right of tilling land given to the actual tillers. They include mainly private individuals, but also state economic enterprises, cooperatives, domestic—foreign joint ventures and other organizations. Upon application by peasant households, village people's councils allocated parcels of land to farmers with a maximum duration of 30 years, but renewable for lifetime, and decided who should till the land after their death. Thus small land-holders have been dominant. (Silverstein 1997: 634—5. Steinberg 1981: 125; 1987: 273. Kyi Win 1997)

During 1962—86, there was a compulsory state rice procurement quota system. In principle, the state had a *monopoly* of all major commercial sales of rice, inter-township paddy shipment, and exports. Quotas were set for procurement from individual farms. The farms could retain fixed amounts for home consumption plus a small amount for seeds and ceremonial activities, were required to sell most of the surplus up to the quotas to the state agency, and could then sell the residual to any individual consumer within the township (in specified rice surplus townships, also beyond the township) (like 'bao *gan* dao hu', the major form of the Household Contract System in China). The state procurement prices, although raised several times, were generally lower than the market prices, hence a Dual Track Price System for rice (analogous to but implemented before the Chinese practice). *During 1987—88*, the state liberalized the marketing of rice, first by allowing cooperatives to operate alongside the state agency, and then, in September 1987, by opening trade to private agents. Their introduction, however, coincided with a decline in paddy production and a period of rapidly rising rice prices which contributed to growing unrest in urban areas in 1988. Thus, *since 1989*, the compulsory state rice procurement quota system has been reintroduced. In 1990—91, the state purchased about 15% of total paddy

---

[1] The framework of this chapter has been published by the Food and Agriculture Organization of the United Nations in Zhou, Jian-Ming [1996] (1997), with abstract by CABI; and an earlier version of it in Zhou, Jian-Ming (March 1998), accepted by the Fifth Conference of the European Association for Comparative Economic Studies (10—12 September 1998), with abstract by CABI.

output, cooperatives bought around 7%, and the rest was open to private agents (similar to China too). Although the quota prices were lower than the market prices, the state provided fertilizer and credit at subsidized prices to farmers. (Steinberg 1981: 133; 1987: 274. Vokes 1997: 646)

Rice still dominates the economy, and is the main source of employment and principal export earner. Production is dependent on the weather. As a result, Myanmar remains one of the poorer countries in Asia. (Vokes 1997: 645–6). Its land tenure system, which is quite similar to feature 1 of the Chinese model, has avoided new landlessness in the low wage economy, could control inefficient land-holding in the high wage economy, and has guaranteed a basic food security via the state compulsory procurement quota system. But it also is currently under revision in order to realize a more market-oriented rural development (Kyi Win 1997).

Level 3: Cambodia, Laos and Vietnam

In contrast to China and Myanmar, Cambodia (1981), Laos (1988) and Vietnam (1993) founded a nominal state - but *de facto* private - land ownership.

In *Cambodia*, agricultural cooperatives under the rigid centrally planned economy were replaced in 1979 by *krom samaki* (solidarity groups), each composed of 10–15 households, with three different classes. In class 1, production was fully collectivized. No matter whether they were shirking or working hard, members could gain the produce according to the man-days they worked (like that in the Chinese communes). In class 2, the major means of production were collectively owned, but only limited work was conducted collectively. Land was divided into parcels allocated on a family basis corresponding to the number of family members, and managed by families. In class 3, land officially belonged to the state but all the other means of production were privately owned, and families were engaged wholly in individual production. While in 1981, 20% of the *krom samaki* were in class 1, and 60% in class 2, by 1989, almost 90% were in class 3. In the same year, it also was decided to abandon the *krom samaki*. Rural residential land was turned to private ownership and could be sold and bought. Farmland belonged to the state but possession was given to peasant households with tax to be paid for using it. If farmland was not used for one year, the authorities could take it away. The possession of farmland was also salable and farmland could be converted into residential land, both subject to the approval of government offices. (Summers 1997: 187. Kusakabe; Wang & Kelkar 1995: 87–90)

Laos halted the establishment of new agricultural cooperatives in 1979, and abandoned them in 1986. In 1988, long-term usufructuary rights to land were granted to peasant households, inheritable and salable to natural and legal persons. This was confirmed in the 1991 new Constitution which also made clear that all land belongs to the state. (Gainsborough 1997: 538–9. Hijmans 1997). Any land left idle could in theory be retrieved by the village chief and reallocated, on a temporary basis, to another family. Since 1993, the state has required that villages pay land tax in cash, while refusing the traditional payments in paddy. (Groppo; Mekouar; Damais & Phouangphet 1996: 14–5)

In *Vietnam*, before 1979, a workpoints system was carried out in agricultural cooperatives (as in the Chinese communes) which resulted in equalitarianism rather than incentives. In that year, it was supplanted by a system of contracting output quotas to households and linking the fulfillment with workpoints which were then linked to remuneration (similar to 'bao *chan* dao hu', the minor form of the Household Contract System in China). To achieve equality in land quality, quantity and distance, land given to households was fragmented (which was not necessarily consolidated in the later reforms). The tenure length was three to 15 years. By 1988, it was further replaced by a system of contracting output quotas to households, leaving the total residuals to them without the involvement of workpoints (analogous to 'bao *gan* dao hu', the major form of the Household Contract System in China). In 1988–89, the compulsory procurement quotas were displaced by a land tax of 10% of normal output (as average in the past)2 and land use rights were given for 15 years to households which agreed their own contracts for the sale of whatever crops they chose to cultivate. (Demaine 1997: 1057. Hayami 1994: 1, 9–10, 13, 19). The Land Law adopted on 14 July and enforced on 14 October 1993, declared that all land was formally owned by the state but households were given land use rights (Article 1) which were further exchangeable, transferable (salable), leasable (maximum three years normally - Article 78), inheritable, and mortgageable for loans (Article 3). The local administrations (such as the people's committee of communes and districts) were supposed to judge the need for land sellers or lessors to reduce their land-holdings and also to assess the capacity of buyers or lessees to use the increased holdings efficiently (Hayami 1994: 14–5). The limit of agricultural land for annual crops of each household was 3 ha (Article 44). The use period was 20 years for planting annual crops and aquaculture, 50 for perennial crops, and renewable if

---

[2] But Haque and Montesi (1997 Part One: 9) report that the land-use tax rate is fixed at 7% of the average value of output achieved during the previous three years. The tax rates vary from 50 kg per ha to 550 kg per ha for various categories of annual cropland, and up to 650 kg per ha for perennial cropland. Once defined, the land categories remain unchanged for 10 years.

lawfully used (Article 20). If the land was not used for one year, it could be withdrawn by the state (Article 26). If the state needed to recover land for public interest, compensation would be given to the households affected (Article 27). (LLV [1993] 1994: 40, 43, 45, 49, 56). In order to record and protect private land use rights, the government has been conducting a nation-wide cadastral survey and land registration and has begun to issue Land Use Right Certificates (LURC). But this would need 15 years to complete and is extremely costly. (Hayami 1994: 9, 12)

Because in these three countries, since the new land tenure reforms, the state-owned farmland could be used as if it were private land, there is no state compulsory procurement quota, the possession of land could be sold and bought like private property, and in Cambodia residential land became privately owned and salable, such land use rights have *'become little different from private land property rights* in modern market economies in their effects on resource allocations, even though "state ownership of land" is maintained' (Hayami 1994: 9).

Level 4: North Korea

In North Korea, agricultural land is either collectively owned (more than 90%) or state-owned. A centrally planned economy is still in place. In 1995–96, a new emphasis was placed on the transformation of collective farms to state ownership. Since 1991, output has declined and serious food shortages have occurred, especially since 1993 due to floods (FEA 1995: 466; 1997: 488). Rice was an important export commodity until the mid-1980s, but has had to be imported, together with wheat, in the 1990s. Although the labor force in agriculture was reduced to 32.6% of the total labor force in 1991 (FAO-YP 1993: 29), this did not mean that it had completed the first transition, but rather it reflected a relative labor scarcity in an economy disproportionately engaged in heavy industry and with a large military. In fact, the armed forces had to be deployed to help agricultural work in 1996. (Chung 1997: 481–3)

A few signs of economic reform have, however, also become apparent. Industrial joint ventures with foreign - including capitalist - countries, following the Chinese-style special economic zones, started in 1984, although with limited success. In 1994–96, emphasis was switched from heavy industry to agriculture, light industry and foreign trade. (Chung 1997: 481–3). More significantly, in 1996, the state allowed 30 pyong (0.0099 ha)3 of backyard cultivation for each civilian household and 100 pyong (0.033 ha)

---

[3] 1 pyong = 0.00033 ha = 0.033 are = 3.3 square meters = 0.00495 mu.

for a soldier's family (Shim Jae Hoon 1996: 30), which were similar to the family plots of China, and it was reported in 1997 that massive collective farms have been reduced in size; in 1998, land was contracted to groups - a level between collective farm and households, and surplus grain beyond quotas could be disposed of by contractors and sold (approaching feature 1 of the Chinese model: institutional changes for a small-scale farming and collective–individual mixed economy). It also was reported that some farmers have been permitted to plant crops twice a year (double-cropping) which had long been forbidden (both feature 4: multiple cropping of grains and feature 5: diversified cropping). Peasants in the hard-hit northern provinces have been told to fend for themselves, allowing them to trade privately with China (feature 2: market-oriented government policies). With help from the UN Development Program, there have been a few scattered experiments, providing credit to individual households to buy chickens or goats and allowing them to sell eggs or milk on the open market (feature 5: non-crop agriculture). (Richburg 1997: 4. APET 1998).

Further encouraging is that in his visit of China during 29–31 May 2000, the North Korean leader Jong Il Kim (Kim, Jong Il) praised and supported China's reform and open-door policies initiated by Xiao-Ping Deng (Deng, Xiao-Ping) in 1978. He indicated that parallel with China's construction of a socialism with Chinese characteristics, North Korea is building a socialism of North Korean style according to its own domestic situations, implying a breakaway from the previous orthodox and stubborn socialism. (XHNA June 2000). He invited South Korean businessmen to make more investments in the North following the historic conciliatory meeting between the leaders of the two Koreas in Pyongyang during 13–15 June 2000 (Taiwan Media 2000). In general, North Korea is still at the beginning stage of the Chinese model of rural development.

8.2 An Analysis of the Nominal State - But *De Facto* Private - Land Ownership

Although the abolition of the centrally planned economy in the rural areas of Cambodia, Laos and Vietnam has raised production, the designers and advocates of the nominal state - but *de facto* private - land ownership either did not expect or excluded the ensuing problems, especially the following two.

(1) New landlessness in the low wage economy. As indicated in Chapter 2, in monsoon Asia, when yields of rice and other grains are low, and rural infrastructure, diversified cropping, non-crop agriculture, and off-farm employment not yet developed, peasants can find few employment

opportunities in non-grain production. Thus their income is very low. In such a low wage economy, their ability to cope with problems in production and living is also very weak. In both the Chinese and Japanese models, however, new landlessness after the land reform of Japan of 1946—50 and the land tenure reform of China of 1978—83 has been avoided mainly by feature 1 (institutional changes for an individual—cooperative or collective—individual mixed economy), showing *two major differences* in comparison with Cambodia, Laos and Vietnam.

The First is prohibition of or strongly restricted private land ownership. In *China*, after the land tenure reform, private ownership of either residential or any other land is not allowed. Everybody is guaranteed land for the state, self-sufficiency and market under the Equal Land System and self-sufficiency land under the Dual Land System. The possession of responsibility land is not equal to private property because there are state compulsory procurement quotas. The possession of any land does not entail that it can be sold and bought, although contracted land can be transferred and the transferor can charge remuneration for the improvement he (she) has made. Under the Single Land System, those who have left farmland to earn an income higher than that from small-scale farming are sold self-consumed grain at lower prices and given family plots for vegetables. In *Japan*, after the land reform to introduce individual ownership, until the 1960s—70s, land sale and lease, although allowed, were seriously restricted by a 3 ha ceiling on land-holding, protection of tenants from eviction, and control of land rent at a very low level.

The Second is collective support to individual farms. In *China*, land is under village—household dual level operation. The households are the basic level, but the village has the duty to provide services and support to them, and reduce or waive their state procurement quotas in the event of natural disasters. In *Japan*, during the 1950s, when peasants were still poor and weak, the national rural cooperatives network provided extensive collective services and support to individual households. Therefore, poverty due to weak single household operation of land and emergence of new landlessness have been avoided in both China and Japan.

By contrast, in Cambodia, Laos and Vietnam, where most rural areas are still in the low wage economy, the permission to sell state-owned but individually possessed land opened up the *possibility* that peasants might be forced to sell land to cope with natural disasters, diseases, debts (including gambling losses) and other difficulties, or be induced to sell land to industrial and urban developers/dwellers in order to earn easy and high short-term profits, thus becoming newly landless. The marginalization or abolition of the agricultural cooperatives together with their services and support to individual households resulted in single individual household system of operation which is weak when peasants are still poor. The difficulties they incurred reinforced the *necessity* for them to sell land and become newly landless.

In Cambodia. Agriculture remains the mainstay of the economy. Employment opportunities outside agriculture are extremely limited. Agriculture itself is dominated by rice subsistence farming. Production is vulnerable to adverse weather conditions. Irrigation systems remain usually inoperable. In 1996, 38% of households were below the poverty line. Cambodia is one of the poorest countries in Asia and the world. (FAO/WFP 1996: 2)

When the *krom samaki* were abolished, land was distributed to member households according to their family size at that time and was to be registered at the district land office. Under the new system, privately owned residential land could be sold and bought with the permission of the district land office. State-owned but privately possessed farmland could also be sold and bought, and converted into residential land, with the permission of the provincial land office. But the management of land by the authorities was not serious. Some people tried to record more land than they had and when the officers came to check, they borrowed others' land temporarily. Many peasants got farmland without registering it with the district land office at all so as not to pay the registration fee. Even so, they could still sell their possessed land with the signatures of the local authority. In one case, a poor woman's farmland was partially occupied by her neighbors, but she could not win justice from the village committee because she could not afford to invite the officers for meals and drinks. Hence the superficial and arguably chaotic land management in the young Cambodian market economy after the abolition of the cooperatives. (Kusakabe; Wang & Kelkar 1995: 88–91)

Eradicated with the *krom samaki* was also their support to individual households. Owing to the loss of men in the wars, women make up 54% of the adult population over 15, head 20% of rural households and hold possession title to substantial paddy land. Peasants in general do not want to sell land, as a group of women cried: 'If I sell land, where shall I live?' (Summers 1997: 189. Kusakabe; Wang & Kelkar 1995: 89–91)

But due to difficulties from the weak individual land operation, poverty, illness, and even gambling losses, many peasant families, especially those headed by widows, were forced to sell their possession of farmland. A widow sold land because her family could not afford to keep the land after three years' bad rice yield and their income from fishing was not sufficient. Although sale of land formally requires all the relevant people's signatures, this regulation seemed unimportant in practice. Owing to gambling losses, a man sold the possession of his family's farmland without even informing his wife, although it had been registered under both of their names. There were also women who, due to marriage, separated from their parents but found that the latter refused to give them farmland owing to family unhappiness, so that they had to work as wage laborers in other farms. They all became poor newly landless. (Kusakabe; Wang & Kelkar 1995: 89–91)4

On the other hand, there were people who sold residential land and possession of farmland along the roads at high prices to earn more money, and thus also joined the newly landless. They could not easily survive if they have spent the easy money while still having not found secure jobs in non-agricultural production which as yet is underdeveloped in the poor rural areas. A widow sold land and bought weaving machines to weave silk skirts to be sold in Phnom Penh. But it was unclear how she and her family could live if market demand fell. (Kusakabe; Wang & Kelkar 1995: 89–91)

In Laos. The agricultural sector is continuously vulnerable to adverse weather and pests. The country is landlocked, with a poorly developed infrastructure and a serious shortage of skilled labor. Economic disparities between the more developed areas, especially the Vientiane Plain and the Southern Mekong towns on one hand, and the rest of the country on the other, have increased since the reform of the late 1980s. Laos is also one of the poorest countries in Asia and the world. (Gainsborough 1997: 539)

Cultivable land is scarce, while population pressure is increasing. The early settlers and their heirs have occupied more land, leaving less or no land for the villages to distribute to the new families. Inheritance also made land more fragmented. (Groppo; Mekouar; Damais & Phouangphet 1996: 11, 17, 31). Because salability of land requires the individually possessed public land to be fixed to the possessors, officials have no means to take a part of land from those households possessing more public land and allocate it to those

---

[4] Looking down upon political economy in non-econometrical approach, some economists favoring econometrics which dominates current economics may doubt whether such anecdotes were representative, because according to them, only large quantities of events upon which regressions can be run can reveal an economic trend or the effect of an economic system. However, such economists or policy makers may be regarded as 'failures' if they have to wait for the appearance of large numbers of new landlessness before seeing the vital shortcomings of a land tenure system which resulted in them. Responsible economists or policy makers would prevent such human tragedies - even one occurrence should be too much. Thus, they should be able to anticipate, or at least soon perceive through a few occurrences, such vital shortcomings. At least in this respect, political economists in a non-econometrical approach may show a superiority over those economists relying on sufficient data for running regressions and drawing conclusions. For example, the author expected that the establishment of the nominal state - but *de facto* private - land ownership in Vietnam would lead to newly landless, thus sent an email to the FAO Representative in Vietnam, and immediately got his confirmation that 'I fully agreed with you that newly landless has appeared in the transition of agriculture in Vietnam' (Messier 1997), although actually the author did not know this real situation.

households holding less or no land below the subsistence level, or to consolidate fragmented parcels.

With the salability of the state-owned but individually possessed land, from 1993—94 on, property transactions near Vientiane mainly involved the sale of agricultural land, mostly along or near roads, to urban dwellers. Peasants with a large land area (5 to 10 ha) have been able to sell at high prices, thus rapidly increasing their capital investment potential while still retaining sufficient agricultural land. In contrast, families with little land (1 to 2 ha) have been unable to sell any land and were having problems meeting their basic requirements on the farm as they were below the sustainability threshold. The social gap has been widening. In the present context of greater market integration and gradual economic opening up, they will probably find it difficult to avoid proletarianization or poverty. (Groppo; Mekouar; Damais & Phouangphet 1996: 16—8)

Land sale to urban dwellers was for high prices reflecting future industrial profits rather than agricultural earnings, thus those farmers who really needed land for survival could not afford to buy it at all. While few villages still have land to allocate to new population, the property market has absorbed a large land area. For example, in one village with 15 landless families and no land to allocate because there was none left, no less than 75 ha have been sold in barely two years. (Groppo; Mekouar; Damais & Phouangphet 1996: 17). Meanwhile, the obligation to sell land due to difficulties in the weak single household operation, natural disasters, diseases, debts, gambling losses, etc. has occurred.

As a result, landless families as a *new* category of inhabitants - agricultural proletariat - began to emerge in many villages. Around Vientiane, it accounted for about 10—15% of the total rural families. In one village, 71.6% of the households were landless. In another village, five families held no land but lived with their parents-in-law, who possessed a fair amount of land. The possibilities for these families to possess land are virtually nil. There is insufficient agricultural land for rent to alleviate the lack of appropriate land. Those who could not rent in land had to rely exclusively on wage labor in the village or in Vientiane. (Groppo; Mekouar; Damais & Phouangphet 1996: 11, 23, 42)

In Vietnam. In 1994, 6.8 million or 17% of the labor force were either unemployed or underemployed. There are sharp contrasts in development between different regions, especially lowlands and uplands. Infrastructure is still backward. (Demaine 1997: 1056—7, 1063). More than half of the 75 million people still live under the poverty line, although major cities have become much richer (*Economist* 1997: 66).

However, during 1988—94, over 2,950 agricultural cooperatives (17.4% of the total) had been dissolved. By the end of 1994, a total of 16,243 agricultural cooperatives still existed, covering about 64% of all farm households. But there were great differences in their operational performance. An estimated 15.5% of those that had recorded good performance in the past (*'good'* cooperatives) were still able to provide necessary services to member households. *'Middle'* performing cooperatives accounted for 40.4% of them and were mainly engaged in providing irrigation facilities and services. They did not have sufficient capital and funds to cover increased expenses, and many members have quit. Thus lots of them have become dormant and nominal. Non-operational (*'bad'*) cooperatives accounted for 43.3% of the total. Although the leadership of these cooperatives remained in place, they neither carried out economic activities nor provided any services to members. The management costs were mainly paid out of debt recovered from the members. In many regions, however, members refused to provide any additional funds. As a result, the number of *'bad'* cooperatives has been increasing. In the South, cooperatives have generally disappeared. The farm tasks that require group actions, such as irrigation management, have had to rely on voluntarily formed production teams, which appeared in both the North and South. (Harms 1996: 1–3. Hayami 1994: 11). Therefore, the majority of farm households are carrying out single household operation of land which is weak.

Under such circumstances, following the permission to sell the individually possessed state-owned land in 1993, new landlessness has appeared. In early 1997, the government raised its concern about this issue during a meeting of provincial leaders in the Mekong Delta. No overall official data relating to this situation was yet available, but a survey on the new landlessness in the Mekong Delta was being carried out. (Messier 1997). An interview with officials of Southern Vietnam in November 1999 revealed that by that time about 20% of peasants there had become newly landless and had to be wage laborers or tenants (Zhang, Heather Xiao-Quan 2000). As a result, even Duc Luong Tran (Tran, Duc Luong 1998: 16), President of Vietnam, has conceded that economic reforms have produced only limited benefits for rural Vietnamese.

Hayami (1994: 15), one of the chief designers and advocates of the nominal state - but *de facto* private - land ownership in Vietnam, however, has excluded the possibility of new landlessness and the related trend of polarization, stating: 'The highly polarized agrarian structure and oppressive landlordism observed in some developing countries have emerged mainly as the result of colonial exploitation policies, including exclusive land allocations to colonial elites. This situation is diametrically different from that of Vietnam today. Therefore, it is not necessary to be overly concerned about such an inequitable agrarian structure emerging in this country'. But Hayami may not know that 'the highly polarized agrarian structure and oppressive landlordism observed in some developing countries' in monsoon Asia had emerged *well before* the colonial era [e.g., before the late 1940s they existed in Japan which was never colonized, in China for about 2,000 years which incorporated Vietnam in 112 BC for 1,000 years (Smith 1997: 1046), no later than the sixth century in Cambodia (Summers 1997: 176) and the eighth century in Laos (Stuart-Fox 1997: 532)]. The incorrectness of Hayami's statement is also shown by the immediate appearance of the new landlessness after the setting-up of the nominal state - but *de facto* private - land ownership in these three countries although they are currently not colonized.

(2) Inefficient land-holding in the high wage economy. As analyzed in Chapters 4–7, in monsoon Asia, once yields of rice and other grains are raised, and rural infrastructure, diversified cropping, non-crop agriculture, and off-farm employment developed, peasants can find sufficient employment in non-grain agriculture and off-farm activities. Their income is greatly increased and there is no need for them to rely on grain production. If land were fixed to the possessors, then, in such a high wage economy, there would be a tendency for the possessors to become *part-time and absent farmers* and keep the land just as an asset without tilling it efficiently, nor selling and leasing it to the full-time farmers who wish to concentrate on grain production. Even in those rural areas which still remain in the low wage economy, many peasants may go to cities or other rural areas which have entered the high wage economy to earn more income, while still holding their land without efficient use and even leaving the land desolated. The newly rich peasants may change farmland into residential land for more housing. *Moreover,* urban developers, who have bought agricultural land when its prices were relatively low in comparison with its future value, may leave the land idle for years without making construction, or repeatedly sell the land between speculators in expectation of continually higher prices.

While the Japanese model, due largely to its reliance on free market forces, has not been able to overcome the fragmented small farms inefficiently held by part-time and absent small farmers as the last obstacle, the Chinese one has, by implementing variable mixed economies. Besides controlling inefficiently used land in agriculture, China has also established mechanisms to prevent collectively owned farmland transferred for non-agricultural development from being idled. As mentioned in Chapter 7, if a piece of farmland already approved for non-agricultural construction is not to be used so within one year, it should be cultivated and harvested (if this is possible) by the original collective or individuals, or by other farmers organized by the constructing unit; if it has been idled for more than one year, the constructing unit should pay an idling fee; if it has been continuously idled for two years without proper approval, the land should be withdrawn to the original collective by the county government without remuneration to the constructing unit. Similarly, the government can impose an idling fee on the real estate developer of the state-owned urban land if the construction has not started one year after the date specified in the contract, and withdraw the land free of payment if it has been idled for two years.

Unexceptionally, the inefficient land-holding has occurred immediately after the setting up of the nominal state - but *de facto* private - land ownership, at least in *Laos* near cities where wages are much higher. It has been mentioned in the above that around Vientiane from 1993—94 on, following the salability of the state-owned but individually possessed land, much agricultural land, mostly along or near roads, was sold mainly to the rich urban dwellers. But much purchased land was just left idle. Although in theory unused land is to be withdrawn by the village, the mechanism to prevent inefficient land-holding and land desolation is neither sufficient, nor effective. (Groppo; Mekouar; Damais & Phouangphet 1996: 17, 44)

A free market solution or variable mixed economies? Overlooking the two major problems above, however, Hayami argues that free market forces should be allowed to play a much greater, and even full, role. He criticizes the 1993 Land Law of Vietnam for putting private land transactions under several regulations (such as the maximum ceiling on land-holding, justification by local officials of the need for land sellers or lessors to reduce their land-holdings and the capacity of buyers or lessees to use the increased holdings efficiently), on the grounds that in his judgement of the experiences of other countries, such regulations, once strongly enforced, became a source of extremely large inefficiency (e.g., in Japan) (Hayami 1994: 14—5).

Hayami's solution (1994: 2) is that 'The proper policy design should limit application of the regulations on land market to the cases in which significant externalities or social costs, such as water pollution, are involved. Land transactions involving no such costs to society should be approved *automatically*'. In short, public land should first be solidly possessed by individuals, and then land transactions among individuals should not be restricted.

However, Hayami does not note a dilemma in his free market recipe, i.e., certain strongly enforced regulations in the land transaction market in the low wage economy may become a source of inefficient land-holding in the high wage economy; but without them, newly landless would appear in the low wage economy. Hayami is unlikely to find any solution to this dilemma within the free market system. Evidence for its solution is found only in *variable* mixed economies, such as in the Chinese model, especially the evolution from feature 1 to feature 9.

Therefore, it was correct for Cambodia, Laos and Vietnam to abandon the centrally planned economy, but *incorrect* to turn to the opposite extreme -

largely relying on free market forces and paying little (at least insufficient) attention to the intervention by government, and management and support by villages and cooperatives.

Hayami (1994: 4) acclaims the nominal state - but *de facto* private - land ownership (in Vietnam) as '*beyond* China's reform in assigning and protecting of private land rights'. But the fact that new landlessness appeared immediately after the land tenure reforms in the low wage economy in Cambodia, Laos and Vietnam already shows that this model is inferior to the Chinese. In the high wage economy, if the state failed to oblige the part-time and absent small farmers to transfer their land to full-time and expert farmers due to the high transaction costs in dealing with the peasants who hold strong bargaining power by possessing LURC (Land Use Right Certificates), then it would fall into feature 9 of the Japanese model in front of the last obstacle, and thus also be second to the Chinese model. If the state, to the contrary, by its ownership right, succeeded in effecting such a transfer, this still would not be beyond the Chinese model (albeit specific methods could be different).

Although Hayami (1994: 9) claims that the nominal state - but *de facto* private - land ownership (in Vietnam) 'may serve as a model, which many other countries in transition to market-oriented economies may well be advised to follow', Diouf, Director-General of FAO, comments (1997) just to the opposite: 'The tremendous achievements of China in realizing food security have attracted world-wide attention. The Chinese experience should be taken into account by other developing countries'. Therefore, countries like Cambodia, Laos, Vietnam, may well be advised to study the Chinese model, especially its features 1 and 9, as a means for overcoming not only poverty, but also 'the last obstacle'.

8.3 Conjectural Proposals 8.1, 8.2 and 8.3

Proposal 8.1. In order to achieve market-oriented rural development in Cambodia, Laos and Vietnam, it was justifiable to retain the state ownership of land, rather than privatizing it. But it should be noted that a nominal state but *de facto* private land ownership system may still lead a part of the peasantry into landlessness in the low wage economy, and part-time and absent small farmers to hold land for inefficient use in the high wage economy.

In particular, both the Chinese experiences and those of these countries have shown that for a market-oriented rural development under public land ownership, (1) private land sale and mortgage are not only unnecessary, but may also be harmful, as they make new landlessness possible; (2) strongly enforced conditions for land-holding are necessary for the efficient land use;

(3) cadastral certification for a *de facto* private land ownership would be unnecessary, because there are other means to maintain the stability of the household-held land, and detrimental, since it not only incurs high costs (in money, time, human resources, etc.) and disputes (Gordillo de Anda 1997: 3), but also tends to fix the land to the possessors and hinders land transfer from inefficient holders to full-time farmers in the high wage economy; (4) state compulsory procurement of grain in quotas is beneficial and may even be a necessary condition of guaranteeing a minimum grain security for the whole country.

It therefore is recommended that Cambodia, Laos and Vietnam draw these lessons, abolish the nominal state - but *de facto* private - land ownership and pursue the Chinese model.

Proposal 8.2. In the revision of the present land tenure system for a more market-oriented rural development in Myanmar, establishing a nominal state - but *de facto* private - land ownership would not be in its fundamental or long-term interests. Rather, it would be beneficial for it to follow features 2– 13 of the Chinese model.

Proposal 8.3. North Korea is the only rice-based economy in monsoon Asia - and the last country in the world - still implementing the centrally planned economy. It is advised to begin land tenure reform and rural development with feature 1, in particular, land should be contracted further down to households, and then proceed with other features, of the Chinese model. Neither privatization of land ownership, nor establishment of a nominal public - but *de facto* private - land ownership would be suitable, as shown by the Japanese model and the experiences of Cambodia, Laos and Vietnam respectively.

Since Proposal 5.1 may be exercised not only for private land ownership, but also for private possession under public ownership of land, it could also be adopted in Myanmar; Cambodia, Laos and Vietnam; and North Korea. In particular, it could be considered in Vietnam now that Land Use Right Certificates have been issued.

The Chinese model of rural development and Proposal 5.1 might be relevant to those economies based upon public land ownership *outside* monsoon Asia in the process of transition towards a market economy as well.

PART FOUR

APPLICATIONS OF THE NEW MODEL
BEYOND MONSOON ASIA

9. The American Model and the Crowding Out of Small Farmers

In contrast with Japan - where from 1960 large-scale farmers were unable to dominate over the inefficient system of land management by small-scale farmers - and with China - where large-scale farmers have increased farm size as small farmers from the early 1980s gradually transferred to non-grain agriculture and off-farm activities while still retaining some basic social welfare rather than being squeezed out from agriculture - in the United States of America, large farmers have consistently dominated over small farmers who have proved too weak to compete. Thus ever since 1935 farm numbers have been in decline with the trend towards larger but fewer farms. Despite the many books, articles, conferences, and bills passed and revised on the subject, a feasible solution to help *both strengthen large and retain small farms* has yet to be found. In this context it is not appropriate to repeat the analyses, or examine each aspect of the problem in detail. Instead a possible solution which would prevent small farmers from being crowded out while still strengthening large farmers will be explored in Chapter 10. However, in order to put such a solution on an evolutionary and logical basis, and in view of the fact that many readers outside the USA may not be familiar with the key features, it is perhaps useful to provide a brief explanation of the historical context in which this situation has evolved in this chapter.

9.1 The General Trend in the USA

Stanton (1993: 46–9, 51–3, 58–61, 64–6) cites four variables commonly used in the study of structural changes in US agriculture: (1) farm size distribution measured in *acreage*,1 (2) farm size distribution measured in *gross sales*, (3) type of *business organization* [i.e., sole proprietorship (individual or family), partnership, corporation] and (4) type of *land tenure*

---

[1] In the USA, acre (= 0.4047 ha = 40.47 are = 4,047 square meters = 6.07 mu) is the basic unit of land area.

of operators (i.e., full owner, part owner, tenant).2 While variables (1)–(3) are examined in this section, (4) will mainly be discussed later.

Farm size is commonly measured in acreage and value of sales (gross value of products sold).3 Both measures have limitations. The acreage criterion conceals the varying quality of land over the same number of acres. But in a composite picture of farms country-wide, it does give an indication of the way in which the use of basic land resource changes with varying technology and economic conditions and the direction of agricultural structure. The gross sales measure is largely accepted for the sake of convenience, but in particular because it is a method used internationally to compare firms both within and between industries. For this reason, the gross sales measure was adopted and retained throughout the second half of the 20th century. (Hornbaker & Denault 1993: 72. Stanton 1993: 51)

The gross sales measure is, however, *influenced by inflation.* Inflation shifts some farms with constant real sales volume from one pecuniary sales class to another. Thus, rigid adherence to a dollar guideline implies that volatile agricultural product prices can mean that a farm is categorized as 'small' one year and 'large' the next. In fact, farmers are particularly vulnerable to inflation because their costs are likely to rise faster than revenues. Price changes obscure logical comparisons across time. (Gebremedhin & Christy 1996: 60). The gross sales measure may also be *affected by other factors*, for example, when changes in technical efficiency have occurred and altered the prices of both outputs and inputs (Stanton 1993: 53).

Some of the commonly recognized problems related to the use of gross sales as a measure of farm size in any given year are that: (1) the effects of changing price levels are not easily accounted for in comparison between years; (2) changes in crops or livestock inventories are not considered, so that a farm's sales in one year may be higher than its current year output as reducing inventory or lower than its current year output as increasing the

---

[2] Farm workers are divided by three occupations: (1) farmers (operators), (2) managers, and (3) laborers; and include (1) family workers: (i) farmers or operators (usually husband), (ii) co-operators (usually wife), (iii) self-employed managers (husband and/or wife), (iv) self-employed laborers (usually wife and children), and (v) unpaid laborers (usually wife and children); and (2) hired workers: (i) hired managers, and (ii) hired laborers (compiled from Ilg 1995: 3, 7–9).

[3] According to Wunderlich (January 1999), a third measure could be the farm real estate - value of land and buildings. It represents 75–80% of farm assets and reflects the differences in types and productivity of land. It is reported in size classes of Census of Agriculture, but without size breakdown in SAUS (the unique source for systematic US statistics available to the author).

inventory; (3) government subsidies are not included as a source of income (e.g., in the Census of 1987); (4) crop failure or livestock losses understate the size of a business when there are relatively few sales, although many acres, workers, or expenses may be involved. Despite these problems, the gross sales measure nevertheless persists as one of the most commonly used methods of describing farm size and presenting size distributions. (Gebremedhin & Christy 1996: 60. Stanton 1993: 53)

In order to avoid the problems related with the gross sales measure, and taking into account that farm size is measured in acreage in Japan and China and other economies analyzed in the book, *farm size in the USA will refer to acreage* in Chapters 9 and 10 unless specified.

The Trend Measured by Acreage

In the USA, the number of farms has been decreasing since 1935,4 the total acreage of farms reducing since 1954, but the average farm acreage increasing since 1910, as Table 9.1 shows.5 Of the total population, the percentage of rural population decreased from 60% in 1900 to 24.8% in 1990, and that of farming population from 34.9% in 1910 to 1.8% in 1990. The urban population increased from 40.6% in 1900 to 75.2% in 1990. (SAUS 1939: 605; 1956: 617; 1958: 23; 1982–83: 649; 1993: 652; 1997: 44)

Within the general reduction of farm number and acreage, it was the

---

[4] Stanton (1993: 43–4) states that 'the fall in farm numbers which started in the decades of the 20s was slowed by the depression of the 30s' according to Census of Agriculture (whose data may not always be the same as in SAUS). But Brown, Christy and Gebremedhin (1994: 51) also present that 'The number of US farms has been declining since 1935 when it reached an all-time high of 6.8 million'.

[5] A census of agriculture was first taken in 1840 as part of the sixth decennial census of population, and conducted from 1840 to 1950 as part of the decennial census. A separate mid-decade census of agriculture was made in 1925, 1935 and 1945. From 1954 to 1974, it covered the years ending in 4 and 9, and since 1978–82, years ending in 2 and 7. (NASS 1998. Powers 1999)

The current definition of farm 'any place from which $1,000 or more of agricultural products were produced and sold or normally would have been sold during the census year' began in 1974. In 1969, 1964 and 1959, a farm was a place with sales of $250 or more if having less than 10 acres, $50 or more if 10 acres or more; while in 1954 and 1950, place with sales of $150 or more if less than 3 acres, sales and home use of $150 or more if 3 acres or more. For 1925–45, a place was a farm if with (1) 3 acres or more of agricultural operations, and (2) less than 3 acres if $250 of products being for sale or home use. 1910–20 was similar to 1925 except a sum less than $250 if in continuous operation. There were no limits in 1900 as long as under continuous management. In 1870, 1880 and 1890 only places of 3 acres or more unless they sold $500 or more agricultural products. 1860 no definition. 1850 no acreage but $100 of value of products were required. (NASS 1998. Wunderlich April 1999)

small (under 50 acres) and some medium farms (50–259 acres) which have

Table 9.1 Number, Total and Average Acreage of Farms in the
USA 1850–1992

Year	No. of farms (1,000)	Change over last year %	Total acreage of farms (million acres)	Change over last year %	Average acreage of farms (acre)	Change over last year %
1850	1,449		299		203	
1860	2,044	41.06	407	36.12	199	–1.97
1870	2,670	30.63	408	0.25	153	–23.12
1880	4,009	50.15	536	31.37	134	–12.42
1890	4,565	13.87	623	16.23	137	2.24
1900	5,737	25.67	839	34.67	146	6.57
1910	6,362	10.89	879	4.77	**138**	–5.48
1920	6,448	1.35	956	8.76	148	7.25
1930	6,546	1.52	987	3.24	151	2.03
1935	**6,814**	4.09	1,055	6.89	155	2.65
1940	6,350	–6.81	1,061	0.57	167	7.74
1950	5,648	–11.06	1,202	13.29	213	27.54
1954	4,798	–15.05	**1,206**	0.33	251	17.84
1959	4,105	–14.44	1,183	–1.91	288	14.74
1964	3,457	–15.79	1,146	–3.13	332	15.28
1969	3,000	–13.22	1,108	–3.32	369	11.14
1974	2,795	–6.83	1,084	–2.17	388	5.15
1978	2,436	–12.84	1,045	–3.60	429	10.57
1982	2,241	–8.00	987	–5.55	440	2.56
1987	2,088	–6.83	964	–2.33	460	4.55
1992	1,925	–7.81	946	–1.87	498	8.26

Sources: *1850–1910*: SAUS 1920: 138. *1920*: SAUS 1949: 613. *1930–78*: SAUS 1984: 652.
1982–92: SAUS 1997: 665.

been decreasing since their peak years 1935 (2,694,426 farms and 59,020,000 acres) and 1910–20 (1,474,745 farms in 1920 and 108,121,000 acres in 1910) respectively (SAUS 1939: 613; 1962: 610; 1979: 687; 1992: 645; 1997: 665), though other medium and some large farms have also quit (Perry 1999). Moreover, 'Yesterday's large farms have become today's small farms' (Gebremedhin & Christy 1996: 60) - the numbers of farms of 260–499 acres and 500–999 acres actually started to decline from their peak in 1954 (482,246) and 1978 (213,000) respectively (SAUS 1962: 610; 1992: 645). Thus they are here accordingly downgraded from large to medium farms after these two peak years respectively, those with 50–259 acres being defined as lower medium farms, and those with 260–999 acres as upper medium farms (this dynamic classification by the author is not seen in the literature).6 In contrast, regarding large farms of 1,000–1,999 and 2,000 acres or over, their numbers and total acreage have been increasing ever since 1900 and 1920 respectively (SAUS 1939: 613; 1979: 687; 1992: 645; 1997: 665). The polarization in number, acreage, percentage in the total between small and large farms has been demonstrated in Tables 9.2 and 9.3 (the peak number in each row is in bold).

In particular, as Bollman, Whitener and Tung (1995: 25) observe, families on mid-sized farms in general have farms too small to provide high levels of net farm income while the time commitments often preclude full-time off-farm work. Historically, therefore, the adjustment among individual farming families has been either to expand or to diminish the size of the farm operation. In view of the decreasing numbers of both small and medium farms, Chapters 9 and 10 will refer generally to large and small-medium farms, or simply large and small farms for convenience.

In the context of the above changes in farm size measured by acreage, a general trend may be seen: farms have become fewer in number and larger in average size. In both number and size, small and medium farms have been reducing, while large farms increasing. Within the group of large farms, in both number and size, some grow even larger thus increasing, while others become relatively smaller hence declining and downgrading into medium farms. Small and medium farms account for the numerical majority, but have minor shares in total farm acreage, while the reverse is true for large farms.

---

[6] Stanton invariably classifies farms of 260–499 acres and 500–999 acres as large farms from 1900 through 1987 (Stanton 1993: 49–50). Such a method may overlook the dynamic changes of farm size distributions.

Table 9.2 Percentage in Farm Number by Farm Size (acre) in the USA 1910–92

	Size	1910	1935	1950	1959	1969	1978	1987	1992
Small	<10	5.3	8.4	**9.0**	6.5	5.9	6.7	8.8	8.6
	10–49	30.1	**31.1**	27.5	21.9	17.3	17.4	19.7	20.2
Small subtotal	<50	35.4	**39.5**	36.5	28.4	23.2	24.1	28.5	28.8
Lower medium	50–259	**54.8**	49.7	49.1	49.8	47.9	44.0	40.1	39.3
Upper medium	260–499				12.7	15.3	**15.4**	13.7	13.2
	500–999							9.6	**9.7**
Medium subtotal		(50–259) 54.8	(50–259) 49.7	(50–259) 49.1	(50–499) 62.5	(50–499) 63.2	(50–499) 59.4	(50–999) **63.4**	(50–999) 62.2
Small–medium subtotal		(<260) 90.2	(<260) 89.2	(<260) 85.6	(<500) 90.9	(<500) 86.4	(<500) 83.5	(<1,000) **91.9**	(<1,000) 91.0
Large	260–499	7.0	6.9	**8.9**					
	500–999	2.0	2.5	3.4	5.4	7.9	**9.4**		
	1,000–1,999	0.8	1.3	2.3	3.7	3.3	4.3	4.9	**5.3**
	>1,999					2.2	2.8	3.2	**3.7**
Large subtotal		(>259) 9.8	(>259) 10.7	(>259) 14.6	(>499) 9.1	(>499) 13.4	(>499) **16.5**	(>999) 8.1	(>999) 9.0

Sources: 1910–35: SAUS 1939: 613. 1950–59: SAUS 1962: 610. 1969: SAUS 1979: 687. 1978: SAUS 1992: 645. 1987–92: SAUS 1997: 665.

Table 9.3 Percentage in Farm Acreage by Farm Size (acre) in the USA 1910–92

	Size	1910	1935	1950	1959	1969	1978	1987	1992
Small	<10	**1.00**	0.29	0.21	0.09	0.06	0.06	0.07	0.07
	10–49	5.2	**5.3**	3.4	1.9	1.3	1.1	1.2	1.1
Small subtotal	<50	**6.2**	5.6	3.6	2.0	1.4	1.2	1.3	1.2
Lower medium	50–259	35.1 [a]	**38.6**	28.5	21.7	16.4	13.0	11.3	10.4
Upper medium	260–499				**14.9**	14.0	12.3	10.7	9.7
	500–999							**14.4**	13.7
Medium subtotal		(50–259) 35.1	(50–259) **38.6**	(50–259) 28.5	(50–499) 36.5	(50–499) 30.4	(50–499) 25.3	(50–999) 36.4	(50–999) 33.8
Small–medium subtotal		(<260) 41.3	(<260) **44.2**	(<260) 32.1	(<500) 38.5	(<500) 31.8	(<500) 26.5	(<1,000) 37.7	(<1,000) 35.0
Large	260–499	30.2 [b]	15.6	14.4			**14.5**		
	500–999	9.5	10.8	10.9	12.3	13.9	13.1		
	1,000–1,999	19.0	29.4	42.6	49.2	11.6	46.1	14.4	**14.7**
	>1,999					42.7		48.0	**50.4**
Large subtotal		(>259) 58.7	(>259) 55.8	(>259) 67.9	(>499) 61.5	(>499) 68.2	(>499) **73.7**	(>999) 62.4	(>999) 65.1

Notes: a.   50–174 acres.   b.   175–499 acres.

Sources: *1910–35*: SAUS 1939: 613. *1950–59*: SAUS 1962: 610. *1969*: SAUS 1979: 687. *1978*: SAUS 1994: 665. *1987–92*: SAUS 1997: 665.

The Trend Measured by Gross Sales

Table 9.4 reveals that there has been a coincidence between acreage and gross sales, in that the changes of farm size measured in gross sales (value of sales) show the same general trend as that measured in acreage (numbers in bold represent categories, while those in italic denote synthetic data for large farms). *Statically* in each year of 1949, 1969, 1959, 1978, 1987 and 1992, the larger in acreage, the larger in gross sales. Large farms in acreage were minority in farm number (except in 1949), but held major shares in total gross sales, which meant that small and medium farms in acreage held majority in farm number, but possessed minor percentage in total gross sales (although gross sales data for small farms in acreage were unreported in SAUS). *Dynamically*, large farms in gross sales are classified as $5,000 or more in 1949, $20,000 or more in 1959 and 1969, $40,000 or more in 1978, and $100,000 or more from 1987 on (this dynamic categorization by the author is not found in the literature). Therefore, large farms have become larger not only in acreage as mentioned above, but also in gross sales. In general, large farms in acreage are large farms in gross sales too. But they may also not match. Efficient management and other factors can lead some smaller farms in acreage to achieving higher gross sales, but some larger farms may do the opposite.

In 1992, as argued by Gebremedhin and Christy (1996: 58) and shown in Table 9.4, large farms in acreage with annual gross sales of $100,000 or more and accounting for only 17.3% in total farm number were *commercial*, while small and medium farms in acreage with annual gross sales below $100,000 but making up 82.7% in total farm number were *non-commercial*. 7 To simplify, farms with annual gross sales below $5,000 in 1949, $20,000 in 1959 and 1969, $40,000 in 1978, and $100,000 from 1987 on are called here non-commercial farms (corresponding to small and medium farms), and those with these or higher amounts commercial (equivalent to large farms).

Peterson and Brooks (1993: 1, 3–7) point out that during 1940–87, the minimum number and proportion of farms required to produce a third of gross sales have declined significantly from 312,939 to 32,023 and from 5.2% to 1.5% respectively; while the total acreage operated by these largest

---

7 Brooks and Kalbacher (1990) define farms with gross sales less than $25,000 as rural residence farms; $25,000 to $99,999 as small commercial farms; $100,000 to $499,999 moderate commercial farms; $500,000 to $999,999 large commercial farms; and $1,000,000 or more very large commercial farms. Their classification is not much different from that by Gebremedhin and Christy. In contrast, USDA (1998) describes small farms as with annual gross sales below $250,000. But it recognizes that this amount may not sound small and in fact may be high for some commodities. Actually they include medium farms.

producers fell, their average acreage increased from 989 acres to 3,921 acres, revealing an increasing *concentration* in both gross sales and acreage of farms from the small to large farms. The *specialization* fields of these few largest farms include livestock (excluding dairy and poultry), cash grains/ field crops and poultry, although their production notably shifted from cash grains/field crops towards vegetables, fruits and poultry. See Table 9.5.

Family Based Business Organization

In the USA, data reports on the business organization of farms began in 1969, and in more detail from 1974, as presented in Tables 9.6 and 9.7. In farm number, acreage and gross sales, sole proprietorship (individual or family) farms have constituted the majority, although the percentages have been declining while partnership and corporate farms have been in the minority but increasing in proportion. Even within the category of corporate farms, family-held ones were the majority and with rising percentages, while other corporations were in a minority with decreasing shares. Most family corporations are formed by father/son, or immediate family members to distribute taxes and legal responsibilities (Perry & Banker 1999). Therefore, the business organization of the US farms is mainly based on families, just as in Japan and China as reviewed in Chapters 4–7.

Although population and thus employment in farming declined, prior to 1970, the ratio of hired worker to family labor (self-employed and unpaid) was constant (about 0.3–0.35, i.e., a family of three employing one), but has since increased (0.55 in 1980–85 and 0.45 in 1990, i.e., a family of two hiring one). This is in accordance with the general trend, because as farm size increases, more workers need to be hired. However, family workers still account for the larger proportion of labor. (Bollman; Whitener & Tung 1995: 22–4). Since most farms are small and can be operated by family workers, this reveals that even large farms only employ a small number of workers, although more in busy seasons.

It is noteworthy that while both sole proprietorship and non-family corporation farms have reduced their percentages, both partnership and family-held corporation farms increased their counterparts. The increasing percentages of large partnership and corporate farms and declining shares of small sole proprietorship farms in total farm number, acreage and gross sales are also in accordance with the general trend.

In general, sole proprietor farms are small, corporate farms are large, while partnership farms are in between in size (Knoeber 1997: 151. Goodwin & Featherstone 1995: 39, 48–9). Farms with annual gross sales below $25,000 (accounting for 62.8% in total farm number, but only 4.9% in total gross sales; 62.3% had operators working off-farm; and 28.9% had operators

Table 9.4 Farm Number, Acreage and Value of Sales by Size of Sales in the USA 1949–92

Value of products sold ($)	Farm No. (1,000)	%	Acreage (acre)			Value of sales ($)		
			Total (mil.)	Average per farm	% of total	Total (mil.)	Average per farm (1,000)	% of total
1949								
2,500 & more	2,087	**100**	850	407	**100**	18,919	9.1	**100**
2,500–4,999	882	42.3	169	191 medium	19.9	3,093	3.5	16.3
5,000–9,999	721	34.5	215	298 large	25.3	4,894	6.8	25.9
10,000 & more	484	23.2	466	963 large	54.8	10,932	22.6	57.8
5,000 & more large		*57.7*		*298–963 large*	*80.1*			*83.7*
1959								
2,500 & more	2,067	**100**	940	455	**100**	29,003	14.0	**100**
2,500–4,999	618	29.9	119	192 lo-med	12.6	2,275	3.7	7.8
5,000–9,999	654	31.6	189	288 up-med	20.1	4,723	7.2	16.3
10,000–19,999	483	23.4	215	445 up-med	22.9	6,705	13.9	23.1
20,000–39,999	210	10.2	166	791 large	17.7	5,648	26.8	19.5
40,000 & more	102	4.9	252	2,466 large	26.8	9,652	94.5	33.3
20,000 & more large		*15.1*		*791–2,466 large*	*44.5*			*52.8*
Below 2,500	1,638	**100**	140	86	**100**	1,514	0.9	**100**
50–2,499	349	21.3	37	106 lo-med	26.4	461	1.3	30.4
Abnormal	3	**100**	43	14,007	**100**	109	36.3	**100**

Value of products sold ($)	Farm No. (1,000)	%	Acreage (acre)			Value of sales ($)		
			Total (mil.)	Average per farm	% of total	Total (mil.)	Average per farm (1,000)	% of total
1969								
2,500 & more	1,734	**100**	918	530	**100**	44,476	25.6	**100**
2,500–4,999	395	22.8	76	192 lo-med	8.3	1,346	3.4	3.0
5,000–9,999	390	22.5	107	274 up-med	11.6	2,814	7.2	6.3
10,000–19,999	395	22.8	171	433 up-med	18.6	5,693	14.4	12.8
20,000–39,999	331	19.1	207	626 large	22.6	9,267	28.0	20.8
40,000–99,999	170	9.8	185	1,092 large	20.2	10,073	59.3	22.6
100,000 & more	52	3.0	172	3,304 large	18.7	15,282	293.8	34.5
20,000 & more large		*31.9*		*626–3,304 large*	*61.5*			*77.9*
Below 2,500	994	**100**	90	90	**100**	935	0.9	**100**
50–2,499	193	19.4	19	96 lo-med	20.8	188	1.0	20.1
Abnormal	2	**100**	55	26,174	**100**	153	72.3	**100**
1978								
2,500 & more	1,865	**100**	927	497	**100**	107,164	57.5	**100**
2,500–4,999	332	17.8	37	112 lo-med	4.0	1,191	3.6	1.1
5,000–9,999	331	17.7	56	168 lo-med	6.0	2,361	7.1	2.2
10,000–19,999	310	16.6	84	272 up-med	9.1	4,425	14.3	4.1
20,000–39,999	306	16.4	133	435 up-med	14.3	8,788	28.7	8.2

Table 9.4 continued

Value of products sold ($)	Farm No. (1,000)	%	Acreage (acre)			Value of sales ($)		
			Total (mil.)	Average per farm	% of total	Total (mil.)	Average per farm (1,000)	% of total
40,000–99,999	363	19.5	245	675 large	26.4	23,059	63.5	21.5
100,000 & more large	223	12.0	372	1,669 large	40.1	67,339	302.0	62.8
40,000 & more large		*31.5*		*675– 1,669 large*	*66.5*			*84.3*
Below 2,500	612	**100**	47	77 lo-med	**100**	705	1.2	**100**
Abnormal	2	**100**	56	24,309	**100**	245	106.4	**100**
1987 total	2,088	**100**	965	462	**100**	136,049	65.2	**100**
10,000 & more	1,060	50.8	829	782	86.1	132,645	125.2	97.5
10,000–24,999	326	15.6	92	283 up-med	9.6	5,244	16.1	3.9
25,000–49,999	220	10.5	111	504 up-med	11.5	7,869	35.8	5.8
50,000–99,999	218	10.4	162	743 up-med	16.8	15,661	71.8	11.5
100,000–249,000	203	9.7	225	1,111 large	23.3	31,178	153.9	22.9
250,000–499,999	61	2.9	114	1,858 large	11.8	20,740	339.2	15.2
500,000–999,999	21	1.0	63	3,002 large	6.5	14,076	672.5	10.3
1,000,000 & more	11	0.5	63	5,655 large	6.5	37,876	3,414.4	27.8
100,000 & more large		*14.1*		*1,111– 5,655 large*	*48.1*			*76.2*
Below 10,000	1,028	49.2	135	132	14.0	3,404	3.3	2.5
Below 2,500	490	23.5	60	122 lo-med	6.2	498	1.0	0.4

Value of products sold ($)	Farm No. (1,000)	%	Acreage (acre)			Value of sales ($)		
			Total (mil.)	Average per farm	% of total	Total (mil.)	Average per farm (1,000)	% of total
2,500– 4,999	263	12.6	30	114 lo-med	3.1	946	3.6	0.7
5,000– 9,999	275	13.2	46	166 lo-med	4.7	1,960	7.1	1.4
1992 total	1,925	**100**	946	491	**100**	162,608	84.5	**100**
10,000 & more	1,019	52.9	822	807	86.9	159,565	156.6	98.1
10,000– 24,999	302	15.7	82	271 up-med	8.7	4,841	16.0	3.0
25,000– 49,999	195	10.1	91	477 up-med	9.7	6,967	35.7	4.3
50,000– 99,999	188	9.8	134	713 up-med	14.2	13,517	72.0	8.3
100,000– 249,000	208	10.8	228	1,094 large	24.1	32,711	157.0	20.1
250,000– 499,999	79	4.1	131	1,666 large	13.8	26,914	342.7	16.6
500,000– 999,999	31	1.6	81	2,598 large	8.5	20,953	675.4	12.9
1,000,000 & more	16	0.8	76	4,751 large	8.0	53,663	3,377.2	33.0
100,000 & more large		*17.3*		*1,094– 4,751 large*	*54.4*			*82.6*
Below 10,000	907	47.1	124	136	13.1	3,043	3.4	1.9
Below 2,500	423	22.0	56	132 lo-med	5.9	411	1.0	0.3
2,500– 4,999	232	12.1	27	116 lo-med	2.8	836	3.6	0.5
5,000– 9,999	252	13.1	41	162 lo-med	4.3	1,797	7.1	1.1

* Large, lower medium (lo-med) and upper medium (up-med) sizes in acreage as in Table 9.2.
Sources: *1949*: SAUS 1964: 615. *1959*: SAUS 1976: 635. *1969–78*: SAUS 1981: 663. *1987*: SAUS 1991: 648. *1992*: SAUS 1997: 666.

Table 9.5 Characteristics of the Minimum Number of Largest Farms Needed to Produce a Third of Total Gross Sales in the USA 1940–87 [a]

Item	Unit	1940	1969	1987
Number of farms	1	312,939	51,995	32,023
Share of all	%	5.2	1.9	1.5
Sales	Million $	2,804	15,327	51,952
Share of all	%	35.9	34.4	38.1
Average per farm	$	8,960	294,784	1,622,343
Acres in farms	1,000	309,479	171,832	125,552
Share of all	%	29.2	16.2	13.0
Average per farm	1	989	3,305	3,921
Value of land & buildings	Million $	8,491	29,780	77,972
Share of all	%	25.2	14.4	12.9
Average per farm	$	28,558	572,752	2,434,883
Expenses	Million $	1,179	13,666	42,406
Average per farm	$	3,766	26,283	1,324,284
Machinery value	Million $	–	2,619	8,759
Average per farm	$	–	5,037	273,510
Operator's average age	Year	48.5	48.1	50.6
Specialization in share of all farms	%	100	100	100
Cash grain/ field crop	%	38.3	14.8	17.1
Vegetable	%	2.6	4.1	5.0
Fruit	%	6.8	5.4	14.5
Livestock [b]	%	30.5	40.5	31.8
Dairy	%	16.5	9.6	11.4
Poultry	%	5.3	16.4	16.7
Miscellaneous	%	–	9.2	3.5

Constant $ value [c]				
Sales	Million $	16,208	32,200	51,952
Average per farm	$	51,792	619,294	1,622,343
Value of land & buildings	Million $	49,081	62,563	77,972
Average per farm	$	165,075	1,203,260	2,434,883
Expenses	Million $	6,815	28,710	42,406
Average per farm	$	21,769	55,216	1,324,284

Notes:

a. Gross sales are defined as the gross market value before taxes and production expenses of all agricultural products sold or removed from farms. Gross sales include net Commodity Credit Corporation (CCC) loans but exclude direct payments and farm-related income from the government.

b. Excludes dairy and poultry.

c. 1987 = 100.

Sources: Peterson & Brooks (1993: 6) according to relevant issues of Census of Agriculture.

65 years old or over in 1992) were mostly *sole proprietorships* rather than partnerships; were operated by full owners of land rather than part owners or tenants; and on average the operators of these farms had negative net income from farming alone but earned supplementary off-farm income. Large farms also carry out farming in an industrial style (Table 9.4. Brooks & Kalbacher 1990. Tweeten 1994. Tweeten & Amponsah 1996: 89, 91).

Therefore, there are on one hand commercial, industrial, specialized and corporate farms small in number but large in acreage and gross sales, and on the other non-commercial, ordinary and sole proprietorship farms large in number but small in acreage and gross sales.

Crowding Out of Small Farmers

The shifting structure of agricultural production, which is characterized by technological and economic changes, has *forced* many small farmers either to expand, seek off-farm work to maintain farming activities, or abandon farming altogether (Gladwin & Zabawa 1985). While a few small farmers have enlarged, many more of them have been *squeezed* to the margin or out

Table 9.6 Farm Number, Acreage and Value of Sales by Type of Organization in the USA 1974–92

Item	Year	Total	Sole proprietorship (individual, family)	%	Partnership	%	Corporation						Other	%
							No.	%	Family-held %	Non-Family %				
Number (1,000)	1974	1,695	1,518	89.5	145	8.6	29	1.7	1.3	0.4			4	0.2
	1978	2,476	2,175	87.8	241	9.7	51	2.1	1.8	0.2			8	0.3
	1982	2,239	1,946	86.9	223	10.0	60	2.7	2.4	0.3			–	–
	1987	2,088	1,809	86.7	200	9.6	67	3.2	2.9	0.3			–	–
	1992	1,925	1,653	85.9	187	9.7	73	3.8	3.4	0.4			–	–

	1974	906	678	74.9	124	13.7	97	10.7	7.9	2.8	6	0.7
Acreage (million acres)	1978	974	687	70.5	159	16.3	120	12.3	10.6	1.6	8	0.8
	1982	932	642	68.9	152	16.3	127	13.6	12.1	1.5	–	–
	1987	964	628	65.1	153	15.9	119	12.4	11.0	1.4	–	–
	1992	946	604	63.9	153	16.2	123	13.0	11.7	1.3	–	–
Value of farm products sold (billion dollars)	1974	81	55	67.6	11	13.9	14	17.9	9.0	9.0	0.4	0.5
	1978	108	66	61.6	17	16.1	23	21.6	15.0	6.5	0.7	0.6
	1982	132	78	59.2	22	16.4	31	23.9	17.4	6.5	–	–
	1987	136	77	56.3	23	17.1	35	25.6	19.5	6.1	–	–
	1992	163	88	54.1	29	18.0	44	27.2	21.2	6.0	–	–

Sources: *1974:* SAUS 1979: 684–5. *1978:* SAUS 1984: 653. *1982:* SAUS 1987: 623. *1987–92:* SAUS 1991: 647; 1997: 666.

Table 9.7 Characteristics of Corporate Farms in the USA 1974–92

Year	Family-held corporations						Other corporations					
	Total farms	%	1–10 stock-holders	%	Over 10 stock-holders	%	Total farms	%	1–10 stock-holders	%	Over 10 stock-holders	%
1974	21,758	76.5	–		–		6,684	23.5	–		–	
1978	45,418	88.6	44,143	86.1	1,275	2.5	5,852	11.4	4,707	9.2	1,145	2.2
1982	52,652	88.1	50,842	85.0	1,810	3.0	7,140	11.9	5,997	10.0	1,143	1.9
1987	60,771	90.7	59,599	89.0	1,172	1.8	6,198	9.3	5,379	8.0	819	1.2
1992	64,528	88.9	62,755	86.5	1,773	2.4	8,039	11.1	6,914	9.5	1,125	1.6

Sources: *1974*: SAUS 1979: 685. *1978*: SAUS 1984: 653. *1982*: SAUS 1987: 623. *1987*: SAUS 1991: 647. *1992*: SAUS 1997: 666.

of agriculture (Boulding 1974: 4).**8**

Among the small farms, those operated by African-Americans have decreased the most. The Land Loss Fund observes that in 1920, one in every seven farmers was black, while in 1982, this ratio fell to one in every 67. In 1910, black farmers owned 15.6 million acres of farmland, whilst in 1982, only 3.1 million acres. In 1950, black farmers in North Carolina owned 500,000 acres, but by 1982, they owned as little as 40,000 acres. The US farms operated by blacks dropped from 926,000 in 1920 to 33,000 by 1982, and are still steadily declining. Almost half of all black-operated farms are smaller than 50 acres. In the late 1980s, there were less than 200 black farmers in the whole country under the age of 25. Blacks are losing land at a rate of 9,000 acres per week. (Land Loss Fund 1998)

Many small farmers relied on off-farm income in order to maintain farming. Families operating small farms usually depend more on off-farm employment than those operating large farms (USDA 1993. Tweeten 1995a). Hallam (1993: 2) notes that while national per capita income, total food production and income and wealth per *commercial* farm (i.e., large farm) have all increased dramatically, numerous rural areas are still impoverished, and hunger in the United States stubbornly persists.**9**

---

[8] One may think that the structure was only a result of the declining small farmers. But it could also be a cause. As improvements and changes in farm technology reduced the labor utilization, agriculture comprised larger, fewer, more specialized and capital-intensive farms. The efficient use of new (usually costly) technologies was often impractical on small farms. Many operators of these farms, unable to adapt and compete, were *forced* to abandon farming entirely, while other farmers purchased the technologies and expanded their operations. Relatively high costs of land and equipment have restricted access to farming for many. (Ilg 1995: 3–4). This point will be elaborated later.

[9] The USDA report 'Household Food Security in the United States 1999' defines a food insecure household as one that is uncertain of having, or unable to acquire, adequate food to fully meet their basic needs because of inadequate resources. Households that are food insecure with hunger are those in which one or more members experienced hunger because of inadequate resources at least some time during the year.

The report, issued annually since 1997, claims that during of the economic booming period of 1995–99, the number of US households confronted with food insecurity declined by about 12%, and the number of households encountering hunger reduced by 24%. Nevertheless, in 1999: (1) 31 million Americans lived in food insecure households; (2) 7.8 million people - 5.1 million adults and 2.7 million children - subsisted in households that suffered hunger; (3) among households of single mothers with children, nearly 30% were food insecure, and 8% food insecure with hunger; (4) black and Hispanic households faced greater food-related hardship than the national average, with both groups registering rates of food insecurity with hunger of about 6%; and (5) more than one-third of households with income below the federal poverty line were food insecure, and 12% food insecure with hunger. (USDA 2000). It would not be difficult to imagine that in the economic slowdown period, food insecurity and hunger would be more serious.

Most small farmers have migrated to cities. They have been attracted by higher incomes, better jobs, improved educational opportunities and other public services in cities - compared with limited employment opportunities, lower relative farm wages, and low returns in agriculture in rural areas (Gebremedhin & Christy 1996: 58–9). It is true however that while many may have realized their expectations, others have encountered serious problems in their new urban surroundings. In fact, urban unemployment, over-crowding, strained social services, miserable conditions in housing, slums, schools, hospitals, homelessness, crimes, etc. have been caused in part by this massive country-to-city migration. (Ritchie 1979: 1, 28)

The demise of small farms has drawn much attention. Ritchie (1979: 1) claims that few social issues have received such widespread concern as the '*loss of our family farms*', and the subsequent destruction of much of the rural society. Bollman, Whitener and Tung (1995: 25) note that the decline of the small family farm continues to receive media attention. This is because small farms are regarded as more socially and environmentally desired (Ahearn 1996: 96).

Many small farms contribute to the economic activity in local rural areas more than fewer large farms do, thereby stimulating the economy (Ahearn 1996: 96). Despite the relatively meager farming income, small farmers are positive and substantial contributors to both the agribusiness and consumer industries of rural communities (Brown; Christy & Gebremedhin 1994: 52). A small farm structure provides a higher personal and community quality of life and social stability. Another positive externality of a small farm structure is the scenic value of the rural landscape and recreational value for city folk, which have been recognized by Europeans explicitly much earlier. (Ahearn 1996: 96–7). In fact, recent studies have shown a substantial population growth in rural and small towns, as a result of the search for a better quality of life and the prospects for economic opportunities, even though employment growth in the nation's rural and small towns is expected to continue lagging behind that in urban areas (Tweeten 1995a).

For small farmers, loss of land ownership also means loss of self-worth (Brown; Christy & Gebremedhin 1994: 53).

Therefore, preservation of rural communities and traditions is viewed as important (Just; Rausser & Zilberman 1993: 40). In fact, 80% of a random sample of adults in 1987 expressed that 'the family farm (not referring to large family corporate farm) is an essential part of our heritage and must be preserved' (Jordan & Tweeten 1987: 3), and the small farms 'are exactly the farms that the American public seems most eager to protect' (Gardner 1995: 277). Thus, the imperative task is to preserve small farms while not creating obstacles to the large farmers.

9.2 The Underlying Economic Forces

What have been the major causes of the above-mentioned general trend? This section discusses the underlying economic forces. Because 'many of the forces that transformed the US economy and US agriculture during the 20th century were set in motion in the 18th and 19th centuries' (Peterson & Brooks 1993: 1), it is important to study the historical and evolutionary context. The author hereby devises and illustrates the American model of rural development with eight distinct features below, which is not seen in the literature.10

Feature 1 of the American Model of Rural Development: Institutional Changes for an Individual Land Ownership (1783)

After the American Revolution through the War for Independence from Britain (1775–83), the feudalistic quit-rents (paid to absentee landlords in England in exchange for the use right of their land by farmers in the Atlantic coastal areas), prohibition of settlement west of the Alleghenies to protect British land speculators, and tax on the trade of the colonial farm products were abolished. Mainly formulated by Jefferson, Western lands were sold with fee simple titles (Rasmussen & Stanton 1993: 31–2). The English settlers then advanced into the West and almost extinguished Indians.

Jefferson initiated a system of agrarianism which has influenced farmers and farm policy throughout the US history. He believed that a wide distribution of land ownership provides the backbone for a democratic government (Harris & Gilbert 1985: 31). It still 'remains an American belief today' (Brewster 1979). Jefferson's ideal farmer '*yeoman*' provided for his (her) family from his own land by his own efforts and achieved self-sufficiency. He (she) carried on a self-dependent agriculture, buying and selling as little as possible. He did not rent in his land but owned it in fee simple. He did his own work. As an independent, self-supporting member of the society, he was his own boss, responsible for his own managerial

---

[10] These eight features of the American model of rural development were raised in the paper accepted by 'The Second National Small Farm Conference' organized by the US Department of Agriculture, with abstract being published in the proceedings and text posted by the University of Minnesota in its electronic library (Zhou, Jian-Ming October 1999).

decisions. (Rasmussen & Stanton 1993: 32. USDA 1998).11 Therefore, after the War for Independence, an *individual land ownership* was established in the North.

The Civil War (1861–65) liberated the black slaves and extended the individual land ownership to the South. The Homestead Act of 1862 provided 160 acres of unoccupied public land to each homesteader on payment of a nominal fee after five years of residence; land could also be acquired after six months of residence at $1.25 an acre (Chernow & Vallasi 1993: 1261). Most blacks remained in farming because there were few off-farm employment opportunities. Without land, capital or farming resources, many blacks became share-croppers.12 The land owning employers provided them with land and capital and performed most of the managerial functions. This form of share-cropping typically involved unequal distribution of risk and rewards between share-cropping farmers and their employers. It kept the share-cropper indebted to the land owning employer and served to extend the slave–master relationship. However, over the years, blacks were able to acquire more land - in 1910 they farmed 15.6 million acres as owners, as mentioned above. But under either share-cropping or individual ownership, their farm size tended to be smaller than that of the whites. (Brown; Christy & Gebremedhin 1994: 58–9)

Feature 2: Government Policies Supporting Agriculture

The 1862 laws also set up the Department of Agriculture (USDA) to develop and circulate useful information to farmers, and the land-grant colleges to educate young farmers the new farming methods. A transcontinental railroad was financed partly to provide better access to lands opened up under the Homestead Act, and to facilitate farmers' marketing of products. (Rasmussen & Stanton 1993: 33). Such supportive policies continued.

---

[11] According to Wunderlich (2000), Jefferson also stated that when opportunities were superior outside of agriculture, farmers should and would move out (Letter to John Jay, Paris, 23 August 1785), but this point has been paid little attention.

[12] In the USA share-cropping is an employer–employee relationship arising out of the plantation culture following the Civil War, which is often confused with crop sharing, that is a lease relationship between landlord and tenant (Wunderlich January 1999).

Feature 3: Commercialization of the Individual Farming Units Promoting Large Farmers and Driving Small Farmers to an Inferior Position

Once the individual land ownership system had been established, the evolution of the farm structure diverged from the Jeffersonian model of self-dependency. Even though many farmers acquired ownership to land under the Jefferson sponsored ordinances, there also immediately appeared both investors and speculators who bought land and leased it to farmers (a few of these early large landed estates, regularly leased to tenants, are still found scattered across the country today). From the beginning, there were already important differences in the ways household farming, businesses, ownership and control of agricultural resources were organized. (Rasmussen & Stanton 1993: 32)

As the economy expanded and industrialized, functions not directly related with the biological nature of farming moved away from the farm, first to local blacksmiths and then to specialized factories. Large investments were necessary for the efficient production of new machinery. As farmers found the new machines to be worthwhile, their need for cash and reliance on markets grew. (Peterson & Brooks 1993: 1)

The increased commercialization of agriculture resulting from the opening of Western lands led to high growth in production and recurring market surpluses. Large-scale corporate farms were experimented with in the West. (Rasmussen & Stanton 1993: 33)

Around the Civil War, increased demand for food products led to commercialization of Northern agriculture, a temporary diversification of Southern agriculture, and substantial shifts of crops from one area to another in the South (Peterson & Brooks 1993: 2).

In the North, the Civil War led many farmers to increase production by expanding farms and replacing manual labor with horse-drawn machines. As a result, they were caught up in commercial agricultural production in order to pay for the land and machinery. The Civil War resulted in high growth of production and continuous market surpluses in the South too. (Rasmussen & Stanton 1993: 33)

Infrastructure created by the expanding railroads enabled major food processors, wholesalers and retailers to expand (Chandler 1977). In the early 20th century, not only steam and but also gasoline power began to replace horse-power, again leading to an increase in productivity. A larger share of farm production was market destined. Adoption of mechanical technologies made farmers more dependent on markets and credit. (Peterson & Brooks 1993: 2)

Around WWII, farmers intensified their substitution of capital for labor, greatly improving labor efficiency. Non-farm firms provided machinery, fertilizers and other agro-chemicals, petroleum and finance. Farmers bought more inputs from non-farm firms, increasing their need for cash and dependence on markets. (Peterson & Brooks 1993: 2)

Since WWII, farmers have continued to be less self-dependent; and more of the inputs of production have had to be purchased (Rasmussen & Stanton 1993: 39).

The significance of the commercialization of the individual farming units is that in terms of inputs, farmers had to turn to industry-made machines and other inputs and borrow credits, thus no more self-dependency. In terms of outputs, surplus was sold to markets, hence beyond self-sufficiency. If small farmers' costs were higher than those of large ones, they could not sell outputs competitively, and thus could not buy inputs to maintain farming. In this case they would have to turn to either earning off-farm income to supplement farming or abandoning it altogether. The disadvantages experienced by small farms will be examined in more detail later.

Feature 4: Technological Progress, Managerial Resources, Rural Development, Procurement and Marketing Facilities Further Strengthening Large Farmers

Ahearn, Whittaker and El-Osta (1993: 107) claim that 'It is a commonly held belief that economies of size exist in US agricultural production and that these economies have been a significant factor, perhaps the most significant factor, in explaining our current agricultural structure', and 'the most economically efficient size of farms will prosper and other farms will tend to exit or gravitate to that farm size.' Underlying production technologies drive the relationship (Heady 1952). Technological change usually is regarded as of prime importance in explaining farm structure (Batte & Johnson 1993: 315).

Technological progress

Traditional technologies. When the first white settlers came to America, the traditional technologies which featured wheel, simple hand tools, irrigation, domestication of plants and animals, and lasted for thousands of years, were still in use (Tweeten 1986: 1).

Technologies of the First Industrial Revolution. Labor scarcity was the main problem experienced by US agriculture during the 19th century leading to major technological innovations during this period in the form of labor saving devices such as reapers, threshers, combines, and steel plows

(Cochrane 1979). They were made possible by the technologies of the First Industrial Revolution of the 18th/19th century characteristic of steel farm implements and steam-powered machines as well as railroads (Tweeten 1986: 1). These innovations allowed for fast expansion of the land base with relatively small numbers of settlers. While the yields per year of the major crops (wheat, corn, etc.) did not change much during the 19th century, US output grew substantially as acreage increased. (Cochrane 1979)

Technologies of the Second Industrial Revolution. As most of the continent was settled towards the end of the 19th century, not only was labor still in relative shortage, but land also became increasingly scarce and costly. Yield-raising innovations and practices thus became the major source of increased agricultural output (Cochrane 1979). Contributing to this process were the technologies of the Second Industrial Revolution which started in the early decades of the 20th century, primarily mechanical, chemical and biological in nature, with main features of rural electrification, electricity/ gas-driven machines, the modern tractor and its complement of machinery; chemical fertilizers and pesticides; improved plant varieties (e.g., hybrid corn) and animal genetic material (Tweeten 1986: 1). Research and extension activities accelerated their introduction and adoption (Cochrane 1979).

Further stimulation for the dissemination of new technologies was provided by a series of wage increases following immigration restrictions brought in as a result of strong pressure from the American Federation of Labor, combined with the pent-up demand for manufactured products from WWI (Oshima 1987: 53–4). After WWII, the industrial and service sectors expanded, resulting in the movement of individuals and families from rural areas to towns and cities (Peterson & Brooks 1993: 2).

The relative scarcity of labor and the technologies of the Second Industrial Revolution lowered machinery costs far below the labor costs. Large farms using big machinery and achieving lower production costs gained competitive superiority over small farms. This led to the development of capital-intensive equipment and practices for the application of new inputs and the continuous introduction of labor saving tillage and harvesting technologies (Cochrane 1979).

Technologies since the late 1970s. Technological change has been largely responsible for the continuous increase in agricultural supply, the increased capital intensity of agriculture, and the growing dependency on chemical inputs. But in the last quarter of the 20th century, it has been noticed that agricultural resources (such as water and topsoil) and environmental quality are becoming more scarce. The increase in the value of these inputs suggests the development and adoption of innovations to conserve water and reduce soil erosion and pesticide use. Scientific breakthroughs in genetics and biochemistry and a substantial reduction in computing costs since the late

1970s have made the wider use of biotechnology and computers possible. (Just; Rausser & Zilberman 1993: 4). But even in the context of environmental protection, large farms - assisted by economies of scale and robotic innovations (US Congress 1986) - have in general achieved superiority over small farms, as will be shown later.

Therefore, the technologies of the First Industrial Revolution, and especially those of the Second, plus those since the late 1970s, embodied a tremendous potential to substitute capital for labor and/or land (Tweeten 1986: 1). The advantages enjoyed by large farms are dealt with in more detail below.

Superiority of large over small farms

Technologies favor large farms. (1) *Mechanical technologies.* Labor shortages induced mechanization which in turn led to farm enlargement. Mechanical technologies have been embodied in *indivisible* and durable assets, and larger machines have lower costs per unit of capacity. Hence, immediately upon adoption of machinery, farmers have the incentive to expand farm size. By more fully utilizing the capacity of the machinery set, average fixed costs can be lowered, thereby reducing average total costs. Moreover, often the capacity of the new technology (machine complement) substantially exceeds that of the existing farm, thus farmers are compelled to expand farm size to utilize the capacity of machinery available at a low per unit cost. In fact, labor-saving technologies such as tractors (and recently robots) have influenced farm structure in the USA more than have output-increasing technologies such as hybrid seed. (Batte & Johnson 1993: 314, 320–1, 329)

In contrast, small farmers cannot mechanize effectively and are forced to quit farming if they cannot increase farm size (Donaldson & McInerney 1973). Also, small farmers, especially blacks, have little access to modern machinery both because the high initial outlay is prohibitive and the machinery is not adapted to small scale farming (Brown; Christy & Gebremedhin 1994: 60. Ilg 1995: 4, 7).

(2) *Divisible technologies.* Large farms have advantages even in technologies that are completely divisible. Technologies such as pesticides and livestock growth stimulants are highly divisible and are often described as size-neutral. But larger farms have achieved higher adoption rates, which can be explained partly by the learning cost (Feder & Slade 1984). The fixed cost of learning to use a complex technology can be justified by the number of units over which it can be used. When learning costs are considered, even divisible inputs have a fixed component that makes the technology scale biased in favor of large farms. Only when learning costs are negligible can a divisible technology be truly size-neutral. (Batte & Johnson 1993: 314)

Risk bearing plays an important part.

* *Information acquisition costs.* Risk perceptions may influence farmers' willingness to expand business size. A farmer's choice of technology is based on his subjective prediction of gains and losses and hence also on acquired information regarding new technologies. Because information acquisition costs are invariant with output, the economics of information acquisition favors large farms. (Batte & Johnson 1993: 315)

* *Treadmill theory.* This theory may explain the process of economic adjustment by farms to technological progress. Farmers have incentives to adopt new technologies that are made profitable by increased productivity or reduced cost. The innovative and early adopters of technology, to the extent that they correctly identify appropriate new technology, could reap pure profits which may then be reinvested to increase farm size or other inputs. As others also adopt the technology, the increased supply of product, coupled with an inelastic aggregate demand, results in a lower commodity price, eliminating the profit in a short run. Later adopters are thus caught in a treadmill, because they also have to bear learning costs and other investments, but cannot capture the 'adoption rents', as if they were peddling on a treadmill but could not move forward. They may even be forced into economic loss and out of business. (Cochrane 1979: 387–90). Therefore, the farm size structure is affected not only by technological changes but also by the rate of adoption of these changes (Batte & Johnson 1993: 316).

* *Attitudes towards risks.* Early adopters, however, may also face risks. Adoption of inappropriate technologies may produce substantial capital losses, especially for capital-embodied technologies. New capital-embodied technologies may be at high cost due to low manufacturing volume and high production costs. There also is a learning cost associated with complex technologies. Because large farms' ability to bear risks is higher, they are typically more leveraged than small farms, and can afford greater exposure to financial risks. In fact, innovators or early adopters tend to be younger, better educated, with more specialized operations, farming larger areas, able to distribute the fixed learning cost over larger units, and are thus likely less risk averse than the later adopters. Therefore larger farms may adopt technologies more quickly than do smaller farms. (Batte & Johnson 1993: 315–7. Rogers 1983)

(3) *Biotechnologies and environmental protection* have the following aspects.

* *Treadmill process.* Many of the emerging biotechnologies are cost-reducing, output-increasing and relatively scale-neutral. The voluntary or regulation-forced movement away from chemical controls of crop and animal pests to more complex control strategies may have an effect on farm structure. (Batte & Johnson 1993: 323, 325). Kalter and Tauer hold that

biotechnology developments will continue the long-term decline in real agricultural prices. This, together with the fact that the continuous technological change often results in chronic excess resources, may result in low returns for agriculture (Heady 1949). But the low returns are only an average for all producers. The early adopters probably will receive returns above average, with laggards earning below average. Thus, even though biotechnologies are likely to be embodied in divisible inputs and should be inherently size-neutral, early adopters will still gain over later ones who, just as in a treadmill, could not advance, and may even fall behind. (Kalter & Tauer 1987: 423). Just as argued above, the early adopters of new technologies tend to be larger farmers. Therefore there is a risk that they could crowd out smaller ones.

* *Lead versus lag in protecting the environment.* Larger farms tend to take better care of land than smaller farms for several reasons. (1) Large farms use new chisel plows, field cultivators, no-till drills, and other equipment for conservation-friendly cultivation, while small farms often rely on older, used machinery such as moldboard plows and conventional drills and planters. (2) Large livestock farms are monitored by the Environment Protection Agency, but waste disposal on smaller family farms is not so supervised. Small farmers often spread manure without turning it into the soil, and thus effluent runoff becomes a problem with heavy rainfall or snow melt off frozen fields. (3) Precision farming with Global Positioning Systems (GPS) presents new challenges for small farms. Technical and environmental gains from tailoring fertilizers and pesticides to meet the precise needs of every spot in each field can be considerable. Such systems require sizable investment in capital and know-how that must be spread over large acreage to be economically efficient, in which, large farms are also superior to small ones. (Tweeten & Amponsah 1996: 91). (4) Similarly, Geographic Information Systems (GIS) can be used to adjust chemical applications as they move across large fields. But it also requires huge investment which small farms may not be able to afford. (5) Since most small farmers rely on off-farm employment for most of their income, they have less time and incentive to take care of their land. (Henry 1996: 85–6). Therefore small farms often lag behind in protecting the environment (Tweeten 1995b).[13]

* *Cost restrictions.* Although many commercial and non-commercial farms supply organic products, smaller farms often have an advantage in the high labor and management intensity characteristic of organic production. Free-range livestock and poultry, preferred by some consumers over products

---

[13] There is a view that small farms make more contributions to protecting the environment (Thompson 1986, D'Souza & Ikerd 1996), which is analyzed and criticized by Henry (1996).

produced in confinement systems, are also well suited to the labor intensity characteristic of many smaller farms. (Tweeten & Amponsah 1996: 91). Medium farms, where a full-time operator supplies both management and labor, are very adept at decision making requiring close coordination between monitoring biological phenomena and daily or hourly decision making responses (Batte & Johnson 1993: 323). However, the higher costs and prices of products by small and medium farms often restrict their potential advantages.**14**

Managers prefer large farms. The number of hired managers on farms is tiny (Perry & Banker 1999). Nevertheless, Seckler and Young (1978) argue that superior managers, as represented by higher profitability, not only have the ability but also, due to the desire to increase net income and reputation, the incentives to expand farm business size and leave the inferior and high-cost smaller farms. Their superior management would strengthen the competitiveness of large farms by reducing costs.

Rural development facilities promote large farms. (1) *Research and extension*. The Agricultural Research Service and Cooperative Extension Service of the USDA have provided the basis for highly innovative agriculture which is designed for capital-intensive and large-scale farming. Most research was conducted by land-grant institutions with the belief that the benefits would filter down, and small farmers would also be able to use the results. This trickle-down has not occurred. Rather, the research has strengthened the concentration process. While the USDA and the land-grant institutions have made a limited effort to solve problems impeding the improvement of small farms, they have not provided the assistance small farmers need to adjust to the changes brought about by such research. In general, established means of communication, both in research and extension, have failed to work for low-income farmers. (Hightower 1972. Marshall & Thompson 1976. Singh & Williamson 1985. Gebremedhin & Christy 1996: 64)

(2) *Credit*. It is difficult for beginners to take up farming due to high land prices, cost of farm equipment, and lack of credit (Penn 1979: 17. Brown; Christy & Gebremedhin 1994: 54). The incumbent small farmers also are continuously plagued by credit problems. Without an adequate source of credit, they cannot invest in land or modern technology to increase

---

[14] Batte and Johnson (1993: 326–8) also hold that the adoption rates of information technologies (broadly defined as including all those developments designed to measure, store, retrieve, process and communicate data or information) are higher for large than small farms. But as computer technology that allows anyone to get on and work spreads quickly, currently about one-third of farmers use computers, much the same as the general population, and that share is growing rapidly (Perry & Banker 1999).

production and expand the farm base. The capital investment possibility has become a question of survival for many small farms. (Gebremedhin & Christy 1996: 62)

In particular, credit constraints tend to limit the adoption of technologies, especially for indivisible, but also for divisible, ones (Feder; Just & Zilberman 1985). Capital in the form of accumulated savings or access to capital markets is typically more available to larger farms. Thus, credit availability may create a size bias in the technology adoption pattern. (Batte & Johnson 1993: 315)

Only a few lending agencies currently have the ability and the mandate to serve start-up or low-equity farmers. In general, many lending institutions seek only large borrowers in order to minimize their service costs per dollar loaned. The small farmers are usually disqualified for farm credit because of their disadvantaged economic conditions - they can offer little security due to low equity positions. (Gebremedhin & Christy 1996: 62)

In cases where small farmers have got credit, these lending institutions often impose rigid rules in order to fully protect the loan, thereby restricting the risk of loss. To obtain a loan, the small producers may have to bear a higher interest rate. Since most small farmers possess limited information about available sources of credit, they usually do not compare interest charges or other measures of the true cost of credit. (Gebremedhin & Christy 1996: 62). Even though they have realized that the interest rate is too high, they do not have many other choices but to accept if they want the loan.

Among those small farmers who have got credit, some have to cut back production by selling land when faced with a huge debt and with no other alternatives (Gebremedhin & Christy 1996: 62). Many blacks have been known to respond to financial stress by hastily disposing of land and other assets to settle overdue financial obligations, in anticipation of the threat of foreclosure (Jones 1994: 46).

(3) *The insufficiency of other rural development facilities* for small, especially black, farmers also puts them in an unfavorable position. Many black farmers have expended adequate physical labor, but without the managerial skills to operate a successful farming business (Huffman 1981). This is partly due to the discrimination in the quality and quantity of educational opportunities (e.g., formal school, dissemination of information by the Cooperative Extension Service). The lack of adequate amounts of land, capital and management caused black farmers to fall in a vicious circle of poverty. They farmed the less productive land continuously, often depleting the soil, which made them even poorer. (Brown; Christy & Gebremedhin 1994: 54, 60)

Procurement and marketing facilitate large farms. (1) *Procurement.* The price paid for inputs varies among individual farms. Large farms typically can buy inputs at lower prices than small ones, not only because a large farm's size yields simple market power in the supplier's market, but also because the supplier charges actual lower costs for moving a large volume to an individual farm. (Gebremedhin & Christy 1996: 63). Thus, larger farms can enjoy pecuniary economies of size. Pecuniary economies are savings achieved by input suppliers due to volume sales, a part of which can be passed on to large volume purchasing farmers in the form of reduced input costs. Therefore, farmers may expand business size further in order to capture higher pecuniary economies of size. (Batte & Johnson 1993: 314)

In contrast, small farmers, especially the blacks, have to bear higher input costs relative to large farmers because they do not buy bulk amounts of farm inputs (Brown; Christy & Gebremedhin 1994: 60).

(2) *Marketing* includes three main aspects.

* *Marketing facilities.* Responding to the development of highly efficient communication and pricing systems, the market structure for most farm products has changed, which includes developments in transportation, storage, the advent of mass retailing patterns, accompanying volume and standardization requirements, integration of segments in the production and marketing systems, and public regulation of marketing activities. As the decentralized marketing system changed to a centralized system, areas capable of amassing large quantities for shipment and specializing on individual farms have gained superiority. (Gebremedhin & Christy 1996: 63). Marketing firms have increasingly turned to large farms or have developed an integrated system which bypasses the small ones (West 1979).

The new methods, which have replaced organized open markets, set volume requirements so high that small producers are often excluded. They are unable to utilize mass retailing, product standardization and volume specialization and thus further lose competitiveness to large farms. Therefore these developments have significant impact upon the survival of small farms and have created serious problems for them. Lack of markets is a growing concern. (Gebremedhin & Christy 1996: 63)

Small farmers have thus been forced to seek other means to obtain access to the centralized system, such as pooling products to form a large volume. They also have to use other marketing outlets for their products, which however are severely limited. (Gebremedhin & Christy 1996: 63). Direct marketing outlets, such as roadside markets, farmers' markets, and pick-your-own operation, have increased market access for some small farms only to some extent (West 1979).

* *Bargaining power.* Unlike large farmers, the small ones, especially the blacks, do not produce enough output to influence prices (Brown; Christy & Gebremedhin 1994: 60. Gebremedhin & Christy 1996: 63).

* *Information.* Also disadvantaged compared to large farmers, the small

producers lack information on the advantages and disadvantages of each market outlet, and the relationships of price levels among and within outlets. Variation in prices in each market outlet translates directly into income variation. Since most small farmers have very little reserve to carry through a bad year, price variation seriously affects their survival. (Gebremedhin & Christy 1996: 63)

Consequences

Larger farms have lower costs than smaller farms. The above mentioned economic forces have promoted large farms while putting small ones in an unfavorable position. In the USA, corn is the most important agricultural product, followed by soybean and wheat (Ahearn; Whittaker & El-Osta 1993: 119, 128, 134). Tables 9.8–9.13 demonstrate that for corn in 1987, and soybean and wheat in 1986, larger farmers enjoyed lower economic costs measured by dollars per bushel15, were younger, and less dependent on off-farm income; while smaller farmers had higher economic costs, were older, and more reliant on off-farm income [economic costs refer to the value of all inputs in production, whether owned, rented in or financed (Ahearn; Whittaker & El-Osta 1993: 117), thus are a more general indicator for costs than any single item of costs]. Figures 9.1 and 9.2 further show that there is an L-shaped relationship between economic costs (dollar per bushel) and farm size measured by economic class (gross income) in Tables 9.8, 9.10 and 9.12, and by acreage in Tables 9.9, 9.11 and 9.13 respectively. This relationship was not incidental for these crops in 1986 and 1987 only. In fact, since Madden's (1967) notable article on economies of size in agriculture, most economists have confirmed such an L-shaped relationship between costs and output level and concluded that it is a result of economies of size (Ahearn; Whittaker & El-Osta 1993: 108).

The lower costs enjoyed by larger farms and caused by the underlying economic forces have fostered their competitiveness and contributed to the general trend. They have given empirical support to the tenet 'that the costs of agricultural products fall as the size of the production unit in agriculture increases', simply converse to Schultz's assumption as stated in Chapter 1.

9.3 Government Interventions

Between 1908 and 1932, the government had already made preliminary interventions. The first federal effort to examine the farming structures and

---

[15] As a dry measure for capacity, 1 bushel = 35.238 litre (in the USA) = 36.368 litre (in the UK).

Table 9.8 Corn Costs of Farms and Operator Characteristics by Economic Class * in the USA in 1987

Item	Below $40,000	$40,000– $99,999	$100,000– $249,999	$250,000 & more	All farms
No. of farms	206,164	123,713	105,833	46,790	482,500
Share of all farms	43	26	22	10	100%
Share of corn output	11	21	33	35	100%
Corn acres/farm	33	85	145	344	101
Variable cash costs					
Dollar/acre	102.98	104.84	115.68	132.77	117.24
Dollar/bushel	1.07	0.91	0.94	1.06	0.99
Fixed cash costs					
Dollar/acre	48.46	46.11	46.86	49.05	47.65
Dollar/bushel	0.51	0.40	0.38	0.39	0.40
Capital replacement					
Dollar/acre	17.12	18.09	18.27	18.93	18.29
Dollar/bushel	0.18	0.16	0.15	0.15	0.15
Economic costs					
Dollar/acre	242.55	243.07	255.75	264.13	253.96
Dollar/bushel	2.53	2.12	2.08	2.10	2.15
Over 65 years	27	11	14	3	18%
Farming as major	64	89	96	97	80%

* Economic class is based on the sum of sales (value of product removed), government payments and other farm-related income.

Source: USDA [1987] 1993: 115, 120–1.

farm life was represented by the Country Life Commission appointed by President Theodore Roosevelt in 1908. The Commission reported that agriculture was generally prosperous, but rural life was deficient. Many of its recommendations were then implemented, such as the establishment of land banks and a nation-wide agricultural extension service. In the 1920s,

Table 9.9 Corn Costs of Farms and Operator Characteristics by Corn Acreage Class in the USA in 1987

Item	Below 25 acres	25–99 acres	100–499 acres	500 & more acres	All farms
No. of farms	124,683	207,256	135,244	15,317	482,500
Share of all farms	26	43	28	3	100%
Share of corn output	2	20	54	23	100%
Corn acres/farm	12	53	190	675	101
Variable cash costs					
Dollar/acre	108.09	110.56	115.11	130.97	117.24
Dollar/bushel	1.19	1.04	0.95	1.03	0.99
Fixed cash costs					
Dollar/acre	57.87	46.73	46.88	49.05	47.65
Dollar/bushel	0.64	0.44	0.39	0.38	0.40
Capital replacement					
Dollar/acre	14.94	17.08	18.71	19.03	18.29
Dollar/bushel	0.16	0.16	0.15	0.15	0.15
Economic costs					
Dollar/acre	239.01	243.11	255.37	264.20	253.96
Dollar/bushel	2.64	2.29	2.10	2.07	2.15
Over 65 years	25	20	9	5	17%
Farming as major	61	83	92	99	80%

Source: USDA [1987] 1993: 123–4.

farm management specialists and other agricultural economists prompted farmers to analyze their costs and returns and to reorganize their farms in order to get the highest returns in the face of the depressed farm economy. However, many of the problems the Commission discussed still exist nowadays. (Rasmussen & Stanton 1993: 34). The interventions were highly strengthened after the Great Depression of 1929–33.

Table 9.10 Soybean Costs of Farms and Operator Characteristics by Economic Class in the USA in 1986

Item	Below $40,000	$40,000–$99,999	$100,000–$249,999	$250,000 & more	All farms
No. of farms	99,953	68,931	77,288	21,497	267,669
Share of all farms	37	26	29	8	100%
Share of soybean output	13	25	41	22	100%
Soybean acres/farm	61	142	215	391	153
Variable cash costs					
Dollar/acre	44.85	50.22	45.83	52.13	48.03
Dollar/bushel	1.55	1.43	1.34	1.40	1.40
Fixed cash costs					
Dollar/acre	37.82	32.35	38.04	36.88	36.04
Dollar/bushel	1.31	0.92	1.11	0.99	1.06
Capital replacement					
Dollar/acre	11.18	10.47	10.78	10.85	10.78
Dollar/bushel	0.39	0.30	0.31	0.29	0.31
Economic costs					
Dollar/acre	159.33	162.83	150.17	154.31	155.42
Dollar/bushel	5.50	4.63	4.38	4.14	4.53
Over 65 years	18	10	6	3	11%
Farming as major	64	86	95	95	81%

Source: USDA [1986a] 1993: 129–30.

Feature 5: Government Protective Safety Net (1933–96) Failing to Avert the Trend towards Fewer But Larger Farms since 1935 and Prevent Small Farmers from Being Crowded Out from Agriculture

The Great Depression affected farms so severely that the federal government was compelled to intervene to alleviate the enormous financial stress being

Table 9.11 Soybean Costs of Farms and Operator Characteristics by Soybean Acreage Class in the USA in 1986

Item	Below 25 acres	25–99 acres	100–499 acres	500 & more acres	All farms
No. of farms	39,105	108,905	106,369	13,290	267,669
Share of all farms	15	41	40	5	100%
Share of soybean output	1	16	59	23	100%
Soybean acres/farm	13	59	213	855	153
Variable cash costs					
Dollar/acre	62.97	50.17	46.30	49.61	48.03
Dollar/bushel	1.70	1.40	1.26	1.73	1.40
Fixed cash costs					
Dollar/acre	52.80	40.36	37.95	30.37	36.40
Dollar/bushel	1.42	1.13	1.03	1.06	1.06
Capital replacement					
Dollar/acre	12.74	10.32	10.90	10.71	10.78
Dollar/bushel	0.34	0.29	0.30	0.37	0.31
Economic costs					
Dollar/acre	200.40	176.46	159.38	133.73	155.42
Dollar/bushel	5.40	4.93	4.34	4.68	4.53
Over 65 years	10	18	5	3	11%
Farming as major	54	81	89	97	81%

Source: USDA [1986a] 1993: 131–2.

experienced by farmers (Jones 1994: 27). A priority for President Franklin
D. Roosvelt and Secretary of Agriculture Wallace, the Agricultural
Adjustment Act of 1933 was signed on 12 May, as a part of the New Deal
(Rasmussen & Stanton 1993: 34).

This intervention and the resulting policies were the forerunners of many
federal agricultural programs and other measures. Criticism persisted from

Table 9.12 Wheat Costs of Farms and Operator Characteristics by
Economic Class in the USA in 1986

Item	Below $40,000	$40,000–$99,999	$100,000–$249,999	$250,000 & more	All farms
No. of farms	106,991	84,835	65,696	23,323	280,846
Share of all farms	38	30	23	8	100%
Share of wheat output	12	24	39	25	100%
Wheat acres/farm	70	162	310	502	190
Variable cash costs					
Dollar/acre	36.70	38.34	44.63	55.13	44.19
Dollar/bushel	1.34	1.26	1.32	1.49	1.35
Fixed cash costs					
Dollar/acre	19.19	21.24	21.30	23.83	21.54
Dollar/bushel	0.70	0.70	0.63	0.65	0.66
Capital replacement					
Dollar/acre	11.36	10.85	11.27	10.70	11.05
Dollar/bushel	0.41	0.36	0.33	0.29	0.34
Economic costs					
Dollar/acre	110.42	111.82	112.36	123.91	114.48
Dollar/bushel	4.03	3.68	3.33	3.35	3.50
Over 65 years	35	9	6	5	18%
Farming as major	71	90	96	88	84%

Source: USDA [1986b] 1993: 136–7.

the very beginning and through the following decades. Investigations, fine tunings, improvements, major modifications and reforms had repeatedly been made, and new programs established to replace old 'new programs' which had failed. (Jones 1994: 25, 27. Ritchie 1979: 1). Below is a summary of the major federal agricultural programs and other measures, mainly according to Jones (1994: 29–35), followed by a discussion of the effects of chiefly the commodity programs, with the focus on domestic problems, rather than

Table 9.13 Wheat Costs of Farms and Operator Characteristics by Wheat Acreage Class in the USA in 1986

Item	Below 25 acres	25–99 acres	100–499 acres	500 & more acres	All farms
No. of farms	71,236	93,072	88,807	27,731	280,846
Share of all farms	25	33	32	10	100%
Share of wheat output	2	10	39	49	100%
Wheat acres/farm	13	54	238	946	190
Variable cash costs					
Dollar/acre	55.00	50.48	44.35	42.47	44.19
Dollar/bushel	1.63	1.46	1.36	1.31	1.35
Fixed cash costs					
Dollar/acre	28.68	25.13	21.33	20.77	21.54
Dollar/bushel	0.85	0.73	0.65	0.64	0.66
Capital replacement					
Dollar/acre	11.79	10.07	11.32	10.99	11.05
Dollar/bushel	0.35	0.29	0.35	0.34	0.34
Economic costs					
Dollar/acre	166.30	130.50	117.36	107.23	114.48
Dollar/bushel	4.92	3.78	3.60	3.31	3.50
Over 65 years	30	17	12	9	18%
Farming as major	80	75	93	93	94%

Source: USDA [1986b] 1993: 138–9.

foreign trade.

Major programs and measures

Commodity programs. * *Price support programs* were designed to maintain agricultural prices above equilibrium levels in order to assure producers a reasonable price for their commodities. These programs were financed by the Commodity Credit Corporation (CCC), administered by the Agricultural Stabilization and Conservation Service (ASCS), and implemented through non-recourse loans and direct commodity purchases.

- *Non-Recourse Loans.* ASCS extended CCC loans to eligible farmers,

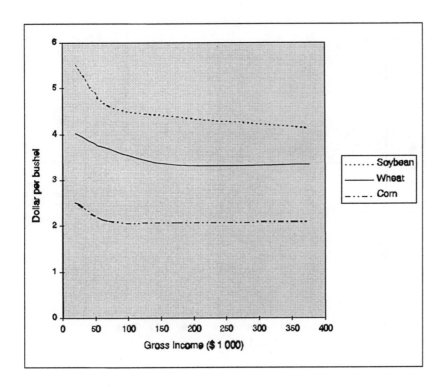

Sources: Tables 9.8, 9.10 and 9.12.

Figure 9.1   Economic Costs for Corn, Soybean and Wheat by Gross Income in the USA 1986–87

using their stored crops as collateral. The loan amount was based on a fixed rate (loan rate) per unit (bushel, pound) of commodity. If the market price reached or rose above the loan rate, a farmer could simply sell his commodity and pay off the loan and accumulated interest; however, if the market price remained below the loan rate, the farmer could forfeit or deliver the commodity to the government to discharge the loan obligation in full. The term 'non-recourse loans' derived from the obligation for the government to accept the crops as repayment (Roberts & Doyle 1996: 211). These loans gave farmers a price floor and provided them with income to meet financial obligations. Eligible commodities for this program included

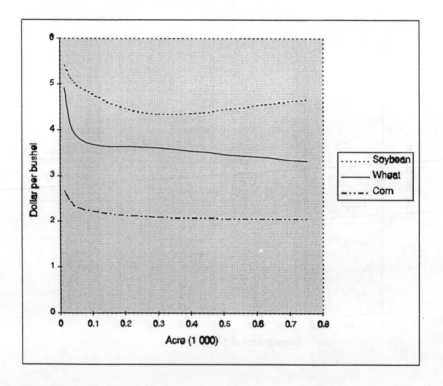

Sources: Table 9.9, 9.11 and 9.13.

Figure 9.2 Economic Costs for Corn, Soybean and Wheat by Acreage in the USA 1986–87

cotton, feed grain, food grain, peanuts, sugar, tobacco, milk, mohair, and wool (Gardner 1995: 22).

For example, the 1990 Farm Bill stipulated that basic loan rates be calculated as 85% of the five-year moving average of producers' price (excluding the highest and lowest years), but a reduction, up to 20%, could be made for some commodities under certain conditions.

- *Direct Purchases*. This was the acquisition of commodities from the market through direct purchases to remove sufficient quantities to enable commodity prices to rise above market clearing prices. In essence, the government agreed to purchase any amount of the product offered for sale at the market clearing prices. The overall plan was to remove excess commodities in periods of above-average production and return them to the market when production was below normal, thus reducing price fluctuation. Commodities that were eligible for this program included sugar, milk and dairy products. Under the dairy price support program, for example, CCC bought surplus butter, cheese and non-fat dry milk from processors at announced prices, in order to maintain prices at support levels.

* *Income support programs* were aimed to stabilize farm income and ease financial stress, and implemented through government *deficiency payments*, which were given directly to farmers in response to low farm prices. A 'target price' was determined by the government for selected commodities, including cotton, feed grain, rice and wheat. (1) When the market price was above or at the target price and above the loan rate, farmers sold products in the market and received no deficiency payment. (2) When the market price was under the target price but over or equal to the loan rate, farmers also sold products in the market but could get a payment equivalent to the gap between the target price and the market price. (3) When the market price was even below the loan rate, farmers sold products to the *government* at the loan rate and could acquire a payment equivalent to the discrepancy between the target price and the loan rate.**16** Thus the deficiency payment was the difference between the target price and the higher of the market price and the loan rate (Gardner 1995: 157). The relationship among the deficiency

---

[16] When explaining the deficiency payments and target prices, Jones (1994: 32) claims that 'Products are sold in the market', while Edgmand, Moowaw and Olson (1996) state that 'Unlike price supports, there is no surplus associated with the target price. A potential surplus does develop, but it is sold on the market'. They may have only noted cases (1) and (2), but not (3) where products were sold to the government, therefore may not be able to explain the existence of high government stocks, as cited by Gardner (1995: 23). But even Gardner does not point out case (3). Thus readers of his book may not be able to understand how the huge government storage could appear with the implementation of the deficiency payments. Hopefully this point has been made clear by the author here.

payment, target price, loan rate and market price is illustrated in Table 9.14.

* *Supply control programs* were developed in the early 1930s to contain expenditures on commodity programs and increase program effectiveness by reducing production of program commodities. In the 1990s, they included the Acreage Reduction Program and the Paid Land Diversion Program.

- *Acreage Reduction Program (ARP)* was a voluntary land retirement program, conducted by CCC, in which participating farmers idled a prescribed portion of their crop acreage base for wheat, feed grain, cotton or rice. It was devised to limit supplies of these commodities and was implemented whenever projected supply was considered excessive. Farmers were not given direct payments from ARP participation, but must comply with the program announced by the Secretary of Agriculture for that crop to be eligible for government loans, purchases and/or payments. Under ARP, the acreage that might be planted to a crop (permitted acreage) was uniformly reduced from the crop acreage base as specified for each crop and might vary from year to year, depending on stock-to-use ratios and year-end stocks for the preceding year.

- *Paid Land Diversion Program (PLD)* was designed to limit supplies of certain commodities including wheat, feed grain, cotton and rice, and permit payment to farmers for reducing the acreage planted to any of these crops, if the Secretary of Agriculture determined that acreage planted should be further reduced. This program may be implemented whether or not an ARP was in effect, if a PLD would assist in adjusting the total national acreage

Table 9.14 Relationship among Deficiency Payment, Target Price, Loan Rate and Market Price in the USA up to 1996

	Case (1)		Case (2)		Case (3)
High	Market price		Target price		Target price
Middle	Target price	Market price = target price	Market price		Loan rate
Low		Loan rate	Loan rate	Market price = loan rate	Market price
	Sell to market, get no deficiency payment		Sell to market, receive deficiency payment = gap between target price and market price		Sell to government, acquire deficiency payment = gap between target price and loan rate

Source: This table is the author's own formulation.

to desirable goals. However, total acreage diverted in any county must be limited so that the local economy was not adversely affected. Diverted land must be devoted to approved conserving use.

Assistance programs. * *Disaster assistance program* was developed to grant relief to farmers who suffered losses through natural disasters such as droughts, hail and other adverse weather conditions. Disaster assistance was supplied when the Secretary of Agriculture determined that, due to a natural disaster, producers have been prevented from planting a portion of their base, or a producer's total yield was less than a certain amount.

* *Farm credit assistance programs* were to satisfy the unmet credit needs of high risk and limited resource farmers, and farmers who have experienced losses from drought and other disasters. These special government programs were contrived to provide direct credit assistance in the form of emergency or supervised financing. This assistance was afforded through the Farmers Home Administration (FmHA) as *Farmers Home Administration Loans*. FmHA channelled credit to farmers, rural residents and communities. The purpose of loans to farmers was to help build the family farm system, the economic and social base of many rural communities. These loans included: *Farm Ownership Loans* for buying land; refinancing debts; constructing, repairing or improving buildings and developing farmland. *Farm Operating Loans* for buying livestock, equipment, feed, seed, fertilizer, birds or supplies for farm and home operations; refinancing debts or paying interest on loans. *Farm Emergency Loans* for covering losses from natural disasters that are not otherwise compensated so farmers may continue their operations with credit from other sources. *Soil and Water Conservation Loans* for financed land and water development measures, afforestation, drainage of farmland, irrigation, pasture improvement and related land and water use adjustment.

* *Emergency Feed Assistance Program* provided for the sale of CCC-owned grain at 75% of the basic county loan rate to livestock producers whose feed fell below normal because of drought or excessive moisture. The Secretary of Agriculture must declare the county a natural disaster area before this program could be implemented and livestock producers were eligible only if their available feed was insufficient to preserve and maintain their breeding stocks.

* *Crop insurance* was set up by the Federal Crop Insurance Corporation (FCIC) founded in 1938 after private attempts to provide all-risk crop insurance failed. The programs were expanded in 1980 when the federal government was required to pay up to 30% of premiums to private companies who acted as agents for the FCIC (Halcrow 1984: 243). Insurance was available for many commodities, including most of the price-supported crops. Farmers may choose to insure 50%, 65%, or 75% of their normal yields, or a market price. (Gardner 1995: 35–6)

Export promoting programs. The USA has been the largest exporter of grains and cotton, and both an important importer and exporter of dairy products and beef. It has imported sugar for refining and export. Before 1985, the policies were oriented to supporting domestic producers' incomes through maintaining relatively high prices as well as supplementing their incomes through deficiency payments. In the mid-1980s, policy makers were concerned that high loan rates were lowering US competitiveness. Thus, since 1985, policies have changed towards ensuring the competitiveness of agricultural export industries. The 1985 Farm Bill was enacted to reduce target prices by about 10% and loan rates, and set up several new subsidy mechanisms. (Roberts & Andrews 1994: 216–8, 220. Vande Kamp & Runge 1994: 321)

　　* *Marketing loans* were to allow US products to be sold below the loan rate. This enabled farmers to repay their commodity loans at rates below the loan rate when world prices were below the loan rate. The difference represented a direct subsidy which virtually ensured that exports and domestic sales would always be price competitive and that large stocks would not accumulate. Marketing loans were first applied to cotton and rice, then extended to wheat and feed grains in 1993. As the USA was a price leader in these commodities, the marketing loan mechanism has had the potential to depress world prices of the relevant commodities. (Roberts & Andrews 1994: 220)

　　* *Export Enhancement Program (EEP)* extended subsidies to exporters to ship specified quantities to designated markets. This enabled exporters to sell at subsidized prices on those markets. EEP has been used predominantly for wheat but has also given support to barley, rice and livestock products, particularly poultry. (Roberts & Andrews 1994: 220)

　　* *Dairy Export Incentive Program (DEIP)* extended export subsidies for dairy products. In addition, considerable funding has been contributed for export credit guarantee programs. (Roberts & Andrews 1994: 220). Besides, the dairy and sugar industries have been supported by measures which kept domestic prices above world market levels by restricting quantities on the internal market. Tariff quotas on imports and minimum prices (loan rates) were applied to diary and sugar. (Roberts & Doyle 1996: 212)

Conservation programs. The 1985 Farm Bill also initiated a number of soil conservation programs to encourage land users to adopt soil conservation measures in order to reduce the threat that soil erosion posed to the future of agriculture. The Soil Conservation Service (SCS) extended technical help as well as cost sharing, and in some cases, ASCS also afforded cost sharing.

　　* *Conservation Reserve Program (CRP)* discouraged farmers from growing crops on crop land designed by SCS as highly erodible. Farmers were encouraged to plant grass or trees on these lands and were paid an

annual rent for 10 years. Cost shares were also available to help establish the permanent planting of grass, legumes, trees and/or windbreaks. However, the CRP has also been used as a *de facto* supply control program, with some farming land enrolled which was not very environmentally sensitive (Osborn & Heimlich 1994).

* *Agricultural Conservation Program (ACP)* was schemed to alleviate soil, water and related resource problems through cost sharing. Through this program ASCS helped farmers and ranchers all over the country to implement conservation practices including terraces, grass covers, and other erosion control measures.

* *Forestry Incentive Program (FIP)* was to increase the supply of timber products from private non-industrial forest land. It was devised for forest operators with at least 10 but not more than 1,000 acres, and provided cost share for tree planting, timber stand improvement or natural regeneration of forests. It offered cost share up to 65% of actual cost with a payment limit of $10,000. Forest land under FIP must produce at least 20 cubic feet of timber per acre per year.

* *Wetlands Reserve Program (WRP)* allowed ASCS to purchase easements, in lump sum payments, from owners of qualifying cropland who were willing to restore and protect wetlands and adjacent areas previously converted to farmlands, for the purpose of restoring the hydrology and vegetation and protecting the functions and values of wetlands for wildlife habitat, water quality improvement, flood water retention, ground water recharge, etc. (Vande Kamp & Runge 1994: 322)

* *Conservation Compliance Provisions (CCP)* linked conservation programs with the commodity programs. CCP required certain environmental plans on farms as a condition of eligibility for commodity program payments, and arguably could achieve environmental targets without expending additional federal funds. All farmers with fields designated as highly erodible land were required to produce an approved conservation plan by 1990 and to implement it by 1 January 1995. Failure to do so would result in loss of future benefits such as price support payments, crop insurance, disaster payments, conservation reserve payments, storage and commodity loans and subsidized agricultural loans. (Vande Kamp & Runge 1994: 323)

Federal tax policies. Federal tax policies gave breaks that represented subsidies to land and capital and allowed farmers to acquire expensive equipment and shift the cost to the government (Brown; Christy & Gebremedhin 1994: 61).

State bans on non-family corporate farming. Some mid-Western states have inhibited corporations from owning farmland or conducting farm operations. Laws banning corporate farming were adopted first by Kansas and North Dakota in the 1930s, and followed by Iowa, Minnesota, Missouri, Nebraska, Oklahoma, South Dakota and Wisconsin in the early 1970s. It is, however, noteworthy that family-held corporations have been exempted in each state. (Knoeber 1997: 151)

A discussion on the commodity programs and other relevant measures
The federal agricultural programs initiated in the 1930s (i.e., commodity and assistance programs) have had two primary policy goals: *supporting farm income* and *stabilizing agricultural prices* (Jones 1994: 25). The 1977 Food and Agriculture Act reaffirmed the historical aim of the commodity programs as *fostering the family farm system* (Tweeten 1993: 336). The state bans on non-family corporate farming also intended to preserve and protect the family farm as the basic unit of production (Krause 1983: 4). The CCP further linked the conservation with the commodity programs and tried to reach both of their aims. Have these purposes been achieved? What have been the effects of these policy measures on family farms and national economy? The discussion below will focus on the commodity programs because they have been the most criticized (Jones 1994: 25), and other relevant measures.17

There have been conflicting views, i.e., that the commodity programs have (1) reduced farm numbers, (2) preserved farms, and (3) had no impact on farm numbers (Tweeten 1993: 337–8). Without wishing to enter too deeply into this debate, it is useful to make a simple observation: on one hand, 'family farm' is not equal to 'small' farm, since there are also large family-held corporate farms which have been increasing; on the other, many small family farms have been exiting farming. The overall result of the 60-year implementation of the commodity programs was larger but fewer farms. Thus, the original aims of the commodity programs have not been reached. Tweeten and Amponsah (1996: 90) also claim that commodity programs saved many small farms in the short-run by intervening in markets to reduce the number of farm failures, especially in times of financial crises such as in 1982–86; but in the long-run, they have not preserved small farms. Hence government policies have both helped and harmed small farms.

Actual discrimination by the commodity programs. The purpose of the commodity programs was to keep agricultural prices, hence farmers' incomes, high (Hurst 1995: 48). But the price support programs tended to encourage increased production, depress prices, and raise government spending, thus production control had to be combined (Jones 1994: 27–30).

---

17 A more general analysis and criticism of the OECD governments' protective policies can be found in OECD (1998c: 64–72).

The measure was that a percentage of the land of a farm should be idled, then, output on the rest of the land would get government subsidies proportionately. Because a larger farm had larger acreage, after a percentage was idled, the used land was still larger, and output higher, than those of a smaller farm. Thus more subsidies went to larger farms. Moreover, larger farms could put more poor land in the idled part, and implement intensive farming to increase yield on the used land, thus the total output might not be affected very much (Just; Rausser & Zilberman 1993: 16). In contrast, the idled part of smaller farms might have to include more good land, since the scope of choosing which land to be idled was very limited. Thus, their total output might be more greatly affected. Accordingly, larger farms would receive more subsidies due to higher output.

Why not then place a ceiling on the production of the used land so as to reduce excessive output and subsidies? The answer is that cutting off payments at a specific ceiling would encourage farmers to undertake esoteric legal maneuvering that could, overnight, produce thousands of new farms that qualified for their own additional payments (in the name of spouses or children) (Hurst 1995: 48–9).

The CRP also favored larger farmers. The first 10-year contracts agreed under the CRP, which commenced in 1986, included 2 million acres, and were to expire in 1995. A total of 22 million contract acres would expire in 1996 and 1997. Secretary of Agriculture Espy announced in August 1994 that landowners who had CRP land due to expire in 1995 which could be brought back to production in 1996 would have the option of extending the contract for one additional year. (Vande Kamp & Runge 1994: 322). Thus, by the mid-1990s, there had been a large area idled under the CRP (36.4 million acres, or 10% of the whole crop area), but the area idled under the ARP had declined to be small both in absolute terms and historical standards, and even zero for wheat in 1992–93. Therefore, CRP has been largely offset by a reduction in ARP. Moreover, the rate at which land entered the CRP markedly declined in the late 1980s and early 1990s. (USDA 1994. Roberts & Andrews 1994: 221–2, 232). The acreage of large farms was not affected very much by the introduction of the CRP in 1985 because they could transfer the land idled under the ARP to the CRP to enjoy the rent paid by the government. Such a transfer could be easier for large farms because they had more land, thus also more poor land which would be erodible. In contrast, such a transfer would be more difficult for small farmers because their limited land idled under the ARP, if not erodible, could not be changed to the CRP according to the rules (although in practice some non-erodible land also entered the CRP). As a result, non-participation of the CRP among small farmers in Louisiana, for example, remained high (McLean-Meyinsse; Hui & Joseph 1994: 383).

The fact that larger acreage and higher output would receive more subsidies in turn encouraged large farmers to buy more land and increase size. Because the *federal tax policies* favored land and capital, large farmers profited from them and could purchase more land and equipment, while small farmers who relatively had more labor but less land and capital could not afford to increase farm size. Thus the tax policies benefited large at the expenses of small farms. (Brown; Christy & Gebremedhin 1994: 61). Moreover, because land could receive subsidies, the commodity programs resulted in significant increase of land value (Johnson 1996: 1327), which made it more difficult for small farmers to increase farm size and for potential ones to enter farming. The *assistance programs* did not provide sufficient credit for them to do so. There also were small and black farmers who sold land for windfall profits, thus losing land as a potentially permanent source of revenue and quitting farming. In so doing, the commodity programs accelerated land loss by small farmers. (Jones 1994: 41). After spending the short-term profits, they would meet difficulties in living if they had not found a stable job.

A part of small, especially black, farmers did not even participate in the commodity programs, thus receiving no subsidies at all. Jones (1994: 40, 44–5) summarizes the major reasons as (1) poor farming managerial ability caused by inferior education opportunities, lack of contact with the Cooperative Extension Service and information (e.g., the inability to produce the right commodity mix in order to receive program benefits), and high involvement in off-farm activities; (2) too high an opportunity cost for idling a portion of already very small acreage; (3) production costs higher than standard costs for target prices due to small size, marginal land, inefficiency, low productivity, limited quantity and low quality of products; (4) lack of information; (5) indifference; and (6) racial discrimination in the implementation of the assistance programs.

Therefore, only about 33% and 30% of all farmers participated in and received direct benefits from the commodity programs in 1978 and early 1990s respectively (Lin; Johnson & Calvin 1981. Zinsmeister 1995: 44).

Among those who participated, in 1977, 10% of farmers as the largest ones received nearly half, while the smallest 50% obtained only 10%, of the commodity program payments (Lin; Johnson & Calvin 1981). In 1992, large farms with annual sales of $100,000 and over accounted for only 17.3% of all farms, but acquired 67% of the commodity program payments (Table 9.4. Roberts & Andrews 1994: 229).

Thus, Jones (1994: 36) claims that although the commodity programs were declared as without regard to race, sex, size of operations or any other unique characteristic, they actually discriminated against small, especially black, farmers and favored large ones.

State bans on non-family corporate farms could be evaded by large farmers through moving to other states which do not ban them. Family farmers will feel the same price competition from low-cost, integrated operations whether these operations are located within the state or elsewhere. This has also deprived local families of the opportunity to remain on the small farm by producing for integrators under contract, receiving cheap fertilizer (manure), or supplementing income through working in integrators' feed mills or processing plants. (Tweeten & Amponsah 1996: 91). Such bans are not imposed on family-held corporate farms which account for the majority of large corporate farms. Therefore, large farms have not been affected much, but small ones have.

Major results of the commodity programs are summarized as follows.

* *Reinforcement for larger but fewer farms.* Gardner (1995) argues that the commodity programs made rich farmers richer. Dodson (1994: 1, 5, 16) reports that during 1987–91, large, specialized farms earned the greatest profits, while small farms showed most losses, as one-third (which were small ones) of all farms had negative incomes. Goetz and Debertin (1996: 529) claim that the commodity programs not only failed to stem, but even led to higher migration out of rural areas.

* *Bureaucracy.* Each year, participating farmers must go to the local federal agency to receive permission to plant the strictly allotted crop acreage, re-measure or even re-organize the fields so that the idled and used acres fell within the bounds of the programs, and revisit the agency to certify that they complied with the rules. Officials may have to check the fields to avoid cheating. Debating in the Congress, and between it and the government, planning, calculating and implementing the programs at all levels of governments cost much time, energy, money and created bureaucracy. (Hurst 1995: 49). In 1983–92, there were 828 federal programs (USGAO 1994). The managerial efficiency was quite low with the enormous number of complicated administrative procedures (OECD 1998c: 69).

* *Market distortions.* Under *price support programs*, through *non-recourse loans*, and under case (3) of deficiency payments within *income support programs*, when market price was lower than the artificial loan rate, farmers could forfeit or deliver the commodity to the government to discharge the loan obligation, so as to reduce supply in the market and maintain prices at a level higher than or at least equal to the loan rate. Via *direct purchases* of commodities at the market clearing price, the government tried to make commodity price rise above the market clearing level. Therefore, commodity prices would be raised artificially.

In contrast, case (2) of deficiency payments within *income support programs* allowed farmers to sell products to the market while obtaining deficiency payments when market price fell below the artificial target price but still higher than or equivalent to the loan rate. This would create surplus in the market.

In order to avoid excessive supply, ARP (which has largely been replaced by CRP since 1985) was combined, so as to reduce production and keep or lead prices to be higher. But farmers could still produce the maximum on the permitted production land, even if the market did not need so much. Actually, the 1977 Farm Bill and 1981 Farm Bill set guaranteed minimum grain prices at well-above-market levels, which affected not only domestic consumers, but also external competition. Thus the 1985 Farm Bill reduced target prices and loans rates, but the principle was the same: the government still tried to keep the artificial prices high, and farmers still produced the highest output on the used land no matter whether the market needed it or not. (Hurst 1995: 50–1)

* *High storage.* The government buying of commodities created huge stocks (Ritchie 1979: 8), with significant storage cost. On one hand, pressures arose to reduce the surplus stocks. This was usually done by subsidized disposal: food grant, subsidized food stamps and school lunch programs to domestic consumers; food aid and subsidized sales to foreign countries. (Gardner 1995: 23). On the other, if stocks were dumped in the market, prices would be lowered (Hurst 1995: 49–50). Thus, producers reacted negatively to the disposal of purchased commodities in the market (Jones 1994: 31). Hence a dilemma in handling stocks. Of course, stocks may fluctuate. For example, in 1995–96, the world grain prices rose to record highs and world stocks fell to their lowest levels in 25 years, as global consumption outpaced production. Domestically, in 1995 and early 1996, both corn and wheat suffered from adverse weather, reduction in area planted and harvested, and lower yields (the two crops together accounted for the majority of commodity program spending; within 23 million acres of all program bases, the largest area was in wheat - 10.8 million acres, or one-seventh of the total wheat plantings). Meanwhile land held out of production under the CRP with contract since 1985 which largely replaced ARP could not be brought back to production. Thus stocks fell and prices rose by large margins. (Stuart & Runge 1997: 129–30. USDA 1994). This shows another side of ARP and CRP: they could also restrict supply rigidly when market demand was high and raise prices artificially.

* *Budget pressure.* Agriculture was one of the most heavily subsidized economic sectors in the USA (Gardner 1995). The cost of farm programs increased phenomenally from slightly over $10 billion in 1981 to approximately $29 billion in 1986 (Knutson; Penn & Boehm 1990), which has contributed to the high federal budget deficit (Goodwin & Featherstone 1995: 39), although agricultural support was relatively a small part of the budget and gross domestic product (Roberts & Andrews 1994: 229).

* *Weaker external competitiveness and heavier burden on taxpayers and consumers.* The external competitiveness of US farm products was lowered by the high domestic prices before 1985, and raised since then by the export promoting programs which allowed farmers to repay commodity loans at rates below the loan rate when world prices were below it. But this was at the expenses of heavier burden on the federal budget or taxpayers. (Jones 1994: 25. Roberts & Andrews 1994: 220). Sugar and dairy produce as import competing commodities have been supported mainly through import barriers which maintained domestic prices well above world prices, and dairy price support has been reinforced by export subsidies. Therefore, most support for program crops has been taxpayer financed, whereas most support for sugar and dairy produce has been consumer financed (Roberts & Doyle 1996: 211) (for details of support arrangements, see Roberts; Andrews; Doyle; Cannan; Connell & Hafi 1995).

Pressure to crowd small farmers and phase commodity programs out
Although benefiting from the commodity programs, large farmers still felt constrained in production, disliked the protection of small farmers who were less efficient in using resources and other drawbacks mentioned above, and pressed to squeeze small farmers and phase the commodity programs out.

In 1942 the Committee for Economic Development (CED) was formed by the presidents of several large corporations and university economists. The aim was to create a two-tier system of agriculture, with a few large corporate farms (25% of farms and 80% of output) and most farmers on part-time farming with off-farm work or on welfare (75% of farms and 20% of output) (Ritchie 1979: 2, 15. CED [1974] 1979: 25). The means was to squeeze, as stated by Samuelson (1970) - farmers should be both forced and attracted out of farming, and by Boulding (1974: 4) - 'The only way I know to get toothpaste out of a tube is to squeeze, and the only way to get people out of agriculture is likewise to squeeze. . . . If you can't get people out of agriculture easily, you are going to have to do farmers severe injustice in order to solve the problem of allocation' - both were members of the Research Advisory Board of the CED (Ritchie 1979: 10, 12).

In Ritchie's view, this was the overall strategy for agriculture that has been enforced since 1946. Even the Democratic Party, which was regarded as more sympathetic to small farmers, initiated the federal agricultural programs in the 1930s and controlled one or both houses of the Congress during 1955–94 (Paarlberg & Orden 1996: 1305), also cooperated with the CED and its strategy. For example, Dale Hathaway, advisor to the Subcommittee of the CED, was appointed as member of the President's Council of Economic Advisors not only for Eisenhower in 1955–56 but also for Kennedy in 1961–63, and Assistant Secretary of Agriculture in charge of the commodity programs for Carter in 1977–81. (Ritchie 1979: 10–2)

Thus, the recommendation to move 2 million small farmers out of a total of 5.5 million farmers and fend off new entrants during a five-year period from 1962 by reducing price supports for crops to below parity level by the CED in 1962 was accepted by the government. By 1974, the reduction of farmers had been accomplished. (CED [1962] 1979: 42, 59; [1974] 1979: 24. Ritchie 1979: 6–8, 15). The higher decreasing rates of farms in 1964 and 1969 in Table 9.1 may be illustration of this point.

Large farms also provided a considerable quantity of campaign funds for members of Congress to phase out the commodity programs, while the lobbying power of small farmers reduced due to their declining number and economic strength (Tweeten & Amponsah 1996: 90–1). As a result, in the early 1990s, the total costs of farm programs had been cut by half. In fact, farm subsidies were the only major domestic program to receive less funding in absolute terms than a decade before. (Hurst 1995: 50)

The Canadian/United States Trade Agreement (CUSTA) was signed in 1988 and stipulated that neither country would use direct export subsidies on agricultural products being sold to one another. The North American Free Trade Agreement (NAFTA) ratified in 1993 by Canada, Mexico and the USA followed the spirit of CUSTA. (CUSTA 1988. Zepp; Plummer & McLaughlin 1995: 175). The GATT Uruguay Round of 1993 prescribed that, among other items, the USA reduce its volume of subsidized exports by 21% and the value of subsidies on those exports by 36% from the averages of 1986–90. The reductions were to be phased in over six years starting from 1995. (Roberts & Andrews 1994: 226). Therefore, the USA had to change its policy of maintaining higher domestic prices while subsidizing exports.

As a result, after the Republicans, who traditionally favored large competitive farmers, had gained a majority in Congress in November 1994, they strengthened their battle against the agricultural programs, which eventually led to the 1996 Farm Bill (Paarlberg & Orden 1996: 1305–6).

Feature 6: Government Market-Driven Measures since 1996 Leaving Small Farmers More Exposed to Free Market Forces

The 1996 Farm Bill - Federal Agricultural Improvement and Reform Act, or FAIR Act - was signed by President Clinton on 4 April 1996 (Clinton 1996). Some of the most relevant aspects of this Act are reviewed below.

Regarding the commodity programs, deficiency payments and ARP were replaced by *Agricultural Market Transition Program* that offered eligible farmers (those who had either participated or certified acreage in the cotton, feed grains, rice and wheat programs in any one of the past five years) a *seven-year production flexibility contract* with the USDA, which nearly all accepted. The contracts guaranteed declining annual payments until 2002 regardless of kinds, prices and production quantities of commodities and areas planted, provided that farmers complied with the conservation requirements. Acre payments would come to an end after 2002. (Roberts & Doyle 1996: 212. Stuart & Runge 1997: 117–9. USDA 1996a)

The fiscal year total payments were limited to $5.6 billion in 1996, $5.4 billion 1997, $5.8 billion 1998, $5.6 billion 1999, $5.1 billion 2000, $4.1 billion 2001, and $4 billion 2002. Spending was prorated on the basis of the previous crop-specific base area, so that 26.26% of total funds went to acres formerly enrolled as wheat base, 46.22% as corn, 5.11% as sorghum, 2.16% as barley, 0.15% as oats, 11.63% as upland cotton, and 8.47% as rice. Farmers would receive production flexibility contract payments on a payment area as 85% of their farm's contract acreage (which is the farm's program base under previous legislation) plus base land taken out of CRP minus base land entered CRP. The payments would be allocated to individual farmers on the basis of a unit payment rate multiplied by the payment area multiplied by the farm's commodity program yield, subject to the aggregate payment limit. It freed producers of program commodities from a system of crop-specific base acre accounting, merged these accounts into a single 'whole farm base', and allowed production of any crop (with limitations only on fruit and vegetables) on their contract acreage, hence 'freedom to farm'. An example of the allocation of available funds is given in Table 9.15. (Roberts & Doyle 1996: 212. Stuart & Runge 1997: 117–8, 122)

Payments per farmer under production flexibility contracts were limited to $40,000. To maximize such payments, farmers would have an incentive to split their farms into several business entities. Thus a 'three-entity rule' capped such payments on a maximum of three entities. Payments for a farmer on his first entity were limited to $40,000 but those on his second and third restricted to $20,000 each. Thus, the maximum payment is effectively $80,000 per person. (USDA 1996b)

Contract holders remained eligible for non-recourse loans and marketing loans as under the 1990 Farm Bill. However, the FAIR Act capped the wheat and corn loan rates at relatively low 1995 levels and set correspondingly low loan rates for barley, cotton, oats, oilseeds, rice, sorghum and soybeans. Government minimum price guarantees were retained as loan rate floor prices, $0.50 per pound of cotton and $6.50 per hundredweight of rice. Individual producers of these crops faced maximum marketing loan gains of $150,000 under the 'three-entity rule'. However, because the loan rates were so low and the 1996 market prices so high, these payments would generally be small or zero. (Stuart & Runge 1997: 123)

Table 9.15 Example of the Production Flexibility Contract Payment in the USA 1996–2002

At aggregate level	
Total payments for 1998	$5.8 billion
Percentage stipulated for corn	46.22%
Payment limit for corn	$2.68 billion
Estimated production for payment [a]	6.537 billion bushels
Estimated payment rate	41 cents per bushel
At individual farm level	
Farmer's corn base	500 acres
Farmer's payment acres	425 acres (500 x 85%)
Farm's program yield [b]	105 bushels per acre
Farmer's 1998 payment	$18,296 [c]

Notes:

a. Estimated as follows: 81.5 million base acres x 85% x 90% participation x program yield 105 bushels per acre (these figures would need to be adjusted for areas of corn base land which move into or out of CRP).

b. The program yield differs from farm to farm. In this example, it is assumed that it corresponds with the national average.

c. Payment estimated as follows: 425 x 105 x 41 cents.

Source: USDA April 1996.

Concerning the assistance programs, the FAIR Act stipulated that delinquent borrowers of credit would face tighter restructuring rules, collection practices and expedited sales of forfeited property. To qualify for emergency loan assistance, the FAIR Act required farmers to have held hazard insurance at the time of the loss. It limited emergency assistance loan amounts to $500,000 per farmer. (Stuart & Runge 1997: 127–8)

In respect of the export promoting programs, the FAIR Act capped the expenditure on EEP at $3.185 billion for the whole seven fiscal years (July–June), with $350 million for 1996, $250 million 1997, $500 million 1998, $550 million 1999, $579 million 2000, $478 million for each of 2001 and 2002 (USDA 1996a). As a result, aggregate EEP subsidy funding would be much lower than in most recent previous years. For example, the average annual EEP subsidy for wheat alone was $769 million during 1990 and 1993 (exceptionally, in mid-1995, EEP subsidy was suspended due to increasing world market prices and decreasing US exportable supplies). (Roberts & Doyle 1996: 218)

As for the conservation programs, the FAIR Act capped the maximum allowed CRP area at 36.4 million acres and strengthened the criteria regarding eligible land. Responding to the low stocks and high prices and the corresponding pressure to bring much of this land back into production, it provided an 'early out' option to enable those areas which are not environmentally sensitive but have been in CRP for at least five years to be withdrawn. It also capped WRP area at 975,000 acres. (Roberts & Doyle 1996: 213. Stuart & Runge 1997: 126. USDA 1996a). Accordingly, it would be possible to limit the government expenditures as well.

The FAIR Act has yielded positive effects. From the above-analyzed evolution of the US farm policy, one can see that it underwent dramatic change in 1996 (Paarlberg & Orden 1996: 1305). It was the first major change since the 1930s and denoted a watershed (Roberts & Doyle 1996: 224) and new era (Drabenstott 1996: 77).

Market orientation. As President Clinton (1996) points out, 'The hallmark of the bill's commodity title is the planting flexibility provisions. At long last, farmers will be free to plant for the market, not for government programs. The expansion of planting flexibility will improve US competitiveness in world markets.' The abolition of the deficiency payments and ARP eliminated their distortions on markets, as the production flexibility contract payments have been decoupled with kinds, quantities, prices of the commodities and areas planted (Roberts & Doyle 1996: 215, 217). The decrease of loan rates, marketing loans and EEP subsidies reduced their distortions on markets. The 'early out' option from CRP has made supply more flexible to meet higher market demand.

Fixation on government expenditures. The payments under production flexibility contracts have a ceiling at both national and individual farmer levels, rather than open-ended, as could be the case with the deficiency payments (Roberts & Doyle 1996: 216). The expenditures on emergency assistance loans, EEP, CRP and WRP have also been limited. Such fixations have contributed to turning budget deficits to surplus after 1996.

The FAIR Act has also had negative aspects. Distortions on both domestic and international markets, although reduced, still exist in the form of the non-recourse loans rates, marketing loans, EEP, etc. (Roberts & Doyle 1996: 215, 217. Stuart & Runge 1997: 133).

Eligibility for the production flexibility contract was limited to those who had participated or certified acreage in the cotton, feed grains, rice and wheat programs in one of the past five years. Those who had not done so (most of whom were small farmers as argued before) could not enjoy the seven-year contract payments. Among those eligible, *largest benefits went to large farmers* (Stuart & Runge 1997: 131). According to Table 9.2, from 1992 on, small farms are classified as with 1–49 acres, lower medium farms 50–259 acres, upper medium 260–999 acres and large 1,000 acres or more. Thus, according to Table 9.15, even if no crop is produced, a farm of 25 acres would in 1998 receive from the government 25 x 0.85 x 105 x 0.41 (dollars) = 25 x 36.5925 = $915; 50 acres, $1,830; 260 acres, $9,514; 1,000 acres, $36,593; and 2,186.24 acres, $80,000 as maximum for one claimer under the three-entity rule. A family of four with 8,744.96 acres might divide the land legally but not physically into 12 farms, each member claiming three, thus receiving $320,000 altogether, but actually still operate them as one farm.

A freedom to gain and also to fail has been given to farmers upon this fixed payment. Farmers would receive a windfall under favorable market conditions, and possibly deficient income support under unfavorable ones. The non-recourse loans, etc. as the remnants of the safety net that since the 1930s has supported farm incomes and reduced the risk of farming, are too low to offer any real security in the event of downturn. After 2002, even the production flexibility contract payment would be stopped, as planned. The tighter restructuring rules, collection practices and expedited sales of forfeited property for delinquent borrowers of credit, and the limit to the emergency assistance loan, would speed up the bankruptcy of small farmers. As a result, this would reinforce the concentration of resources towards large farmers with more capital, advanced technology and management, lower costs, and other advantages. (Stuart & Runge 1997: 118, 132–3. Drabenstott 1996: 77)

Therefore, political realists doubt that the end of the seven-year contract will actually terminate subsidy transfers to these producers as announced (Stuart & Runge 1997: 118). In fact, President Clinton (1996) declares that 'I am signing H.R. 2854 [1996 Farm Bill] with reservation because I believe the bill fails to provide an adequate safety net for family farmers. The fixed payments in the bill do not adjust to changes in market conditions, which would leave farmers, and the rural communities in which they live, vulnerable to reductions in crop prices or yields. I am firmly committed to submitting legislation and working with the Congress next year to strengthen the farm safety net.' The continuous Republican control of the Congress since 1994 has prevented him from doing so. But even if the Democrats did gain control of the Congress in the near future and restore the safety net, two vital dilemmas would still not be solved: (1) *For raising domestic efficiency and international competitiveness, large farms should be promoted, while for conserving environmental landscape, rural communities and democracy roots, and reducing rural poverty, small farms should be preserved. These two goals seem contradictory.* (2) Full or partial restoration of the previous protective safety net would not only bring back its drawbacks (market distortions, etc. as analyzed above), but also, even such a net could not change the trend towards fewer but larger farms as proved since 1933, while without such a net, small farmers would face stronger squeezing power of free market forces. No solution has ever been found to stop the swinging between these two unworkable extremes.**18** Therefore, Browne, Allen and Schweikhardt (1997) lament that 'the road to agricultural policy reform has a long way to go'.

---

[18] Here is a recent example of such swinging. Driven by low crop prices (corn and soybean were forecast to fetch the lowest farm-gate prices since the agricultural recession of the mid-1980s, and a global grain glut has depressed demand for US exports), bad weather (floods, drought, etc.) in many parts of the country, and arcane farm–state politics, after the Senate's approval, President Clinton on 22 October 1999 signed into law a record $8.7 billion emergency aid to farmers, which is part of a $69 billion spending bill to finance agriculture and food programs in the current fiscal year. The aid package includes $5.54 billion in cash that will be directly paid to grain and cotton growers. The money would be a substantial part of direct federal payments to farmers that could exceed $22 billion in 1999, the highest ever. This is the second successive year that the Congress and government have spent billions of dollars to bail farmers out of financial trouble, raising doubt about the political practicality of applying free-market principles to US farmers. (NYT 1999: 3. Reuters 1999: 3)

10. Application of the New Model in the USA

10.1 Seeking a Possible Solution [1]

In order to find a solution to both strengthening large and preserving small farms, let us first look at the performance of part owners of land.

Feature 7: Part Ownership of Land Tenure Dominating since 1950 But Never Being Promoted as a Policy Direction or a New Round of Institutional Changes

The US land tenure structure includes three types of tenure of operators: full owners who operate only land they own; part owners who operate both land they own and rent in (as part ownership and part tenancy); and tenants who operate only land they rent in (as full tenancy) (Janssen 1993: 473). More specifically, there are full owner operators (operating their own land and not renting in or out any land), full owner operator landlords (operating some of their own land and renting out some of it, but not renting in any land), part owner operators (operating their own land and land rented in, not renting out land), part owner operator landlords (operating some of their own land and renting out some of it, and operating land rented in), tenant owner operators (owning land but not operating it and not renting it out, only operating land rented in), tenant owner operator landlords (owning land but not operating it, renting out some or all of their own land, only operating land rented in), nonoperator landlords (not operating any land, but renting out some or all of their own land), and nonoperator nonlandlords (reporting the ownership of

---

1 A paper based on the earlier version of this section has been accepted by 'The Second National Small Farm Conference' organized by the US Department of Agriculture, with abstract being published in the proceedings and text posted by the University of Minnesota in its electronic library (Zhou, Jian-Ming October 1999).

land, but not operating it or any other land, and not renting it out) (Harris & Gilbert 1985: 34–5).

Trend in the evolution of the land tenure structure. Table 10.1 shows that during 1900–92, the number of farms under full owners and full tenants decreased from 1920 and 1935 respectively, while that of farms under part owners, though reduced from 1950, was still higher in 1992 than in 1900. Table 10.2 indicates that the acreage of farms under full ownership and full tenancy dropped from 1910 and 1935 respectively, while that of farms under part owners, although declined from 1978, was nevertheless much larger in

Table 10.1 Farm Number (1,000) under Different Tenure of Operator (1,000) in the USA 1900–92

Year	Total No.	Full owner	%	Part owner	%	Full tenant [a]	% [a]
1900	5,737	3,202	55.8	451	7.9	2,084	36.3
1910	6,362	3,355	52.7	594	9.3	2,413	37.9
1920	6,448	**3,367**	52.2	559	8.7	2,523	39.2
1935	**6,812** [b]	3,210	47.1	689	10.1	**2,913**	**42.8**
1940	6,097 [b]	3,084	50.6	615	10.1	2,398	39.3
1950	5,382 [b]	3,090	57.4	**825**	15.3	1,468	27.3
1959	3,711 [bc]	2,119	57.1	811	21.9	760	20.5
1969	2,730 [b]	1,706	**62.5**	672	24.6	353	12.9
1978	2,479 [b]	1,451	58.6	714	28.8	314	12.7
1982	2,241	1,326	59.2	656	29.3	259	11.5
1987	2,088	1,239	59.3	609	29.2	240	11.5
1992	1,925	1,112	57.7	597	**31.0**	217	11.3

Notes:
a. 1900–59 include managers.
b. Original data slightly different from those in Table 9.1.
c. Includes managers.

Sources: *1900–35*: SAUS 1939: 615. *1940–50*: SAUS 1964: 618. *1959–78*: SAUS 1984: 653. *1987–92*: SAUS 1997: 665.

1992 than in 1900; and since 1950, part ownership has been the major form of land tenure in terms of acreage (peak numbers in columns of Tables 10.1 and 10.2 are in bold). Table 10.3 demonstrates that from 1978 to 1992, the percentage of farms under full owners in all farms fell, while that of farms under part owners grew continuously, paralleling the increase of farm acreage; within small farms (1–49 acres) and lower medium farms (50–179 acres), full owners were the majority; in medium farms of 180–499 acres, they were still more than part owners (the data did not distinguish lower medium farms of 180–259 acres and upper medium farms of 260–499 acres); but for upper medium farms (500–999 acres in 1987–92) and large

Table 10.2   Farm Acreage (1,000,000 acres) under Different Tenure of Operator (1,000) in the USA 1900–92

Year	Total acreage	Full owner	%	Part owner	%	Full tenant [a]	% [a]
1900	839	431	51.4	125	14.9	283	33.7
1910	879	**465**	**52.9**	134	15.2	280	31.9
1920	956	461	48.3	176	18.4	319	33.4
1935	1,055	391	37.1	266	25.2	**397**	**37.7**
1940	1,061	382	36.0	300	28.3	378	35.6
1950	**1,159** [b]	419	36.2	422	36.4	317	27.4
1959	1,124 [bc]	349	31.0	498	44.3	167	14.9
1969	1,063 [b]	375	35.2	550	51.8	138	13.0
1978	1,030 [b]	341	33.1	**565**	54.9	124	12.0
1982	987	342	34.7	531	53.8	114	11.6
1987	964	318	32.9	520	53.9	127	13.2
1992	946	296	31.3	527	**55.7**	123	13.0

Notes:
a. 1900–59 include managers.
b. Original data slightly different from those in Table 9.1.
c. 1959 includes managers.

Sources: *1900–35*: SAUS 1939: 615. *1940–50*: SAUS 1964: 618. *1959–78*: SAUS 1984: 653. *1982–92*: SAUS 1997: 665.

farms (500–999 acres in 1978, and 1,000 and more acres in all years), it was part owners who were in the majority; in contrast, full tenants were the minority in all categories of farms. Thus, the trend in the US land tenure structure has experienced the reduction of full owners and full tenants, but an increase and dominance of part owners.

Superiority of part owners over full owners and full tenants. The major reason why part owners could have gained increase and dominance is that they have achieved larger acreage and could thus benefit from economies of scale, lower production costs in general, and be competitively stronger, as already argued in Chapter 9 and further revealed in Table 10.4 (numbers in bold are costs of part owners lower than those of full owners). This is a further supporting empirical evidence to the tenet 'that the costs of agricultural products fall as the size of the production unit in agriculture increases', as contrasting to Schultz's conviction indicated in Chapter 1.

Advantages in increasing farm size by part ownership. How could the part owners achieve larger acreage? Here an analysis of the major advantages and disadvantages of the full ownership, full tenancy and part ownership of farmland is useful.

The main advantages of full farmland ownership by farm operators include (1) greater security of tenure, (2) greater managerial freedom and independence, (3) earlier purchase of farmland could avoid the impact of further price rises, (4) farmland can be used for loan collateral, (5) land ownership reflects prestige, may be a family heritage, and can be passed on to heirs. The chief disadvantages are (1) reduced working capital due to farmland debt servicing, (2) mortgage payments may exceed net returns from the purchased land, (3) compared with investment in farm machinery, livestock or operating inputs, capital for buying land may bring lower current rate of return, and (4) farmers with limited capital and sole reliance on farmland ownership often find it difficult to increase farm size. (Kay 1981: 252)

The principal benefits from full tenancy of farmland by operators consist of (1) higher flexibility in deciding farm size, (2) more elastic financial obligations, compared to typical land purchase arrangements (mortgage or installment), and (3) greater working capital for buying machinery, livestock, or operating inputs. The key shortcomings are (1) farm size reduction due to dis-renewal of lease, (2) poor facilities and reluctance of lessors and lessees to invest in land improvement (Kay 1981: 252), (3) fragmentation owing to non-adjacency of leased parcels.

Part ownership permits operators to acquire the right to use farmland without obtaining ownership, which allows them to increase farm size while conserving capital from purchasing land (Janssen 1993: 470, 476), and avoiding the disadvantages of full tenancy.

Part owners have already owned some land, upon which the problems of withdrawal and low incentive of investment in land improvement could be avoided, and fragmentation could be solved by joining parcels through land consolidation. In contrast, full tenants do not have such a base.

Upon the leased land, how to avoid the problems of withdrawal and low incentive of investment in land improvement? In 1986, a common questionnaire for farmland leasing was mailed to 5,800 Nebraska and 4,100 South Dakota landlords and lessees - a random sample of 5% of the total in

*Table 10.3 Farm Number (1,000) and Percentage by Tenure of Operator in Different Farm Acreage in the USA 1978–92 ***

Size (acre)	Total	Full owner	%	Part owner	%	Full tenant	%
1978	2,479	1,451	58.6	714	28.8	314	12.7
Under 50	690	532	77.1	74	10.8	84	12.2
50–179	814	563	69.2	157	19.3	94	11.5
180–499	596	262	43.9	247	41.4	87	14.7
500–999	215	57	26.5	128	59.5	30	14.0
1,000 & over	161	36	22.4	107	66.2	18	11.4
1982	2,241	1,326	59.2	656	29.3	259	11.5
Under 50	637	505	79.3	68	10.7	63	9.9
50–179	711	489	68.7	144	20.2	79	11.1
180–499	526	232	44.1	221	42.0	73	13.8
500–999	204	57	27.9	120	58.8	27	13.2
1,000 & over	161	41	25.4	103	64.0	17	10.6
1987	2,088	1,239	59.3	609	29.2	240	11.5
Under 50	596	483	81.1	59	9.9	53	9.0
50–179	645	449	69.6	130	20.1	66	10.3
180–499	478	217	45.3	195	40.8	67	13.9
500–999	200	53	26.3	117	58.3	31	15.4
1,000 & over	169	37	22.1	108	64.2	23	13.7

Size (acre)	Total	Full owner	%	Part owner	%	Full tenant	%
1992	1,925	1,112	57.7	597	31.0	217	11.3
Under 50	554	444	80.1	58	10.5	52	9.4
50–179	584	395	67.6	130	22.3	59	10.1
180–499	428	190	44.4	183	42.8	55	12.8
500–999	186	48	25.8	111	59.7	27	14.5
1,000 & over	173	35	20.2	114	65.9	24	13.9

* Earlier data unavailable.

Sources: *1978*: SAUS 1984: 653. *1982*: SAUS 1989: 629. *1987*: SAUS 1994: 666. *1992*: SAUS 1997: 665.

Table 10.4 Average Variable Cash and Economic Costs for Corn (1987), Soybean (1986), Wheat (1986) Production by Tenure of Operator in the USA

Tenure	Average variable cash costs ($/bushel)			Average economic costs ($/bushel)		
	Corn	Soybean	Wheat	Corn	Soybean	Wheat
Full owner	0.98	1.45	1.74	2.06	4.71	4.41
Part owner	1.00	**1.43**	**1.30**	2.17	**4.61**	**3.38**
Some share, no cash	**0.91**	**1.22**	**1.20**	2.20	**4.41**	**3.30**
Some cash, no share	1.13	1.71	**1.38**	2.24	5.09	**3.52**
Both cash & share	**0.96**	**1.37**	**1.32**	2.07	**4.32**	**3.32**

Sources: USDA [1986a] (1993): 135; [1986b] (1993): 144; [1987] (1993): 127.

the two states, and completed by 1,615 Nebraska and 1,155 South Dakota respondents (Johnson; Janssen; Lundeen & Aiken 1987. Lundeen & Johnson 1987. Peterson & Janssen 1988). The survey provided useful answers.

There were two major methods for resolving the problem of withdrawal. *The first was multiple leasing* - leasing land from more than one landlord by farm operators. This has been the rule rather than exception. Also, most operators with multiple leasing combined cash and share leases [common types of farmland leasing arrangements in the USA are crop sharing, cash rent, and livestock sharing (Janssen 1993: 470)]. Thus, a sophisticated process of land resource control via farmland rental was adopted by lessees. In so doing, their risks related with losing any one parcel have been reduced. It also suggested that many lessees may have more knowledge of and experience with farmland rental agreements than many landlords.

The second method was informal and short-term, but de facto long-term leasing. Despite a 27% of absentee landlord ownership (residing in another state) and multiple leasing among lessees, most leasing agreements were relatively informal (verbal) and short-term (annual). This facilitated not only dis-renewal of leasing but also adjustment of rental rates.

In cropland leasing of these two states, crop sharing was dominant. In almost all cases, landlords could get one-third, two-fifths or a half of crop output, depending on the region, quality of land and crops grown.

Of crop share lease respondents, 75% reported that the landlord and tenant shared expenses for one or more variable inputs, but less than 10% stated sharing expenses of all variable inputs. In almost all crop share leases, the proportion of input sharing was the same as in output sharing. Fertilizer was the most commonly shared input, followed by insecticide or herbicide. Input costs were more likely to be shared on tracts with relatively high per acre input costs.

Cash leases completely dominated rangeland and pasture leases, with cash rent per acre or per animal. Cash leases also accounted for 40% in South Dakota and 28% in Nebraska of cropland acres leased. Cash rental rates changed annually.

While 75% of lessees were highly dependent on net farm income, rent accounted for less than 30% of total household income for most landlords.

However, except for the annual changes of cash rental rates, the incidence of change in the details of share and cash agreements were infrequent. Moreover, the typical lease agreement had been in effect for more than a decade and most respondents reported considerable satisfaction with their leasing agreements.

Therefore, although the leasing agreements were informal and short-term, the result was a *de facto* long-term leasing. This, in the author's view, was chiefly because the informal and short-term agreements gave incentives to tenants to cherish the leasing, removed the concern of landlords that leased land may not be taken back, and facilitated the adjustment of rental rates to a balanced satisfaction of both lessors and lessees.

On the leased land, how is it possible to overcome the obstacle of low incentive of investment in land improvement by both lessors and lessees? The answer already exists in the above account. In principle, because the leasing contract was informal and short-term, in order to obtain its renewal, the lessee would have the incentive to improve the land. In specific measures, sharing input costs in the same proportion as sharing crop output between landlord and tenant joined them together to improve the land for their common interests.

How to solve the issue related to fragmentation due to the non-adjacency of leased parcels? Physically, it would not always be possible to join leased parcels together, since the same parcels might be leased to other tenants, which would lead to re-split of the united ones. However, as Table 9.2 has shown, in 1992, only 8.6% of the US farms were smaller than 10 acres (= 4.047 ha = 60.7 mu) which are very large farms in monsoon Asia, and 28.8% of farms under 50 acres (= 20.235 ha = 303.5 mu) which are normally unimaginable in monsoon Asia. Therefore, even if parcels are not adjacent, each parcel may still be large enough to use large machinery, and fragmentation would not cause a serious problem.

Being able to achieve the advantages of full ownership and tenancy while avoiding their disadvantages, part owners tend to rent in more acres than full tenants, as a comparison between the 1951 survey of farmland rental market in Nebraska and South Dakota and the above-mentioned 1986 survey in the same states shows (Hurlburt 1954. Janssen & Johnson 1989). Thus part owners could realize larger farm size than full owners and full tenants.

Senilization and feminization of nonoperator landlords. Landlords in many cases are reluctant to sell farmland because it is a family heritage. Many of them were raised on farms, have some farm management experience and are more familiar with farmland as an investment opportunity. Rates of return to farmland ownership (current rates plus expected capital appreciation) have been competitive with many other long-term investments. (Janssen 1993: 476). Moreover, many landlords are unwilling to rent out land.

The 1986 survey in Nebraska and South Dakota discovered that nonoperator landlords were often near or past retirement age - 84% of women respondents were nonoperator landlords and a majority were over 65 years of age; women were 40% of nonoperator landlords and only 10% of farm operator respondents. Full tenants were the youngest group. Between these two extremes were part owner operators and full owner operator landlords.

Similarly, beyond these two states, Harris and Gilbert (1985) have made a comparison between the 1946 and 1978 nation-wide Land Ownership Survey by the USDA and found that nonoperator landlords were the oldest group, followed by full owner operator landlords, full owner operators, and part owner operators, with full tenants as the youngest. The majority of male landowners were full owner operators and the majority of female landowners were nonoperator landlords.

The above data of tenure by age may be explained to some extent by the ordinary life cycle of farm occupation. Start-up farmers may rent in land when their capital is short, the successful part of them may later buy some land, then purchase more, further expand by renting in more, when aging cut operations to their owned land, and finally rent out land first on crop sharing and then cash leasing. (Wunderlich January 1999). Therefore, a tendency could be perceived that as long as landowners are physically still able-bodied, they would be reluctant to rent out land. In contrast, because old and female landowners are not or less able-bodied, they are more willing to lease land.

Successful black farmers - examples of part owners. It has been mentioned in the above that in general small farmers have been in a worse situation, and black farmers the worst. But some black farmers have been successful in farming.

In the summer of 1976, Brown and Larson (1979: 153, 158, 162) interviewed 13 black farmers, dispersed among 10 communities in eight counties of three states - seven in one Southern state (South Atlantic census division), four in another Southern state (East South Central division), and two in a Northern state (East North Central division). In racial composition the counties varied from one where blacks accounted for less than 1% of the population in 1970 to two where blacks were the majority.

Brown and Larson discover their common key factors as: (1) preference for farming as an occupation, (2) strong work orientation, (3) access to land resources, (4) commitment to learn and development of managerial skills, (5) effective linkages with farm and non-farm organizations and activities, and (6) strong family support and high educational aspirations for their children.

Concerning access to land resources, as Table 10.5 demonstrates, the owned land of these farmers ranged from small (40 acres) to upper medium size (290 acres) (not including two much larger jointly owned farms with 400 and 700 acres respectively) in terms of acreage as classified in Table 9.2 for 1959–86. Three farmers older than 70 did not rent in land, while all the others did (EL did not do so but operated land owned by other family members, hence equivalent to leasing), thus becoming *part owners*. On average 52% of land were rented in and the farm size was enlarged from lower medium (210 or 180 acres) to upper medium size (376 acres). As a result, most of them achieved annual gross sales of $40,000 or more, the remainder $20,000–$39,999, both entering large farms in terms of gross sales as defined in Table 9.4 for 1959–77.

There have also been recent cases of highly successful black farmers in Louisiana. McLean-Meyinsse and Brown (1994) made a survey to a sample of 15 of the 46 outstanding black farmers listed by the US Soil Conservation

Table 10.5 Age, and Acreage Owned and Leased of
Some Successful Black Farmers in the USA in 1976

Farmer	Age	Acreage in farm		
		Owned	Leased	Total
NN	76	185 lower medium	–	185 [a] lower medium
EN	74	216 lower medium	–	216 [b] lower medium
LE	71	50 lower medium	–	50 lower medium
LY	70	132 lower medium	350	482 upper medium
EL	66	400 [c] upper medium	–	400 upper medium
CD	65	185 lower medium	200	385 upper medium
ES	63	90 lower medium	85	175 lower medium
ME	60	700 [d] large	800	1,100 [e] large
TS	60	189 lower medium	160	349 upper medium
EE	59	40 small	400	440 upper medium
ND	48	40 small	400	440 upper medium
DN	44	212 lower medium	100	312 upper medium
SR	36	290 upper medium	70	360 upper medium
Total acres		2,729 [f] (2,329)	2,565	4,894
Average acres		210 [f] (180) lower medium		376 upper medium

Notes:

a. The acreage for NN applies to the time before he retired from farming. Upon retirement he sold 80 acres. He has continued to live on the remaining 105-acre farm, some of which a son and grandson operate on a part-time farming basis.

b. Includes the part of the pasture land which EN currently rents out to another farmer.

c. Farm jointly owned with brothers and sisters. However, farmer EL is the sole operator of the farm.

d. Farm jointly owned with brothers, each farming a portion; farmer ME, however, individually rents in 800 acres.

e. 400 acres are deducted without explanation in the original table, but by inference should be operated by brothers of ME, and are also deducted in the sum of the total acres in brackets.

f. Includes the land in the two farms jointly owned.

Sources: Brown and Larson 1979: 162. Table 9.2.

Service in Louisiana. They mainly produced soybean, sugarcane, rice and wheat. Respectively in 1986, 1987 and 1988, they achieved average gross sales of $95,000, $84,000 and $78,000 (the lower sales in 1988 were attributed to the drought), thus equalling large farms in gross sales; 20%, 33% and 40% of them even realized gross sales over $100,000. In contrast, in 1987, the gross sales of 64.8% of all farms and 91% of all black-operated farms in the USA were below $25,000, and of a typical black farmer in Louisiana only $15,551 (Table 9.4. BCUS 1987). Due to their higher farming income, less than 30% of the sample resorted to off-farm activities, while 74% of all black farmers in Louisiana had to do so (BCUS 1987).

McLean-Meyinsse and Brown find that their sample farmers' success was related to (1) younger age [80% of the sampled farmers were below 50 years old, while a typical black farmer in Louisiana was aged 57.6 in 1987 (BCUS 1987)], (2) a better level of education (40% of them had completed high school and three obtained some college education), (3) good management, (4) early adoption of new technology, (5) love of farming with the desire to be one's own boss and sound work ethics, (6) strong family support (which provided the bulk of labor; some of them hired labor mainly in the planting and harvesting seasons), (7) participation of government programs, and (8) larger farm size [80% of them on average operated 488 acres while a typical black farmer in Louisiana only 110 acres in 1987 (BCUS 1987)].

How did these black farmers achieve larger farm size? 13 owned part of the land, from 19 to 270 acres, with nine owning less than 50 acres as small farmers (1—49 acres), and four owning 50—270 acres as lower medium (50—259 acres) or upper medium (260—999 acres) farmers in terms of land owned. Most of the average 488 acres were however rented in. Therefore, they were *part owners* (but McLean-Meyinsse and Brown do not include this concept in their article). Their average 488 acres reached through part ownership and part tenancy made them enter upper medium farms, thus being able to benefit from economies of scale and achieve success in farming.

Part ownership has never been promoted as a policy direction. There are economists who have noted the contribution of part ownership of farmland to the success of both large and small farmers, but ignored it. The typical example is the above-cited McLean-Meyinsse and Brown who revealed that part ownership (although they do not possess this term) was one of the factors of the highly successful black farmers in Louisiana who were small farmers in terms of land owned. However, part ownership did not get a place in the 'Policy Recommendations' of their article. Rather, in the 'Summary and Conclusions', they emphasize that 'potential black farmers must be aware of available opportunities to borrow funds to *purchase* land'. (McLean-Meyinsse & Brown 1994: 79—82)

Interestingly and puzzlingly, even these black farmers in Louisiana themselves disregarded part ownership, as 'they indicated that although their future in farming appeared favorable, they would not actively encourage their children to continue farming. To them, the main farm problems today were lack of land at affordable prices, and high costs of getting started in farming.' (McLean-Meyinsse & Brown 1994: 78–9). It is true that land is and will still be very expensive to purchase, but why can their children not inherit their own small, and rent in other, land to enjoy the similar 'favorable future'?

There are also economists who slightly recommend part ownership. For instance, Janssen (1993: 476, 495) notices 'the dominant trend to part ownership since 1950' and elaborates it. However, in the overall conclusion, he merely states that 'Farm management, resource and policy economists should continue: (1) to monitor ongoing changes in land tenure, ownership and rental market; (2) to examine probable socio–economic consequences of alternative changes in tenure and ownership patterns; and (3) to recommend specific changes which improve efficiency and equity of leasing agreements.' Apparently, he does not raise part ownership to such a high position as a deliberate policy direction or a new round of institutional changes. Similarly, although Brown and Larson (1979: 162–3, 172–3) recognize the role played by leasing in the successful farming of the above-mentioned black farmers, they stress the importance of owning land in drawing policy implications from their experiences.

Most recommendations advocate the unsustainable full owners and less stable full tenants. For example, very recently, a comprehensive report 'A Time to Act' by the National Commission on Small Farms of the USDA in January 1998, dedicated to 'Thomas Jefferson, who envisioned the "yeoman" farmer as the bedrock of American democracy', provides a considerable amount - 145 - recommendations on promoting small farmers. Although it sporadically mentions extending credit and tax exempt to beginning farmers to buy and lease land, its aim was to foster full owners and full tenants, rather than promoting part ownership (in fact there is no such a term in the text).

Feature 8: The Development in Recent Decades of Off-Farm Employment Pursued as Subordinate to the Loss-Making Independent Small Farming Resulting in Inefficient Land-Holding by Part-Time and Absent Small Farmers while Only Slowing But Not Halting Small Farmers' Exiting Farming

The second issue to examine for finding a solution to both strengthening large and preserving small farms is the major effects of off-farm activities on small farmers.

Off-farm income helped maintain loss-making small farming. Off-farm work exists among operators of all farm sizes. On average, off-farm income contributed to 31% of total farm household income in 1950, 55% in 1970, 62% in 1982, and 87% in 1993 (US Congress 1986. Tweeten 1995a).

Specifically, a few large farms could gain farm earnings as the largest proportion of their family income, while the large number of small farm families have had little or no farm income and received almost all their income from off-farm sources (Bollman; Whitener & Tung 1995: 24). The lower the total income of farm families, the more dependent they are on off-farm income to maintain family well-being. In many cases, off-farm employment is crucial to the continuation of small farming. (Gebremedhin & Christy 1996: 63–4). Compared to white farmers, the outlook for black farmers seems bleak because they are slightly older, operate a much smaller farm and have much lower gross sales. The survival strategy of many black operators is to work more days off-farm. (Jones 1994: 27)

As a result, expanding off-farm employment opportunities in rural communities have enabled families operating small farms to improve their incomes while continuing farming (Peterson and Brooks 1993: 13). Many (perhaps most) small farms exist only because of off-farm income. Thus, rural development is an important means to sustain small farms. (Tweeten & Amponsah 1996: 93). In fact, an econometric analysis using county-level data from 2,323 rural (nonmetro) counties (excluding those in Alaska and Hawaii, and Virginia municipalities) for 1980–90 found that those counties in which off-farm income was relatively important had stabilized or even increased rural population (Goetz & Debertin 1996: 518, 528–9).

A perception could be comprehended that small farmers seek off-farm employment relatively passively due to no other choice and as an income source supplementary and subordinate to the independent small farming which, although loss-making, is still pursued as their major occupation.

It is important to note that, unlike Schultz's conception presented in Chapter 1, *inefficient land-holding* by part-time small farmers has also appeared, for many of them 'get most of their income from off-farm sources and continue to subsidize their way of life even through multi-years of not making any money on the farm' (Perry 1999).

Small farmers could not satisfactorily combine farming and off-farm work. Although most small farm families make their living by combining farm and off-farm activities (Ahearn 1996: 95), this does not ensure the survival of their farm operation on one hand, because it reduces their time available for farm work, causes decreased productivity and limits farm expansion (Jones 1994: 27); on the other, by the same rationale, part-time farming also cuts down their time available for off-farm work, constrains them on learning advanced knowledge and hinders them from obtaining posts with higher pay.

In fact, some small farm operators hold full-time jobs in the cities and do farming only at night and on weekends, thus unable to take care of land and production. Many of them work in the secondary labor market of the small rural towns, receiving low wages corresponding to their educational backgrounds and practical experience. (Gebremedhin & Christy 1996: 64).[2]

Part-time farming by small farmers did not prevent their eventual exiting farming. Although part-time farming has resisted to some extent the general trend towards fewer but larger farms, it has neither reversed nor even halted it. Thus Peterson and Brooks (1993: 13) envisage that the farm sector will continue to move in the direction of greater concentration in the remaining years of the 20th century and the next.

In conclusion, many small farmers have chosen farming as an occupation because of the values they attach to farm work, including the opportunity to be one's own boss (Gebremedhin & Christy 1996: 64). As a result, as mentioned in Chapter 9, small farms with annual gross sales below $25,000 (accounting for 62.8% in total farm number, but only 4.9% in total gross sales; 62.3% had operators who worked off-farm; and 28.9% had operators 65 years old or over in 1992) were operated by *full owners* of land rather than part owners or tenants; and on average the operators of these farms had negative net income from farming alone.

Thus, the preference to be one's own boss led to full owners, who were unable to expand small farms, that resulted in loss-making farming, and

---

[2] Quantitatively, in the literature no data have been found to indicate that at least some small farmers are making economically irrational decisions with land they own (farming it when they could earn a higher return by renting it out). But there may be two causes for no data on a phenomenon: (1) this phenomenon does not exist at all; (2) it exists, but no data have yet been collected. With the reports of Ahearn, Jones, Gebremedhin and Christy cited above, one may think that (2) would be a more possible cause for the shortage of data. If so, Proposal 10.1 below at least could arouse the society to pay more attention to this phenomenon and start to collect relevant data.

further required supplementary off-farm work, which has only slowed but not prevented their gradual and eventual being crowded out from agriculture.3

Off-farm activities have been promoted only as a subordinate occupation. The promotion of off-farm employment has been supported by many, almost without disagreement. But it is still generally regarded as subordinate to the independent small farming, which, although a loss-making enterprise, is upheld as the major occupation for small farmers. Hence it is a relatively passive and reluctant engagement.

Conjectural Proposal 10.1

In the above analysis, we can see that, as surmised in Chapter 1, and reverse to Schultz's judgements, now that so many part-time and absent small farmers have been engaged in off-farm activities, it would be logical for them to rent out a part of their land to full-time farmers, so that the latter could increase farm size and benefit from the functioning of the tenet 'that the costs of agricultural products fall as the size of the production unit in agriculture increases', while they could earn rent and gain more time on and income from off-farm employment. We have also seen that if a back-up basic social welfare (such as the private land ownership) could be kept and appropriate remuneration paid so as to relieve their rational concern over direct interests in security, then some landowners (not excluding some part-time and absent small farmers) would be agreeable to transfer their inefficiently held land in various suitable forms to full-time farmers for effective use, but others would still be reluctant to do so, even though land property rights have been well defined and market transactions facilitated. Their inefficient land-holding has made it more difficult for full-time farmers to increase farm size, even if the knowledge and other conditions are available for producing the same output with fewer resources or a larger output from the same resources, whereas the weak small farmers could not be prevented from gradually being crowded out of agriculture. Therefore at least some of the part-time and absent small farmers are not so rational to the society's and their own fundamental interests. Consequently, proper land tenure systems in variable mixed economies should be designed to promote the transfer of their inefficiently held land. However, this does not as yet seem like a commonplace idea, partly or perhaps even mainly because such knowledge is generally unavailable to the society particularly in the USA.

3
    Secretary of Agriculture Glickman confirms again on 22 October 1999 the long-running decline in the number of family farms and the development of large-scale commercial farm operations in the USA (Reuters 1999: 3).

In order to find a way out of oscillating between the two unfunctionable extremes of protective safety net (1933−96) and free market forces (1996−), to achieve the two necessary but seemingly contradictory aims of not only strengthening large but also preserving small farms, a new round of institutional changes is proposed here. This would focus on the *promotion of part ownership of land and off-farm activities with either a Dual Land System or Single Land System*, i.e., small farmers, being engaged in off-farm activities, retain self-sufficiency land (under the Dual Land System) or family plots (under the Single Land System) as small farms, and lease production land for market to competent farmers (including competent small farmers) as part owners (who either are already, or could become, large farmers) to strengthen the existing, or form new, large farms (bearing in mind that in Chapters 9 and 10, unless specified, small farmers include medium farmers as opposed to large farmers). Small farmers would thus hold a triple status or possess three principal occupations: off-farm workers, bosses of self-operated small farms, and landlords in leasing to part owners.

Dual Land System. Where off-farm activities are not yet highly developed and most small farmers working there have not secured jobs, their farmland could be divided into *self-sufficiency land* to be kept for producing food grains and vegetables for the family, and *production land for market* to be leased to competent farmers as part owners.

Single Land System. Alternatively, where off-farm activities are highly developed and most small farmers have secured jobs there, they could keep a *family plot* for growing vegetables to accommodate farmers' tradition of not buying them from the market, and lease the rest of farmland as production land for market to competent farmers as part owners. Small farmers would not need to retain self-sufficiency land because they could use off-farm income and land rent to buy food. Since a family plot would be much smaller than self-sufficiency land, from a quantitative point of view, agricultural land is no longer divided into the Dual Land. Hence a Single Land System. Reducing self-sufficiency land to family plots correspondingly makes the farming scale of the production land for market rented in by part owners much larger than under the Dual Land System. Nevertheless, family plots for self-use by small farmers still constitute small farms. (The elaboration of the Dual Land System and Single Land System have been made in Chapter 5 and is thus not repeated here.)

The Dual Land System and Single Land System could co-exist in one locality, if some small farmers are already willing to concentrate on off-farm activities and only retain the smaller family plots, while others still wish to keep the larger self-sufficiency land. Following the development of off-farm activities to higher levels, more and more small farmers could secure jobs there and lease more land to part owners, the Dual Land System would evolve into the Single Land System.

Although physically it would be unimaginable that someday the whole of American farmland would be merged into one super-large farm, and legally the US anti-trust law would not allow such a situation, the general trend towards fewer but larger farms may still continue, due to domestic and international competitive pressure. Yesterday's large farms may still become today's small farms. But, in this dynamic process, part owners could become larger through merging and renting in more land, and small farmers as landlords would not be crowded out but integrated.

Considering the old and female landowners are already willing to rent out land, able-bodied male small farmers should be emphatically encouraged to do so. Of course, among them, those who are competent could rent in land to become large farmers.

Small farmers' housing land together with their houses would constitute part of the small farms, dotted in the landscape.

Absentees could choose to lease the whole land without keeping any for self-use. But absenteeism is not advocated here, taking into account both American small farmers' traditional preference to be one's own boss on land and the need for small farms as part of the environmental landscape.

Of course, if some small farmers are willing (not forced) to transfer land ownership and quit farming for better full-time off-farm jobs, this should be encouraged, just as Jefferson states in 1785 but overlooked by many.

The interventions of the federal, state and local governments should be reoriented chiefly in two dimensions: (1) Not to foster independent small farming, but guide, encourage and help small farmers to lease production land for market to part owners to form large farms; it is essential to lead small farmers to realize that independent small farming would be unsustainable, and no government assistance could be strong enough to rescue them, hence 'joining or perishing'; favorable tax and credit treatment and transitory direct income support may be given to those who rent out land and develop off-farm activities. (2) To guide small farmers to treat off-farm employment, not passively because of no other choice and as a subordinate engagement, but actively as one of their three principal occupations; and help them to actively develop overall off-farm activities to generate more employment opportunities and construct rural communities. Vigorous experiments are both beneficial and necessary.

The land tenure structure in Proposal 10.1 may be summarized as large–small farmers mixed economy.

Proposal 10.1 may have the following implications. Large farms would be strengthened since leasing the production land for market by small farmers to competent farmers as part owners could increase their farm size, and accordingly their domestic and international competitiveness. Numerous small areas of land, which are loss-making when operated by small farmers, would become profitable after they are leased to part owners. Land resources are thus better allocated and utilized.

Small farmers would share the reinforced strength of part owner large farmers. Technologies (mechanical, divisible, biochemical, environmental, etc.), managerial resources, rural development, procurement and marketing facilities which have thus far mainly favored large farmers (as reviewed in Chapter 9) would no more be antagonistic to small farmers but could be enjoyed by them because they are now also a part of the large farmers. By joining large farmers and sharing their strength, small farmers would no longer be vulnerable and could retain ownership of their small farmland and receive land rent permanently. Improving the quality and productivity of farmland which small farmers have neither time nor resources to carry out due to being engaged in off-farm work and weak capacity could now be performed by large farmers, since part owners not only would gain incentives to do so through informal short-term but actual long-term leasing, and shared investment in input costs, but also possess advanced technologies, managerial resources and sufficient capital to do so. Small farmers could thus release more time to gain advanced knowledge in order to obtain better off-farm employment. They are not only still their own bosses on the self-sufficiency land or family plots, but also become bosses of others, i.e., part owners who rent in their land, and could thus exert power of ownership control. The dynamic process of farms' becoming fewer and larger would not be at the expenses of squeezing out small farmers, as they would be integrated by part owner large farmers through merging and renting in more land.

Inefficient land-holding by small farmers could be resolved, for the many small farmers who 'get most of their income from off-farm sources and continue to subsidize their way of life even through multi-years of not making any money on the farm' (as cited above) could lease the part of the loss-making farm beyond self-consumption need to part owners, so that part owners could use land efficiently and achieve economies of scale, while they could earn rent.

Landscape, rural communities and democracy roots would be conserved, as the small farms including their houses constitute environmental scenes, the development of off-farm activities strengthens rural communities, and the preservation of small farmers also preserves their votes.

The government would be relieved from the unbearable burden of small farmers. The traditional interventions provided small farmers with *Farm Ownership Loans* for buying land, *Farm Operating Loans* for buying equipment, refinancing debts, etc. They were impotent, however, in the face of the overwhelming strength of large farmers. It would be impractical to increase such loans to so many small farmers to such an extent that they could resist large farmers or become large themselves. The safety net designed to protect small farmers during 1933–96 ended up with assisting large farmers more than those it was devised to help and therefore failed. The 1996 Farm Bill introduced in a stronger bias in favor of large and against small farmers, but even here the production flexibility contract payments would be stopped after 2002. In contrast, according to Proposal 10.1, the government subsidies, the cost of which has been borne by taxpayers and consumers, would be partially or even fully replaced by land rent paid by large farmers to small farmers and increased off-farm income both of which are yielded within rural areas and could be permanent.

The two-tier or bimodal system of agriculture, including a few large corporate farms and most farmers on part-time farming with off-farm work or on welfare as advocated by the Committee for Economic Development (CED) could be integrated, with the difference that the land rent and increased off-farm income may partly or even completely replace the government welfare provisions.

Therefore, by solving the first vital dilemma, i.e., realizing the two seemingly contradictory aims of preserving small while strengthening large farms, Proposal 10.1 would accordingly also resolve the second, i.e., the government's swaying between protective safety net and free market forces. Proposal 10.1 would thus lead to the achievement of the essential and interdependent goals of sustainable agricultural and rural development as defined by FAO in 1991 'Food security, to be obtained by ensuring an appropriate and sustainable balance between self-sufficiency and self-reliance; employment and income generation in rural areas, particularly to eradicate poverty; and natural resource conservation and environmental protection' as introduced in Chapter 1.

A new Columbus's tragedy? In 1492, Columbus disembarked on a new continent but still believed it to be the India of Asia. Until the 1950s, full ownership by farm families was considered the 'ideal' system of land tenure (Janssen 1993: 473). But since then, small farmers, economists and policy makers have seen the success of part owners as their performance has been regularly reported. Why do they still stick to the declining independent small farming? Isn't it a new Columbus's tragedy? If so, the old one may be excused as Columbus had little time to make research. But how to explain that after 50 years of intensive studies by so many, part ownership is still not promoted and is even ignored?

The new Columbus's tragedy has mainly been caused by the failure to solve two fundamental contradictions. First, on one hand, in order to realize Jefferson's spirit of retaining democracy roots, small farmers should be preserved. On the other, the 'ideal' full owners in Jefferson's 'yeoman' model have been too weak to sustain. Thus even 'Jefferson himself operated a commercial plantation with slave labor, producing crops for market, and importing goods from England', and 'the structure of American agriculture never followed the Jeffersonian model' (Rasmussen & Stanton 1993: 32). As the 'yeomen' being crowded out, the democracy roots also have been cut. Therefore, Jefferson's specific 'yeoman' model is the exact opposite to his spirit. But, in the USA, no one dared oppose Jefferson's spirit (at least openly). Many politicians have even been eager to show their fervent belief in it in order tọ win votes. Thus, although it is apparent that promotion of independent small farming would not be feasible and halt the cutting of democracy roots, being unable to resolve this contradiction, people have to stick to it. Now Proposal 10.1 may provide a solution: Jefferson's model is simply modified from 'yeomen' to small farmers, because these two concepts are not necessarily the same. By retaining self-sufficiency land or family plots and leasing the rest of farmland as production land for market to part owners, small farmers are maintained, and hence also the roots of democracy, although they are no more full owner 'yeomen' as before.

The second contradiction may be related to the American small farmers' traditional preference to be one's own boss. On one hand, if they rent land out, they would lose this status. On the other, if they operate land themselves, they would make a loss and be crowded out. Many old and female small farmers choose to be nonoperator landlords, because they are not able-bodied. But most able-bodied male small farmers, being unable to overcome this contradiction, stick to operating land themselves, and earn supplementary off-farm income, but still cannot avoid the fate of being squeezed out. Proposal 10.1, by separating small farmers' land into self-sufficiency land or family plots upon which they are still their own bosses and the rest of land as production land for market which is leased to part owners, may also settle this contradiction. In so doing, the promotion of part ownership and maintenance of small farmers could be combined, and small and large farmers integrated.

Proposal 10.1 in fact is the application of the principles of the new model for sustainable rural development raised in Proposal 5.1. Proposal 5.1 recommended village-wide corporate ownership of physically unwithdrawable but financially salable private land shares for Japan and other rice-based economies under private land ownership in monsoon Asia because leasing is largely unsuitable both due to subjective reluctance of small landowners and objective barrier of extreme fragmentation; but leasing is objectively feasible in the USA thanks to the use of multiple leasing and much larger farmland areas than those in monsoon Asia. Thus Proposal 10.1 suggested a different form of amalgamation. Proposal 10.1 is actually one of the various possible forms of the new model.

10.2 A Comparison among the American, Japanese, Chinese Models and the New Model

A brief and general comparison among the American, Japanese, Chinese and the new models of rural development follows.

Feature 1 of the American model of rural development - institutional changes for an individual land ownership was similar to the land reforms in Japan (1946–50) and China (1949–53), and the Chinese land tenure reform (1978–83) for establishing individual land units upon collectively owned land.

Both the two general methods in the evolution, adjustment or change of property rights structures examined in Chapter 3 were adopted. The first general method, *gradual* changes in social mores and common law precedents happened as the resentment against the British feudal and Southern states slave systems accumulated. This contributed to the use of the second general method, *conscious* (collective) endeavor, such as a major reform or revolution at a certain stage of the gradual changes in the first general method - the War for Independence (1775–83) and Civil War (1861–65). The analogous processes can be seen in the Japanese and Chinese land reforms and the Chinese land tenure reform.

Approach 4 to assigning property rights - reorganization of property rights structures without market exchange through a political or legal process, i.e., the authorities awarding the relevant property rights to the externality-receiving party, was implemented in the US land reform after the two wars respectively, just as in the Chinese land reform. In comparison, the Japanese land reform exercised Approach 3 - reform of property rights structures through a political or legal process, followed by exchange at prices lower than the market levels, while the Chinese land tenure reform Approach 1 - permission for the relevant parties to exchange property rights through a political or legal process, followed by market exchange.

Institutional changes - the American land reform - as one of the two long-term ultimate causes for economic development, paved the way for the later rural development, showing its keystone role, as pointed out in Chapter 1. The same was true for the Japanese and Chinese land reforms and the Chinese land tenure reform.

Melmed-Sanjak and Lastarria-Cornhiel (1998: 5) indicate that after the cold war, although the situations which led to land reforms in past decades are still present, the general policy agenda has removed land reform, and relied on land markets as the means of peasant access to development. In Chapter 9, we have seen that the so-called largest free market of the world - the USA - began actually with a land reform over 200 years ago. Therefore, policy makers and academics should really rethink whether land reform should be excluded in the current developing countries.

Feature 2 of the American model of development - government policies supporting agriculture reveals that mixed economies started from the very beginning of rural development, the same as in the Japanese and Chinese models. This is a further evidence that market forces should be fostered by the government, as argued in Chapter 2.

Feature 3 - commercialization of the individual farming units promoting large farmers and driving small farmers to an inferior position, and *feature 8* - the development in recent decades of off-farm employment pursued as subordinate to the loss-making independent small farming resulting in inefficient land-holding by part-time and absent small farmers while only slowing but not halting small farmers' exiting farming, are studied together.

Large farmers could be formed through land transfer as a result of commercialization of individual farming units even with the existing technologies in the USA. As already elaborated in Chapters 2, 4 and 5, in both Japan and China, immediately after the land reform, most peasants were still very poor. Due to various difficulties in production and living, the self-dependent households had to resort to the market. If credits or other help were unavailable or interest rates too high, they might be forced to sell land, while a few people would gather more land. Because large-scale farming was impossible owing to the unavailability of electricity/gas-powered technologies of the Second Industrial Revolution in the 1950s in monsoon Asia, these new large farmers in terms of land ownership would have to rent out land to small tenants. As more and more landless peasants competed for tenancy, the landlords would raise rent to very high and exploitative levels, hence becoming feudal landlords. This trend emerged in China immediately after the land reform. In order to prevent feudalism from restoration, Japan implemented a 3 ha land-holding ceiling until 1962 and China guided peasants first to mutual aid teams, then to elementary and advanced cooperatives which prohibited land sale and tenancy. Therefore, large farmers in terms of both ownership and operation were not formed. In contrast, in the USA there was no restriction on land purchase or sale, and large-scale farming was facilitated by the American climate and geography even with the horse-driven and steam-powered technologies. Thus large farmers in terms of both ownership and operation were formed.

Large farms could also be established through land reclamation in the USA. At the time of the land reform of 1780s in the North and 1860s in the South, there was much open land with few inhabitants in the USA. Thus, even without buying land from small farmers, large farmers could be formed by reclaiming new land. The newly established large farmers could then reduce prices, make the small farmers less competitive and eventually crowd them out. In contrast, in Japan and China, at the time of the land reform in the late 1940s — early 1950s, the easy reclamation of land had already come to an end as a result of increasing population over more than 40 centuries, which made it difficult to form large farmers through land reclamation.

Large farms could be strengthened before and during the development of off-farm activities in the USA. In Japan and China, after small peasants gained incentives through the land tenure reforms (1946–50, 1949–53 and 1978–83 respectively), both labor and land productivity was raised. They developed higher yields and multiple cropping of rice and other grains, diversified cropping and non-crop agriculture, and then small rural enterprises for processing and transporting agricultural goods, even directly producing industrial goods, and providing services in the form of off-farm activities. The rural enterprises absorbed many peasants, filling the vacuum between urban industry and agriculture, although there were also many peasants migrating to cities. The part-time and absent small farmers treated off-farm employment as their major occupation because of its higher income, and farming as subordinate. But they were largely unwilling to transfer land, even though the land-holding ceiling was lifted in 1962 and termination of land lease legalized in the 1970s in Japan and transfer of land use allowed ever since 1978 in China. Thus the formation of large farmers was blocked by small farmers.

In contrast, in the USA, because large farmers could be formed initially after the land reform, they could process agricultural goods in an industrial style which used more machines and less workers, rather than relying on the establishment of small rural enterprises. Therefore, before the mid-20th century, off-farm activities were little, and there was a vacuum between urban industry and agriculture. Once small farmers could not maintain farming activities competitively, they had to leave for cities, rather than for rural off-farm posts. Since the mid-20th century, however, off-farm activities gradually developed, which boosted small farmers' survival, slowed their land transfer, and resulted in their inefficient land-holding, similar to Japan and China. Here, we can see the role that proximate *sources* (labor, capital, education, structural change, etc.) played in development as discussed in Chapter 1. However, since off-farm activities in the USA are not as highly developed as in Japan and China, large farmers are too strong, also because small farmers regard the loss-making independent farming as their ideal and primary occupation and off-farm employment as subordinate, thus causing a relatively passive attitude in the development of off-farm activities, it has not been possible to avoid the crowding out process.

In *feature 4* - technological progress, managerial resources, rural development, procurement and marketing facilities further strengthening large farmers, we can not only see the causal effect of both technologies as another ultimate *cause* and proximate *sources* in development, but also the role played by institutions. In Japan, in the latter half of the 1950s, agricultural mechanization with small machinery released peasants from farming. As more peasants left farming with their land under-utilized or just idled, and with the introduction of the technologies of the Second Industrial Revolution, agricultural mechanization with large machinery became both necessary and possible in order to achieve technological Pareto efficiency reviewed in Chapter 3, i.e., large farms could produce more output with the same inputs or the same output with less inputs through economies of scale of land, thus becoming superior to small farms. But it could not be realized because the formation of large farms was hindered by small landowners.

In the USA, because large farms could be formed, large machinery could be used and economies of scale realized - in this sense Pareto efficiency has been realized. But the technological progress has had a detrimental effect on small farmers. Pareto efficiency has not been achieved in the sense that although large farmers were better off, small farmers became worse off rather than being unaffected. In contrast, in China, agricultural mechanization with small machinery was performed as peasants left farming, which was similar to Japan. But part-time and absent small farmers could not succeed in blocking the formation of large farms as they were obliged to transfer their inefficiently used production land for state and market to full-time and expert farmers while retaining self-sufficiency land or family plots. Thus the Chinese model may arguably be superior to the Japanese one. It might even be better than the American model, as large farms have been formed gradually following the transfer of small peasants to off-farm activities, rather than crowding them out (of course, China should also learn from the American model especially in technological progress, infrastructure construction, agricultural education, farm management, rural services, procurement and marketing facilities, agro-food processing, external trade promotion, environmental protection, anti-corruption, etc.). However, the Chinese model is based on public land ownership, which may not be acceptable to many other economies. Hence the application of the principles of the new model which could prevent small farmers from hampering the formation of large farmers as in the Japanese model as one extreme, and keep small farmers from being crowded out by large farmers as in the American model as the other extreme, while still retaining private land ownership which is different from the Chinese model, thus would be more suitable to various economies around the world in achieving efficient use of land and sustainable rural development.

Feature 5 - government protective safety net (1933–96) failing to avert the trend towards fewer but larger farms since 1935 and prevent small farmers from being crowded out from agriculture, *feature 6* - government market-driven measures since 1996 leaving small farmers more exposed to free market forces, and *feature 7* - part ownership of land tenure dominating since 1950 but never being promoted as a policy direction or a new round of institutional changes, are discussed together here.

Even at the beginning of the 20th century, when agriculture in monsoon Asia was still dominated by free market forces, the US government already was aware of their harmful results as argued in Chapter 2, and implemented interventions. Following the Great Depression, it further established a protective safety net to small farmers during 1933 and 1996. Just contrary to laissez-fair, the government introduced the strongest intervention and protection measures ever seen in agriculture of the USA, the so-called largest free market of the world. In fact, agriculture was one of the most regulated sectors (Gardner 1995). Thus the question is not whether to implement mixed economies and government interventions, but how.

Why did the government interventions in this period fail? Except for market distortions, etc. as already analyzed, there were two major reasons: (1) they did not generate income within rural areas, but relied instead on outside government subsidies the cost of which was borne by taxpayers and consumers and thus unsustainable; (2) they did not touch institutional changes in the land tenure structure. This was similar to the Japanese government interventions which have provided a huge amount of subsidies but not reformed the land tenure system, and hence have been unsuccessful in overcoming the inefficient land-holding by part-time and absent small farmers and accordingly the fragmented small farms problem as the last obstacle in sustainable rural development of monsoon Asia. Here again we can see that institutional changes play the keystone role. In contrast, the Chinese central government intervened much less but largely encouraged and guided local governments and peasants to carry out experiments in land tenure reform, thus achieving success in overcoming the last obstacle.

The 1996 Farm Bill reduced the financial burden of the government, but again, institutional changes were not touched. It simply forced the already very weak small farmers to be more exposed to free market forces; the planned termination of subsidies after 2002 would make them more vulnerable. Therefore, in line with the variable mixed economies concept, a new round of institutional changes is needed.

Part ownership has been growing and become dominant from 1950 onwards. It could achieve Pareto efficiency in the sense that small land cannot be taken care of by small farmers due to their part-time off-farm engagement and is loss-making (the same as in Japan and China), but if leased to part owners, both large and small farmers could get benefits from the increased economies of scale. Multiple leasing could avoid the problems related to withdrawal. The informal, short-term (annual) and renewable leasing resulted in *de facto* long-term leasing, which is similar to that presented in Chapter 7, i.e., the renewable short-term (annual) use contracts in some Chinese villages also gave contractors incentives to improve land. Sharing input costs as output between the landlords and part owners further gave both of them incentives for investment in land improvement.

However, most nonoperator landlords have been old and female, similar to the Japanese case where, since 1985, old and part-time farmers lacking young successors for farming have been more willing to lease land, as presented in Chapter 4. Most able-bodied American small farmers would rather earn off-farm income to maintain the loss-making independent farming, but may not be able to avoid being finally crowded out of agriculture. Part ownership has never been a specific policy direction. Thus, even more active development of part ownership is technically possible, it may not be promoted. This is a further evidence that it is the institutional component that is the most important in the interaction of institutions and technologies underlying the growth as argued in Chapter 1.

Proposal 10.1, as an application of the principles of the new model raised in Proposal 5.1 for Japan and other rice-based economies under private land ownership in monsoon Asia, may turn feature 7 to be a feasible new policy direction and way out of the US government's unending oscillation between features 5 and 6.

Last but definitely not least, it would be worthwhile noticing that food overproduction has never been resolved in the American model. As introduced in Chapter 9, over the years since the 1930s, the US government has implemented the supply control programs [including the Acreage Reduction Program (ARP) and Paid Land Diversion Program (PLD)], and the conservation programs [containing the Conservation Reserve Program (CRP), Agricultural Conservation Program (ACP), Forestry Incentive Program (FIP), Wetlands Reserve Program (WRP), and Conservation Compliance Provisions (CCP)], by giving financial benefits to the participating farmers. But because land is privately owned, if farmers did not join the programs, the government could not oblige them to do so, not to mention those large farmers who left inferior land aside to enjoy the financial benefits yet still increased food production on the rest of the land. The similar programs and results could be found in other developed countries. In contrast, the Chinese model based on public land ownership could mobilize farmers to convert erodible cultivated land back to forestry, grassland, lake land and wetland, by awarding them food subsidy allocated from the surplus food produced on normal land, so that a national balance between the supply of and demand for food could be reached, food overproduction prevented and the environment improved. Similarly, the new model based on private land ownership may also achieve these ends.

11. Implementations of the New Model in the OECD, EU, CEECs, CIS, and Rest of the World

As conjectured in Chapter 5, the new model for sustainable rural development, either in its specific form as in Proposal 5.1, or in other forms adapted to varied local conditions according to its principles, may have a global applicability beyond monsoon Asia and the USA. A brief illustration of possible applications follows.

11.1 In Rural Areas at Different Wage Economies

In the low wage economy. The new model could be exercised in various forms when rural areas are still in the low wage economy, land consolidation upon private land ownership has not been conducted, cooperative services are very weak, off-farm activities are not yet developed, and the first transition (agriculture—industry) has not been completed. Here, although the fragmented small farms may not have emerged as the last obstacle, a consolidated structure would be better. In fact, such subsistence farms exist in numerous developing countries in Africa, Central and West Asia, the Pacific, Latin America, and Central and Eastern Europe. Easy references are various issues of *Africa South of the Sahara* (ASS), *The Middle East and North Africa* (MENA), *South America Central America and the Caribbean* (SACAC), *The Far East and Australasia* (FEA), *Eastern Europe and the Commonwealth of Independent States* (EECIS), *Central and South-Eastern Europe* (CSEE), *Eastern Europe, Russia and Central Asia* (ERCA), and *Agricultural Policies in Emerging and Transition Economies - Monitoring and Evaluation* (OECD).

In the co-existence of the low and high wage economies. The new model could be used in different methods under the situation that many peasants are seeking higher off-farm income in their own rural areas which are still in the low wage economy but developing towards the high wage economy, or in other rural areas which have already entered the high wage economy, or cities and abroad, while still holding land in inefficient use. This phenomenon exists in many developing countries - see the above-cited references.

In the high wage economy. The new model might also be applied in diverse patterns when rural areas have entered the high wage economy, land consolidation upon private land ownership has been tried or conducted (either partially or completely), cooperative services are sound, off-farm activities are developed, the first transition has been completed, the fragmented small farms have become the last obstacle, large farmers are weak but part-time and absent small farmers strong. Typical examples can be found in the four Southern European countries: Greece, Italy, Portugal and Spain. For instance, in Portugal, 'the growth of part-time farming in some regions . . . fossilized the farm structure, with the off-farm income allowing families to retain small, uneconomic holdings'. (Yannopoulos 1993: 287. Stevenson 1993: 345. Willams 1993: 464. Harrison 1993: 495)

Once food shortage has been replaced by food self-sufficiency and further by *food overproduction*, the new model could be implemented to prevent it from becoming chronic, which has never been realized in developed countries, and further *improve the environment*.

This new model may also be practiced under *public* land ownership. In order to raise individual incentives for production, publicly owned land should and can be distributed for private use or possession. In such cases, the term '*private* land shares' in the new model is replaced by '*individual* land shares'. In fact, in Africa and Latin America, there does exist public ownership of agricultural land.

11.2 In OECD and EU Countries in General [1]

Proposal 10.1 as one of the various forms of the new model according to its principles might be adopted for preserving small farmers while still strengthening large farmers in many other OECD (Organization for Economic Cooperation and Development, which includes EU - the European Union) countries where there exists a large versus small bimodal farm structure similar to the USA's. The Canadian case is analyzed, inter alia, in the Special Issue of *Canadian Journal of Agricultural Economics* (CJAE 1995). In the United Kingdom, large farms are very competitive, but 'the

---

[1] The earlier version of this section was included in the paper accepted by 'The Second National Small Farm Conference' organized by the US Department of Agriculture, with abstract being published in the proceedings and text posted by the University of Minnesota in its electronic library (Zhou, Jian-Ming October 1999).

squeeze on agriculture is likely to be felt most keenly by the small, poorer farms, and this in turn raises another issue: that of the effect of agricultural decline on social and economic life in rural communities' (Gowland & James 1993: 580). In OECD and EU countries in general, there has been a trend towards larger but fewer farmers. Although until the mid-1990s, many governments maintained protective safety nets aimed at helping small farms, the subsidies derived from taxpayers and consumers largely went to the few large farmers while markets had been distorted and budget burdens increased. The development of off-farm activities has had the positive result of slowing small farmers' exiting, but also the negative consequences of decreasing land mobility towards more efficient farmers. Since the mid-1990s, many governments have begun to adopt market-oriented policies, by reducing market-distorting protection of prices, etc., and providing transitory direct income support, with the long-term aim of establishing a *'farming without subsidies'* [e.g., in March 1998 the Commission of the European Union made this its Agenda 2000 (EC DG VI 1998a; 1998b)]. The market-oriented measures would be unfavorable to the already weak small farmers, and more exiting by them could be anticipated. Thus governments wish to both strengthen large farmers and retain small farmers in agriculture and rural areas because urban unemployment has already been so high and homeless people so many, but no effective measures have yet been found to match these two seemingly contradictory goals. Although part ownership of land tenure has developed, it has not been recommended as a new policy direction. (OECD 1998c: 15–87). Therefore, Proposal 10.1 might be useful to other relevant OECD and EU countries with a bimodal farm structure too.

In particular, some EU member countries (e.g., Italy) once adopted laws to oblige part-time and absent farmers to lease their inefficiently held land to full-time farmers for more efficient use. But such laws ceased to function in order to comply with the EU's common agricultural policy of reducing food overproduction. (Omodei Zorini 2001). Hence the EU faces a dilemma: if such land were more efficiently used, food overproduction would be strengthened; if not, the EU farmers would not be able to increase farm size in order to be more competitive in the international markets especially in front of the much larger US farms with much lower costs. Here, the author wishes to point out that it is the ecologically weak land which should be converted back to forestry, grassland, lake land and wetland, so as to both decrease food overproduction and protect the environment, while the inefficiently held normal land should still be turned over to full-time farmers for more efficient use, so that they could increase farm size and lower costs, as indicated in the principles of the new model in Chapter 5.

11.3 In CEECs and the CIS (27 Countries) [2]

In the FSU (former Soviet Union) since 1917, the land had been owned by the state but distributed for use first to individual producers and then in the 1930s to state farms *sovkhozes* with state owned (non-land) assets and collective farms *kolkhozes* with collectively owned assets without significant practical difference between them. Both state and collective farms gave household plots to families for subsidiary production and sale of any surplus on the town markets. In CEECs (Central and Eastern European Countries), in the late 1940s after WWII, Albania nationalized land ownership; in all the other countries, land was never completely turned over to public ownership, but joined together for collective operation, with household plots to families [the major exceptions were Poland and former Yugoslavia, where collectivization either failed or was not initiated; about 80% of the total agricultural land was cultivated by small individual family farms, with the rest by a few large state farms; for example, Slovenia had a small 'socially owned' sector of agriculture and a large number of part-time small farmers, occupying over 90% of agricultural area (EC DG VI 1998: 18. Mathijs & Swinnen 1999: 5. Bozic 1997: 75)]. In both the FSU and CEECs, the state and collective farms were based on the Soviet farm model of operating thousands of hectares of land with large machines and employing hundreds of people (differences existed among the composing economies but cannot be elaborated in this brief account) which led to low incentives and other inefficiencies, supplemented by subsistence-oriented individual farming based on household plots of less than 1 ha (Lerman January 1999: 2). Since the 1960s reform had been attempted but never succeeded under the centrally planned economy. (Csaki & Lerman 1997: 429–30, 433. Serova 1998: 20)

Since the late 1980s and early 1990s, with the abolition of the centrally planned economy, CEECs and the FSU have carried out land privatization or farm restructuring. Their major method was either restitution of land to former owners or distribution of land (and asset) shares to farm members (some land shares stay as 'paper shares', and when the owners withdraw them for individual farming, physical parcels are given), with the choice for them to either set up individual farms or remain in the collectively operated

---

[2] Papers based on the earlier versions of this section have been accepted by three international conferences on transition organized by the Russian Education Ministry (Zhou, Jian-Ming 9–10 December 1999), Greek universities with text being published in the proceedings and abstract to be published by CABI (Zhou, Jian-Ming 16–18 December 1999), and European Association for Comparative Economic Studies with text being published in the proceedings (Zhou, Jian-Ming 7–9 September 2000) respectively.

large farms. In CEECs, *Albania* distributed land equally to farm members for private ownership (with state bonds to former owners as compensation), resulting in fragmented small individual farms. The *Czech Republic, Hungary, Romania* and *Slovakia* mixed restitution with compensation to some extent to former owners, and granted land to current farm members for private ownership in the interest of social equity (EC DG VI 1998: 18. Lerman January 1999: 3). In other CEECs, restitution to former owners was made, and agricultural workers have had priority in acquiring land, but they have to purchase it in full payment (Lerman January 1999: 3). In CEECs (except Albania), the common results after land privatization were (1) individual farms, (2) collectively operated large farms with joined private land shares,3 and (3) household plots (variations also existed among the component countries but cannot be detailed in this general review). In the FSU, the three Baltic states (*Estonia, Latvia* and *Lithuania*) adopted restitution of land (or mixed with compensation) to former owners, protected use rights of current farm members, ending up with (1) individual farms, (2) collectively operated large farms with joined private land shares, and (3) household plots. Other 12 republics joined the CIS (Commonwealth of Independent States) in which restitution was impossible mainly due to missing records. Thus, land was allocated in 'a perfectly equitable manner' (Lerman January 1999: 3). *Armenia* and *Georgia* distributed land to farm members for private ownership, creating fragmented small individual farms. *Azerbaijan, Kyrgyzstan,4 Moldova, Russia (federation but not all republics), Turkmenistan,5* and *Ukraine* established private land ownership, causing (1) individual farms, (2) collectively operated large farms with joined private land shares, and (3) household plots. *Kazakhstan* developed (1) individual farms with publicly owned but privately possessed land shares, (2) collectively operated large farms with joined publicly owned but privately possessed land shares, while allowed (3) privately owned household plots.

3
   Such large farms may rent in land from individual landowners for collective operation without calling such land as land shares. But in the sense that revenue is distributed among rents to land, dividends to capital shares and wages to labor, such land may be regarded as de facto land shares.
4
   Kyrgyzstan held a referendum on 17 October 1998 in which 90.09% of the participants voted for privatization and free selling of land with 4.43% against (PD 1998). But it immediately imposed a five-year moratorium on all land transactions (Lerman 8 January 2001).
5
   In Turkmenistan private land ownership is purely notional without any rights of transfer (Lerman January 1999: 3). Although this seems a very special case because of the gap between the narrow interpretation of the legal language and the substance of the law (Lerman 9 January 2001), it may reflect the reservation towards private land ownership.

Tajikistan and Uzbekistan did not permit private land ownership, generating (1) individual farms with publicly owned but privately possessed land shares, (2) collectively operated large farms with joined publicly owned but privately possessed land shares, and (3) publicly owned but privately possessed household plots. *Belarus* (1) permitted publicly owned but privately possessed land for individual farms, (2) did not restructure the large-scale state and collective farms by giving land (and asset) shares to members, and (3) allowed privately owned household plots. (Csaki & Lerman 1997: 433–7. Serova 1998: 22. Mathijs & Swinnen 1999: 23). [Belarus, Kazakhstan, Russia and Ukraine are the most important food producers and consumers of the CIS - for example, in 1997 they accounted for about 90% of the grain, meat and milk produced (OECD 1998b: 99). Armenia, Azerbaijan, Georgia, Kazakhstan, Kyrgyzstan, Tajikistan, Turkmenistan, and Uzbekistan are in Central Asia]. The general results are shown in Tables 11.1–11.4, and classified as follows.

Classification 1: Overwhelming Fragmented Small Individual Farms (Nine Countries)

In Albania and Armenia, the former state and collective farms have completely, and in Georgia almost completely, been divided into individual family farms. Their reform was thus the most radical among CEECs and the CIS (this way of distribution was quite similar to that of China during 1978–83 because of the allocation of publicly owned land to households; but considering that it was different from China's keeping public land ownership, it would be more analogous to that of Japan during 1946–50 since it also resulted in individual land ownership).

Albania distributed agricultural land of the collective and state farms in 1991 and 1992 respectively for private ownership to households living there according to family size with equalized composition in terms of land quality, quantity and distance, while giving financial compensation to the pre-1945 landowners or their heirs in 1993 (Beka 1998: 11. Marku 1997: 48). As a result, the average area of an individual farming unit was 1.08 ha *fragmented* into 3.41 parcels in 1996 (AMOAF 1996).

In *Armenia*, during 1991–92, two-thirds of arable land was privatized, while nearly one-third of arable land and virtually all pastures remained in state ownership but were available for leasing to individuals (Lerman; Lundell; Mirzakhanian; Asatrian & Kakosian 1999: 1). The state and collective farms were eliminated in 1991–92, but the members had the option of maintaining the previous operation structure. In practice, however, the members opted for individual farming, and most collective and state farms were dismantled in 1992–93. Some state farms remained for specific purposes, such as seed production, animal breeding, experimental stations, etc. (they are therefore not considered as normal farms in Table 11.3) (Lerman 1996: vii, 2). According to two surveys of small individual farms conducted in different counties, the average area of an individual farming unit was 1.28 ha, including 73.4% as arable, 13.3% under perennials

Table 11.1 Percentage in Agricultural Land of Collectively Operated Large Farms and Individual Farms in 13 CEECs 1991–98

	State		Cooperative		Other corporate[a]	Individual [b]		Year of census or source
	pre-tran-sition	post-tran-sition	pre	post	post	pre	post	
Albania	22	0	74	0	–	4	100 [c]	96/97
Bos & Hz	–	–	–	–	–	94	94	1997
Bulgaria	29	6	58	42	0	13	52	95/96
Croatia	–	–	–	–	–	62.8	73.5	1998
Czech R.	38	2	61	43	32	0	23	1996
Estonia	37	0	57	0	37	6	63	1997
Hungary	14	4	80	28	14	6	54	05.96
Latvia	41	1	54	0	4	5	95	1997
Lithuania	91	33	0	0	0	9	67	1996
Poland	19	7	4	3	8	77	82	1996
Romania	29	21	59	12	0	12	67	1997
Slovakia	26	15	69	60	20	5	5	1994
Slovenia	8	4	0	0	0	92	96	1997
Average	–	–	–	–	–	26	71	1996

Notes:
a. Joint stock, limited liability companies and other business entities.
b. Including household plots.
c. 20% of agricultural land in Albania was refused land in 1993–97.

Sources: *Albania*: Kodderitzsch 1998. AMOAF 1996 & 1997. *Bosnia and Herzegovina*: Numic 1997: 65. *Croatia*: Bozic 1997: 75; 1998: 16; 1999: 10. *Others*: EC DG VI 1998: 19.

(orchards and vineyards) and 13.3% under hay meadows and pasture, which implies *fragmentation* (Aghamian 1997: 56–7).

In *Georgia*, at the beginning of 1996, 49% of cultivated land was privatized, and 51% remained under state ownership but leasable to individual farms. The state and collective farms have virtually ceased

Table 11.2 Average Size of Collectively Operated Large Farms and Individual Farms in 13 CEECs 1991–98 [a]

	State		Cooperative		Other corporate [b]	Individual [c]	
	pre-tran-sition	post-tran-sition	pre	post	post	pre	post
Albania	1,070	–	1,024	–	–	–	1.1
Bos & Hz	–	–	–	–	–	3.1	3.1
Bulgaria	1,615	735	4,000	637	–	0.4	1.4
Croatia	–	–	–	–	–	3.6 [d]	2.8 [e]
Czech R.	9,443	521	2,578	1,447	690	5.0	34.0
Estonia	4,206	–	4,060	–	449	0.2	19.8
Hungary	7,138	7,779	4,179	833	204	0.3	3.0
Latvia	6,532	340	5,980	–	309	0.4	23.6
Lithuania	2,773	372	–	–	–	0.5	7.6
Poland	3,140	620	335	222	333	6.6	7.0
Romania	5,001	3,657	2,374	451	–	0.5	2.7
Slovakia	5,186	3,056	2,667	1,509	1,191	0.3	7.7
Slovenia	470	371	–	–	–	3.2	4.8

Notes:
a. Year of census or source for each country as in Table 11.1.
b. Joint stock, limited liability companies and other business entities.
c. Including household plots.
d. 1960.
e. 1991.

Sources: *Albania*: AMOAF 1996 & 1997. *Bosnia and Herzegovina*: Numic 1997: 65. *Croatia*: Bozic 1998: 9. *Others*: EC DG VI 1998: 19.

production, and only some collective farms were still functioning producers. The average area of an individual farming unit was 0.9 ha. Privately owned land was usually divided into two parcels: one around the house and the other at the perimeter of the village. Leased land was typically also separated into two. Thus farms with leased land were *fragmented* into four parcels. (Lerman 1996b: vii, 1, 5, 8, 14, 16. Serova 1998: 22)

The fragmented small farms remain a long-term structural handicap in Poland, and still dominate in former Yugoslavia: Bosnia and Herzegovina, Croatia, Macedonia, Slovenia and Yugoslavia (EC DG VI 1998: 20. OECD 1998b: 29).

Table 11.3 Percentage in Agricultural Land by Collectively Operated Large Farms and Individual Farms in 11 CIS Countries in the 1990s

	Year	Collective farms	Individual farms
Armenia	1996	–	100
Azerbaijan	01.1996	77.4	22.6
Belarus	1998	84	16
Georgia	1996	–	Over 90
Kazakhstan	1997	88	12
Kyrgyzstan *	1995	59	24
Moldova	1995	85	15
Russia	1997	91	9
Turkmenistan	1995	92	8
Ukraine *	1995	80	15
Uzbekistan	1995	86	14

*   Data original, cannot be added to 100%.

Sources: *Armenia*: Lerman 1996a: vii, 2. *Azerbaijan*: Shikhaliev 1997: 59. *Belarus*: Petkevich 1998: 16. *Georgia*: Lerman 1996b: vii, 1, 5. *Kazakhstan*: Suleimenov 1998: 9. *Russia*: OECD 1998d: 16–7. *Others*: Csaki & Lerman 1997: 436.

Classification 2: Persistence of Collectively Operated Large Farms with Privately Owned Land Shares (14 Countries)

The common results of land privatization in Bulgaria, the Czech Republic, Estonia, Hungary, Latvia, Lithuania, Romania, Slovakia among CEECs, and Azerbaijan, Kyrgyzstan, Moldova, Russia (federation but not all republics), Turkmenistan, and Ukraine of the CIS were (1) individual farms, (2) collectively operated large farms with joined private land shares, and (3) household plots. Russia's case is illustrated below.

Russia began to privatize agricultural land and non-land assets belonging to the large state and collective farms in the form of shares to their employees, pensioners and social workers in 1991. By October 1997, over 90% of landowners had received certificates. By November 1997, of the total 221 million ha of agricultural land, 38% or 84 million ha were *not privatized* due to various reasons, including 9% owned by municipalities, 3% as state land reserve, 9% in land redistribution fund, 2% in forestry fund, 15% or

Table 11.4 Average Size of Collectively Operated Large Farms, Household Plots and Individual Farms in Eight CIS Countries in the 1990s

	Collective				House-hold	Indi-vidual
	Year	ha	Year	ha	ha	ha
Armenia	–	–	1997	–	–	1.28
Azerbaijan	–	–	01.1996	75	–	11.4
Belarus	1990	3,448.5	1998	2,940.5	1	20.6
Georgia	–	–	1996	–	–	0.9
Kazakhstan	1990	100,000	1997	3,746	–	–
Moldova	1990–91	2,800	1995–96	2,000	–	–
Russia	1990–91	9,500	1997	3,569	0.4	48
Ukraine	1990–91	3,700	1995–96	3,100	–	26 *

* Beginning of 1998.

Sources: *Armenia*: Aghamian 1997: 56. *Azerbaijan*: Shikhaliev 1997: 59. *Belarus*: Petkevich 1998: 13. *Georgia*: Lerman 1996b: 8, 14. *Kazakhstan*: Suleimenov 1998: 9. *Moldova*: OECD 1999v1: 69. *Russia*: OECD 1999v1: 69; Serova 1998: 21. *Ukraine*: OECD 1999v1: 69; 1998b: 142.

33.2 million ha as state owned land but used by collectively operated large farms; 62% or 137 million ha were *privatized*, containing 3% or 6.6 million ha as 16 million household plots averaging 0.4 ha per household mainly for food self-sufficiency rather than market supply (Serova 1998: 21), 6% or 13.3 million ha by 285,600 individual farms averaging 48 ha at the beginning of 1998, and 53% or 117.1 million ha by collectively operated large farms. The collectively operated large farms included production cooperatives, partnerships and joint stock companies, etc. (Serova 1998: 22). Of 68% (15% publicly owned and 53% privately owned) or 150.3 million ha of land under these large farms, about 8% or 18 million ha were under 14,000 ones *averaging 1,300 ha*, and about 60.6% or 134 million ha under 27,000 ones *averaging 4,950 ha* in January 1997. (OECD 1998d: 14–7, 86). Thus collectively operated large farms dominated.

Even under private land ownership, the large corporate farms amalgamated private land and capital shares for collective use. Managers were selected in a 'one member one vote' system. Profits were to be distributed to land and capital shares and labor. These aspects are similar to the content of Proposal 5.1, but other parts are different: profits were actually paid predominantly to labor, since managers were reluctant or unable to pay them to shareholders; land was operated on a collective basis, rather than contracted/leased to families; members also have the right to withdraw land physically, which may cause reduction in size and lead to fragmented small farms (e.g., in 1995 in Nizhny-Novgorod region which has dense population and poor land quality, the average size of individual farms was only 25 ha, and yield and profits were also low). In fact, the volume of agricultural production of the whole country fell by 36% during 1990–97. Thus in Russia the collectively operated large farms under both public and private land ownership needed to be converted into viable, and business oriented enterprises. (OECD 1998d: 13, 15–6, 18, 277)

Classification 3: Domination of Collectively Operated Large Farms with Publicly Owned But Privately Possessed Land Shares (Three Countries)

The major difference between Kazakhstan, and Tajikistan and Uzbekistan (all CIS countries) is that household plots in Kazakhstan are privately owned but in the others still publicly owned. The major similarity between them is that they all have (1) individual farms with publicly owned but privately possessed land shares, and (2) collectively operated large farms with joined publicly owned but privately possessed land shares. Furthermore, sale, exchange, mortgage and gifting of publicly owned but privately possessed land shares have been allowed in Kazakhstan hence a nominal public but *de facto* private land ownership, or *nominal public–individual mixed economy*, but not in Tajikistan and Uzbekistan (Csaki & Lerman 1997: 437). Below is the example of Kazakhstan.

In Kazakhstan, the *state owned* all farmland in 1990, but only 3% in 1997, following the reform in 1993. *Private farmland ownership* was allowed only for small household plots. Most state farms have been transformed into collective farms, and at the end of 1997, traditional state farms only operated about 5% of agricultural land. Overwhelming areas of farmland were turned over to *ownership by collective farms*. Shares for land and non-land assets were allocated to current and former farm workers and managers according to their wages. Land could be given to members of collective farms for temporary use (up to three years) or long-term use (three to 99 years). Land use rights could be sold, granted, leased, exchanged, used as collateral, inherited, joined for partnerships and cooperatives. (OECD 1998b: 120. Suleimenov 1998: 8–9). Hence a nominal collective but *de facto* private land ownership.

Most shareholders of collective farms put their individual land shares together to form *joint stock companies* or limited partnerships (similar to Proposal 5.1) in collective (other than family) operation (different from Proposal 5.1). A significant number of collective farms were broken into smaller entities. During 1990–97, the number of farms has increased from 2,200 to 58,825 and the average farm size reduced from 100,000 ha to 3,746 ha. But there was no real change in institutional structures, management practices or agricultural techniques. Shareholders remained paid workers by the management expecting some dividends by the end of the year. (OECD 1998b: 120. Suleimenov 1998: 5, 9)

Household plots accounted for a large proportion of potato, fruit and vegetable and livestock production. The contribution of household plots to total meat, milk, egg and wool production has increased continuously since 1995. (OECD 1998b: 120). *Individual farms* have also been set up as some shareholders exploited their shares of collective land separately (Suleimenov 1998: 5–7, 9).

Classification 4: Predomination of Collectively Operated Large Farms under Public Ownership without Land Shares (One Country)

Belarus permitted publicly owned but privately possessed land for individual farms up to 100 ha, did not restructure the large-scale state and collective farms by giving land and asset shares to members, but allowed private ownership for household plots up to 1 ha (as well as cooperative gardens up to 0.1 ha) (Petkevich 1998: 6, 10).

Household plots continued to supply over 80% of all wool, potatoes, fruit and vegetables, which was made possible, however, largely due to substantial input supplies from large state and collective farms. *Individual farms* have played a minor role, occupying merely 0.7% of arable land. Their number increased by 1.4% to 3,020, while their average size remained at 20.6 ha during 1997. The government promoted the individual farms. Thus on 3 March 1998, it increased their size limit from 50 ha to 100 ha, called to allocate good quality land to those workers who wished to leave large farms, and allowed private farmers to rent in buildings and machinery from large farms without paying rent during the first two years. But as off-farm activities have not yet developed, the government also actively encouraged large farms to act as the last resort in employment, thus hidden unemployment has increased, and real incomes have been declining in rural areas. (OECD 1998b: 112, 115). In fact, in 1998 nearly 99% of farmers were employed by large farms, with only 1% by individual ones (Petkevich 1998: 5–6).

Although the average size of the state farms decreased from 3,488 ha to 2,825 ha, and that of the collective farms from 3,409 ha to 3,056 ha during 1990–98 (Petkevich 1998: 13), these *collectively operated* large farms have made few managerial reforms since the Soviet era. The unprofitable ones were merely merged with other farms or agro-service and processing enterprises, without solving the underlying problems of lacking incentive in performance, poor technology and low productivity. (OECD 1998b: 114, 116)

The land market was not developed. Buying and selling have been allowed for privately owned land (household plots and cooperative gardens) but not for public land; inheritance of privately owned land and individual farms permitted; and leasing also legalized (Petkevich 1998: 10–2). Agro-food prices remained highly regulated by the government (OECD 1998b: 115).

The First Possible Dilemma

On one hand, fragmented small farms have been characteristic of the individual farms and household plots under both *private land ownership* in Classification 1, 2, 3 (privately owned household plots in Kazakhstan) and 4 (privately owned household plots in Belarus) and *public ownership but private possession of land* in Classification 3 (individual farms with publicly owned but privately possessed land shares in all the three countries; and publicly owned but privately possessed household plots in Tajikistan and

Uzbekistan), and 4 (individual farms with publicly owned but privately possessed land), with the exceptions that the average individual farm size was 34 ha in the Czech Republic, 23.6 ha in Latvia, and 19.8 ha in Estonia as shown in Table 11.2. Most small farms in CEECs were non-viable as full-time units (OECD 1998b: 30).

On the other hand, low individual incentives and other inefficiencies could be attributed to the collectively operated large farms with either merged privately owned land shares in Classification 2, or joined publicly owned but privately possessed land shares in Classification 3, or publicly owned land without shares in Classification 4.

Thus, although variations and exceptions exist among countries and localities, CEECs and the CIS are facing a possible *dilemma*: turning to individual farming would lead to fragmented small farms; but retaining collective operation of large farms would continue the low individual incentives of members and other problems of the old system. As Csaki and Lerman write (1997: 449):

> The former socialist countries in Europe have made significant progress on the road of market reforms in agriculture, including land privatization and farm restructuring. Yet, as the years go by and the process of reform unfolds throughout the region, it is becoming increasingly clear that the actual achievements do not match the original expectations of politicians and experts, both domestic and international. Initially, market reforms were expected to produce a quick supply response, leading to rapid increase in production; in reality, production has declined precipitously in most countries [see Table 11.5]. Land privatization was expected to be a fast and easy process; in reality, although the state has relinquished its monopoly on land, most [much] land remains in collective, not individual ownership [operation]. Private family farming was expected to achieve a rapid dominant position in agriculture; in reality, private farming is developing slowly and its contribution to agricultural output is still very low. Finally, the traditional large-scale farms were expected to be dismantled within a year; in reality, the majority [many] of members opted to remain under the safety umbrella of cooperation and large-scale farming, not family farms, dominates the agricultural sector in ECE and FSU. [Brackets added by the author for more accurate descriptions.]

The main reasons why many farm workers have decided not to withdraw their individual land shares from the collectively operated large corporate farms to establish *individual farming* included: (1) difficult macroeconomic conditions; (2) legislative and political uncertainty (reservation and even resentment towards private ownership and selling of land in some republics of Russia and other CIS countries and controversy over them in CEECs and certain other CIS countries); (3) lack of tradition and experience with

Table 11.5 Percentage Change from Previous Year of Gross Agricultural Output in 12 CEECs and 12 CIS Countries 1990–98 (in current prices)

	1990	1991	1992	1993	1994	1995	1996	1997	1998 [a]
Albania	-2.00	-17.40	17.10	18.60	8.30	13.20	3.30	1.00	6.00
Bulgaria	-6.60	4.50	-12.90	-18.30	6.80	15.40	-13.10	30.20	-6.20
Croatia	-3.00	-5.00	-5.00	-5.00	-3.00	0.70	1.20	2.10	-1.40
Czech R.	-2.30	-8.90	-12.10	-2.30	-6.00	5.30	-0.90	-5.90	-1.30
Estonia	-13.10	-5.80	-19.50	-12.20	-12.90	-0.90	-6.30	-1.50	-0.50
Hungary	-4.70	-6.20	-20.00	-9.70	3.20	2.60	4.90	-0.60	-0.26
Latvia	-10.20	-3.90	-15.60	-22.20	-20.60	-6.00	-7.40	-2.40	-4.00
Lithuania	-4.42	-5.76	-23.45	-5.41	-20.18	6.04	10.32	6.45	-3.33
Poland	-5.50	-1.60	-10.70	8.00	-10.80	16.30	-8.90	-0.70	3.80
Romania	-2.90	0.80	-13.30	10.20	0.20	4.50	1.80	1.60	-7.60
Slovakia	-7.10	-7.00	-12.80	-7.20	9.30	2.10	4.10	-0.80	-0.80
Slovenia	3.50	0.40	-5.50	-1.00	9.10	1.30	1.10	-2.60	-1.50 [b]

Armenia	—	0.00	−13.00	24.00	3.00	5.00	2.00	—	—
Azerbaijan	—	0.00	−25.00	−15.00	−13.00	−7.00	3.00	—	—
Belarus	—	−5.00	−9.00	4.00	−14.00	−5.00	2.00	−5.00	−0.40
Georgia	—	−36.00	−13.00	−12.00	11.00	13.00	6.00	—	—
Kazakhstan	—	−10.00	1.00	−5.00	−20.00	−23.00 [c]	−10.00 [c]	−0.80	−19.00
Kyrgyzstan	—	−10.00	−5.00	−10.00	−18.00	−2.00 [c]	15.00 [c]	—	—
Moldova	—	−10.00	−16.00	10.00	−25.00	3.00	−13.00 [c]	—	—
Russia	−3.60	−5.00	−9.00	−4.00	−12.00	−8.00	−7.00	2.00	−12.30
Tajikistan	—	−4.00	−27.00	−4.00	−8.00	—	—	—	—
Turkmenistan	—	−4.00	−9.00	8.00	−11.00	−18.00	−2.00	—	—
Ukraine	—	−13.20	−8.30	1.50	−16.50	−5.60	−9.50	−1.90	−8.30
Uzbekistan	—	−1.00	−6.00	1.00	−8.00	3.00	−6.00	—	—

Notes:
a. Preliminary.
b. Estimate.
c. In 1994 prices.
Sources: OECD 1999v1: 244. Serova 1998: 43.

individual farming; (4) shortage of capital, credits, information and access to markets; (5) concern over prospects for fragmented small individual farms; (6) worry about market risks faced by individual farming after losing large farms' employment;6 (7) fear of losing access to large farms' infrastructure (storage, repair service, grain drying facilities, etc.) [even *household plots* heavily relied on their large mother farms for inputs, services, etc. (Serova 1998: 21)]; (8) reliance on large farm managers' accumulated expertise while bearing the brunt of their vested interests against deep restructuring in order to retain power, etc. These factors all affected agricultural productivity. (OECD 1998d: 17. Csaki & Lerman 1997: 445–6, 449–50)

The Second Possible Dilemma

The first side of the second possible dilemma is that some poor peasants due to difficulties in production and living would have to sell land parcels or shares and become newly landless, and land has been concentrated towards powerful people at the *low wage economy* (Van Eldijk 2000); and the second side is that part-time and absent small farmers earning higher off-farm income in rural areas (including those still saddled with traditional agriculture) developing towards the *high wage economy*, or cities and abroad, may have little incentive to lease or sell land to the remaining full-time (or mainly agriculture-engaged) farmers, resulting in inefficient land-holding.

Regarding the first side, in general, the rural areas of the four major countries of the CIS - Belarus, Kazakhstan, Russia and Ukraine - lacked off-farm employment opportunities and remained at a low wage economy. Although agriculture's contribution to GDP has been sharply declining, its share in total employment stayed high (and even growing), with increasing hidden unemployment. The collectively operated large farms continued to dominate grain, fodder and sugar beet production, while the numerous tiny household plots held by large farm members provided the majority of total milk, meat, potatoes, fruits and vegetables. Output per worker of large farms was declining, financial situation of large farms deteriorating, and wages

---

6 In the Czech Republic, Estonia, Hungary and Slovakia, there are collectively operated large farms which are sufficiently independent and restructured. Their managers, by laying off unproductive workers, have been able to cut their labor input more effectively and radically than individual farms. This could raise efficiency but also would have made them jobless considering these workers in particular have insufficient qualifications for other jobs. In fact, about 5% and 10–12% of the fired workers in the Czech Republic and Slovakia respectively became unemployed during 1989–97. (OECD 1999-10: 8, 12, 16–7. Mathijs 1999). The similar situation has happened in some Russian large farms (OECD 1999v1: 174–5).

were low, which have forced some Russian large farm managers to reduce the number of farm employees, that consequently raised the question of how they could then survive. (OECD 1999v1: 174–5)

For the new landlessness and land concentration phenomenon, the typical example is Kazakhstan. In Kazakhstan, there was a high rate of unemployment in urban areas, prevalent hidden unemployment and lack of non-agricultural employment in rural areas, although part-time farming has been increasing. Land privatization did not bring about incentives for farmers to work harder. On the contrary, farming has become an unprofitable business. There were many (hidden) unemployed young people in rural areas, some of whom were trying to move to cities. As a result, there were huge areas of abandoned and idled land. The government, however, did not regard the abandonment of farmland as a public concern but instead tried to justify it as an optimization process of crop sown areas, and an adjustment measure towards a market-driven economy. The overall agricultural situation has been worsening progressively. (Suleimenov 1998: 5–7, 9–10. OECD 1998b: 117)

The indebtedness of the ill-functioning collectively operated large farms stimulated changes in their possession and management of land. An important feature in the past few years was that input suppliers and grain traders (which have been privatized since 1992) were gaining control over the assets of these large farms, usually through a purchase of rights to either use or manage the farm's land. In some cases this happened without any formal arrangements, when creditors established *de facto* control over an indebted farm. Nine companies were reported to own land use rights for 641,000 ha and management rights for 591,000 ha in 1998, of which, a single grain trading company held use and management rights for 518,000 ha. (OECD 1999v2: 62; 1998b: 120)

Another notable phenomenon over the past few years was a growth in the number of collectively operated large farms whose managers controlled most land shares. As unique feasible buyers, managers not only gathered land shares from the ethnic Germans and Russians leaving Kazakhstan, but also, more vitally, from other holders who due to poverty and need for cash were induced to sell land shares, hence new landlessness on one hand and land concentration on the other. (OECD 1999v2: 62. Van Eldijk 2000)

There was also a trend of concentration of non-land assets. While non-land assets of collective farms *kolkhozes* have been considered as collectively owned, those of state farms *sovkhozes* were due to be privatized and the privatization was virtually completed in 1996. In several cases this process implied substantial changes in the structure of ownership and management. For example, about 20 state farms were sold at closed auctions to restricted groups (mainly farm managers, input suppliers and foreign investors) and another 33 were taken over by their directors who received 51% of non-land assets. (OECD 1999v2: 62)

The second side, inefficient land-holding by part-time and absent small farmers earning higher off-farm income, seems more ostensible and widespread.

Development of off-farm activities and appearance of part-time and absent small farmers who are young, skilled and dynamic. Not every region in other CEECs and CIS countries has quickly entered the high wage economy. Where the social welfare systems were not well developed, access to farmland provided households with a way to seek food security. It has restrained the labor outflow from agriculture or even resulted in an inflow. This has happened in Albania, Bosnia and Herzegovina, Bulgaria, Latvia, Lithuania, Eastern areas of Poland, Romania, and Armenia. For example, land restitution in Bulgaria made it possible for many urban or semi-urban households to produce food. In Armenia, following land distribution, a massive labor inflow to agriculture in order to achieve household food security led to an increase of 80% in the agricultural labor force during the war of 1990–93. In Bosnia and Herzegovina, during and after the war in the early 1990s, many former industrial workers turned to agriculture as the unique possibility of finding a job. In contrast, in Hungary, there has been not only a strong labor outflow from agriculture, but also, the generous early retirement schemes encouraged older workers to leave the payroll of farms. (OECD 1999-10: 15, 19. Numic 1997: 66)

Nevertheless, in both regions at low and high wage stages in transition economies, part-time and absent small farmers seeking higher off-farm income are notable. A large part of those young, most skilled and dynamic have left agriculture during the transition for other sectors in both rural and urban areas. It was estimated that in most CEECs up to 20% of family farms have off-farm activities. The share was considerably higher in some countries, such as Poland and Slovenia which have had a high ratio of part-time small farmers. The proportion of off-farm income in total farm household incomes varied but could be more than half in some regions. In 1996, only 38% of agricultural families in Poland took farming as the main source of income. In Albania, non-agricultural incomes were very important and included mainly service activities and remittance payments to rural households from post-1991 emigrants, mostly working in Greece and Italy. Remittance payments were also important in other countries, especially in regions close to the EU which allowed for daily or weekly commuting. For instance, a considerable number of migrants and commuters from the Czech Republic, Hungary, Poland and Slovakia worked in construction and services of Western Europe. (OECD 1999-10: 10–1, 16)

Active women. 'Although some reports suggest that women in agriculture are particularly affected by the negative impacts of transition as they are typically less mobile than men, the available data do not confirm this'. During 1980–97, the ratio of women in total agricultural employment was high in all countries: women contributed more than 30% of total labor in all countries, and around 50% in Albania, Romania and Ukraine. In most of CEECs and the CIS the proportion of women in total agricultural employment has changed little during the past two decades and transition. (OECD April 1999-10: 7)

A possible explanation for the phenomenon that women are as active as men in off-farm activities is that in the previous socialist systems both men and women, including those in rural areas, had relatively equal access to education. This contrasts sharply with the experience of many developing countries with a strong bias against women. (Kwiecinski 2001)

Senilization. Those left in agriculture are usually less educated, typically older workers with relatively few skills to offer outside agriculture. The share of older people in agriculture was especially large in countries such as Romania, where pensions have been falling so that small-scale farming became an essential element of the social security system for elderly people. In the Czech Republic, Estonia and Belarus, the ratio of agricultural labor force older than 55 increased by about 2% during 1990–95 to 11.5%, 28% and 36.9% respectively. In Croatia and Romania more than half of the agricultural labor force was older than 50 years, while in Estonia 29% was above 55 years. (OECD 1999-10: 7–8, 16, 19)

Could a free land market promote land transactions effectively? Yes, according to orthodox theory, as Lerman (April 1999: 20) presents:

Once land has been allocated to individuals through the various processes of restitution and distribution, the new owners may immediately sense a need for adjustment of their holdings. Some landowners have no inclination to farm their land: they are too old, too frail, have better jobs outside agriculture, or do not have sufficient knowledge to become successful farmers. The optimal course of action for these landowners may be to get rid of their land. Other individuals, who know how to farm efficiently, may wish to increase their holdings in order to achieve higher earnings and greater welfare. The optimal course of action for these individuals is to acquire more land. The land market provides a meeting place where both groups of agents may enter into appropriate transactions for adjustment of land-holdings through transfer of ownership rights (buying and selling of land) or use rights (leasing of land). The economic role of land markets as a stage for farm size optimization explains the considerable interest in this issue in transitional economies, where the new farm sizes are decided abruptly and quite arbitrarily through administrative and political processes.

In reality, however, *land buy–sale has occurred at very low percentages*, as Table 11.6 demonstrates. 'Even in Armenia, where buying and selling of land has been completely legal since 1992, two large surveys covering 6,000 farms in 1996 and 1998 did not detect any significant transfers of land ownership through market mechanism' (Lerman April 1999: 22).

Leasing is widespread as Table 11.6 reveals. Now that there are so many part-time and absent small farmers, 'in principle there could be a market for leasing among individuals in the village (including villagers with off-farm jobs and of course pensioners)' (Lerman 2000). But in fact, most land leased is from the governments, some (not all) city dwellers who were restituted land but only till a small part for subsistence due to lacking agricultural experience and capital to establish their own farms, and some old peasants, rather than from part-time and absent small farmers (Schulze December 1999). '*Family farms with privately owned land generally lease relatively little land*' (Schulze May 1999: 2). (But even if small farmers were willing to rent out land, owned and leased land of the lessees is usually fragmented into several small parcels.)

For further evidence in specific countries, let us first look at the three 'leader' or 'star' countries acclaimed so for their agriculture's impressive gains after privatization - Armenia, Georgia and Albania (Lerman January 1999: 12).

In *Armenia*, the growth rate of gross agricultural output dropped from 24% in 1993 to 2% in 1996 (see Table 11.5), became negative in 1997 to about 1990 level, and the agricultural production in 1997 was still about 20% below its 1985 level (Lerman; Lundell; Mirzakhanian; Asatrian & Kakosian 1999: 10–1). Its agriculture faced the following major problems: deteriorating food security; reduction in production owing to inadequate irrigation, shortage of farm inputs, lack of credit, farm power, etc.; and limited outlets for produce due to unavailability of markets, transport and storage, and declining purchasing power. The Farm households on average consumed 60–70% of the produce and sold the surplus, slightly beyond subsistence. Off-farm activities have developed and part-time farming appeared. The average family was composed of four, and farming employed two to three members mostly on a part-time basis. Households gained a substantial share of earnings from off-farm sources, as in 51% of households farming provided less than 50% of income. Although small farms based on manual work will still dominate in the near future, the task of *unifying small parcels* and creating efficient farms has been raised in the present policy, which was expected to occur *without ownership transfer* according to the characteristics of Armenian farmers. (Aghamian 1997: 55–7). In fact, a 1998 survey conducted by the World Bank and Armenian government found that about 20% of respondents would like to increase their land-holdings. But only 1% of respondents reported that they leased land to other users (on average only half of their private holdings and mainly for a short-term of around one year). 'The land lease market in Armenia is thus *strictly one-way*: the private farmers lease land from the state (through the village council)', normally for one to three years, but 15% reported lease terms

Table 11.6 Land Buy—Sale and Lease in Nine CEECs and Three CIS Countries 1996—98

Country	Year	Land buy—sale	Area (ha)	Share in agricultural land (%)	Area leased in agricultural land (%)
Albania	Before 08.98	1,200	–	–	–
Bulgaria	1998	Hardly any	–	–	70–80
Czech R.	1996	Sale —	8,800	0.21	ca. 90
Hungary	1998	–	–	–	> 70
Lithuania	1998	–	–	–	56
Poland	1996	Sale —	367,900	1.99	20
	1997	Sale —	307,900	1.67	
Romania	Before 09.98	Intra-village sale 33,742	9,210	0.062	7.2
		Extra-village sale 3,268	13,231	0.089	–
Slovakia	1998	Sale —	7,000	0.29	> 96
Slovenia	1998	5,000	2,000 –2,500	0.25 –0.32	7.9
Kazakhstan	1998	–	–	–	11.9 *
Russia	1996	Sale 218,759	33,621.6	0.016	1.4
		Gift 34,094	8,270.3	0.004	–
		Devise 132,171	128,447.7	0.062	–
Ukraine	1.1.98	–	–	–	445,000 ha (= 1.3%) in public sector * 86,000–146,000 ha leased by private farmers

* Maybe under free use rather than leasing.

Sources: *Lithuania*: Duzinskas 1998: 8. *Others*: Schulze May 1999: 8–9.

longer than five years. The average size of farms with leased land reached 3.21 ha (with 2.06 ha owned and 1.16 ha leased), larger than that of farms without leased land - 1.98 ha. (Lerman; Lundell; Mirzakhanian; Asatrian & Kakosian 1999: 13–4).

In *Georgia*, gross agricultural output grew by 11% in 1994, 13% in 1995 and 6% in 1996 (see Table 11.5). Nevertheless, in the summer of 2000, an unprecedented drought devastated most crops, and the country faced famine. The President of State had to appeal to many international organizations and countries for aid. (XHNA September 2000). Hence the vulnerability of its agriculture. A 1996 rural survey by the World Bank and Georgian government discovered that farming was the main source of family income for fewer than 10% of respondents, provided less than half the family earnings for 60%, constituted between half and three-quarters of family budget for 20%, and 4.5% received financial assistance from family members employed abroad (Lerman 1996b: 6). Although the national average farm size was less than 1 ha, a World Bank team has recently disclosed some 3,000 farms (about 1% of all farming households) with more than 10 ha of land, most of which was however leased from the state for one or two years, although the Georgian law of land leasing allows much longer lease terms (Lerman April 1999: 23). Only a negligible percentage of respondents reported leasing from other individuals (Lerman 2000).

How about *Albania*, 'one of the few economies in transition to have experienced positive agricultural growth early in the reform process, but since 1995 output growth has stagnated' (OECD 1999v2: 7)? The situation in this country, besides what has been mentioned above, was that agriculture accounted for 64.5% of national employment in 1997, and remained a critical sector of the economy. Farming was primarily for subsistence, and the poorest tenth of rural population was unable to meet its staple food requirements. Thus, farmers have had to seek off-farm income. After the collapse of the financial pyramid schemes at the end of 1996 and the resulted turmoil in the first half of 1997, emigration to cities and abroad increased significantly. Consequently, a large number of farmers worked part-time. Although land consolidation and expansion have been raised as a policy direction, fragmentation of land-holdings remained the norm. The fragmented small farms with traditional technology have seriously hampered the growth of agricultural output, which was further aggravated by land idling. Although land leasing was made legal in 1994, so was buying, selling and mortgaging in 1995, and some leasing has been carried out (data unavailable), inefficient land-holding and -idling have occurred. In most cases, land held by the emigrants became fallow rather than being used by the remaining farmers. In 1998, for example, the potentially highly productive agricultural area near Greece lied idle. (Beka 1998: 7, 9–11, 14, 17–8. OECD 1998b: 37–8;

1999v1: 44. Marku 1997: 48)

Former Yugoslavia and Poland, where collectivization either failed or was not initiated after WWII, and about 80% of the total agricultural land had been cultivated by small individual family farms, with the rest by a few large state farms even before the transition, provide further evidence.

In *Croatia* - take an example from former Yugoslavia - before the transition, there was already a bimodal farm structure with numerous small private farms and a few large state farms (Bozic 1997: 75). The legal maximum private land-holding was 10 ha, but no ceiling has existed at all since 1984 (Bozic 1998: 9). By 1998, the state owned land had been privatized by 7%, but still accounted for 30% (962,400 ha) of the total agricultural land (3,208,000 ha), 70% being owned privately (2,245,600 ha). Small and part-time farms played the leading role in agriculture. (Bozic 1997: 75; 1998: 16). The average size of privately owned farm reduced from 3.6 ha in 1960 to 2.8 ha in 1991, fragmented into five parcels, with low production potential. Most farms were not specialized and market oriented, but only produced for their own consumption. During 1981–91, of the total population, while rural population only declined from 49.2% to 45%, farming population decreased from 15.2% to 9.1%; of all the rural households, those with farming as the unique source of income fell from about 25% to 15%, but those with off-farm income increased from 50% to almost 70%. Young, male and vital people have left farming, with the old and female remaining. Although the Law on Farmland has authorized local governments to let arable agricultural land that has not been cultivated in the previous vegetation season for three years, desertion of land was still a public problem. (Bozic 1998: 9–11, 15–6)

According to the World Bank, there were already large-scale farmers - of the total roughly 500,000 households with privately owned land, 33% owned below 1 ha and only 2.6% over 10 ha; about 400,000 were part-time farmers holding sub-subsistence unit below 3 ha and with a growing labor constraint due to age, and around 100,000 active full-time farmers owning 3 ha or over (34% had below 5 ha and about 60% 5–20 ha) and renting in extra land, usually through annual lease arrangements. The lessors, however, were not young and able-bodied part-time farmers, but *aged* small farmers (who would not sell land, as it provided security). (World Bank 1996: 4–5). Farmland owned by the state can also be leased to domestic and foreign legal and physical persons for 3–10 years. By 1998, the Ministry of Agriculture and Forestry had rented out state-owned land of 111,970 ha in total value of 48.4 million kunas through tendering to the most favorable offers (Bozic 1999: 10) (thus 73.5% of total agricultural land were operated privately - 3.5% as leased state-owned land plus 70% as privately owned land). Although the World Bank (1996: 4) optimistically expected that

'These [small] farms will gradually be absorbed by the progressive farmers who already form the production core of the future' (note: not the present), and the Strategy for Sustainable Agricultural Development of the Croatian government in 1994 intended to change the present agrarian structure through enlarging family farms by land purchase or leasing from the state or other landowners, 'this process is proceeding slowly' (Bozic 1997: 76).

The most recent situation of *Slovenia* - another example in former Yugoslavia - is presented by an OECD report. Slovenia to a large extent is still a rural country with rural areas holding 89% of the territory and 57% of the population. Agricultural area occupies 44% of the territory, and agriculture accounts for around 3% of the GDP and about 5% of the employment - these shares have fallen since the beginning of the 1990s and are expected to decrease further, mostly due to the growth of non-agricultural sectors. (OECD 2000: 8)

After WWII, a small part of land which had been owned by large landowners, private companies, banks, churches and expelled Germans and Italians was nationalized and turned over to a few large-scale collective farms, with poor economic results; most land owned by fragmented small farms remained privately owned - thus the farm structure was still dual. The land market was limited but functioning, with free prices. During 1960–91, fragmentation was notable with a growing share of very small farms below 1 ha and decreasing share of farms over 1 ha in the total private farm number. Before the transition, large-scale collective farms held about 10% of land and around one-third of gross output in agriculture; and fragmented small private farms (usually part-time) about 90% of land and around two-thirds of gross output. (OECD 2000: 11, 55–7, 60)

In 1991, it was decided to restitute nationalized land and properties to the former owners or their heirs. If restitution would lead to fragmentation of land into economically unmanageable pieces, no physical parceling of land to individual owners was allowed, and all individuals could obtain land ownership rights only in co-ownership of a whole consolidated parcel. There was an adjustment period of five years from the establishment of the co-ownership to December 1998 (Bojnec and Swinnen 1997). Only afterwards did original owners have the right to physically possess the land and use it. The Fund for Agricultural Land and Forests (FALF) was established to manage the state agricultural and forest land, and to carry out restitution. FALF comprised about 26% of total utilized agricultural area, which was partly used by former socially-owned farms, and individual farms, with the rest being idled or protected areas. By 1 January 2000, FALF still controlled 22% of all agricultural land. There were 90,611 private family farms, accounting for 94% of total agricultural land and about two-thirds of gross agricultural output. The average farm size was 9.4 ha, with 4.8 ha under cultivation. Almost 60% of these farms, occupying about one-third of agricultural land, cultivated only 1–5 ha. (OECD 2000: 12, 57)

Private traditional family farms are predominantly located in areas unfavorable to agricultural production. Their production potential is low also due to limited land and capital. The average yields of major crops are far below the EU levels. By the end of the 1990s, the share of *part-time farms increased* to about 75% of the total private farm number and 70% of land in private farms. There was also a marked increase of farms operated by *retirees*, as the agricultural population is aging and more land has shifted into the hands of elderly persons during the 1990s. Less than 12% of private farms were full-time. Many farms were poorly linked with the markets: a considerable share of their production was used for home consumption or on-farm sales. (OECD 2000: 12–3, 23)

Large-scale farms represent a small segment of agriculture. In 2000 there were 208 large agricultural companies, as formerly socially-owned farms (about 100 of them being, e.g., pig and poultry complexes, possessing no agricultural land). In 1998, they operated 6% of agricultural land. Most of them are located in the plain areas favorable to production. They carried out intensive farming and generally benefited from economies of scale. However, many of them were unprofitable. Some have accumulated substantial arrears in paying land rents. The better-off companies were reluctant to modernize, make new investments or undertake any restructuring due to uncertainties related to the forthcoming restitution of the land under their operation. Thus their future as land users is uncertain. (OECD 2000: 13)

By 1991, the major constraints to land trade among citizens - the preemptive right of large-scale farms to buy land, and upper size limit for private farms - were abolished, and individuals became the first among preferential claimants, although some restrictions still exist (e.g., in 1996 some control was stipulated over land re-sales, speculation and 'unreasonable increases' in land prices). Just as before the transition, land continues to be a low-tradable asset. It is estimated that in 1997 the marketed land area comprised less than 0.5% of utilized agricultural land with an average size per transaction of about 0.4 ha. Most transactions concerned land of low quality (permanent grassland, land for permanent plantations, etc.), whereas high quality land was in short supply. The land market was only slightly invigorated by the process of restitution, partly as many beneficiaries of restitution could only possess their parcels and sell them after 1998 when the adjustment period for co-ownership ended, and partly due to insufficient information, but more importantly because land has been regarded by most owners as an important economic 'safeguard'. (OECD 2000: 57, 60–1)

Given the limited land market and high land prices, the demand for leased land from the family farms is considerable, and land leasing may remain the principal means of agricultural land reallocation in the nearest future. The minimum contract terms have been determined by law according to a standard depreciation period for investments in land, i.e., 10 years for arable land and 15 years for permanent plantations, in order to both prevent over-exploitation of land by tenants, and protect investments in land. Agricultural companies usually have formal lease contracts, but the practice of informal short-term leases is widespread among private farmers. The 1997 Farm Structure Survey found that one-quarter or so of family farms rented in land, representing around 13% of utilized agricultural area in the private farm sector. Two-thirds of the land rented in by family farms was in 5–20 ha. The *principal lessors*, however, were not family farmers (which only rented out around 20% of all land leased to family farms), but the *state* via FALF (about 40%), and *non-farm landowners* (around 40%). (OECD 2000: 61–2)

For *Poland*, the 2000 World Bank survey gives the newest information. Poland is among the largest agrarian economies in CEECs. In 1997, it held 18.5 million ha of agricultural land (reduced from 20.4 million ha in 1950), accounting for 60% of the total land area. After WWII, its agriculture was never fully collectivized. As shown in Table 11.7, in 1990, state farms owned 24% of agricultural land but only used 20%, while cooperative (or collective) farms owned and also used 4%. During the transition up to 1997, both privatized 2%. The pre-1944 private land of 6 million ha was not restituted to large landowners (with holdings over 50–100 ha) mainly because it was partitioned and distributed during 1944–50 or sold afterwards to individuals. Thus of the remaining 22% of state owned land, the state (via Agricultural Property Agency - APA, part of the State Treasury) leased out 64% (half to individual farms and half to private corporate farms all of which were privatized state or cooperative farms) and used 36%. (Csaki & Lerman 2000: 1, 3, 14)

As Table 11.7 displays, in 1996–97, 83% of agricultural land were in individual farms and household plots averaging 7 ha and 0.4 ha respectively. In the 2,835 households surveyed (60% of which owned land, 53% cultivated land, but 47% did not farm), 5% of respondents reported owning 31–115 ha, and 13% owning 20 ha or more; while for 50% of respondents, owned farm was up to 3.7 ha, split into 1–5 parcels (median number of parcels 3 and mean 4.5), and distance of the farthest parcel to the house was 1–4 km (median distance 2 km and mean 3.1 km). Hence domination of fragmented small farms. 'Respondents perceive considerable deterioration in their standard of living during the transition decade': from 1990 to 2000, those who characterized their existence as not better than subsistence increased from 11% to 45%, while those who reported comfortable or better living decreased from 60% to 21%. In 1997, agriculture has employed 4.4 million people (or 27% of the total employed of the country), as a result of an

Table 11.7 Ownership and Use of Agricultural Land and Average Farm Size in Poland 1990–97

	Owned land %		Used land %		Number of units	Average size (ha)	Used land %
	1990	1997	1990	1997		1996	1996
Individual							
Household plot	72	76	76	83	975,000	0.4	2.1
Individual farm				7	2,100,000	7	79
Private corporate farm	–	–	–	7	2,000	620	6.7
Cooperative	4	2	4	2	–	–	2 *
State	24	22	20	8	–	–	8 *
Unused land	–	–	–	–	–	–	2.2
Total	100	100	100	100	–	–	100

* 1997.

Sources: *1990 and 1997*: PASY [1998] 2000: 1–2. *1996*: PCBS [1996] 2000: 4.

annual increase by nearly 2% since 1990, even though agricultural land has been reducing. Rural population reached 15 million, almost 40% of the whole population. Yet agriculture contributed to only 6% of GDP, demonstrating a substantially lower productivity, profitability and efficiency than in the rest of the economy. (Csaki & Lerman 2000: 1, 17–9, 25, 37)

In contrast, off-farm activities appeared profitable. Thus, as mentioned above, many peasants have been seeking off-farm employment. Of total family incomes surveyed, off-farm income accounted for over 50% in farms of 1–10 ha, less than 40% in farms of 10–20 ha, and below 20% in farms of 20 ha and more. Hence the smaller (larger) the farm size, the higher (lower) engagement in off-farm activities. In this largely subsistence economy, families combining farming with off-farm jobs earned higher total incomes than those not cultivating land. Thus prevalence of part-time farming. Even though, the survey found that almost 15% of landowners did not farm, and during 1997–99, 26% of decreased land were *idled*, compared with 9% as gifted, 16% rented out, 26% sold, and 22% disposed by other means. (Csaki & Lerman 2000: 19, 23, 27–8, 31)

In 1990, land transactions were freed, as any person may acquire agricultural land without any restriction on total holdings and penalties on 'irrational use' or 'non-use' of land, although transaction costs were still relatively high. However, during 1995–99, only about 5% of respondents bought or sold land, whereas 'land leasing is a relatively infrequent phenomenon'. Moreover, 'landowners who lease out land are *older*, have smaller families, and control a smaller land endowment than those who do not lease out land'. Actually, 'the number of farms that reduce their size and thus supply land through the land market is much smaller than the number of farms that generate the demand for land: between 1990–1996 more than 14% of farms increased their size by acquiring additional land, while less than 6% of farms acted as land suppliers. Private land is thus insufficient to meet the full demand.' It is the state which has played the major role in supplying land through leasing: 60–80% in Western and Northern parts, and 30–40% in Central-Eastern and Southern zones of the country. The average lease was around 15 ha in the former, and below 5 ha in the rest of the country. Private corporate farms did not own any, but rented in, land from the state and reached a large average farm size of 620 ha, as presented in Table 11.7. The state also rented out more than 100,000 ha to nearly 300 companies with majority foreign ownership. According to the estimates of the Polish Institute of Agricultural and Food Economics, during 1992–98, the average lease of state land was 10.6 ha, while that of private land only 3 ha, and private land buy and sale merely 2.6 ha, thus 'transactions in state land are on average substantially larger than transactions in private land' and 'the average leasing transaction is generally larger than the average land purchase transaction'. (Csaki & Lerman 2000: 3–4, 8–9, 12–3, 20–1, 23)

Theoretical Discussion

Basic land operation at families. Collectively operated large farms with public land ownership have not been successful (as proved previously in China, the FSU, CEECs under the centrally planned economy and currently in Classification 4), converting them to publicly owned but privately possessed land shares has not either (as evidenced in Classification 3), further reforming them to operate with privately owned land shares is still not (as witnessed in Classification 2), even after the centrally planned economy had been abolished. Thus, the basic operation level as a collective consisting of many households would not work, no matter if it were based on public or private land ownership, under the centrally planned economy or free market system.

In line with the author's three-phase hypothesis outlined in earlier chapters, the basic operation level at single household farms should be the major form of farming, and at units including a small number of households the minor form. In short, family operation is a necessity for successful farming. This has been confirmed in Japan and the USA under private land ownership and China under public land ownership for both small and large-scale farming as already analyzed. Interesting enough, China privatized the basic operation level of land rather than land ownership itself, and thus succeeded. In contrast, many CEECs and CIS countries privatized land ownership rather than its basic operation level, and hence failed. Therefore, it is the basic operation level, other than ownership, of land which is decisive.

Individualization. In order to avoid the drawbacks of the collectively operated large farms, many CEECs and CIS countries took one step further and established individual farms with either private or public (*de facto* private) land ownership, but were then confronted with fragmented small farms. As Lerman (January 1999: 1) correctly points out, 'individualization is not a sufficient condition of success'. Under private land ownership, landowners may not realize the relevant rights they are supposed to enjoy, which to the contrary may be effected under public ownership with village–household dual level operation of land, as the following OECD report (1999-11: 4) emphasizes:

> In China, there is no private ownership of land. However, there is a hierarchy of rights under which village leaders are granted rights to allocate land among households. In many cases, households have enough faith in their exclusive access to the land, and in the possibility of bequeathing such access to the next

generation, that they are prepared to invest in the land. By contrast, although land is privately owned in most transition countries it is often fragmented. Moreover, land markets are underdeveloped and usually governed by short-term lease. Given the difficulty of consolidating the land into economically viable plots, the actual rights of landowners, as manifested in their ability to exploit their land for economic purposes, are thus severely restricted.

Therefore, public ownership with village—household dual level operation of land may lead family farms to be productive, while individual farms under private land ownership may not be viable. Here again, it is the operation system, rather than ownership, of land which is fundamental.

At the low wage economy. Under private or nominal public but *de facto* private land ownership, when rural areas are still at the low wage economy, free buying and selling of land may lead poor peasants to become newly landless and powerful people to gather land. It has not been prevented in the USA under individual land ownership established in 1783 (analyzed in Chapters 9 and 10), but was precluded in Japan by the land-holding ceiling and tenant protection under individual land ownership in the early 1950s (Chapter 4), emerged in China in the early 1950s, but stopped by the prohibition of land sale in the elementary cooperatives under individual land ownership in the mid-1950s, excluded by the advanced cooperatives and people's communes under collective land ownership afterwards, and the Household Contract System under collective land ownership since 1978 (Chapters 5— 7), but still being experienced in Cambodia, Laos and Vietnam since the 1980s—90s under the nominal public - but *de facto* private - land ownership (Chapter 8). It has now also happened at least in Kazakhstan in the late 1990s.

Towards the high wage economy. At this stage, part-time and absent small farmers seeking higher off-farm income tend to hold land in inefficient use, while full-time farmers may not be able to enlarge farm size. This shows that inefficient land-holding by part-time and absent small farmers constitutes the last, or one of the last, obstacle(s) in sustainable rural development not only in monsoon Asia, but also in CEECs and the CIS. Even in the USA and many other OECD countries where large farmers due to historical and other reasons have been formed and are much stronger, inefficient land-holding by part-time and absent small farmers is also a serious problem. Indeed, it is a world-wide phenomenon. It reveals that the land reform which simply transfers ownership, even with clear property rights, to individual farmers may not necessarily result in greater efficiency in economies of scale, and may eventually lead to inefficiency in land utilization. This also provides another evidence for the author's argument stressed in Chapter 3 that after the former centrally planned economies have adopted a market economy, and most capitalist countries have implemented deregulation, it is negative *pecuniary* externalities which would be the major negative externalities. They may outweigh negative technological externalities in the current real world but are unfortunately neglected in the literature. Of course, in CEECs and the CIS, some restrictions in the land markets may still exist, e.g., in Slovenia, and transaction costs may still be relatively high, e.g., in Poland, as mentioned above. But even the restrictions and transaction costs were substantially reduced, land sales subsidized and land leases encouraged, they may still not happen very much, basically because landowners may not have enough incentive to do so, as evidenced in Japan and analyzed in Chapter 4.

Unfeasibility of the Western European model. One may wish that the size of the individual farms in CEECs and the CIS be increased through free market transactions just as in Western Europe previously. But as discussed in Chapter 4, in Western Europe, a market solution - emigration, and two non-market solutions - primogeniture and enclosure of land, have promoted land transactions (thus they were not so free and democratic). It is however unperceivable that they could be exercised in today's CEECs and the CIS, just as not in Japan, Taiwan Province of China and South Korea. Moreover, unlike the situation in the 1950s, the present rural areas may enjoy the similar facilities as in the cities, transportation and services become convenient, and most importantly, people attach much more value to the precious and primitive rural environment. The improvement in rural conditions would prompt part-time and absent small farmers to keep land with them from selling and leasing.

Initial success. Although Lerman (January 1999: 12) perceives that 'the three "stars" *happen* to be the smallest countries in the region', and Swinnen (1999) cheers that 'in the countries where reform was most radical, agricultural production has increased!', this initial achievement in Albania, Armenia and Georgia was neither accidental nor surprising if we compare them with Japan and China. Both of them, similar to these three countries, distributed land into fragmented small individual farms and had experienced positive agricultural growth early in the reform process - Japan during 1950–60 and China during 1978–84. But China upheld collective land ownership and was then able to overcome the fragmented small farms as the 'last obstacle' maintained by the inefficient land-holding of the part-time and absent small farmers, while Japan kept individual land ownership and was unable to surpass it. It would be interesting to see whether Albania, Armenia and Georgia would follow the trajectory of the Japanese model: the setting-up of the individual land ownership initially led to the increase of agricultural production, which released labor to off-farm activities, but much land is still held by part-time and absent small farmers in inefficient use rather than being sold or leased to the remaining full-time small farmers, who as a result could not easily survive on, nor expand, their limited land, and national food self-sufficiency would only be kept at subsistence level or could not even be maintained without large amount of government subsidies.

Land leasing to private farmers by the state. Such practices in Armenia, Georgia, Croatia, Slovenia and Poland are very meaningful. In Armenia, it is the state owned land (nearly one-third of arable land and virtually all pastures), rather than the individually owned one (two-thirds of arable land), which constituted the strictly one-way source of land leasing - through the village councils - to private farmers. In Georgia, it is the state owned cultivated land (51%), other than the individually owned one (49%), that provided almost all of the land rented out to private large-scale farmers. In Croatia, the state-owned agricultural land (30%) has been partly rented out through tendering to the most favorable offers, while the lessors in the private sector have not been part-time and absent small farmers, but aged small farmers. In Slovenia, the so many part-time private family farms have contributed a minor source of land leasing to private family farmers, the principal source being the state-owned agricultural land (22%) which is also the almost unique source of land leasing to the large agricultural companies. In Poland, the state-owned agricultural land (22%) has played the major role in supplying land through leasing - 14% have been leased out to individual farms and private corporate farms, while individual lessors are older and their leasings infrequent. In these five countries, the remaining state owned land is actually vestige of the former socialist public land ownership system and should have been privatized in view of the free market advocates [e.g., the World Bank report demands quick privatization of the remaining state-owned land in Poland (Csaki & Lerman 2000: 34–5), while the restitution of the land still owned by the state in Slovenia is ongoing]. But ironically, it is such despised vestige of publicly owned land that has been facilitating effective land use (in Slovenia it has the potential to do so), while the much acclaimed privatized land is hampering efficient land use. The success of competitive leasing of publicly owned land to individuals in promoting efficient land utilization and large-scale farming in these countries is just in accordance with the Chinese model of rural development based on public land ownership and market socialism, while the inefficient holding of individually owned land by part-time and absent small farmers exactly reflects the failure of the Japanese model and free market system.

Therefore, the OECD report (2000: 23) correctly recommends the Slovenian state agency FALF, which now has no significant influence on the management decisions of its tenants including indebted ones, and thus faces a lack of clarity in business and development objectives and also moral hazard, to review all leasing contracts with agricultural enterprises, discontinue those with dilatory tenants, and reallocate the country's most fertile land to more efficient producers. In contrast, the World Bank has reported and noticed the widespread inefficient holding of land by part-time and absent small farmers from renting it out in CEECs and the CIS such as in Armenia, Georgia, Croatia, Poland, etc., but still advocates that the state-owned land be privatized, state agency removed from land leasing, and leasing decisions made by the new private owners in an open lease market, e.g., in Poland. It also accuses the now abolished pre-transition penalties on 'irrational use' or 'non-use' of land in Poland as *draconian* (Csaki & Lerman 2000: 8, 34–5), leading to an impression as if 'irrational use' or 'non-use' of land either should be sustained or could be removed by free market forces.

Land consolidation under private farmland ownership has been pursued as priority in many of CEECs and the CIS (Riddell 2000. Lapse 1999. Csaki & Lerman 2000: 37–8). However, it is neither sufficient, since after fragmented parcels have been joined together, part-time and absent small farmers may still not have incentive to lease out land (as analyzed in Chapter 4), nor necessary, because it incurs very high transaction costs (as indicated in Chapter 3) which could otherwise be avoided if Proposal 5.1 could be adopted.

A mixed economy. After establishing individual farms, the small peasants in CEECs and the CIS also may have lost the access to the infrastructure, services, managers' expertise, employment safety of large farms and be exposed to market risks directly. This in turn persuaded other potential individual farmers not to leave their collectively operated large farms although they have had the freedom to do so. Ironically, collectivization was regarded as having been forced on peasants against their will in the 1930s and 1940s in the FSU and CEECs respectively. But now in contrast many peasants voluntarily joined their privately owned or possessed land shares for collective operation. This would appear to sustain the argument that there are some benefits in the collective operation of large farms.

Cochrane (1999: 1) stresses that 'nearly all CEECs intervene in their markets far less than many OECD countries'. We have seen in this book that the governments of OECD's developed member countries - Japan, the USA, Canada and EU, contrary to the world-wide propagandized impression of implementing a *free* market economy, have all intervened extensively in agriculture for decades. Therefore the question is not whether, but how, to intervene appropriately and establish a mixed economy. It is time for CEECs and the CIS to realize that a free market economy cannot work for their good.

This chapter has also given evidence to the author's surmise in Chapter 1 that, contrary to Schultz's assertions, in (1) the low income countries still saddled with traditional agriculture, (2) the low income countries developing towards the high income economy [many rural areas in CEECs and the CIS are still in (1) and (2)], and (3) the high income countries, the part-time and absent small farmers are not so efficient. They hold land in inefficient use, even though land property rights have been well defined and market transactions facilitated, and it would be logical for them to transfer land to the remaining full-time farmers for increasing farm size, so that they could earn remuneration and gain more time on and income from off-farm activities, while the society and full-time farmers could benefit from the functioning of the tenet 'that the costs of agricultural products fall as the size of the production unit in agriculture increases' (as the large-scale farming in Armenia, Georgia, Croatia, Slovenia, Poland, etc. may imply). The inefficient land-holding by the part-time and absent small farmers may be out of their rational concern over direct interests in security. Thus if they could be guaranteed with a back-up basic social welfare (such as the privately owned, or publicly owned but privately possessed, land shares) and provided with appropriate remuneration, then some of them would be agreeable to transfer their inefficiently held land in various suitable forms to the full-time farmers for effective use (e.g., leasing by the aged small farmers in Croatia and Poland), yet others would still be reluctant to do so. As a result, the remaining full-time small farmers, largely non-viable as the economy develops into the high wage stage, could not easily get the inefficiently held resources for effective use, although the knowledge and other conditions are available to both the full-time, and part-time and absent small farmers that would permit them to produce the same output with fewer resources or a larger output from the same resources. Therefore at least some of the part-time and absent small farmers are not so rational to the society's and their own fundamental interests. Consequently proper land tenure systems in variable mixed economies should be devised to effect the transfer of their inefficiently held land. But this does not as yet seem like a commonplace idea in CEECs and the CIS.

A Proposed Third Way

Following the above analysis, a third way beyond the centrally planned economy and free market system, and between the collective land operation and fragmented small individual farming, which could build on the benefits of collectively operated large farms and individual farms but avoid their shortcomings, would be desirable. Hence Proposal 5.1: village-wide corporate ownership of physically unwithdrawable but financially salable private land shares (with the term village being replaced by large corporate farm, and private land shares by individual land shares, i.e., either privately owned or publicly owned but privately possessed land shares in the context of CEECs and the CIS, it becomes here *large farm corporate ownership of physically unwithdrawable but financially salable individual land shares*).

Because the use of land in various forms is guaranteed, the concern that the physical unwithdrawability of land shares would lead to the loss of land could be removed and such unwithdrawability would be acceptable to land shareholders.

Proposal 5.1 recommended a village—individual dual level of land operation, with the basic operation level at one household as the major form or at a unit including a small number of households as the minor form. Considering the lack of tradition of individual farming in CEECs and the CIS, would family operation be feasible? The answer should be yes.

* The success of household plot operation has already provided a basis, showing that members of collective land operation are not so 'lacking' in the tradition of individual farming. (For a long time in pre-reform China, policy makers and economists puzzled over the fact that while lazy and lowly-productive in collective land operation, the same peasants at the same time were very industrious and highly-productive in family plot production. This hinted at the potential ability of peasants in individual farming. Hence the reform of contracting land to households.)

* Why have household plots generally been more successful than individual farms in CEECs and the CIS? This was mainly because household plot operators are still members of the collectively operated large farms and could use the latter's facilities and services, while individual farmers could not. Thus if these members could contract/lease land units larger than the household plots from the large corporate farms, but still keep the membership and entitlement to use the latter's facilities and services, their family operation of larger land units could also be successful.

* The market economy should and could be fostered as reviewed in Chapter 2, so as the tradition of individual farming. The Japanese cooperative services and Chinese village—household dual level operation presented in Chapters 4–7 respectively are successful examples. Thus, if the large corporate farms were not dismantled in order that they could still provide facilities, services and general management to member households as the basic land operation units, individual farming could also succeed in CEECs and the CIS. (During the reform, the collectively operated large state farms in China were not disbanded. Just like villages, they contracted land to member households, and provided them with facilities, services and general management, and hence were a success, as mentioned in Chapters 6 and 7.)

Other concerns or impediments to transforming the collectively operated large farms may also be removed or alleviated. (1) The large corporate farms could and should help their individual farming member households in obtaining capital, credits, information and access to markets. (2) The individual farming member households would certainly face market risks directly, but not alone, because they could get assistance from their large mother farms. (3) Distribution of fragmented small farms for individual farming could be avoided by contracting/leasing large land units to member households in compact form. (4) In the low wage economy, before the establishment of an effective welfare system, the right or obligation for land shareholders to retain some minimum land shares would protect them from becoming newly landless. (5) In the high wage economy, land under-utilization or idling due to peasants' increasing engagement in off-farm employment could be prevented by transferring their production land for market to the fewer remaining full-time or expert farmers along the four categories of the Dual Land System and finally the Single Land System. (6) Splitting of the large corporate farms and loss of economies of scale of land owing to quitting of members could be excluded by the mechanism of financial salability but physical unwithdrawability of the individual land shares. (7) The accumulated expertise of large farm managers could be accessed since they would still exercise general management of the large corporate farms. (8) But their vested interests against deep restructuring in order to retain power would no longer pose a problem because member households would hold management autonomy in the land they possess, and the distribution of the production land for market in Category 4 of the Dual Land System and Single Land System would be via a tendering system. Their arbitrariness and corruption could be controlled since major decisions concerning the adjustment of individual land within its contractual period or change of the contract content should be agreed by 51% or two-thirds of the members or their representatives of the large corporate farm, and law suits and court settlement allowed. (9) There should be no need for members to worry about losing employment in the large farms because, as in the different categories of the Dual Land System and Single Land System, their access to self-sufficiency land, family plots and production land for market to varying extents would be guaranteed. Those members who have voluntarily given all land back to their large corporate farms and become absentees or retirees could still keep individual land shares (as well as capital shares) and enjoy annual dividends permanently. (10) It would be easier for both those who favor and resent private ownership and selling of land to accept Proposal 5.1 as a third way building on the merits but avoiding drawbacks of both collectively operated large farms and individual farms, so that a legislative and political stability could be promoted which is conducive to a macroeconomic environment favorable to agricultural and rural development.

For those farmers who have already withdrawn individual land shares from large farms and established individual farms, adopting Proposal 5.1 would be more difficult, but still possible, recalling that the Japanese owners of fragmented small farms voluntarily organized village-wide production cooperatives (joining physically withdrawable land shares) since the 1970s, just one step towards Proposal 5.1 (with physically unwithdrawable land shares), as analyzed in Chapters 4 and 5.

Adopting Proposal 5.1 would promote EU enlargement. As pointed out above, having borne a heavy burden of subsidizing farmers, the EU intends to replace market-distorting protection of prices, etc., by transitory direct income support, with the long-term aim of establishing a *'farming without subsidies'*, as announced in the 'Agenda 2000'. However, this has encountered strong protests by farmers since 1998 in order to keep their vested interests. With this old burden difficult to shed, the EU faces a new one, i.e., to render the similar protection and subsidies to farmers of the incoming members from CEECs and the CIS, which it cannot afford and has thus become a barrier in EU enlargement. If, however, Proposal 5.1 could be implemented in farms of CEECs and the CIS, then, rather than relying on the EU price protection or income subsidies, they would be able to stand on their own feet. The EU could instead give financial and other supports to help these farms to strengthen rural development. Moreover, they would succeed in preventing food overproduction which may appear at a later stage of rural development, and has never been solved even by the EU itself, through converting erodible land back to forestry, grassland, lake land and wetland, and giving surplus food produced in the normal land as transitory subsidies to the shareholders of the erodible land to foster them to gain income from non-grain agriculture and off-farm activities, as presented in Proposal 5.1. In so doing, they would steadily and finally achieve sustainable agricultural and rural development as defined by FAO and introduced in Chapter 1, i.e., 'food security, to be obtained by ensuring an appropriate and sustainable balance between self-sufficiency and self-reliance; employment and income generation in rural areas, particularly to eradicate poverty; and natural resource conservation and environmental protection'.

Bibliography

1. Abler, Ronald; Adams, John S. and Gould, Peter (1971): *Spatial Organization: The Geographer's View of the World*, Englewood Cliffs, New Jersey: Prentice Hall.
2. Abramovitz, Moses (March 1981): 'Welfare Quandaries and Productivity Concerns', *American Economic Review*, Vol. 71, No. 1: 1–17.
3. Abramovitz, Moses and David, Paul A. (May 1973): 'Reinterpreting Economic Growth: Parables and Realities', *American Economic Review*: 428–39.
4. AD (8 March 2000): 'Anhui Province Will Take the Lead in Implementing the Reform of Replacing Fees with Taxes in Rural Areas', *Anhui Daily*. (In Chinese)
5. Agarwal, S. K. (1971): *Economics of Land Consolidation in India*, New Delhi: S. Chand.
6. Agarwala, Narmal (1983): *The Development of A Dual Economy*, Calcutta: K P Bagchi.
7. Aghamian, Levon (1997): 'Country Report of National Experience in Reforms and Adjustment - Armenia', *Agricultural Reforms in the Transition Economies of Central and Eastern Europe*, Subregional Office for Central and Eastern Europe, Food and Agriculture Organization of the United Nations, Rome.
8. Ahearn, Mary C. (July 1996): 'Alternatives for Small Farm Survival: Government Policies versus the Free Market: Discussion', *Journal of Agricultural and Applied Economics*, Vol. 28, No. 1: 95–8.
9. Ahearn, Mary C.; Whittaker, Gerald W. and El-Osta, Hisham (1993): 'The Production Cost–Size Relationship: Measurement Issues and Estimates for Three Major Crops', in Hallam, Arne (ed.) *Size, Structure, and Changing Face of American Agriculture*, Boulder, Colorado: Westview Press.
10. Ahmad, Ehtisham; Dreze, Jean; Hills, John and Sen, Amartya (1991): 'Preface', in Ahmad, Ehtisham; Dreze, Jean; Hills, John and Sen, Amartya (eds.) *Social Security in Developing Countries*, Oxford: Clarendon Press.

11. Ahmed, Iftikhar and Timmons, John F. (February 1971): 'Current Land Reforms in East Pakistan', *Land Economics*, Vol. 47, No. 1: 55–64.

12. Ai, Chen (14 February 2001): 'International Observation: The West Is Implementing Which Kind of Foreign Policies towards North Korea', *China Youth Daily* [Zhong Guo Qing Nian Bao], <http://news.sohu.com/20010214/file/1515,002,100046.html> (In Chinese).

13. Alchian, A. (1974): 'Foreword' to Furubotn, E.G. and Pejovich, S. (eds.) *The Economics of Property Rights*, Cambridge, Massachusetts: Ballinger.

14. Amato, Giuliano (5 November 2000): Email, Prime Minister, Italy.

15. AMOAF - Albanian Ministry of Agriculture and Food (1996): *1996 Annual Agricultural Survey*, Service of Statistics, Tirana.

16. AMOAF - Albanian Ministry of Agriculture and Food (1997): *1997 Annual Agricultural Survey*, Service of Statistics, Tirana.

17. ANGOC - Asian NGO Coalition for Agrarian Reform and Rural Development (1997): 'Agrarian Reform in the Philippines', *Agrarian Reform, Land Settlement and Cooperatives*, Food and Agriculture Organization of the United Nations, Rome, No. 1: 96–9.

18. APET (13 October 1998): *Asian–Pacific Economic Times*.

19. APL (4 April 1989): *Administrative Procedural Law of the People's Republic of China*, <http://www.stc.sh.cn/falu/faz/faz21404.htm>. (In Chinese)

20. Arrow, K. J. (1963): 'Uncertainty and the Welfare Economics of Medical Care', *American Economic Review*, No. 53: 941–73.

21. Ash, Robert (1976): *Land Tenure in Pre-Revolutionary China: Kiangsu [Jiangsu] Province in the 1920s and 1930s*, Contemporary China Institute, School of Oriental and African Studies, University of London.

22. ASS (various issues): *Africa South of the Sahara*, London: Europa Publications.

23. Aubert, Claude (1996): 'The Chinese Rural Economy in 1995', *China Review*, Hong Kong: Chinese University Press: 315–41.

24. Aubert, Claude (Spring 1999): 'Rural Reform', *China Review*, Great Britain–China Center, Issue 12: 13–8.

25. Bai, You-Guang; Zhao, Shu-Feng and Pei, Chang-Hong (1988): 'The Form of Economies of Scale in Beijing's Agriculture', *Chinese Rural Economy*, No. 6: 41–2. (In Chinese)

26. Barker, Randolph; Herdt, Robert W. with Rose, Beth (1985): *The Rice Economy of Asia*, Washington DC: Resources for the Future.

27. Barsony, J. (1982): 'Tibor Liska's Concept of Socialist Entrepreneurship', *Acta Oeconomica*, Vol. 28, Nos. 3–4.

28. Baru, Sanjaya (1997): 'Economy - India', *Far East and Australasia*

1997, London: Europa Publications.

29. Batte, Marvin T. and Johnson, Roger (1993): 'Technology and Its Impact on American Agriculture', in Hallam, Arne (ed.) *Size, Structure, and Changing Face of American Agriculture*, Boulder, Colorado: Westview Press.

30. BCS - Bureau of the Census and Statistics (1965): 'Summary Report', *Census of the Philippines 1960: Agriculture*, Manila, the Philippines, Vol. 2.

31. BCUS - Bureau of Census, US Department of Commerce (1987): *1987 Census of Agriculture*, Washington DC.

32. Beaumond, Hans-Christian (11 June 1999): Email, Directorate-General for Agriculture (DG VI), Commission of the European Union, Brussels.

33. Beka, Ismail (28–30 October 1998): *Albania: Impacts of the Asian Crisis on Agricultural Trade and the Agricultural Financial Situation, Policy Reform and Labor Adjustment, and Agricultural Land Reform and Farmland Markets*, Emerging Market Economy Forum, Forum on Agricultural Policies in Non-Member Countries, Organization for Economic Cooperation and Development, Paris.

34. Beres, Bela (11 May 2000): Fax, Ministry of Agriculture and Regional Development, Hungary.

35. Berglof, Erik (27 May 1999): Email, Stockholm Institute of Transition Economics and East European Economies (SITE), Stockholm School of Economics.

36. Berry, R. Albert and Cline, William R. (1979): *Agrarian Structure and Productivity in Developing Countries*, Baltimore, Maryland: Johns Hopkins University Press.

37. Binns, Bernard O. (September 1950): 'General', in Binns, Bernard O. (ed.) *The Consolidation of Fragmented Agricultural Holdings*, Food and Agriculture Organization of the United Nations, Washington DC.

38. Binswanger, Hans P.; Deininger, Klaus and Feder, Gershon (1993): *Power, Distortions, Revolt, and Reform in Agricultural Land Relations*, World Bank Working Paper 1164.

39. Blarel, Benoit; Hazell, Peter; Place, Frank and Quiggin, John (1992): 'The Economics of Farm Fragmentation: Evidence from Ghana and Rwanda', *World Bank Economic Review*, Vol. 6, No. 2: 233–54.

40. Bo, Yi-Bo (June 1991): *Review of Some Important Decisions and Events*, Beijing: Publishing House of the Party School of the Central Committee of the Communist Party of China, Vol. 1. (In Chinese)

41. Bojnec, S. and Swinnen, Johan, E. M. (1997): 'Agricultural Privatization and Farm Restructuring in Slovenia', in Swinnen, Johan, E. M. (ed.) *Agricultural Privatization, Land Reform and Farm Restructuring in*

Central and Eastern Europe, Aldershot, UK: Ashgate.

42. Bollman, Ray D; Whitener, Leslie A. and Tung, Fu-Lai (1995): 'Trends and Patterns of Agricultural Structural Change: A Canada–U.S. Comparison', *Canadian Journal of Agricultural Economics*, Special Issue: 15–28.

43. Bonner, Jeffrey P. (1987): *Land Consolidation and Economic Development in India - A Study of Two Haryana Villages*, Riverdale, Maryland: Riverdale Company.

44. Boulding, Kenneth (27 March 1974): *American Agriculture News*.

45. Bowman, Mary Jean (1983): Endorsement Quote, in Schultz, Theodore W. [1964] *Transforming Traditional Agriculture*, reprinted in (1983), Chicago: University of Chicago Press.

46. Bozic, Miroslav (1997): 'Country Report of National Experience in Reforms and Adjustment - Croatia', *Agricultural Reforms in the Transition Economies of Central and Eastern Europe*, Subregional Office for Central and Eastern Europe, Food and Agriculture Organization of the United Nations, Rome.

47. Bozic, Miroslav (26–28 October 1998): *Croatia: Impacts of the Asian Crisis on Agricultural Trade and the Agricultural Financial Situation, Policy Reform and Labor Adjustment, and Agricultural Land Reform and Farmland Markets*, Emerging Market Economy Forum, Forum on Agricultural Policies in Non-Member Countries, Organization for Economic Cooperation and Development, Paris.

48. Bozic, Miroslav (28–30 April 1999): *Review of Agricultural Policy, Market and Trade in 1998 - Report from the Republic of Croatia*, Emerging Market Economy Forum, Forum on Agricultural Policies in Non-Member Countries, Organization for Economic Cooperation and Development, Paris.

49. Bray, Francesca (1986): *The Rice Economies - Technology and Development in Asian Societies*, Oxford: Basil Blackwell.

50. Brewster, David (1979): 'Historical Notes on Agricultural Structure' and 'The Family Farm: A Changing Concept', *Structure Issues of American Agriculture*, Economic Research Service, US Department of Agriculture, Washington DC, Agricultural Economics Report No. 438.

51. Brooks, N. and Kalbacher, J. (1990): 'Profiling the Diversity of America's Farms', in *Americans in Agriculture: Portraits of Diversity* (1990 Yearbook of Agriculture), US Department of Agriculture, Washington DC: 18–23.

52. Brown, T. Louise (1997): 'Economy - Nepal', *Far East and Australasia 1997*, London: Europa Publications.

53. Brown, Minnie M. and Larson, Olaf F. (1979): 'Successful Black

Farmers: Factors in Their Achievement', *Rural Sociology* 44 (1): 153–75.

54. Brown, Adell, Jr.; Christy, Ralph D. and Gebremedhin, Tesfa G. (Spring 1994): 'Structural Changes in U.S. Agriculture: Implications for African American Farmers', *Review of Black Political Economy*: 51–71.

55. Browne, W. P.; Allen, K. and Schweikhardt, D. B. (1997): 'Never Say Never Again: Why the Road to Agricultural Policy Reform Has a Long Way to Go', *Choices - the Magazine of Food, Farm, and Resources Issues*, No. 4: 4–9.

56. Buck, John Lossing [1937]: *Land Utilization in China: A Study of 16,786 Farms in 168 Localities, and 38,256 Farm Families in Twenty-Two Provinces in China, 1929–1933*, University of Nanjing, 2nd printing (1964), New York: Paragon Book Reprint Corp.

57. Byres, Terence J. (November 1995): Presentation of the Rural Situation in India, School of African and Oriental Studies, London.

58. Callender, G. S. (November 1902): 'The Early Transportation and Banking Enterprises of the States in Relation to the Growth of Corporation', *Quarterly Journal of Economics*, Vol. 17: 111–62.

59. Cao, Yin-Kang (11 August 2000): 'The Internet Is Changing the Modes of Production and Living of the Chinese Peasants', *People's Daily (overseas edition)*. (In Chinese)

60. Cao, Meng-Jiao and Liu, Zong-Xiao (1987): 'A Survey of Adopting Appropriate Scale of Management in Langfang Prefecture', *Chinese Rural Economy*, No. 1: 32–6. (In Chinese)

61. Carre, J. J.; Dubois, P. and Malinvaud, E. (1975): *French Economic Growth*, Palo Alto, California: Stanford University Press.

62. Casler, George L. (1993): 'Use of Firm-Level Agricultural Data Collected and Managed at the State Level for Studying Farm Size Issues', in Hallam, Arne (ed.) *Size, Structure, and Changing Face of American Agriculture*, Boulder, Colorado: Westview Press.

63. CCCPC - Central Committee of the Communist Party of China [31 December 1982]: 'Some Issues Concerning the Current Rural Economic Policies', issued on 2 January 1983, reprinted in Research Section of Documents of the Central Committee of CPC and Development Research Center of the State Council (eds.) (1992) *Important Documents on Agriculture and Rural Work of the New Era*, Beijing: Publishing House for Documents of the Central Committee of CPC and Central Government. (In Chinese)

64. CCCPC - Central Committee of CPC [1 January 1984]: Document No. 1 'Notification on Rural Work in 1984', reprinted in Research Section of Documents of the Central Committee of CPC and Development

Research Center of the State Council (eds.) (1992) *Important Documents on Agriculture and Rural Work of the New Era*, Beijing: Publishing House for Documents of the Central Committee of CPC and Central Government. (In Chinese)

65. CCCPC - Central Committee of CPC [1993]: Document No. 11, in Zhang, Shi-Yun (1996) 'Difficulties in the Ongoing Reform of Rural Agrarian System', *Problems of Agricultural Economy*, No. 3: 16—9. (In Chinese)

66. CCCPC - Central Committee of CPC [1994]: Document No. 6, cited in Zhang, Shi-Yun (1996) 'Difficulties in the Ongoing Reform of Rural Agrarian System', *Problems of Agricultural Economy*, No. 3: 16—9. (In Chinese)

67. CCCPC and SC - Central Committee of CPC and State Council [29 September 1984]: 'Notification on Helping the Poor Areas Change Situation Soon', reprinted in Research Section of Documents of the Central Committee of CPC and Development Research Center of the State Council (eds.) (1992) *Important Documents on Agriculture and Rural Work of the New Era*, Beijing: Publishing House for Documents of the Central Committee of CPC and Central Government. (In Chinese)

68. CCCPC and SC - Central Committee of CPC and State Council (July 2000): 'Some Opinions on Promoting the Healthy Development of Small Towns', in (5 July 2000) *Guangming Daily (electronic edition)*, <http://news.sohu.com/20000705/100164.html> (In Chinese).

69. CCJ (11 June 1996): 'Harvesters Failed in Wheat Fields When Yield Exceeded 500 kg', *China Commercial Journal* [Zhong Guo Shang Bao]. (In Chinese)

70. CED - Committee for Economic Development of the USA [1962]: *An Adaptive Program for Agriculture*, cited in Ritchie, Mark (1979): *The Loss of Our Family Farms*, San Francisco, California: Center for Rural Studies: 6—8, 15, 32.

71. CED - Committee for Economic Development of the USA [1974]: *A New U.S. Farm Policy for Changing World Needs*, cited in Ritchie, Mark (1979): *The Loss of Our Family Farms*, San Francisco, California: Center for Rural Studies: 2, 15, 32.

72. CEDIC (1980): *A Chinese—English Dictionary*, Beijing: Commercial Publishing House.

73. CEST - 'Cooperative Economy' Study Team (Research Group on 'Rural Cooperation Economy'), Ministry of Agriculture (1991): 'China's Rural Land Contract Management System and Operation of Cooperative Organizations in 1990', *Problems of Agricultural Economy*, No. 8: 33—40. (In Chinese)

74. CEST - 'Cooperative Economy' Study Team (Research Group on 'Rural Cooperation Economy'), Ministry of Agriculture (1993): 'Land Contract System in Rural China and the Functioning of Cooperative Organizations', *Problems of Agricultural Economy*, No. 11: 45–53. (In Chinese)

75. CEST - 'Cooperative Economy' Study Team (Research Group on 'Rural Cooperation Economy'), Ministry of Agriculture (1996): 'The Land Contract Management System in Rural China and Functions of Cooperatives', *Problems of Agricultural Economy*, No. 2: 38–43. (In Chinese)

76. Chandler, Alfred D. (1977): *The Invisible Hand*, Cambridge, Massachusetts: Belknap Press of Harvard University.

77. Chang, T. T.; Vegara, B. S. and Yoshida, S. (1976): *Proceedings of the Symposium on Climate and Rice*, International Rice Research Institute, Los Banos, the Philippines.

78. Chen, Dong-Qiang (1996): 'On the Centralization Mechanism of Farm Land in China', *Chinese Rural Economy*, No. 3: 23–6. (In Chinese)

79. Chen, Jian-Bo (5–7 January 2000): Presentation, Sixth European Conference on Agricultural and Rural Development in China, organized by University of Leiden, the Netherlands.

80. Chen, Rui-Hua (28 February 2000): 'Converting Cultivated Land to Forestry in Guangxi Zhuang Autonomous Region', *People's Daily (overseas edition)*. (In Chinese)

81. Chen, Yun [1978]: 'Stabilize the Part of Peasants First', reprinted in Research Section of Documents of the Central Committee of CPC and Development Research Center of the State Council (eds.) (1992) *Important Documents on Agriculture and Rural Work of the New Era*, Beijing: Publishing House for Documents of the Central Committee of CPC and Central Government. (In Chinese)

82. Chen, Wei and Zhang, Yan (21 September 2000): *The Area of the Natural Reservations Has Reached 50% of the Whole Area of Qinghai Province*, China News Agency, <http://news.sohu.com/20000921/file/021,001,100014.html> (In Chinese).

83. Chen, Yun-Ling; Cai, Ji-Suo and Jin, You-Xin (19 June 2000): 'Land Yields Gold in the Internet', *People's Daily (overseas edition)*. (In Chinese)

84. Chen, Ji-Yuan; Chen, Jia-Ji and Yang, Xun (1993): *The Social and Economic Vicissitudes in Rural Areas of China*, Taiyuan: Shanxi Economy Publishing House. (In Chinese)

85. Cheng, Shy-Hwa (1994): 'A Study of Full-Time Farm Families in Minimum Scale for Rice Crop Growing in Taiwan', *Journal of Agricultural Economics*, Vol. 56: 77–95. (In Chinese with English

Summary)

86. Chernow, Barbara A. and Vallasi, George A. (eds.) (1993): *The Columbia Encyclopedia*, 5th edition, New York: Houghton Mifflin.

87. Chisholm, Michael (1962): *Rural Settlement and Land Use: An Essay in Location*, London: Hutchinson.

88. Chui, Rong-Hui (14 February 2001): 'Six Major Causes of Land Desolation in Rural Areas of China', *China Economic Times* [Zhong Guo Jing Ji Shi Bao], <http://news.sohu.com/20010214/file/0937,003, 100028.html> (In Chinese).

89. Chung, Joseph S. (1997): 'Economy - the Democratic People's Republic of Korea', *Far East and Australasia 1997*, London: Europa Publications.

90. Chung, Joseph S. (2000): 'Economy - the Democratic People's Republic of Korea', *Far East and Australasia 2000*, London: Europa Publications.

91. C-I-A (12 July 1994): *Countries with the Most Computers Year-End 1993*, Computer Industry Almanac, <http://www.c-i-a.com/199407cc. htm>.

92. C-I-A (12 November 1997): *Top 25 Countries with the Most Computers*, Computer Industry Almanac, <http://www.c-i-a.com/19971125.htm>.

93. C-I-A (28 September 1998): *Over 300 Million Internet Users in Year 2000*, Computer Industry Almanac, <http://www.c-i-a.com/199809iu. htm>.

94. C-I-A (3 November 1998): *Nearly 600 Million Computers-in-Use in Year 2000*, Computer Industry Almanac, <http://www.c-i-a.com/19981103. htm>.

95. C-I-A (23 March 1999): *Top 15 Countries in PCs-in-Use Worldwide at Year-End 1998*, Computer Industry Almanac, <http://www.c-i-a.com/ 199903pcuse.htm>.

96. C-I-A (30 April 1999): *Over 150 Million Internet Users Worldwide at Year-End 1998*, Computer Industry Almanac, <http://www.c-i-a.com/ 199904iu.htm>.

97. CJAE (1995): *Canadian Journal of Agricultural Economics*, Special Issue.

98. Clinton, William J. (4 April 1996): *Statement by the President on the Farm Bill Signing*, <http://www.usda.gov/farmbill/state.htm>.

99. Clout, Hugh (1984): *A Rural Policy for the EEC?*, London and New York: Methuen.

100. CNA - China News Agency (30 March 2000): *The Central Government Gives Grain Subsidy for Converting 5,150,000 mu of Cultivated Land to Forests in the Western Areas*, <http://news.sohu.com/20000330/

100268.html> (In Chinese).

101. CNA - China News Agency (15 April 2000): *The Ministry of Land and Natural Resources Issues Warning to those Provinces and Municipalities Which Have Not Yet Reached a Balance between Occupied Cultivated Land and Reclaimed Wasteland*, <http://news.sohu.com/20000415/100211.html> (In Chinese).

102. CNA - China News Agency (28 January 2001): *China Will Stabilize the Grain Planting Area this Year*, <http://news.sohu.com/20010128/file/0936,001,100032.html> (In Chinese).

103. Coase, R. H. (November 1937): 'The Nature of the Firm', *Economica*, Vol. 4, No. 16: 386–405.

104. Coase, R. H. (October 1960): 'The Problem of Social Cost', *Journal of Law and Economics*, Vol. 3: 1–44.

105. Cochrane, Nancy (28–30 April 1999): *Policy Response of Central and Eastern Europe to the Global Market Shocks of 1998*, Emerging Market Economy Forum, Forum on Agricultural Policies in Non-Member Countries, Organization for Economic Cooperation and Development, Paris.

106. Cochrane, W. W. (1979): *The Development of American Agriculture: An Historical Analysis*, Minneapolis: University of Minnesota Press.

107. Constitution (20 September 1954): *Constitution of the People's Republic of China*, <http://web4.peopledaily.com.cn/item/xianfa/01.html>. (In Chinese)

108. Copeland, E. B. (1924): *Rice*, London: Macmillan.

109. CPCOSP - Changzhi Prefectural Commissioner's Office, Shanxi Province (1952): 'Achievements and Experiences of Ten Experimental Agricultural Producers' Cooperatives', *China Agriculture Journal*, No. 3. (In Chinese)

110. Csaki, Csaba and Lerman, Zvi (1997): 'Land Reform and Farm Restructuring in East Central Europe and CIS in the 1990s: Expectations and Achievements after the First Five Years', *European Review of Agricultural Economics*, No. 24: 428–52.

111. Csaki, Csaba and Lerman, Zvi (15 December 2000): *Poland Rural Factor Markets Study: Land Module*, World Bank, Washington DC, ECSSD Working Paper (Working Draft - Revised).

112. CSEE (various issues): *Central and South-Eastern Europe*, London: Europa Publications.

113. CSY [1984]: *China Statistical Yearbook 1984*, State Statistical Bureau of China, China Statistical Publishing House, cited in Nolan, Peter (1988) *The Political Economy of Collective Farms*, Cambridge, England: Polity Press: 83, 254.

114. CSY (1988): *China Statistical Yearbook 1988*, State Statistical Bureau of China, Beijing: China Statistical Publishing House.
115. CSY (1989): *China Statistical Yearbook 1989*.
116. CSY (1990): *China Statistical Yearbook 1990*.
117. CSY (1991): *China Statistical Yearbook 1991*.
118. CSY (1992): *China Statistical Yearbook 1992*.
119. CSY (1993): *China Statistical Yearbook 1993*.
120. CSY (1995): *China Statistical Yearbook 1995*.
121. CSY (1996): *China Statistical Yearbook 1996*.
122. CSY (1997): *China Statistical Yearbook 1997*.
123. CSY (1998): *China Statistical Yearbook 1998*.
124. CSY (1999): *China Statistical Yearbook 1999*.
125. CUSTA (January 1988): 'The Canadian/United States Free Trade Agreement', *International Legal Materials*, Vol. 27: 281–402.
126. CVJ (28 August 2000): 'Continuous Bumper Crops of Rice in Recent Years in Japan Have Worried the Government', *Daily Voice of China (electronic edition)* [Hua Sheng Bao Daily], <http://news.sohu.com/20000828/file/018,002,100096.html> (In Chinese).
127. CYC [1989]: *Commercial Yearbook of China 1989*, Ministry of Commerce, cited in Zhu, Ling and Jiang, Zhong-Yi (1993) 'From Brigade to Village Community: the Land Tenure System and Rural Development in China', *Cambridge Journal of Economics*, No. 17: 441–61.
128. De A. Samarasinghe, S. W. R. (1997): 'Economy - Sri Lanka', *Far East and Australasia 1997*, London: Europa Publications.
129. Debreu, G. (1959): *The Theory of Value*, New York: Wiley.
130. Demaine, Harvey (1997): 'Economy - Vietnam', *Far East and Australasia 1997*, London: Europa Publications.
131. Demaine, Harvey (2000): 'Economy - Vietnam', *Far East and Australasia 2000*, London: Europa Publications.
132. Demsetz, H. [May 1967]: 'Toward a Theory of Property Rights', *American Economic Review* 57: 347–59, reprinted in Furubotn, E.G. and Pejovich, S. (eds.) (1974) *The Economics of Property Rights*, Cambridge, Massachusetts: Ballinger.
133. Demsetz, H. (1988): *Ownership, Control, and the Firm*, Oxford: Basil Blackwell.
134. Deng, Xiao-Ping [1983]: 'All Work Should be Conducive to Constructing Socialism with China's Characteristics', reprinted in Research Section of Documents of the Central Committee of CPC and Development Research Center of the State Council (eds.) (1992) *Important Documents on Agriculture and Rural Work of the New Era*,

Beijing: Publishing House for Documents of the Central Committee of CPC and Central Government. (In Chinese)

135. Deng, Xiao-Ping [1990]: cited in Sun, Zhong-Hua and Li, Shao-Hua (1997) 'Studying Xiao-Ping Deng's Ideas on Agricultural Issues in China', *Chinese Rural Economy*, No. 3: 6–7. (In Chinese)

136. DGAA - Directorate-General of Agricultural Administration, Ministry of Agriculture (1952): 'Some Issues in the Current Development of Agricultural Producers' Cooperatives', *Journal of Chinese Agriculture*, No. 7. (In Chinese)

137. Ding, Xian-Jie; Wei, Xin; Yang, Zu-Zeng and Sang, Wen-Hua (1995): 'Optimization for Management Scale in Grain Production in Zhejiang Province', *Problems of Agricultural Economy*, No. 5: 22–7. (In Chinese)

138. Diouf, Jacques (12 September 1997): 'Speech in Meeting with the Chinese Prime Minister Peng Li (Li, Peng) in Beijing', *People's Daily (overseas edition)*. (In Chinese)

139. Dixon, Chris (1997): 'Economy - Thailand', *Far East and Australasia 1997*, London: Europa Publications.

140. Dodson, Charles B. (1994): *Profitability of Farm Businesses: A Regional, Farm Type, and Size Analysis*, Economic Research Service, US Department of Agriculture, Washington DC, SB-884.

141. Donaldson, G. F. and McInerney, J. P. (1973): 'Changing Machinery Technology and Agricultural Adjustment', *American Journal of Agricultural Economics* 55: 829–39.

142. Drabenstott, Mark (1st Quarter 1996): 'The Outlook for U.S. Agriculture: Entering a New Era', *Economic Review*, Federal Reserve Bank of Kansas City: 77–97.

143. Dreze, Jean (1990): 'Famine Prevention in India', in Dreze, Jean and Sen, Amartya (eds.) *The Political Economy of Hunger*, Oxford: Clarendon Press, Vol. 2.

144. Dreze, Jean and Sen, Amartya (1991): 'Public Action for Social Security: Foundations and Strategy', in Ahmad, Ehtisham; Dreze, Jean; Hills, John and Sen, Amartya (eds.) *Social Security in Developing Countries*, Oxford: Clarendon Press.

145. D'Souza, Gerard and Ikerd, John (July 1996): 'Small Farms and Sustainable Development: Is Small More Sustainable?', *Journal of Agricultural and Applied Economics*, Vol. 28, No. 1: 73–83.

146. Du, Deng-Bin (17 January 2001): 'The State Administration on Industry and Commerce Raised Six Measures on Strengthening Surveillance and Management of the Food Procurement Markets', *China Economic Times* [Zhong Guo Jing Ji Shi Bao], <http://news.sohu.com/20010117/file/0937,001,100023.html> (In Chinese).

147. Du, Run-Sheng (September 1985): *Rural Economic Reforms of China*, Beijing: China Social Sciences Publishing House. (In Chinese)

148. Duzinskas, Raimundas (28–30 October 1998): *Lithuania: Impacts of the Asian and Russian Crises on Agricultural Trade and the Agricultural Financial Situation, Policy Reform and Labor Adjustment, and Agricultural Land Reform and Farmland Markets*, Emerging Market Economy Forum, Forum on Agricultural Policies in Non-Member Countries, Organization for Economic Cooperation and Development, Paris.

149. EC DG VI - Commission of the European Union, Directorate General for Agriculture (March 1998a): *Agenda 2000 - Agricultural Part*, Brussels, <http://europa.eu.int/comm/dg06/ag2000/index/index_en/htm>.

150. EC DG VI - Commission of the European Union, Directorate General for Agriculture (March 1998b): *Agenda 2000 - Commission Proposals - Fact Sheets - Rural Development*, Brussels, <http://europa.eu.int/comm/dg06/ag2000/fact/rudev/index_en/htm>.

151. EC DG VI - Commission of the European Union, Directorate General for Agriculture (June 1998): *Agricultural Situation and Prospects in the Central and Eastern European Countries - Summary Report*, Brussels, <http://europa.eu.int/comm/dg06/index_en.htm>, 'Publications', 'Hypertext version', '2.3 Farm structures'.

152. Economist (24 September 1996): 'The Flourishing Business of Slavery', *Economist*: 45–6.

153. Economist (13 September 1997): 'Vietnam - Rural Descent', *Economist*: 65–6.

154. ED (6 January 1988): *Economic Daily*, cited in Li, Xiang-Zhang (1989) 'On Double Dual Structure and Agricultural Development: Transition Path of Dual Economy in China', *Chinese Rural Economy*, No. 2: 10. (In Chinese)

155. ED [5 January 1994]: Investigation at Fixed Observation Posts throughout the Country, *Economic Daily*, cited in Zhang, Shi-Yun (1996) 'Difficulties in the Ongoing Reform of Rural Agrarian System', *Problems of Agricultural Economy*, No. 3: 17. (In Chinese)

156. Edgmand, Michael; Moowaw, Ronald and Olson, Kent (eds.) (1996): 'III. Politics, Government, and the Farm Problems', 'Chapter 3', *Economics and Contemporary Issues*, 3rd edition, Fort Worth, Texas: Dryden Press, <http://www.nd.edu/~cwilber/econ504/504book/outln3c.html>.

157. Edwards, Chris (1997): 'Economy - Malaysia', *Far East and Australasia 1997*, London: Europa Publications.

158. EECIS (various issues): *Eastern Europe and the Commonwealth of Independent States*, London: Europa Publications.

159. EIN - European Internet Network (13 January 2001): *China Stands Firm on Agricultural Demands at WTO Talks*, <http://insidechina.com/news.php3?id=254291>.

160. Elder, Joseph W. (1962): 'Land Consolidation in an Indian Village: A Case Study of the Consolidation of Holdings Act in Uttar Pradesh', *Economic Development and Cultural Change*, Vol. 11, No. 1: 14–40.

161. Elvin, Mark (1973): *The Pattern of the Chinese Past*, Palo Alto, California: Stanford University Press.

162. ER (1965): *Economic Research*, No. 7. (In Chinese)

163. ERCA (various issues): *Eastern Europe, Russia and Central Asia*, London: Europa Publications.

164. ESJ (1955–56): *Economic Survey of Japan (1955–1956)*, Economic Planning Board, Japanese Government, Tokyo.

165. ESJ (1960–61): *Economic Survey of Japan (1960–1961)*, Economic Planning Agency, Japanese Government, Tokyo: Japan Times.

166. Fals-Borda, Orlando (1955): 'A Sociological Study of the Relationship between Man and the Land in the Department of Boyaca, Colombia', PhD Thesis, University of Florida.

167. Fan, Hong [year unspecified]: *The Development of the Xishan Agricultural Producers' Cooperatives*, Beijing: Sanlian Publishing House, cited in Su, Xing (October 1980): *The Socialist Transformation in Agriculture of Our Country*, Beijing: People's Publishing House: 116. (In Chinese)

168. Fan, Kun-Tian (1987): 'Development of Large-Scale Farming and Agricultural Mechanization through Mutual Promotion', *Chinese Rural Economy*, No. 2: 63. (In Chinese)

169. Fan, Xiao-Gui and Zhou, Hao-Zhi (1994): 'Some Thoughts on the Reform of the Property Rights System of the Rural Land', *Reference Materials for the Reform*, No. 8: 15–8. (In Chinese)

170. FAO (1981): *1970 World Census of Agriculture - Analysis and International Comparison of the Results*, Food and Agriculture Organization of the United Nations, Rome.

171. FAO-PY (1972): *FAO Production Yearbook 1972*, Food and Agriculture Organization of the United Nations, Rome.

172. FAO-SDE (1997): *Report on the 1990 World Census of Agriculture - International Comparison and Primary Results by Country (1986–1995)*, Food and Agriculture Organization of the United Nations, Rome, FAO Statistical Development Series 9.

173. FAO/WFP (February 1996): *Special Report: FAO/WFP Crop and Food Supply Assessment Mission to Cambodia*, Economic and Social Department Dimensions in the Internet, Food and Agriculture

Organization of the United Nations, Rome, <http://www.fao.org>, 'Economics', 'GIEWS', 'Special Reports and Alerts', '1996'.

174. FAO-YP (1991): *FAO Yearbook: Production 1991*, Food and Agriculture Organization of the United Nations, Rome.

175. FAO-YP (1993): *FAO Yearbook: Production 1993*, Food and Agriculture Organization of the United Nations, Rome.

176. FAO-YP (1996): *FAO Yearbook: Production 1996*, Food and Agriculture Organization of the United Nations, Rome.

177. FEA (1975–76): *Far East and Australasia 1975–76*, London: Europa Publications.

178. FEA (1976–77): *Far East and Australasia 1976–77*, London: Europa Publications.

179. FEA (1977–78): *Far East and Australasia 1977–78*, London: Europa Publications.

180. FEA (1979–80): *Far East and Australasia 1979–80*, London: Europa Publications.

181. FEA (1980–81): *Far East and Australasia 1980–81*, London: Europa Publications.

182. FEA (1981–82): *Far East and Australasia 1981–82*, London: Europa Publications.

183. FEA (1982–83): *Far East and Australasia 1982–83*, London: Europa Publications.

184. FEA (1986): *Far East and Australasia 1986*, London: Europa Publications.

185. FEA (1989): *Far East and Australasia 1989*, London: Europa Publications.

186. FEA (1992): *Far East and Australasia 1992*, London: Europa Publications.

187. FEA (1995): *Far East and Australasia 1995*, London: Europa Publications.

188. FEA (1997): *Far East and Australasia 1997*, London: Europa Publications.

189. FEA (various issues): *Far East and Australasia*, London: Europa Publications.

190. Feder, Gershon and Slade, Roger (1984): 'The Acquisition of Information and the Adoption of New Technology', *American Journal of Agricultural Economics*, 66: 312–20.

191. Feder, Gershon; Just, Richard E. and Zilberman, David (1985): 'Adoption of Agricultural Innovations in Developing Countries: A Survey', *Economic Development and Cultural Change*, 33: 255–98.

192. FEER (4 November 1999): 'India', *Far Eastern Economic Review*.

193. Fei, Xiao-Tong (1990): 'Agricultural Modernization and the Deepening Reform', *Problems of Agricultural Economy*, No. 2: 3—6. (In Chinese)

194. Fewsmith, J. (July—August 1985): 'Rural Reforms in China: Stage Two', *Problems of Communism*, Vol. 34, No. 4: 48—55.

195. Figes, Orlando (1996): *A People's Tragedy: the Russian Revolution 1891—1924'*, New York: Viking.

196. Floyd, Barry (December 1964): 'Terrace Agriculture in Eastern Nigeria: the Case of Maku', *The Nigerian Geographical Journal*, VII, No. 2: 91—108.

197. Franceschetti, Giorgio (6 November 2000): Email, Department of Territory and Agro-Forest Systems, University of Padua, Italy.

198. Francks, Penelope (1984): *Technology and Agricultural Development in Pre-War Japan*, New Haven, Connecticut: Yale University Press.

199. Francks, Penelope (1996): *Agricultural Adjustment and the East Asian Development Model: the Japanese Example*, University of Leeds, Leeds East Asia Paper No. 34.

200. Fre-Gov - Government of the French Republic (September 1950): 'Consolidation of Agricultural Holdings in France', in Binns, Bernard O. (ed.) *The Consolidation of Fragmented Agricultural Holdings*, Food and Agriculture Organization of the United Nations, Washington DC.

201. Friedman, Milton (14 May 1990): 'Four Steps to Reform', *National Review*, No. 42: 33—6.

202. Furubotn, E. G. and Pejovich, S. (1974): *The Economics of Property Rights*, Cambridge, Massachusetts: Ballinger.

203. G & G - Group on Land Project of the Center for Development Studies of the State Council of China and Group on Land Project of University of Hohenheim of Germany (1992): in Group on Land Project of the Center for Development Studies of the State Council (ed.) *Farmland Scale and Agricultural Development*, Haikou: Nanhai Publishing Company. (In Chinese)

204. Gainsborough, Martin (1997): 'Economy - Laos', *Far East and Australasia 1997*, London: Europa Publications.

205. Gainsborough, Martin (2000): 'Economy - Laos', *Far East and Australasia 2000*, London: Europa Publications.

206. Gao, Yi (1983): 'Responsibility Systems in Agricultural Production in 1959', *Study of the History of the Communist Party of China*, No. 1: 39—44. (In Chinese)

207. Gao, Hong and Liu, Xue-Yao (1984): 'On the Farmland Specialized Management under the Socialist Conditions', *Problems of Agricultural Economy*, No. 11: 18—21. (In Chinese)

208. Gao, Shu-Hua and Wang, Zuo-Kui (17 January 2000): '"Beidahuang"

Has Stopped Reclamation', *People's Daily (overseas edition)*. (In Chinese)

209. Gardner, B. Delworth (1995): *Plowing Ground in Washington: The Political Economy of U.S. Agriculture*, San Francisco, California: Pacific Research Institute for Public Policy.

210. GD (14 August 2000): 'Professors of the Agricultural University of Inner Mongolia Question the Increase Numbers of Livestock', *Guangming Daily (electronic edition)*, <http://news.sohu.com/20000814/100385.html> (In Chinese).

211. Gebremedhin, Tesfa G. and Christy, Ralph D. (July 1996): 'Structural Changes in U.S. Agriculture: Implications for Small Farms', *Journal of Agricultural and Applied Economics*, Vol. 28, No. 1: 57–66.

212. Geng, Yan-Ling (23 November 1952): 'The Experiences of Carrying Out Planting in Line with Local Conditions in Yu Luo-Shan Agricultural Producers' Cooperative', *Hebei Daily*. (In Chinese)

213. Gillis, Malcolm; Perkins, Dwight H.; Roemer, Michael and Snodgrass, Donald R. (1992): *Economics of Development*, 3rd edition, New York: W. W. Norton.

214. Ginsburg, N.; Brush, J. E.; McCune, S.; Philbrick, A. K.; Randall, J. R. and Weins, H. J. (1958): *The Pattern of Asia*, Englewood Cliffs, New Jersey: Prentice Hall.

215. Giordano, Mark and Raney, Terri (1993): 'Thailand', *Asia 1993*, US Department of Agriculture, Washington DC.

216. Gladwin, C. H. and Zabawa, R. (1985): 'Survival Strategies of Small Part-Time Farmers: A Response to Structural Change', in *Strategy for Survival of Small Farmers - International Implications*, Human Resources Development Center, Tuskegee Institute, Tuskegee Alabama.

217. GO - General Office of the Central Committee of the CPC (1956): *The Socialist High Tide in the Chinese Countryside*, 3 volumes, Beijing: People's Publishing House.

218. Goetz, Stephan J. and Debertin, David L. (August 1996): 'Rural Population Decline in the 1980s: Impacts of Farm Structure and Federal Farm Programs', *American Journal of Agricultural Economics*: 517–29.

219. Gong, Jing and Wang, Feng-Shan (29 August 1995): 'Peasants of Panshidian Have a New Move: Leasing 300 mu of Land to a Foreigner', *People's Daily (overseas edition)*. (In Chinese)

220. Goodwin, Barry K. and Featherstone, Allen M. (1995): 'An Empirical Analysis of Participation in US Government Farm Programmes', *Applied Economics*, No. 27: 39–50.

221. Gordillo de Anda, Gustavo (10–12 March 1997): 'The State and the Market: the Missing Link', 'International Seminar on Agriculture and

Sustainable Development in the Mediterranean', Montpellier, France, *Sustainable Development Dimensions in the Internet*, Food and Agriculture Organization of the United Nations, Rome, <http://www. fao.org>, 'Sustainable Development', 'Rural Administration and Cooperatives', 'Analysis'.

222. Gowland, D. H. and James, S. (1993): 'Economy - United Kingdom', *Western Europe 1993*, London: Europa Publications.

223. Grist, D. H. (1975): *Rice*, 5th edition, London: Longman.

224. Groppo, P.; Mekouar, M. A.; Damais, G. and Phouangphet, K. (July 1996): *Land Regularization Policy for Sustainable Agriculture in the Lao PDR*, United Nations Development Program and Food and Agriculture Organization of the United Nations, Rome.

225. GT - Group on Transfer of Rural Labor Force and Agricultural Modernization, Rural Research Center of the State Council and Research Center of the State Science Commission (1988): 'Evolution in Scale Operation of Rural Land and Some Issues Faced in Zhongshan City', *Chinese Rural Economy*, No. 12: 16–22. (In Chinese)

226. Guo, Wei (12 October 2000): 'The Target of Eliminating Poverty Will Be Basically Achieved', *People's Daily (overseas edition)*: 2. (In Chinese)

227. Haack, Barry and English, Richard (1996): 'National Land Cover Mapping by Remote Sensing', *World Development*, Vol. 24, No. 5: 845–55.

228. Halcrow, Harold G. (1984): *Agricultural Policy Analysis*, New York: McGraw-Hill.

229. Hallam, Arne (1993): 'The Importance of Size and Structure in U.S. Agriculture, in Hallam, Arne (ed.) *Size, Structure, and Changing Face of American Agriculture*, Boulder, Colorado: Westview Press.

230. Hamilton, C. (1986): *Capitalist Industrialization in South Korea*, Boulder, Colorado: Westview Press.

231. Handley, Paul (29 April 1993): 'Thai Farm Policy Faces Long-Term Choices', *Far Eastern Economic Review*: 46–8.

232. Hao, Meng-Bi and Duan, Hao-Ran (October 1984): *60 Years of the Communist Party of China*, Beijing: Publishing House of the People's Liberation Army, Vol. 2. (In Chinese)

233. Haque, T. and Montesi, L. (25 July 1997): 'Tenurial Reforms and Agricultural Development in Viet Nam', *Sustainable Development Dimensions in the Internet*, Food and Agriculture Organization of the United Nations, Rome, <http://www.fao.org>, 'Sustainable Development', 'Land Tenure', 'Land Reform 1996'.

234. Harms, Bernd (10 May 1996): 'Toward a New Cooperative System in Viet Nam', *Sustainable Development Dimensions in the Internet*, Food

and Agriculture Organization of the United Nations, Rome, <http://www.fao.org>, 'Sustainable Development', 'Rural Administration and Cooperatives', 'Analysis'.

235. Harris, Craig K. and Gilbert, Jess (1985): 'Measuring the Social Dimensions of Land Ownership and Control', in Moyer, D. David and Wunderlich, Gene (eds.) *Transfer of Land Rights*, Oak Brook, Illinois: Farm Foundation.

236. Harrison, Alan (ed.) (1982): 'Factors Influencing Ownership, Tenancy, Mobility and Use of Farmland in the Member States of the European Community', *Information on Agriculture*, Commission of the European Union, Brussels, No. 86.

237. Harrison, Joseph (1993): 'Economy - Spain', *Western Europe 1993*, London: Europa Publications.

238. Hayami, Yujiro (1988): *Japanese Agriculture under Siege*, New York: St. Martin's Press.

239. Hayami, Yujiro (1994): 'Strategies for the Reform of Land Policy Relations', in *Agricultural Policy Analysis for Transition to a Market-Oriented Economy in Vietnam*, Food and Agriculture Organization of the United Nations, Rome, FAO Economic and Social Development Paper 123.

240. Hayami, Yujiro and Yamada, Saburo (1991): *The Agricultural Development of Japan - A Century's Perspective*, Tokyo: University of Tokyo Press.

241. He, Dao-Feng et al. (1992): 'Investigation on Land Utilization and Land Institution in Wugong County', in Group on Land Project of the Center for Development Studies of the State Council (ed.) *Farmland Scale and Agricultural Development*, Haikou: Nanhai Publishing Company. (In Chinese)

242. He, Tian-Wen and Ding, Wen-Jie (8 August 2000): 'Guizhou Completely Prohibited Land Reclamation', *People's Daily (overseas edition)*. (In Chinese)

243. Heady, Earl O. (1949): 'Basic Economic and Welfare Aspects of Farm Technological Advance', *Journal of Farm Economics*, 31: 292–316.

244. Heady, Earl O. (1952): *Economics of Agricultural Production and Resource Use*, Englewood Cliffs, New Jersey: Prentice Hall.

245. Henry, Mark S. (July 1996): 'Small Farms and Sustainable Development: Is Small More Sustainable? Discussion', *Journal of Agricultural and Applied Economics*, Vol. 28, No. 1: 84–7.

246. Heston, Alan and Kumar, Dharma (1983): 'The Persistence of Land Fragmentation in Peasant Agriculture: An Analysis of South Asian Cases', *Explorations in Economic History*, Vol. 20, No. 2: 119–220.

247. Hightower, J. (1972): *Hard Tomatoes, Hard Times: The Failure of the*

Land Grant College Complex, Agri-Business Accountability Project, US Department of Agriculture, Washington DC.

248. Hijmans, Peer (11 July 1997): Laws in Laos, Email, Representative in Laos, Food and Agriculture Organization of the United Nations.

249. Hjort, Kim and Landes, Rip (1993): 'Indonesia', *Asia 1993*, US Department of Agriculture, Washington DC.

250. Hobohm, Sarwar O. H. (1997): 'Economy - Indonesia', *Far East and Australasia 1997*, London: Europa Publications.

251. Hodgkinson, Edith (1996): 'Economy - the Philippines', *Far East and Australasia 1996*, London: Europa Publications.

252. Hodgkinson, Edith (1997): 'Economy - the Philippines', *Far East and Australasia 1997*, London: Europa Publications.

253. Holland, Stuart (1976a): *Capital versus the Regions*, London: Macmillan.

254. Holland, Stuart (1976b): *The Regional Problem*, London: Macmillan.

255. Holland, Stuart (26 March 1993): *Welfare, States and Europe*, paper for the seminar 'L'Etat, le Souverain, la Finance et le Social', organized by IRIS-TS, University of Paris, Dauphine, Paris.

256. Holland, Stuart (1994): *Towards a New Bretton Woods - Alternatives for the Global Economy*, Nottingham, England: Spokesman.

257. Hornbaker, Robert H. and Denault, Steven R. (1993): 'Recent Changes in Size and Structure of Agriculture: A Survey of Selected States in the North Central Region', in Hallam, Arne (ed.) *Size, Structure, and Changing Face of American Agriculture'*, Boulder, Colorado: Westview Press.

258. Howe, Christopher (1997): 'Economy - China', *Far East and Australasia 1997*, London: Europa Publications.

259. Howe, Christopher (1998): 'Economy - China', *Far East and Australasia 1998*, London: Europa Publications.

260. Hu, Sheng (August 1991): *70 Years of the Communist Party of China*, Beijing: Publishing House of the History of the Communist Party of China. (In Chinese)

261. Hu, Xue-Lai; Yu, Qian et al. (1988): 'An Experiment on Large-Scale Farming on Self-Sufficiency Land', *Chinese Rural Economy*, No. 5: 63. (In Chinese)

262. Huang, Chieh (1967): *Farm Consolidation in Taiwan*, Taipei: Taiwan Provincial Government.

263. Huang, Qiang-Hua (1980a): 'Explanations to Questions about the First Volume of "Capital" by Marx', Political Economy Section, Political Education Department, East China Normal University. (In Chinese)

264. Huang, Qiang-Hua (1980b): Lessons on Marx's 'Capital', Political

Economy Section, Political Education Department, East China Normal University. (In Chinese)

265. Huang, Xi-Yuan (November 1986): *The Modern and Contemporary History of the Agricultural Economy of China*, Zhengzhou: Henan People's Publishing House. (In Chinese)

266. Huang, Zu-Hui; Xu, Jia; Zhang, Zhong-Gen and Ni, Ai-Juan (1996): 'Attitudes of Farmer Households to Operating Optimal Scale of Grain Field and Their Behavior in Coastal Areas and Enlightenments for Policy', *Chinese Rural Economy*, No. 6: 57–64. (In Chinese)

267. Huffman, William (March 1981): 'Black–White Human Capital Differences: Impact on Agricultural Productivity in the U.S. South', *American Economic Review*, Vol. 71, No. 1: 94–107.

268. Hurlburt, Virgil (1954): *Farm Rental Practices and Problems in the Midwest*, Iowa State University, North Central Regional Publication No. 50.

269. Hurst, Blake (July/August 1995): 'A Farmer's Plea: Trade, Not Subsidies', *American Enterprise*: 48–51.

270. Hussain, T. (1995): *Land Rights in Bangladesh*, Dhaka: University Press.

271. Hyodo, Setsuro (1956): 'Aspects of Land Consolidation in Japan', in Parsons, Kenneth H.; Penn, Raymond J. and Raup, Philip M. (eds.) *Land Tenure*, Madison: University of Wisconsin Press.

272. Ilg, Randy E. (April 1995): 'The Changing Face of Farm Employment', *Monthly Labor Review*: 3–12.

273. Ire-Gov - Government of the Republic of Ireland (September 1950): 'Relief of Rural Congestion in Ireland', in Binns, Bernard O. (ed.) *The Consolidation of Fragmented Agricultural Holdings*, Food and Agriculture Organization of the United Nations, Washington DC.

274. Ishikawa, Shigeru (1967): *Economic Development in Asian Perspective*, Tokyo: Kinokuniya Bookstore.

275. Ishikawa, Shigeru (1981): *Essays on Technology, Employment and Institutions in Economic Development: Comparative Asian Experience*, Tokyo: Kinokuniya Bookstore.

276. Janssen, Larry (1993): 'Empirical Analysis of Tenure Patterns and Farm Structure', in Hallam, Arne (ed.) *Size, Structure, and Changing Face of American Agriculture*, Boulder, Colorado: Westview Press.

277. Janssen, Larry and Johnson, Bruce B. (1989): 'Farmland Leasing and Land Tenure in South Dakota and Nebraska, NC-181 Proceedings', in Hallam, Arne (ed.) *Determinants of Farm Size and Structure*, Ames: Iowa State University.

278. JFEC (4 February 2000): 'The Replacement of Fees with Taxes Will Be Popularized in All Rural Areas Next Year', *Journal of Finance and*

Economy of China [Zhong Guo Cai Jing Bao]. (In Chinese)

279. Jia, Quan-Xin (5 July 2000): 'Conversion of Erodible Cultivated Land Back to Forestry in the Yangtze and Yellow River Valleys Has Achieved Remarkable Success', *People's Daily (overseas edition).* (In Chinese)

280. Jiang, Ji-Fen (1986): 'Scale Economy in Agricultural Management Based on the Specific Local Conditions', *Problems of Agricultural Economy*, No. 7: 22–6. (In Chinese)

281. Jiang, Ze-Min (13 March 2000): 'Strategic Adjustment Must Be Made in the Agricultural Structures and Reform and Difficulty-Relief of State Enterprises Be Well Grasped by the Whole Party with Concerted Efforts', in (14 March 2000) *People's Daily (overseas edition).* (In Chinese)

282. Jiang, Zhong-Yi et al. (1992a): 'Investigation on Land Utilization and Land Institution in Songjiang County', in Group on Land Project of the Center for Development Studies of the State Council (ed.) *Farmland Scale and Agricultural Development*, Haikou: Nanhai Publishing Company. (In Chinese)

283. Jiang, Zhong-Yi et al. (1992b): 'Investigation on Land Utilization and Land Institution in Yuyao City', in Group on Land Project of the Center for Development Studies of the State Council (ed.) *Farmland Scale and Agricultural Development*, Haikou: Nanhai Publishing Company. (In Chinese)

284. Jiang, Zhong-Yi et al. (1992c): 'Investigation on Land Utilization and Land Institution in Changshu City', in Group on Land Project of the Center for Development Studies of the State Council (ed.) *Farmland Scale and Agricultural Development*, Haikou: Nanhai Publishing Company. (In Chinese)

285. Jiang, Zhong-Yi; He, Dao-Feng and Wang, Xi-Yu et al. (1992): 'Research on the Management of Chinese Farm Scale', in Group on Land Project of the Center for Development Studies of the State Council (ed.) *Farmland Scale and Agricultural Development*, Haikou: Nanhai Publishing Company. (In Chinese)

286. JMAFF - Japanese Ministry of Agriculture, Forestry and Fisheries (1988): *Results of Investigation on the Thinking of Farm Households*, Tokyo: JMAFF. (In Japanese)

287. JMAFF (November 1992): 'The Basic Direction of New Policies for Food, Agriculture and Rural Areas', *Japan's Agricultural Review*, Tokyo: JMAFF, Vol. 21.

288. JMAFF (1994): *Rice Production Cost Survey 1994* [Kome Seisanhi Chosa], Tokyo: JMAFF. (In Japanese)

JMAFF (1995): *Statistical Appendix to the 1995 Agricultural*

White Paper [Heisei 7 Nendo Nogyo Hakusho Fuzoku Tokei Hyo], Tokyo: JMAFF. (In Japanese)

289. JMAFF (1996): *Statistical Appendix to the 1996 Agricultural White Paper* [Heisei 8 Nendo Nogyo Hakusho Fuzoku Tokei Hyo], Tokyo: JMAFF. (In Japanese)

290. JMAFF (18 April 1997): *Situation of Food, Agriculture and Rural Areas*, <http://www.maff.go.jp>, 'Basic Statistics', 'Office of the Minister'. (In Japanese)

291. JMAFF (1998): 'Production Costs for Rice (Farm Households)', *Farm Economy Survey 1998*, <http://www.maff.go.jp>, 'English', 'List of Statistics on Agriculture, Forestry and Fisheries', 'Preliminary Statistical Report on Agriculture, Forestry and Fisheries'.

292. JMAFF (a - various issues): *Census of Agriculture and Forestry* [Noringyo Census], Tokyo: JMAFF. (In Japanese)

293. JMAFF (b). 'Census of Agriculture and Forestry [Noringyo Census]', 'Agricultural Survey [Nogyo Chosa]', *Statistical Appendix to the 1986 Agricultural White Paper* [Showa 61 Nendo Nogyo Hakusho Fuzoku Tokei Hyo]: 137, Tokyo: JMAFF. (In Japanese)

294. JMAFF (c - various issues). *Rice Production Cost Survey* [Kome Seisanhi Chosa], Tokyo: JMAFF. (In Japanese)

295. JMAFF (d - various issues). *Statistics of Cultivated Land and Areas Planted in Crops* [Kochi Oyobi Sakutsuke Menseki Tokei], Tokyo: JMAFF. (In Japanese)

296. Johnson, D. Gale (1983): Endorsement Quote, in Schultz, Theodore W. [1964] *Transforming Traditional Agriculture*, reprinted in (1983), Chicago: University of Chicago Press.

297. Johnson, D. Gale (December 1996): 'Explaining U.S. Farm Policy in 1996 and Beyond: Changes in Party Control and Changing Market Conditions: Discussion', *American Journal of Agricultural Economics*: 1327–8.

298. Johnson, Bruce B.; Janssen, Larry; Lundeen, Michael and Aiken, J. David (1987): *Agricultural Land Leasing and Rental Market Characteristics: A Case Study of South Dakota and Nebraska*, Completion Report to US Department of Agriculture, Washington DC.

299. Johnston, Donald (7 November 2000): Email, Organization for Economic Cooperation and Development, Paris.

300. Jones, Hezekiah S. (Spring 1994): 'Federal Agricultural Policies: Do Black Farm Operations Benefit?', *Review of Black Political Economy*: 25–50.

301. Jones, L. and Mason, E. (1982): 'Roles of Economic Factors in Determining the Size and Structure of the Public-Enterprise Sector in Less-Developed Countries with Mixed Economies' in Jones, L. (ed.):

Public Enterprises in Less Developed Countries, New York: Cambridge University Press.

302. Jones, L. and Sakong, I. (1980): *Government, Business and Entrepreneurship in Economic Development: The Korean Case*, Cambridge, Massachusetts: Harvard University Press.

303. Jordan, B. and Tweeten, L. (1987): *Public Perceptions of Farm Problems*, Agricultural Experiment Station, Oklahoma State University, Research Report No. P-894.

304. Jorgenson, D. W. (June 1961): 'The Development of a Dual Economy', *Economic Journal*, Vol. 71, No. 282: 309–34.

305. JRG (1987): Joint Research Group on the Subject of 'the Proper Management Scale of Planting': 'A Study of the Problems in Developing the Scale of Agricultural Management (1)', *Chinese Rural Economy*, No. 1: 26–31, inside back cover. (In Chinese)

306. JSY (1977): *Japan Statistical Yearbook 1977*, Statistical Bureau of Japan, Tokyo: Japan Statistical Association.

307. JSY (1978): *Japan Statistical Yearbook 1978*.

308. JSY (1979): *Japan Statistical Yearbook 1979*.

309. JSY (1980): *Japan Statistical Yearbook 1980*.

310. JSY (1981): *Japan Statistical Yearbook 1981*.

311. JSY (1982): *Japan Statistical Yearbook 1982*.

312. JSY (1983): *Japan Statistical Yearbook 1983*.

313. JSY (1984): *Japan Statistical Yearbook 1984*.

314. JSY (1985): *Japan Statistical Yearbook 1985*.

315. JSY (1986): *Japan Statistical Yearbook 1986*.

316. JSY (1987): *Japan Statistical Yearbook 1987*.

317. JSY (1988): *Japan Statistical Yearbook 1988*.

318. JSY (1989): *Japan Statistical Yearbook 1989*.

319. JSY (1990): *Japan Statistical Yearbook 1990*.

320. JSY (1991): *Japan Statistical Yearbook 1991*.

321. JSY (1992): *Japan Statistical Yearbook 1992*.

322. JSY (1993/94): *Japan Statistical Yearbook 1993/94*.

323. JSY (1995): *Japan Statistical Yearbook 1995*.

324. JSY (1996): *Japan Statistical Yearbook 1996*.

325. JSY (1997): *Japan Statistical Yearbook 1997*.

326. JSY (1998): *Japan Statistical Yearbook 1998*.

327. JSY (1999): *Japan Statistical Yearbook 1999*.

328. JSY (2000): *Japan Statistical Yearbook 2000*.

329. Just, Richard E.; Rausser, Gordon C. and Zilberman, David (1993): *A Framework for Analyzing Specific Agricultural Policy Reform*, Department of Agricultural and Resource Economics, University of

California at Berkeley, Working Paper No. 647.

330. Kalter, Robert J. and Tauer, Loren W. (May 1987): 'Potential Economic Impacts of Agricultural Biotechnology', *American Journal of Agricultural Economics*', Vol. 69, No. 2: 420–5.

331. Kanda, Mohan (28–30 October 1998): *India: Impacts of the Asian Crisis on Agricultural Trade and the Agricultural Financial Situation, Policy Reform and Labor Adjustment, and Agricultural Land Reform and Farmland Markets*, Emerging Market Economy Forum, Forum on Agricultural Policies in Non-Member Countries, Organization for Economic Cooperation and Development, Paris.

332. Kattoulas, Velisarios (18 February 1997): 'An Army of Homeless Rises Up in Tokyo', *International Herald Tribune*: 2.

333. Kay, Ronald D. (1981): *Farm Management: Planning, Control and Implementation*', New York: McGraw-Hill.

334. Kayo, N. (ed.) (1977): *The Basic Statistics of Japanese Agriculture* [Kaitei Nihon Nogyo Kiso Tokei], revised edition, Tokyo: Norin Tokei Kyokai. (In Japanese)

335. Keeler, Murray E. and Skuras, Dimitrios G. (1990): 'Land Fragmentation and Consolidation Policies in Greek Agriculture', *Geography*, Vol./Part 75, Issue 326: 73–6.

336. Khan, Mushtaq (1997): 'Economy - Bangladesh', *Far East and Australasia 1997*, London: Europa Publications.

337. Khanal, D. R. (1995): *Land Tenure System and Agrarian Structure of Nepal*, Food and Agriculture Organization of the United Nations, Rome.

338. King, F. H. (1911): *Farmers of Forty Centuries*, Emmaus, Pennsylvania: Rodale Press.

339. Knoeber, Charles R. (January 1997): 'Explaining State Bans on Corporate Farming', *Economic Inquiry*: 151–66.

340. Knutson, Ronald D.; Penn, J. B. and Boehm, William T. (1990): *Agricultural and Food Policy*, 2nd edition, Eaglewood Cliffs, New Jersey: Prentice Hall.

541. Kodderitzsch, S. (1998): *Reforms in Albanian Agriculture: Assessing a Sector in Transition*, World Bank, Washington DC, ECSSD Sector Series Paper No. 2.

342. Kojima, Reeitsu (December 1988): 'Agricultural Organization: New Forms, New Contradictions', *China Quarterly*: 706–35.

343. Koppel, Bruce (1993): 'Land Policy Problems in East Asia: Understanding the Past and Moving toward New Choices', in Koppel, Bruce and Kim, D. Young (eds.) *Land Policy Problems in East Asia - Toward New Choices - A Comparative Study of Japan, Korea and*

Taiwan, East West Center (Honolulu, US) and Korea Research Institute for Human Settlements (Kyounggi-Do, South Korea).

344. Krause, Kenneth R. (1983): *Corporate Farming: Importance, Incentives, and State Restrictions*, Economic Research Service, US Department of Agriculture, Washington DC, Agricultural Economics Report No. 506.

345. Kristof, Nicholas D. (3 January 1996): 'Japanese Family Farm: A Way of Life in Crisis', *International Herald Tribune*: 1, 4.

346. Kung, J. (1986): 'Beyond Subsistence: The Role of Collectivization in Rural Economic Development in Post-Mao China', unpublished paper, cited in Nolan, Peter (1988) *The Political Economy of Collective Farms*, Cambridge, England: Polity Press: 147.

347. Kung, James Kai-Sing and Liu, Shou-Ying (July 1997): 'Farmers' Preferences Regarding Ownership and Land Tenure in Post-Mao China: Unexpected Evidence from Eight Counties', *China Journal*, No. 38: 33–64.

348. Kurita, Akiyoshi (1994): 'Conditions for Achieving Effective Land Use by Diversifying "Individual Farm Management Bodies": Case Studies of Large-Scale Rice-and-Wheat Cropping Farms in Saitama Prefecture', *Journal of Science of Labor*, Vol. 70, No. 11: 511–29. (In Japanese with English Summary)

349. Kusakabe, Kyoko; Wang, Yun-Xian and Kelkar, Govind (28 October 1995): 'Women and Land Rights in Cambodia', *Economic and Political Weekly*: 87–92.

350. Kuznets, Simon [1954]: 'Underdeveloped Countries and the Pre-Industrial Phase in the Advanced Countries - An Attempt at Comparison', in *Proceedings of the World Population Conference* of the United Nations, Papers Vol. 5, reprinted in Agarwala, Amar Narain; and Singh, Sampat Pal (eds.) (1958) *The Economics of Underdevelopment*, Oxford: Oxford University Press.

351. Kuznets, Simon (1960): 'Present Underdeveloped Countries and Past Growth Patterns', in Nelson, E. (ed.) *Economic Growth: Rationale, Problems, Cases*, Austin: University of Texas Press.

352. Kuznets, Simon (1966): *Modern Economic Growth: Rate, Structure, and Spread*, New Haven, Connecticut: Yale University Press.

353. Kuznets, Simon (1971): *Economic Growth of Nations*, Cambridge, Massachusetts: Belknap Press of Harvard University Press.

354. Kwiecinski, Andrzej (9 November 1999): Email, Directorate-General for Agriculture, Food and Fisheries, Organization for Economic Cooperation and Development, Paris.

355. Kwiecinski, Andrzej (9 January 2001): Email, Directorate-General for Agriculture, Food and Fisheries, Organization for Economic Cooperation and Development, Paris.

356. Kyi Win (3 September 1997): Materials on Land Utilization in Myanmar, Myanmar Delegation to the Food and Agriculture Organization of the United Nations, Rome.

357. Laffont, J. J. (1987): 'Externalities', in Eatwell, John; Milgate, Murry and Newman, Peter (eds.) *The New Palgrave - A Dictionary of Economics*, London: Macmillan.

358. Land Loss Fund (15 January 1998): <http://members.aol.com/tillery/llf.html>.

359. Lapse, Janis (20 August 1999): Fax and Email, Ministry of Agriculture, Latvia.

360. LD (27 May 1996): 'Peasants in Hougu Village of Liaoyang City Have No Land to Till', *Liaoning Daily*. (In Chinese)

361. Leach, Edmund R. (1961): *Pul Eliya: A Village in Ceylon*, Cambridge, England: Cambridge University Press.

362. Leacock, E. (1954): 'The Montagnes "Hunting Territory" and the Fur Trade', *American Anthropologist*, No. 56.

363. Lehrer, P. L. (June 1964): 'African Agriculture in Kenya: A Study of a Changing System of Subsistence Farming', *The Nigerian Geographical Journal*, Vol. 7, No. 1: 24–33.

364. Lerman, Zvi (1996a): *Land Reform and Private Farms in Armenia: 1996 Status*, Europe and Central Asia Region, Natural Resources Management Division, World Bank, Washington DC, EC4NR Agriculture Policy Note No. 8.

365. Lerman, Zvi (1996b): *Land Reform and Private Farms in Georgia: 1996 Status*, Europe and Central Asia Region, Natural Resources Management Division, World Bank, Washington DC, EC4NR Agriculture Policy Note No. 6.

366. Lerman, Zvi (January 1999): *Agriculture in ECE and CIS: From Common Heritage to Divergence*, World Bank, Washington DC.

367. Lerman, Zvi (28–30 April 1999): *Record of Land Reform in Transition Economies*, Emerging Market Economy Forum, Forum on Agricultural Policies in Non-Member Countries, Organization for Economic Cooperation and Development, Paris.

368. Lerman, Zvi (18 January 2000): Email, World Bank, Washington DC.

369. Lerman, Zvi (8 January 2001): Email, Department of Agricultural Economics and Management, Hebrew University, Israel.

370. Lerman, Zvi (9 January 2001): Email, Department of Agricultural Economics and Management, Hebrew University, Israel.

371. Lerman, Zvi; Lundell, Mark; Mirzakhanian, Astghik; Asatrian, Paruir and Kakosian, Ashot (November 1999): *Armenia's Private Agriculture: 1998 Survey of Family Farms*, EU PHARE ACE and the World Bank/ECSSD/DECRG, Working Paper Series on Micro Economic Analysis

of Rural Households and Enterprises in Transition Countries, Working Paper No. 2.

372. Levin, Carol (1993): 'Agriculture's Diverse Role in the Economies of Asia and the Pacific Rim', *Asia and Pacific Rim - Situation and Outlook Series 1993*, US Department of Agriculture, Washington DC.

373. Lewis, W. Arthur (May 1954): 'Economic Development with Unlimited Supplies of Labor', *Manchester School of Economic and Social Studies*, Vol. 22: 139–91.

374. Li, Da-Dong (13 August 1996): 'A Warm Tide of Reclamation of Waste Land Has Appeared in the Western Frontier', *People's Daily (overseas edition)*. (In Chinese)

375. Li, Ji-Ping (20 January 1956): 'Advanced Cooperatives Can Also Be Set Up Faster, More and Run Better', *People's Daily*. (In Chinese)

376. Li, Jian-Guo (15 February 2000): 'Grasp Firmly the Opportunity of Developing the Western Areas in a Vast Scale', *People's Daily*. (In Chinese)

377. Li, Wan-Dao (1988): 'What Does the Returning of Land Distribution from "Concentration" to "Equalization" Imply', *Problems of Agricultural Economy*, No. 9: 57–8. (In Chinese)

378. Li, Lin and Tang, Ning (14 September 2000): 'Entering the Western Areas', *People's Daily (overseas edition)*. (In Chinese)

379. Li, Feng; Liu, Pu-Quan and Zhang, Yun-Chang (6 April 2000): 'Sowing a Large Green Shade', *People's Daily (overseas edition)*. (In Chinese)

380. Liaison (1989): Liaison Team of Ministry of Agriculture in Shunyi County 'An Investigation on Optimal Size of Agricultural Operation in Shunyi County', *Chinese Rural Economy*, No. 6: 34–40. (In Chinese)

381. Liang, Juan (22 January 2000): 'The Ecological Environment around the Qinghai Lake Has Been Improving', *People's Daily (overseas edition)*. (In Chinese)

382. Liang, Xiao-Qin (20 March 2000): 'The Project of Converting Cultivated Land to Forests in Sichuan Province Has Progressed Smoothly', *People's Daily (overseas edition)*. (In Chinese)

383. Liang, Zhen-Hua and Wang, Yan-Ming (1988): 'A Review on the Scale of Economy in Agricultural Management', *Problems of Agricultural Economy*, No. 3: 15–8. (In Chinese)

384. Lin, Cong-Jun (1987): 'Specialization and Optimal Management Scale: Essential to Development of Rural Economy in Beijing Suburbs', *Problems of Agricultural Economy*, No. 12: 18–20. (In Chinese)

385. Lin, Zi-Li and Tao, Hai-Su (1983): 'A New Important Progress in the Renewal of Agricultural Mode of Production', *Problems of*

Agricultural Economy, No. 9: 3–8. (In Chinese)

386. Lin, William; Johnson, James and Calvin, Linda (1981): *Farm Commodity Programs, Who Participates and Who Benefits*, Economic Research Service, US Department of Agriculture, Washington DC, Agricultural Economics Report No. 474.

387. Liska, Tibor (1963): 'Critique and Construction. Theses for a Reform of the Economic Mechanism', *Kozgazdasagi Szemle*, No. 9.

388. LISVE (30 August 1999): 'Law on Individual Single Venture Enterprises of the People's Republic of China', cited in (1 September 1999) 'A New Stride Forward in the Development of Private Economy', *China Youth Daily* [Zhong Guo Qing Nian Bao]. (In Chinese)

389. Liu, Cheng-Guo (6 August 2000): 'China Will Further Adjust Its Agricultural Structures', in (7 August 2000) *People's Daily (overseas edition)*. (In Chinese)

390. Liu, Hui (25 February 2000): 'Nearly 100 000 Persons Have Left Poverty for Richness through Tourism in Hubei Province', *People's Daily (overseas edition)*. (In Chinese)

391. Liu, Wei (5 October 2000): 'Farmers in the Suburbs of Beijing Enter the Internet to Solve Problems in Cultivation', *Beijing Evening Paper*, <http://news.sohu.com/20001005/file/064,004,100146.html> (In Chinese).

392. Liu, Zong-Xiao (1987): 'Observing Conditions and Timing for the Scale Operation of Land from the Practices of a Township', *Chinese Rural Economy*, No. 6: 64. (In Chinese)

393. Liu, Yu-Qing and Hu, Liang-Zhong (1982): 'On the Production Responsibility System during the Period of Agricultural Cooperation of our Country', *Study of the History of Communist Party of China*, No. 5: 30–8, 61. (In Chinese)

394. Liu, Guang-Yu and Song, Pei-Qin (1987): 'Some Contradictions in Improving the Management Scale in the Economically Developed Regions', *Problems of Agricultural Economy*, No. 12: 26–8, 61. (In Chinese)

395. Liu, Yi-Shun and Zhou, Duo-Li (1983): 'The Issue of the "Responsibility Land" in Anhui Province in 1961', *Study of the History of the Communist Party of China*, No. 5: 35–40. (In Chinese)

396. Liu, Chan-Xing; Kong, Yu-Lan and Liu, He-Fen (3 October 1995): 'Today's New Peasants in Jiangyin County', *People's Daily (overseas edition)*. (In Chinese)

397. LLV [14 July 1993]: 'Land Law of Vietnam', reprinted in (1994) *Agricultural Policy Analysis for Transition to a Market-Oriented Economy in Vietnam*, Food and Agriculture Organization of the United

Nations, Rome, FAO Economic and Social Development Paper 123.

398. LML [25 June 1986]: 'Land Management Law of the People's Republic of China', reprinted in Land Administration of Shanghai (ed.) (July 1989) *Selected Documents on Land Management*, Vol. 2: 24–38. (In Chinese)

399. LML [29 August 1998]: 'Land Management Law of the People's Republic of China', reprinted in (March 1999) *New Laws and Regulations Monthly* offprint. (In Chinese)

400. Lockwood, B. (1987): 'Pareto Efficiency', in Eatwell, John; Milgate, Murry and Newman, Peter (eds.) *The New Palgrave - A Dictionary of Economics*, London: Macmillan.

401. Lu, Nong (1988): 'The Progressiveness of Optimizing Scale of Land Management', *Problems of Agricultural Economy*, No. 5: 42. (In Chinese)

402. Lu, Sheng (28 November 1953): 'Why is the Output of Rural Producers' Cooperatives Higher?', *People's Daily*. (In Chinese)

403. Lu, Xiu-Jun (1989): 'Intensive Operation Is a Basic Way of Agricultural Development', *Chinese Rural Economy*, No. 3: 52–8. (In Chinese)

404. Lu, Jonathan J. and Chang, Te-Tzu (1980): 'Rice in Its Temporal and Spatial Perspective', in Luh, Bor Shiun *Rice: Production and Utilization*, Westport, Connecticut: AVI Pub.

405. Lu, Gen-Ming and Li, Jia-Hao (1987): 'Two Cruxes in Land Scale Management in Economically Developed Regions and Their Solutions', *Problems of Agricultural Economy*, No. 10: 33–5. (In Chinese)

406. Lu, Yong-Jian and Zhao, Cheng (25 January 2000): 'China Has Lowered Target Output of Grain and Cotton', *People's Daily (overseas edition)*. (In Chinese)

407. Lu, Xing-He; Gao, You-Yuan and Li, Hui-Zhen (1995): 'Modern Agriculture in Xishan City Is Already in Embryonic Form', *Xin Hua Daily*, No. 16851, reprinted in (7 September 1995) *People's Daily (overseas edition)*. (In Chinese)

408. Lu, Xing-He; Li, Hui-Zhen and Zou, Jian-Feng (1996): 'Five Villages of Xishan City Have Taken the Lead in Implementing the "Single Land System"', *Xin Hua Daily*, No. 17209, reprinted in (4 September 1996) *People's Daily (overseas edition)*. (In Chinese)

409. Lundeen, Michael and Johnson, Bruce (1987): *Farmland Leasing in Nebraska*, University of Nebraska, Agricultural Economics Report No. 152.

410. Ma, Bing-Quan (1988): 'To See the New Development of the Output-Related Contract System from the Change of Land Management System', *Chinese Rural Economy*, No. 4: 46–8. (In Chinese)

411. Madden, J. Patrick (1967): *Economies of Size in Farming*, Economic Research Service, US Department of Agriculture, Washington DC, Agricultural Economics Report No. 107.

412. Mao, Ze-Dong [1926]: 'An Analysis on All Classes of the Chinese Society', reprinted in (November 1967) *Volumes 1–4 of Selected Works of Ze-Dong Mao*, pocket edition, Beijing: People's Publishing House. (In Chinese)

413. Mao, Ze-Dong [1933]: 'How to Analyze the Rural Classes', reprinted in (November 1967) *Volumes 1–4 of Selected Works of Ze-Dong Mao*, pocket edition, Beijing: People's Publishing House. (In Chinese)

414. Mao, Ze-Dong [1955]: 'On Issues of the Agricultural Cooperation', reprinted in (April 1977) *Selected Works of Ze-Dong Mao*, Beijing: People's Publishing House, Vol. 5. (In Chinese)

415. Marku, Menka (1997): 'Country Report of National Experience in Reforms and Adjustment - Albania', *Agricultural Reforms in the Transition Economies of Central and Eastern Europe*, Subregional Office for Central and Eastern Europe, Food and Agriculture Organization of the United Nations, Rome.

416. Marshall, Alfred [1887]: 'Evidence before the Gold and Silver Commission', reprinted in Keynes, J. M. (ed.) (1926) *Official Papers by Alfred Marshall*, London: Macmillan.

417. Marshall, R. and Thompson, A. (1976): *Status and Prospects of Small Farmers in the South*, Atlanta Southern Regional Council, Atlanta.

418. Marx, Karl [1887]: *Capital*, reprinted in (1977), English edition, London: Lawrence & Wishart, Vol. 1.

419. Mathijs, Erik (20 July 1999): Email, Department of Agricultural and Environmental Economics, Catholic University of Leuven, Belgium.

420. Mathijs, Erik and Swinnen, Johan, E. M. (9–11 May 1999): *Efficiency Effects of Land Reforms in East Central Europe and the Former Soviet Union*, International Seminar on Land Ownership, Land Markets and their Influence on the Efficiency of Agricultural Production in Central and Eastern Europe, organized by Institute for Agriculture in Central and Eastern Europe (IAMO) and Food and Agriculture Organization of the United Nations, Halle/Saale, Germany.

421. Matthews, R. C. et al. (1982): *British Economic Growth: 1856–1973*, Palo Alto, California: Stanford University Press.

422. McLean-Meyinsse, Patricia E. and Brown, Adell Jr. (Spring 1994): 'Survival Strategies of Successful Black Farmers', *Review of Black Political Economy*: 73–83.

423. McLean-Meyinsse, Patricia E.; Hui, Jian-Guo and Joseph, Randolph, Jr. (December 1994): 'An Empirical Analysis of Louisiana Small Farmers' Involvement in the Conservation Reserve Program', *Journal of*

Agricultural and Applied Economics, Vol. 26, No. 2: 379—85.

424. Meadows, Donella H.; Meadows, Dennis L.; Randers, Jorgen and Behrens, William W. (1974): *The Limits to Growth: A Report for the Club of Rome's Project on the Predicament of Mankind*, London: Pan Books.

425. Melmed-Sanjak, Jolyne and Lastarria-Cornhiel, Susana (1998): 'Land Access, Off-Farm Income and Capital Access in Relation to the Reduction of Rural Poverty', *Land Reform, Land Settlement and Cooperatives*, Food and Agriculture Organization of the United Nations, Rome, No. 1: 5—18.

426. MENA (various issues): *Middle East and North Africa*, London: Europa Publications.

427. Meng, Fan-Qi (1988): 'The Prospects of Agricultural Scale Economy and Choices of Land Tenure Systems in Our Country', *Chinese Rural Economy*, No. 12: 11—6. (In Chinese)

428. Menon, M. S. (1956): 'Cooperative Farming in India', in Parsons, Kenneth H.; Penn, Raymond J. and Raup, Philip M. (eds.) *Land Tenure*, Madison: University of Wisconsin Press.

429. Messier, Marcel (15 August 1997): New Landlessness in Vietnam, Email, Representative in Vietnam, Food and Agriculture Organization of the United Nations.

430. Michael, W. Don (1953): *Revolution without R*, Associated Newspapers of Ceylon, Colombo.

431. Milgrom, Paul and Roberts, John (1992): *Economics, Organization and Management*, Eaglewood Cliffs, New Jersey: Prentice Hall International.

432. Milward, Alan (1 February 2001): Presentation on Farming in Western Europe since the 1950s, Department of History and Civilization, European University Institute, Italy.

433. Mises, Ludwig von (1951): *Socialism - An Economic and Sociological Analysis*, translation by Kahane, J., Indianapolis, Indiana: Liberty Classics.

434. MLURE (5 July 1994): 'Management Law on Urban Real Estate of the People's Republic of China', reprinted in (1994) *New Laws and Regulations Monthly*, No. 9: 19—31. (In Chinese)

435. Monke, Eric; Avillez, Francisco and Ferro, Manuela (1992): 'Consolidation Policies and Small-Farm Agriculture in Northwest Portugal', *European Review of Agricultural Economics*, No. 19: 67—83.

436. Myers, Ramon H. (1996): 'Economy - China (Taiwan)', *Far East and Australasia 1996*, London: Europa Publications.

437. Myrdal, Gunnar (1957): *Economic Theory and Under-developed*

Regions, London: Gerald Duckworth.

438. Myrdal, Gunnar (1972): *Asian Drama*, Allen Lane, London: the Penguin Press.

439. NASS - National Agricultural Statistics Service, US Department of Agriculture (1998): *What is the Census of Agriculture?* Washington DC, <http://www.nass.usda.gov/census/>.

440. National Survey [31 October 1996], cited in Zou, Qing-Li (5 July 2000) 'Our Country Has for the First Time Ascertained the Land Resources', *People's Daily (overseas edition)*. (In Chinese)

441. NECD (1985): *A New English-Chinese Dictionary*, Shanghai: Shanghai Translations Publishing House.

442. Nelson, Shayne (1993): *Computer + Farmers = Better Cadastres*, Ceres 139, Food and Agriculture Organization of the United Nations, Rome, Vol. 25, No. 1: 23–5.

443. Ni, Si-Yi and Li, Nu-Er (5 November 1998): 'Guaranteeing the Democratic System by Democratic Legislation', *People's Daily (overseas edition)*. (In Chinese)

444. Nie, Chuan-Qing and Tang, Ning (6 October 2000): 'Shepherds Who Have Descended from Mountains', *People's Daily (overseas edition)*. (In Chinese)

445. NIRA - National Institute for Research Advancement, Tokyo (1995): *Study of How to Eradicate the Problem of Farmland That Is Small in Scale, Geographically Scattered, and Mixed Together in Terms of Its Ownership*, NIRA Research Report No. 950057. (In Japanese with English Summary)

446. Nishimura, Kiyohiko G. and Sasaki, Shinya (1993): 'Agricultural Land Reform and the Japanese Farm Land Market', in Koppel, Bruce and Kim, D. Young (eds.) *Land Policy Problems in East Asia - Toward New Choices -A Comparative Study of Japan, Korea and Taiwan*, East West Center (Honolulu, US) and Korea Research Institute for Human Settlements (Kyounggi-Do, South Korea).

447. Niu, Ting-Xiang and Yu, Zhen-Hai (28 October 1998): 'Peasants of Shanxi Province Say: We Have Had "Long-Term Effective Heart-Ease Pill"', *People's Daily (overseas edition)*. (In Chinese)

448. Nolan, Peter (1988): *The Political Economy of Collective Farms*, Cambridge, England: Polity Press.

449. North, Douglass C. (1990): *Institutions, Institutional Change and Economic Performance*, Cambridge, England: Cambridge University Press.

450. Numic, Refik M. (1997): 'Country Report of National Experience in Reforms and Adjustment - Bosnia and Herzegovina', *Agricultural Reforms in the Transition Economies of Central and Eastern Europe*,

Subregional Office for Central and Eastern Europe, Food and Agriculture Organization of the United Nations, Rome.

451. Nurkse, Ragnar (May 1952): 'Some International Aspects of the Problem of Economic Development', *American Economic Review*, Vol. 42, No. 2 (papers and proceedings): 571–83.

452. Nurkse, Ragnar (1953): *Problems of Capital Formation in Underdeveloped Countries*, Oxford: Basil Blackwell.

453. Nuti, Domenico Mario (1988): 'Competitive Valuation and Efficiency of Capital Investment in the Socialist Economy', *European Economic Review*, Vol. 32: 459–64.

454. Nuti, Domenico Mario (1992): 'Market Socialism: the Model That Might Have Been - But Never Was', in Aslund, Anders (ed.) *Market Socialism or the Restoration of Capitalism?*, Cambridge, England: Cambridge University Press.

455. NYT (15 October 1999): 'Another Bailout for US Farmers', *New York Times*, in *International Herald Tribune*: 3.

456. OECD (1995): *Agricultural Policy Reform and Adjustment in Japan*, Organization for Economic Cooperation and Development, Paris.

457. OECD (1998a): *Adjustment in OECD Agriculture - Reforming Farmland Policies*, Organization for Economic Cooperation and Development, Paris.

458. OECD (1998b): *Agricultural Policies in Emerging and Transition Economies - Monitoring and Evaluation 1998*, Organization for Economic Cooperation and Development, Paris.

459. OECD (1998c): *Agricultural Policy Reform and the Rural Economy in OECD Countries*, Organization for Economic Cooperation and Development, Paris.

460. OECD (1998d): *Review of Agricultural Policies - Russian Federation*, Organization for Economic Cooperation and Development, Paris.

461. OECD (1999v1): *Agricultural Policies in Emerging and Transition Economies 1999*, Organization for Economic Cooperation and Development, Paris, Vol. 1.

462. OECD (1999v2): *Agricultural Policies in Emerging and Transition Economies 1999*, Organization for Economic Cooperation and Development, Paris, Vol. 2.

463. OECD (28–30 April 1999-6): *A Review of Recent Developments in Agricultural Policies, Markets and Trade in the CEECs*, Emerging Market Economy Forum, Forum on Agricultural Policies in Non-Member Countries, Organization for Economic Cooperation and Development, Paris, CCNM/EMEF/CA(99)6.

464. OECD (28–30 April 1999-10): *The Impacts of Policy Reform on Labor*

Adjustment in Agriculture, Emerging Market Economy Forum, Forum on Agricultural Policies in Non-Member Countries, Organization for Economic Cooperation and Development, Paris, CCNM/EMEF/CA(99)10.

465. OECD (28–30 April 1999-11): *Agricultural Land Reform and the Development of Farmland Markets*, Emerging Market Economy Forum, Forum on Agricultural Policies in Non-Member Countries, Organization for Economic Cooperation and Development, Paris, CCNM/EMEF/CA(99)11.

466. OECD (13–15 November 2000): *Review of Agricultural Policies: Slovenia*, Emerging Market Economy Forum, Forum on Agricultural Policies in Non-Member Countries, Organization for Economic Cooperation and Development, Paris, CCNM/EMEF/CA(2000)21.

467. OECD (various issues): *Agricultural Policies in Emerging and Transition Economies - Monitoring and Evaluation*, Organization for Economic Cooperation and Development, Paris.

468. OED (1989): *Oxford English Dictionary*, 2nd edition, Oxford: Clarendon Press, Vol. 13.

469. Ohkawa, Kazushi and Rosovsky, Henry (1973): *Japanese Economic Growth*, Palo Alto, California: Stanford University Press.

470. Oi, Jean Chun (1989): *State and Peasant in Contemporary China*, Berkeley: University of California Press.

471. Oi, Jean Chun (September 1999): 'Two Decades of Rural Reform in China: An Overview and Assessment', *China Quarterly*: 616–28.

472. Oldenburg, Philip (1990): 'Land Consolidation as Land Reform, in India', *World Development*, Vol. 18, No. 2: 183–95.

473. Omodei Zorini, Luigi (7 February 2001): Presentation of More Efficient Use of Land versus Food Overproduction in the European Union, Department of Agricultural and Forest Economics, University of Florence, Italy.

474. Osborn, T. and Heimlich, R. (July 1994): 'Changes ahead for Conservation Reserve Program', *Agricultural Outlook*: 26–8.

475. Oshima, Harry T. (1st Semester 1971): 'Seasonality and Unemployment in Monsoon Asia', *Philippine Economic Journal*, Vol. 10, No. 1: 63–97.

476. Oshima, Harry T. (March 1984): 'The Growth of US Factor Productivity: The Significance of New Technologies in the Early Decades of the Twentieth Century', *Journal of Economic History*: 161–70.

477. Oshima, Harry T. (1987): *Economic Growth in Monsoon Asia*, Tokyo: University of Tokyo Press.

478. Oshima, Harry T. (1993): *Strategic Processes in Monsoon Asia's*

Economic Development, Baltimore, Maryland: Johns Hopkins University Press.

479. Ou, Yang and Yan, Mei (24 February 2000): 'Jiangxi Province Heavily Promotes Brands of Green Products', *People's Daily (overseas edition)*. (In Chinese)

480. Paarlberg, Robert and Orden, David (December 1996): 'Explaining U.S. Farm Policy in 1996 and Beyond: Changes in Party Control and Changing Market Conditions', *American Journal of Agricultural Economics*, 78: 1305–13.

481. Padar, Ivari (14 September 1999): Letter, Ministry of Agriculture, Estonia.

482. Pareto, Vilfredo [1927]: *Manual of Political Economy*, translation (1971), London: Macmillan.

483. PASY [1998]: *Poland Agricultural Statistical Yearbook 1998*, cited in Csaki, Csaba and Lerman, Zvi (15 December 2000) *Poland Rural Factor Markets Study: Land Module*, World Bank, Washington DC, ECSSD Working Paper (Working Draft - Revised): 1–2.

484. PCBS - Polish Central Bureau of Statistics (GUS) [1996]: *Uzytkowanie i jakosc gruntow, Powszechny Spis Rolny, str 6*, cited in Csaki, Csaba and Lerman, Zvi (15 December 2000) *Poland Rural Factor Markets Study: Land Module*, World Bank, Washington DC, ECSSD Working Paper (Working Draft - Revised): 4.

485. PD [12 May 1995]: *People's Daily*, cited in Li, Xue-Liang (1996) 'Practices and Thinking on the Reform of the Land Property Rights Systems under the Market Economy Conditions', *Problems of Agricultural Economy*, No. 6: 51. (In Chinese)

486. PD (22 October 1998): 'Kyrgyzstan Held a Referendum on Land Privatization', *People's Daily (overseas edition)*. (In Chinese)

487. PD (13 October 1999): 'Polyandry Still Exists in India', *People's Daily (overseas edition)*. (In Chinese)

488. PD (14 March 2000): 'Records of Free Talking by Deputies to the National People's Congress', *People's Daily (overseas edition)*. (In Chinese)

489. Pei, Chang-Hong et al. (1992): 'Investigation on Land Utilization and Land Institution in Shunyi County', in Group on Land Project of the Center for Development Studies of the State Council (ed.) *Farmland Scale and Agricultural Development*, Haikou: Nanhai Publishing Company. (In Chinese)

490. Peng, Jun-Xiang; Zhang, Xue-Nian and Yang, Shu-Lun (1988): 'Analysis to Present Situation and Countermeasures of Moderate Scale Management of Land', *Chinese Rural Economy*, No. 11: 16–21. (In

Chinese)
491. Penn, J. B. (1979): 'The Structure of Agriculture: An Overview of the Issue', in *Structure Issues of American Agriculture*, Agricultural Economics Report 438, Economic Research Service, US Department of Agriculture, Washington DC.

492. Perry, Janet (29 April 1999): Comments on the US part of the manuscript of this book.

493. Perry, Janet and Banker, David (23 March 1999): Comments on the US part of the manuscript of this book.

494. Peterson, R. Neal and Brooks, N. (July 1993): *The Changing Concentration of U.S. Agricultural Production during the 20th Century: 14th Annual Report to the Congress on the Status of the Family Farm*, Agricultural and Rural Economy Division, Economic Research Service, US Department of Agriculture, Washington DC, Agriculture Information Bulletin No. 671.

495. Peterson, Scott and Janssen, Larry (December 1988): *Farmland Leasing in South Dakota*, South Dakota State University, Agricultural Experiment Station B 704.

496. Petkevich, Sergei (26–8 October 1998): *Belarus: Impacts of the Asian Crisis on Agricultural Trade and the Agricultural Financial Situation, Policy Reform and Labor Adjustment, and Agricultural Land Reform and Farmland Markets*, Emerging Market Economy Forum, Forum on Agricultural Policies in Non-Member Countries, Organization for Economic Cooperation and Development, Paris.

497. Pigou, A. C. (1920): *The Economics of Welfare*, London: Macmillan.

498. Pio, Louis Albert Francois (4 November 1871): 'Om vore Landboforhold', *Socialisten*, Copenhagen: No. 17.

499. POSC - Press Office of the State Council (17 February 2000): '50 Years of Development of Human Rights in China - A White Paper', in (18 February 2000) *People's Daily (overseas edition)*: 1, 6. (In Chinese)

500. Powers, Sharon (1 April 1999): Covering Years of Census of Agriculture, Email, National Agricultural Statistics Service, US Department of Agriculture, Washington DC.

501. Preobrazhensky, Evgeny A. [1924]: *The New Economics*, translation by Pearce, B. (1965), Oxford: Clarendon Press.

502. Prosterman, Roy; Hanstad, Tim and Li, Ping (1995): 'The Reform on the Land System in China's Countryside: An On-the-Spot Report', *Chinese Rural Economy*, No. 3: 38–44. (In Chinese)

503. Prosterman, Roy; Hanstad, Tim and Li, Ping (July 1996): *Land-Scale Farming in China: An Appropriate Policy?*, Rural Development Institute, Seattle, Washington, RDI Reports on Foreign Aid and

Development No. 90.

504. Prosterman, Roy; Hanstad, Tim and Li, Ping (November 1996): 'Can China Feed Itself?' *Scientific American*: 90–6.

505. Putterman, Louis (1993): *Continuity and Change in China's Rural Development*, Oxford: Oxford University Press.

506. Qian, Wei-Zeng (1987): 'On Economy of Scale in Farming (A Case Study in South Jiangsu)', *Problems of Agricultural Economy*, No. 4: 15–8. (In Chinese)

507. Qian, Shui-Fa; Shi, Gao-Zheng and Xie, Zhi-Qiang (1996): 'An Investigation Report on the Changes in Using System of Grain Production Fields and the Effects and Problems in Huangjiabu Town, Yuyao City, Zhejiang Province', *Chinese Rural Economy*, No. 3: 27–33. (In Chinese)

508. Qin, Jing-Wu (27 July 2000): 'The Ministry of Land and Natural Resources Has Successfully Employed the Remote Sensing Technology', *People's Daily (overseas edition)*. (In Chinese)

509. Qin, Jing-Wu (17 August 2000): 'A New Business Opportunity: Invest in the Restoration of Cultivated Land of China', *People's Daily (overseas edition)*. (In Chinese)

510. Qin, De-Wen and Wang, Huai-Zhong (1995): 'Institutional Innovation as a Strong Stimulus to Agricultural Development', *Problems of Agricultural Economy*, No. 3: 42–6. (In Chinese)

511. Qiu, Wei-Lian (1987): 'Seriation of Farm Machinery: An Effective Way to Raise Food Production in South Jiangsu', *Problems of Agricultural Economy*, No. 9: 28–9. (In Chinese)

512. Qiu, Wei-Lian (1988): 'Scale Operation of Land Is Not Suitable for the Conditions of People in Southern Jiangsu Province', *Chinese Rural Economy*, No. 7: 63. (In Chinese)

513. Qu, Xian-Yun; Chen, Heng-Feng and Bao, Xue (1982): 'To See the Perspective of Bao Gan Dao Hu from the Emergence of Specialized Households', *Forum of Yangtze River and Huai River Area* [Jiang Huai Lun Tan], No. 5: 33–8, in (1982) 'Reprinted Materials of Journals' [Fu Yin Bao Kan Zi Liao] of People's University of China, No. 24: 53–8. (In Chinese)

514. Ran, Ming-Quan and Yang, Jing-Lun (1985): 'Land Desolation: Situation, Causes and Policy', *Problems of Agricultural Economy*, No. 3: 15–20. (In Chinese)

515. Ranis, Gustav and Fei, John C. H. (September 1961): 'A Theory of Economic Development', *American Economic Review*, Vol. 51: 533–65.

516. Rasmussen, Wayne D. and Stanton, B. F. (1993): 'The Structure of Agriculture on an Historical Context', in Hallam, Arne (ed.) *Size,*

Structure, and Changing Face of American Agriculture, Boulder, Colorado: Westview Press.

517. RCRD - Research Center for Rural Development of the State Council [1989]: 'A National Sample Survey on the State Compulsory Purchase System', cited in Zhu, Ling and Jiang, Zhong-Yi (1993) 'From Brigade to Village Community: the Land Tenure System and Rural Development in China', *Cambridge Journal of Economics*, No. 17: 441–61.

518. RCSC - Research Center of the State Council (1996), cited in Zhang, Shi-Yun (1996) 'Difficulties in the Ongoing Reform of Rural Agrarian System', *Problems of Agricultural Economy*, No. 3: 16–9. (In Chinese)

519. Ren, Pei-Wu [3 April 1955]: 'Xiangyin County Has Solved the Problem of Finding a Way Out for Surplus Labor Force', *Rural Areas of Hunan Province*, No. 110, in General Office of the Central Committee of the CPC (ed.) (1956) *The Socialist High Tide in the Chinese Countryside*, Beijing: People's Publishing House, Vol. 2. (In Chinese)

520. Reuters (23–24 October 1999): 'Clinton Signs Bill to Rescue Farmers', *International Herald Tribune*: 3.

521. RFSBP [7 December 1991]: 'Regulations on Fees and Services Born by Peasants' of the State Council, reprinted in (1992) *New Laws and Regulations Monthly*, No. 3: 11–7. (In Chinese)

522. RG - Research Group of Appropriate Management Scale of Farming (1987): 'A Study of Some Problems Concerning the Development of Agricultural Scale Management', *Chinese Rural Economy*, No. 2: 17–21. (In Chinese)

523. Ricardo, David [1817]: *The Principles of Political Economy and Taxation*, reprinted in (1973), London: J. M. Dent & Sons.

524. Richardson, Michael (21 March 1997): 'Poverty Marches to Forefront in Thailand', *International Herald Tribune*: 1, 12.

525. Richburg, Keith B. (20 October 1997): 'A Rare Look at North Korea Reveals Ubiquitous Signs of Collapse', *International Herald Tribune*: 4.

526. Riddell, James C. (August 1996): Information on Land Consolidation from a Mission to Slovenia, Food and Agriculture Organization of the United Nations, Rome.

527. Riddell, James C. (1–5 April 1997): 'Introduction' to the 'High-Level Technical Seminar: Private and Public Sector Cooperation in National Land Tenure Development in Eastern and Central Europe', Bertinoro, Italy, *Sustainable Development Dimensions in the Internet*, Food and Agriculture Organization of the United Nations, Rome, <http://www.fao.org>, 'Sustainable Development', 'Land Tenure', 'Forum'.

528. Riddell, James C. (22 May 2000): Email, Food and Agriculture

Organization of the United Nations, Rome.

529. Ritchie, Mark (1979): *The Loss of Our Family Farms*, San Francisco, California: Center for Rural Studies.

530. RO - Research Office of the Yueyang Prefectural Party Committee of Hunan Province (1984): 'An Exploration of the Questions Concerning the Households Specializing in Grain Production', *Problems of Agricultural Economy*, No. 1: 14–7. (In Chinese)

531. Roberts, Ivan and Andrews, Neil (June 1994): 'Perspectives on Support Programs', *Australian Commodities*, Vol. 1, No. 2: 216–33.

532. Roberts, Ivan and Doyle, Suzanne (June 1996): 'US Federal Agricultural Improvement and Reform Act of 1996', *Australian Commodities*, Vol. 3, No. 2: 210–24.

533. Roberts, Ivan; Andrews, Neil; Doyle, Suzanne; Cannan, F.; Connell, P. and Hafi, A. (1995): *US Agricultural Policies on the Eve of the 1995 Farm Bill*, Canberra, ABARE Policy Monograph No. 5.

534. Roche, Jean (1956): 'Important Aspects of Consolidation in France', in Parsons, Kenneth H.; Penn, Raymond J. and Raup, Philip M. (eds.) *Land Tenure*, Madison: University of Wisconsin Press.

535. Rogers, Everett (1983): *Diffusion of Innovations*, London: Macmillan.

536. Rothacher, Albrecht (1989): *Japan's Agro-Food Sector*, London: Macmillan.

537. RPMF [18 August 1994]: 'Regulations on the Protection of the Main Farmland' of the State Council, reprinted in (1995) *New Laws and Regulations Monthly*, No. 9: 12–5. (In Chinese)

538. RRL [21 October 1988]: 'Regulations on the Restoration of Land' of the State Council, reprinted in Land Administration of Shanghai (ed.) (July 1989) *Selected Documents on Land Management*, Vol. 2: 194–9. (In Chinese)

539. RSO - Rural Survey Office, Rural Development Research Center, State Council (1990): 'Micro Perspective on Grain Production 1984 through 1988', *Chinese Rural Economy*, No. 3: 16–24. (In Chinese)

540. RT - Research Team of Rural Economic Development and Model Comparative Study (1991): 'A Study on the Optimal Size of Agricultural Operation in the Southern Part of Jiangsu Province', *Chinese Rural Economy*, No. 1: 23–7. (In Chinese)

541. RWDAC - Rural Work Department, CPC Committee of Anguang County, Jilin Province [25 March 1955]: 'The Experience of Fixing Production Team and Exercising Contracting Work and Output in Siyi Agricultural Producers' Cooperative of Anguang County', in General Office of the Central Committee of the CPC (ed.) (1956) *The Socialist High Tide in the Chinese Countryside*, Beijing: People's Publishing House, Vol. 1. (In Chinese)

542. RWDFJ - Rural Work Department, CPC Committee of Fujian Province [1954]: Investigation to Four Elementary Cooperatives, cited in Su, Xing (October 1980): *The Socialist Transformation in Agriculture of Our Country*, Beijing: People's Publishing House. (In Chinese)

543. RWDWX - Rural Work Department, CPC Committee of Wuxi City, Jiangsu Province (1984): 'The Relative Concentration of Farmland Is the Starting Point for the Realization of Specialized Grain Production', *Problems of Agricultural Economy*, No. 9: 30–3. (In Chinese)

544. SACAC (various issues): *South America Central America and the Caribbean*, London: Europa Publications.

545. Sahi, I. D. N. (April 1964): 'Consolidation of Holdings', *Journal of the National Academy of Administration*, Vol. 9, No. 2.

546. Saito, Harumi; Fukukawa, Kazuhiko; Tada, Hiromitsu and Kajiya, Tsuyoshi (1995): 'Proposal on the New Land Consolidation Project System with Participation of Core Farmers', *Collection of Theses of the Society for Agricultural Construction* [Nogyo-doboku-gakkai-ronbunshu], translation of JSIDRE, Vol. 2, No. 175: 81–6. (In Japanese with English Summary)

547. Samuelson, Paul Anthony (1970): *Economics*, 8th edition, New York: McGraw-Hill.

548. SAUS (1920): *Statistical Abstract of the United States 1920*, Bureau of Census, US Department of Commerce, Washington DC: Government Printing Office.

549. SAUS (1939): *Statistical Abstract of the United States 1939*.

550. SAUS (1949): *Statistical Abstract of the United States 1949*.

551. SAUS (1956): *Statistical Abstract of the United States 1956*.

552. SAUS (1958): *Statistical Abstract of the United States 1958*.

553. SAUS (1962): *Statistical Abstract of the United States 1962*.

554. SAUS (1964): *Statistical Abstract of the United States 1964*.

555. SAUS (1976): *Statistical Abstract of the United States 1976*.

556. SAUS (1979): *Statistical Abstract of the United States 1979*.

557. SAUS (1981): *Statistical Abstract of the United States 1981*.

558. SAUS (1982–83): *Statistical Abstract of the United States 1982–83*.

559. SAUS (1984): *Statistical Abstract of the United States 1984*.

560. SAUS (1987): *Statistical Abstract of the United States 1987*.

561. SAUS (1989): *Statistical Abstract of the United States 1989*.

562. SAUS (1991): *Statistical Abstract of the United States 1991*.

563. SAUS (1992): *Statistical Abstract of the United States 1992*.

564. SAUS (1993): *Statistical Abstract of the United States 1993*.

565. SAUS (1994): *Statistical Abstract of the United States 1994*.

566. SAUS (1997): *Statistical Abstract of the United States 1997*.

567. SBNESDC [1999]: '1999 Statistical Bulletin for National Economy and Social Development of China', (28 February 2000) State Statistical Bureau of China, in (29 February 2000) *Daily Voice of China (electronic edition)* [Hua Sheng Bao Daily], <http://news.sohu.com/20000229/100246.html> (In Chinese).

568. SC - State Council (23 January 2000): 'Seize the Opportune Moment to Advance the Development of the Western Areas in a Vast Scale', in (24 January 2000) *People's Daily (overseas edition)*. (In Chinese)

569. Schaede, Ulrike (1994): 'Economy - Japan', *Far East and Australasia 1994*, London: Europa Publications.

570. Schaede, Ulrike (1997): 'Economy - Japan', *Far East and Australasia 1997*, London: Europa Publications.

571. Schiller, Otto (1956): 'Aspects of Land Consolidation in Germany', in Parsons, Kenneth H.; Penn, Raymond J. and Raup, Philip M. (eds.) *Land Tenure*, Madison: University of Wisconsin Press.

572. Schultz, Theodore W. [1964]: *Transforming Traditional Agriculture*, reprinted in (1983), Chicago: University of Chicago Press.

573. Schulze, Eberhard (9–11 May 1999): *Comparison of the Development of Land Markets in European Transition Countries*, International Seminar on Land Ownership, Land Markets and their Influence on the Efficiency of Agricultural Production in Central and Eastern Europe, organized by Institute for Agriculture in Central and Eastern Europe (IAMO) and Food and Agriculture Organization of the United Nations, Halle/Saale, Germany.

574. Schulze, Eberhard (29 December 1999): Email, Institute for Agriculture in Central and Eastern Europe (IAMO), Halle, Germany.

575. SCL (12 May 1994): *State Compensation Law of the People's Republic of China*, <http://www.spp.gov.cn/falv/default.htm>. (In Chinese)

576. SDD-FAO (22–24 November 1995): *Current Thinking and Activities*, paper prepared for the Oversight Panel on Sustainable Development, Sustainable Development Department, Food and Agriculture Organization of the United Nations, Rome.

577. Seckler, David and Young, Robert A. (1978): 'Economic and Policy Implications of the 160-Acre Limitation in Federal Reclamation Law', *American Journal of Agricultural Economics*, Vol. 60, No. 4: 575–88.

578. Serova, Eugenia (1998): *Agri-Food Development in the CIS in the 1990s*, manuscript for the Food and Agriculture Organization.

579. Sharma, K. L. (1986): 'General Discussion (of paper by Simons)', *Agriculture in a Turbulent World Economy*, Aldershot, Hampshire: Gower.

580. Shaw, Brian (1997): 'Economy - Bhutan', *Far East and Australasia*

1997, London: Europa Publications.

581. Shen, Shou-Ye (1987): 'Fluctuating Situation of the Specialized Grain Producers and the Land Scale', *Problems of Agricultural Economy*, No. 10: 27–30. (In Chinese)

582. Shi, Jing-Tang (1957): *Historical Materials of the Agricultural Cooperative Movements of China*, Beijing: Sanlian Publishing House, Vol. 2. (In Chinese)

583. Shi, Yu-Wen (26 August 2000): 'To Prevent Desertification of Beijing, Rong-Ji Zhu (Zhu, Rong-Ji) Ordered to Slaughter Sheep to Protect Grasses', *Taiwan Today News Network*, <http://www.ttnn.com/cna/000826/b03.html> (In Chinese).

584. Shi, Xun-Ru and Zhang, Jun-Ren (1987): 'Land Productivity as the Major Technical and Economic Indicator in Agricultural Scale Management', *Problems of Agricultural Economy*, No. 12: 21–5. (In Chinese)

585. Shi, Yong-Hong; Zhu, Zhong-Liang and Zhang, Qi-Zhi (1 August 1996) 'The Yangtze River Delta Is Striding towards Agricultural Modernization', *People's Daily (overseas edition)*. (In Chinese)

586. Shikhaliev, Ashraf A. (1997): 'Country Report of National Experience in Reforms and Adjustment - Azerbaijan', *Agricultural Reforms in the Transition Economies of Central and Eastern Europe*, Subregional Office for Central and Eastern Europe, Food and Agriculture Organization of the United Nations, Rome.

587. Shim Jae Hoon (10 October 1996): 'Darkness at Noon', *Far Eastern Economic Review*: 26–30.

588. Shitang [11 June 1955]: CPC Committee of Shitang District of Feidong County of Anhui Province: 'Surplus Labor Force Has Found a Way Out', *Communications of Rural Work* of Anhui Province, No. 58, in General Office of the Central Committee of the CPC (ed.) (1956) *The Socialist High Tide in the Chinese Countryside*, Beijing: People's Publishing House, Vol. 2. (In Chinese)

589. Shonfield, Andrew (1969): *Modern Capitalism - the Changing Balance of Public and Private Power*, Oxford: Oxford University Press.

590. Silverstein, Josef (1997): 'History - Myanmar', *Far East and Australasia 1997*, London: Europa Publications.

591. Singh, S. P. and Williamson, H. Jr. (1985): *Perspectives on the Small Farm (Small, Low-Income Farms in Tennessee)*, Cooperative Research Program, School of Agricultural and Home Economics, Tennessee State University.

592. Skovgaard, K. (September 1950): 'Consolidation of Agricultural Land in Denmark', in Binns, Bernard O. (ed.) *The Consolidation of*

Fragmented Agricultural Holdings, Food and Agriculture Organization of the United Nations, Washington DC.

593. Smith, Ralph (1997): 'History - Vietnam', *Far East and Australasia 1997*, London: Europa Publications.

594. Smith, T. Lynn (June 1959): 'Fragmentation of Agricultural Holdings in Spain', *Rural Sociology*, Vol. 24, No. 2: 140–9.

595. Smith, Thomas C. (1966): *The Agrarian Origins of Modern Japan*, New York: Atheneum.

596. Spencer, Joseph E. and Thomas, William L. (1971): *Asia, East by South*, 2nd edition, New York: Wiley.

597. SQD (5 April 1998): *San Qin Daily* [San Qin Du Shi Bao - Daily of Cities of Shaanxi Province]. (In Chinese)

598. SQD (1 February 2001): 'Our Country Will Use the Strictest Measures to Protect the Cultivated Land', *San Qin Daily* [San Qin Du Shi Bao - Daily of Cities of Shaanxi Province], <http://news.sohu.com/20010201/file/0950,001,100521.html>. (In Chinese)

599. Stanton, B. F. (1993): 'Changes in Farm Size and Structure in American Agriculture in the Twentieth Century', in Hallam, Arne (ed.) *Size, Structure, and the Changing Face of American Agriculture*, Boulder, Colorado: Westview Press.

600. Steinberg, David I. (1981): *Burma's Road toward Development*, Boulder, Colorado: Westview Press.

601. Steinberg, David I. (1987): 'Economy - Burma', *Far East and Australasia 1987*, London: Europa Publications.

602. Stevenson, Andrew (1993): 'Economy - Italy', *Western Europe 1993*, London: Europa Publications.

603. Stuart, Kimberly and Runge, C. Ford (1997): 'Agricultural Policy Reform in the United States: An Unfinished Agenda', *Australian Journal of Agricultural and Resource Economics*, 41:1: 117–36.

604. Stuart-Fox, Martin (1997): 'History - Laos', *Far East and Australasia 1997*, London: Europa Publications.

605. Suleimenov, Mekhlis (26–8 October 1998): *Kazakhstan: Impacts of the Asian Crisis on Agricultural Trade and the Agricultural Financial Situation, Policy Reform and Labor Adjustment, and Agricultural Land Reform and Farmland Markets*, Emerging Market Economy Forum, Forum on Agricultural Policies in Non-Member Countries, Organization for Economic Cooperation and Development, Paris.

606. Summary [December 1981]: 'Summary of the Meeting on Rural Work of the Whole Country', reprinted in Research Section of Documents of the Central Committee of CPC and Development Research Center of the State Council (eds.) (1992) *Important Documents on Agriculture*

and *Rural Work of the New Era*, Beijing: Publishing House for Documents of the Central Committee of CPC and Central Government. (In Chinese)

607. Summers, Laura (1997): 'History and Economy - Cambodia', *Far East and Australasia 1997*, London: Europa Publications.

608. Summers, Laura (2000): 'History and Economy - Cambodia', *Far East and Australasia 2000*, London: Europa Publications.

609. Sun, Yong-Zheng (1996): 'Appropriate Scale of Land Operation: the Way to Transfer of Agricultural Growth Pattern', *Chinese Rural Economy*, No. 10: 21–5. (In Chinese)

610. Swi-Gov - Federal Government of Switzerland (September 1950): 'Consolidation of Land in Switzerland', in Binns, Bernard O. (ed.) *The Consolidation of Fragmented Agricultural Holdings*, Food and Agriculture Organization of the United Nations, Washington DC.

611. Swinnen, Johan, E. M. (1 June 1999): Email, Directorate-General for Economic and Financial Affairs (DG II), Commission of the European Union, Brussels.

612. SY [1989]: 'Statistical Yearbook 1989', cited in Zhang, Chao-Zun (July 1991): *Economic Problems of Socialist Land of China*, Beijing: Press of People's University of China. (In Chinese)

613. SYAP (1970): *Statistical Yearbook for Asia and Pacific 1970*, Economic Commission for Asia and the Far East of the United Nations, Bangkok.

614. SYC (1984): *Statistical Yearbook of China 1984*: State Statistical Bureau of China, Beijing: China Statistical Publishing House.

615. SYC (1986): *Statistical Yearbook of China 1986*.

616. SYC [1989]: *Statistical Yearbook of China 1989*, State Statistical Bureau of China, Beijing: China Statistical Publishing House, cited in Zhu, Ling and Jiang, Zhong-Yi (1993) 'From Brigade to Village Community: the Land Tenure System and Rural Development in China', *Cambridge Journal of Economics*, No. 17: 441–61.

617. SYC (1994): *Statistical Yearbook of China 1994*.

618. Tabata, Tamotsu (1990): *Agricultural Problem Facing Japan: A Perspective from Agricultural Structure*, National Research Institute of Agricultural Economics, Ministry of Agriculture, Forestry and Fisheries.

619. Tabata, Tamotsu [year unspecified]: cited in Tsuge, Norio (13 May 1998) Email, Department of Economics, Tohoku University, Japan.

620. Taiwan Media (30 June 2000): *The 'Modern Group' of South Korea Will Actively Develop the Jingang Mountain Special Economic Zone of North Korea*, <http://news.sohu.com/20000701/100137.html> (In

Chinese).

621. Takahashi, Akira (1993): 'The Evolution of Japan's Land Policies in the East Asian Context', in Koppel, Bruce and Kim, D. Young (eds.) *Land Policy Problems in East Asia - Toward New Choices - A Comparative Study of Japan, Korea and Taiwan*, East West Center (Honolulu, US) and Korea Research Institute for Human Settlements (Kyounggi-Do, South Korea).

622. Tao, Xiao-Yong (1986): 'The Contract Management System in the Zhujiang (Pearl) River Delta', *Problems of Agricultural Economy*, No. 10: 16–8, 61. (In Chinese)

623. Taylor, David (1997): 'Economy - Pakistan', *Far East and Australasia 1997*, London: Europa Publications.

624. Taylor, Donald C. (1981): *The Economics of Malaysian Paddy Production and Irrigation*, the Agriculture Development Council, Bangkok.

625. Thamilarasan, M. (11 November 1999): Email, Department of Sociology, Bharathidasan University, India.

626. Thomas, Binu S. (8 April 1993): 'Long Days and Short Nights in India's Mud without Pay', *International Herald Tribune*.

627. Thompson, E. Jr. (1986): *Small Is Beautiful: The Importance of Small Farms in America*, American Farmland Trust, Washington DC.

628. Tran, Duc Luong (5 March 1998): 'Regional Briefing - This Week - Vietnam', *Far Eastern Economic Review*: 16.

629. Tribe, K. (1987): 'List, Friedrich', *The New Palgrave: A Dictionary of Economics*, London: Macmillan.

630. Trivedi, K. D. and Trivedi, Kamla (1973): 'Consolidation of Holdings in Uttar Pradesh', *Journal of Administration Overseas*, Vol. 12, No. 2: 179– 87.

631. TRPE (25 June 1988): 'Temporary Regulations on Private Enterprises' of the State Council, reprinted in (1988) *New Laws and Regulations Monthly*, No. 8: 10–7. (In Chinese)

632. Tsuge, Norio (17 March 1997): Materials on Japan, Department of Economics, Tohoku University, Japan.

633. Tsuge, Norio (13 May 1998): Materials on Japan, Department of Economics, Tohoku University, Japan.

634. Tsuge, Norio (28 December 1998): Materials on Japan, Department of Economics, Tohoku University, Japan.

635. Tweeten, Luther G. (1986): *Agricultural Technology - The Potential Socio–Economic Impact*, Department of Agricultural Economics, Oklahoma State University, Paper AE8680.

636. Tweeten, Luther G. (1993): 'Government Commodity Program Impacts on Farm Numbers', in Hallam, Arne (ed.) *Size, Structure, and the*

Changing Face of American Agriculture, Boulder, Colorado: Westview Press.

637. Tweeten, Luther G. (1994): 'Is It Time to Phase Out Commodity Programs?' in Tweeten, Luther (ed.) *Countdown to 1995: Perspective for a New Farm Bill*, Department of Agricultural Economics, Ohio State University, Anderson Chair Publications No. ESO 2122.

638. Tweeten, Luther G. (2nd Quarter 1995a): 'The Twelve Best Reasons for Commodity Programs: Why None Stands Scrutiny', *Choices - the Magazine of Food, Farm, and Resources Issues*: 4–7, 43–4.

639. Tweeten, Luther G. (1995b): 'The Structure of Agriculture: Implications for Soil and Water Conservation', *Journal of Soil and Water Conservation*, Vol. 50, No. 4: 347–51.

640. Tweeten, Luther G. and Amponsah, William A. (July 1996): 'Alternatives for Small Farm Survival: Government Policies versus the Free Market', *Journal of Agricultural and Applied Economics*, Vol. 28, No. 1: 88–94.

641. US Congress (March 1986): Office of Technology Assessment: *Technology, Public Policy, and the Changing Structure of American Agriculture*, Washington DC: Government Printing Office, Pub. No. OTA-F-285.

642. USDA - US Department of Agriculture [1986a]: '1986 Soybean version, Farm Costs and Return Survey', cited in Ahearn, Mary C.; Whittaker, Gerald W. and El-Osta, Hisham (1993) 'The Production Cost–Size Relationship: Measurement Issues and Estimates for Three Major Crops', in Hallam, Arne (ed.) *Size, Structure, and Changing Face of American Agriculture*, Boulder, Colorado: Westview Press.

643. USDA - US Department of Agriculture [1986b]: '1986 Wheat version, Farm Costs and Return Survey', cited in Ahearn, Mary C.; Whittaker, Gerald W. and El-Osta, Hisham (1993) 'The Production Cost–Size Relationship: Measurement Issues and Estimates for Three Major Crops', in Hallam, Arne (ed.) *Size, Structure, and Changing Face of American Agriculture*, Boulder, Colorado: Westview Press.

644. USDA - US Department of Agriculture [1987]: '1987 Corn version, Farm Costs and Return Survey', cited in Ahearn, Mary C.; Whittaker, Gerald W. and El-Osta, Hisham (1993) 'The Production Cost–Size Relationship: Measurement Issues and Estimates for Three Major Crops', in Hallam, Arne (ed.) *Size, Structure, and Changing Face of American Agriculture*, Boulder, Colorado: Westview Press.

645. USDA - US Department of Agriculture, Economic Research Service (1993): *Economic Indicators of the Farm Sector: National Financial Summary 1992*, Washington DC: Government Printing Office.

646. USDA - US Department of Agriculture, Economic Research Service

(1994): 'CRP at 36.4 Million Acres, But First Contracts Expire Soon', *RTD Updates*, Washington DC: No. 2.

647. USDA - US Department of Agriculture (1996a): *1996 Farm Bill*, Washington DC, <http://www.usda.gov/farmbill/title0.htm>.

648. USDA - US Department of Agriculture (1996b): *Federal Agricultural Improvement and Reform Act of 1996: A Description of US Farm Commodity Programs under the 1996 Farm Bill*, Briefing Booklet, Washington DC.

649. USDA - US Department of Agriculture (April 1996): '1996 FAIR Act Frames Farm Policy for 7 Years', *Agricultural Outlook Supplement*, Washington DC: 1–21.

650. USDA - US Department of Agriculture, National Commission on Small Farms (January 1998): *A Time to Act*, Washington DC, <http://www.reeusda.gov/agsys/smallfarm/report.htm>.

651. USDA - US Department of Agriculture, Office of Communications (8 September 2000): *New Report Shows Improvement in Hunger, But Challenges Remain*, News Release, Release No. 0301.00, Washington DC, <http://www.usda.gov/news/releases/2000/09/0301.htm>.

652. USGAO - US General Accounting Office (1994): *Rural Development: Patchwork of Federal Program Needs to Be Reappraised*, Washington DC, GAO/RECD-94-165.

653. Van Eldijk, Abraham (4 January 2000): Introduction of the New Landlessness and Land Concentration in CEECs and the CIS, Wageningen Agricultural University, the Netherlands.

654. Van Rossem, Jan M. (1956): 'Aspects of Consolidation Work in the Netherlands', in Parsons, Kenneth H.; Penn, Raymond J. and Raup, Philip M. (eds.) *Land Tenure*, Madison: University of Wisconsin Press.

655. Vande Kamp, Philip and Runge, C. Ford (December 1994): 'Trends and Developments in United States Agricultural Policy: 1993–1995', *Review of Marketing and Agricultural Economics*, Vol. 62, No. 3: 317–35.

656. Vander Meer, Paul (1982): *Farm Plot Dispersal, Luliao Village, Taiwan, 1967*, Taipei: Chinese Materials Center.

657. Vander Meer, Canute and Vander Meer, Paul (November 1968): 'Land Property Data on Taiwan', *Journal of Asian Studies*, Vol. 28, No. 1: 144–50.

658. Vanderpol, Philine R. (1956): 'Reallocation of Land in the Netherlands', in Parsons, Kenneth H.; Penn, Raymond J. and Raup, Philip M. (eds.) *Land Tenure*, Madison: University of Wisconsin Press.

659. Varian, Hal R. (1987): *Intermediate Microeconomics - A Modern Approach*, New York: W. W. Norton.

660. Varian, Hal R. (1992): *Microeconomic Analysis*, 3rd edition, New York:

W. W. Norton.

661. Vokes, Richard (1997): 'Economy - Myanmar', *Far East and Australasia 1997*, London: Europa Publications.

662. Vokes, Richard (2000): 'Economy - Myanmar', *Far East and Australasia 2000*, London: Europa Publications.

663. Wade, Robert (1990): *Governing the Market - Economic Theory and the Role of Government in East Asian Industrialization*, Princeton, New Jersey: Princeton University Press.

664. Walker, Kenneth R. (1966): 'Collectivization in Retrospect: The "Socialist High Tide" of Autumn 1955 — Spring 1956', *China Quarterly*, Vol. 26: 1–43.

665. Wallis, John J. and North, Douglass C. (1986): 'Measuring the Transaction Sector in the American Economy, 1870–1970', in Engerman, S. L. and Gallman, R. E. (eds.) *Long-Term Factors in American Economic Growth*, Chicago: University of Chicago Press.

666. Wan, Li [1982]: 'Further Develop the Already Started New Situation in Agriculture', reprinted in Research Section of Documents of the Central Committee of CPC and Development Research Center of the State Council (eds.) (1992) *Important Documents on Agriculture and Rural Work of the New Era*, Beijing: Publishing House for Documents of the Central Committee of CPC and Central Government. (In Chinese)

667. Wang, Chun-Zheng (14 June 1999): 'Perfectizing Policy Measures and Continuing to Deepen Reforms', *Xin Hua Daily Telegraph* [Xin Hua Mei Ri Dian Xun]. (In Chinese)

668. Wang, Gui-Chen (1989): 'Speech in the Seminar on Optimal Operation Size of Agriculture', *Chinese Rural Economy*, No. 4: 16. (In Chinese)

669. Wang, Jing (8 August 2000): 'Over Three Million Poor Peasants in China Have Benefited from the Minimum Living Standard Guarantee System', *People's Daily (overseas edition)*. (In Chinese)

670. Wang, Shi-Yuan (26 November 1999): 'Our Country Has for the First Time Applied Satellite Remote Sensing to Monitor the Dynamic Change in Land Use ', *Journal of Land and Natural Resources*. (In Chinese)

671. Wang, Song-Pei (1989): 'Necessity of Transformation from Resource Exploitative Agriculture to Resource Conservative Agriculture', *Chinese Rural Economy*, No. 4: 32–6. (In Chinese)

672. Wang, Wei-Jia (1987): 'Multiple Forms in the Operation of Agricultural Machinery', *Chinese Rural Economy*, No. 6: 35. (In Chinese)

673. Wang, Xue-Xi (1995): 'Seven-Year Experiments in Reforming the Land System in Shaanxi Province', *Problems of Agricultural Economy*, No. 7: 22– 6. (In Chinese)

674. Wang, Yun-Feng (4 December 1996): 'Large and Medium Enterprises of Guangdong Province "Stretch Legs into Fields"', *People's Daily (overseas edition).* (In Chinese)

675. Wang, Zhi-Bao (15 February 2000): 'China's Forestry Has Been Continuously Increasing in Contrast to the Downsizing Trend of the Forest Resources of the Whole World', *People's Daily (overseas edition).* (In Chinese)

676. Wang, Xi-Yu and Ma, Su-Yuan (1990): 'Ponderation upon the Problems of Land System Construction', *Problems of Agricultural Economy*, No. 2: 33–7. (In Chinese)

677. Wang, Lai-Xi and Wang, Jian-Hua (24 December 1998): '"Handing Farm" Creating Miracles', *People's Daily (overseas edition).* (In Chinese)

678. WE (1993): *Western Europe 1993*, London: Europa Publications.

679. Weitzman, Martin L. and Xu, Cheng-Gang (1993): *Chinese Township and Village Enterprises as Vaguely Defined Cooperatives*, Center for Economic Performance, London School of Economics and Political Science, Discussion Paper 601.

680. West, G. G. (July 1979): 'Agricultural Economics Research and Extension Needs of Small-Scale, Limited-Resource Farmers', *American Journal of Agricultural Economics*, Vol. 61, No. 1: 49–56.

681. Wickizer, V. D. and Bennett, M. K. (1941): *The Rice Economy of Monsoon Asia*, Food Research Institute, Palo Alto, California: Stanford University.

682. Willams, Allan M. (1993): 'Economy - Portugal', *Western Europe 1993*, London: Europa Publications.

683. Wilson, T. B. (1958): 'Part I: Land Tenure, Rents, Land Use and Fragmentation', *The Economics of Padi Production in North Malaya*, Department of Agriculture, Kuala Lumpur, Bulletin No. 103.

684. World Bank (1976): *The Philippines, Priorities and Prospect for Development*, World Bank, Washington DC.

685. World Bank (1993): *The East Asian Miracle - Economic Growth and Public Policy*, Oxford: Oxford University Press.

686. World Bank (February 1996): *Staff Appraisal Report: Republic of Croatia, Farm Support Services Project*, World Bank, Washington DC, Report No. 14398-HR.

687. WTO - World Trade Organization (18 December 2000): *Agriculture: Explanation - Domestic support*, <http://www.wto.org/english/tratop_e/agric_e/ag_intro03_domestic.htm>, and *Agriculture Negotiations: Backgrounder - Domestic support*, <http://www.wto.org/english/tratop_e/agric_e/negs_bkgrnd05_domestic_e.htm>.

688. Wu, Wei-Han (1989): 'On Validity of Household Contract System', *Chinese Rural Economy*, No. 1: 20–6. (In Chinese)

689. Wu, Cheng-Liang and Hu, Guang-Ming (1995): 'Practice of Land Optimum Scale Operation in Leqing County, Zhejiang Province', *Chinese Rural Economy*, No. 6: 41–4. (In Chinese)

690. Wu, Cheng-Liang; Yu, Xue-Ping and Zhu, Qi-Ren (1996): 'The Only Way of Agricultural Modernization', *Problems of Agricultural Economy*, No. 7: 14–5. (In Chinese)

691. Wu, Yu-Ming; Xu, Ting-Zhu; Tian, Wei and Bai, Guo-Ping (1988): 'Competing for Contracted Land Plots: A Survey', *Problems of Agricultural Economy*, No. 5: 36–9. (In Chinese)

692. Wunderlich, Gene (12 January 1999): Comments on the US part of the manuscript of this book.

693. Wunderlich, Gene (2 April 1999): Farm Definitions in Census of Agriculture, Email.

694. Wunderlich, Gene (2000): 'Two on Jefferson', in Thompson, Paul and Hilde (eds.) *Agrarianism and Pragmatism in America*, Nashville, Tennessee: Vanderbilt University Press.

695. XHD (29 May 1998): *Xin Hua Daily*. (In Chinese)

696. XHNA - Xin Hua News Agency (11 June 1998): 'China Promulgates and Implements the Regulations on Procurement of Grain', in (12 June 1998) *People's Daily (overseas edition)*. (In Chinese)

697. XHNA - Xin Hua News Agency (13 January 2000): 'China Has Effectively Protected Wild Animals and Plants', in (14 January 2000) *People's Daily (overseas edition)*. (In Chinese)

698. XHNA - Xin Hua News Agency (28 May 2000): 'Further Implement and Perfectize the Reform of the Grain Circulation System and Accelerate the Strategic Adjustment of the Structures of Agriculture and Food Production', in (29 May 2000) *People's Daily (overseas edition)*. (In Chinese)

699. XHNA - Xin Hua News Agency (1 June 2000): 'Ze-Min Jiang (Jiang, Ze-Min) and Jong Il Kim (Kim, Jong Il) Held Meetings', in (2 June 2000) *People's Daily (overseas edition)*. (In Chinese)

700. XHNA - Xin Hua News Agency (5 September 2000): 'Georgia Is Facing the Threat of Famine', <http://news.sohu.com/20000905/file/724,002,100138.html> (In Chinese).

701. Xiang, Zhen-Hua (9 April 1999): 'Going well, Private Economy', *People's Daily (overseas edition)*. (In Chinese)

702. Xie, Guo-Ji and Gao, Shu-Hua (3 December 1998): 'A Historic Stride 20 Years Later', *People's Daily (overseas edition)*: 1, 4. (In Chinese)

703. Xin, Si and Zhao, Xiangru (25 June 1996): '"Feeding Back' Agriculture by Enterprises Has Become a Style in Shaoxing County', *People's*

Daily (overseas edition). (In Chinese)

704. Xu, He (November 1973): *Introduction to Political Economy*, Beijing: People's Publishing House. (In Chinese)

705. Xu, Hui (7 July 1998): in Huang, Zhi-Hao and Zhu, Man-Ting (26 August 1998) 'A Chinese Star Shining in Peru - Interview with Victor Hui Xu, Chairman of Foreign Affairs Committee of the Peruvian Congress', *People's Daily (overseas edition)*: 1, 5. (In Chinese)

706. Yang, Wen-Bo (1995): 'Stabilizing and Perfectizing Contractual Land Relationship is a Realistic Choice for Solving Agricultural Problems', *Problems of Agricultural Economy*, No. 7: 43–4. (In Chinese)

707. Yang, Yong-Zhe (1995): 'The Actual Conditions and Enhancement of Management Efficiency as the Keys to an Enlarged Management Scale', *Problems of Agricultural Economy*, No. 5: 15–8. (In Chinese)

708. Yang, Zuo-Hua (1995): 'Deliberation on Further Establishing Peasants' Position as the Main Land Users', *Problems of Agricultural Economy*, No. 2: 48–50. (In Chinese)

709. Yang, Xun and Liu, Jia-Rui (1987): *The Road of Rural Reform in China*, Beijing: Press of University of Beijing. (In Chinese)

710. Yannopoulos, G. N. (1993): 'Economy - Greece', *Western Europe 1993*, London: Europa Publications.

711. Yao, Shi-An et al. (19 March 1952): 'The Agricultural Producers' Cooperative under the Leadership of Chang-Suo Geng (Geng, Chang-Suo', *People's Daily*. (In Chinese)

712. Ye, Yu-Fang and Liu, Run-Sheng (30 January 1956): 'The Change of Gushan Advanced Agricultural Producers' Cooperative from Semi-Socialism to Complete Socialism', *Fujian Daily*. (In Chinese)

713. YLS (1963): *Yearbook of Labor Statistics 1963*, International Labor Office, Geneva.

714. YLS (1978): *Yearbook of Labor Statistics 1978*, International Labor Office, Geneva.

715. Ytterborn, G. R. (1956): 'Consolidation of Holdings in Sweden', in Parsons, Kenneth H.; Penn, Raymond J. and Raup, Philip M. (eds.) *Land Tenure*, Madison: University of Wisconsin Press.

716. Zaheer, M. (September 1975): 'Measures of Land Reform: Consolidation of Holdings in India', *Behavioural Sciences and Community Development*, Vol. 9, No. 2: 87–121.

717. Zeddies, Jurgen (1992): 'Increasing Potentiality of Chinese Agriculture at Current Input Level', in Group on Land Project of the Center for Development Studies of the State Council (ed.) *Farmland Scale and Agricultural Development*, Haikou: Nanhai Publishing Company. (In Chinese)

718. Zepp, Glenn; Plummer, Charles and McLaughlin, Barbara (1995):

'Potatoes: A Comparison of Canada–U.S. Structure', *Canadian Journal of Agricultural Economics*, Special Issue: 165–76.

719. Zhai, Wei (5 October 2000): *Throughout the Country 6.17 Million Urban and Rural Residents Have Received a Minimum Living Standard Guarantee Payment*, Xin Hua News Agency, <http://news.sohu.com/20001005/file/724,001,100078.html> (In Chinese).

720. Zhang, Chao-Zun (July 1991): *Economic Problems of Socialist Land of China*, Beijing: Press of People's University of China. (In Chinese)

721. Zhang, Heather Xiao-Quan (5–7 January 2000): Presentation, Sixth European Conference on Agricultural and Rural Development in China, organized by University of Leiden, the Netherlands.

722. Zhang, Shi-Rong [20 October 1955]: 'Standing-Up Cooperative Stood Up within One Year', *Communications of Rural Work* of Anhui Province, No. 68, in General Office of the Central Committee of the CPC (ed.) (1956) *The Socialist High Tide in the Chinese Countryside*, Beijing: People's Publishing House, Vol. 2. (In Chinese)

723. Zhang, Shi-Yun (1996): 'Difficulties in the Ongoing Reform of Rural Agrarian System', *Problems of Agricultural Economy*, No. 3: 16–9. (In Chinese)

724. Zhang, Rong-Hua and Hou, Jiang-Hong (1995): 'For Another Set of Land Contract Policy', *Problems of Agricultural Economy*, No. 4: 23–7. (In Chinese)

725. Zhang, Ren-Yuan and Xing, Ming-Bao (1985): 'Optimum Size: the Key to Success for the Big Grain Producers', *Problems of Agricultural Economy*, No. 7: 53–5. (In Chinese)

726. Zhang, Qi-Hua; Liu, Chang-Jiang and Zhang, Ba-Xing (1989): 'Introducing a Regulatory Act on Income Distribution to Stabilize the Land Contract System', *Problems of Agricultural Economy*, No. 4: 34–6. (In Chinese)

727. Zhang, Yun-Qian; Wang, Xi-Yu and Guo, Yong-Li (1987): 'On Optimal Management Scale in Agricultural Production', *Problems of Agricultural Economy*, No. 12: 15–7. (In Chinese)

728. Zhang, Qi-Zhi; Zhu, Zhong-Liang and Shi, Yong-Hong (12 June 1996): 'Foreign Businessmen Hold Good Prospects for Agriculture in the Yangtze River Delta', *People's Daily (overseas edition)*. (In Chinese)

729. Zhao, Cheng (27 May 2000): 'The Adjustment of the Agricultural Structures in All Parts of the Country Has Made a Big Stride', *People's Daily (overseas edition)*. (In Chinese)

730. Zhao, Cheng (14 June 2000): 'The Forest Resources of Our Country Have Been Found Out', *Liberation Daily*, <http://news.sohu.com/20000614/100074.html> (In Chinese).

731. Zhao, Fang-Chun (17 November 1955): 'Seeing from the Investigation

in Three Villages the Necessity of Actively Developing the Movement of Agricultural Cooperation Currently', *Jilin Daily*. (In Chinese)

732. Zhao, Xiang-Ru and Zhou, Hong-Yang (21 February 2000): 'General Thinking for Adjusting Afforestation in Our Country', *People's Daily (overseas edition)*. (In Chinese)

733. Zheng, Ke-Feng (1996): 'Approach to Improvement and Development of Optimal Scale of Farm Land in Zhejiang Province', *Chinese Rural Economy*, No. 4: 67–70. (In Chinese)

734. Zheng, Rong-Lai (4 January 2000): 'Standing on the Relic Field of Mount Chengtou', *People's Daily (overseas edition)*. (In Chinese)

735. Zhong, Yong-Ling and Cai, Xue-Rue (1997): 'Contracting via Tendering: An Effective Form of Land Management', *Chinese Rural Economy*, No. 2: 54–7. (In Chinese)

736. Zhou, Da-Fu (1987): 'Carry Out the "Two Field" System, Perfect the Contract Responsibility Management System of Land', *Chinese Rural Economy*, No. 12: 28–31. (In Chinese)

737. Zhou, Jian-Ming [9–13 April 1996]: 'Agrarian Reform and Rural Development Strategies in China, Japan and Other Rice-Based Economies of Monsoon Asia', in Food and Agriculture Organization of the United Nations (ed.) (1997) *Rural Development: International Workshop*; <http://www.fao.org>, search 'Jian-Ming Zhou'. Abstract No. 3313, (June 1998) *World Agricultural Economics and Rural Sociology Abstracts*, Commonwealth Agricultural Bureau International (CABI), Vol. 40, No. 6.

738. Zhou, Jian-Ming (22 November 1996): *Proposals for Land Consolidation and Expansion in Japan*, European University Institute, EUI Working Paper ECO No. 96/36; <http://www.iue.it>, 'Department of Economics', 'Working Papers'. Abstract No. 5508, (October 1997) *World Agricultural Economics and Rural Sociology Abstracts*, Commonwealth Agricultural Bureau International (CABI), Vol. 39, No. 10.

739. Zhou, Jian-Ming (1 October 1997): 'A New Proposal for Land Consolidation and Expansion in Japan and Other Economies', *Sustainable Development Dimensions in the Internet*, Food and Agriculture Organization of the United Nations, Rome (voted *Internet's No. 1 website* - leading 78 top sites - on sustainable development by Lycos visitors, March 1998), <http://www.fao.org>, search 'Jian-Ming Zhou'.

740. Zhou, Jian-Ming (December 1997): 'Overcoming the Last Obstacle in Sustainable Rural Development of Monsoon Asia - The Japanese and Chinese Models and a Proposed New Model', PhD Thesis in

Economics, European University Institute.

741. Zhou, Jian-Ming (1998): 'Land Consolidation in Japan and Other Rice-Based Economies under Private Land Ownership in Monsoon Asia', *Land Reform, Land Settlement and Cooperatives*, Food and Agriculture Organization of the United Nations, Rome, No. 1: 123–34; <http://www.fao.org>, search 'Jian-Ming Zhou'.

742. Zhou, Jian-Ming (10 March 1998): *Is Nominal Public But De Facto Private Land Ownership Appropriate? - A Comparative Study among Cambodia, Laos, Vietnam; Japan, Taiwan Province of China, South Korea; China, Myanmar; and North Korea*, European University Institute, EUI Working Paper ECO No. 98/12; <http://www.iue.it>, 'Department of Economics', 'Working Papers'; accepted by the Fifth Conference of the European Association for Comparative Economic Studies, in Bulgarian Academy of Sciences, Golden Sands, Varna, Bulgaria (10–12 September 1998). Abstract No. 1422, (March 1999) *World Agricultural Economics and Rural Sociology Abstracts*, Commonwealth Agricultural Bureau International (CABI), Vol. 41, No. 3.

743. Zhou, Jian-Ming (January 1999): *How to Carry Out Land Consolidation - An International Comparison*, European University Institute, EUI Working Paper ECO No. 99/1; <http://www.iue.it>, 'Department of Economics', 'Working Papers'.

744. Zhou, Jian-Ming (12–15 October 1999): *Preserving Small while Strengthening Large Farmers in the USA and OECD*, Second National Small Farm Conference, organized by the US Department of Agriculture, St. Louis, Missouri, with abstract being published in the proceedings; posted by University of Minnesota in its electronic library: <http://agecon.lib.umn.edu/>, search 'Jian-Ming Zhou'.

745. Zhou, Jian-Ming (9–10 December 1999): 'Present Situation and Solution for Farm-Restructuring in the CIS and CEECs', Conference of 'The Present and the Future of the Russian Economy: Problems, Approaches, Solutions', organized by the Ministry of General Education and Vocational Training of Russian Federation, and Department of Economic Theory and World Economy, Faculty of Economics, Perm State University, Perm, Russia.

746. Zhou, Jian-Ming (16–18 December 1999): *A New Proposal for Agricultural Transition in the CEECs and CIS*, European Integration and Economies in Transition Conference, organized by the Journal *East–West Cooperation in Economics*, Department of Economics of University of Crete, and Department of Business Administration of University of the Aegean, Chios, Greece, with text being published in the proceedings and abstract to be published in *World Agricultural*

Economics and Rural Sociology Abstracts, Commonwealth Agricultural Bureau International (CABI).

747. Zhou, Jian-Ming (5–7 January 2000): *Land Consolidation and Expansion in China in the Reform Era*, Sixth European Conference on Agricultural and Rural Development in China, organized by University of Leiden, the Netherlands.

748. Zhou, Jian-Ming (7–9 September 2000): *A Third Way for Farm-Restructuring in the CIS and CEECs*, Sixth Conference of the European Association for Comparative Economic Studies, in Faculty of Economics, University of Barcelona, Spain, with text being published in the proceedings.

749. Zhou, Jian-Ming (2000): 'Principal Forms of Land Consolidation and Expansion in China', *Land Reform, Land Settlement and Cooperatives*, Food and Agriculture Organization of the United Nations, Rome, No. 1: 88–107; <http://www.fao.org>, search 'Jian-Ming Zhou'. Abstract (2001 forthcoming) *World Agricultural Economics and Rural Sociology Abstracts*, Commonwealth Agricultural Bureau International (CABI).

750. Zhou, Jian-Ming (2001 forthcoming): 'Functioning of the Appropriate Large-Scale Farming in China', *Land Reform, Land Settlement and Cooperatives*, Food and Agriculture Organization of the United Nations, Rome, No. 1; <http://www.fao.org>, search 'Jian-Ming Zhou'.

751. Zhou, Jian-Ming (2002 forthcoming): Abstract of 'Sustainable Development in Asia, America and Europe with Global Applications: A New Approach to Land Ownership', *World Agricultural Economics and Rural Sociology Abstracts*, Commonwealth Agricultural Bureau International (CABI).

752. Zhou, Xiao (1984): 'China's Farm Mechanization Has Entered a New Stage of Development', *Problems of Agricultural Economy*, No. 9: 34–5. (In Chinese)

753. Zhou, Xin-Jing (1988): 'Scale of Economy in Agriculture: A Case Study in Beijing', *Problems of Agricultural Economy*, No. 3: 7–11. (In Chinese)

754. Zhu, Qi-Zhen (1996): 'Attitudes to Farmland of Rural Migrants to Cities', *Chinese Rural Economy*, No. 3: 34–6. (In Chinese)

755. Zhu, Rong-Ji (7 July 1997): 'Purchase Grain at Protective Quota Prices and Negotiable Prices - Speech at the National Meeting via Television and Telephone on the Grain Purchase and Sale', in (9 July 1997) *People's Daily (overseas edition)*. (In Chinese)

756. Zhu, Rong-Ji (6 March 2000): 'Adjusting Agricultural Structures and Raising Peasants' Incomes', in (7 March 2000) *People's Daily (overseas edition)*. (In Chinese)

757. Zhu, Rong-Ji (15 March 2000): 'Answering Questions in Press

Conference', in (16 March 2000) *People's Daily (overseas edition)*. (In Chinese)

758. Zhu, Rong-Ji (31 July 2000): 'Actively and Safely Conduct Experiments by Strengthening Leadership and Paying Attention to the Actual Results - Speech at the Symposium on the Experiments of Converting Erodible Cultivated Land Back to Forestry and Grassland in the Central and Western Areas', *People's Daily (overseas edition)*. (In Chinese)

759. Zhu, Ling and Jiang, Zhong-Yi (1993): 'From Brigade to Village Community: the Land Tenure System and Rural Development in China', *Cambridge Journal of Economics*, No. 17: 441–61.

760. Zinsmeister, Karl (July/August 1995): 'Can Americans Farm without Subsidies?', *American Enterprise*: 43–8.

761. Zou, Qing-Li (5 July 2000): 'Our Country Has for the First Time Ascertained the Land Resources', *People's Daily (overseas edition)*. (In Chinese)

762. Zou, Hui-Feng; Yan, Yin-Long and Shi, Xun-Ru (1984): 'Exploration on the Part-Time Operation in Economically Developed Areas', *Problems of Agricultural Economy*, No. 11: 22–6. (In Chinese)

763. Zuo, Chun-Tai and Song, Xin-Zhong (April 1988): *A Brief History of the Socialist Finance of China*, Beijing: China Finance and Economy Publishing House. (In Chinese)

Index

1977 Farm Bill 362
1981 Farm Bill 362
1985 Farm Bill 356, 357,
  362
1990 Farm Bill 353, 366
1996 Farm Bill
  see also FAIR Act 365,
  388, 395

'A Time to Act' 25, 382
abandoning
  agriculture 186, 222
  cooperatives 297, 298
  farming 47, 55, 156, 328,
  336
  land 32, 138, 139, 164,
  171, 197, 414
  rice production 131, 149
Abramovitz, Moses 61
Abs, Herman 58
absentee 123, 155, 157, 333,
  376, 387, 433
ACP (Agricultural
  Conservation Program)
  357, 396
afforestation 194, 287, 356
Afghanistan 31
Africa 25, 31, 32, 44, 45,
  146, 396, 397
African-Americans 331
agrarianism 333
agricultural market transition

program 365
Ahearn, Mary C. 336, 384
Ahmad, Ehtisham 176, 189
Albania 16, 399-404, 410,
  415, 417-419, 428
Allen, K. 370
Amato, Giuliano 24
American model of rural
  development 15, 30,
  313, 333, 391, 394, 396
American Revolution 333
Amponsah, William A. 359
animal husbandry 5, 45, 46,
  48, 158, 202, 203, 211,
  257, 280, 283
Approach 1 to assigning
  property rights 82, 86,
  88, 91, 94, 151, 205,
  289, 391
Approach 2 to assigning
  property rights 86-88,
  91, 289
Approach 3 to assigning
  property rights 88,
  127, 182, 391
Approach 4 to assigning
  property rights 90, 94,
  103, 391
Approach 5 to assigning
  property rights 90
approaches to assigning
  property rights 13, 21,

86, 90-92, 103
Armenia 16, 400-402, 404,
    405, 406, 411, 415-417,
    428-431
ARP (Acreage Reduction
    Program) 354, 355,
    360, 362, 363, 365,
    368, 396
Arrow, K. J. 73
ASCS (Agricultural
    Stabilization and
    Conservation Service)
    352, 357
Ash, Robert 52
'Asian comfort women' 80,
    90, 91
assistance programs 355,
    358, 360, 361, 367
Aubert, Claude 195, 201,
    202, 212, 213, 215
Australasia 396
Australia 11, 142, 146, 147,
    149, 258
Austria 11, 28, 147, 148
Azerbaijan 16, 400, 401,
    404, 405, 406, 411

back-up basic social welfare
    29, 89, 97, 137, 155,
    158, 163, 212, 217,
    220, 221, 222, 226,
    235, 243, 248, 289,
    385, 431
Bangladesh 3, 7, 14, 53, 187
bao chan dao hu 18, 168,
    175, 197, 251, 298
bao gan dao hu 18, 176,
    191, 197-199, 296, 298
bao gong dao lao (hu)
    see also contracting work
        to laborers (households)
    197, 252

bargaining power 10, 14, 73,
    75, 83, 86, 88, 90, 91,
    96, 99, 127, 152, 180,
    181, 289, 290, 308, 344
Barker, Randolph 19, 23, 34
Barone, Enrico 73
Batte, Marvin T. 341
Beaumond, Hans-Christian
    27
beginning farmers
    see also start-up farmers
    382
Belarus 16, 401, 404-406,
    408, 409, 411, 413, 416
Belgium 11, 28, 117, 147,
    148
Bennett, M. K. 22, 33, 52
Beres, Bela 27
Berglof, Erik 27
Berry, R. Albert 51
Bhutan 3, 7, 14, 53, 187,
    188
Binns, Bernard O. 22
Binswanger, Hans P. 51
biotechnology 338, 340
black farmers 331, 343, 360,
    378, 379-383
blacks 331, 334, 338, 342,
    343, 344, 378
Bollman, Ray D. 317, 332
Bosnia and Herzegovina 16,
    403, 404, 415
Boulding, Kenneth 364
Bray, Francesca 8, 36, 48,
    49, 51, 62, 149
brigade 18, 175, 191, 199,
    217, 226, 249, 252,
    271, 272
Britain 19, 147, 149, 333
Brooks, N. 320, 384
Brown, Adell, Jr. 315, 379,
    380, 381

Brown, Minnie M. 378, 382
Browne, W. P. 370
Bulgaria 16, 402, 403, 405,
    410, 415, 418
Burma
    see also Myanmar 3

CABI (Commonwealth
    Agricultural Bureau
    International) 22-26,
    31, 108, 123, 185, 223,
    296, 399
Cambodia 3, 11, 14, 15, 24,
    52, 149, 295, 297, 299,
    300, 301, 302, 306,
    308, 309, 310, 427
Canada 11, 147, 259, 365,
    430
Cao, Lan-Mu
    Cooperative 170
capital construction 194
capital shares 66, 68, 97,
    157, 162, 165, 168,
    400, 406, 433
Caribbean 396
Carter, Jimmy 364
CCC (Commodity Credit
    Corporation) 327, 352,
    353, 354, 356
CEECs (Central and Eastern
    European Countries)
    16, 20, 25, 26, 178,
    396, 399-403, 405, 409,
    410, 414, 415, 418,
    423, 425-432, 434
ceiling on land-holding 53,
    65, 76, 82, 123, 133,
    151, 159, 194, 222,
    301, 307, 359, 368,
    392, 393, 420, 427
Central America 31, 32, 44,
    396

Central Asia 16, 26, 179,
    396
Central Europe 16, 25, 26,
    179, 290, 396, 399
centrally planned economy
    8, 12, 14, 15, 21, 60,
    61, 70, 75, 164, 171,
    177, 184, 191, 205,
    223, 278, 292, 295,
    297, 299, 300, 308,
    309, 399, 400, 425-427,
    431
Ceylon
    see also Sri Lanka 39
Chen, Yao-Xi 250
Chen, Zong-Tong 258
China 3, 7, 10, 11, 17, 18,
    24, 27, 30, 31, 33, 34,
    37, 38, 39, 43, 45, 47,
    48, 49, 52, 60, 65, 69,
    70, 71, 76, 86, 89, 95,
    96, 97, 98, 100, 102,
    104, 106, 107, 109,
    142, 146, 149, 150,
    159, 160, 165, 167,
    169, 175-179, 184, 189,
    192, 193, 199-207, 209,
    210, 211-214, 216, 218,
    219, 221-223, 226-229,
    232, 235-238, 242-245,
    247, 248, 254, 255,
    257-260, 262-264, 266,
    267, 268-270, 274, 276,
    278, 279-281, 284-298,
    300, 301, 306, 307,
    308, 313, 315, 321,
    391-394, 396, 401, 425,
    426-428, 432
Chinese model of rural
    development 8, 10-12,
    14, 15, 19, 21, 22,
    23-25, 30, 71, 108,

189, 191, 206, 207,
209, 223, 231, 259,
264, 278, 292-295,
297, 300, 308, 309,
310, 394, 396, 429
Christy, Ralph D. 315, 320,
384
CIS (Commonwealth of
Independent States) 16,
20, 25, 26, 178, 396,
399, 400, 401, 404,
405, 407, 409, 410,
413, 414, 415, 418,
426, 427-432, 434
Civil War of the USA 80,
83, 90, 91, 103, 334,
335, 391
climate 3, 31, 44, 45, 48,
392
Cline, William R. 51
Clinton, William J. 365, 368,
369, 370
Coase, R. H.
theorem 13, 22, 71, 77,
81, 83, 84, 151
transaction costs approach
21, 92, 94, 96, 99, 179,
180, 184, 289
Cochrane, Nancy 430
collective farm 1 250, 253
collective farm 2 251, 253,
256
collective farm 3 252
collectively operated large
farms 16, 178, 400,
401, 403, 405-407, 409,
410, 412-414, 425, 426,
430, 431-433
Columbus, Christopher
new tragedy 389
commercial farm 331, 384
commercialization of

individual farming
units 15, 335, 336,
392
commodity programs 350,
352, 354, 358-362, 364,
365
commune 18, 60, 124, 175,
199, 200, 217, 221,
249, 252, 271, 297,
298, 427
compact land units 9, 84, 85,
88, 96, 97, 118, 122,
132, 135, 155, 157,
161, 162, 179, 223,
224, 229, 234, 235,
241, 260, 433
competitiveness 13, 341,
344, 345, 356, 363,
368, 370, 387
compulsory land
consolidation 91, 111,
112
computer 22, 64, 109, 114,
120, 122, 148, 187,
263, 338, 341
concentration
of land towards expert
farmers 244
of land towards large
farms 321, 342, 384
of land towards powerful
people 16, 26, 413,
414
of non-land assets towards
powerful people 414
of resources towards large
farms 369
conservation programs 357,
358, 368, 396
constructing agriculture by
industry 272, 274
construction of rural

infrastructure 5, 9, 19, 71, 103, 125, 170, 200

contracting work to laborers (households) 197, 252

conversion of erodible cultivated land back to forestry, grassland, lake land and wetland 158, 166, 280-284, 287, 290, 291, 294, 357, 397

convert idled non-agricultural land back to farmland 307

cooperative 4, 6, 7, 12, 13, 18, 21-23, 57, 60-63, 66-70, 76, 82, 86, 88, 94, 96, 97, 100, 111, 123-125, 127, 132, 135, 138, 142, 148, 151, 153, 157, 158, 163, 164, 166-175, 177, 178, 179-182, 184, 188, 194, 204-206, 239, 249, 295, 296-298, 301, 302, 305, 308, 341, 343, 361, 392, 396, 397, 402, 403, 406, 408, 409, 423, 424, 427, 432, 434

core farmers 137

corn 16, 32, 34, 37, 170, 172, 265, 266, 268, 275, 276, 337, 344-346, 351, 352, 363, 366, 367, 370, 374

corporate farms 321, 327, 329, 335, 359, 361, 364, 389, 406, 410, 423, 425, 429, 432, 433

Corporate-Holding System 9, 14, 96, 97, 104, 177, 234, 235, 243, 244

Croatia 16, 402-404, 410, 416, 420, 428-431

crop insurance 356, 358

crop sharing 334, 376, 378

crowding out small farmers *see also* squeezing out small farmers 15, 24, 30, 166, 177, 189, 207, 313, 328, 332, 340, 348, 364, 384-386, 389, 390, 392-396

CRP (Conservation Reserve Program) 357, 360, 362, 363, 366-368, 396

Csaki, Csaba 410

cun ti liu *see also* village reserved fees 194

CUSTA (Canadian/United States Trade Agreement) 365

Czech Republic 11, 16, 400, 405, 409, 412, 415, 416

Debertin, David L. 362

Debreu, G. 73

deficiency payments 353, 354, 356, 362, 365, 368

Deininger, Klaus 51

DEIP (Dairy Export Incentive Program) 357

demand for labor 3, 43, 46, 124, 148

democracy 112, 147, 247, 370, 382, 388-390

Democratic Party 179, 364

Democratic People's Republic of Korea *see also* North Korea 3

Demsetz, H. 22, 64, 72, 75, 77, 79-81, 85, 86, 101

Deng, Xiao-Ping 221, 244,

300
Denmark 11, 28, 100, 109,
    111, 147, 148
desolation of land 197, 214,
    216, 218, 240, 248,
    306, 307
dilemma 16, 26, 59, 150,
    308, 363, 369, 389,
    398, 409, 413
Diouf, Jacques 308
direct purchases 353, 362
direct subsidy 219, 233, 252,
    265, 270-274, 294, 356
disaster assistance program
    355
discrimination 343, 359, 361
disguised unemployment 4,
    28, 35, 48, 54, 126,
    170, 171
diversified cropping 5, 9, 19,
    50, 71, 103, 125, 128,
    131, 170, 171, 188,
    200, 202, 211, 233,
    300, 301, 306, 393
Dodson, Charles B. 361
Dreze, Jean 63, 176, 187,
    189
dual economy 4, 12, 36, 57,
    127
Dual Land on Account
    System 97, 225
Dual Land System 9, 10, 14,
    16, 76, 85, 90, 96, 97,
    99, 104, 155, 157, 158,
    161, 166, 177, 181,
    192, 223, 224, 226-233,
    239, 241-245, 271, 273,
    289, 291, 301, 385,
    386, 433

East Asia 3, 31, 62, 201,
    160

Eastern Europe 26, 60, 179,
    208, 209, 290, 396
economies of scale 6, 7, 14,
    45, 47, 48, 136-138,
    153, 156, 158, 164,
    166, 171, 174, 179,
    188, 201, 221, 223,
    225, 226, 244, 257,
    274, 293, 338, 381,
    388, 394, 396, 422,
    427, 433
economies of size 336, 343,
    345
Edgmand, Michael 354
EDMS (Electronic Distance
    Measuring System)
    120
EEP (Export Enhancement
    Program) 356, 357,
    367, 368
efficiency
    see also Pareto 10, 13,
    62, 63, 66, 67, 70-78,
    81-84, 86, 87, 89, 95,
    103, 104, 125, 127,
    151, 152, 180-182, 205,
    206, 208, 223, 226,
    292, 293, 314, 336,
    362, 370, 381, 394,
    395, 412, 424, 427
Eisenhower, Dwight David
    364
El-Osta, Hisham 336
electricity/gas-powered
    technologies and
    machines 47, 48, 51,
    55, 102, 103, 125, 392
Elvin, Mark 49
environment 5, 11, 13, 14,
    24, 33, 73, 139, 149,
    156, 158, 164, 166,
    178, 193, 202, 277,

278, 280, 281, 284,
290, 293, 294, 340,
341, 397, 399, 428,
434
environmental improvement
71
environmental protection 5,
115, 150, 162, 284,
294, 295, 338, 340,
389, 394, 434
Equal Land System 8, 10,
97, 191, 192, 210, 212,
216, 217, 224, 232-235,
240, 243, 244, 249,
274, 291, 301
ERP (externality-receiving
party) 92-94
Espy, Mike 360
Estonia 16, 26, 27, 400, 402,
403, 405, 409, 410,
412, 416
EU
see also European Union
11, 16, 24-27, 149, 178,
396, 397, 398, 415,
422, 430, 434
European Union
see also EU 11, 149, 288,
398
exiting farming by small
farmers 16, 336, 359,
382, 384, 392, 398
expert farmer 9, 14, 88, 97,
156, 157, 162, 164,
166, 182, 192, 193,
217, 221, 224, 226,
227, 229-235, 238, 239,
244, 246, 248, 249,
251, 252, 266, 272,
289, 291, 308, 394, 433
export promoting programs
356, 363, 367

external and foreign venture
258, 259, 292, 293
externality 13, 21, 71-83, 86,
87, 88-94, 100-104,
117, 127, 150-153, 172,
180, 181-184, 206, 209,
222, 289, 291, 292,
308, 332, 391, 427
EYP (externality-yielding
party) 92-94

FAIR Act (Federal
Agricultural
Improvement and
Reform Act)
see also 1996 Farm Bill
365, 366-368
family farm system 355, 358
family plot 9, 88, 99, 154,
157, 158, 161, 162,
166, 168, 191, 192,
231, 232, 234, 289,
291, 300, 301, 385,
386, 388, 390, 394,
432, 433
family-held corporation farms
321
fan zu dao bao
see also inverse leasing or
contracting 235
FAO (Food and Agriculture
Organization of the
United Nations) 3-5,
22, 23, 24, 31, 33, 44,
150, 299, 302, 303,
308, 389, 434
Far East 396
farm credit assistance
programs 355
farm operating loans 355,
388
farm ownership loans 355,

388

farm size 6, 7, 23, 30, 44,
51, 52, 54, 95-97, 115,
118, 122, 124, 128,
129, 131-135, 138, 149,
151, 163, 174, 178,
179, 180, 184, 185,
212, 219, 221, 244,
260, 264-266, 313, 314,
315, 317, 318, 320,
321, 334, 336, 338,
339, 345, 360, 375,
377, 379-381, 385, 387,
398, 399, 408, 409,
416, 419, 422, 424,
425, 427, 431

farming community
see also rural community
120

farming in an industrial style
327

farming unit 3, 15, 124, 127,
157, 168, 197, 226,
227, 246, 256, 273,
335, 336, 392, 402, 404

FCIC (Federal Crop
Insurance Corporation)
356

Feder, Gershon 51

federal tax policies 358, 360

fee simple 333, 334

Fei, J. C. H. 35

feminization 35, 127, 139,
151, 212, 377

feudal 3, 8, 24, 36, 40, 52,
55, 56, 68, 89, 90, 104,
107, 123, 126, 127,
132, 167, 391, 392

feudalism 47, 53, 127, 392

feudalistic 333

Finland 11, 147

FIP (Forestry Incentive

Program) 357, 396

First Industrial Revolution
46, 48, 50, 51, 55, 102,
125, 148, 337, 338

fishery 5, 45, 72, 124, 125,
158, 202, 203, 211,
214, 232, 257, 259

FmHA (Farmers Home
Administration) 355

food security 5, 150, 160,
166, 174, 182, 206,
207, 295, 297, 308,
331, 389, 415, 417, 434

forestry 5, 31, 45, 115, 124,
125, 132, 158, 162,
166, 202, 203, 211,
257, 280-285, 287, 288,
290, 294, 357, 396-398,
405, 420, 421, 434

fragmentation 3, 4, 7, 14,
39, 40-43, 96, 104, 109,
112, 121-124, 131, 132,
138, 147, 149, 151,
174, 210, 225, 235,
236, 239, 246, 375-377,
390, 403, 419, 421

fragmented small farms 4, 6,
7, 8, 10, 12, 13, 19-23,
25, 26, 30, 36, 39, 43,
51, 55, 60, 61, 63, 70,
71, 84, 94-96, 99,
102-104, 121, 126, 131,
142, 146, 150-152, 154,
163, 164, 165, 167,
176-179, 184, 186-188,
192, 201, 209, 210,
211, 212, 218, 221,
222, 223, 243, 289,
290, 292, 293, 295,
307, 395-397, 404, 407,
409, 419, 421, 424,
426, 428, 433, 434

France 11, 19, 28, 57, 58,
110, 111, 112, 117,
121, 147, 148
Franceschetti, Giorgio 31
Francks, Penelope 8
free market forces 12, 15,
21, 22, 25, 36, 55, 57,
87, 91, 127, 135, 146,
152, 153, 179, 183,
222, 295, 307, 308,
365, 370, 385, 389,
395, 430
free market system 8, 12,
60, 61, 70, 165, 177,
184, 191, 205, 292,
295, 308, 426, 429, 431
freedom to gain and also to
fail 369
Friedman, Milton
free market system 209,
290
FSU (Former Soviet Union)
see also USSR, Soviet
Union 399, 400, 410,
425, 430
full owner 314, 327, 370,
371, 372-375, 377, 378,
382, 384, 389, 390
full ownership 371, 375,
377, 389
full tenancy 370, 371, 375
full-time farmers 6, 9, 11,
29, 30, 76, 82, 83, 88,
89, 90, 95, 97, 134,
135, 137, 138, 148,
163, 181, 212, 217,
219, 220, 231, 236,
244, 247, 248, 289,
292, 306, 309, 385,
398, 399, 420, 427, 431
Furubotn, E. G. 22, 64, 83,
84, 87, 88, 100, 101

Gao, De-Ming 249
Gao, Gui-Lan 241
Gao, Wan-Nian 240
Gardner, B. Delworth 354,
361
GATT (General Agreement
on Tariffs and Trade)
142, 294, 365
GDP (gross domestic
product) 295, 413,
421, 424
Gebremedhin, Tesfa G. 315,
320, 384
Georgia 16, 400, 401, 403,
404, 405, 406, 411,
417, 419, 428-431
Germany 11, 28, 58, 80, 90,
118, 147, 148, 258
Gillis, Malcolm 17
GIS (Geographic Information
Systems) 120, 341
Glickman, Dan 384
GNP (gross national product)
295
Goetz, Stephan J. 362
Gordillo de Anda, Gustavo
63
government 4, 7, 8, 12, 15,
19, 22, 25, 26, 28, 29,
46, 51, 57, 59, 61-63,
65, 77, 80, 84, 87,
88-91, 95, 96, 98, 99,
109-112, 115, 117, 120,
121-123, 125, 127, 132,
133, 142, 143, 149,
150-152, 155, 159, 160,
163-166, 174, 175, 182,
183, 187, 188, 189,
192, 194, 196, 199-201,
205, 207, 208-210, 220,
221, 239, 243, 246,
247, 248, 266, 272,

278, 282, 285-287,
290-295, 297, 299,
300, 305, 307, 308,
315, 327, 333, 334,
345, 348, 353-356,
358-360, 362, 364,
365, 366, 368-370,
380, 387, 388, 389,
391, 392, 394, 395,
396, 398, 408, 409,
414, 417, 419, 420,
421, 428, 430
GPS (Global Positioning
Systems) 340
grain rations land
see also self-sufficiency
land 192
Great Depression 347, 348,
395
Greece 11, 27, 113, 118,
147, 397, 415, 419
gross sales
see also value of sales
314, 315, 319-322, 326,
327, 379, 380, 383, 384

Hallam, Arne 331
halt excessive grazing 283
handicraft 45-48, 54, 106,
171
Handing
'Farm' 262, 263
Haque, T. 298
Hathaway, Dale 364
Hayami, Yujiro 24, 306-308
Hayek, Friedrich A.
free market system 290
Hegel, Georg Wilhelm
Friedrich 107
Henry, Mark S. 341
Herdt, Robert W. 19, 23, 34
Hicks, John Richard 73

high wage economy 6, 7, 9,
13, 16, 22-24, 26, 30,
71, 95, 104, 131, 151,
158, 159, 164, 174,
176, 177, 178, 181,
186, 188, 201, 210,
212, 218, 222, 265,
292, 295, 297, 306,
308, 309, 397, 413,
414, 427, 433
Hills, John 176, 189
holding 3, 4, 6-9, 13, 14, 16,
19, 22, 24-26, 30, 39,
40, 44, 45, 52, 53, 63,
65, 66, 76, 82, 84, 94,
95, 96, 97, 99, 103,
104, 108, 110, 112,
113, 119, 123, 124,
126, 131, 133, 135,
146, 148, 150-152, 154,
158, 159, 161, 164,
166, 177, 178, 186,
188, 189, 200, 214,
218, 219, 222, 223,
227, 234, 235, 242-244,
246, 247, 289, 290,
293, 295, 297-299, 301,
304, 306, 307, 308,
309, 382, 383, 385,
388, 392, 393, 395,
397, 413, 414, 416,
417, 419-421, 423, 425,
427, 428, 429, 431
Holland, Stuart
variable mixed economies
12, 35, 57, 58, 70, 71,
104, 291
homeless 10, 155, 160, 161,
183, 213, 332, 398
Homestead Act, 1862 334
horse-powered technologies
and tools 170, 335,

392
Household Contract System
18, 19, 60, 66, 168,
176, 191, 197, 199,
205, 206, 207, 226,
251, 252, 282, 296,
298, 427
Howe, Christopher 221
Huang, Zhi-Hua 232
Hungary 11, 16, 23, 27, 400,
402, 403, 405, 411,
412, 415, 418
hunting 5, 45, 102, 103
hypothesis for overcoming
fragmented small farms
obstacle 12, 13, 28, 60,
70, 71, 104, 153, 164,
179, 184, 295, 426

Iceland 11
idling land 10, 76, 98, 136,
138, 150, 153, 164,
188, 216, 217, 222,
247, 258, 286, 287,
292, 298, 306, 307,
354, 359-362, 394, 414,
419, 421, 425, 433
incentive 4, 8, 13, 19, 26,
51, 59, 60, 64, 66-71,
76, 87, 88, 90, 95, 98,
124, 127, 133, 134,
135, 159, 163, 167,
176, 178, 181, 182,
196, 198, 214, 221,
231, 239, 240, 252,
259, 271, 292, 298,
338, 339, 341, 357,
366, 375-377, 388, 393,
396, 397, 399, 409,
410, 413, 428, 430
income support programs
353, 362

India 3, 7, 14, 24, 31, 38,
39, 45, 47-49, 52, 54,
109, 110, 111, 113,
114, 118, 120, 121,
177, 187-189, 292, 389
Indians of North America
102, 103, 333
indirect subsidies 219, 272,
273, 277, 293, 294
individual farming 15, 26,
124, 127, 168, 197,
226, 293, 317, 335,
336, 392, 399, 400,
402, 404, 409, 410,
412, 431-433
individual farms 16, 112,
124, 178, 296, 301,
343, 400-409, 412, 421,
423, 426-434
individual household farm
249, 251, 253, 254,
259, 292
individual land ownership 9,
15, 95, 127, 167, 201,
204, 333-335, 391, 401,
427, 428
individual—cooperative mixed
economy 4, 21, 123
Indonesia 3, 7, 14, 31, 45,
48, 53, 186, 187
industrialization 4, 24, 47,
58, 134, 186, 187, 201,
202, 233, 235, 243,
244, 245, 291
inefficiency 71, 72, 84, 134,
307, 361, 427
inefficient land-holding 6-8,
13, 14, 16, 19, 22, 24,
25, 26, 30, 63, 95, 99,
104, 124, 126, 131,
146, 150, 152, 154,
158, 164, 186, 188,

223, 247, 289, 290,
293, 295, 297,
306-308, 382, 383,
385, 388, 392, 393,
395, 413, 414, 419,
427-429, 431
inefficient use of land 6, 7,
9, 14, 29, 90, 96, 138,
178, 212, 213, 218,
220, 248, 289, 293,
307, 309, 394, 397,
427, 428, 431
inflation 89, 106, 123, 127,
200, 314
information 120, 124, 187,
263, 276, 334, 339,
341, 342-344, 361, 412,
423, 433
inheritance 3, 39, 121, 147,
160, 304, 409
institution 3, 16, 17, 19, 20,
22, 48, 57, 58, 62, 64,
66, 83, 87, 99, 149,
152, 176, 180, 207,
208, 292, 341, 342,
394, 396
institutional changes 4, 5, 8,
9, 15, 19, 20, 22, 70,
71, 123, 125, 127, 152,
167, 180, 191, 200,
201, 207, 221, 292,
293, 300, 301, 333,
370, 381, 385, 391, 395
internalizing externalities 21,
73, 74, 77-81, 86, 88,
90, 93, 100-103, 127,
151, 184, 209, 291
Internet 148, 263, 264, 276
intervention 12, 22, 35, 58,
63, 87-89, 111, 113,
122, 127, 147, 149,
165, 166, 182, 183,

205, 207, 246, 290,
291, 308, 345, 347,
349, 387, 388, 395
inverse leasing or contracting
235
Ireland 11, 28, 109, 147, 148
Ishikawa, Shigeru 20, 36, 56
Italy 11, 24, 31, 57, 58, 89,
147, 230, 397, 398, 415

Janssen, Larry 381
Japan 3, 4, 7, 9-11, 14, 17,
19, 20, 21, 23, 28, 30,
31, 37-39, 43, 46, 47,
49, 51, 52, 55-58, 65,
69, 70, 76, 84, 86, 89,
91, 94-96, 99, 102, 104,
109, 113, 118, 126-128,
131-133, 136, 137, 139,
141, 143, 146, 147-150,
154, 155, 159, 160,
164-166, 174, 176,
177-179, 182, 184, 185,
186, 201, 204, 205,
209, 210, 218, 221,
222, 223, 245, 246,
257, 258, 260, 263,
284, 288-290, 292, 293,
301, 306, 307, 313,
315, 321, 390-394, 396,
401, 426, 427, 428, 430
Japanese model of rural
development 4, 5, 7, 9,
10, 13-15, 19, 21-23,
30, 56, 69, 71, 121,
123, 126, 130, 150,
152, 185-189, 201, 205,
209, 230, 292, 293,
295, 307-309, 394, 428,
429
Jefferson, Thomas
yeoman 333-335, 382,

387, 389, 390
Ji, Shu-En 215
Jiang, Ze-Min 278, 280
Jing, Xue-Rong 249
jobless 161, 183, 213, 412
Johnson, Roger 341
Johnston, Donald 24
Jones, Hezekiah S. 350, 354,
    361, 384
Jorgenson, D. W. 35

Kai, Ming-Yi
  Standing-Up Cooperative
    172, 173
Kalbacher, J. 320
Kalter, Robert J. 340
Kazakhstan 16, 401, 404,
    405, 406, 407, 409,
    411, 413, 414, 418, 427
Kennedy, John F. 364
Kim, Jong Il 300
King, F. H. 49
Kojima, Reeitsu 176
kolkhozes (collectively owned
    farms) 399, 414
kou liang tian
    see also self-sufficiency
    land, grain rations land
    192
krom samaki
    see also solidarity groups
    297, 302
Kuznets, Simon 17, 20, 55,
    61
Kwiecinski, Andrzej 27
Kyrgyzstan 16, 400, 401,
    405, 411

L-shaped relationship 344,
    345
labor accumulation man-days
    98, 194, 210

labor-intensive 3, 36, 38, 43,
    45, 48, 50, 51, 54, 55,
    125, 126
Laffont, J. J. 22, 72, 75
land consolidation 6, 10, 13,
    22, 26, 84, 85, 91, 94,
    96, 99, 104, 108-110,
    113, 117, 120, 121,
    132, 135, 146, 151,
    152, 164, 165, 177,
    178, 181, 182, 188,
    198, 289-291, 376, 396,
    397, 419, 430
land reform 4, 8, 17, 24, 52,
    53, 57, 59, 65, 69, 70,
    89, 90, 109, 112, 123,
    124, 127, 132, 134,
    146, 160, 167, 172,
    173, 185, 189, 204,
    301, 391-393, 427
land share 12, 13, 21, 60,
    61, 66, 68-70, 76, 82,
    88, 89, 96, 97, 99, 100,
    108, 153, 154, 158-166,
    168, 169, 174, 177,
    178, 180-184, 234, 235,
    291, 295, 390, 397,
    400, 401, 405, 407,
    408-410, 414, 426, 430,
    431-434
landless 14, 16, 24, 26, 53,
    108, 160, 172, 176,
    183, 295, 297, 301-306,
    308, 309, 392, 413,
    414, 427, 433
landlord 3, 8, 36, 40, 52-56,
    68, 82, 89, 90, 109,
    123, 126, 127, 132,
    134, 147, 151, 167,
    172, 173, 333, 334,
    370, 371, 376-378, 386,
    390, 392, 396

landscape 149, 332, 370, 387, 388
lao dong ji lei gong
  see also labor
    accumulation man-days
    194
Laos 3, 11, 14, 15, 24, 149, 295, 297, 298, 300, 301, 303, 304, 306-310, 427
Lapse, Janis 26
large machinery 6, 7, 9, 14, 19, 24, 30, 51, 71, 102, 103, 115, 131, 132, 135, 162, 189, 201, 212, 250, 259-264, 273, 275, 293, 377, 394, 399
large-scale farm 6, 14, 16, 24, 26, 27, 30, 50, 51, 132, 134, 178, 227, 240, 249, 250, 259-262, 264, 265, 274, 293, 317, 318, 320, 321, 327, 331, 332, 337, 338-341, 343, 344, 360, 361, 365, 370, 377, 379, 380, 382, 385, 386, 387, 389, 392, 393, 394, 398, 400, 401-410, 412-414, 422, 425, 426, 430-434
large-scale farmer 14-16, 25, 30, 178, 188, 189, 228, 231, 235, 238, 239, 243, 246, 248, 255, 259, 260-262, 265, 266, 271, 272-274, 276, 277, 292, 293, 294, 313, 333, 335, 336, 343, 344, 360, 361, 364, 369, 385-388, 390, 392, 393, 394, 396-398,

420, 427, 429
large-scale farming 9, 12, 14, 19, 21, 24, 30, 36, 40, 48-51, 55, 61, 70, 76, 88, 103, 104, 126, 128, 134, 135, 151, 153, 166, 177, 184, 189, 199, 201, 221, 223, 224, 228, 233, 235, 242-244, 246-249, 251, 253, 256, 260, 262, 273, 274, 277, 289, 291-293, 295, 341, 392, 410, 426, 429, 431
large-scale farming and
  collective—individual
  mixed economy 14, 24, 223, 274, 291, 292
large—small farmers mixed
  economy 16, 21
Larson, Olaf A. 378, 382
last obstacle 8, 10, 12-14, 21, 22-24, 60, 64, 70, 94, 95, 99, 104, 123, 150, 166, 177, 178, 181, 184, 188, 189, 191, 209, 218, 221-223, 243, 246-248, 278, 289, 290, 295, 307-309, 395-397, 428
Lastarria-Cornhiel, Susana 391
Latin America 25, 396, 397
Latvia 16, 26, 400, 402, 403, 405, 409, 411, 415
Leacock, E. 101
Leasing System 9, 14, 96, 104, 177, 229, 243, 244
Lerman, Zvi 410, 416, 428
Lerner, Abba 73
Lewis, W. Arthur 28, 35
li tu bu li xiang

see also quit the land
without quitting the
countryside 201
Li, Mei 264
Li, Zheng-Xiang 217
Liska, Tibor 60
List, Friedrich
protection to 'infant
industries' 149
Lithuania 16, 400, 402, 404,
405, 411, 415, 418
Liu, Cheng-Guo 280
livestock 3, 42, 45, 124, 125,
158, 175, 233, 261,
280, 283, 288, 315,
321, 327, 339-341, 355,
356, 357, 375, 376, 408
loan rate 353-356, 362, 363,
366
loss-making independent
small farming 16, 382,
383, 384, 387, 388,
392, 393, 396
low wage economy 7, 13,
16, 22, 24, 26, 30, 102,
159, 164, 172, 174,
176, 177, 186, 188,
201, 218, 222, 292,
295, 297, 301, 306,
308, 309, 396, 397,
413, 427, 433
LURC (Land Use Right
Certificate) 299, 308
Luxembourg 11, 147

Macedonia 16, 404
Madden, J. Patrick 345
making-over 196
Malaya 39, 47
Malaysia 3, 7, 14, 39, 53,
186, 222
male principal persons

engaged mainly in
farming 136
market distortions 362, 370,
395
market socialism 12, 58-60,
69, 70, 181, 182, 205,
292, 429
market-driven economy 414
market-driven measures 15,
365, 395
marketing 15, 52, 59, 125,
196, 207, 239, 263,
279, 283, 296, 335,
336, 343, 344, 356,
366, 368, 387, 393, 394
marketing loans 356, 366,
368
Marshall, Alfred 149
Marx, Karl 50, 104-107
McLean-Meyinsse, Patricia E.
379, 380, 381
mechanization 5, 9, 14, 19,
37, 43, 71, 125, 128,
131, 171, 201, 221,
232, 246, 259, 262,
264, 265, 266, 275,
293, 338, 394
Meiji 46, 47, 51, 55, 58,
123, 147
Melmed-Sanjak, Jolyne 391
Mexico 11, 365
Middle East 396
migration 5, 9, 19, 35, 47,
71, 115, 125, 128, 142,
170, 186, 200, 202,
212, 332, 362
Milgrom, Paul 22, 64, 66,
67, 72, 75, 83, 86
Ministry
of Agriculture and
Forestry, Croatia 420
of Agriculture and

Regional Development, Hungary 27
of Agriculture, China 279
of Agriculture, Estonia 27
of Agriculture, Forestry and Fisheries, Japan 132
of Agriculture, Latvia 26
of Agriculture, the Netherlands 113
of General Education and Vocational Training, Russia 26, 399
of Land and Natural Resources, China 285, 286
Mises, Ludwig von 59
mixed economy 4, 6, 8, 9, 12, 13, 14, 16, 18-22, 24, 29, 31, 55, 57, 58, 60, 61, 64, 70, 71, 90, 91, 104, 108, 117, 122, 123, 125-127, 152, 153, 163, 164, 166, 167, 179, 180, 183, 184, 189, 191, 199, 201, 204-206, 208, 221-223, 238, 274, 289-293, 295, 300, 301, 307, 308, 385, 387, 391, 395, 407, 430, 431
Moldova 16, 400, 405, 406, 411
Mongolia 10, 31, 279, 283
Monnet, Jean 58
monsoon Asia 3, 5-8, 11-17, 20-25, 31, 32, 34, 35, 36, 39, 41-45, 48, 50-52, 54, 55, 56, 60-62, 64, 70, 91, 94, 95, 99, 102, 107, 125, 126, 128, 146, 147, 150, 154, 164, 178, 179, 184-186, 188, 189, 209, 230, 238, 240, 289, 295, 301, 306, 309-311, 377, 390, 392, 395, 396, 427
Montesi, L. 298
Moowaw, Ronald 354
multiple cropping 5, 9, 19, 39, 49, 50, 62, 71, 125, 127, 170, 172, 173, 200, 216, 249, 300, 393
mutual aid teams 167, 172, 173, 175, 204, 392
Myanmar 3, 11, 14, 15, 38, 52, 149, 295-297, 309, 310
Myrdal, Gunnar 20, 35, 56

NAFTA (North American Free Trade Agreement) 365
National Commission on Small Farms of USDA 25, 382
natural reserves 162, 284, 285
Nepal 3, 7, 14, 53, 54, 187, 188
Netherlands 5, 11, 24, 28, 110, 111-113, 118, 147, 148, 223
new model for sustainable rural development 13, 14, 15, 16, 22, 23, 25, 26, 30, 61, 64, 63, 108, 121, 154, 163, 165, 166, 177, 178, 188, 311, 370, 390, 394, 396, 397, 396, 397, 399

New Zealand 11, 146, 147
Nolan, Peter 176, 207, 208,
    213, 215, 238, 246, 260
nominal public–individual
    mixed economy 407
non-commercial farms 320,
    341
non-crop agriculture 5, 9, 19,
    71, 103, 125, 128, 131,
    170, 171, 188, 200,
    202, 211, 233, 300,
    301, 306, 393
non-family corporation farms
    321
non-recourse loans 352, 353,
    362, 366, 368, 369
nong cun yi wu gong
    see also rural obligatory
    man-days 194
nonoperator landlords 370,
    377, 378, 390, 396
nonoperator nonlandlords
    371
North Africa 396
North America 31, 32, 44,
    146
North Korea 3, 11, 14, 15,
    52, 149, 295, 299, 300,
    309, 310
North, Douglass C. 83, 85
Northwest Europe 28, 148
Norway 11, 28, 31, 147, 148
Nuti, Domenico Mario
    model of market socialism
    12, 58-60, 69, 70, 205,
    292

Oceania 31, 32, 44
OECD (Organization for
    Economic Cooperation
    and Development) 8,
    11, 16, 20, 24, 25, 27,

30, 31, 109, 112,
    141, 142, 147, 178,
    359, 362, 396-398,
    401, 404, 405,
    406-409, 412-416,
    419, 421-423, 426,
    427, 429, 430
off-farm activities 6, 7, 10,
    13, 14, 16, 30, 45, 83,
    95, 96, 146, 155-158,
    163, 166, 171, 173,
    177, 178, 188, 189,
    209, 211, 212, 214,
    215-218, 223-226, 230,
    232, 234, 238, 242-244,
    246, 248, 257, 263,
    266, 271, 272, 277,
    291, 293, 306, 313,
    361, 380, 382, 383-388,
    393, 394, 396, 397,
    398, 408, 414, 415-417,
    424, 425, 428, 431, 434
off-farm employment 5, 7, 9,
    15, 19, 30, 39, 43, 62,
    71, 103, 125, 128, 131,
    133, 155, 156, 166,
    170, 172, 200, 202,
    213, 217, 218, 224-226,
    230, 231, 246, 247,
    301, 306, 331, 334,
    341, 382, 383, 384,
    385, 387, 388, 392,
    393, 413, 424, 433
off-farm income 16, 26, 76,
    95, 133, 134, 159, 177,
    327, 331, 336, 344,
    382, 383, 386, 389,
    390, 396, 397, 413-415,
    419, 420, 424, 427
Oi, Jean Chun 195, 208,
    211, 212, 213, 215,
    217, 238, 242, 246, 260

Olson, Kent 354

Oshima, Harry T. 17, 19, 20, 23, 36, 39, 49-52, 61, 62, 123, 230
approach of narrative analysis or analytical description 20

overproduction of food 11, 13, 14, 23, 24, 29, 30, 77, 143, 152, 158, 164, 166, 178, 202, 207, 220, 277, 278, 281, 282, 288-290, 293-295, 396-399, 434

owner-peasant 3, 40, 64, 69, 111, 172

ownership 3, 4, 6-16, 18, 21, 22, 23-27, 30, 36, 52, 53, 55, 57-61, 63-70, 84, 85, 88, 89, 91, 94-97, 99, 100, 102, 104, 105-109, 112, 117, 122, 123, 124, 126, 127, 132, 134, 135, 137, 138, 146, 149, 152, 153, 154, 160, 161, 163-168, 172, 174, 175-182, 184, 185, 188, 191, 200, 201, 204-206, 209, 223, 234, 256-258, 289-292, 294-297, 299-301, 303, 306, 307, 308-310, 332, 333, 334, 335, 355, 370, 371, 372, 375, 376, 377, 378, 381, 382, 385, 387-392, 394-397, 396-403, 406-410, 414, 416, 417, 421, 422, 424, 425, 426-433

Pacific 25, 396

Padar, Ivari 27

paddy 31, 33, 34, 36-39, 45, 49, 51, 53, 54, 123, 125, 231, 250, 296-298, 302

pai jia
see also quota prices 192

Pakistan 3, 7, 14, 31, 39, 45, 53, 54, 187

Pareto, Vilfredo
efficiency 13, 66, 67, 70, 71, 72-78, 80-84, 86, 87, 89, 95, 127, 151, 152, 180-182, 205, 223, 292, 293, 394, 395

parity prices 195

part owner 314, 327, 370, 371, 372-375, 377-379, 381, 384-390, 396

part ownership 15, 16, 370, 372, 375, 381, 382, 385, 389, 390, 395, 396, 398

part-time and absent small farmers 6-11, 14, 16, 19, 22, 24-26, 28-30, 63, 71, 76, 82, 83, 88-90, 95-97, 99, 104, 124, 126, 131, 133, 134, 137, 146, 148, 150, 152-154, 163, 164, 178, 181, 186, 188, 212, 216-220, 222, 223, 231, 235, 238, 242, 247, 248, 289, 290, 292, 306-309, 382, 385, 392-395, 397, 398, 413, 414, 415, 417, 427, 428-431

part-time farming 29, 88, 133, 138, 214, 364, 380, 383, 384, 389,

397, 413, 417, 425
partnership farms 321
pecuniary externalities 21,
    72, 74-76, 82, 83, 87,
    152, 153, 181, 182,
    222, 289, 292, 314,
    343, 427
Pejovich, S. 22, 64, 83, 84,
    87, 88, 100, 101
Perkins, Dwight H. 17
persons engaged in farming
    136, 137, 139, 141
persons engaged mainly in
    farming 28, 136, 137,
    140
Peterson, R. Neal 320, 384
Philippines 3, 7, 14, 37, 39,
    48, 51, 53, 186, 187
Pigou, A. C.
    Pigouvian tax 74, 90
ping jia
    see also parity prices 195
Pio, Louis Albert Francois
    puzzle 13, 21, 23, 100,
    179, 180, 181
PLD (Paid Land Diversion
    Program) 354, 355,
    396
Poland 11, 16, 399, 403,
    404, 411, 415, 418,
    420, 423, 424, 427-431
policy 4, 8, 15, 16, 19, 20,
    26, 28, 31, 35, 57, 59,
    60, 63, 91, 113, 124,
    125, 132, 158, 196,
    200, 207, 208, 213,
    239, 259, 271, 274,
    294, 300, 303, 306,
    307, 333-335, 349, 356,
    358, 359, 360, 365,
    368, 370, 381, 382,
    389, 391, 395, 396,

398, 417, 419, 432
population 3, 4, 14, 17, 18,
    28, 30, 36, 38, 39, 43,
    44, 45-47, 50, 54-56,
    61, 97, 121, 122, 126,
    127, 136, 137, 141,
    148, 169, 176, 191,
    192, 202, 207, 210,
    218, 224-226, 228, 240,
    244-246, 258, 259, 262,
    278-280, 283, 284, 289,
    302, 304, 315, 316,
    321, 332, 341, 378,
    383, 393, 407, 419,
    420-422, 424
Portugal 11, 113, 147, 149,
    397
possession 13-15, 64-68, 87,
    94, 105, 167, 178, 276,
    297, 299, 301-303, 310,
    397, 409, 414
poverty 4, 5, 12, 13, 18, 20,
    35, 36, 48, 52-55, 62,
    87, 98, 109, 126-128,
    151, 158, 160, 161,
    163, 173, 174, 182,
    183, 187, 188, 202,
    206, 287, 289, 292,
    295, 301, 302, 304,
    305, 309, 331, 343,
    370, 389, 414, 434
Preobrazhensky, Evgeny A.
    35
price support programs 352,
    359, 362
principal persons engaged
    mainly in farming 136,
    137, 140
principles
    of market competition 12,
    156, 290
    of sustainable rural

development 183
of the new model 14, 16,
    25, 166, 177, 390, 394,
    396, 397
private land ownership 4, 6,
    7, 10, 13-15, 21-23, 30,
    65, 66, 89, 94, 96, 99,
    100, 108, 124, 134,
    135, 137, 149, 152-154,
    163, 164, 167, 174,
    177-182, 185, 188, 201,
    205, 257, 258, 290,
    291, 295, 301, 309,
    310, 385, 390, 394,
    396, 397, 396, 397,
    401, 406-409, 426, 427
production flexibility contract
    365, 366, 368, 369, 388
production land for market
    88, 99, 154-158, 161,
    162, 164-166, 385-387,
    390, 433
property rights 13, 21, 29,
    40, 63, 64, 66, 70, 77,
    81, 82-93, 100-104,
    126, 127, 151, 152,
    181, 182-184, 205, 206,
    220, 238, 289, 291,
    295, 299, 385, 391,
    427, 431
Proposal 5.1 13-16, 25, 26,
    85, 88, 89, 95, 99, 100,
    104, 108, 154, 165,
    177, 234, 291, 310,
    390, 396, 406, 408,
    430, 431-434
Proposal 5.2 14, 188
Proposal 8.1 15, 309
Proposal 8.2 15, 309
Proposal 8.3 15, 309
Proposal 10.1 16, 25, 384,
    387, 388-390, 396-398

protective safety net 15, 25,
    348, 370, 385, 389,
    394, 395, 398
proximate sources of
    development 11, 17,
    19, 127, 207, 393, 394
public land ownership 4, 7,
    10, 11, 12, 14, 15, 22,
    23, 24, 25, 30, 61, 66,
    85, 89, 94-97, 99, 108,
    163, 166, 178, 181,
    256, 258, 292, 295,
    309, 310, 394, 396,
    397, 401, 425, 426, 429
public—individual mixed
    economy 12, 21, 61,
    70, 184, 295, 407
Putterman, Louis 175, 176,
    200, 201, 207, 211, 212

quit the land without quitting the
    countryside 201
quit-rents 333
quota prices 192-195, 206,
    207, 224, 226, 231,
    232, 234, 275, 297

Ranis, G. 35
rationality
    of small farmers 11, 28,
    29, 77, 89, 111, 118,
    137, 152, 163, 220,
    221, 235, 238, 385, 431
reclamation 3, 10, 39, 62,
    168, 193, 283-285, 392,
    393
Ren, Si-De 250
Republic of Korea
    see also South Korea 3
Republican Party 365, 369
residual 157, 196, 231, 282,
    298, 68, 69, 199, 206,

231, 296
claim 60, 205
claimant 65-67, 205
control 64, 66-68, 95, 205
decisions 67, 205
output 191, 194
returns 65-68, 95, 205
responsibility land 9, 97,
191, 192, 193, 212,
224, 225-231, 239, 242,
243, 244-246, 249, 252,
264, 271, 272, 291, 301
Ricardo, David
comparative advantage
149
rice 3-14, 16, 17, 19-24, 31,
32, 33-39, 41, 43, 45,
47, 48-56, 71, 76, 94,
95, 99, 102, 107, 118,
125, 126-128, 131, 134,
135, 141-146, 149-152,
154, 156, 160, 164,
170, 172, 173, 178,
179, 185, 186, 187-189,
200, 201, 203, 207,
209, 210, 212, 215,
226, 231, 249, 253,
257, 260, 261, 262,
264, 265, 266, 268,
273, 277, 278, 279,
288, 295, 296, 297,
299, 301, 302, 303,
306, 309, 353, 354,
356, 357, 365, 366,
369, 380, 390, 393, 396
rice-based economies 3, 4, 6,
7, 8, 10, 11, 13, 14, 16,
17, 21-24, 39, 51, 56,
94, 99, 100, 107, 126,
154, 160, 178, 185,
186, 188, 189, 209,
295, 390, 396

Riddell, James C. 63
Ritchie, Mark 332, 364
Roberts, John 22, 64, 66, 67,
72, 75, 83, 86
Roemer, Michael 17
Romania 16, 400, 403-405,
411, 415, 416, 418
Roosevelt, Theodore 346
Roosvelt, Franklin D. 349
Rose, Beth 19, 23, 34
rural areas 5-7, 10, 16, 18,
26, 28, 35, 39, 45, 48,
53, 98, 124, 125, 127,
132, 139, 148, 155,
160, 163, 164, 166,
169, 172, 176-178, 182,
186, 188, 196, 200,
201, 202, 206, 210,
213, 214, 219, 222,
231, 239, 243, 244,
248, 259, 260, 263,
295, 300, 301, 303,
306, 331, 332, 337,
362, 389, 395, 396,
397, 398, 409, 413,
416, 421, 427, 428,
430, 434
rural community
see also farming
community 56, 142,
166, 332, 355, 369,
370, 383, 387, 388, 398
rural development 4, 5, 8-13,
15, 19, 21-25, 31, 36,
55-57, 60, 64, 63, 69,
70, 87, 91, 95, 109,
115, 117, 122, 123,
125, 126, 127, 130,
146, 150, 152, 154,
160, 163, 166, 167,
170, 174, 177, 179,
182, 183-189, 191,

192, 197, 198, 200,
202, 206, 207, 209,
210, 218, 221-223,
225, 242, 259, 264,
271, 272, 278, 289,
292, 293, 295, 297,
300, 309, 310, 333,
336, 341, 343, 383,
387, 389-396, 427,
429, 434
rural obligatory man-days
98, 194, 210
Russia 16, 27, 109, 112,
264, 396, 400, 401,
405, 406, 407, 410,
411, 413, 418

Samuelson, Paul Anthony
73, 364
Schiller, Otto 148
Schultz, Theodore W. 11,
27, 28-30, 76, 131, 152,
219, 244, 265, 288,
345, 375, 383, 385, 430
Schweikhardt, D. B. 370
SCS (Soil Conservation
Service) 357
Seckler, David 341
Second Industrial Revolution
47, 48, 51, 55, 103,
125, 337, 392, 394
self-dependency by yeoman
334, 335, 336, 392
self-reliance
by large-scale farmers 14,
265, 295
in food production 5, 150,
160, 182, 206, 295,
389, 434
self-sufficiency
of food 5, 13, 30, 143,
150, 155, 157, 158,

160, 182, 206, 214,
215, 217, 218, 224,
244, 288, 295, 334,
336, 397, 406, 434
of foods except rice and
whale 143
of rice 5, 7, 125, 126,
131, 142, 145, 150
of whale 145
self-sufficiency land
see also grain rations land
9, 88, 90, 96, 97, 99,
154, 155-158, 161, 162,
166, 192, 212, 223-231,
242, 243, 245, 252,
271, 289, 291, 301,
385, 386, 388, 390,
394, 433
self-sufficient 145, 150, 273
Sen, Amartya 63, 176, 189
senilization 35, 127, 139,
151, 212, 377, 416
shareholder 58, 66, 68, 99,
100, 154, 162, 163,
181, 182, 234, 407,
408, 432-434
shareholding 27, 60, 66, 67,
70, 82, 94, 100, 162,
181, 234, 250
shortage
of agricultural labor 3, 5,
126, 142, 221, 337, 338
of capital, credits,
information, and access
to market 412
of food 30, 56, 158, 288,
299, 397
of labor in peak seasons
36, 38, 55, 126
of land 53
of local agricultural labor
37, 238, 239

of local skillful
    able-bodied agricultural
    labor 260
of skilled agricultural labor
    303
shun jia
    see also streamline prices
    195
Singapore 3, 258
Single Land System 9, 10,
    14, 16, 85, 96, 97, 99,
    104, 157, 158, 161,
    166, 177, 181, 230,
    232, 233, 235, 239,
    241, 243, 244, 274,
    277, 289, 291, 301,
    385, 386, 433
size-neutral technologies
    339, 340
slavery 53, 54, 79, 80, 83
slave—master relationship
    334
Slovakia 16, 400, 403-405,
    411, 412, 415, 418
Slovenia 16, 112, 399, 403,
    404, 411, 415, 418,
    421, 427-429, 431
slum 24, 189, 207, 213, 222,
    332
small machinery 5, 9, 19,
    125, 128, 131, 171,
    201, 394
small-scale farm 4, 6-8, 10,
    12, 13, 19-23, 25, 26,
    30, 36, 39, 43, 50-52,
    55, 60, 61, 63, 70, 71,
    84, 94-96, 99, 102, 103,
    104, 121, 124, 126,
    131, 134, 142, 146,
    150-152, 154, 163, 164,
    165, 167, 176, 177-179,
    184, 186, 187, 188,

192, 197, 201,
    209-212, 218, 221,
    222, 223, 243, 259,
    264, 265, 289, 290,
    292, 293, 295, 307,
    313, 317, 318, 320,
    331, 332, 333,
    336-338, 340-342,
    344, 359, 360-362,
    369, 370, 372,
    382-388, 394-398,
    404, 407, 409, 417,
    419, 421, 424, 426,
    428, 433, 434
small-scale farmer 6-11, 14,
    15, 16, 19, 21, 22, 24,
    25, 26, 29, 30, 63, 65,
    71, 76, 77, 82, 83,
    88-90, 95-97, 99, 104,
    112, 124, 126, 131,
    133, 134, 137, 148,
    150, 152-154, 163, 164,
    166, 177, 178, 181,
    187, 188, 211, 216,
    217, 218-223, 235, 238,
    242, 247, 248, 272,
    273, 289, 290, 292,
    295, 307-309, 313, 328,
    331, 332, 335, 336,
    338, 340-344, 348, 360,
    361, 364, 365, 369,
    370, 378, 381, 382,
    383-390, 392, 393,
    394-399, 413, 414, 415,
    417, 420, 427, 428-431
small-scale farming 8, 18,
    21, 180, 191, 199, 205,
    206, 260, 300, 301, 416
small-scale farming and
    collective—individual
    mixed economy 18,
    180, 205, 206, 300

Snodgrass, Donald R. 17
soil and water conservation
    loans 356
soil erosion 281, 284, 288,
    338, 357
sole proprietor farms 321
solidarity groups
    see also krom samaki 297
South Africa 146, 396
South America 31, 44, 146,
    396
South Asia 3, 31, 53, 54, 56
South Korea 3, 7, 11, 14,
    52, 57, 59, 160, 176,
    185, 186, 300, 428
Southeast Asia 3, 31, 37, 56,
    160
Southern Europe 25, 397
Soviet Union
    see also FSU, USSR 26,
    209, 399, 409
sovkhozes (state owned
    farms) 399, 414
soybean 16, 344, 347, 348,
    351, 352, 370, 374, 380
Spain 11, 147, 397
specialized teams 253, 254
speculative behavior on land
    159, 182
speculators for land 306,
    333, 335
squeezing out small farmers
    see also crowding out
        small farmers 30, 222,
        223, 266, 291, 313,
        328, 364, 370, 388,
        390, 398
Sri Lanka 3, 7, 14, 39, 41,
    47, 53, 187
Stanton, B. F. 313, 315, 317
start-up farmers
    see also beginning farmers

378
state bans on non-family
    corporate farming 358
State Council of China 106,
    193, 194-196, 280, 285,
    286
steam-powered technologies
    and machines 46, 48,
    50, 51, 55, 102, 125,
    337, 392
streamline prices 195, 196,
    279
sub-contracting 196
sub-village
    individual–collective
    mixed economy 12,
    21, 60, 70, 153, 179,
    184, 295
subsidizing agriculture by
    industry 271, 272
subsidy 7, 14, 26, 29, 77,
    91, 95, 125, 142, 143,
    145, 150, 152, 158,
    163, 166, 182, 199,
    200, 207, 219, 220,
    233, 252, 265, 270-274,
    277, 281, 282, 293,
    294, 295, 315, 356,
    357-361, 363, 365, 368,
    369, 388, 395, 397,
    398, 428, 434
superiority
    of 'bao gan dao hu' 199
    of large farms over small
        farms 337, 338, 340,
        341, 394
    of part owners over full
        owners and full tenants
        373
    of the Chinese model over
        the American model
        394

of the Chinese model over
the Japanese model 10,
22, 293, 394
of the Household Contract
System 206
supply control programs 354,
396
sustainable rural development
5, 10-13, 19, 21-23, 31,
36, 55, 57, 60, 64, 70,
87, 91, 126, 127, 146,
152, 154, 160, 163,
174, 177, 179, 183,
184, 189, 218, 221,
222, 289, 293, 295,
390, 394-396, 427
Sweden 11, 28, 113, 147,
148
Swinnen, Johan, E. M. 428
Switzerland 11, 109, 111,
147

Tabata, Tamotsu 23, 166,
167
Tajikistan 16, 401, 407, 409,
412
target price 353-355, 362
Tauer, Loren W. 340
tax 18, 50, 74, 87, 90, 98,
148, 151, 159, 168,
173, 181, 182, 193,
196, 197, 200, 210,
215, 224, 252, 257,
259, 274, 289, 297,
298, 321, 327, 333,
358, 360, 382, 387
Taylor, Donald C. 36
team 18, 167, 172, 173, 175,
199, 200, 204, 217,
239, 252-254, 262, 271,
305, 392, 419
technological efficiency

see also Pareto 13, 70,
71, 127
technological progress 5, 9,
15, 48, 71, 123, 125,
127, 200, 215, 277,
284, 336, 337, 339,
393, 394
technology 3, 7, 10, 16, 17,
19, 20, 22, 31, 36, 38,
48, 49-51, 59, 62, 70,
71, 97, 102, 103, 109,
119, 122, 152, 166,
168, 173, 179, 184,
185, 187, 198, 201,
206, 207, 214, 215,
219, 232, 239, 241,
257, 258, 259, 262,
272, 273, 275, 276,
288, 291, 292, 314,
331, 336-342, 369, 380,
387, 388, 392, 393,
394, 396, 409, 419
tenant 3, 40, 51, 52, 62, 65,
68, 69, 82, 109, 110,
123, 124, 132, 134,
147, 172, 189, 301,
305, 314, 327, 334,
335, 370-374, 376-378,
382, 384, 392, 423,
427, 429
tenet
costs fall as farm size
increases 11, 29, 30,
131, 219, 244, 265,
345, 375, 385, 431
Thailand 3, 7, 14, 37, 38,
53, 142, 186, 258
third way beyond the
centrally planned
economy
and free market system 8,
12, 60, 61, 70, 164,

177, 184, 191, 205,
292, 295, 431, 433
three-entity rule 366, 369
town 5, 9, 19, 52, 71, 125,
128, 133, 148, 171,
200, 201, 202, 210,
212, 215, 216, 218,
226, 227, 231, 232,
234, 235, 238, 239,
241, 242, 245-248, 257,
258, 260, 261, 265,
266, 271-273, 303, 332,
337, 383, 399
township 82, 98, 167, 170,
171, 172, 174, 175,
193, 194, 199, 200,
208, 210, 215, 216,
224, 227, 230, 231,
233, 240, 247-249, 252,
253, 266, 271, 274,
275, 290, 294, 296
township unified finance fees
98, 194, 210, 271
traditional agriculture 11, 26,
27, 28, 29, 35, 127,
186, 222, 413, 430
Tran, Duc Luong 305
transition
1st, agriculture to industry
5, 57, 62, 126, 146,
166, 177, 178, 185,
186, 202, 230, 299,
396, 397
2nd, industry to services
5, 126, 146, 166, 185,
202, 230
countries 27, 426
economics 27
economies 396, 415, 416
low wage economy to high
wage economy 158,
174

small-scale farming to
large-scale farming
199, 223
stages 20
towards market economy
15, 26, 178, 208, 303,
308, 310, 399, 403,
415, 419-421, 423, 424,
428
treadmill
process 340
theory 339
Tsuge, Norio 137
Tudors
autocratic rule 147
Tung, Fu-Lai 317, 332
Turkey 11, 147
Turkmenistan 16, 401, 405,
412
TVE (Township and Village
Enterprise) 82, 200,
213, 219, 232, 233,
240, 251-253, 271, 273,
277
Tweeten, Luther G. 359

UK
see also United Kingdom
11, 28, 147, 148, 344
Ukraine 16, 401, 405, 406,
412, 413, 415, 418
ultimate cause of
development 11, 17,
19, 126, 127, 152, 207,
292, 391, 394
under-utilizing land 29, 77,
138, 150, 152, 220,
394, 433
unemployment 4, 10, 28, 35,
48, 54, 62, 126, 155,
170, 171, 188, 221,
332, 398, 409, 413

United Kingdom
    see also UK 398
United States of America
    see also USA 313, 331,
        365
urban unemployment 188,
    332, 398
urban–rural joint enterprise
    201, 256, 259, 292, 293
Uruguay Round 142, 294,
    365
US Department of
    Agriculture 333, 370,
    397
    see also USDA 25, 334
USA 7, 11, 15, 16, 19, 20,
    24, 25, 30, 37, 58, 59,
    142, 147, 149, 178,
    240, 258, 259, 313-316,
    318, 321, 322, 326,
    328, 329, 334, 338,
    344-352, 354, 356, 363,
    365, 366, 370-374, 376,
    379, 380, 384, 385,
    389-396, 398, 426, 427,
    430
USDA
    see also US Department of
        Agriculture 320, 341,
        342, 365, 378, 382
USSR (Union of Soviet
    Socialist Republics)
    see also FSU, Soviet
        Union) 16, 27, 44, 60,
        290
utilization rate of land 139,
    276
Uzbekistan 16, 401, 405,
    407, 409, 412

value of sales
    see also gross sales 314,

        320, 322-325, 328
variable mixed economies
    12, 13, 20-22, 29, 31,
    57, 58, 60, 64, 70, 71,
    91, 104, 126, 152, 153,
    164, 166, 179, 180,
    184, 221, 222, 238,
    291, 293, 295, 307,
    308, 385, 395, 431
Varian, Hal R. 22, 70, 72,
    73, 75, 77, 78, 81, 82
vicious circle of poverty 4,
    12, 20, 35, 36, 52, 54,
    55, 87, 126-128, 202,
    343
Vietnam 3, 11, 14, 15, 24,
    49, 52, 149, 295, 297,
    298, 300, 301, 303,
    305-310, 427
village 4-6, 8, 9, 12, 13, 19,
    21, 22, 39, 41, 46, 47,
    52, 60, 61, 65, 70, 71,
    82, 84, 85, 88, 89, 91,
    95, 96-100, 109-115,
    117, 118, 120, 121,
    125, 128, 132-135, 137,
    138, 148, 149, 152-172,
    174-184, 189, 191-194,
    196-200, 202, 205, 206,
    208, 210-216, 218, 222,
    224, 225, 226-236,
    238-246, 248-253, 255,
    257, 258, 260-263, 265,
    266, 271-275, 277, 289,
    290, 291, 294-296, 298,
    301, 302, 304, 305,
    307, 308, 390, 396,
    404, 417, 418, 426,
    429, 431, 432, 434
village reserved fees 98,
    194, 210, 242, 271
village-wide

corporate—individual
mixed economy 21,
163
village-wide
individual—collective
mixed economy 12,
21, 61, 70, 153, 184,
295
villagers' democratic
participation 14, 99,
292
villagers' group 199, 207,
210, 224, 239, 253

Wade, Robert 59
wage economies 25, 396
wage labor 105, 163, 172,
260, 264, 305
wage laborers 3, 97, 104,
105, 106-108, 132, 157,
172, 293, 303, 305
Walker, Kenneth R. 167
Wallace, Henry A. 349
Wallis, John J. 85
Wan, Xian-Jian 250
Wan, Xian-Yu 250
Wan, Ying-Gan 265
Wang, Li-Zhong 263
War for Independence from
Britain 333, 334, 391
War of Anti-Japanese
Invasion 80, 90, 91
water conservancy 62, 115,
162, 194, 257, 258, 274
Weitzman, Martin L. 82
West Asia 25, 396
Western Europe 30, 48, 146,
149, 415, 428
whale 144, 145, 150
wheat 16, 32, 34, 37, 45,
134, 144, 156, 231,
249, 253, 264-266,

268, 273, 275-278,
299, 337, 344,
349-354, 356, 357,
360, 363, 365, 366,
368, 369, 374, 380
Whitener, Leslie A. 317, 332
Whittaker, Gerald W. 336
Wickizer, V. D. 22, 33, 52
WRP - Wetlands Reserve
Program 357, 368, 396
wu bao hu 194
Wunderlich, Gene 314, 334

xiang tong chou fei
see also township unified
finance fees 194
Xu, Cheng-Gang 82

yeoman 334, 382, 389, 390
yi gong bu nong
see also subsidizing
agriculture by industry
271, 272
yi gong jian nong
see also constructing
agriculture by industry
272
yield 5, 9, 19, 23, 32-34, 36,
37, 38, 39, 49-51, 54,
64, 71-73, 100, 125,
127, 142, 170, 171,
173, 175, 200, 215,
241, 245, 251, 252,
257, 258, 264, 265,
268, 269-271, 273-277,
279, 280, 284, 288,
301, 303, 306, 337,
343, 355, 356, 359,
363, 366, 367, 369,
393, 407, 422
Young, Robert A. 341
Yu, Luo-Shan

Cooperative 171
Yugoslavia 16, 399, 404,
    420, 421

ze ren tian
    see also responsibility land
    191
Zhang, Li-Ming 287
Zhang, Ren-Huai
    Standing-Up Cooperative
    172, 173
Zheng, Nong-Mu
    Cooperative 174
Zhu, Rong-Ji 195, 243, 279
zhuan bao
    see also sub-contracting
    196
zhuan rang
    see also making-over 196
zi liu di
    see also family plot 191